ETHICAL THEORY AND SOCIAL ISSUES
HISTORICAL TEXTS AND CONTEMPORARY READINGS

ETHICAL THEORY AND SOCIAL ISSUES

HISTORICAL TEXTS AND CONTEMPORARY READINGS

DAVID THEO GOLDBERG
Drexel University

Holt, Rinehart and Winston, Inc.
New York   Chicago   San Francisco
Philadelphia   Montreal   Toronto
London   Sydney   Tokyo

Cover Art   Reproduced by courtesy of the Trustees of the British Museum

Library of Congress Cataloging-in-Publication Data

Ethical theory and social issues.

Includes bibliographies and index.
1. Ethics.   2. Social ethics.   I. Goldberg, David
Theo.
BJ1012.E8834   1988   170   88-13687

ISBN 0-03-014194-X

Copyright © 1989 Holt, Rinehart and Winston, Inc.
All rights reserved. No part of this publication may be
reproduced or transmitted in any form or by any means,
electronic or mechanical, including photocopy, recording, or
any information storage and retrieval system, without
permission in writing from the publisher.

Requests for permission to make copies of any part of the
work should be mailed to:
Copyrights and Permissions Department
Holt, Rinehart and Winston, Inc.
Orlando, FL 32887

Printed in the United States of America

9 1 0 2 090 9 8 7 6 5 4 3 2 1

Holt, Rinehart and Winston, Inc.
The Dryden Press
Saunders College Publishing

For Alena and for the future of Gabriel Dylan

Preface

Ethics touches everyone, which suggests one reason why ethics courses are currently popular among college students. Student curiosity about ethics is prompted in the main by an interest in discussing pressing social and professional issues. Course instructors tend to rely on several basic pedagogical methods. One alternative places emphasis upon the more traditional philosophical concern with ethical theory. Another tends to tackle directly the contemporary social issues that form the focus of student concern. Those employing a methodological mix usually proceed in either of two ways: They may begin by presenting ethical theories in their historical setting, and then turn to discuss contemporary issues; or they may tease out the underlying theoretical considerations from a direct discussion of the social issues.

Textbooks available for ethics courses reflect these methodological dispositions. Some textbooks include only chronologically ordered selections from the history of ethics. These usually open with Plato and close, perhaps, with Rawls. Other textbooks include only articles about contemporary social problems. Recently a few texts have sought to combine theoretical and applied readings. Yet they tend to be restricted to covering only those theories or traditions that in one way or another are currently fashionable. Finally, there are those books that are structured thematically, rather than historically or topically. These tend, by contrast, to restrict the material on contemporary social problems.

Ethical Theory and Social Issues includes ethical theory and contemporary applications within the covers of a single text. It sets out to provide instructors and students with a wide range of selections covering the history of ethical theory and analysis of contemporary moral and legal issues. There is a concern to illustrate, as far as feasible, the relevance of ethical theory to an understanding of the social issues covered. Thus this text has two primary aims. The first is to provide a clear picture of the historical development of ethical theory; the second is to provide a firm theoretical foundation on the basis of which contemporary moral problems may be addressed. Instructors preferring to concentrate exclusively upon historical material may encourage students to pursue the contemporary material on their own. Correspondingly, instructors concentrating primarily upon applied ethics will be able to refer students back to the underlying theoretical arguments.

The book is divided into two parts. Part I includes substantial selections from the work of Plato through that of contemporary moral theorists. Though divided into six groups, the selections are chronologically ordered. Part II covers eight topics of current moral relevance: distributive justice, affirmative action, censorship and pornography, sexual morality and AIDS, abortion, euthanasia, punishment and the death penalty, and political violence. In particular, the section on political violence represents a break from the norm. Many ethics textbook anthologies include articles on war or the nuclear debate. Yet I know of none that explicitly addresses the pressing problems of political violence. Where relevant, each of the chapters in Part II includes extracts from majority and dissenting opinions in leading legal cases. A brief glossary may be found at the back of the book. For those more interested in pursuing a thematically ordered course curriculum, an alternative Contents is furnished largely as a substitute for Part I.

Economic considerations dictate that a book of this sort omit something. I have been guided in my choices by the desire to make available to readers a wide and full range of selections; to reflect the interplay between theory and its application; and to provide an even mixture of familiar and challenging texts. I have restricted the section introductions to allow for greater scope in the selections. In any introduction to texts of this sort, the choice is between (some mixture of) the philosophical or social context of the issues covered in the selections; a survey of the arguments selected; and critical discussion of the arguments. Presentation of arguments is logically prior to their criticism. Thus I have set out some background context and a summary of the central points of the arguments. These should be taken as guides for readers, whose task becomes the philosophical one of reconstructing the argumentation. Discussion of criticisms is limited to those that are considered central to interpretation and understanding. I have also noted interrelations between theory and social applications wherever this can be done without too much explanation.

The bibliographies that follow each section are ordered to offer some guidance for further reading and research. I have also added suggestions for discussion. These questions are not intended as traditional study guides for the selections. Rather, their aim is to encourage thinking about the connections between theory and application: how theoretical considerations might determine social decisions, or be challenged by them; and what theoretical considerations underlie a given decision. These questions are suggestions for class discussion, for conversations students might pursue, or for philosophy club topics.

I take pleasure in extending my gratitude to the many colleagues and friends whose thoughtful comments, criticisms, kind advice, and encouragement were of great benefit in completing the book. Correspondence with C.A.J. Coady and Professors Hugo Bedau, Philippa Foot, and Howard McGary improved the sections in which their articles appear. The comments of Jacques Catudal, Michael Edwards, Mark Halfon, Frances Kamm, Steven Mandell, Martha Montgomery, Burton Porter, Rosamond Rhodes, Sara Ruddick, Bill Vitek, and Ben Zipursky brought to my notice points I might otherwise have overlooked. Many conversations with Bernard Baumrin and Bill Ruddick helped me to clarify points large and small. I am especially grateful to Alena Luter: her critical eye and her material and emotional support, despite a busy schedule, ensured that the book was considerably improved. In addition, I would like to thank my reviewers: Fred J. Blomgren, Monroe Community College; Douglas Browning, University of Texas at Austin; Patricia K. Curd, Purdue University; Leslie P. Francis, University of Utah; Richard T. Lambert, Carroll College; Sharon Lloyd, University of Southern California; Robert Hollinger, Iowa State University; John Murray, County College of Morris; Nelson Potter, University of Nebraska–Lincoln; Robert T. Radford, Oklahoma State University; and John P. Tobin, Edison Community College. Though one always takes issue with one's critical reviews, many of their suggestions have been incorporated into the text. I thank also Karen Dubno, my editor at Holt, Rinehart and Winston, for her care and precision in putting the project together. Of course, gratitude is no substitute for responsibility in the case of error, which remains entirely mine.

D.T.G.

NOTE TO STUDENTS

The bibliographies at the end of each part are intended as guides to further reading or research. The lists are alphabetically ordered, and each entry is qualified in terms of its kind (survey, interpretation, or critical analysis) and its level of difficulty (introductory, intermediate, or advanced). *Survey* indicates a general summary of the main points at issue; *interpretation* indicates a detailed reconstruction and explanation of the arguments making up the text; *critical analysis* indicates a discussion and assessment of the strengths and weaknesses of the arguments at issue. When a given text is taken to fit more than one category, this is specified. The only nonannotated bibliographical entries are primary historical references.

Table of Contents

Part II. Social Issues: Contemporary Readings   221

7. Distributive Justice   225

8. Affirmative Action (Race and Sex)   258

Thematic
Table of Contents
TYPES OF ETHICAL THEORY

ETHICAL THEORY AND SOCIAL ISSUES

HISTORICAL TEXTS AND CONTEMPORARY READINGS

GENERAL
INTRODUCTION

In January 1988 a prominent medical journal published an account by a young hospital doctor who claimed to have injected a patient dying of a very painful cancer with a lethal dose of morphine. In causing the woman to die, was the doctor simply ending her unbearable suffering? Did he thus perform a permissible act, if not one required of him as his moral duty? Or, in killing the patient, is he to be blamed for having done an act that is morally impermissible? Doctors have a duty, as human beings and especially in their professional capacity, to diminish suffering whenever they can; but they also have a duty to respect life.

Where a person can fulfill one moral duty only by violating another, he or she is faced by a moral dilemma. Here apparently convincing reasons can be given for choices that mutually exclude each other: Choosing to do one act excludes the possibility of doing the other. Yet, at least on the face of it, both seem morally compelling. If the doctor leaves the woman to die of natural causes, he fails in his duty to reduce suffering (assuming that no painkilling drug will help); and if he causes her death, he fails to respect life. So choosing either alternative seems to imply doing something that is from one point of view right, and from another wrong.

Resolving dilemmas of this sort requires ethical analysis of the relevant facts, concepts, and theoretical principles, and of how they inform action. Persons confronted by ethical dilemmas need to make judgments about what they are required, or at least permitted, to do in the given circumstances. Of course, the questions "How ought I to act here?" or "What am I required or permitted to do?" are not posed only for moral dilemmas: they may be asked of a wide variety of circumstances human beings face. Practical deliberation or reasoning, if properly done, is supposed to tell one what one is required or permitted to do. Theoretical reasoning about ethics involves formulating the principles, rules, and reasons that underlie and support moral judgments and choices in particular circumstances. Practical reasoning should inform the doctor whether or not he ought to inject the patient with morphine; theoretical analysis reveals the principles in terms of which the proper practical judgment in this matter can be reached. In keeping with this distinction Part I of this book covers the major historical contributions to ethical theory. Part II illustrates the application of various and often competing principles elaborated in Part I, in establishing what it is right to do in the case of numerous and pressing social issues.

Moral Concepts   Ethical judgments loom large in our lives, and especially in our relations with others. We often judge some belief, rule, or act to be good or right or proper or just; and we sometimes wonder whether someone has the right to act in a given way. These judgments may be made about acts that are done or intended, about hypothetical or institutional rules, or about possible or actual beliefs. One might ask, "Was I right to break my appointment without notice?" or "Should I keep the book or jacket I borrowed?" We may be taught that it is *good* to be kind or that it is *just* to help the homeless, that these are the things we *ought* or have an *obligation* to do. We tend to think that we have a *duty* to care for the elderly or not to steal. Like George Washington, we might believe that *it is right* never to lie, but that *we have a right* to express ourselves freely. More general judgments are made about *character*. In renting an apartment or applying for a job, one is likely to be asked for character references: "What kind of person is he?" or "Can she be trusted with sensitive information?" At a moral level even more general than this, we make judgments about the *justice* of a given institution or society. We argue over how social goods like health care should be allocated; about the principles of distributing or redistributing wealth; about the rights a society ought to extend to its members or the duties it should command.

Ethics and Morality   Some features of ethical or moral judgments must be noted. Perhaps most basically, the terms *ethics* and *morality* have different roots, and correspondingly different popular usages. The word *ethics* derives from the classical Greek terms *ethos* and *ta ethika*; *morality* stems from the Latin term *mores*. To the ancient Greeks, *ethos* meant personal character, and *ta ethika* signified investigation into the nature of the virtuous life or the right way to live. In Latin, *mores* means social habits or customs. These distinctions in meaning are sometimes reflected in contemporary popular usage. We might refer to someone's "personal ethics" or character, while "morality" is often used in discussions about social conventions and custom. However, contemporary philosophers generally take the terms to be synonymous. So we use the terms here interchangeably to denote philosophical inquiry into the problems of and judgments about acceptable human conduct and character.

Descriptive Ethics   This inquiry can be approached in different ways. One way is simply *to describe* how some person, members of a culture, or society address the sorts of moral issues raised above, what customs they have, and so how they are accustomed to behave. This is called *descriptive ethics*, and it is largely a concern of cultural anthropologists and sociologists. The philosopher's focus upon ethics differs from this. The fundamental philosophical concerns have to do not with how people and cultures in fact behave, but with how we *ought* to treat and be treated by others, what kind of life we should live, and what sort of society we should strive to institute.

Metaethics   Two kinds of questions can be asked about ethical judgments. We can ask for the *meanings* of the moral terms employed. These terms include *good* and *bad* (or *evil*), *right* and *wrong, propriety* and *impropriety, duties* and *rights, obligations* and *claims*, and *justice* and *injustice*. Here we are concerned to understand the use of these terms, their logical form, and the "objects" to which they refer. What, in short, are the logical and conceptual differences between ethical language and other forms of linguistic expression? This analysis of moral language is called *metaethics*.

Normative Ethics   A different kind of question concerns whether acts, principles, or rules are (morally) right or wrong, what characteristics make a person virtuous or vicious, and what reasons can be given for these judgments. This inquiry into the norms or principles of justifiable behavior and the values they embody is called *normative ethics*. It is on the basis of these norms, principles, and values that conduct is judged permissible or impermissible. A fundamental mark of moral justification is the claim that social beliefs, principles, policies, and conduct not be arbitrary. Citing reasons to support moral beliefs, principles, policies, and conduct is required as a test of their nonarbitrariness and justifiability. Reasons embody the grounds on which some intuition, policy, or conduct is considered morally permissible or not. Of course, simply citing reasons to support some belief or bit of behavior is not sufficient grounds to make it moral. The reasons must be relevant, and they must be impartially convincing. In other words, reasons must be acceptable to any reasonable person who has no vested interest in the matter at hand.

Thus anyone concerned with the grounds of ethical analysis must be careful to distinguish among the three kinds of undertakings we have identified here. The question "Do members of some society believe that capital punishment, say, or pornography is wrong?" is one posed by descriptive ethics. "What does it mean for members of that society to say that capital punishment or pornography is wrong?" is a metaethical question. Questions of normative ethics are more direct: "Is capital punishment or pornography right or wrong, and what are the grounds for believing so?" The primary concern of this book is with normative ethical issues: in general, what kinds of acts are right or permissible, what kind of life is good, and what sort of society just? Social justice is interpreted widely to include not only inquiry into the principles of distributive justice but also the permissibility of such practices as affirmative action, censorship, abortion, euthanasia, and capital punishment. We focus, in particular, upon the reasoned grounds offered to justify the answers to these questions. Clearly, normative concerns touch upon descriptive and metaethical considerations, and these are incorporated wherever relevant.

Explanation and Justification   The distinction between explanation of behavior and its justification is one way in which the difference between descriptive and normative (or evaluative) ethics is manifested. Explanation of some bit of behavior involves factual investigation and analysis of what gave rise to it, what caused it to come about, perhaps what function it was intended to serve. Justification involves evaluating the adequacy of reasons supporting the propriety or permissibility of the belief, act, or rule at issue. Generally, a belief or an act may be justified in terms of a rule or principle, and these in turn are justified in terms of a moral theory or system of principles. One of the primary aims of a normative moral theory, then, is to establish in a principled way how we ought or ought not to act.

Fact and Value   These distinctions between description and explanation, on one hand, and evaluation and justification, on the other, rest upon the underlying distinction between fact and value. A fact is an event, occurrence, or act that has taken place; a value is that quality of a thing or act which makes it worthy or desirable. Facts concern the way things actually are; evaluations are judgments about how things *ideally* are or ought to be. *If* abortion causes pain to the fetus, then that is a fact for which there must be some physical evidence, and we should be able to explain it physiologically. Yet even if some pain is suffered by the fetus, this alone does not amount to justification of a principle that abortions ought not to be permitted. Some convincing reasons or adequate argument must be provided showing that the pain in cases of this kind is unwarranted, unacceptable, or impermissible. And this can only be done by appealing to some more general moral principle, ideal, or value, such as "It is wrong to cause harm to the innocent." Whether *this* principle, or the value it embodies, is sufficient to justify the impermissibility of abortion will depend upon whether there are any relevant exceptions to it; that is, whether it can be overridden by any competing principle, and whether a fetus is in the relevant sense innocent.

Relativism   One popular form that ethical justification often assumes is *relativism*. There are a number of related claims basic to the theory of relativism: Ethical values and principles are taken to vary from one society, generation, or individual to another; the values of one society, generation, or individual have no privileged claim to truth; and moral truth or objectivity is restricted to the shared values of the society or generation. There are two views here. *Cultural relativism* holds that an act, rule, or practice which is *thought* wrong by one culture may be *thought* right by another; whereas *ethical relativism* holds that an act, rule, or practice which *is* right for one society, culture, or individual may actually *be* wrong for another. Where a basic ethical value of one society or individual conflicts with that of another, ethical relativism insists that there is no principled way of judging between them, for there are no universal, transcultural, or absolute moral values. The values of each society or individual are considered to be equally acceptable. "Right" or "good" or "valuable" acquire content only relative to a given society or individual.

Clearly, different societies have different practices, and correspondingly different values: It may be thought permissible, in the Netherlands, say, for a doctor to inject a terminally ill patient with a lethal dose of morphine, but impermissible in another country, such as the United States. One normative implication of this is that members of one society should not object to practices of those in another. This has some appeal, for it seems to undermine social chauvinism or the condemnation of other societies just because they are different. Nevertheless, we are prevented by the same token from asking whether there is a right way to act that is independent of culture; and we are restricted in criticizing other societies for practices, such as racial discrimination, that we find genuinely abhorrent.

Simple forms of cultural relativism face a basic theoretical objection. Because an act may be right relative to the values or ideals of one society or culture and wrong according to those of another, the relativist appears committed to the apparent contradiction that the same act is both right and wrong. A relativist may counter that the values according to which the act is thought right differ from those in terms of which it is wrong: The doctor's lethal injection may be considered permissible in the Netherlands in terms of the value of ending unnecessary suffering, but impermissible in the United States in virtue of taking an innocent life. An act may be deemed right in terms of value *V1* in one society or culture, but wrong in terms of *V2* in the other. Though different, *V1* and *V2* need not be contradictory values. So the relativist seems not to be committed to a contradiction. Yet an inconsistency may arise elsewhere: In claiming that it is wrong to object to practices of a society different from one's own, the relativist is forced to use a notion of "wrong" that is no longer relative but transcultural. It is for reasons of these kinds that philosophers have tended to reject the simpler forms of relativism as justification for ethical principles. (Nevertheless, Alasdair MacIntyre has offered a sophisticated defense of ethical relativism that escapes these shortcomings; see Part I, Chapter 6.)

Moral Conflict   A basic concern of ethical analysis in its practical applications is to clarify the nature of moral disagreements or conflicts, with the goal of resolving them. Moral conflicts may be a function of disagreements concerning *facts* or *concepts* or *values*. Where the conflict is factual, ethical analysis may be able to resolve the problem by uncovering and encouraging agreement on all the relevant facts. For example, proponents of capital punishment often appeal to the claimed fact that the death penalty deters violent crime. If the evidence shows that the rate of violent crime is either unchanged or increases when the death penalty is in place, then appeal to its deterrent effect can no longer serve as justification for capital punishment and proponents would have to claim some other justification or renounce their support.

Sometimes moral conflict turns on underlying or hidden conceptual disagreement. Resolution may then depend upon establishing agreement about the meanings of relevant concepts in use. Conflict concerning the permissibility of abortion often involves the concept of a person. There may be agreement on the principle that one ought never to harm an innocent person, but disagreement over whether the fetus is a person (and not simply a human being in the physical or genetic sense). No factual evidence will resolve this issue; and calling the fetus a baby simply assumes what has to be established by argument. Conceptual clarification is required. Similarly, parties may agree that legitimate freedom fighters ought as a matter of political morality to be given aid, while terrorist groups should be strongly opposed. Whether the African Nationalist Congress in South Africa deserves our support should accordingly depend upon whether it meets reasonable and impartial criteria for being a liberation movement, and this is clearly a conceptual and not an ideological issue.

Finally, disagreement may concern moral rules, principles, or values. Parties may disagree about norms or principles that ought morally to be endorsed, or they may disagree about the values to be considered primary. For example, some may consider the Offense Principle (that restriction of a person's liberty can be justified to prevent offense to others) sufficiently strong to limit freedom of expression, while others may reject this principle (cf. Chapter 9). The former may appeal to offensiveness in trying to justify the impermissibility of homosexuality, while the latter will reject the principle in accepting the freedom of homosexuals to express their sexual preference. One attempt to resolve this conflict at the level of institutional principles has been to encourage proponents of the Offense Principle to acknowledge its limits, in light of the more compelling principle of Respect for Persons, that is, that persons are owed respect as autonomous agents (cf. Chapter 3).

Thus moral philosophers aim to get agreement on the facts, to clarify the definition of relevant concepts, and to analyze justifications offered for underlying values. Should moral disagreement persist, it is likely to concern the basic source or grounds of moral value; for example, whether an act's value is taken to be determined by its consequences or its intrinsic worth.

The complexity of such issues as affirmative action, censorship and pornography, abortion, or capital punishment does not consist simply in the fact that persuasive arguments can be offered for conflicting points of view. These issues are by nature social; they must be resolved, accordingly, at the level of social policy. Social policies, in the form of institutional rules, regulations, and laws, direct individual conduct, and they often clash with individuals' convictions. It is important, then, to get clear about the theoretical basis and scope of moral judgments, and about the application of ethical principles in determining social policy and practice. The application of laws and the underlying legal analysis may lead to different constraints on social action than does moral inquiry.

Law and moral principles do not always coincide. It is unlikely that every law will meet moral constraints; nor will every moral principle or rule be embodied in a law. Laws can be altered or added by legislation; moral obligations and rights are not so easily created or destroyed. Indeed, laws can be critically evaluated and attacked on the basis of moral principles; yet we do not ordinarily criticize a moral principle or value in terms of some given law. So where a given law clashes with a moral principle, especially if they constrain us to act in mutually exclusive ways, morality may require that we oppose the law. For example, Rosa Parks rightly and courageously opposed the racist statute in Montgomery, Alabama, that required blacks to occupy only the rear seats in public buses. Opposition to unjust or immoral laws will not always require civil disobedience, though in extreme cases like the one facing Ms. Parks and others it did. In less severe circumstances, opposition can take the form of lobbying or letter-writing, peaceful protests or voting. Discussions of the legal and moral problems in Part II draw at many points and in many ways on the theoretical moral principles developed and discussed in Part I. The general aim is to furnish a forum for readers to construct for themselves reasoned and critical dispositions to moral action for each of the social topics at issue.

FURTHER READING

Hudson, W.D. *Modern Moral Philosophy*. London: Macmillan, 1970. (Interpretation, critical analysis; intermediate)

Journal of American Medical Association "It's All Over, Debbie," 259, 2 (Jan. 8, 1988): 272.

Krausz, M., and Meiland, J. eds. *Relativism, Cognitive and Moral*. South Bend: University of Notre Dame Press, 1982. (Interpretation, critical analysis; advanced)

Ladd, J., ed. *Ethical Relativism.* Belmont, Calif.: Wadsworth, 1973. (Interpretation, critical analysis; intermediate)

Lyons, D. *Ethics and the Rule of Law.* Cambridge: Cambridge University Press, 1984. (Interpretation, critical analysis; introductory)

MacIntyre, A. *A Short History of Ethics.* New York: Macmillan, 1966. (Survey, critical analysis; introductory)

Nielsen, K. *Ethics Without God.* London: Pemberton, 1973. (Interpretation, critical analysis; intermediate)

Norman, R. *The Moral Philosophers.* Oxford: Clarendon Press, 1973. (Survey; introductory)

Olson, G. *The Morality of Self-Interest.* New York: Harcourt, 1965. (Interpretation, critical analysis; intermediate)

Outka, G., and Reeder, J., eds. *Religion and Morality.* New York: Anchor Books, 1973. (Interpretation, critical analysis; intermediate)

Rachels, J. *The Elements of Moral Philosophy.* New York: Random House, 1986. (Survey, critical analysis; introductory)

Raphael, D. D. *Moral Philosophy.* Oxford: Oxford University Press, 1981. (Survey, critical analysis; introductory)

Stoljar, S. *Moral and Legal Reasoning.* New York: Harper & Row, 1980. (Critical analysis; intermediate)

Toulmin, S. *Reason in Ethics.* Cambridge: Cambridge University Press, 1971. (Interpretation, critical analysis; intermediate)

Williams, B. *Morality: An Introduction.* New York: Harper & Row, 1972. (Survey, critical analysis; introductory)

PART

I

□

ETHICAL THEORY: HISTORICAL TEXTS

Ethical Theory: Introduction

Criteria of Evaluation An act, policy, or institution that is right, good, or just shares some characteristic features or properties with other acts, policies, or institutions that are similarly characterized. Normative ethical theories set out to establish just what these shared features or properties are. In evaluating ethical theories, it is useful to bear in mind the following set of criteria. First, the principles of the theory must be *consistent:* they must be capable of being jointly true. Further, implications to which the theory gives rise must be consistent with every principle of the theory. Second, *the wider the scope* of the theory—that is, the more moral data it is capable of accounting for—the more acceptable it will be. Third, the theory must provide a *decision procedure* for establishing what act is morally permissible or required in any given act context. A theory that fails to specify what act is required, or at least a range of permissible acts, will be useless. Fourth, *the fewer the basic moral precepts* of the theory, the better. Of two theories equally wide in scope, the simpler one will be more appealing. Two theories that have great historical and contemporary influence, Kant's deontology (see Chapter 3) and utilitarianism (see Chapter 4), specify one fundamental ethical principle each. Particular rules of behavior in actual act contexts are supposed to be derivable from the basic principle. Finally, the theory must be capable of rendering moral judgments that *conform with* a set of widely held, carefully considered, and reasonable *moral intuitions* about what is right and wrong. A viable theory might challenge some popular moral beliefs. However, no acceptable theory will endorse such acts as murder, such practices as political torture, or such institutions as slavery. There are good reasons for considering such acts, practices, and institutions to be morally unacceptable.

These criteria are unlikely to establish a single prevailing moral theory to the exclusion of all others. Nevertheless, they will reduce the field of viable alternatives to a manageable handful. Moreover, those theories that may be considered viable are unlikely to be flawless. In this respect, moral theories mirror scientific ones: we adopt the best available, adapting and revising it in accordance with the test of experience.

Classification of Theories   The ethical theories included in Part I are given below chronologically. It is possible also to order them thematically, and it may help to give a brief characterization of each thematic category listed in the alternative Contents. *Virtue* theories take the basic inquiry of morality to concern the moral *character* of individuals, rather than the rightness or wrongness of *actions*. The fundamental question for virtue theories concerns what sort of person one should be or what sort of character one should develop in order to be virtuous, rather than what sort of action one ought to do. *Natural Law* theories hold that moral principles or laws reflect the nature or rational order of things. For human laws and actions to be moral, they must conform with the natural law. (Note that while Hobbes is included in this category, he imputes a different sense to the concept of natural law, and may be interpreted as challenging traditional Natural Law theories.) *Deontological* theories reject the claim that the moral rightness or wrongness of an act is to be defined in terms of its production of goodness or badness. Rather, acts will be right if they are implied or commanded by some binding or overriding moral principle(s) or system of duties. *Intuitionism* is the theory that ethical concepts like good or right are apprehended, and ethical judgments properly concluded, by a direct moral insight or intuition. *Social contract* theories take morality to consist in a set of rules establishing how members of a society ought to treat each other. The rules are those that would be (contractually) agreed to by any rational member of the society, if all members accepted them, because these rules would maximize their mutual benefits. *Utilitarian* theories judge the moral worth of actions or rules solely in terms of the goodness or badness of their consequences. Accordingly, an act or rule will be right if it produces greater goodness in general, or perhaps greater goodness for each person affected by it, than any alternative. *Right-based* theories take the basic concept of morality to be rights; that is, freedoms and claims. These theories attempt to derive a general system of rights, goals, and duties from one fundamental right or from a small number of basic rights. Theories of *justice* offer principles of fairness or rightness to guide rules, policies, and actions in the distribution and exchange of goods, in the formation of sociopolitical institutions, and in the punishment of wrongs committed. Finally, the category of *moral critics* differs from the others, for it does not include positive formulations about the nature of moral rightness or goodness. Rather, it involves critical attacks on the traditional forms of moral justification, and upon the social uses to which theories of moral justification have been put.

1

□

Plato, Aristotle, and Aquinas

PLATO (427–347 B.C.): THE IDEAL GOOD

Plato and Socrates   Plato developed the philosophical legacy of his teacher, Socrates (c. 470–399 B.C.). Both were primarily concerned with the question "What is the good or virtuous life?" In *The Republic*, as in Plato's other mature dialogues, the literary figure of Socrates represents Plato's philosophical views. Plato's overriding concern in *The Republic* was with the nature of justice. So this question of the life most worthy of human pursuit assumes a fundamentally social character. Human beings are social by nature, and the just or right way to live can be defined only in terms of their relations with others.

The Sophists   Plato criticized philosophical and social views commonly expressed in classical Greece, especially those of the Sophists. The Sophists were a loosely related class of professional teachers, representing a variety of subjects, who accepted payment for their instruction. Their primary social importance lay in teaching activities central to Greek political life. These skills included management of family and estate, and rhetoric or the art of persuasion to one's opinion without concern for the truth. Though there is no single set of Sophistic views, it may be possible to establish a common theme in Sophistic thinking about the nature of virtue. The Sophists considered virtue to be relative to common opinion about it. Thus it was thought that virtue is not innate, and that it can be taught. Some Sophists appear also to have supported the dictum that "might makes right," that justice is determined by those who have power. In short, the Sophists insisted that morality and justice are a matter not of nature, human or cosmic, but of social convention, custom, and tradition.

Plato's Criticism of the Sophists   Plato's Socrates attacks a version of this view, as represented by the Sophist Thrasymachus, in the opening book of *The Republic*, excerpted below. Thrasymachus defined justice or right as what the stronger parties take to be in their own interests. Socrates shows that this definition of justice involves a contradiction, and is accordingly false. Thrasymachus then contends that injustice pays while justice does not, and so that doing what is morally wrong must be superior to justice. In response, Socrates demonstrates that because effective injustice necessitates some cooperation, injustice is inevitably self-defeating. Hence, justice must be superior to injustice.

Justice and Reason   In addition to these criticisms of Thrasymachus's views, Socrates argues positively that the proper performance of reason is a necessary condition for all *human* functions. Persons will be just if their ideas are, and their lives will thus be good. For Plato, reason is fundamental to establishing what ought to be done; it is central to living the good and just life. This is highlighted in the extracts from *The Republic,* Books VI and VII, which concern Plato's views about reality and how we acquire knowledge of it.

Plato held that beliefs or opinions grounded in sense perceptions of physical objects do not amount to knowledge. The proper objects of knowledge are not physical; rather, they are abstract universal Forms. These Forms or Ideas— representing essences of things—exist for Plato in an independent idealized realm. They are real, but do not exist in and are independent of the physical world. Reason, equally universal and immortal, is that faculty of the soul capable of contemplating and knowing these eternally true ideal objects. Nevertheless, human beings need sense perceptions. The senses assist in the development of the soul, which is necessary for rational contemplation or knowledge of these ideal Forms. On Plato's view, sense perceptions of like objects lead us to conceive the ideal or formal properties in virtue of which the perceived objects can be judged alike. Learning, then, is a matter of bringing these Forms from the cavelike darkness of the soul to the light of reason's "eye." The Form represents the Good (in the sense of "best") for each class of object or quality. Thus, Plato holds that the value of objects or qualities is not established contextually or by social convention; rather, value is determined by the degree to which objects or qualities embody the formal properties of constancy, purity, and truth.

To know the Good, for Plato, is ultimately to have complete knowledge; that is, knowledge that is the best, true, and most stable. A knowledgeable person will accordingly do good acts. By contrast, immoral acts imply ignorance; the ignorant person is one who failed to know what was truly or essentially good in the instance at hand. Plato drew the important moral distinction between undertaking the right *act*, thereby acting justly, and being a just or virtuous *person* because one has done the act *for the right reason.* For example, it is right to remove a dangerous weapon from the reach of a person bent on doing harm. Yet if one removes the weapon with a view also to using it oneself to commit some other harm, the act of removal is done for the wrong reason and one would be unjust. Plato thought that because philosophers alone have knowledge of the Good and of justice, they should rule the Republic or ideal state. Philosophers would rule for the good of all classes in the state, and not out of self-concern.

Justice and the State   Elsewhere in *The Republic*, Plato defined a just state as one in which the members of each class do what they *know* best, for the good of all, and mind their own business: workers produce, soldiers defend, and guardians rule. Members of one class do not impose upon members of other classes their ill-informed *opinions* of how the latter ought to perform their respective functions. As justice individually is the harmony among parts of the soul (the appetitive, the spirited, and the rational), so social justice consists in this special cooperation among classes of the state.

Plato set the standard for moral reasoning. Whatever views one holds about the nature of morality, reasons must be cited to support them if others are to agree or be convinced. If the reasons are poor or overridden by better ones supporting another belief or act, commitment to the former view must be given up. Plato encourages us to think deeply about the relation among our moral beliefs, the acts we undertake, the kinds of persons we are, and the sort of society we live in. Socrates underscores these concerns in his famous remark that "the unexamined life is not worth living."

ARISTOTLE (384–323 B.C.): VIRTUES AND PRACTICAL REASONING

Aristotle's Teleology   Like Plato, with whom he studied for many years, Aristotle considered the life of contemplation to be the essential human good. Aristotle's conception of nature, including human nature, is *teleological*; that is, each class or kind of thing has an end (*telos*). To bring this *telos* about is its natural function. A member of the class or kind will be more or less good to the extent that it fulfills the natural function of its kind. The function of hearts, say, is to pump blood. A good heart is one that pumps well; it fulfills its function.

Eudaimonia   Aristotle began and ended his study of ethics (*Nicomachean Ethics,* Books I and X) by inquiring into the nature of the good for human beings. He claimed that the goal of human beings is to live well or happily. (*Eudaimonia*, the term Aristotle uses, is probably best translated as "well-being.") It is not uncommon to equate happiness with pleasure. Nevertheless, Aristotle was careful to distinguish between them, arguing that a life of happiness, unlike one of pleasure, will be self-sufficient, complete, and chosen for its own sake (see Book I). Thus pleasure is rejected as the proper *telos* of human acts.

It should be noted that although Aristotle's view of human nature is teleological, his account of how we decide what is right or wrong is not consequentialist; that is, he does not consider an act to be moral or immoral on the basis of the pleasurable or painful consequences it effects. (In this, Aristotle's view differs fundamentally from utilitarianism; see Part I, Chapter 4).

Reason and the Virtues   Aristotle was concerned to spell out the conditions of a life worth living. Unlike Plato, for whom the most worthy life is strictly contemplative, Aristotle stressed that human life is by nature social and active, and that human virtue or excellence should reflect this. Reason, for Aristotle, has both intellectual and practical states, and so there are intellectual and practical virtues (excellences). The moral or practical virtues are accordingly the conclusions to excellent practical reasoning in given contexts. For example, generosity is the moral virtue established by excellent practical reasoning in the case of giving or taking property; courage is the virtue in battle. Vices in each context are extremes either of excess or insufficiency (defect). In the case of property, the excessive vice is wastefulness and the defect is stinginess; for battle, they are foolhardiness and cowardice, respectively. For a particular act to be virtuous or vicious, it must be voluntary. A set of criteria for distinguishing between voluntary and involuntary acts is laid out in Book III. Where the moving principle of the act is outside the agent—an act done from imposed force, for example—it will be involuntary. A voluntary act is one for which the determining cause is in the agent, when he or she could have done otherwise. Voluntary acts are praiseworthy or blameworthy; involuntary acts, by contrast, are pardonable.

Practical Reasoning The moral virtues require right choice. On Aristotle's account, the intellectual virtue of correct practical reasoning effects right choice: its aim is to act well. So correct practical reasoning or deliberation underlies the moral virtues. The virtue of practical deliberation is analyzed in Book VI. Excellence in deliberation involves the right process of reasoning, leading in conclusion to a timely choice of the right act, and with the view to bringing about the right end. Good choice requires that the reasoning be true and that desire follow what reason determines (Aristotle accordingly calls choice either "desiderative reason" or "ratiocinative desire").

Right reason concerns the proper relation between universal and particular premises. *Universal premises* express value judgments about the general class of object under consideration; for example, "Drunk driving is dangerous." *Particular premises* are factual claims about the concrete circumstances in which the agent stands: "A friend offers me a ride home; he is drunk." For Aristotle, practical ethical choices cannot be reduced to a set of universal rules. *Perception* of the agent's particular circumstances is crucial, and this may prompt a revision of the universal rules or laws. The conclusion to the practical reasoning, then, is not a tendency or conviction to act in some way. The reasoning ends in actually bringing about the act; in our example, "I take the keys and drive my friend home" or "I call a cab." Error in deliberation leading to the wrong or vicious act may involve a mistake either in the universal or particular premise of the practical reasoning. My decision to accept a ride home with my drunk friend may follow from a mistaken universal premise, "Drunk driving is not dangerous," or from a false impression of my friend's sober state.

Incontinence (*Weakness of the Will*) In Book VII, Aristotle addressed the problem of how one may judge correctly and yet act *incontinently* or without restraint. It may be recalled that Socrates thought bad action is a function of ignorance: one cannot do wrong *knowingly*. Plato explained incontinence or weakness of the will (*akrasia*) by claiming that though one apparently has knowledge, an irrational appetite blinds one to it. On Plato's view, this meant that the agent fails to possess real knowledge but only has mere opinion. Aristotle rejected both views as an inadequate account of all the facts. He insisted that one can clearly commit a wrong knowingly, and he identified various ways agents may do something they know they ought not.

Justice In contrast to the intellectual virtue of practical deliberation, justice—like courage—is a moral virtue, and injustice a moral vice. In Book V, Aristotle distinguished between two senses of justice (the lawful and the fair) and two senses of injustice (the unlawful and the unfair). The lawful is equivalent to the whole of virtue; the unlawful, to the whole of vice. For Aristotle, the notion of the law is a collection of wise or rational judgments about excellent or virtuous actions in all kinds of circumstances. As a summary of past experience, laws guide choice. Thus to act in terms of the appropriate law in every case is to be completely virtuous. Nevertheless, it should be stressed that good judgment in the actual situation confronting agents involves properly identifying their given circumstances, and this is a matter of what Aristotle called *perception*.

Justice as fairness, by contrast, is a particular virtue, and the unfair is a particular vice. Aristotle distinguished between two kinds of fairness: distributive and rectificatory. *Distributive* justice involves establishing principles for proportionate equality or fairness in distributing goods among citizens. *Rectificatory* or corrective justice concerns setting right or "equalizing" harms for injuries done, whether these harms are a matter of unfair distributions of goods or of injurious acts. Equality is to be restored either by way of a redistribution of goods or by corrective punishment.

Much of the contemporary moral concern about social problems is tied up with the notion of justice in both of Aristotle's senses. The general questions that are raised for each of the social issues in Part II of this book were part of Aristotle's primary focus: "What is the right action for me to do here, and how do I decide this?" But questions can be asked also about the justice of institutions basic to any social fabric. These include concerns about the principles of just distribution of social resources (see Part II, Chapter 7) and the principles of punishment (see Chapter 13). Aristotle's view represents one way to set about answering both sets of questions. However, his historical importance is perhaps wider in scope, for he furnished the very terms of the debate.

Aristotle's philosophical thought, including his moral theory, exerted tremendous influence upon later thinkers. This was especially so in the case of medieval Christian philosophers. Aristotle's writings were to secular questions in the Middle Ages what Scriptures were to religious questions: virtually the ultimate and unchallenged authority concerning the truth. Moral questions were considered to display both religious and secular dimensions. Thus ethical theory as reflected in the work of St. Thomas Aquinas, the most important medieval philosopher, is a marriage of Christian and Aristotelian outlooks.

ST. THOMAS AQUINAS (c. A.D. 1225–1274): THE NATURAL LAW

Stoicism Aquinas's interpretation of Aristotle's moral theory in light of prevailing Christian doctrine was also influenced by Stoic thought. The Stoic school of philosophy lasted approximately from 300 B.C. in Greece to A.D. 200 in Rome. The Stoics held that social convention or custom ought to be shunned in favor of following universal principles of nature. Rationality was considered the distinctive feature of human nature; to follow human nature implied following reason. Reason was thought to provide an unchanging natural law.

Aquinas's Conception of Law Aquinas held that the law in general is a dictate or rule of reason that commands or forbids. He distinguished between three kinds of law: Eternal, Natural, and Human. The Eternal Law, given by Divine Reason, is "the plan of the divine wisdom . . . directing all the acts and motions" of things. Divine Reason is timeless, and so too are its products. Thus God's Law is eternal: it rules everything subject to God's power. The eternal Divine Law determines the proper function of all things and directs them to the attainment of their proper ends. The proper performance of each thing that is determined in this way is its *natural* one.

Nature Here the *nature* of a thing is taken to mean its essential properties, those characteristics without which it would not be that thing. Things are thought to be divided into natural kinds, which are distinguished from each other by their own inner essences. The essence specifies the proper end for the kind, and by extension for each thing of that kind. The virtue or goodness of each thing, accordingly, is supposed to be tied to the fulfillment of its "natural" end.

Human nature consists of those characteristics that are essential to humans as a kind, and that differentiate them from all other kinds of thing. All bodies and creatures below human or rational beings on the hierarchical scale, according to Aquinas, cannot act otherwise than they do. They are not free to act contrary to the laws of their own nature. Human beings, however, are free to follow or disobey the dictates of practical reason. Hence, they are free to establish the rational principles of morality and to choose to follow them. The Natural Law of morality is the Eternal Law as applied to human affairs. The Natural Law is established by human beings rather than imposed from above. To recognize the rationality of the Natural Law is also recognition of its binding force. Thus for Aquinas, actions are wrong not because they are prohibited by God's Eternal Law; rather, they are prohibited because they are inherently wrong. In other words, they are contrary to human nature, and so they violate the rational principles of the moral law.

Natural Law Aquinas argued that the law of human nature requires action in accordance with reason. The effect of this law on action is to make humans good. Accordingly, the first principle of Natural Law is the teleological one that good is to be done and evil avoided. All other precepts of Natural Law are rationally derivative from this one. Acts of virtue are good as such, and the Natural Law commands them. Acts of vice are evil, and the law of reason forbids them as contrary to nature. Some acts by nature are indifferent, neither distinctly good nor bad: these the law may permit. It follows that reason establishes what kinds of acts are virtuous and so commanded, or what are evil and so forbidden.

This rational determination of good and bad acts is refined by Aquinas's distinction between the external and internal features of an act. Externally, an act is good according to whether it brings about the rationally determined human good or *telos*. Internally, act and agent are both good according to whether the agent *intended* to bring about this good or end. Circumstances beyond the agent's rational control may cause her act to lead to bad consequences, yet we commend her good effort. Similarly, though an agent's act effects good consequences, he may not be praiseworthy because his intention in so acting was bad. For example, we commend the efforts of a doctor who intends to cure and believes she is taking reasonable steps to do so, though the unsuccessful liver transplant surgery she performs on a patient with terminal liver disease causes the patient's death. And we think poorly of the business journalist who intended to mislead the public, though the misinformation he provides leads to an increase in the price of stocks we are holding.

Finally, Aquinas argued that the Natural Law provides only general, eternal principles of nature. Reason is supposed to establish how these general principles apply in particular circumstances. Nevertheless, human reason is imperfect and open to error. So temporal or Human Laws are devised to govern these more particular cases. Yet in practical human matters there are differences of judgment; errors may be committed. The Natural Law, on Aquinas's view, reflects God's Eternal Law and cannot be mistaken. If there are mistakes in the law, they must occur in the temporal dictates or Human Law, which are made by those charged with care of the community. Though particular human laws may aim for the common good, their failure to bring it about means that they must be mistaken. Thus the Natural Law theory of morality makes the Law of Nature the ultimate arbiter of moral good.

Natural Law theory underlies traditional Roman Catholic thought, though the theory is not limited to theology. It stresses that the good to be pursued (or evil avoided) is given by the characteristic or universal inclinations or tendencies of human nature that are taken to promote (or undermine) human flourishing. These characteristic human goods include life and health, pursuit of knowledge, procreation, promotion of children and the innocent, and love of fellow humans. What is morally right or required for any social issue such as abortion, euthanasia, sexual relations, pornography, or punishment, on the Natural Law view, must at least be consistent with the goods basic to human flourishing.

Plato

The Republic

Book I

... That I learn of others, I replied, is quite true; but that I am ungrateful I wholly deny. Money I have none, and therefore I pay in praise, which is all I have; and

From *The Republic*, trans. by Benjamin Jowett, *The Dialogues of Plato* (Oxford University Press, 1892).

how ready I am to praise any one who speaks well you will very soon find out when you answer, for I expect that you will answer well.

Listen, then, [Thrasymachus] said; I proclaim that might is right, justice the interest of the stronger. But why don't you praise me?

Let me first understand you, I replied. Justice, as you say, is the interest of the stronger. Now what, Thrasymachus, is the meaning of this? You cannot mean to say that because Polydamas, the pancratiast, who is stronger than we are, finds the eating of beef for his interest, that this is equally for our interest who are weaker than he is?

That's abominable of you, Socrates; why you are just taking the words in the way which is most damaging to the argument.

Not at all, my good sir, I said; I am trying to understand them; and I wish that you would be a little clearer.

Well, he said, I suppose you know that forms of government differ; there are tyrannies, and there are democracies, and there are aristocracies?

Yes, I know that.

And the government is that which has power in each State?

Certainly.

And the different forms of government make laws democratical, aristocratical, tyrannical, with a view to their several interests; and these laws, which are made by them for their interests, they deliver to their subjects as justice, and punish him who transgresses them as a breaker of the law, and unjust. And that is what I mean when I say that in all States there is the same principle of justice, which is neither 339   more nor less than the interest of the government; and as the government must be supposed to have power, the reasonable conclusion is, that everywhere there is one principle of justice, which is the interest of the stronger.

Now I understand you, I said; and whether you are right or not I will try to learn. But let me first remark, that you have yourself said "interest," although you forbade me to use that word in answer. I do not, however, deny that in your definition the words are added "of the stronger."

A slight addition, that you must allow, he said.

Great or small, never mind that; the simple question is, whether what you are saying is the truth. Now we are both agreed that justice is interest of some sort, but we are not agreed as to the additional words "of the stronger"; and this is the point which I will now examine.

Proceed.

That I will; and first tell me, Do you admit that it is just for subjects to obey their rulers?

I do.

But are the rulers of States absolutely infallible, or are they sometimes liable to err?

To be sure, he replied; they are liable to err.

Then in making their laws they may sometimes make them rightly, but they are not always right?

True.

When they make them rightly, they make them agreeably to their interests; when they are mistaken, contrary to their interests—that is what you would say?

Yes.

And the laws which they make must be obeyed by their subjects—and that is what you call justice?

Doubtless.

Then justice, according to your argument, is not only the interest of the stronger but the reverse?

What are you saying? he asked flurriedly.

I am only saying what you were saying, I believe. But let us consider. Have we not admitted that the rulers may be mistaken about their own interests in what they command, and also that to obey them is justice? Has not that been admitted?

Yes.

Then you must also have acknowledged that justice is not the interest of the stronger, when the rulers who are stronger unintentionally command that which is to their own injury. For if, as you say, justice is the obedience which the subject renders to their commands, then in the case supposed, O thou wisest of men, is there any escape from the conclusion that justice is the injury and not the interest of the stronger, which is imposed on the weaker?

Nothing can be clearer, Socrates, said Polemarchus.

340   Yes, said Cleitophon, interposing, if you are admitted as his witness.

But there is no need of any witness, said Polemarchus, for Thrasymachus himself acknowledges that rulers command what is not for their own interest, and that to obey them is justice.

Yes, Polemarchus—Thrasymachus said that for subjects to do what was commanded by the rulers was just.

Yes, but he also said that justice was the interest of the stronger, and, while admitting both these propositions, he further admitted that the stronger commands what is not for his own interest; whence follows that justice is the injury quite as much as the interest of the stronger.

But, said Cleitophon, he meant by the interest of the stronger what the stronger thought to be for his interest.

That was not the statement, said Polemarchus.

Never mind, I said; let us accept the new statement, if Thrasymachus has changed his opinion.

Tell me then, I said, Thrasymachus, did you mean by justice what the stronger thought to be his interest, whether really so or not?

Certainly not, he said. Do you suppose that I call him who is mistaken the stronger at the time when he is mistaken?

Yes, I said, that I supposed to be your meaning when you admitted that the ruler was not infallible and might be mistaken.

You are a sharper, Socrates, in argument. Pray do you imagine that he who is mistaken about the sick is a physician in that he is mistaken and at the time that he is mistaken? or that he who errs in arithmetic or grammar is an arithmetician or grammarian in that he is mistaken and at the time that he is mistaken? True, we say that the arithmetician or grammarian or physician has made a mistake, but this is only a way of speaking; for the fact is that neither the grammarian nor any other person of skill ever makes a mistake in as far as he is what his name implies: they all of them err only when their skill fails them. No craftsman or sage or ruler errs at the time when he is what he is called, though he is commonly said to err; and after this manner I answered you. But the more precise expression, since you will have 341 precision, is that the ruler, as ruler, is unerring, and, being unerring, always commands that which is for his own interest; and the subject is required to execute this: and therefore, as I said at first and now repeat, justice is the interest of the stronger.

. . . Is the physician, in that strict sense of which you are speaking, a healer of the sick or a maker of money? And remember that I am now speaking of the true physician.

A healer of the sick, he replied.

And the pilot—that is to say, the true pilot—is he a captain of sailors or a mere sailor?

A captain of sailors.

The circumstance that he sails in the ship is not to be reckoned; this is an accident only, and has nothing to do with the name pilot, which is significant of his skill and of his authority.

Very true, he said.

Now, I said, each of these has an interest?

Certainly.

And the art has to find and provide for this interest?

Yes, that is the aim of the art.

And the interest of each of the arts is the perfection of each of them; nothing but that?

What do you mean?

I mean what I may illustrate negatively by the example of the body. Suppose you were to ask me whether the body is self-sufficing or has wants, I should reply: Certainly the body has wants; for the body may be ill and require to be cured, and has therefore interests to which the art of medicine ministers; and this is the origin and intention of medicine, as you will acknowledge. Am I not right in saying that?

Quite right, he replied.

342 But is the art of medicine or any other art faulty or deficient in any quality in the same way that the eye may be deficient in sight or the ear fail of hearing, and, in consequence of this defect, require another art to provide for the interest of seeing and hearing? Has art, I say, any similar liability to fault or defect, and does every art require another supplementary art to provide for its interests, and that another and another without end? Or may the arts be said to look after their own interests? Or have they no need of either—having no faults or defects, they have no need to correct them, either by the exercise of their own art or of any other—that is not required of them for the preservation of their interest; they have only to consider the interest of their subject-matter, for every art remains pure and faultless while remaining true—that is to say, while perfect and unimpaired? Is not all this clear? And I would have you take the words in your precise manner.

Yes, that is clear.

Then medicine does not consider the interest of medicine, but the interest of the body.

True, he said.

Nor does farriery consider the interests of farriery, but the interests of the horse; neither do any other arts care for themselves, for they have no needs, but they care only for that which is the subject of their art?

True, he said.

But surely, I added, the arts are the superiors and rulers of their own subjects: you will admit that, Thrasymachus?

To this he assented with a good deal of reluctance.

Then, I said, no science or art considers or enjoins the interest of the stronger or superior, but only the interest of the subject and weaker?

He acquiesced in this after a feint of resistance.

Then, I continued, no physician, in as far as he is a physician, considers his own good but the good of the patient; for the true physician is also a ruler having the human body as a subject, and is not a mere money-maker; that has been admitted?

Yes.

And the pilot likewise, in the strict sense of the term, is a ruler of sailors and not a mere sailor?

That has been admitted.

And such a pilot and ruler will provide and prescribe for the interest of the sailor who is under him, and not for his own or the ruler's interest?

He gave a very reluctant "Yes."

Then, I said, Thrasymachus, there is no one in any rule who, in as far as he is a ruler, considers or enjoins that which is for his own interest, but always that which is for the interest of his subject and of his art; to that he looks, and that alone he considers in everything which he says and does.

343   When we had got to this point in the argument, and every one saw that the definition of justice had been completely reversed, Thrasymachus ... said ... you further imagine that the rulers of States, who are true rulers, never think of their subjects as sheep, and that they are not studying their own advantage day and night. O, no; and so entirely astray are you in the very rudiments of justice and injustice as not even to know that justice and the just are in reality another's good; that is to say, the interest of the ruler and stronger, and the loss of the subject and servant; whereas the reverse holds in the case of injustice; for the unjust is lord over the truly simple and just: he is the stronger, and his subjects do what is for his benefit, and minister to his happiness, which is very far from being their own. Consider further, most foolish Socrates, that the just is always a loser in comparison with the unjust. First of all in their private dealings: whenever the unjust is the partner of the just the conclusion of the affair always is that the unjust man has more and the just less. Next in their dealings with the State: when there is an income tax the just man will pay more and the unjust less on the same amount of income; and when there is anything to be received the one gains nothing and the other much. Observe also that when they come into office, there is the just man neglecting his affairs and perhaps suffering other losses, but he will not compensate himself out of the public purse because he is just; moreover he is hated by his friends and relations for refusing to serve them in unlawful ways. Now all this is reversed in the case of the unjust man. I am speaking of injustice on a large scale in which the advantage of the unjust is most apparent, and my meaning will be most

344   clearly seen in that highest form of injustice the perpetrator of which is the

happiest of men, as the sufferers or those who refuse to do injustice are the most miserable—I mean tyranny, which by fraud and force takes away the property of others, not retail but wholesale; comprehending in one, things sacred as well as profane, private and public; for any one of which acts of wrong, if he were detected perpetrating them singly, he would be punished and incur greater dishonor; for they who are guilty of any of these crimes in single instances are called robbers of temples, and man-stealers and burglars and swindlers and thieves. But when a man has taken away the money of the citizens and made slaves of them, then, instead of these dishonorable names, he is called happy and blessed, not only by the citizens but by all who hear of his having achieved the consummation of injustice. For injustice is censured because the censurers are afraid of suffering, and not from any fear which they have of doing injustice. And thus, as I have shown, Socrates, injustice, when on a sufficient scale, has more strength and freedom and mastery than justice; and, as I said at first, justice is the interest of the stronger, whereas injustice is a man's own profit and interest.

... So far am I from agreeing with Thrasymachus that justice is the interest of the stronger. That, however, is a question which I will not now further discuss; but when Thrasymachus says that the life of the unjust is more advantageous than that of the just, this new statement of his appears to me to be a far more serious matter. Which of us is right, Glaucon? And which sort of life do you deem most advantageous?

The life of the just, he answered.

348   Did you hear all the advantages of the unjust which Thrasymachus was rehearsing?

Yes, I heard him, but I was not convinced by him.

And would you desire to convince him, if we can only find a way, that he is saying what is not true?

Most certainly, he replied.

If, I said, he makes a set speech, and we make another set speech and tell our friend all the good of being just, and he answers and we rejoin, there must be a numbering and measuring of the goods that are claimed on either side, and the end will be that we shall want judges to decide; but if we proceed in our inquiry as we lately did, by a method of mutual agreement, we shall unite the office of judge and advocate in our own persons.

Very good, he said.

And which method do I understand you to prefer? I said.

That which you propose.

Well then, Thrasymachus, I said, suppose that you begin at the beginning and answer me. Your statement is that perfect injustice is more gainful than justice?

Yes, that is my statement, the grounds of which I have also stated.

And you would call one of them virtue and the other vice?

Certainly.

I suppose that you would call justice virtue and injustice vice?

That is a charming notion and so likely, seeing that I affirm injustice to be profitable and justice not.

What else then?

The opposite, he replied.

And would you call justice vice?

No, I would rather say sublime simplicity.

And would you call injustice malignity?

No; I would rather say discretion.

And do the unjust appear to you to be wise and good?

Yes, he said; at any rate this is true of those who are able to be perfectly unjust, and who have the power of subduing States and nations; but I dare say that you imagine me to be talking of cutpurses. Even that, if undetected, has advantages though they are hardly worth mentioning when compared with the other.

I do not think that I misapprehend your meaning, Thrasymachus, I replied; but still I cannot hear without amazement that you class injustice with wisdom and virtue, and justice with the opposite.

Certainly, that is the way in which I do class them.

Now, I said, you are on more substantial and almost unanswerable ground; for if the injustice which you were maintaining to be profitable had been admitted by you or by other men to be vice and deformity, an answer might have been given to you on received principles; but now I perceive that you will call injustice strong and honorable, and to the unjust you will assign all the qualities which were assigned by us before to the just, seeing that you do not hesitate to place injustice on the side of wisdom and virtue.

That is exactly the truth, he replied.

Now, I said, I see that you are speaking your mind, and therefore I do not shrink from the argument; for I do believe, Thrasymachus, that you are in earnest, and are not amusing yourself at our expense.

What is it to you, he said, whether I am in earnest or not? Your business is to refute the argument.

Very true, I said; and will you be so good as to answer another question?—Does the just man try to gain any advantage over the just?

Far otherwise; if he did he would not be the simple amusing creature which he is.

And does he try to gain more than his just share in action?

He does not.

And how would he regard the attempt to gain an advantage over the unjust man or action; would that be considered by him as just or unjust?

He would think that just, and would try to gain the advantage. But he could not.

Whether he could or could not, I said, is not the question. I simply asked whether the just man, while refusing to have more than another just man, would wish and claim to have more than the unjust?

Yes, he would.

And what of the unjust—does he claim more than the just man and more than the just action?

Of course, he said, he claims to have more than all men.

And the unjust man will desire more than the unjust man and action, and will strive to get more than all?

True.

Let us put the matter thus, I said; the just does not desire more than his like but more than his unlike, whereas the unjust desires more than both like and unlike.

Nothing, he said, can be better than that statement.

And the unjust is good and wise, and the just is neither?

Good again, he said.

And is not the unjust like the wise and good and the just unlike them?

Of course, he said, he who is just is like the just, and the unjust is like the unjust.

Each of them, I said, is such as his like is?

Certainly, he replied.

Then now, Thrasymachus, I said, let us try these statements by the analogy of the arts. You would admit that one man is a musician and another not a musician?

Yes.

And the musician is wise, and he who is not a musician is unwise?

True.

And in that he is wise he is good, and in that he is unwise he is bad?

Yes.

And you would say the same sort of thing of the physician?

Yes.

And do you think, my excellent friend, that a musician when he adjusts the lyre would desire or claim to be in excess of a musician in the tightening or loosening the strings?

I do not think that he would.

But he would claim to be in excess of the non-musician?

Of course.

350   And what would you say of the physician? In prescribing meats and drinks would he wish to go beyond another physician or beyond the art of medicine?

He would not.

But he would wish to exceed the non-physician?

Yes.

And about knowledge and ignorance in general; see whether you think that any man of intelligence whatsoever would wish to have the choice of saying or doing more than another man of intelligence. Would he not rather say or do the same as his like in the same case?

That I suppose is not to be denied.

And what would you say of the unintelligent? Would he not desire to have more than either intelligent or unintelligent?

That, I suppose, must be as you say.

And the intelligent is wise?

Yes.

And the wise is good?

True.

Then the wise and good will not desire to gain more than his like, but more than his unlike?

That is evident.

Whereas the bad and ignorant will desire to gain more than both?

Yes.

But were you not saying, Thrasymachus, that the unjust exceeds both his like and unlike?

Yes, I did say that.

And you also said that the just will not exceed his like but his unlike?

Yes, he said.

Then the just is like the wise and good, and the unjust like the evil and ignorant?

That is the inference.

And each of them is such as his like is?

That was admitted.

Then the just has turned out to be wise and good and the unjust evil and ignorant. . .

. . . that the just are clearly wiser and better and abler than the unjust, and that the unjust are incapable of common action—this has been already shown; nay more, when we speak thus confidently of gangs of evil-doers acting together, this is not strictly true, for if they had been perfectly unjust, they would have laid hands upon one another; but there must evidently have been some remnant of justice in them, or they would have injured one another as well as their victims, and then they would have been unable to act together; they were but semi-villainous, for had they been whole villains, wholly unjust, they would have been wholly incapable of action. That, as I believe, is the truth of the matter, and not what you said at first. But whether the just have a better and happier life than the unjust is a further question which we also proposed to consider. I think that they have, and for the reasons which I have given; but still I should like to examine further, for this is no light matter, concerning nothing less than the true rule of life.

Proceed.

I will proceed by asking a question: Would you not think that a horse has some end or use?

I should.

And that would be the end or use of a horse or anything which could not be accomplished, or not so well accomplished, by any other thing?

I do not understand, he said.

Let me explain then. Can you see, except with the eye?

Certainly not.

Or hear, except with the ear?

No.

These then are the uses or ends of these faculties?

They are.

353 But you can cut off a vine-branch with a carving-knife or with a chisel?

Of course.

And yet not so well as with a pruning-hook made for the purpose?

True.

May we not say, then, that this is the use of the pruning-hook?

We may.

Then now I think you will have no difficulty in understanding my meaning when I said that the end or use of anything was that which could not be accomplished, or not so well accomplished, by any other thing?

I understand your meaning, he said, and assent.

And as all things have ends, have they not also excellence? Need I ask again whether the eye has an end?

It has.

And has not the eye an excellence?

Yes.

And the ear has an end and an excellence also?

True.

And the same is true of all other things; they have each of them an end and a special excellence?

That is so.

Well, and can the eyes fulfill their end if they are wanting in their own proper excellence and have a defect instead?

How can they, he said, if they are blind?

You mean to say, if they have lost their proper excellence, which is sight; but I have not arrived at that point yet. I would rather ask the question more generally, and only inquire whether the things which fulfill their ends fulfill them by their own proper excellence, and fail of fulfilling them by their proper defect?

Yes, I assent to that, he replied.

I might say the same of the ears; when deprived of their own proper excellence they cannot fulfill their end?

True.

And the same may be said of all other things?

I agree.

And has not the soul an end which nothing else can fulfill? for example, to provide and command and advise, and the like. Are not these peculiar to the soul, and can they rightly be assigned to any other?

To no other.

And is not life to be reckoned among the ends of the soul?

Assuredly, he said.

And has not the soul an excellence also?

Yes.

And can she or can she not fulfill her ends or uses when deprived of that excellence?

She cannot.

Then an evil soul must necessarily be an evil ruler, and a good soul a good ruler?

Yes, that must be as you say.

And we have admitted that justice is the excellence of the soul, and injustice the defect of the soul?

That has been admitted.

Then the just soul and the just man will live well, and the unjust man will live ill?

That is involved in your argument.

354   And he who lives well will be blessed and happy, and he who lives ill the reverse of happy?

Certainly.

Then the just is happy, and the unjust miserable?

Granted.

But happiness and not misery is profitable. Then, my blessed Thrasymachus, injustice can never be more profitable than justice.

Book VI

... You have to imagine, then, that there are two ruling powers, and that one of them is set over the intellectual world, the other over the visible. I do not say heaven, lest you should fancy that I was refining about the name (οὐρανός, ὁρατός). May I suppose that you have this distinction of the visible and intelligible fixed in your mind?

I have.

Now take a line which has been cut into two unequal parts, and divide each of them again in the same proportion, and suppose the two main divisions to answer, one to the visible and the other to the intelligible, and then compare the subdivisions as to their relative clearness and want of clearness, and you will find that the first section in the sphere of the visible consists of images. And by images I mean, in the first place, shadows, and in the second place, reflections in water 510 and in solid, smooth and polished bodies, and all that sort of thing, as you understand.

Yes. I understand.

Imagine now, the other section, of which this is only the resemblance, to include ourselves and the animals, and everything in nature and everything in art.

Very good.

Would you not admit that this latter section has a different degree of truth, and that the copy is to the object which is copied as the sphere of opinion is to the sphere of knowledge?

Most undoubtedly.

Next proceed to consider the manner in which the sphere of the intellectual is to be divided.

In what manner?

As thus: there are two subdivisions, in the lower of which the soul uses the figures given by the former division as images; the inquiry can only be hypothetical, and instead of going upwards to a principle descends to the other end; in the higher of the two, the soul passes out of hypotheses, and goes up to a principle which is above hypotheses, making no use of images as in the former case, but proceeding only in and by the ideas themselves.

I do not quite understand your meaning, he said.

I will try again. I said: for you will understand me better now that I have made these preliminary remarks. You are aware that students of geometry, arithmetic, and the kindred sciences assume the odd and the even and the figures and three kinds of angles and the like in their several branches of science; these are their hypotheses, which everybody is supposed to know, and of which therefore they do not deign to give any account either to themselves or others; but they begin with these, and go on until they arrive at last, and in a consistent manner, at their conclusion?

Yes, he said, I know that.

And do you know also that although they use and reason about the visible forms, they are thinking not of these, but of the ideals which they resemble; not of the figures which they draw, but of the absolute square and the absolute diameter, and so on: and, while using as images these very forms which they draw or make, and which in turn have their shadows and reflections in the water, they are really seeking for the things themselves, which can only be seen with the eye of the mind?

511   That is true.

And of this kind I still spoke as intelligible, although in inquiries of this sort the soul is compelled to use hypotheses; not proceeding to a first principle because unable to ascend above hypotheses, but using as images the objects of which the shadows are resemblances in a still lower sphere, they having in relation to the shadows a higher value and distinctness.

I understand, he said, that you are speaking of geometry and the sister arts.

And when I speak of the other division of the intellectual, you will also understand me to speak of that knowledge which reason herself attains by the power of dialectic, using the hypotheses not as first principles, but only as hypotheses—that is to say, as steps and points of departure into a region which is above hypotheses, in order that she may soar beyond them to the first principle of the whole; and clinging to this and then to that which depends on this, by successive steps she descends again without the aid of any sensible object, beginning and ending in ideas.

I understand you he replied; not perfectly, for the matter of which you speak is too great for that; but, at any rate, I understand you to say that knowledge and being, which the science of dialectic contemplates, are clearer than the notions of the arts, as they are termed, which proceed from hypotheses only: these are also contemplated by the understanding, and not by the senses: yet, because they start from hypotheses and do not ascend to a principle, those who contemplate them appear to you not to exercise the higher reason upon them, although when a first principle is added to them they are cognizable by the higher reason. And the habit which is concerned with geometry and the cognate sciences I suppose that you would term understanding and not reason, as being intermediate between opinion and reason.

You have quite conceived me, I said; and now, corresponding to these four sections, let there be four faculties in the soul—reason answering to the highest, understanding to the second, faith or persuasion to the third, and knowledge of shadows to the last—and let there be a scale of them, and let us suppose that the several faculties have clearness in the same degree that their objects have truth.

I understand, he replied, and give my assent, and will arrange them as you say.

Book VII

After this, I said, imagine the enlightenment or ignorance of our nature in a figure: Behold! human beings living in a sort of underground den, which has a mouth open towards the light and reaching all across the den; they have been here from their childhood, and have their legs and necks chained so that they cannot move, and can only see before them; for the chains are arranged in such a manner as to prevent them from turning round their heads. At a distance above and behind them the light of a fire is blazing, and between the fire and the prisoners there is a raised way; and you will see, if you look, a low wall built along the way, like the screen which marionette players have before them, over which they show the puppets.

I see, he said.

And do you see, I said, men passing along the wall carrying vessels, which appear over the wall; also figures of men and animals, made of wood and stone and 515 various materials; and some of the passengers, as you would expect, are talking, and some of them are silent?

That is a strange image, he said, and they are strange prisoners.

Like ourselves, I replied; and they see only their own shadows, or the shadows of one another, which the fire throws on the opposite wall of the cave?

True, he said; how could they see anything but the shadows if they were never allowed to move their heads?

And of the objects which are being carried in like manner they would only see the shadows?

Yes, he said.

And if they were able to talk with one another, would they not suppose that they were naming what was actually before them?

Very true.

And suppose further that the prison had an echo which came from the other side, would they not be sure to fancy that the voice which they heard was that of a passing shadow?

No question, he replied.

There can be no question, I said, that the truth would be to them just nothing but the shadows of the images.

That is certain.

And now look again, and see how they are released and cured of their folly. At first, when any one of them is liberated and compelled suddenly to go up and turn his neck round and walk and look at the light, he will suffer sharp pains; the glare will distress him, and he will be unable to see the realities of which in his former state he had seen the shadows; and then imagine some one saying to him, that what he saw before was an illusion, but that now he is approaching real being and has a truer sight and vision of more real things—what will be his reply? And you may further imagine that his instructor is pointing to the objects as they pass and requiring him to name them,—will he not be in a difficulty? Will he not fancy that the shadows which he formerly saw are truer than the objects which are now shown to him?

Far truer.

And if he is compelled to look at the light, will he not have a pain in his eyes which will make him turn away to take refuge in the object of vision which he can see, and which he will conceive to be clearer than the things which are not being shown to him?

True, he said.

And suppose once more, that he is reluctantly dragged up a steep and rugged ascent, and held fast and forced into the presence of the sun himself, do you not think that he will be pained and irritated, and when he approaches the light he will have his eyes dazzled, and will not be able to see any of the realities which are not affirmed to be the truth?

Not all in a moment, he said.

He will require to get accustomed to the sight of the upper world. And first he will see the shadows best, next the reflections of men and other objects in the water, and then the objects themselves; next he will gaze upon the light of the moon and the stars; and he will see the sky and the stars by night, better than the sun, or the light of the sun, by day?

Certainly.

And at last he will be able to see the sun, and not mere reflections of him in the water, but he will see him as he is in his own proper place, and not in another, and he will contemplate his nature.

Certainly.

And after this he will reason that the sun is he who gives the seasons and the years, and is the guardian of all that is in the visible world, and in a certain way the cause of all things which he and his fellows have been accustomed to behold?

Clearly, he said, he would come to the other first and to this afterwards.

And when he remembered his old habitation, and the wisdom of the den and his fellow-prisoners, do you not suppose that he would felicitate himself on the change, and pity them? . . .

Yes, he said, I think that he would rather suffer anything than live after their manner.

Imagine once more, I said, that such an one coming suddenly out of the sun were to be replaced in his old situation, is he not certain to have his eyes full of darkness?

Very true, he said.

And if there were a contest, and he had to compete in measuring the shadows with the prisoners who have never moved out of the den, during the time that his 517 sight is weak, and before his eyes are steady (and the time which would be needed to acquire this new habit of sight might be very considerable), would he not be ridiculous? Men would say of him that up he went and down he comes without his eyes; and that there was no use in even thinking of ascending: and if any one tried to loose another and lead him up to the light, let them only catch the offender in the act, and they would put him to death.

No question, he said.

This allegory, I said, you may now append to the previous argument; the prison is the world of sight, the light of the fire is the sun, the ascent and vision of the things above you may truly regard as the upward progress of the soul into the intellectual world; that is my poor belief, to which, at your desire, I have given expression. Whether I am right or not God only knows; but, whether true or false, my opinion is that in the world of knowledge the idea of good appears last of all, and is seen only with an effort; and, when seen, is also inferred to be the universal author of all things beautiful and right, parent of light and the lord of light in this world, and the source of truth and reason in the other: this is the first great cause which he who would act rationally either in public or private life must behold.

I agree, he said, as far as I am able to understand you.

I should like to have your agreement in another matter, I said. For I would not have you marvel that those who attain to this beatific vision are unwilling to descend to human affairs; but their souls are ever hastening into the upper world in which they desire to dwell; and this is very natural, if our allegory may be trusted.

Certainly, that is quite natural. . .

518   Any one who has common sense will remember that the bewilderments of the eyes are of two kinds, and arise from two causes, either from coming out of the light or from going into the light, which is true of the mind's eye, quite as much as of the bodily eye; and he who remembers this when he sees the soul of any one whose vision is perplexed and weak, will not be too ready to laugh; he will first ask whether that soul has come out of the brighter life, and is unable to see because unaccustomed to the dark, or having turned from darkness to the day is dazzled by excess of light. And then he will count the one happy in his condition and state of being, and he will pity the other; or, if he have a mind to laugh at the soul which comes from below into the light, there will be more reason in this than in the laugh which greets the other from the den.

That, he said, is a very just remark.

But if this is true, then certain professors of education must be mistaken in saying that they can put a knowledge into the soul which was not there before, like giving eyes to the blind.

Yes, that is what they say, he replied.

Whereas, I said, our argument shows that the power is already in the soul; and that as the eye cannot turn from darkness to light without the whole body, so too, when the eye of the soul is turned round, the whole soul must be turned from the world of generation into that of being, and become able to endure the sight of being, and of the brightest and best of being—that is to say, of the good.

Very true.

Aristotle

Nicomachean Ethics

Book I

1 Every art and every inquiry, and similarly every action and pursuit, is thought to aim at some good; and for this reason the good has rightly been declared to be that at which all things aim. But a certain difference is found among ends; some are activities, others are products apart from the activities that produce them. Where

From *Ethica Nicomachea,* trans. by W. D. Ross for *The Oxford Translation of Aristotle,* edited by W. D. Ross, vol. 9 (1925). Reprinted by permission of Oxford University Press.

there are ends apart from the actions, it is the nature of the products to be better than the activities. Now, as there are many actions, arts, and sciences, their ends also are many; the end of the medical art is health, that of shipbuilding a vessel, that of strategy victory, that of economics wealth. But where such arts fall under a single capacity—as bridle-making and the other arts concerned with the equipment of horses fall under the art of riding, and this and every military action under strategy, in the same way other arts fall under yet others—in all of these the ends of the master arts are to be preferred to all the subordinate ends; for it is for the sake of the former that the latter are pursued. It makes no difference whether the activities themselves are the ends of the actions, or something else apart from the activities, as in the case of the sciences just mentioned.

2 If, then, there is some end of the things we do, which we desire for its own sake (everything else being desired for the sake of this), and if we do not choose everything for the sake of something else (for at that rate the process would go on to infinity, so that our desire would be empty and vain), clearly this must be the good and the chief good. Will not the knowledge of it, then, have a great influence on life? Shall we not, like archers who have a mark to aim at, be more likely to hit upon what is right? If so, we must try, in outline at least to determine what it is, and of which of the sciences or capacities it is the object. It would seem to belong to the most authoritative art and that which is most truly the master art. And politics appears to be of this nature: for it is this that ordains which of the sciences should be studied in a state, and which each class of citizens should learn and up to what point they should learn them; and we see even the most highly esteemed of capacities to fall under this, e. g. strategy, economics, rhetoric; now, since politics uses the rest of the sciences, and since, again, it legislates as to what we are to do and what we are to abstain from, the end of this science must include those of the others, so that this end must be the good for man. For even if the end is the same for a single man and for a state, that of the state seems at all events something greater and more complete whether to attain or to preserve; though it is worth while to attain the end merely for one man, it is finer and more godlike to attain it for a nation or for city-states. These, then, are the ends at which our inquiry aims, since it is political science, in one sense of that term. . . .

5 . . . To judge from the lives that men lead, most men, and men of the most vulgar type, seem (not without some ground) to identify the good, or happiness, with pleasure; which is the reason why they love the life of enjoyment. For there are, we may say, three prominent types of life—that just mentioned, the political, and thirdly the contemplative life. Now the mass of mankind are evidently quite slavish in their tastes, preferring a life suitable to beasts, but they get some ground for their view from the fact that many of those in high places share the tastes of Sardanapallus. A consideration of the prominent types of life shows that people of superior refinement and of active disposition identify happiness with honour; for this is, roughly speaking, the end of the political life. But it seems too superficial to what we are looking for, since it is thought to depend on those who bestow honour rather than on him who receives it, but the good we divine to be something proper to a man and not easily taken from him. Further, men seem to pursue honour in order that they may be assured of their goodness: at least it is by men of practical wisdom that they seek to be honoured, and among those who know them, and on the ground of their virtue; clearly, then, according to them, at any rate, virtue is better. And perhaps one might even suppose this to be, rather than honour, the end of the political life. But even this appears somewhat incomplete; for possession of virtue seems actually compatible with being asleep, or with lifelong inactivity, and, further, with the greatest sufferings and misfortunes: but a man who was living so no one would call happy, unless he were maintaining a thesis at all costs. But enough of this; for the subject has been sufficiently treated even in the current discussions. Third comes the contemplative life, which we shall consider later.

The life of money-making is one undertaken under compulsion, and wealth is evidently not the good we are seeking; for it is merely useful and for the sake of something else. And so one might rather take the aforenamed objects to be ends; for they are loved for themselves. But it is evident that not even these are ends; yet many arguments have been thrown away in support of them. Let us leave this subject, then.

6 We had perhaps better consider the universal good and discuss thoroughly what is meant by it, although such an inquiry is made an uphill one by the fact that the Forms have been introduced by friends of our own. Yet it would perhaps be thought to be better, indeed to be our duty, for the sake of maintaining the truth even to destroy what touches us closely, especially as we are philosophers or lovers of wisdom; for, while both are dear, piety requires us to honour truth above our friends. . . .

. . . Clearly, then, goods must be spoken of in two ways, and some must be good in themselves, the others by reason of these. Let us separate, then, things good in themselves from things useful, and consider whether the former are called good by reference to a single Idea. What sort of goods would one call good in themselves? Is it those that are pursued even when isolated from others, such as intelligence, sight, and certain pleasures and honours? Certainly, if we pursue these also for the sake of something else, yet one would place them among things good in themselves. Or is nothing other than the Idea of good good in itself? In that case the Form will be empty. But if the things we have named are also things good in themselves, the account of the good will have to appear as something identical in them all, as that of whiteness is identical in snow and in white lead. But of honour, wisdom, and pleasure, just in respect of their goodness, the accounts are distinct and diverse. The good, therefore, is not some common element answering to one Idea. . . .

7 Let us again return to the good we are seeking, and ask what it can be. It seems different in different actions and arts; it is different in medicine, in strategy, and in the other arts likewise. What then is the good of each? Surely that for whose sake everything else is done. In medicine this is health, in strategy victory, in architecture a house, in any other sphere something else, and in every action and pursuit the end; for it is for the sake of this that all men do whatever else they do. Therefore, if there is an end for all that we do, this will be the good achievable by action, and if there are more than one, these will be the goods achievable by action.

So the argument has by a different course reached the same point; but we must try to state this even more clearly. Since there are evidently more than one end, and we choose some of these (e.g., wealth, flutes, and in general instruments) for the sake of something else, clearly not all ends are final ends; but the chief good is evidently something final. Therefore, if there is only one final end, this will be what we are seeking, and if there are more than one, the most final of these will be what we are seeking. Now we call that which is in itself worthy of pursuit more final than that which is worthy of pursuit for the sake of something else, and that which is never desirable for the sake of something else more final than the things that are desirable both in themselves and for the sake of that other thing, and therefore we call final without qualification that which is always desirable in itself and never for the sake of something else.

Now such a thing happiness, above all else, is held to be; for this we choose always for itself and never for the sake of something else, but honour, pleasure, reason, and every virtue we choose indeed for themselves (for if nothing resulted from them we should still choose each of them), but we choose them also for the sake of happiness, judging that by means of them we shall be happy. Happiness, on the other hand, no one chooses for the sake of these, nor, in general, for anything other than itself.

From the point of view of self-sufficiency the same result seems to follow; for the final good is thought to be self-sufficient. Now by self-sufficient we do not mean that which is sufficient for a man by himself, for one who lives a solitary life, but also for parents, children, wife, and in general for his friends and fellow citizens, since man is born for citizenship. But some limit must be set to this; for if we extend our requirement to ancestors and descendants and friends' friends we are in for an infinite series. Let us examine this question, however, on another occasion; the self-sufficient we now define as that which when isolated makes life desirable and lacking in nothing; and such we think happiness to be; and further we think it most desirable of all things, without being counted as one good thing among others —if it were so counted it would clearly be made more desirable by the addition of even the least of goods; for that which is added becomes an excess of goods, and of goods the greater is always more desirable. Happiness, then, is something final and self-sufficient, and is the end of action.

Presumably, however, to say that happiness is the chief good seems a platitude, and a clearer account of what it is is still desired. This might perhaps be given, if we could first ascertain the function of man. For just as for a flute-player, a sculptor, or any artist, and, in general, for all things that have a function or activity, the good and the 'well' is thought to reside in the function, so would it seem to be for man, if he has a function. Have the carpenter, then, and the tanner certain functions or activities, and has man none? Is he born without a function? Or as eye, hand, foot, and in general each of the parts evidently has a function, may one lay it down that man similarly has a function apart from all these? What then can this be? Life seems to be common even to plants, but we are seeking what is peculiar to man. Let us exclude, therefore, the life of nutrition and growth. Next there would be a life of perception, but *it* also seems to be common even to the horse, the ox, and every animal. There remains, then, an active life of the element that has a rational principle; of this, one part has such a principle in the sense of being obedient to one, the other in the sense of possessing one and exercising thought. And, as "life of the rational element" also has two meanings, we must state that life in the sense of activity is what we mean; for this seems to be the more proper sense of the term.

Now if the function of man is an activity of soul which follows or implies a rational principle, and if we say "a so-and-so" and "a good so-and-so" have a function which is the same in kind, e.g., a lyre-player and a good lyre-player, and so without qualification in all cases, eminence in respect of goodness being added to the name of the function (for the function of a lyre-player is to play the lyre, and that of a good lyre-player is to do so well): if this is the case, [and we state the function of man to be a certain kind of life, and this to be an activity or actions of the soul implying a rational principle, and the function of a good man to be the good and noble performance of these, and if any action is well performed when it is performed in accordance with the appropriate excellence: if this is the case,] human good turns out to be activity of soul in accordance with virtue, and if there are more than one virtue, in accordance with the best and most complete.

But we must add "in a complete life." For one swallow does not make a summer, nor does one day; and so too one day, or a short time, does not make a man blessed and happy.

Let this serve as an outline of the good. . . .

8 . . . Another belief which harmonizes with our account is that the happy man lives well and does well; for we have practically defined happiness as a sort of good life and good action. . . .

With those who identify happiness with virtue or some one virtue our account is in harmony; for to virtue belongs virtuous activity. But it makes, perhaps, no small difference whether we place the chief good in possession or in use, in state of mind or in activity. For the state of mind may exist without producing any good result, as in a man who is asleep or in some other way quite inactive, but the activity cannot; for one who has the activity will of necessity be acting, and acting well. And as in the Olympic Games it is not the most beautiful and the strongest that are crowned but those who compete (for it is some of these that are victorious), so those who act win, and rightly win, the noble and good things in life.

Their life is also in itself pleasant. For pleasure is a state of *soul,* and to each man that which he is said to be a lover of is pleasant; e.g., not only is a horse pleasant to the lover of horses, and a spectacle to the lover of sights, but also in the same way just acts are pleasant to the lover of justice and in general virtuous acts to the lover of virtue. Now for most men their pleasures are in conflict with one another because these are not by nature pleasant, but the lovers of what is noble find pleasant the things that are by nature pleasant; and virtuous actions are such, so that these are pleasant for such men as well as in their own nature. Their life, therefore, has no further need of pleasure as a sort of adventitious charm, but has its pleasure in itself. For, besides what we have said, the man who does not rejoice in noble actions is not even good; since no one would call a man just who did not enjoy acting justly, nor any man liberal who did not enjoy liberal actions; and similarly in all other cases. If this is so, virtuous actions must be in themselves pleasant. But they are also *good* and *noble,* and have each of these attributes in the highest degree, since the good man judges well about these attributes; his judgment is such as we have described. Happiness then is the best, noblest, and most pleasant thing in the world, and these attributes are not severed . . . For all these properties belong to the best activities; and these, or one—the best—of these, we identify with happiness.

Yet evidently . . . it needs the external goods as well; for it is impossible, or not easy, to do noble acts without the proper equipment. In many actions we use friends and riches and political power as instruments; and there are some things the lack of which takes the lustre from happiness, as good birth, goodly children, beauty; for the man who is very ugly in appearance or ill-born or solitary and childless is not very likely to be happy, and perhaps a man would be still less likely if he had thoroughly bad children or friends or had lost good children or friends by death.

9 For this reason also the question is asked, whether happiness is to be acquired by learning or by habituation or some other sort of training, or comes in virtue of some divine providence or again by chance. Now if there is *any* gift of the gods to men, it is reasonable that happiness should be god-given, and most surely god-given of all human things inasmuch as it is the best. But this question would perhaps be more appropriate to another inquiry; happiness seems, however, even if it is not god-sent but comes as a result of virtue and some process of learning or training, to be among the most god-like things; for that which is the prize and end of virtue seems to be the best thing in the world, and something god-like and blessed. . . .

The answer to the question we are asking is plain also from the definition of happiness; for it has been said to be a virtuous activity of soul, of a certain kind. Of the remaining goods, some must necessarily pre-exist as conditions of happiness, and others are naturally co-operative and useful as instruments. And this will be found to agree with what we said at the outset; for we stated the end of political science to be the best end, and political science spends most of its pains on making the citizens to be of a certain character, viz. good and capable of noble acts.

It is natural, then, that we call neither ox nor horse nor any other of the animals happy; for none of them is capable of sharing in such activity. For this reason also a boy is not happy; for he is not yet capable of such acts, owing to his age; and boys who are called happy are being congratulated by reason of the hopes we have for them. For there is required, as we said, not only complete virtue but also a complete life, since many changes occur in life, and all manner of chances, and the most prosperous may fall into great misfortunes in old age, as is told of Priam in the Trojan Cycle; and one who has experienced such chances and has ended wretchedly no one calls happy.

13 Since happiness is an activity of soul in accordance with perfect virtue, we must consider the nature of virtue; for perhaps we shall thus see better the nature of happiness. . . . [C]learly the virtue we must study is human virtue; for the good we were seeking was human good and the happiness human happiness. By human virtue we mean not that of the body but that of the soul; and happiness also we call an activity of soul. . . .

Of the irrational element one division seems to be widely distributed, and vegetative in its nature, I mean that which causes nutrition and growth; for it is this kind of power of the soul that one must assign to all nurslings and to embryos, and this same power to full-grown creatures; this is more reasonable than to assign some different power to them. Now the excellence of this seems to be common to all species and not specifically human. . . .

There seems to be also another irrational element in the soul—one which in a sense, however, shares in a rational principle. For we praise the rational principle of the continent man and of the incontinent, and the part of their soul that has such a principle, since it urges them aright and towards the best objects; but there is found in them also another element naturally opposed to the rational principle, which fights against and resists that principle. For exactly as paralyzed limbs when we intend to move them to the right turn on the contrary to the left, so is it with the soul; the impulses of incontinent people move in contrary directions. But while in the body we see that which moves astray, in the soul we do not. No doubt, however, we must none the less suppose that in the soul too there is something contrary to the rational principle, resisting and opposing it. In what sense it is distinct from the other elements does not concern us. Now even this seems to have a share in a rational principle . . . at any rate in the continent man it obeys the rational principle —and presumably in the temperate and brave man it is still more obedient; for in him it speaks, on all matters, with the same voice as the rational principle.

Therefore the irrational element also appears to be twofold. For the vegetative element in no way shares in a rational principle, but the appetitive, and in general the desiring element in a sense shares in it, in so far as it listens to and obeys it; this is the sense in which we speak of "taking account" of one's father or one's friends, not that in which we speak of "accounting" for a mathematical property. That the irrational element is in some sense persuaded by a rational principle is indicated also by the giving of advice and by all reproof and exhortation. . . .

Virtue too is distinguished into kinds in accordance with this difference; for we say that some of the virtues are intellectual and others moral, philosophic wisdom and understanding and practical wisdom being intellectual, liberality and temperance moral. For in speaking about a man's character we do not say that he is wise or has understanding but that he is good-tempered or temperate; yet we praise the wise man also with respect to his state of mind; and of states of mind we call those which merit praise virtues.

Book II

1 Virtue, then, being of two kinds, intellectual and moral, intellectual virtue in the main owes both its birth and its growth to teaching (for which reason it requires experience and time), while moral virtue comes about as a result of habit, whence also its name *ethike* is one that is formed by a slight variation from the word *ethos* (habit). From this it is also plain that none of the moral virtues arises in us by nature; for nothing that exists by nature can form a habit contrary to its nature. . . . Neither by nature, then, nor contrary to nature do the virtues arise in us; rather we are adapted by nature to receive them, and are made perfect by habit.

. . . [T]he virtues we get by first exercising them, as also happens in the case of the arts as well. For the things we have to learn before we can do them, we learn by doing them, e.g., men become builders by building and lyre-players by playing the lyre; so too we become just by doing just acts, temperate by doing temperate acts, brave by doing brave acts.

This is confirmed by what happens in states; for legislators make the citizens good by forming habits in them, and this is the wish of every legislator, and those who do not effect it miss their mark, and it is in this that a good constitution differs from a bad one.

Again, it is from the same causes and by the same means that every virtue is both produced and destroyed, and similarly every art; for it is from playing the lyre that both good and bad lyre-players are produced. And the corresponding statement is true of builders and of all the rest; men will be good or bad builders as a result of building well or badly. For if this were not so, there would have been no need of a teacher, but all men would have been born good or bad at their craft. This, then, is the case with the virtues also; by doing the acts that we do in our transactions with other men we become just or unjust, and by doing the acts that we do in the presence of danger, and being habituated to feel fear or confidence, we become brave or cowardly. The same is true of appetites and feelings of anger; some men become temperate and good-tempered, others self-indulgent and irascible, by behaving in one way or the other in the appropriate circumstances. Thus, in one word, states of character arise out of like activities. This is why the activities we exhibit must be of a certain kind; it is because the states of character correspond to the differences between these. It makes no small difference, then, whether we form habits of one kind or of another from our very youth; it makes a very great difference, or rather *all* the difference.

2 Since, then, the present inquiry does not aim at theoretical knowledge like the others (for we are inquiring not in order to know what virtue is, but in order to become good, since otherwise our inquiry would have been of no use), we must examine the nature of actions, namely how we ought to do them; for these determine also the nature of the states of character that are produced, as we have said. Now, that we must act according to the right rule is a common principle and must be assumed—it will be discussed later, i.e., both what the right rule is, and how it is related to the other virtues. But this must be agreed upon beforehand, that the whole account of matters of conduct must be given in outline and not precisely. . . .

But though our present account is of this nature we must given what help we can. First, then, let us consider this, that it is the nature of such things to be destroyed by defect and excess, as we see in the case of strength and of health (for to gain light on things imperceptible we must use the evidence of sensible things); both excessive and defective exercise destroys the strength, and similarly drink or food which is above or below a certain amount destroys the health, while that which is proportionate both produces and increases and preserves it. So too is it, then, in the case of temperance and courage and the other virtues. For the man who flies from and fears everything and does not stand his ground against anything becomes a coward, and the man who fears nothing at all but goes to meet every danger becomes rash; and similarly the man who indulges in every pleasure and abstains from none becomes self-indulgent, while the man who shuns every pleasure, as boors do, becomes in a way insensible; temperance and courage, then, are destroyed by excess and defect, and preserved by the mean.

But not only are the sources and causes of their origination and growth the same as those of their destruction, but also the sphere of their actualization will be the same; for this is also true of the things which are more evident to sense, e.g., of strength; it is produced by taking much food and undergoing much exertion, and it is the strong man that will be most able to do these things. So too is it with the virtues; by abstaining from pleasures we become temperate, and it is when we have become so that we are most able to abstain from them; and similarly too in the case of courage; for by being habituated to despise things that are terrible and to stand our ground against them we become brave, and it is when we have become so that we shall be most able to stand our ground against them.

4 The question might be asked, what we mean by saying that we must become just by doing just acts, and temperate by doing temperate acts; for if men do just and temperate acts, they are already just and temperate, exactly as, if they do what is in accordance with the laws of grammar and of music, they are grammarians and musicians.

Again, the case of the arts and that of the virtues are not similar; for the products of the arts have their goodness in themselves, so that it is enough that they should have a certain character, but if the acts that are in accordance with the virtues have themselves a certain character it does not follow that they are done justly or temperately. The agent also must be in a certain condition when he does them; in the first place he must have knowledge, secondly he must choose the acts, and choose them for their own sakes, and thirdly his action must proceed from a firm and unchangeable character. These are not reckoned in as conditions of the possession of the arts, except the bare knowledge; but as a condition of the possession of the virtues knowledge has little or no weight, while the other conditions count not for a little but for everything, i.e., the very conditions which result from often doing just and temperate acts.

Actions, then, are called just and temperate when they are such as the just or the temperate man would do; but it is not the man who does these that is just and temperate, but the man who also does them *as* just and temperate men do them. It is well said, then, that it is by doing just acts that the just man is produced, and by doing temperate acts the temperate man; without doing these no one would have even a prospect of becoming good.

But most people do not do these, but take refuge in theory and think they are being philosophers and will become good in this way, behaving somewhat like patients who listen attentively to their doctors, but do none of the things they are ordered to do. As the latter will not be made well in body by such a course of treatment, the former will not be made well in soul by such a course of philosophy.

5 Next we must consider what virtue is. Since things that are found in the soul are of three kinds—passions, faculties, states of character, virtue must be one of these. By passions I mean appetite, anger, fear, confidence, envy, joy, friendly feeling, hatred, longing, emulation, pity, and in general the feelings that are accompanied by pleasure or pain; by faculties the things in virtue of which we are said to be capable of feeling these, e.g., of becoming angry or being pained or feeling pity; by states of character the things in virtue of which we stand well or badly with reference to the passions, e.g., with reference to anger we stand badly if we feel it violently or too weakly, and well if we feel it moderately; and similarly with reference to the other passions.

Now neither the virtues nor the vices are *passions,* because we are not called good or bad on the ground of our passions, but are so called on the ground of our virtues and our vices, and because we are neither praised nor blamed for our passions (for the man who feels fear or anger is not praised, nor is the man who simply feels anger blamed, but the man who feels it in a certain way), but for our virtues and our vices we *are* praised or blamed.

Again, we feel anger and fear without choice, but the virtues are modes of choice or involve choice. Further, in respect of the passions we are said to be moved, but in respect of the virtues and the vices we are said not to be moved but to be disposed in a particular way.

For these reasons also they are not *faculties;* for we are neither called good nor bad, nor praised nor blamed, for the simple capacity of feeling the passions; again, we have the faculties by nature, but we are not made good or bad by nature; we have spoken of this before.

If, then, the virtues are neither passions nor faculties, all that remains is that they should be *states of character.*

Thus we have stated what virtue is in respect of its genus.

6 We must, however, not only describe virtue as a state of character, but also say what sort of state it is. We may remark, then, that every virtue or excellence both brings into good condition the thing of which it is the excellence and makes the work of that thing be done well; e.g., the excellence of the eye makes both the eye and its work good; for it is by the excellence of the eye that we see well. Similarly the excellence of the horse makes a horse both good in itself and good at running and at carrying its rider and at awaiting the attack of the enemy. Therefore, if this is true in every case, the virtue of man also will be the state of character which makes a man good and which makes him do his own work well.

How this is to happen we have stated already, but it will be made plain also by the following consideration of the specific nature of virtue. In everything that is continuous and divisible it is possible to take more, less, or an equal amount, and that either in terms of the thing itself or relatively to us; and the equal is an intermediate between excess and defect. By the intermediate in the object I mean that which is equidistant from each of the extremes, which is one and the same for all men; by the intermediate relatively to us that which is neither too much nor too little—and this is not one, nor the same for all. For instance, if ten is many and two is few, six is the intermediate, taken in terms of the object; for it exceeds and is exceeded by an equal amount; this is intermediate according to arithmetical proportion. But the intermediate relatively to us is not to be taken so; if ten pounds are too much for a particular person to eat and two too little, it does not follow that the trainer will order six pounds; for this also is perhaps too much for the person who is to take it, or too little—too little for Milo, too much for the beginner in athletic exercises. The same is true of running and wrestling. Thus a master of any art avoids excess and defect, but seeks the intermediate and chooses this—the intermediate not in the object but relatively to us.

If it is thus, then, that every art does its work well—by looking to the intermediate and judging its works by this standard (so that we often say of good works of art that it is not possible either to take away or to add anything, implying that excess and defect destroy the goodness of works of art, while the mean preserves it; and good artists, as we say, look to this in their work), and if, further, virtue is more exact and better than any art, as nature also is, then virtue must have the quality of aiming at the intermediate. I mean moral virtue, for it is this that is concerned with passions and actions, and in these there is excess, defect, and the intermediate. For instance, both fear and confidence and appetite and anger and pity and in general pleasure and pain may be felt both too much and too little, and in both cases not well; but to feel them at the right times, with reference to the right objects, towards the right people, with the right motive, and in the right way, is what is both intermediate and best, and this is characteristic of virtue. Similarly with regard to actions also there is excess, defect, and the intermediate. Now virtue is concerned with passions and actions, in which excess is a form of failure, and so is defect, while the intermediate is praised and is a form of success; and being praised and being successful are both characteristics of virtue. Therefore virtue is a kind of mean, since, as we have seen, it aims at what is intermediate.

Again, it is possible to fail in many ways (for evil belongs to the class of the unlimited, as the Pythagoreans conjectured, and good to that of the limited), while to succeed is possible only in one way (for which reason also one is easy and the other difficult—to miss the mark easy, to hit it difficult); for these reasons also, then, excess and defect are characteristic of vice, and the mean of virtue;

For men are good in but one way, but bad in many.

Virtue, then, is a state of character concerned with choice, lying in a mean, i.e., the mean relative to us, this being determined by a rational principle, and by that principle by which the man of practical wisdom would determine it. Now it is a mean between two vices, that which depends on excess and that which depends on defect; and again it is a mean because the vices respectively fall short of or exceed what is right in both passions and actions, while virtue both finds and chooses that which is intermediate. Hence in respect of its substance and the definition which states its essence virtue is a mean, with regard to what is best and right an extreme.

But not every action nor every passion admits of a mean; for some have names that already imply badness, e.g., spite, shamelessness, envy, and in the case of actions adultery, theft, murder; for all of these and suchlike things imply by their names that they are themselves bad, and not the excesses or deficiencies of them. It is not possible, then, ever to be right with regard to them; one must always be wrong. Nor does goodness or badness with regard to such things depend on committing adultery with the right woman, at the right time, and in the right way, but simply to do any of them is to go wrong. It would be equally absurd, then, to expect that in unjust, cowardly, and voluptuous action there should be a mean, an excess, and a deficiency; for at that rate there would be a mean of excess and of deficiency, an excess of excess, and a deficiency of deficiency. But as there is no excess and deficiency of temperance and courage because what is intermediate is in a sense an extreme, so too of the actions we have mentioned there is no mean nor any excess and deficiency, but however they are done they are wrong; for in general there is neither a mean of excess and deficiency, nor excess and deficiency of a mean.

7 We must, however, not only make this general statement, but also apply it to the individual facts. For among statements about conduct those which are general apply more widely, but those which are particular are more genuine, since conduct has to do with individual cases, and our statements must harmonize with the facts in these cases. We may take these cases from our table. With regard to feelings of fear and confidence courage is the mean; of the people who exceed, he who exceeds in fearlessness has no name (many of the states have no name), while the man who exceeds in confidence is rash, and he who exceeds in fear and falls short in confidence is a coward. With regard to pleasures and pains—not all of them, and not so much with regard to the pains—the mean is temperance, the excess self-indulgence. Persons deficient with regard to the pleasures are not often found; hence such persons also have received no name. But let us call them "insensible." . . .

9 That moral virtue is a mean, then, and in what sense it is so, and that it is a mean between two vices, the one involving excess, the other deficiency, and that it is such because its character is to aim at what is intermediate in passions and in actions, has been sufficiently stated. Hence also it is no easy task to be good. For in everything it is no easy task to find the middle, e.g., to find the middle of a circle is not for every one but for him who knows; so, too, any one can get angry—that is easy—or give or spend money; but to do this to the right person, to the right extent, at the right time, with the right motive, and in the right way, *that* is not for every one, nor is it easy; wherefore goodness is both rare and laudable and noble.

But we must consider the things toward which we ourselves also are easily carried away; for some of us tend to one thing, some to another; and this will be recognizable from the pleasure and the pain we feel. We must drag ourselves away to the contrary extreme; for we shall get into the intermediate state by drawing well away from error, as people do in straightening sticks that are bent.

Now in everything the pleasant or pleasure is most to be guarded against; for we do not judge it impartially. We ought, then, to feel towards pleasure as the elders of the people felt towards Helen, and in all circumstances repeat their saying; for if we dismiss pleasure thus we are less likely to go astray. It is by doing this, then (to sum the matter up), that we shall best be able to hit the mean.

But this is no doubt difficult, and especially in individual cases; for it is not easy to determine both how and with whom and on what provocation and how long one should be angry; for we too sometimes praise those who fall short and call them good-tempered, but sometimes we praise those who get angry and call them manly. The man, however, who deviates little from goodness is not blamed, whether he do so in the direction of the more or of the less, but only the man who deviates more widely; for *he* does not fail to be noticed. But up to what point and to what extent a man must deviate before he becomes blameworthy it is not easy to determine by reasoning, any more than anything else that is perceived by the senses; such things depend on particular facts, and the decision rests with perception. So much, then, is plain, that the intermediate state is in all things to be praised, but that we must incline sometimes towards the excess, sometimes towards the deficiency; for so shall we most easily hit the mean and what is right.

Book III

1 Since virtue is concerned with passions and actions, and on voluntary passions and actions praise and blame are bestowed, on those that are involuntary pardon, and sometimes also pity, to distinguish the voluntary and the involuntary is presumably necessary for those who are studying the nature of virtue, and useful also for legislators with a view to the assigning both of honours and of punishments.

Those things, then, are thought involuntary, which take place under compulsion or owing to ignorance; and that is compulsory of which the moving principle is outside, being a principle in which nothing is contributed by the person who is acting or is feeling the passion, e.g., if he were to be carried somewhere by a wind, or by men who had him in their power.

But with regard to the things that are done from fear of greater evils or for some noble object (e.g., if a tyrant were to order one to do something base, having one's parents and children in his power, and if one did the action they were to be saved, but otherwise would be put to death), it may be debated whether such actions are involuntary or voluntary. Something of the sort happens also with regard to the throwing of goods overboard in a storm; for in the abstract no one throws goods away voluntarily, but on condition of its securing the safety of himself and his crew any sensible man does so. Such actions, then, are mixed, but are more like voluntary actions; for they are worthy of choice at the time when they are done, and the end of an action is relative to the occasion. Both the terms, then, "voluntary" and "involuntary," must be used with reference to the moment of action. Now the man acts voluntarily; for the principle that moves the instrumental parts of the body in such actions is in him, and the things of which the moving principle is in a man himself are in his power to do or not to do. Such actions, therefore, are voluntary, but in the abstract perhaps involuntary; for no one would choose any such act in itself. . . .

What sort of acts, then, should be called compulsory? We answer that without qualification actions are so when the cause is in the external circumstances and the agent contributes nothing. But the things that in themselves are involuntary, but now and in return for these gains are worthy of choice, and whose moving principle is in the agent, are in themselves involuntary, but now and in return for these gains voluntary. They are more like voluntary acts; for actions are in the class of particulars; and the particular acts here are voluntary. What sort of things are to be chosen, and in return for what, it is not easy to state; for there are many differences in the particular cases.

But if some one were to say that pleasant and noble objects have a compelling power, forcing us from without, all acts would be for him compulsory; for it is for these objects that all men do everything they do. And those who act under compulsion and unwillingly act with pain, but those who do acts for their pleasantness and nobility do them with pleasure; it is absurd to make external circumstances responsible, and not oneself, as being caught by such attractions, and to make oneself responsible for noble acts but the pleasant objects responsible for base acts. The compulsory, then, seems to be that whose moving principle is outside, the person compelled contributing nothing.

Everything that is done by reason of ignorance is *not* voluntary; it is only what produces pain and repentance that is *in*voluntary. For the man who has done something owing to ignorance, and feels not the least vexation at his action, has not acted voluntarily, since he did not know what he was doing, nor yet involuntarily, since he is not pained. Of people, then, who act by reason of ignorance he who repents is thought an involuntary agent, and the man who does not repent may, since he is different, be called a not voluntary agent; for, since he differs from the other, it is better that he should have a name of his own.

Acting by reason of ignorance seems also to be different from acting *in* ignorance; for the man who is drunk or in a rage is thought to act as a result not of ignorance but of one of the causes mentioned, yet not knowingly but in ignorance.

Now every wicked man is ignorant of what he ought to do and what he ought to abstain from, and it is by reason of error of this kind that men become unjust and in general bad; but the term "involuntary" tends to be used not if a man is ignorant of what is to his advantage—for it is not mistaken purpose that causes involuntary action (it leads rather to wickedness), nor ignorance of the universal (for *that* men are *blamed*), but ignorance of particulars, i.e., of the circumstances of the action and the objects with which it is concerned. For it is on these that both pity and pardon depend, since the person who is ignorant of any of these acts involuntarily.

Perhaps it is just as well, therefore, to determine their nature and number. A man may be ignorant, then, of who he is, what he is doing, what or whom he is acting on, and sometimes also what (e.g., what instrument) he is doing it with, and to what end (e.g., he may think his act will conduce to some one's safety), and how he is doing it (e.g., whether gently or violently). Now of all of these no one could be ignorant unless he were mad, and evidently also he could not be ignorant of the agent; for how could he not know himself? But of what he is doing a man might be ignorant. . . . The ignorance may relate, then, to any of these things, i.e., of the circumstances of the action, and the man who was ignorant of any of these is thought to have acted involuntarily, and especially if he was ignorant on the most important points; and these are thought to be the circumstances of the action and its end. Further, the doing of an act that is called involuntary in virtue of ignorance of this sort must be painful and involve repentance.

Since that which is done under compulsion or by reason of ignorance is involuntary, the voluntary would seem to be that of which the moving principle is in the agent himself, he being aware of the particular circumstances of the action. Presumably acts done by reason of anger or appetite are not rightly called involuntary. For in the first place, on that showing none of the other animals will act voluntarily, nor will children; and secondly, is it meant that we do not do voluntarily *any* of the acts that are due to appetite or anger, or that we do the noble acts voluntarily and the base acts involuntarily? Is not this absurd, when one and the same thing is the cause? But it would surely be odd to describe as involuntary the things one ought to desire; and we ought both to be angry at certain things and to have an appetite for certain things, e.g., for health and for learning. Also what is involuntary is thought to be painful, but what is in accordance with appetite is thought to be pleasant. Again, what is the difference in respect of involuntariness between errors committed upon calculation and those committed in anger? Both are to be avoided, but the irrational passions are thought not less human than reason is, and therefore also the actions which proceed from anger or appetite are the man's actions. It would be odd, then, to treat them as involuntary.

2 Both the voluntary and the involuntary having been delimited, we must next discuss choice; for it is thought to be most closely bound up with virtue and to discriminate characters better than actions do.

Choice, then, seems to be voluntary, but not the same thing as the voluntary; the latter extends more widely. For both children and the lower animals share in voluntary action, but not in choice, and acts done on the spur of the moment we describe as voluntary, but not as chosen.

What, then, or what kind of thing is [choice] . . . ? It seems to be voluntary, but not all that is voluntary [is] an object of choice. Is it, then, what has been decided on by previous deliberation? At any rate choice involves a rational principle and thought. Even the name seems to suggest that it is what is chosen before other things.

3 Do we deliberate about everything, and is everything a possible subject of deliberation, or is deliberation impossible about some things? We ought presumably to call not what a fool or a madman would deliberate about, but what a sensible man would deliberate about, a subject of deliberation. Now about eternal things no one deliberates, e.g., about the material universe or the incommensurability of the diagonal and the side of a square. But no more do we deliberate about the things that involve movement but always happen in the same way, whether of necessity or by nature or from any other cause, e.g., the solstices and the risings of the stars; nor about things that happen now in one way, now in another, e.g., droughts and rains: nor about chance events, like the finding of treasure. But we do not deliberate even about all human affairs; for instance, no Spartan deliberates about the best constitution for the Scythians. For none of these things can be brought about by our own efforts.

Now every class of men deliberates about the things that can be done by their own efforts. And in the case of exact and self-contained sciences there is no deliberation, e.g., about the letters of the alphabet (for we have no doubt how they should be written); but the things that are brought about by our own efforts, but not always in the same way, are the things about which we deliberate, e.g., questions of medical treatment or of money-making.) And we do so more in the case of the art of navigation than in that of gymnastics, inasmuch as it has been less exactly worked out, and again about other things in the same ratio, and more also in the case of the arts than in that of the sciences; for we have more doubt about the former. Deliberation is concerned with things that happen in a certain way for the most part, but in which the event is obscure, and with things in which it is indeterminate. We call in others to aid us in deliberation on important questions, distrusting ourselves as not being equal to deciding.

We deliberate not about ends but about means. For a doctor does not deliberate whether he shall heal, nor an orator whether he shall persuade, nor a statesman whether he shall produce law and order, nor does any one else deliberate about his end. They assume the end and consider how and by what means it is to be attained; and if it seems to be produced by several means they consider by which it is most easily and best produced, while if it is achieved by one only they consider how it will be achieved by this and by what means *this* will be achieved, till they come to the first cause, which in the order of discovery is last. . . . And if we come on an impossibility, we give up the search, e.g., if we need money and this cannot be got; but if a thing appears possible we try to do it. By "possible" things I mean things that might be brought about by our own efforts; and these in a sense include things that can be brought about by the efforts of our friends, since the moving principle is in ourselves. The subject of investigation is sometimes the instruments, sometimes the use of them; and similarly in the other cases—sometimes the means, sometimes the mode of using it or the means of bringing it about. It seems, then, as has been said, that man is a moving principle of actions; now deliberation is about the things to be done by the agent himself, and actions are for the sake of things other than themselves. For the end cannot be a subject of deliberation, but only the means; nor indeed can the particular facts be a subject of it, as whether this is bread or has been baked as it should: or these are matters of perception. If we are to be always deliberating, we shall have to go on to infinity.

The same thing is deliberated upon and is chosen, except that the object of choice is already determinate, since it is that which has been decided upon as a result of deliberation that is the object of choice. For every one ceases to inquire how he is to act when he has brought the moving principle back to himself and to the ruling part of himself; for this is what chooses. . . . The object of choice being one of the things in our own power which is desired after deliberation, choice will be deliberate desire of things in our own power; for when we have decided as a result of deliberation, we desire in accordance with our deliberation.

We may take it, then, that we have described choice in outline, and stated the nature of its objects and the fact that it is concerned with means.

5 The end, then, being what we wish for, the means what we deliberate about and choose, actions concerning means must be according to choice and voluntary. Now the exercise of the virtues is concerned with means. Therefore virtue also is in our own power, and so too vice. For where it is in our power to act it is also in our power not to act, and *vice versa;* so that, if to act, where this is noble, is in our power, not to act, which will be base, will also be in our power, and if not to act, where this is noble, is in our power, to act, which will be base, will also be in our power. Now if it is in our power to do noble or base acts, and likewise in our power not to do them, and this was what being good or bad meant, then it is in our power to be virtuous or vicious.

The saying that "no one is voluntarily wicked nor involuntarily happy" seems to be partly false and partly true; for no one is involuntarily happy, but wickedness *is* voluntary. . . .

Witness seems to be borne to this both by individuals in their private capacity and by legislators themselves; for these punish and take vengeance on those who do wicked acts (unless they have acted under compulsion or as a result of ignorance for which they are not themselves responsible), while they honour those who do noble acts, as though they meant to encourage the latter and deter the former. But no one is encouraged to do the things that are neither in our power nor voluntary; it is assumed that there is no gain in being persuaded not to be hot or in pain or hungry or the like, since we shall experience these feelings none the less. Indeed, we punish a man for his very ignorance, if he is thought responsible for the ignorance, as when penalties are doubled in the case of drunkenness; for the moving principle is in the man himself, since he had the power of not getting drunk and his getting drunk was the cause of his ignorance. And we punish those who are ignorant of anything in the laws that they ought to know and that is not difficult, and so too in the case of anything else that they are thought to be ignorant of through carelessness; we assume that it is in their power not to be ignorant, since they have the power of taking care.

But perhaps a man is the kind of man not to take care. Still they are themselves by their slack lives responsible for becoming men of that kind, and men make themselves responsible for being unjust or self-indulgent, in the one case by cheating and in the other by spending their time in drinking bouts and the like; for it is activities exercised on particular objects that make the corresponding character. . . .

But not only are the vices of the soul voluntary, but those of the body also for some men, whom we accordingly blame; while no one blames those who are ugly by nature, we blame those who are so owing to want of exercise and care. So it is, too, with respect to weakness and infirmity; no one would reproach a man blind from birth or by disease or from a blow, but rather pity him, while every one would blame a man who was blind from drunkenness or some other form of self-indulgence. Of vices of the body, then, those in our own power are blamed, those not in our power are not. And if this be so, in the other cases also the vices that are blamed must be in our own power. . . .

. . . If, then, as is asserted, the virtues are voluntary (for we are ourselves somehow partly responsible for our states of character, and it is by being persons of a certain kind that we assume the end to be so and so), the vices also will be voluntary; for the same is true of them.

With regard to the virtues in *general* we have stated their genus in outline, viz., that they are means and that they are states of character, and that they tend, and by their own nature, to the doing of the acts by which they are produced, and that they are in our power and voluntary, and act as the right rule prescribes. But actions and states of character are not voluntary in the same way; for we are masters of our actions from the beginning right to the end, if we know the particular facts, but though we control the beginning of our states of character the gradual progress is not obvious, any more than it is in illnesses; because it was in our power, however, to act in this way or not in this way, therefore the states are voluntary. . . .

Book V

1 With regard to justice and injustice we must consider (1) what kind of actions they are concerned with, (2) what sort of mean justice is, and (3) between what extremes the just act is intermediate. Our investigation shall follow the same course as the preceding discussions.

We see that all men mean by justice that kind of state of character which makes people disposed to do what is just and makes them act justly and wish for what is just; and similarly by injustice that state which makes them act unjustly and wish for what is unjust. . . .

Now "justice" and "injustice" seem to be ambiguous. . . . Let us take as a starting-point, then, the various meanings of "an unjust man." Both the lawless man and the grasping and unfair man are thought to be unjust, so that evidently both the law-abiding and the fair man will be just. The just, then, is the lawful and the fair, the unjust the unlawful and the unfair. . . .

Since the lawless man was seen to be unjust and the law-abiding man just, evidently all lawful acts are in a sense just acts; for the acts laid down by the legislative art are lawful, and each of these, we say, is just. Now the laws in their enactments on all subjects aim at the common advantage either of all or of the best or of those who hold power, or something of the sort; so that in one sense we call those acts just that tend to produce and preserve happiness and its components for the political society. And the law bids us do both the acts of a brave man (e.g., not to desert our post nor take to flight nor throw away our arms), and those of a temperate man (e.g., not to commit adultery nor to gratify one's lust), and those of a good-tempered man (e.g., not to strike another nor to speak evil), and similarly with regard to the other virtues and forms of wickedness, commanding some acts and forbidding others; and the rightly-framed law does this rightly, and the hastily conceived one less well.

This form of justice, then, is complete virtue, but not absolutely, but in relation to our neighbor. And therefore justice is often thought to be the greatest of virtues. . . . And it is complete virtue in its fullest sense, because it is the actual exercise of complete virtue. It is complete because he who possesses it can exercise his virtue not only in himself but toward his neighbour also; for many men can exercise virtue in their own affairs, but not in their relations to their neighbour. . . . [J]ustice, alone of the virtues, is thought to be "another's good," because it is related to our neighbor; for it does what is advantageous to another, either a ruler or a copartner. Now the worst man is he who exercises his wickedness both towards himself and towards his friends, and the best man is not he who exercises his virtue towards himself but he who exercises it towards another; for this is a difficult task. Justice in this sense, then, is not part of virtue but virtue entire, nor is the contrary injustice a part of vice but vice entire. What the difference is between virtue and justice in this sense is plain from what we have said; they are the same but their essence is not the same; what, as a relation to one's neighbour, is justice is, as a certain kind of state without qualification, virtue.

2   But at all events what we are investigating is the justice which is a *part* of virtue; for there is a justice of this kind, as we maintain. Similarly it is with injustice in the particular sense that we are concerned. . . .

It is clear, then, that there is more than one kind of justice, and that there is one which is distinct from virtue entire; we must try to grasp its genus and differentia.

The unjust has been divided into the unlawful and the unfair, and the just into the lawful and the fair. To the unlawful answers the afore-mentioned sense of injustice. But since the unfair and the unlawful are not the same, but are different as a part is from its whole (for all that is unfair is unlawful, but not all that is unlawful is unfair), the unjust and injustice in the sense of the unfair are not the same as but different from the former kind, as part from whole; for injustice in this sense is a part of injustice in the wide sense, and similarly justice in the one sense of justice in the other. Therefore we must speak also about particular justice and particular injustice, and similarly about the just and the unjust. The justice, then, which answers to the whole of virtue, and the corresponding injustice, one being the exercise of virtue as a whole, and the other that of vice as a whole, towards one's neighbour, we may leave on one side. And how the meanings of "just" and "unjust" which answer to these are to be distinguished is evident; for practically the majority of the acts commanded by the law are those which are prescribed from the point of view of virtue taken as a whole; for the law bids us practice every virtue and forbids us to practice any vice. And the things that tend to produce virtue taken as a whole are those of the acts prescribed by the law which have been prescribed with a view to education for the common good. . . .

Of particular justice and that which is just in the corresponding sense, (A) one kind is that which is manifested in distributions of honour or money or the other things that fall to be divided among those who have a share in the constitution (for in these it is possible for one man to have a share either unequal or equal to that of another), and (B) one is that which plays a rectifying part in transactions between man and man. Of this there are two divisions; of transactions (1) some are voluntary and (2) others involuntary—voluntary such transactions as sale, purchase, loan for consumption, pledging, loan for use, depositing, letting (they are called voluntary because the origin of these transactions is voluntary), while of the involuntary *(a)* some are clandestine, such as theft, adultery, poisoning, procuring, enticement of slaves, assassination, false witness, and *(b)* others are violent, such as assault, imprisonment, murder, robbery with violence, mutilation, abuse, insult.

3 . . . Now equality implies at least two things. The just, then, must be both intermediate and equal and relative (i.e., for certain persons). And *qua* intermediate it must be between certain things (which are respectively greater and less); *qua* equal, it involves *two* things; *qua* just, it is for certain people. The just, therefore, involves at least four terms; for the persons for whom it is in fact just are two, and the things in which it is manifested, the objects distributed, are two. And the same equality will exist between the persons and between the things concerned; for as the latter—the things concerned—are related, so are the former; if they are not equal, they will not have what is equal, but this is the origin of quarrels and complaints—when either equals have and are awarded unequal shares, or unequals equal shares. . . .

The just, then, is a species of the proportionate (proportion being not a property only of the kind of number which consists of abstract units, but of number in general). For proportion is equality of ratios, and involves four terms at least. . . .

This, then, is one species of the just.

4 The remaining one is the rectificatory, which arises in connexion with transactions both voluntary and involuntary. This form of the just has a different specific character from the former. . . . For it makes no difference whether a good man has defrauded a bad man or a bad man a good one, nor whether it is a good or a bad man that has committed adultery; the law looks only to the distinctive character of the injury, and treats the parties as equal, if one is in the wrong and the other is being wronged, and if one inflicted injury and the other has received it. Therefore, this kind of injustice being an inequality, the judge tries to equalize . . . things by means of the penalty, taking away from the gain of the assailant. For the term "gain" is applied generally to such cases, even if it be not a term appropriate to certain cases, e.g., to the person who inflicts a wound—and "loss" to the sufferer; at all events when the suffering has been estimated, the one is called loss and the other gain. . . . [C]orrective justice will be the intermediate between loss and gain. This is why, when people dispute, they take refuge in the judge; and to go to the judge is to go to justice; for the nature of the judge is to be a sort of animate justice; and they seek the judge as an intermediate, and in some states they call judges mediators, on the assumption that if they get what is intermediate they will get what is just. The just, then, is an intermediate, since the judge is so. Now the judge restores equality. . . .

6 . . . [Political justice] is found among men who share their life with a view to self-sufficiency, men who are free and either proportionately or arithmetically equal, so that between those who do not fulfill this condition there is no political justice but justice in a special sense and by analogy. For justice exists only between men whose mutual relations are governed by law; and law exists for men between whom there is injustice; for legal justice is the discrimination of the just and the unjust. And between men between whom there is injustice there is also unjust action (though there is not injustice between all between whom there is unjust action), and this is assigning too much to oneself of things good in themselves and too little of things evil in themselves. This is why we do not allow a *man* to rule, but *rational principle,* because a man behaves thus in his own interests and becomes a tyrant. The magistrate on the other hand is the guardian of justice, and, if of justice, then of equality also. And since he is assumed to have no more than his share, if he is just (for he does not assign to himself more of what is good in itself, unless such a share is proportional to his merits—so that it is for others that he labours, and it is for this reason that men, as we stated previously, say that justice is "another good"), therefore a reward must be given him, and this is honour and privilege; but those for whom such things are not enough become tyrants. . . .

7 Of political justice part is natural, part legal—natural, that which everywhere has the same force and does not exist by people's thinking this or that; legal, that which is originally indifferent, but when it has been laid down is not indifferent. . . .

Of things just and lawful each is related as the universal to its particulars; for the things that are done are many, but of *them* each is one, since it is universal.

There is a difference between the act of injustice and what is unjust, and between the act of justice and what is just; for a thing is unjust by nature or by enactment; and this very thing, when it has been done, is an act of injustice, but before it is done is not yet that but is unjust. So, too, with an act of justice. . . .

Book VI

2 What affirmation and negation are in thinking, pursuit and avoidance are in desire; so that since moral virtue is a state of character concerned with choice, and choice is deliberate desire, therefore both the reasoning must be true and the desire right, if the choice is to be good, and the latter must pursue just what the former asserts. . . .

The origin of action—its efficient, not its final cause—is choice, and that of choice is desire and reasoning with a view to an end. This is why choice cannot exist either without reason and intellect or without a moral state; for good action and its opposite cannot exist without a combination of intellect and character. Intellect itself, however, moves nothing, but only the intellect which aims at an end and is practical; for this rules the productive intellect as well, since every one who makes makes for an end, and that which is made is not an end in the unqualified sense (but only an end in a particular relation, and the end of a particular operation)—only that which is *done* is that; for good action is an end, and desire aims at this. Hence choice is either desiderative reason or ratiocinative desire, and such an origin of action is a man. (It is to be noted that nothing that is past is an object of choice, e.g., no one chooses to have sacked Troy; for no one *deliberates* about the past, but about what is future and capable of being otherwise. . . .)

5 Regarding *practical wisdom* we shall get at the truth by considering who are the persons we credit with it. Now it is thought to be the mark of a man of practical wisdom to be able to deliberate well about what is good and expedient for himself, not in some particular respect, e.g., about what sorts of thing conduce to health or to strength, but about what sorts of thing conduce to the good life in general. This is shown by the fact that we credit men with practical wisdom in some particular respect when they have calculated well with a view to some good end which is one of those that are not the object of any art. It follows that in the general sense also the man who is capable of deliberating has practical wisdom. Now no one deliberates about things that are invariable, nor about things that it is impossible for him to do. Therefore, since scientific knowledge involves demonstration, but there is no demonstration of things whose first principles are variable (for all such things might actually be otherwise), and since it is impossible to deliberate about things that are of necessity, practical wisdom cannot be scientific knowledge nor art; not science because that which can be done is capable of being otherwise, not art because action and making are different kinds of thing. The remaining alternative, then, is that it is a true and reasoned state of capacity to act with regard to the things that are good or bad for man. For while making has an end other than itself, action cannot; for good action itself is its end. It is for this reason that we think Pericles and men like him have practical wisdom, viz., because they can see what is good for themselves and what is good for men in general; we consider that those can do this who are good at managing households or states. . . .

Practical wisdom, then, must be a reasoned and true state of capacity to act with regard to human goods. But further, while there is such a thing as excellence in art, there is no such thing as excellence in practical wisdom; and in art he who errs willingly is preferable, but in practical wisdom, as in the virtues, he is the reverse. Plainly, then, practical wisdom is a virtue and not an art. There being two parts of the soul that can follow a course of reasoning, it must be the virtue of one of the two, i.e., of that part which forms opinions; for opinion is about the variable and so is practical wisdom. But yet it is not only a reasoned state; this is shown by the fact that a state of that sort may be forgotten but practical wisdom cannot.

7 ... Practical wisdom on the other hand is concerned with things human and things about which it is possible to deliberate; for we say this is above all the work of the man of practical wisdom, to deliberate well, but no one deliberates about things invariable, nor about things which have not an end, and that a good that can be brought about by action. The man who is without qualification good at deliberating is the man who is capable of aiming in accordance with calculation at the best for man of things attainable by action. Nor is practical wisdom concerned with universals only—it must also recognize the particulars; for it is practical, and practice is concerned with particulars. This is why some who do not know, and especially those who have experience, are more practical than others who know; for if a man knew that light meats are digestible and wholesome, but did not know which sorts of meat are light, he would not produce health, but the man who knows that chicken is wholesome is more likely to produce health.

Now practical wisdom is concerned with action; therefore one should have both forms of it, or the latter in preference to the former. But of practical as of philosophic wisdom there must be a controlling kind.

8 ... Further, error in deliberation may be either about the universal or about the particular; we may fail to know either that all water that weighs heavy is bad, or that this particular water weighs heavy. ...

9 ... But excellence in deliberation is a certain correctness of deliberation; hence we must first inquire what deliberation is and what it is about. And, there being more than one kind of correctness, plainly excellence in deliberation is not any and every kind; for (1) the incontinent man and the bad man, if he is clever, will reach as a result of his calculation what he sets before himself, so that he will have deliberated correctly, but he will have got for himself a great evil. Now to have deliberated well is thought to be a good thing; for it is this kind of correctness of deliberation that is excellence in deliberation, viz., that which tends to attain what is good. But (2) it is possible to attain even good by a false syllogism, and to attain what one ought to do but not by the right means, the middle term being false; so that this too is not yet excellence in deliberation—this state in virtue of which one attains what one ought but not by the right means. Again (3) it is possible to attain it by long deliberation while another man attains it quickly. Therefore in the former case we have not yet got excellence in deliberation, which is rightness with regard to the expedient—rightness in respect both of the end, the manner, and the time. (4) Further it is possible to have deliberated well either in the unqualified sense or with reference to a particular end. Excellence in deliberation in the unqualified sense, then, is that which succeeds with reference to what is the end in the unqualified sense, and excellence in deliberation in a particular sense is that which

succeeds relatively to a particular end. If, then, it is characteristic of men of practical wisdom to have deliberated well, excellence in deliberation will be correctness with regard to what conduces to the end of which practical wisdom is the true apprehension.

11   What is called judgment, in virtue of which men are said to "be sympathetic judges" and to "have judgment," is the right discrimination of the equitable. This is shown by the fact that we say the equitable man is above all others a man of sympathetic judgment, and identify equity with sympathetic judgment about certain facts. And sympathetic judgment is judgment which discriminates what is equitable and does so correctly; and correct judgment is that which judges what is true.

Now all the states we have considered converge, as might be expected, to the same point; for when we speak of judgment and understanding and practical wisdom and intuitive reason we credit the same people with possessing judgment and having reached years of reason and with having practical wisdom and understanding. For all these faculties deal with ultimates, i.e., with particulars; and being a man of understanding and of good or sympathetic judgment consists in being able to judge about the things with which practical wisdom is concerned; for the equities are common to all good men in relation to other men. Now all things which have to be done are included among particulars or ultimates; for not only must the man of practical wisdom know particular facts, but understanding and judgment are also concerned with things to be done, and these are ultimates. And intuitive reason is concerned with the ultimates in both directions; for both the first terms and the last are objects of intuitive reason and not of argument, and the intuitive reason which is presupposed by demonstrations grasps the unchangeable and first terms, while the intuitive reason involved in practical reasonings grasps the last and variable fact, i.e., the minor premise. For these variable facts are the starting-points for the apprehension of the end, since the universals are reached from the particulars; of these therefore we must have perception, and this perception is intuitive reason. . . .

Book VII

2   Now we may ask . . . how a man who judges rightly can behave incontinently. That he should behave so when he has knowledge, some say is impossible; for it would be strange—so Socrates thought—if when knowledge was in a man something else could master it and drag it about like a slave. For *Socrates* was entirely opposed to the view in question, holding that there is no such thing as incontinence; no one, he said, when he judges acts against what he judges best—people act so only by reason of ignorance. Now this view plainly contradicts the observed facts, and we must inquire about what happens to such a man; if he acts by reason of ignorance, what is the manner of his ignorance? For that the man who behaves incontinently does not, before he gets into this state, *think* he ought to act so, is evident. But there are *some* who concede certain of Socrates' contentions but not others; that nothing is stronger than knowledge they admit, but not that no one acts contrary to what has seemed to him the better course, and therefore they say that the incontinent man has not knowledge when he is mastered by his pleasures, but opinion. But *if* it is opinion and not knowledge, if it is not a strong conviction that resists but a weak one, as in men who hesitate, we sympathize with their failure to stand by such convictions against strong appetites; but we do not sympathize with wickedness, nor with any of the other blameworthy states. Is it then *practical wisdom* whose resistance is mastered? That is the strongest of all states. But this is absurd; the same man will be at once practically wise and incontinent, but *no one* would say that it is the part of a practically wise man to do willingly the basest acts. Besides, it has been shown before that the man of practical wisdom is one who will *act* (for he is a man concerned with the individual facts) and who has the other virtues. . . .

3   . . . As for the suggestion that it is true opinion and not knowledge against which we act incontinently, that makes no difference to the argument; for some people when in a state of opinion do not hesitate, but think they know exactly. If, then, the notion is that owing to their weak conviction those who have opinion are more likely to act against their judgment than those who know, we answer that there need be no difference between knowledge and opinion in this respect; for some men are no less convinced of what they think than others of what they know: as is shown by the case of Heraclitus. But (*a*), since we use the word "know" in two senses (for both the man who has knowledge but is not using it and he who is using it are said to know), it *will* make a difference whether, when a man does what he should not, he has the knowledge but is not exercising it, or *is* exercising it; for the latter seems strange, but not the former.

  (b) Further, since there are two kinds of premises, there is nothing to prevent a man's having both premises and acting against his knowledge, provided that he is using only the universal premise and not the particular; for it is particular acts that have to be done. And there are also two kinds of universal term; one is predictable of the agent, the other of the object; e.g., "dry food is good for every man," and "I am a man," or "such and such food is dry"; but whether "this food is such and such," of this the incontinent man either has not or is not exercising the knowledge. There will, then, be, firstly, an enormous difference between these manners of knowing, so that to know in one way when we act incontinently would not seem anything strange, while to know in the other way would be extraordinary.

And further (*c*) the possession of knowledge in another sense than those just named is something that happens to men; for within the case of having knowledge but not using it we see a difference of state, admitting of the possibility of having knowledge in a sense and yet not having it, as in the instance of a man asleep, mad, or drunk. But now this is just the condition of men under the influence of passion; for outbursts of anger and sexual appetites and some other such passions, it is evident, actually alter our bodily condition, and in some men even produce fits of madness. It is plain, then, that incontinent people must be said to be in a similiar condition to men asleep, mad, or drunk. The fact that men use the language that flows from knowledge proves nothing; for even men under the influence of these passions utter scientific proofs and verses of Empedocles, and those who have just begun to learn a science can string together its phrases, but do not yet know it; for it has to become part of themselves, and that takes time; so that we must suppose that the use of language by men in an incontinent state means no more than its utterance by actors on the stage.

(*d*) Again, we may also view the cause as follows with reference to the facts of human nature. The one opinion is universal, the other is concerned with the particular facts, and here we come to something within the sphere of perception; when a single opinion results from the two, the soul must in one type of case affirm the conclusion, while in the case of opinions concerned with production it must immediately act (e.g., if "everything sweet ought to be tasted," and "this is sweet," in the sense of being one of the particular sweet things, the man who can act and is not prevented must at the same time actually act accordingly). When, then, the universal opinion is present in us forbidding us to taste, and there is also the opinion that "everything sweet is pleasant," and that "this is sweet" (now this is the opinion that is active), and when appetite happens to be present in us, the one opinion bids us avoid the object, but appetite leads us toward it (for it can move each of our bodily parts); so that it turns out that a man behaves incontinently under the influence (in a sense) of a rule and an opinion, and of one not contrary in itself, but only incidentally—for the appetite is contrary, not the opinion—to the right rule. It also follows that this is the reason why the lower animals are not incontinent, viz., because they have no universal judgment but only imagination and memory of particulars.

The explanation of how the ignorance is dissolved and the incontinent man regains his knowledge, is the same as in the case of the man drunk or asleep and is not particular to this condition; we must go to the students of natural science for it. Now, the last premise both being an opinion about a perceptible object, and being what determines our actions, this a man either has not when he is in the state of passion, or has it in the sense in which having knowledge did not mean knowing but only talking, as a drunken man may mutter the verses of Empedocles. And because the last term is not universal nor equally an object of scientific knowledge with the universal term, the position that Socrates sought to establish actually seems to result; for it is not in the presence of what is thought to be knowledge proper that the affection of incontinence arises (nor is it this that is dragged about as a result of the state of passion), but in that of perceptual knowledge.

This must suffice as our answer to the question of action with and without knowledge, and how it is possible to behave incontinently with knowledge.

Book X

7 If happiness is activity in accordance with virtue, it is reasonable that it should be in accordance with the highest virtue; and this will be that of the best thing in us. Whether it be reason or something else that is this element which is thought to be our natural ruler and guide and to take thought of things noble and divine, whether it be itself also divine or only the most divine element in us, the activity of this in accordance with its proper virtue will be perfect happiness. That this activity is contemplative we have already said.

Now this would seem to be in agreement both with what we said before and with the truth. For, firstly, this activity is the best (since not only is reason the best thing in us, but the objects of reason are the best of knowable objects); and, secondly, it is the most continuous, since we can contemplate truth more continuously than we can *do* anything. And we think happiness has pleasure mingled with it, but the activity of philosophic wisdom is admittedly the pleasantest of virtuous activities; at all events the pursuit of it is thought to offer pleasures marvelous for their purity and their enduringness, and it is to be expected that those who know will pass their time more pleasantly than those who inquire. And the self-sufficiency that is spoken of must belong most to the contemplative activity. For while a philosopher, as well as a just man or one possessing any other virtue, needs the necessaries of life, when they are sufficiently equipped with things of that sort the just man needs people toward whom and with whom he shall act justly, and the temperate man, the brave man, and each of the others is in the same case, but the philosopher, even when by himself, can contemplate truth, and the better the wiser he is; he can perhaps do so better if he has fellow-workers, but still he is the most self-sufficient. And this activity alone would seem to be loved for its own sake; for nothing arises from it apart from the contemplating, while from practical activities we gain more or less apart from the action.... [B]ut the activity of reason, which is contemplative, seems both to be superior in serious worth and to aim at no end beyond itself, and to have its pleasure proper to itself (and this augments the activity), and the self-sufficiency, leisureliness, unweariedness (so far as this is possible for man), and all the other attributes ascribed to the supremely happy man are evidently those connected with this activity, it follows that this will be the complete happiness of man, if it be allowed a complete term of life (for none of the attributes of happiness is *in*complete.

But such a life would be too high for man; for it is not in so far as he is man that he will live so, but in so far as something divine is present in him; and by so much as this is superior to our composite nature is its activity superior to that which is the exercise of the other kind of virtue. If reason is divine, then, in comparison with man, the life according to it is divine in comparison with human life. But we must not follow those who advise us, being men, to think of human things, and, being mortal, of mortal things, but must, so far as we can, make ourselves immortal, and strain every nerve to live in accordance with the best thing in us; ... for man, therefore, the life according to reason is best and pleasantest, since reason more than anything else *is* man. This life therefore is also the happiest.

8 But in a secondary degree the life in accordance with the other kind of virtue is happy; for the activities in accordance with this befit our human estate. Just and brave acts, and other virtuous acts, we do in relation to each other, observing our respective duties with regard to contracts and services and all manner of actions and with regard to passions; and all of these seem to be typically human. Some of them seem even to arise from the body, and virtue of character to be in many ways bound up with the passions. Practical wisdom, too, is linked to virtue of character, and this to practical wisdom, since the principles of practical wisdom are in accordance with the moral virtues and rightness in morals is in accordance with practical wisdom. Being connected with the passions also, the moral virtues must belong to our composite nature; and the virtues of our composite nature are human; so, therefore, are the life and the happiness which correspond to these. The excellence of the reason is a thing apart. . . .

But that perfect happiness is a contemplative activity will appear from the following consideration as well. We assume the gods to be above all other beings blessed and happy; but what sort of actions must we assign to them? Acts of justice? Will not the gods seem absurd if they make contracts and return deposits, and so on? Acts of a brave man, then, confronting dangers and running risks because it is noble to do so? Or liberal acts? To whom will they give? It will be strange if they are really to have money or anything of the kind. And what would their temperate acts be? Is not such praise tasteless, since they have no bad appetites? If we were to run through them all, the circumstances of action would be found trivial and unworthy of gods. Still, every one supposes that they *live* and therefore that they are active; we cannot suppose them to sleep like Endymion. Now if you take away from a living being action, and still more production, what is left but contemplation? Therefore the activity of God, which surpasses all others in blessedness, must be contemplative; and of human activities, therefore, that which is most akin to this must be most of the nature of happiness.

This is indicated, too, by the fact that the other animals have no share in happiness, being completely deprived of such activity. For while the whole life of the gods is blessed, and that of men too in so far as some likeness of such activity belongs to them, none of the other animals is happy, since they in no way share in contemplation. Happiness extends, then, just so far as contemplation does, and those to whom contemplation more fully belongs are more truly happy, not as a mere concomitant but in virtue of the contemplation; for this is in itself precious. Happiness, therefore, must be some form of contemplation.

. . . Now he who exercises his reason and cultivates it seems to be both in the best state of mind and most dear to the gods. For if the gods have any care for human affairs, as they are thought to have, it would be reasonable both that they should delight in that which was best and most akin to them (i.e. reason) and that they should reward whose who love and honour this most, as caring for the things that are dear to them and acting both rightly and nobly. And that all these attributes belong most of all to the philosopher is manifest. He, therefore, is the dearest to the gods. And he who is that will presumably be also the happiest; so that in this way too the philosopher will more than any other be happy.

9 . . . And surely he who wants to make men, whether many or few, better by his care must try to become capable of legislating, if it is through laws that we can become good. For to get any one whatever—any one who is put before us—into the right condition is not for the first chance comer; if any one can do it, it is the man who knows, just as in medicine and all other matters which give scope for care and prudence.

Thomas Aquinas

Summa Theologica

Treatise on Law

1. IN GENERAL

QUESTION XC
OF THE ESSENCE OF LAW

Article 1. *Whether Law Is Something Pertaining to Reason?*

... It would seem that law is not something pertaining to reason.

Obj. 3.   ... the law moves those who are subject to it to act rightly. But it belongs properly to the will to move to act, ... Therefore law pertains, not to the reason, but to the will.... "Whatsoever pleaseth the sovereign has force of law."

On the contrary, It pertains to the law to command and to forbid. But it pertains to reason to command, as stated above.... Therefore law is something pertaining to reason.

I answer that, Law is a rule and measure of acts, by which man is induced to act or is restrained from acting; for *lex* (law) is derived from *ligare* (to bind), because it obliges (*obligare*) one to act. Now the rule and measure of human acts is the reason, which is the first principle of human acts, ... for it belongs to the reason to direct to the end, which is the first principle in all matters of action, according to the Philosopher. Now that which is the principle in any genus, is the rule and measure of that genus; for instance, unity in the genus of numbers, and the first movement in the genus of movements. Consequently, it follows that law is something pertaining to reason.

Reply Obj. 3.   Reason has its power of moving from the will ...; For it is due to the fact that one wills the end that the reason issues its commands as regards things ordered to the end. But in order that the volition of what is commanded may have the nature of law, it needs to be in accord with some rule of reason. And in this sense is to be understood the saying that the will of the Sovereign has the force of law: otherwise the Sovereign's will would savour of lawlessness rather than of law.

From *Summa Theologica,* by St. Thomas Aquinas, trans. Dominican Fathers of English Province (New York: Benzinger, Inc., 1947). Reprinted by permission of Burns and Oates Ltd.

Article 3. *Whether the Reason of Any Man Is Able to Make Laws?*

... It would seem that the reason of any man is able to make laws.

On the contrary, Isidore says ... "A law is an ordinance of the people, whereby something is sanctioned by the Elders together with the Commonalty." Therefore it does not pertain to everyone to make laws.

I answer that, A law, properly speaking, regards first and foremost the order to the common good. Now to order anything to the common good belongs either to the whole people, or to someone who is the vicegerent of the whole people. And therefore the making of a law belongs either to the whole people or to a public personage who has care of the whole people; for in all other fields the directing of anything to the end concerns him to whom the end belongs ...

Thus, from the ... preceding articles, the definition of law may be gathered; and it is nothing other than an ordinance of reason for the common good, made by him who has care of the community, and promulgated. ...

QUESTION XCI
OF THE VARIOUS KINDS OF LAW

Article 1. *Whether There Is an Eternal Law?*

We proceed thus to the First Article: It would seem that there is no eternal law.

Objection 1. Because every law is imposed on someone. But there was not someone from eternity on whom a law could be imposed, since God alone was from eternity. Therefore no law is eternal. ...

On the contrary, Augustine says ... "That Law which is the Supreme Reason cannot be understood to be otherwise than unchangeable and eternal."

I answer that, ... a law is nothing else but a dictate of practical reason emanating from the ruler who governs a perfect community. Now it is evident, granted that the world is ruled by Divine Providence, ... that the whole community of the universe is governed by Divine Reason. Therefore the very Idea of the government of things in God, the Ruler of the universe, has the nature of a law. And since the Divine Reason's conception of things is not subject to time but is eternal, according to Prov. 8. 23, hence it is that this kind of law must be called eternal.

Reply Obj. 1. Those things that are not in themselves exist with God, since they are foreknown and preordained by Him, according to Rom 4. 17: *Who calls those things that are not, as those that are.* Accordingly the eternal concept of the Divine law bears the character of an eternal law, in so far as it is ordained by God to the government of things foreknown by Him.

Article 2. *Whether There Is in Us a Natural Law?*

... It would seem that there is no natural law in us.

Obj. 3. Further, the more a man is free, the less he is under the law. But man is freer than all the animals, on account of free choice, with which he is endowed above all other animals. Since therefore other animals are not subject to a natural law, neither is man subject to a natural law. . . .

I answer that, . . . since all things subject to Divine providence are ruled and measured by the eternal law, as was stated above (A. 1.), it is evident that all things partake somewhat of the eternal law, in so far as, namely, from its being imprinted on them, they derive their respective inclinations to their proper acts and ends. Now among all others, the rational creature is subject to Divine providence in the most excellent way, in so far as it partakes of a share of providence, by being provident both for itself and for others. Therefore it has a share of the Eternal Reason, by which it has a natural inclination to its due act and end; and this participation of the eternal law in the rational creature is called the natural law. . . . It is therefore evident that the natural law is nothing else than the rational creature's participation of the eternal law. . . .

Reply Obj. 3. Even irrational animals partake in their own way of the Eternal Reason, just as the rational creature does. But because the rational creature partakes of it in an intellectual and rational manner, therefore the participation of the eternal law in the rational creature is properly called a law, since a law is something pertaining to reason, as stated above (Q. XC. A. 1). Irrational creatures, however, do not partake of it in a rational manner, and so there is no participation of the eternal law in them, except by the way of likeness.

Article 3. *Whether There Is a Human Law?*

We proceed to the Third Article: It would seem that there is not a human law.

Objection 1. For the natural law is a participation of the eternal law, as stated above (A. 2). Now through the eternal law "all things are most orderly," as Augustine states. . . . Therefore the natural law suffices for the ordering of all human affairs. Consequently there is no need for a human law.

Obj. 2. Further, a law bears the character of a measure, as stated above. . . . But human reason is not a measure of things, but rather vice versa. . . . Therefore no law can emanate from human reason.

Obj. 3. Further, a measure should be most certain. . . . But the dictates of human reason in matters of conduct are uncertain, according to Wisd. 9. 14: *The thoughts of mortal men are fearful, and our counsels uncertain.* Therefore no law can emanate from human reason.

On the contrary, Augustine . . . distinguishes two kinds of law, the one eternal, the other temporal, which he calls human.

I answer that, . . . a law is a dictate of the practical reason. Now it is to be observed that the same procedure takes place in the practical and in the speculative reason, for each proceeds from principles to conclusions, as stated above (*ibid.*). Accordingly we conclude that just as, in the speculative reason, from naturally known indemonstrable principles we draw the conclusions of the various sciences, the knowledge of which is not imparted to us by nature, but acquired by the efforts of reason, so too it is from the precepts of the natural law, as from general and indemonstrable principles, that the human reason needs to proceed to the more particular determination of certain matters. These particular determinations, devised by human reason, are called human laws, provided the other essential conditions of law be observed. . . .

Reply Obj. 1. The human reason cannot have a full participation of the dictate of the Divine Reason, but according to its own mode, and imperfectly. Consequently, as on the part of the speculative reason, by a natural participation of Divine Wisdom; there is in us the knowledge of certain general principles, but not a proper knowledge of each single truth, such as that contained in the Divine Wisdom: so too, on the part of the practical reason, man has a natural participation of the eternal law, according to certain general principles but not as regards the particular determinations of individual cases, which are, however, contained in the eternal law. Hence the need for human reason to proceed further to sanction them by law.

Reply Obj. 2. Human reason is not, of itself, the rule of things; but the principles impressed on it by nature, are general rules and measures of all things relating to human conduct, of which the natural reason is the rule and measure, although it is not the measure of things that are from nature.

Reply Obj. 3. The practical reason is concerned with practical matters, which are singular and contingent, but not with necessary things, with which the speculative reason is concerned. Therefore human laws cannot have that inerrancy that belongs to the demonstrated conclusions of sciences. Nor is it necessary for every measure to be altogether unerring and certain, but according as it is possible in its own particular genus.

2. IN PARTICULAR

QUESTION XCIV
OF THE NATURAL LAW

Article 2. *Whether the Natural Law Contains Several Precepts, or One Only?*

. . . It would seem that the natural law contains not several precepts, but one only.

Objection 1. For law is a kind of precept. . . . If therefore there were many precepts of the natural law, it would follow that there are also many natural laws. . . .

Obj. 3. Further, law is something pertaining to reason. . . . Now reason is but one in man. Therefore there is only one precept of the natural law.

On the contrary, The precepts of the natural law in man stand in relation to practical matters as the first principles to matters of demonstration. But there are several first indemonstrable principles. Therefore there are also several precepts of the natural law.

I answer that, . . . The precepts of the natural law are to the practical reason what the first principles of demonstrations are to the speculative reason; because both are self-evident principles. Now a thing is said to be self-evident in two ways: first, in itself; secondly, in relation to us. Any proposition is said to be self-evident in itself if its predicate is contained in the notion of the subject, although to one who does not know the definition of the subject it happens that such a proposition is not self-evident. For instance, this proposition, Man is a rational being, is, in its very nature, self-evident, since who says man, says a rational being; and yet to one who does not know what a man is this proposition is not self-evident. Hence it is that . . . certain axioms or propositions are universally self-evident to all; and such are those propositions whose terms are known to all, as, Every whole is greater than its part, and, Things equal to one and the same are equal to one another. But some propositions are self-evident only to the wise, who understand the meaning of the terms of such propositions; thus to one who understands that an angel is not a body, it is self-evident that an angel is not circumscriptively in a place; but this is not evident to the unlearned, for they cannot grasp it.

Now a certain order is to be found in those things that are apprehended by man. For that which, before anything else falls under apprehension, is being, the understanding of which is included in all things whatsoever a man apprehends. Therefore the first indemonstrable principle is that the same thing cannot be affirmed and denied at the same time, which is based on the notion of being and not-being; and on this principle all others are based, as is stated in the *Metaphysics*. Now as being is the first thing that falls under the apprehension absolutely, so good is the first thing that falls under the apprehension of the practical reason, which is directed to action; for every agent acts for an end, which has the aspect of good. Consequently, the first principle in the practical reason is one founded on the notion of good, namely, that the good is what all desire. Hence this is the first precept of law, that good is to be pursued and done, and evil is to be avoided. All other precepts of the natural law are based upon this, so that whatever the practical reason naturally apprehends as man's good belongs to the precepts of the natural law as something to be done or avoided.

Since, however, good has the nature of an end, and evil, the nature of a contrary, hence it is that all those things to which man has a natural inclination are naturally apprehended by reason as being good, and consequently as objects of pursuit, and their contraries as evil, and objects of avoidance. Therefore the order of the precepts of the natural law is according to the order of natural inclinations. Because in man there is first of all an inclination to good in accordance with the nature which he has in common with all substances; that is, every substance seeks the preservation of its own being, according to its nature. And by reason of this inclination, whatever is a means of preserving human life and of warding off its obstacles belongs to the natural law. Secondly, there is in man an inclination to things that pertain to him more specially, according to that nature which he has in common with other animals. And in virtue of this inclination, those things are said to belong to the natural law "which nature has taught to all animals," such as sexual intercourse, education of offspring and so forth. Thirdly, there is in man an inclination to good, according to the nature of his reason, which nature is proper to him; thus man has a natural inclination to know the truth about God, and to live in society. And in this respect, whatever pertains to this inclination belongs to the natural law; for instance, to shun ignorance, to avoid offending those among whom one has to live, and other such things regarding the above inclination.

Reply Obj. 1. All these precepts of the law of nature have the character of one natural law because they flow from one first precept. . . .

Reply Obj. 3. Although reason is one in itself, yet it directs all things regarding man, so that whatever can be ruled by reason is contained under the law of reason.

Article 3. *Whether All Acts of Virtue Are Prescribed by the Natural Law?*

. . . It would seem that not all acts of virtue are prescribed by the natural law.

Objection 1. Because, . . . it is essential to a law that it be ordered to the common good. But some acts of virtue are ordered to the private good of the individual, as is evident especially in regard to acts of temperance. Therefore not all acts of virtue are the subject of natural law.

Obj. 2. Further, every sin is opposed to some virtuous act. If therefore all acts of virtue are prescribed by the natural law, it seems to follow that all sins are against nature which, however, applies especially to certain sins.

Obj. 3. Further, those things which are according to nature are common to all. But acts of virtue are not common to all, since a thing is virtuous in one and vicious in another. Therefore not all acts of virtue are prescribed by the natural law.

On the contrary, Damascene says . . . "virtues are natural." Therefore virtuous acts also fall under the natural law.

I answer that, We may speak of virtuous acts in two ways: first, under the aspect of virtuous; secondly, as such and such acts considered in their proper species. If then we speak of acts of virtue considered as virtuous, thus all virtuous acts belong to the natural law. For it has been stated (A. 2) that to the natural law belongs everything to which a man is inclined according to his nature. Now each thing is inclined naturally to an operation that is suitable to it according to its form; thus fire is inclined to give heat. Therefore, since the rational soul is the proper form of man, there is in every man a natural inclination to act according to reason, and this is to act according to virtue. Consequently, considered thus, all acts of virtue are prescribed by the natural law; for each one's reason naturally requires him to act virtuously. But if we speak of virtuous acts, considered in themselves, that is, in their proper species, in this way not all virtuous acts are prescribed by the natural law. For many things are done virtuously to which nature does not incline at first, but which, through the inquiry of reason, have been found by men to be conducive to well-living.

Reply Obj. 1. Temperance is about the natural concupiscences of food, drink and sexual matters, which are indeed ordered to the natural common good, just as other matters of law are ordered to the moral common good.

Reply Obj. 2. By human nature we may mean either that which is proper to man —and in this sense all sins, as being against reason, are also against nature, . . . Or we may mean that nature which is common to man and other animals, and in this sense, certain special sins are said to be against nature; thus contrary to sexual intercourse, which is natural to all animals, is unisexual lust, which has received the special name of the unnatural vice.

Reply Obj. 3. This argument considers acts in themselves. For it is owing to the various conditions of men that certain acts are virtuous for some, as being proportionate and fitting to them, while they are vicious for others, as being not proportioned to them.

Article 4. *Whether the Natural Law Is the Same in all Men? ...*

Obj. 1. It would seem that the natural law is not the same in all.

Obj. 2. Further, "Things which are according to the law are said to be just," as stated in the *Ethics*. But it is stated in the same book that nothing is so just for everybody as not to be subject to change in regard to some men. Therefore even the natural law is not the same in all men.

Obj. 3. Further, ... to the natural law pertains everything to which a man is inclined according to his nature. Now different men are naturally inclined to different things; some to the desire of pleasures, others to the desires of honours, and other men to other things. Therefore there is not one natural law for all.

I answer that ... those things to which a man is inclined naturally pertain to the natural law, and among these it is proper to man to be inclined to act according to reason. Now the process of reason is from the common to the proper.... The speculative reason, however, is differently situated in this matter from the practical reason. For since the speculative reason is busied chiefly with necessary things which cannot be otherwise than they are, its proper conclusions, like the common principles, contain the truth without fail. The practical reason, on the other hand, is busied with contingent matters, about which human actions are concerned: and consequently, although there is necessity in the general principles, the more we descend to matters of detail the more frequently we encounter defects. Accordingly then in speculative matters truth is the same in all men, both as to principles and as to conclusions, although the truth is now known to all as regards the conclusions, but only as regards the principles which are called "common notions." But in matters of action, truth or practical rectitude is not the same for all as to matters of detail, but only as to the common principles; and where there is the same rectitude in matters of detail, it is not equally known to all.

It is therefore evident that as regards the common principles, whether of speculative or of practical reason, truth or rectitude is the same for all, and is equally known by all. As to the proper conclusions of the speculative reason, the truth is the same for all, but is not equally known to all: thus it is true for all that the three angles of a triangle are together equal to two right angles, although it is not known to all. But as to the proper conclusions of the practical reason, neither is the truth or rectitude the same for all, nor, where it is the same, is it equally known by all. Thus it is right and true for all to act according to reason. And from this principle it follows as a proper conclusion that goods entrusted to another should be restored to their owner. Now this is true for the majority of cases, but it may happen in a particular case that it would be injurious, and therefore unreasonable, to restore goods held in trust; for instance, if they are claimed for the purpose of fighting against one's country. And this principle will be found to fail the more according as we descend further into detail, for example if one were to say that goods held in trust should be restored with such a guarantee, or in such and such a way; because the greater the number of conditions added, the greater the number of ways in which the principle may fail, so that it be not right to restore or not to restore.

Consequently, we must say that the natural law, as to first common principles, is the same for all, both as to rectitude and as to knowledge. But as to certain matters of detail, which are conclusions, as it were of those common principles, it is the same for all in the majority of cases, both as to rectitude and as to knowledge; and yet in some few cases it may fail, both as to rectitude, by reason of certain obstacles (just as natures subject to generation and corruption fail in some few cases on account of some obstacle), and as to knowledge, since in some the reason is perverted by passion, or evil habit, or an evil disposition of nature. Thus formerly, theft, although it is expressly contrary to the natural law, was not considered wrong among the Germans, as Julius Caesar relates. . . .

Reply Obj. 2. The saying of the Philosopher is to be understood of things that are naturally just not as common principles, but as conclusions drawn from them, having rectitude in the majority of cases, but failing in a few.

Reply Obj. 3. As in man reason rules and commands the other powers, so all the natural inclinations belonging to the other powers must be directed according to reason. Therefore it is universally right for all men that all their inclinations should be directed according to reason.

Article 5. *Whether the Natural Law Can be Changed?*

. . . It would seem that the natural law can be changed.

Obj. 2. Further, the slaying of the innocent, adultery, and theft are against the natural law. But we find these things changed by God, as when God commanded Abraham to slay his innocent son (Gen. 22. 2); and when He ordered the Jews to borrow and purloin the vessels of the Egyptians (Exod. 12. 35); and when He commanded Osee to take to himself a *wife of fornication* (Osee 1. 2). Therefore the natural law can be changed.

Obj. 3. Further, Isidore says . . . that "the possession of all things in common, and a uniform freedom, are matters of natural law." But these things are seen to be changed by human laws. Therefore it seems that the natural law is subject to change.

I answer that, A change in the natural law may be understood in two ways. First, by way of addition. In this sense nothing hinders the natural law from being changed, since many things for the benefit of human life have been added over and above the natural law, both by the Divine law and by human laws.

Secondly, a change in the natural law may be understood by law of subtraction, so that what previously was according to the natural law ceases to be so. In this sense, the natural law is altogether unchangeable in its first principles. But in its secondary principles, which . . . are certain detailed proximate conclusions drawn from the first principles, the natural law is not changed so that what it prescribes be not right in most cases. But it may be changed in some particular cases of rare occurrence, through some special causes hindering the observance of such precepts. . . .

Reply Obj. 2.   All men alike, both guilty and innocent, die the death of nature, which death of nature is inflicted by the power of God on account of original sin, according to I Kings 2. 6: *The Lord killeth and maketh alive.* Consequently, by the command of God, death can be inflicted on any man, guilty or innocent, without any injustice whatsoever. In like manner adultery is intercourse with another man's wife, who is allotted to him by the law emanating from God. Consequently intercourse with any woman, by the command of God, is neither adultery nor fornication. The same applies to theft, which is the taking of another's property. For whatever is taken by the command of God, to Whom all things belong, is not taken against the will of its owner, which is what theft is. Nor is it only in human things that whatever is commanded by God is right; but also in natural things, whatever is done by God, is, in some way, natural.

Reply Obj. 3.   A thing is said to belong to the natural law in two ways. First, because nature inclines there; for example, that one should not do harm to another. Secondly, because nature did not bring in the contrary: thus we might say that for man to be naked is of the natural law, because nature did not give him clothes, but art invented them. In this sense, "the possession of all things in common and uniform freedom" are said to be of the natural law, because, that is, the distinction of possessions and slavery were not brought in by nature, but devised by human reason for the benefit of human life. Accordingly the law of nature was not changed in this respect, except by addition.

SUGGESTIONS FOR DISCUSSION

1. Plato develops a "natural," as opposed to a "conventional" conception of moral value. What implications might this distinction have for deciding what it is right to do in the case of social issues such as those discussed in Part II?

2. What views about justice does Plato criticize, and what views does he affirm? Would a Platonist endorse any of the contemporary views on distributive justice expressed in Part II, Chapter 7?

3. What are the kinds of justice Aristotle distinguishes? Are these distinctions pertinent to our contemporary conceptions of justice?

4. How, on Aristotle's view, are we to decide what it is virtuous to do when confronted by social problems of the sort discussed in Part II? Is this how we should make our moral decisions?

5. Are moral rules given in rationally determinable, eternal, and unchanging natural laws?

6. Are there circumstances in which the Natural Law theory developed by Aquinas would recognize a woman's right to an abortion (see Part II, Chapter 11) or a person's request of euthanasia (see Chapter 12)?

FURTHER READING

PLATO

Annas, J. *An Introduction to Plato's* Republic. Oxford: Oxford University Press, 1981 (Interpretation; introductory)

Brumbaugh, R. *The Philosophers of Greece.* Albany: SUNY Press, 1981. (Survey; introductory)

Cross, R. C., and Woozley, A. D. *Plato's Republic: A Philosophical Commentary.* London: Macmillan, 1964. (Interpretation, critical analysis; intermediate)

Nettleship, R. L. *Lectures on the Republic of Plato.* London: Macmillan, 1968. (Interpretation; intermediate)

Plato. *The Dialogues of Plato.* 4th ed. Trans. Benjamin Jowett. Oxford: Oxford University Press, 1892.

Vlastos, G., ed. *Plato I and II.* New York: Doubleday, 1971. (Interpretation, critical analysis; advanced)

White, N. *A Companion to Plato's* Republic. Indianapolis: Hackett Publishing Company, 1979 (Interpretation; introductory)

ARISTOTLE

Ackrill, J. L. *Aristotle's Ethics.* New York: Humanities Press, 1973.

Aristotle. *Politics.*

Guthrie, W.K.C. *History of Greek Philosophy.* Vol. III, *(The Sophists and Socrates)*; Vols. IV and V *(Plato)*; Vol. VI *(Aristotle).* Oxford: Clarendon Press, 1969. (Survey; interpretation; introductory)

Hardie, W.F.R. *Aristotle's Ethical Theory.* Oxford: Oxford University Press, 1981. (Interpretation; intermediate)

Kenny, A. *Aristotle's Theory of the Will.* New Haven: Yale University Press, 1979. (Interpretation, critical analysis; advanced)

Lear, T. *Aristotle: The Desire to Understand.* Cambridge: Cambridge University Press, 1988. (Interpretation; introductory)

Lloyd, G.E.R. *Aristotle.* London: Cambridge University Press, 1968. (Survey; introductory)

Randall, J. A. *Aristotle.* New York: Random House, 1960. (Interpretation; introductory)

Rorty, A., ed. *Essays on Aristotle's Ethics.* Berkeley: University of California Press, 1980. (Interpretation, critical analysis; advanced)

Ross, W. D. *Aristotle.* Oxford: Oxford University Press, 1960. (Interpretation; intermediate)

Smith, J. A., and Ross, W. D., eds. *The Works of Aristotle.* Oxford, 1910–52.

Sorabji, R. *Necessity, Cause and Blame.* Ithaca: Cornell University Press, 1980. (Interpretation, critical analysis; advanced)

AQUINAS

Aquinas, Thomas. *Basic Writings of St. Thomas Aquinas.* Ed. A. Pegis. New York: Random House, 1948.

Chesterton, G. K. *St. Thomas Aquinas.* New York: Doubleday, 1933. (Survey; introductory)

Copleston, F. *Aquinas.* London: Penguin, 1955. (Interpretation; introductory)

———. *A History of Philosophy.* Vol. 2. New York: Doubleday, 1962. (Survey; introductory)

———. *Medieval Philosophy.* London: Methuen, 1952. (Interpretation; intermediate)

Kenny, A. *Aquinas.* Oxford: Oxford University Press, 1980. (Critical survey, interpretation, introductory)

O'Connor, D. J. *Aquinas and the Natural Law.* London: Macmillan, 1968. (Interpretation, critical analysis; intermediate)

2

□

Hobbes and Hume

THOMAS HOBBES (1588–1679): THE STATE OF NATURE AND THE SOCIAL CONTRACT

Hobbes's Premises   Thomas Hobbes focused his philosophical attention upon an analysis of political power. Hobbes's theory of power was deeply influenced by both the deductive method of Euclidean geometry and the new heliocentric (or "sun-centered") world view of contemporary scientists, especially that of Galileo (1564–1642). Hobbes set out to develop a deductive science of politics laid upon the foundation of fundamental first principles. He assumed Galileo's antitraditional view that the primary state of all matter is motion, not rest. The principle of *human* self-motion was taken to be desire, and human beings were characterized in terms of two basic principles of voluntary action: appetites and aversions. Appetites were defined as attractions to motion or to what enables motion; and aversions, as repulsions from rest or from what leads to rest. Hobbes considered "good" to be any object of appetite, and "evil" as any object of aversion. Death is the worst of all evils because it is the end of all motion. It follows that the first principle of Hobbes's political theory is that all people fear death: the most basic desire of every person is to live a long life.

Hobbes admitted that there are particular differences, both mental and physical, between individuals. Nevertheless, he argued that human differences are not so great that weaker people could not overcome their natural disadvantages—by cunning, by complicity with others, or by taking up weapons. Further, most persons consider themselves more capable in some respects than everyone else. Hobbes inferred from this that although there are ("material") inequalities, persons can be generally assumed to be ("formally") equal. Hobbes thought that this equality is the foundation for the equality of *hope* among all individuals to obtain the objects of their wants. No matter their diversity, if they are self-interestedly rational, the fact that people have these wants entails that they hope to satisfy their own desires. Given the underlying asumption that human desires as a whole are limitless, it follows that resources will be scarce; at some point there will be insufficient goods to satisfy demand for them. Hobbes concluded that the inevitable outcome is competition for scarce resources. With competition—at least in the absence of rules that are agreed upon and enforced—mistrust of others must arise.

Hobbes's State of Nature This condition of general mistrust Hobbes called "warre." "Warre" would occur whenever there is no common power sufficiently strong to instill the fear of punishment and to maintain order. The state of "warre," elsewhere termed by Hobbes the *state of nature*, is not simply the actual battle of each individual against all the others. In the absence of laws and their adequate enforcement, it is sufficient that the will of some to attack and fight with others be publicly known or assumed. The hypothetical state of nature, then, is one of paranoia ("worry"). In this state, each has a right to everything, including the right to self-protection by whatever means deemed fit; physical strength and mental deception are the fundamental virtues; and the only property would be what one could keep by force or fraud. There would be no products of cooperation: no science, culture, or industry. Life, as Hobbes concluded pessimistically, would be "solitary, poor, nasty, brutish and short." A fundamental implication of this conception of the state of nature is that there is no natural sin or right conduct. Justice and injustice are laid out in laws, which are established by a chosen authority whose task it is to write the laws. On Hobbes's view, where there is no sovereign power there will be no written law.

Laws of Nature and the Social Contract Hobbes thought that everyone fears death and desires to live long. The state of nature is inconsistent with this desire. Rational self-interest suggests to each individual a set of general principles to secure a peaceful social order. These rational principles, or what Hobbes called *laws of nature*, are general rules established by reason. They oblige rational persons to follow them, for the likelihood of a long life would thereby be increased. These laws of nature are to be distinguished from the *right of nature*. The latter is the freedom in the state of nature to do whatever satisfies one's desires. Most fundamentally, one has the right in the state of nature to defend oneself by any means available. Nevertheless, reason commands as the first *law* that one seek peace and preserve it, for this maximizes the possibility of self-preservation. The second law, crucial for peace, requires that one give up as many liberties in the state of nature as one demands that others give up. Here the motivation is twofold: to disadvantage neither oneself nor others, and to oblige all to cease random or self-interested acts of violence. Agents are not simply to renounce these rights but are to transfer them for safekeeping to a party consensually agreed to, a sovereign monarch or body of rulers. This common agreement or mutual promise between individuals in choosing a sovereign ruler is the *social contract*. Hobbes insisted that the designated sovereign ruler must be invested with sufficient power to guarantee security: the sovereign's word must become law. Justice (right) and injustice (wrong) are taken to be *relative* to the particular language of the sovereign at the particular time and place. The only rational grounds for citizens' objections would be the failure of the sovereign to secure social order and peace. Hobbes derived the rest of his nineteen laws of nature deductively from these first three.

Interpreting Hobbes Hobbes's moral and political theories are usually characterized as a rationalization for authoritarianism, in so far as moral and political obligations and rights are made subject to the power of the sovereign. So Hobbes seems to offer a sophisticated and more plausible version of the Sophists' view that "might makes right." However, there is another way in which Hobbes's theory can be read. Here "reason" and the "laws of nature" to which reason gives rise bear the weight of Hobbes's theoretical construct. Reason demands that everyone be treated equally and justly, and that each give up only the *minimum* liberties necessary to guarantee peace. The sovereign is not subject to the particular laws made, for what the sovereign rules the sovereign can alter. Nevertheless, the sovereign or ruling body also consists of persons, and they similarly desire self-preservation. Thus the sovereign body is likewise subject to the rational constraints of the laws of nature. Reason demands that the sovereign restrict no more than what is *minimally* necessary to maintain peace. For example, if peace and security can be promoted without the institution of censorship (see Part II, Chapter 9) or capital punishment (see Chapter 13), then on this reading it would be irrational for the sovereign to require it. As generally recognized, Hobbes criticized the Natural Law tradition promoted by Aquinas. Yet on this alternative interpretation, Hobbes's universal principles commanded by reason tend to undermine crude conceptions of justice that are linked to authoritarianism.

DAVID HUME (1711–1776): A CRITIQUE OF MORAL REASON AND THE THEORY OF MORAL SENTIMENTS

Hobbes's theory was so provocative and his arguments so compelling that for a century and a half British philosophers, theologians, and political theorists felt constrained to address the issues he raised. Almost all British philosophers of the time devoted their philosophical energies largely to moral matters. David Hume was somewhat less concerned with moral matters than other British Moralists (as they have been named). Yet it is perhaps a mark of Hobbes's influence that Hume chose the title of his influential work *Treatise of Human Nature* (1739) from the title of Hobbes's book *Human Nature* (1650).

Hume's Critique of Reason   Hume formulated a consistent critical attack upon the possibility of all forms of claimed knowledge. He raised deep questions about the possibility of acquiring scientific knowledge of the external world, especially of the relation between cause and effect; knowledge of the self; and religious knowledge of God. Hume's moral criticisms are part of this wider critical attack and they are directed primarily against the claims of moral objectivity and against moral knowledge of the distinction between right and wrong. Much as he argued that reason is incapable of establishing the relation between cause and effect, so Hume suggested that the distinction between good and evil cannot be deduced by reason.

The primary target of Hume's moral criticism, then, is the claim that reason is practical. Many philosophers had assumed that good and evil are to be distinguished by rational deliberation, and that to be moral actions must be commanded by practical reasoning. Accordingly, practical reasoning must conclude, as Aristotle noted, with an action (see Aristotle, Part I, Chapter 1). Hume's attack on practical reasoning rests upon two arguments: that reason alone is incapable of motivating an action; and that reason alone cannot oppose the effect on the will of the passions.

For Hume, *impressions* and *ideas* together exhaust the contents of mind. The passions (like hunger or anger) are impressions or original impositions on the mind that motivate or excite the agent to action. Reason, by contrast, has to do only with relations of ideas or matters of fact. So reason is not capable on its own of moving one to action, for it has no impressive force upon the will. In short, while reason is inert and impotent, morality concerns virtuous *action*. Active principles cannot be prompted by inactive ones, and so moral action cannot be a function of reason alone, nor can immoral actions simply be ascribed to irrationality. Despite the claim of many British Moralists, moral rules cannot be conclusions to the deductions of reason, for then they would have no force on their own to affect behavior.

Hume held that, at most, reason can indicate the existence of some end that is desired, or the means best able to achieve that end. Reason is unable to recommend an end as desired or to originate the causal impulse that leads an agent to pursue or avoid something. For example, reason may suggest to me that the surest way to secure my graduation is to study hard; but on Hume's view reason cannot impress upon me the goal of graduation or create in me the desire to study. The originating impulse that disposes an agent to pursue or avoid some end arises from the agent's anticipation of the accompanying pleasure or pain. Only such an impulse can move the will to act or refrain from acting; in the example, to study or not. It follows that reason is also incapable of preventing the will from acting. Because of reason's impotence in the face of the passions, Hume drew his celebrated conclusion that "reason is, and ought to be the slave of the passions."

Fact and Value   Hume inferred a more general lesson from this line of argument. If moral claims are to impel action, they must prescribe behavior. They must command agents to do what they ought or to refrain from doing what they ought not. Moral prescriptions, by definition, involve value claims and so are not matters of fact. They cannot be reduced to factual claims about what is or is not the case. That I *ought* not to lie, say, cannot be derived from any *factual* claim about the harmful consequences of lying. We cannot, in short, deduce "ought" or value claims solely from "is" or factual ones.

Moral Sentiments   If reason is incapable of determining the distinction between virtue and vice or right and wrong, Hume had to argue that the source of these moral distinctions lies elsewhere. By circumscribing the effective power of reason, he evaded the claim that moral rules or judgments are objective, eternal, or universally obligatory. Rather, he took them to have their foundation in people's desires for what is in their common interest. In contrast to those who argued that moral judgments and knowledge of the moral distinctions stem from reason, Hume contended that they spring from ordinary sensations. These sensations he called the *moral sentiments* or moral passions, the most fundamental of which are *sympathy* and *antipathy*.

Hume's theory of sympathy was supposed to explain how an isolated individual with private experiences and feelings can care for the feelings of others. He held that moral sentiments are innate to human nature; and in spite of the seemingly local variations, human beings have a uniform tendency to sympathize with their fellows. As a consequence of social functioning, this results in sympathy for some kinds of objects and antipathy toward others. Hume suggested that we sympathize with the pleasure that we presume an object, quality, or character gives to an agent possessing it. This reflects the paradigm case of the pleasure that one experiences from some object, character, or quality that one owns. Sympathy amounts to—it is identical with—a pleasure (or in the case of antipathy, a pain) that *we* experience. For example, we approve of the courage exhibited by one who performs a daring rescue, for we have experienced the sort of pleasure arising from courageous action and so we can sympathize with the pleasure of the rescuer. Our approval is a function of the pleasure we feel in sympathizing with the rescuer's pleasure.

Hume presumed, with little supporting argument, that this transferred pleasure or pain will suffice to outweigh any direct pleasure or pain we might experience from a competing object, quality, or character directly in our possession; for example, that the rescuer is someone we otherwise despise. He supposed that overcoming this direct pleasure or pain is sufficient to arouse in us disapproval of any unjust self-serving action that we might be considering. Thus Hume rejected the idea, suggested perhaps by Hobbes's general moral law or by the Golden Rule of "doing unto others," that sympathy is a function of impartially imagining ourselves in another's place. On Hume's view, we do not sympathize with other members of our society because to do so is objectively or impartially right or just, but because our social condition and custom have led us to love and identify with them.

Thus for both Hobbes and Hume social considerations play central though different roles in the determination of morality and how we ought to act on any given social issue. For Hobbes, the sovereign's prescription of moral rules and morally acceptable behavior is founded upon a social contract subject to certain rational contstraints. For Hume, moral rules are established in accordance with social condition, custom, and common interests.

Thomas Hobbes

Leviathan

Part I: Of Man

CHAP. XIII
OF THE NATURALL CONDITION OF MANKIND, AS CONCERNING THEIR FELICITY, AND MISERY

Men by nature
Equall

Nature hath made men so equall, in the faculties of body, and mind; as that though there bee found one man sometimes manifestly stronger in body, or of quicker mind then another; yet when all is reckoned together, the difference between man, and man, is not so considerable, as that one man can thereupon claim to himselfe any benefit, to which another may not pretend, as well as he. For as to the strength of body, the weakest has strength enough to kill the strongest, either by secret machination, or by confederacy with others, that are in the same danger with himselfe.

And as to the faculties of the mind (setting aside the arts grounded upon words, and especially that skill of proceeding upon generall, and infallible rules, called Science; which very few have, and but in few things; as being not a native faculty, born with us; nor attained [as Prudence] while we look after somewhat else I find yet a greater equality amongst men, than that of strength. For Prudence, 61 is but Experience; which equall time, equally bestowes on all men, in those things they equally apply themselves unto. That which may perhaps make such equality incredible, is but a vain conceit of ones owne wisdome, which almost all men think they have in a greater degree, than the Vulgar; that is, than all men but themselves, and a few others, whom by Fame, or for concurring with themselves, they approve. For such is the nature of men, that howsoever they may acknowledge many others to be more witty, or more eloquent, or more learned; Yet they will hardly believe there be many so wise as themselves: For they see their own wit at hand, and other men's at a distance. But this proveth rather that men are in that point equall, than unequall. For there is not ordinarily a greater signe of the equall distribution of anything, than that every man is contented with his share.

From Equality
proceeds Dissidence

From this equality of ability, ariseth equality of hope in the attaining of our Ends. And therefore if any two men desire the same thing, which neverthelesse they cannot both enjoy, they become enemies; and in the way to their End (which is principally their owne conservation, and sometimes their delectation only), endeavour to destroy, or subdue one

From Thomas Hobbes, *Leviathan* (London, 1651).

an other. And from hence it comes to passe, that where an Invader hath no more to feare, than an other mans single power; if one plant, sow, build, or possesse a convenient Seat, others may probably be expected to come prepared with forces united, to dispossesse, and deprive him, not only of the fruit of his labour, but also of his life, or liberty. And the Invader again is in the like danger of another.

From Dissidence Warre

And from this diffidence of one another, there is no way for any man to secure himselfe, so reasonable, as Anticipation; that is, by force, or wiles, to master the persons of all men he can, so long, till he see no other power great enough to endanger him: And this is no more than his own conservation requireth, and is generally allowed. Also because there be some, that taking pleasure in contemplating their own power in the acts of conquest, which they pursue farther than their security requires; if others, that otherwise would be glad to be at ease within modest bounds, should not by invasion increase their power, they would not be able, long time, by standing only on their defence, to subsist. And by consequence, such augmentation of dominion over men, being necessary to a mans conservation, it ought to be allowed him.

Againe, men have no pleasure (but on the contrary a great deale of griefe) in keeping company, where there is no power able to over-awe them all. For every man looketh that his companion should value him, at the same rate he sets upon himselfe: And upon all signes of contempt, or undervaluing, naturally endeavours, as far as he dares (which amongst them that have no common power, to keep them in quiet, if far enough to make them destroy each other,) to extort a greater value from his contemners, by dommage; and from others, by the example.

So that in the nature of man, we find three principall causes of quarrell. First, Competition; Secondly, Diffidence; Thirdly, Glory.

62 The first, maketh men invade for Gain; the second, for Safety; and the third, for Reputation. The first use Violence, to make themselves Masters of other mens persons, wives, children, and cattell; the second, to defend them; the third, for trifles, as a word, a smile, a different opinion, and any other signe of undervalue, either direct in their Persons, or by reflexion in their Kindred, their Friends, their nation, their Profession, or their Name.

Out of Civil States, there is always Warre of every one against every one

Hereby it is manifest, that during the time men live without a common Power to keep them all in awe, they are in that condition which is called Warre; and such a warre, as is of every man, against every man. For Warre, consisteth not in Battell onely, or the act of fighting; but in a tract of time, wherein the Will to contend by Battell is sufficiently known; and therefore the notion of *Time*, is to be considered in the nature of Warre; as it is in the nature of Weather. For as the nature of Foule weather, lyeth not in a showre or two of rain; but in an inclination thereto of many dayes together: So the nature of War, consisteth not in actuall fighting; but in the known disposition thereto, during all the time there is no assurance to the contrary. All other time is Peace.

The Incommodities of such a Warre

Whatsoever therefore is consequent to a time of Warre, where every man is Enemy to every man; the same is consequent to the time, wherein men live without other security, than what their own strength, and their own invention shall furnish them withall. In such condition, there is no place for Industry; because the fruit thereof is uncertain: and consequently no Culture of the Earth; no Navigation, nor use of the commodities that may be imported by Sea; no commodious Building; no Instruments of moving, and removing such things as require much force; no Knowledge of the face of the Earth; no account of Time; no Arts; no Letters; no Society; and which is worst of all, continuall feare, and danger of violent death; And the life of man, solitary, poore, nasty, brutish, and short.

It may seem strange to some man, that has not well weighed these things; that Nature should thus dissociate, and render men apt to invade, and destroy one another: and he may therefore, not trusting to this Inference, made from the Passions, desire perhaps to have the same confirmed by Experience. Let him therefore consider with himselfe, when taking a journey, he armes himselfe, and seeks to go well accompanied; when going to sleep, he locks his dores; when even in his house he lockes his chests; and this when he knows there bee Lawes, and publike Officers, armed, to revenge all injuries shall bee done him; what opinion he has of his fellow subjects, when he rides armed; of his fellow Citizens, when he locks his dores; and of his children, and servants, when he locks his chests. Does he not there as much accuse mankind by his actions, as I do by my words? But neither of us accuse mans nature in it. The Desires, and other Passions of man, are in themselves no Sin. No more are the Actions, that proceed from those Passions, till they know a Law that forbids them: which till Lawes be made they cannot know: nor can any Law be made, till they have agreed upon the Person that shall make it.

63   It may peradventure be thought, there was never such a time, nor condition of warre as this; and I believe it was never generally so, over all the world; but there are many places, where they live so now. For the savage people in many places of *America*, except the government of small Families, the concord whereof dependeth on naturall lust, have no government at all; and live at this day in that brutish manner, as I said before. Howsoever, it may be perceived what manner of life there would be, where there were no common Power to feare; by the manner of life, which men that have formerly lived under a peacefull government, use to degenerate into, in a civill Warre.

But though there had never been any time, wherein particular men were in a conditon of warre one against another; yet in all times, Kings, and Persons of Soveraigne authority, because of their Independency, are in continuall jealousies, and in the state and posture of Gladiators; having their weapons pointing, and their eyes fixed on one another; that is, their Forts, Garrisons, and Guns upon the Frontiers of their Kingdomes; and continuall Spyes upon their neighbours; which is a posture of War. But because they uphold thereby, the Industry of their Subjects; there does not follow from it, that misery, which accompanies the Liberty of particular men.

In such a Warre,   To this warre of every man against every man, this also is conse-
nothing is Unjust   quent; that nothing can be Unjust. The notions of Right and Wrong, Justice and Injustice have there no place. Where there is no common Power, there is no Law: where no Law, no Injustice. Force, and Fraud,

are in warre the two Cardinall vertues. Justice, and Injustice are none of the Faculties neither of the Body, nor Mind. If they were, they might be in a man that were alone in the world, as well as his Senses, and Passions. They are Qualities, that relate to men in Society, not in Solitude. It is consequent also to the same conditon, that there be no Propriety, no Dominion, no *Mine* and *Thine* distinct; but onely that to be every mans that he can get; and for so long, as he can keep it. And thus much for the ill condition, which man by meer Nature is actually placed in; though with a possibility to come out of it, consisting partly in the Passions, partly in his Reason.

The Passions that incline men to Peace

The Passions that encline men to Peace, are Feare of Death; Desire of such things as are necessary to commodious living; and a Hope by their Industry to obtain them. And Reason suggesteth convenient Articles of Peace, upon which men may be drawn to agreement. These Articles, are they, which otherwise are called the Lawes of Nature: whereof I shall speak more particularly, in the two following Chapters.

CHAP. XIV
OF THE FIRST AND SECOND NATURALL
LAWES, AND OF CONTRACTS

Right of Nature what

The Right of Nature, which Writers commonly call *Jus Naturale*, is the Liberty each man hath, to use his own power, as he will himselfe, for the preservation of his own Nature; that is to say, of his own Life; and consequently, of doing any thing, which in his own Judgement, and Reason, hee shall conceive to be the aptest means thereunto.

Liberty what

By Liberty, is understood, according to the proper signification of the word, the absence of externall Impediments: which Impediments, may oft take away part of a mans power to do what hee would; but cannot hinder him from using the power left him, according as his judgement, and reason shall dictate to him.

Difference of Right and Law

A Law of Nature (*Lex Naturalis*) is a Precept, or a generall Rule, found out by Reason, by which a man is forbidden to do, that, which is destructive of his life, or taketh away the means of preserving the same; and to omit, that by which he thinketh it may be best preserved. For though they that speak of this subject, use to confound *Jus*, and *Lex*, *Right* and *Law;* yet they ought to be distinguished; because Right, consisteth in liberty to do, or to forbeare; Whereas Law, determineth, and bindeth to one of them: so that Law, and Right, differ as much, as Obligation, and Liberty; which in one and the same matter are inconsistent.

Naturally every man has Right to everything

And because the condition of Man (as hath been declared in the precedent Chapter) is a condition of Warre of every one against every one; in which case every one is governed by his own Reason; and there is nothing he can make use of, that may not be a help unto him, in preserving his life against his enemyes; It followeth, that in such a condition, every man has a Right to every thing; even to one anothers body. And therefore, as long as this naturall Right of every man to every thing endureth, there can be no security to any man (how strong or wise soever he be) of living out the time, which Nature ordinarily alloweth men to live. And consequently it is a precept, or generall rule

The Fundamentall Law of Nature

of Reason, *That every man, ought to endeavour Peace, as farre as he has hope of obtaining it; and when he cannot obtain it, that he may seek, and use, all helps, and advantages of Warre.* The first branch of which Rule, containeth the first, and Fundamentall Law of Nature; which is, *to seek Peace, and follow it.* The Second, the summe of the Right of Nature; which is, *By all means we can, to defend our selves.*

The second Law of Nature

From this Fundamentall Law of Nature, by which men are commanded to endeavour Peace, is derived this second Law; *That a man*
65   *be willing, when others are so too, as farre-forth, as for Peace, and defence of himselfe he shall think it necessary, to lay down this right to all things; and be contented with so much liberty against other men, as he would allow other men against himselfe.* For as long as every man holdeth this Right, of doing any thing he liketh; so long are all men in the condition of Warre. But if other men will not lay down their Right, as well as he; then there is no Reason for any one, to devest himselfe of his: For that were to expose himselfe to Prey (which no man is bound to) rather than to dispose himselfe to Peace. This is that Law of the Gospell; *Whatsoever you require that others should do to you, that do ye to them.* And that Law of all men, *Quod tibi fieri non vis, alteri ne feceris.*

What it is to lay down a Right

To *lay downe* a mans *Right* to any thing, is to *devest* himselfe of the *Liberty*, of hindring another of the benefit of his own Right to the same. For he that renounceth, or passeth away his Right, giveth not to any other man a Right which he had not before; because there is nothing to which every man had not Right by Nature: but onely standeth out of his way, that he may enjoy his own originall Right, without hindrance from him; not without hindrance from another. So that the effect which redoundeth to one man, by another mans defect of Right, is but so much diminution of impediments to the use of his own right originall.

Renouncing a Right what it is

Transferring Right what

Obligation

Duty

Injustice

Right is layd aside, either by simply Renouncing it; or by Transferring it to another. By *Simply* Renouncing; when he cares not to whom the benefit thereof redoundeth. By Transferring; when he intendeth the benefit thereof to some certain person, or persons. And when a man hath in either manner abandoned, or granted away his Right, then is he said to be Obliged, or Bound, not to hinder those, to whom such Right is granted, or abandoned, from the benefit of it: and that he *Ought*, and it is his Duty, not to make voyd that voluntary act of his own: and that such hindrance is Injustice, and Injury, as being *Sine Jure;* the Right being before renounced, or transferred. So that *Injury*, or *Injustice*, in the controversies of the world, is somewhat like to that, which in the disputations of Scholers is called *Absurdity*. For as it is there called an Absurdity, to contradict what one maintained in the Beginning: so in the world, it is called Injustice, and Injury, voluntarily to undo that, which from the beginning he had voluntarily done....

The mutuall transferring of Right, is that which men call Contract.

There is difference, between transferring of Right to the Thing; and transferring, or tradition, that is, delivery of the Thing it selfe. For the Thing may be delivered together with the Translation of the Right; as in buying and selling with ready mony; or exchange of goods, or lands: and it may be delivered some time after.

Covenant what

Again, one of the Contractors, may deliver the Thing contracted for on his part, and leave the other to perform his part at some determinate time after, and in the mean time be trusted; and then the Contract on his part, is called Pact, or Covenant: Or both parts may contract now, to performe hereafter: in which cases, he that is to performe in time to come, being trusted, his performance is called *Keeping of Promise*, or Faith; and the fayling of performance (if it be voluntary) *Violation of Faith*....

CHAP. XV
OF OTHER LAWES OF NATURE

The third Law of Nature, Justice

From that law of Nature, by which we are obliged to transferre to another, such Rights, as being retained, hinder the peace of Mankind, there followeth a Third; which is this, *That men performe their Covenants made;* without which, Covenants are in vain, and but Empty words; and the Right of all men to all things remaining, wee are still in the conditon of Warre.

Justice and Injustice what

And in this law of Nature, consisteth the Fountain and Originall of Justice. For where no Covenant hath preceded, there hath no Right been transferred, and every man has right to every thing; and consequently, no action can be Unjust. But when a Covenant is made, then to break it is *Unjust:* And the definition of Injustice, is no other than *the not Performance of Covenant.* And whatsoever is not Unjust, is *Just.*...

A Rule, by which the Lawes of Nature may easily be examined

... And though this may seem too subtile a deduction of the Lawes of Nature, to be taken notice of by all men; whereof the most part are too busie in getting food, and the rest too negligent to understand; yet to leave all men unexcusable, they have been contracted into one easie sum, intelligible, even to the meanest capacity; and that is, *Do not that to another, which thou wouldest not have done to thy selfe;* which sheweth him, that he has no more to do in learning the Lawes of Nature, but, when weighing the actions of other men with his own, they seem too heavy, to put them into the other part of the ballance, and his own into their place, that his own passions, and selfe-love, may adde nothing to the weight; and then there is none of these Lawes of Nature that will not appear unto him very reasonable.

The Lawes of Nature oblige in Conscience always, but in Effect then onely when there is Security

The Lawes of Nature oblige *in foro interno;* that is to say, they bind to a desire they should take place: but *in foro externo;* that is, to the putting them in act, not alwayes. For he that should be modest, and tractable, and performe all he promises, in such time, and place where no man els should do so, should but make himselfe a prey to others, and procure his own certain ruine, contrary to the ground of all Lawes of Nature, which tend to Natures preservation. . . .

The Lawes of Nature are Eternal;

The Lawes of Nature are Immutable and Eternall; For Injustice, Ingratitude, Arrogance, Pride, Iniquity, Acception of persons, and the rest, can never be made lawfull. For it can never be that Warre shall preserve life, and Peace destroy it.

And yet Easie

The same Lawes, because they oblige onely to a desire, and endeavour, I mean an unfeigned and constant endeavour, are easie to be observed. For in that they require nothing but endeavour; he that endeavoureth their performance, fulfilleth them; and he that fulfilleth the Law, is Just.

David Hume

A Treatise of Human Nature

Book II
Of the Passions.

PART III. *OF THE WILL AND DIRECT PASSIONS.*

SECTION III.
OF THE INFLUENCING MOTIVES OF THE WILL.

Nothing is more usual in philosophy, and even in common life, than to talk of the combat of passion and reason, to give the preference to reason, and to assert that men are only so far virtuous as they conform themselves to its dictates. Every rational creature, 'tis said, is oblig'd to regulate his actions by reason; and if any other motive or principle challenge the direction of his conduct, he ought to oppose

From David Hume, *A Treatise of Human Nature.* First published in 1739 and 1740.

it, 'till it be entirely subdu'd, or at least brought to a conformity with that superior principle. On this method of thinking the greatest part of moral philosophy, ancient and modern, seems to be founded; nor is there an ampler field, as well for metaphysical arguments, as popular declamations, than this suppos'd pre-eminence of reason above passion. The eternity, invariableness, and divine origin of the former have been display'd to the best advantage: The blindness, unconstancy and deceitfulness of the latter have been as strongly insisted on. In order to shew the fallacy of all this philosophy, I shall endeavour to prove *first*, that reason alone can never be a motive to any action of the will; and *secondly*, that it can never oppose passion in the direction of the will.

The understanding exerts itself after two different ways, as it judges from demonstration or probability; as it regards the abstract relations of our ideas, or those relations of objects, of which experience only gives us information. I believe it scarce will be asserted, that the first species of reasoning alone is ever the cause of any action. As its proper province is the world of ideas, and as the will always places us in that of realities, demonstration and volition seem, upon that account, to be totally remov'd, from each other. Mathematics, indeed, are useful in all mechanical operations, and arithmetic in almost every art and profession: But 'tis not of themselves they have any influence. Mechanics are the art of regulating the motions of bodies *to some design'd end or purpose;* and the reason why we employ arithmetic in fixing the proportions of numbers, is only that we may discover the proportions of their influence and operation. A merchant is desirous of knowing the sum total of his accounts with any person: Why? but that he may learn what sum will have the same *effects* in paying his debt, and going to market, as all the particular articles taken together. Abstract or demonstrative reasoning, therefore, never influences any of our actions, but only as it directs our judgment concerning causes and effects; which leads us to the second operation of the understanding.

'Tis obvious, that when we have the prospect of pain or pleasure from any object, we feel a consequent emotion of aversion or propensity, and are carry'd to avoid or embrace what will give us this uneasiness or satisfaction. 'Tis also obvious, that this emotion rests not here, but making us cast our view on every side, comprehends whatever objects are connected with its original one by the relation of cause and effect. Here then reasoning takes place to discover this relation; and according as our reasoning varies, our actions receive a subsequent variation. But 'tis evident in this case, that the impulse arises not from reason, but is only directed by it. 'Tis from the prospect of pain or pleasure that the aversion or propensity arises towards any object: And these emotions extend themselves to the causes and effects of that object, as they are pointed out to us by reason and experience. It can never in the least concern us to know, that such objects are causes, and such others effects, if both the causes and effects be indifferent to us. Where the objects themselves do not affect us, their connexion can never give them any influence; and 'tis plain, that as reason is nothing but the discovery of this connexion, it cannot be by its means that the objects are able to affect us.

Since reason alone can never produce any action, or give rise to volition, I infer, that the same faculty is as incapable of preventing volition, or of disputing the preference with any passion or emotion. This consequence is necessary. 'Tis impossible reason cou'd have the latter effect of preventing volition, but by giving an impulse in a contrary direction to our passion; and that impulse, had it operated alone, wou'd have been able to produce volition. Nothing can oppose or retard the impulse of passion, but a contrary impulse; and if this contrary impulse ever arises from reason, that latter faculty must have an original influence on the will, and must be able to cause, as well as hinder any act of volition. But if reason has no original influence, 'tis impossible it can withstand any principle, which has such an efficacy, or ever keep the mind in suspense a moment. Thus it appears, that the principle, which opposes our passion, cannot be the same with reason, and is only call'd so in an improper sense. We speak not strictly and philosophically when we talk of the combat of passion and of reason. Reason is, and ought only to be the slave of the passions, and can never pretend to any other office than to serve and obey them. As this opinion may appear somewhat extraordinary, it may not be improper to confirm it by some other considerations.

A passion is an original existence, or, if you will, modification of existence, and contains not any representative quality, which renders it a copy of any other existence or modification. When I am angry, I am actually possest with the passion, and in that emotion have no more a reference to any other object, than when I am thirsty, or sick, or more than five foot high. 'Tis impossible, therefore, that this passion can be oppos'd by, or be contradictory to truth and reason; since this contradiction consists in the disagreement of ideas, consider'd as copies, with those objects, which they represent.

What may at first occur on this head, is, that as nothing can be contrary to truth or reason, except what has a reference to it, and as the judgments of our understanding only have this reference, it must follow, that passions can be contrary to reason only so far as they are *accompany'd* with some judgment or opinion. According to this principle, which is so obvious and natural, 'tis only in two senses, that any affection can be call'd unreasonable. First, When a passion, such as hope or fear, grief or joy, despair or security, is founded on the supposition of the existence of objects, which really do not exist. Secondly, When in exerting any passion in action, we chuse means insufficient for the design'd end, and deceive ourselves in our judgment of causes and effects. . . . In short, a passion must be accompany'd with some false judgment, in order to its being unreasonable; and even then 'tis not the passion, properly speaking, which is unreasonable, but the judgment.

The consequences are evident. Since a passion can never, in any sense, be call'd unreasonable, but when founded on a false supposition, or when it chuses means insufficient for the design'd end, 'tis impossible, that reason and passion can ever oppose each other, or dispute for the government of the will and actions. The moment we perceive the falshood of any supposition, or the insufficiency of any means our passions yield to our reason without any opposition. I may desire any fruit as of an excellent relish; but whenever you convince me of my mistake, my longing ceases. I may will the performance of certain actions as means of obtaining any desir'd good; but as my willing of these actions is only secondary, and founded on the supposition that they are causes of the propos'd effect; as soon as I discover the falshood of that supposition, they must become indifferent to me.

Book III.
Of Morals.

PART I.
OF VIRTUE AND VICE IN GENERAL.

SECTION I.
MORAL DISTINCTIONS NOT DERIV'D FROM REASON.

... It has been observ'd, that nothing is ever present to the mind but its perceptions; and that all the actions of seeing, hearing, judging, loving, hating, and thinking, fall under this denomination. The mind can never exert itself in any action, which we may not comprehend under the term of *perception*; and consequently that term is no less applicable to those judgments, by which we distinguish moral good and evil, than to every other operation of the mind. To approve of one character, to condemn another, are only so many different perceptions.

Now as perceptions resolve themselves into two kinds, viz. *impressions* and *ideas*, this distinction gives rise to a question, with which we shall open up our present enquiry concerning morals, *Whether 'tis by means of our* ideas *or* impressions *we distinguish betwixt vice and virtue, and pronounce an action blameable or praise-worthy?* This will immediately cut off all loose discourses and declamations, and reduce us to something precise and exact on the present subject.

Those who affirm that virtue is nothing but a conformity to reason; that there are eternal fitnesses and unfitnesses of things, which are the same to every rational being that considers them; that the immutable measures of right and wrong impose an obligation, not only on human creatures, but also on the Deity himself: All these systems concur in the opinion, that morality, like truth, is discern'd merely by ideas, and by their juxta-position and comparison. In order, therefore, to judge of these systems, we need only consider, whether it be possible, from reason alone, to distinguish betwixt moral good and evil, or whether there must concur some other principles to enable us to make that distinction.

If morality had naturally no influence on human passions and actions, 'twere in vain to take such pains to inculcate it; and nothing wou'd be more fruitless than that multitude of rules and precepts, with which all moralists abound. Philosophy is commonly divided into *speculative* and *practical;* and as morality is always comprehended under the latter division, 'tis supposed to influence our passions and actions, and to go beyond the calm and indolent judgments of the understanding. And this is confirm'd by common experience, which informs us, that men are often govern'd by their duties, and are deter'd from some actions by the opinion of injustice, and impell'd to others by that of obligation.

Since morals, therefore, have an influence on the actions and affections, it follows, that they cannot be deriv'd from reason; and that because reason alone, as we have already prov'd, can never have any such influence. Morals excite passions, and produce or prevent actions. Reason of itself is utterly impotent in this particular. The rules of morality, therefore, are not conclusions of our reason.

No one, I believe, will deny the justness of this inference; nor is there any other means of evading it, than by denying that prinicple, on which it is founded. As long as it is allow'd, that reason has no influence on our passions and actions, 'tis in vain to pretend, that morality is discover'd only by a deduction of reason. An active principle can never be founded on an inactive; and if reason be inactive in itself, it must remain so in all its shapes and appearances, whether it exerts itself in natural or moral subjects, whether it considers the powers of external bodies, or the actions of rational beings. . . .

Reason is the discovery of truth or falshood. Truth or falshood consists in an agreement or disagreement either to the *real* relations of ideas, or to *real* existence and matter of fact. Whatever, therefore, is not susceptible of this agreement or disagreement, is incapable of being true or false, and can never be an object of our reason. Now 'tis evident our passions, volitions, and actions, are not susceptible of any such agreement or disagreement; being original facts and realities, compleat in themselves, and implying no reference to other passions, volitions, and actions. 'Tis impossible, therefore, they can be pronounced either true or false, and be either contrary or conformable to reason.

This argument is of double advantage to our present purpose. For it proves *directly*, that actions do not derive their merit from a conformity to reason, nor their blame from a contrariety to it; and it proves the same truth more *indirectly*, by shewing us, that as reason can never immediately prevent or produce any action by contradicting or approving of it, it cannot be the source of moral good and evil, which are found to have that influence. Actions may be laudable or blameable; but they cannot be reasonable or unreasonable: Laudable or blameable, therefore, are not the same with reasonable or unreasonable. The merit and demerit of actions frequently contradict, and sometimes controul our natural propensities. But reason has no such influence. Moral distinctions, therefore, are not the offspring of reason. Reason is wholly inactive, and can never be the source of so active a principle as conscience, or a sense of morals. . . .

It has been observ'd, that reason, in a strict and philosophical sense, can have an influence on our conduct only after two ways: Either when it excites a passion by informing us of the existence of something which is a proper object of it; or when it discovers the connexion of causes and effects, so as to afford us means of exerting any passion. These are the only kinds of judgment, which can accompany our actions, or can be said to produce them in any manner; and it must be allow'd, that these judgments may often be false and erroneous. A person may be affected with passion, by supposing a pain or pleasure to lie in an object, which has no tendency to produce either of these sensations, or which produces the contrary to what is imagin'd. A person may also take false measures for the attaining his end, and may retard, by his foolish conduct, instead of forwarding the execution of any project. These false judgments may be thought to affect the passions and actions, which are connected with them, and may be said to render them unreasonable, in a figurative and improper way of speaking. But tho' this be acknowledg'd, 'tis easy to observe, that these errors are so far from being the source of all immorality, that they are commonly very innocent, and draw no manner of guilt upon the person who is so unfortunate as to fall into them. They extend not beyond a mistake of *fact*, which moralists have not generally suppos'd criminal, as being perfectly involuntary. I am more to be lamented than blam'd, if I am mistaken with regard to the influence of objects in producing pain or pleasure, or if I know not the proper means of satisfying my desires. No one can ever regard such errors as a defect in my moral character. A fruit, for instance, that is really disagreeable, appears to me at a distance, and thro' mistake I fancy it to be pleasant and delicious. Here is one error. I choose certain means of reaching this fruit, which are not proper for my end. Here is a second error; nor is there any third one, which can ever possibly enter into our reasonings concerning actions. I ask, therefore, if a man, in this situation, and guilty of these two errors, is to be regarded as vicious and criminal, however unavoidable they might have been? Or if it be possible to imagine, that such errors are the sources of all immorality? . . .

Shou'd it be pretended, that tho' a mistake of *fact* be not criminal, yet a mistake of *right* often is; and that this may be the source of immorality: I would answer, that 'tis impossible such a mistake can ever be the original source of immorality, since it supposes a real right and wrong; that is, a real distinction in morals, independent of these judgments. A mistake, therefore, of right may become a species of immorality; but 'tis only a secondary one, and is founded on some other, antecedent to it. . . .

Thus upon the whole, 'tis impossible, that the distinction betwixt moral good and evil, can be made by reason; since that distinction has an influence upon our actions, of which reason alone is incapable. Reason and judgment may, indeed, be the mediate cause of an action, by prompting, or by directing a passion: But it is not pretended, that a judgment of this kind, either in its truth or falshood, is attended with virtue or vice. And as to the judgments, which are caused by our judgments, they can still less bestow those moral qualities on the actions, which are their causes.

But to be more particular, and to shew, that those eternal immutable fitnesses and unfitnesses of things cannot be defended by sound philosophy, we may weigh the following considerations.

If the thought and understanding were alone capable of fixing the boundaries of right and wrong, the character of virtuous and vicious either must lie in some relations of objects, or must be a matter of fact, which is discovered by our reasoning. This consequence is evident. As the operations of human understanding divide themselves into two kinds, the comparing of ideas, and the inferring of matter of fact; were virtue discover'd by the understanding; it must be an object of one of these operations, nor is there any third operation of the understanding, which can discover it. There has been an opinion very industriously propagated by certain philosophers, that morality is susceptible of demonstration; and tho' no one has ever been able to advance a single step in those demonstrations; yet 'tis taken for granted, that this science may be brought to an equal certainty with geometry or algebra. Upon this supposition, vice and virtue must consist in some relations; since 'tis allow'd on all hands, that no matter of fact is capable of being demonstrated. . . .

If you assert, that vice and virtue consist in relations susceptible of certainty and demonstration, you must confine yourself to those *four* relations, which alone admit of that degree of evidence; and in that case you run into absurdities, from which you will never be able to extricate yourself. For as you make the very essence of morality to lie in the relations, and as there is no one of these relations but what is applicable, not only to an irrational, but also to an inanimate object; it follows, that even such objects must be susceptible of merit or demerit. *Resemblance, contrariety, degrees in quality*, and *proportions in quantity and number;* all these relations belong as properly to matter, as to our actions, passions, and volitions. 'Tis unquestionable, therefore, that morality lies not in any of these relations, nor the sense of it in their discovery. . . .

I must, therefore, on this occasion, rest contented with requiring the two following conditions of any one that wou'd undertake to clear up this system. *First*, As moral good and evil belong only to the actions of the mind, and are deriv'd from our situation with regard to external objects, the relations, from which these moral distinctions arise, must lie only betwixt internal actions, and external objects, and must not be applicable either to internal actions, compared among themselves, or to external objects, when placed in opposition to other external objects. For as morality is supposed to attend certain relations, if these relations cou'd belong to internal actions consider'd singly, it wou'd follow, that we might be guilty of crimes in ourselves, and independent of our situation, with respect to the universe: And in like manner, if these moral relations cou'd be apply'd to external objects, it wou'd follow, that even inanimate beings wou'd be susceptible of moral beauty and deformity. Now it seems difficult to imagine, that any relation can be discover'd betwixt our passions, volitions and actions, compared to external objects, which relation might not belong either to these passions and volitions, or to these external objects, compar'd among *themselves.*

But it will be still more difficult to fulfil the *second* condition, requisite to justify this system. According to the principles of those who maintain an abstract rational difference betwixt moral good and evil, and a natural fitness and unfitness of things, 'tis not only suppos'd, that these relations, being eternal and immutable, are the same, when consider'd by every rational creature, but their *effects* are also suppos'd to be necessarily the same; and 'tis concluded they have no less, or rather a greater, influence in directing the will of the deity, than in governing the rational and virtuous of our own species. These two particulars are evidently distinct. 'Tis one thing to know virtue, and another to conform the will to it. In order, therefore, to prove, that the measures of right and wrong are eternal laws, *obligatory* on every rational mind, 'tis not sufficient to shew the relations upon which they are founded: We must also point out the connexion betwixt the relation and the will; and must prove that this connexion is so necessary, that in every well-disposed mind, it must take place and have its influence; tho' the difference betwixt these minds be in other respects immense and infinite. Now besides what I have already prov'd, that even in human nature no relation can ever alone produce any action; besides this, I say, it has been shewn, in treating of the understanding, that there is no connexion of cause and effect, such as this is suppos'd to be, which is discoverable otherwise than by experience, and of which we can pretend to have any security by the simple consideration of the objects. All beings in the universe, consider'd in themselves, appear entirely loose and independent of each other. 'Tis only by experience we learn their influence and connexion; and this influence we ought never to extend beyond experience.

Thus it will be impossible to fulfil the *first* condition required to the system of eternal rational measures of right and wrong; because it is impossible to shew those relations, upon which such a distinction may be founded: And 'tis as impossible to fulfil the *second* condition; because we cannot prove *a priori*, that these relations, if they really existed and were perceiv'd, wou'd be universally forcible and obligatory.

But to make these general reflexions more clear and convincing, we may illustrate them by some particular instances, wherein this character of moral good or evil is the most universally acknowledged. Of all crimes that human creatures are capable of committing, the most horrid and unnatural is ingratitude, especially when it is committed against parents, and appears in the more flagrant instances of wounds and death. This is acknowledg'd by all mankind, philosophers as well as the people; the question only arises among philosophers, whether the guilt or moral deformity of this action be discover'd by demonstrative reasoning, or be felt by an internal sense, and by means of some sentiment, which the reflecting on such an action naturally occasions. This question will soon be decided against the former opinion, if we can shew the same relations in other objects, without the notion of any guilt or iniquity attending them. Reason or science is nothing but the comparing of ideas, and the discovery of their relations; and if the same relations have different characters, it must evidently follow, that those characters are not discover'd merely by reason. . . .

But to chuse an instance, still more resembling; I would fain ask any one, why incest in the human species is criminal, and why the very same action, and the same relations in animals have not the smallest moral turpitude and deformity? If it be answer'd, that this action is innocent in animals, because they have not reason sufficient to discover its turpitude; but that man, being endow'd with that faculty, which *ought* to restrain him to his duty, the same action instantly becomes criminal to him; should this be said, I would reply, that this is evidently arguing in a circle. For before reason can perceive this turpitude, the turpitude must exist; and consequently is independent of the decisions of our reason, and is their object more properly than their effect. According to this system, then, every animal, that has sense, and appetite, and will; that is, every animal must be susceptible of all the same virtues and vices, for which we ascribe praise and blame to human creatures. All the difference is, that our superior reason may serve to discover the vice or virtue, and by that means may augment the blame or praise: But still this discovery supposes a separate being in these moral distinctions, and a being, which depends only on the will and appetite, and which, both in thought and reality, may be distinguish'd from the reason. Animals are susceptible of the same relations, with respect to each other, as the human species, and therefore wou'd also be susceptible of the same morality, if the essence of morality consisted in these relations. Their want of a sufficient degree of reason may hinder them from perceiving the duties and obligations of morality, but can never hinder these duties from existing; since they must antecedently exist, in order to their being perceiv'd. Reason must find them, and can never produce them. This argument deserves to be weigh'd, as being, in my opinion, entirely decisive.

Nor does this reasoning only prove, that morality consists not in any relations, that are the objects of science; but if examin'd, will prove with equal certainty, that it consists not in any *matter of fact*, which can be discover'd by the understanding. This is the *second* part of our argument; and if it can be made evident, we may conclude, that morality is not an object of reason. But can there be any difficulty in proving, that vice and virtue are not matters of fact, whose existence we can infer by reason? Take any action allow'd to be vicious: Wilful murder, for instance. Examine it in all lights, and see if you can find that matter of fact, or real existence, which you call *vice*. In which-ever way you take it, you find only certain passions, motives, volitions and thoughts. There is no other matter of fact in this case. The vice entirely escapes you, as long as you consider the object. You never can find it, till you turn your reflexion into your own breast, and find a sentiment of disapprobation, which arises in you, towards this action. Here is a matter of fact; but 'tis the object of feeling, not of reason. It lies in yourself, not in the object. So that when you pronounce any action or character to be vicious, you mean nothing, but that from the constitution of your nature you have a feeling or sentiment of blame from the contemplation of it. Vice and virtue, therefore, may be compar'd to sounds, colours, heat and cold, which, according to modern philosophy, are not qualities in objects, but perceptions in the mind: And this discovery in morals, like that other in physics, is to be regarded as a considerable advancement of the speculative sciences; tho', like that too, it has little or no influence on practice. Nothing can be more real, or concern us more, than our own sentiments of pleasure and uneasiness; and if these be favourable to virtue, and unfavourable to vice, no more can be requisite to the regulation of our conduct and behaviour.

I cannot forbear adding to these reasonings an observation, which may, perhaps, be found of some importance. In every system of morality, which I have hitherto met with, I have always remark'd, that the author proceeds for some time in the ordinary way of reasoning, and establishes the being of a God, or makes observations concerning human affairs; when of a sudden I am surpriz'd to find, that instead of the usual copulations of propositions, *is*, and *is not*, I meet with no proposition that is not connected with an *ought* or an *ought not*. This change is imperceptible; but is, however, of the last consequence. For as this *ought*, or *ought not*, expresses some new relation or affirmation, 'tis necessary that it shou'd be observ'd and explain'd; and at the same time that a reason should be given, for what seems altogether inconceivable, how this new relation can be a deduction from others, which are entirely different from it. But as authors do not commonly use this precaution, I shall presume to recommend it to the readers; and am persuaded, that this small attention wou'd subvert all the vulgar systems of morality, and let us see, that the distinction of vice and virtue is not founded merely on the relations of objects, nor is perceiv'd by reason.

SECTION II.
MORAL DISTINCTIONS DERIV'D FROM A MORAL SENSE.

Thus the course of the argument leads us to conclude, that since vice and virtue are not discoverable merely by reason, or the comparison of ideas, it must be by means of some impression or sentiment they occasion, that we are able to mark the difference betwixt them. Our decisions concerning moral rectitude and depravity are evidently perceptions; and as all perceptions are either impressions or ideas, the exclusion of one is a convincing argument for the other. Morality, therefore, is more properly felt than judg'd of; tho' this feeling or sentiment is commonly so soft and gentle, that we are apt to confound it with an idea, according to our common custom of taking all things for the same, which have any near resemblance to each other.

The next question is, Of what nature are these impressions, and after what manner do they operate upon us? Here we cannot remain long in suspense, but must pronounce the impression arising from virtue, to be agreeable, and that proceeding from vice to be uneasy. Every moment's experience must convince us of this. There is no spectacle so fair and beautiful as a noble and generous action; nor any which gives us more abhorrence than one that is cruel and treacherous. No enjoyment equals the satisfaction we receive from the company of those we love and esteem; as the greatest of all punishments is to be oblig'd to pass our lives with those we hate or contemn. A very play or romance may afford us instances of this pleasure, which virtue conveys to us; and pain, which arises from vice.

Now since the distinguishing impressions, by which moral good or evil is known, are nothing but *particular* pains or pleasures; it follows, that in all enquiries concerning these moral distinctions, it will be sufficient to shew the principles, which make us feel a satisfaction or uneasiness from the survey of any character, in order to satisfy us why the character is laudable or blameable. An action, or sentiment, or character is virtuous or vicious; why? because its view causes a pleasure or uneasiness of a particular kind. In giving a reason, therefore, for the pleasure or uneasiness, we sufficiently explain the vice or virtue. To have the sense of virtue, is nothing but to *feel* a satisfaction of a particular kind from the contemplation of a character. The very *feeling* constitutes our praise or admiration. We go no farther; nor do we enquire into the cause of the satisfaction. We do not infer a character to be virtuous, because it pleases: But in feeling that it pleases after such a particular manner, we in effect feel that it is virtuous. The case is the same as in our judgments concerning all kinds of beauty, and tastes, and sensations. Our approbation is imply'd in the immediate pleasure they convey to us.

I have objected to the system, which establishes eternal rational measures of right and wrong, that 'tis impossible to shew, in the actions of reasonable creatures, any relations, which are not found in external objects; and therefore, if morality always attended these relations, 'twere possible for inanimate matter to become virtuous or vicious. Now it may, in like manner, be objected to the present system, that if virtue and vice be determin'd by pleasure and pain, these qualities must, in every case, arise from the sensations; and consequently any object, whether animate or inanimate, rational or irrational might become morally good or evil, provided it can excite a satisfaction or uneasiness. But tho' this objection seems to be the very same, it has by no means the same force, in the one case as in the other. For, *first,* 'tis evident, that under the term *pleasure,* we comprehend sensations, which are very different from each other, and which have only such a distant resemblance, as is requisite to make them be express'd by the same abstract term. A good composition of music and a bottle of good wine equally produce pleasure;

and what is more, their goodness is determin'd merely by the pleasure. But shall we say upon that account, that the wine is harmonious, or the music of a good flavour? In like manner an inanimate object, and the character or sentiments of any person may, both of them, give satisfaction; but as the satisfaction is different, this keeps our sentiments concerning them from being confounded, and makes us ascribe virtue to the one, and not to the other. Nor is every sentiment of pleasure or pain, which arises from characters and actions, of that *peculiar* kind, which makes us praise or condemn. The good qualities of an enemy are hurtful to us; but may still command our esteem and respect. 'Tis only when a character is considered in general, without reference to our particular interest, that it causes such a feeling or sentiment, as denominates it morally good or evil. 'Tis true, those sentiments, from interest and morals, are apt to be confounded, and naturally run into one another. It seldom happens, that we do not think an enemy vicious, and can distinguish betwixt his opposition to our interest and real villainy or baseness. But this hinders not, but that the sentiments are, in themselves, distinct; and a man of temper and judgment may preserve himself from these illusions. In like manner, tho' 'tis certain a musical voice is nothing but one that naturally gives a *particular* kind of pleasure; yet 'tis difficult for a man to be sensible, that the voice of an enemy is agreeable, or allow it to be musical. But a person of a fine ear, who has the command of himself, can separate these feelings, and give praise to what deserves it.

Secondly, We may call to remembrance the preceding system of the passions in order to remark a still more considerable difference among our pains and pleasures. Pride and humility, love and hatred are excited, when there is any thing presented to us, that both bears a relation to the object of the passion, and produces a separate sensation related to the sensation of the passion. Now virtue and vice are attended with these circumstances. They must necessarily be plac'd either in ourselves or others, and excite either pleasure or uneasiness; and therefore must give rise to one of these four passions; which clearly distinguishes them from the pleasure and pain arising from inanimate objects, that often bear no relation to us: And this is, perhaps, the most considerable effect that virtue and vice have upon the human mind.

It may now be ask'd *in general,* concerning this pain or pleasure, that distinguishes moral good and evil, *From what principles is it derived, and whence does it arise in the human mind?* To this I reply, *first,* that 'tis absurd to imagine, that in every particular instance, these sentiments are produc'd by an *original* quality and *primary* constitution. For as the number of our duties is, in a manner, infinite, 'tis impossible that our original instincts should extend to each of them, and from our very first infancy impress on the human mind all that multitude of precepts, which are contain'd in the compleatest system of ethics. Such a method of proceeding is not conformable to the usual maxims, by which nature is conducted, where a few principles produce all that variety we observe in the universe, and every thing is carry'd on in the easiest and most simple manner. 'Tis necessary, therefore, to abridge these primary impulses, and find some more general principles, upon which all our notions of morals are founded.

But in the *second* place, should it be ask'd, Whether we ought to search for these principles in *nature,* or whether we must look for them in some other origin? I wou'd reply, that our answer to this question depends upon the definition of the word, Nature, than which there is none more ambiguous and equivocal. If *nature* be oppos'd to miracles, not only the distinction betwixt vice and virtue is natural, but also every event, which has ever happen'd in the world, *excepting those miracles, on which our religion is founded.* In saying, then, that the sentiments of vice and virtue are natural in this sense, we make no very extraordinary discovery.

But *nature* may also be opposed to rare and unusual; and in this sense of the word, which is the common one, there may often arise disputes concerning what is natural or unnatural; and one may in general affirm, that we are not possess'd of any very precise standard, by which these disputes can be decided. Frequent and rare depend upon the number of examples we have observ'd; and as this number may gradually increase or diminish, 'twill be impossible to fix any exact boundaries betwixt them. We may only affirm on this head, that if ever there was any thing, which cou'd be call'd natural in this sense, the sentiments of morality certainly may; since there never was any nation of the world, nor any single person in any nation, who was utterly depriv'd of them, and who never, in any instance, shew'd the least approbation or dislike of manners. These sentiments are so rooted in our constitution and temper, that without entirely confounding the human mind by disease or madness, 'tis impossible to extirpate and destroy them.

But *nature* may also be opposed to artifice, as well as to what is rare and unusual; and in this sense it may be disputed, whether the notions of virtue be natural or not. We readily forget, that the designs, and projects, and views of men are principles as necessary in their operation as heat and cold, moist and dry: But taking them to be free and entirely our own, 'tis usual for us to set them in opposition to the other principles of nature. Shou'd it, therefore, be demanded, whether the sense of virtue be natural or artificial, I am of opinion, that 'tis impossible for me at present to give any precise answer to this question. Perhaps it will appear afterwards, that our sense of some virtues is artificial, and that of others natural....

Mean while it may not be amiss to observe from these definitions of *natural* and *unnatural,* that nothing can be more unphilosophical than those systems, which assert, that virtue is the same with what is natural, and vice with what is unnatural. For in the first sense of the word, Nature, as opposed to miracles, both vice and virtue are equally natural; and in the second sense, as oppos'd to what is unusual, perhaps virtue will be found to be the most unnatural. At least it must be own'd, that heroic virtue, being as unusual, is as little natural as the most brutal barbarity. As to the third sense of the word, 'tis certain, that both vice and virtue are equally artificial, and out of nature. For however it may be disputed, whether the notion of a merit or demerit in certain actions be natural or artificial, 'tis evident, that the actions themselves are artificial, and are perform'd with a certain design and intention; otherwise they cou'd never be rank'd under any of these denominations. 'Tis impossible, therefore, that the character of natural and unnatural can ever, in any sense, mark the boundaries of vice and virtue.

PART III.
OF THE OTHER VIRTUES AND VICES.

SECTION I.
OF THE ORIGIN OF THE NATURAL VIRTUES AND VICES.

...The same principle produces, in many instances, our sentiments of morals, as well as those of beauty. No virtue is more esteem'd than justice, and no vice more detested than injustice; nor are there any qualities, which go farther to the fixing the character, either as amiable or odious. Now justice is a moral virtue, merely because it has that tendency to the good of mankind; and, indeed, is nothing but an artificial invention to that purpose. The same may be said of allegiance, of the laws of nations, of modesty, and of good-manners. All these are mere human contrivances for the interest of society. And since there is a very strong sentiment of morals, which in all nations, and all ages, has attended them, we must allow, that the reflecting on the tendency of characters and mental qualities, is sufficient to give us the sentiments of approbation and blame. Now as the means to an end can only be agreeable, where the end is agreeable; and as the good of society, where our own interest is not concern'd, or that of our friends, pleases only by sympathy: It follows, that sympathy is the source of the esteem, which we pay to all the artificial virtues.

Thus it appears, *that* sympathy is a very powerful principle in human nature, *that* it has a great influence on our taste of beauty, and *that* it produces our sentiment of morals in all the artificial virtues. From thence we may presume, that it also gives rise to many of the other virtues; and that qualities acquire our approbation, because of their tendency to the good of mankind. This presumption must become a certainty, when we find that most of those qualities, which we *naturally* approve of, have actually that tendency, and render a man a proper member of society: While the qualities, which we *naturally* disapprove of, have a contrary tendency, and render any intercourse with the person dangerous or disagreeable. For having found, that such tendencies have force enough to produce the strongest sentiment of morals, we can never reasonably, in these cases, look for any other cause of approbation or blame; it being an inviolable maxim in philosophy, that where any particular cause is sufficient for an effect, we ought to rest satisfied with it, and ought not to multiply causes without necessity....

...The approbation of moral qualities most certainly is not deriv'd from reason, or any comparison of ideas; but proceeds entirely from a moral taste, and from certain sentiments of pleasure or disgust, which arise upon the contemplation and view of particular qualities or characters. Now 'tis evident, that those sentiments, whence-ever they are deriv'd, must vary according to the distance or contiguity of the objects; nor can I feel the same lively pleasure from the virtues of a person, who liv'd in *Greece* two thousand years ago, that I feel from the virtues of a familiar friend and acquaintance. Yet I do not say, that I esteem the one more than the other: And therefore, if the variation of the sentiment, without a variation of the esteem, be an objection, it must have equal force against every other system, as against that of sympathy. But to consider the matter a-right, it has no force at all....

In general, all sentiments of blame or praise are variable, according to our situation of nearness or remoteness, with regard to the person blam'd or prais'd, and according to the present disposition of our mind. But these variations we regard not in our general decisions, but still apply the terms expressive of our liking or dislike, in the same manner, as if we remain'd in one point of view. Experience soon teaches us this method of correcting our sentiments, or at least, of correcting our language, where the sentiments are more stubborn and inalterable. Our servant, if diligent and faithful, may excite stronger sentiments of love and kindness than *Marcus Brutus,* as represented in history; but we say not upon that account, that the former character is more laudable than the latter. We know, that were we to approach equally near to that renown'd patriot, he wou'd command a much higher degree of affection and admiration. Such corrections are common with regard to all the senses; and indeed 'twere impossible we cou'd ever make use of language, or communicate our sentiments to one another, did we not correct the momentary appearances of things, and overlook our present situation. . . .

Thus, to take a general review of the present hypothesis: Every quality of the mind is denominated virtuous, which gives pleasure by the mere survey; as every quality, which produces pain, is call'd vicious. This pleasure and this pain may arise from four different sources. For we reap a pleasure from the view of a character, which is naturally fitted to be useful to others, or to the person himself, or which is agreeable to others, or to the person himself. One may, perhaps, be surpriz'd, that amidst all these interests and pleasures, we shou'd forget our own, which touch us so nearly on every other occasion. But we shall easily satisfy ourselves on this head, when we consider, that every particular person's pleasure and interest being different, 'tis impossible men cou'd ever agree in their sentiments and judgments, unless they chose some common point of view, from which they might survey their object, and which might cause it to appear the same to all of them. Now, in judging of characters, the only interest or pleasure, which appears the same to every spectator, is that of the person himself, whose character is examin'd; or that of persons, who have a connexion with him. And tho' such interests and pleasures touch us more faintly than our own, yet being more constant and universal, they counter-balance the latter even in practice, and are alone admitted in speculation as the standard of virtue and morality. They alone produce that particular feeling or sentiment, on which moral distinctions depend.

As to the good or ill desert of virtue or vice, 'tis an evident consequence of the sentiments of pleasure or uneasiness. These sentiments produce love or hatred; and love or hatred, by the original constitution of human passion, is attended with benevolence or anger; that is, with a desire of making happy the person we love, and miserable the person we hate.

SUGGESTIONS FOR DISCUSSION

1. Can all moral principles be established as a result of a social contract?

2. What policies would a Hobbesian sovereign adopt concerning capital punishment (see Part II, Chapter 13) or political violence and terrorism (see Chapter 14)?

3. Do *facts* play the decisive role in establishing what we *ought* morally to do in given circumstances?

4. What implications, if any, do Hume's positive views on morality have for setting social policy?

FURTHER READING

HOBBES

Baumrin, B., ed. *Hobbes's Leviathan.* San Francisco: Wadsworth, 1969. (Interpretation, critical analysis; advanced)

Brown, K. C. *Hobbes Studies.* Cambridge, Mass: Harvard University Press, 1965. (Interpretation, critical analysis; advanced)

Collingwood, R. G. *The New Leviathan.* Oxford: Clarendon Press, 1942. (Interpretation; advanced)

Gauthier, D. P. *The Logic of Leviathan.* Oxford: Clarendon Press, 1969. (Interpretation, critical analysis; advanced)

Gert, B. *The Moral Rules.* New York: Harper & Row, 1970. (Interpretation, critical analysis; advanced)

Goldsmith, M. M. *Hobbes's Science of Politics.* New York: Columbia University Press, 1966. (Interpretation, critical analysis; intermediate)

Hampton, J. *Hobbes and the Social Contract Tradition.* Cambridge: Cambridge University Press, 1986. (Interpretation, critical analysis; advanced)

Johnston, D. *The Rhetoric of Leviathan.* Princeton: Princeton University Press, 1986. (Interpretation, critical analysis; advanced)

Kavka, G. *Hobbesian Moral and Political Theory.* Princeton: Princeton University Press, 1986. (Interpretation, critical analysis; advanced)

Macpherson, C. B. *The Political Theory of Possessive Individualism.* Oxford: Clarendon Press, 1962. (Interpretation, critical analysis; advanced)

Oakeshott, M. *Rationalism in Politics and Other Essays.* New York: Basic Books, 1962. (Interpretation, critical analysis; advanced)

Peters, R. *Hobbes.* London: Harmondsworth, 1962. (Interpretation, critical analysis; intermediate)

Strauss, L. *Political Philosophy of Hobbes.* Oxford: Clarendon Press, 1936. (Interpretation; advanced)

Taylor, A. E. *Thomas Hobbes.* London: A. Constable, 1908. (Interpretation, critical analysis; advanced)

Warrender, H. *The Political Philosophy of Hobbes.* Oxford: Clarendon Press, 1957. (Interpretation, critical analysis; advanced)

Watkins, J. W. *Hobbes's System of Ideas.* New York: Hilary House, 1965. (Interpretation; critical analysis; advanced)

HUME

Baier, A. *Postures of the Mind.* Minneapolis: University of Minnesota Press, 1985. (Interpretation, critical analysis; advanced)

Bennett, J. *Locke, Berkeley and Hume*. Oxford: Oxford University Press, 1971. (Interpretation, critical analysis; advanced)

Broad, C. D. *Five Types of Ethical Theory*. London: Routledge, 1930. (Interpretation, critical analysis; advanced)

Chappell, V. C., ed. *Hume: A Collection of Critical Essays*. South Bend: University of Notre Dame Press, 1966. (Interpretation, critical analysis; advanced)

Glathe, A. B. *Hume's Theory of the Passions and of Morals*. Berkeley: University of California Press, 1950. (Interpretation, critical analysis; advanced)

Hume, D. *Enquiry Concerning Human Understanding*. London, 1751.

Kemp, J. *Ethical Naturalism: Hume and Hobbes*. London: Macmillan, 1970. (Interpretation, critical analysis; advanced)

Pears, D. F., ed. *David Hume: A Symposium*. London: Macmillan, 1963. (Interpretation, critical analysis; advanced)

Raphael, D. D., ed. *British Moralists, 1650–1800*. Oxford: Oxford University Press, 1979.

———. *The Moral Sense*. London: Oxford University Press, 1947. (Interpretation, critical analysis; advanced)

3

□

Rousseau and Kant

JEAN-JACQUES ROUSSEAU (1712–1778):
THE GENERAL WILL AND THE SOCIAL
CONTRACT

Hobbes and Rousseau Like Hobbes, Jean-Jacques Rousseau was primarily concerned with questions of political morality and the social institutions that would best secure legitimate government. Like Hobbes, again, Rousseau developed his philosophical analysis of legitimate government in terms of concepts like the "state of nature," "right," and the "social contract." However, on Hobbes's conception of human nature individuals fear death, while on Rousseau's view they do not. Nor did Rousseau assume that in an economy of scarce resources, each individual equally desires simply to satisfy self-interests (see Hobbes, Part I, Chapter 2). Rather, Rousseau believed that the state of nature is one of abundance, that human beings are equally interested in and capable of achieving freedom, and that they are motivated by self-love.

Rousseau's State of Nature Schematically, self-interest need not incorporate notions of self-respect and self-esteem, whereas the concept of self-love must include them. So, for its satisfaction, self-love requires recognition *by* others, while self-interest need not. Yet individuals in Rousseau's state of nature are indifferent to each other; they seek only what they find necessary for self-preservation. Accordingly, life in Rousseau's state of nature may not be short, nasty, and brutish but it will lack human fulfillment, for the benefits of social cooperation are lacking.

The Social Contract Rousseau assumed that individuals desire to satisfy their fundamental needs and to fulfill their self-love. Each understands also that if he or she aimed only to satisfy self-interest, everyone would fare worse than if all cooperated. Rousseau held that satisfaction of self-love depends upon actions of others; satisfaction is ultimately possible only under conditions of social interdependence. Moreover, he assumed that each individual has a set of beliefs

98

about the acceptability of claims that can be made upon him or her, and that this set conflicts with the relevant beliefs of others. Given these assumptions, Rousseau sought a form of social cooperation and association that protects the person and property of each, while making possible individual development, education, and expression. It must do so, however, while it maintains individual freedom, rights, and self-determination. The social contract was supposed to furnish this form of association.

For Rousseau, each individual knows that a conception of the "common good" or common interest is shared with all others. What differs among agents, if anything, is not this conception, but their particular views of how best to achieve the common good. That an institution, social arrangement, or law best guarantees the common good is considered by individuals as one among the possible reasons for accepting it. They comprehend that reason requires them to act for the sake of the common good, if they are reasonably confident others will also.

The General Will   Rousseau argued that self-protection, self-expression, and freedom would be maximized by a contractual agreement among members of the state of nature. After all, they share a conception of their common interest. This agreement establishes a *general will*. The general will is constituted by a contract whereby each individual will invests person and power in a common authority and common institutions. Authority is bestowed in the final analysis by the shared conception each contractor has of the good common to all. The general will commands the "supreme" direction, though not the only one. The contract that produces the general will promotes both individual freedom and self-love. Though the conception of the common good is shared, it is the agent's own; it is chosen autonomously. Each citizen accepts the law because in prescribing it for all, each prescribes it for himself or herself. So the rule of the general will is the rule of each individual will. Yet the general will differs from the *will of all;* that is, from the aggregate forces of all separate individuals. The social contract, Rousseau concluded, "leaves [contractors or citizens] as free as before." Further, it is only because the unanimous agreement is among rational agents with common interests that they are prepared to accept the contract. The satisfaction of common interest by contractual agreement, in turn, is a necessary condition for fulfilling self-love.

Morality and Socialization   Rousseau's justification of the general will in terms of the social contract depends upon an analysis of rationality, and the moral principles it identifies, that is independent of any appeal to empirical or factual experience of how the world is. Known as *a priori* analysis, it is to be distinguished from the account Rousseau offered of how citizens in fact acquire social and political principles as they become socialized. These potentially conflicting concerns with moral principles or right, on the one hand, and principles acquired in socialization, on the other, merged for Rousseau in the question of how citizens best acquire and act upon principles of right. Rousseau thought that socialization in a *democratic* state would engender in agents the conception of the general will. This conception was taken to provide citizens with the basis for establishing the principles of moral and political right. In this way, Rousseau merged moral and political inquiry: what it takes to be a moral person is what is required of a good citizen.

IMMANUEL KANT (1724–1804): SELF-DETERMINATION AND THE CATEGORICAL IMPERATIVE

Kant and Hume   The German philosopher Immanuel Kant was deeply troubled by Hume's argument that reason is incapable of originating or inhibiting action. Hume's argument was designed to show that formal principles of reason cannot directly cause human action. These rational principles are in the service of socially formed and changing motivations. Hume's critique of reason effectively undermined the view that moral claims are objectively right or wrong (see Part I, Chapter 2).

Challenged by Hume's critique of reason, Kant appealed to Rousseau's insight that if morality is to be possible on its own terms, self-interest must be governed by moral reason. This required demonstrating that moral reason is necessarily self-motivating: moral reason must be independent of both self-interest and any such moral sentiment as benevolence or sympathy. Kant set out to establish the conditions that must hold for individual agents if moral reason is to provide them with its own motive to act.

He began by assuming that ordinary moral judgments in the Judeo-Christian tradition—for instance, that we ought to keep our promises or pay our debts—may legitimately claim to be true. He set out to establish the conditions that must hold for such claims to be true. Thus Kant represented his undertaking as moving from "common sense morality" to "philosophical morality." In other words, he aimed to show, against Hume, that pure reason can be practical or can cause action. Kant argued that reason is represented, in its application to practical affairs requiring action, by a single unchanging principle of right conduct. If agents are to be held responsible for acting on this morally binding principle, it cannot be imposed upon them by external forces. Thus Kant had to show that the principle of morality is freely chosen by agents themselves.

Morality and Rationality   Kant considered human beings to be only partly rational in constitution. Where sensuous inclinations such as desires or passions present goals or ends to be pursued, Kant acknowledged Hume's point that reason simply services the sensuous by identifying the best means to achieve the given ends. A supreme principle or single standard capable of determining the morality of any act, however, cannot be established empirically by observing actual human behavior. Descriptive psychology and anthropology reveal only facts, and they are unable to establish what acts *ought* to be done. Kant argued also that the Natural Law tradition is mistaken in taking morality to be derivable from human nature, for human nature in general changes over time (on Natural Law, see Aquinas, Part I, Chapter 1). He insisted that only the formal or rational part of human nature is unchanging. Moral action is rational action, and the supreme principle of morality must apply to all rational beings in virtue of their rationality. Analysis of rationality was supposed to reveal how, in being commanded by reason to act morally, rational agents nevertheless remain free and so rationally responsible for their acts.

The Good Will Kant acknowledged that nature, including human nature, functions according to laws. For an act to be moral, it must accord with and be done for the sake of the moral law: Duty must be done for duty's sake. Rational creatures differ from others in that they alone are capable of willing that their actions be done for the sake of the moral law. A will governed always by reason is a *good will*. A good will, for Kant, may be thought of as the self-conscious resolve to act in a way that is morally right, and only for the reason that it is right. A will is not good because of any beneficial consequences it brings about; a good will has intrinsic moral worth independent of its advantages. Indeed, on Kant's view, the good will is the only thing that is good without qualification; it is necessary for the production of any other moral good, including happiness.

Imperatives While the human will may be rational and so good, it is also subject to motivations that are not strictly rational. To the extent that it is motivated by nonrational inclinations like pleasure, the human will is less than perfectly good. So the human will experiences the laws of reason as commands or requirements of what it ought rationally to do. These commands or constraints of reason Kant called "imperatives." Imperatives are commands or requirements issued by reason to act in various ways that may or should be considered valuable. Examples of imperatives may include "Learn to speak Spanish," "You should go to sleep," and "Do not lie."

Hypothetical Imperatives Kant identified two general kinds of imperative, the *hypothetical* and the *categorical*. If an action is commanded as instrumentally necessary for bringing about some further end, the imperative is hypothetical; if it is required as good without qualification, the imperative is categorical. Kant distinguished two sorts of hypothetical imperatives. First, *imperatives of skill* are technical rules of skill necessary for bringing about a given end or goal. Whoever desires the end is rationally constrained to use the technical means appropriate to achieving it: If I wish to work in Argentina, I must become fluent in Spanish. Second, *pragmatic counsels of prudence* advise one how best to achieve those goals that are likely to make one happy. Happiness is indefinite, for it is an ideal of imagination rather than one of reason. Accordingly, the means to its attainment suffer a lack of precision. For example, if I am tired and wish to be rested, I should sleep. The goals specified in hypothetical imperatives depend upon persons' subjective desires. The means ordered by such imperatives reflect the uncertainty of the hypothetical ends aimed at. Should the ends alter, the particular conditional imperative will no longer rationally command the will: if I am no longer tired, reason will not command me to sleep.

The Categorical Imperative The *categorical imperative,* by contrast, commands unconditionally. It constrains all rational agents irrespective of their subjective goals; it commands unqualified obedience to the practical law formulated by reason. The principles of practical reason are universal, impartial, and objective. In commanding me to act in some way, reason requires every rational agent to act alike in suitably similar circumstances. Kant formulated a decision procedure for rational agents to establish what they have a *duty* or a moral obligation to do in each act-context. First, the subjective principle or *maxim* of the act must be specified. For example, I am considering whether to lie to the buyer of my house about the development of the neighboring lot. The maxim of my projected act may be formulated as follows: "I will lie to the buyer of my property in order to secure the success of the sale." Second, in circumstances where this kind of act (in our example, lying to secure personal advantage) is a relevant option, the agent must be willing to have everyone act on the maxim. Finally, the act will be required as a moral duty if and only if the maxim can be willed without inconsistency to be acted on by all those for whom this kind of act is a relevant option. I will have a duty to lie if and only if it can be willed consistently that all individuals lie when it is to their advantage. Kant argued that the maxim of lying to secure advantage cannot be consistently willed to be universally acted upon: for, if everyone acted on it, there would be no institution of truth-telling that the maxim of lying must presuppose were it to be successful. Note that Kant is not appealing here to the bad consequences of lying for advantage. Rather, his argument turns on the claim that the projected consequences of everyone acting in this way are self-defeating. Just as I cannot consistently conceive a square circle, so I cannot conceive that my lie will be believed if people generally lied. The contradiction is contained in any liar's conception *both* that the lie be successful *and* that, once universalized, the lie must fail. So Kant would insist that my advantageous lie, as with lying in general, must be wrong irrespective of its benefits. Thus there is a duty never to lie.

Kant insisted that there is only one categorical imperative or fundamental rule of morality, though he formulated it in various ways. The first formulation is that an act is moral, and so required, if the maxim can be willed rationally, that is, without inconsistency, to become a universal law, a duty for all. Kant's second suggestive formulation, which has been emphasized by commentators, is that rational beings must be treated with the *respect* due them as such. They must be treated, that is, as *ends in themselves* and not merely as means to one's own ends. Humanity, or rational nature in general, has unqualified value that cannot be compared to or traded for anything one otherwise deems beneficial. The capacity of rational beings to determine and pursue their own ends implies that they should be treated as autonomous agents, free to decide rationally what they wish to do as long as they respect the same freedom for others. Though open to considerable interpretation, the notion of *respect* is far less formalistic than *universalizability*. Accordingly, many philosophers have found it germane to the moral domain.

Kant stressed that there is only one categorical imperative or principle of moral law. One might wonder, then, why he offered various formulations of it. He claimed that the first formulation or universalizability principle is a pure law, a formula that can be universally applied. The alternative formulations are offered to render the moral law more accessible to our ordinary grasp or intuition, to demonstrate in terms more readily acceptable what duty requires of us.

Autonomy   Thus Kant claimed to have met Hume's challenge. Duties, or the commands of pure reason in its practical application, constrain the will to undertake impartial action, to act as any rational agent would. Though constrained, actions done from duty are nevertheless free because the principles of duty are self-legislated. They are consistent universalizations of the agent's own motives. This is what Kant means by the claim that if duties are to be morally binding, they must be *autonomously* chosen: Rational agents are free and self-determined. In legislating rationally for themselves, agents legislate for all other rational agents. Kant concluded that rationality is impartial and, against Hume, that it is practical or capable of motivating action. Rousseau's dictum of self-determination, interpreted from the standpoint of the individual rather than the body politic, echoes through Kant's moral theory: "...each one uniting with all obeys only himself and remains as free as before."

Kant rejected all teleological appeals, whether to beneficial ends, pleasure, or happiness, as the grounds for justifying moral claims. Any such appeal would sustain only hypothetical imperatives. In contrast to autonomously chosen moral principles, the latter are imposed upon the agent "heteronomously"; that is, because of various and possibly inconsistent considerations external to acts. In contrast to teleological moral theories, Kant's system of morality is *deontological;* that is, it sets out to establish what rational agents ought morally to do independent of the act's projected consequences, such as its production of goodness.

Kant's attempt to construct a philosophical justification for general moral principles in the Judeo-Christian tradition has exerted considerable and lasting influence upon modern moral philosophy. Contemporary ethics has come to consist largely in the theoretical debate, and its public policy implications, between Kantian-inspired moral philosophy and the view of utilitarianism that developed in the wake of Hume and Kant. It will be seen in the following chapter that utilitarianism consists in interpretations of the principle that moral good consists in maximizing utility or goodness.

Jean-Jacques Rousseau

The Social Contract

Book I

CHAPTER I
THE SUBJECT OF BOOK I

Man was born free, and he is everywhere in chains. Those who think themselves the masters of others are indeed greater slaves than they. How did this transformation come about? I do not know. How can it be made legitimate? That question I believe I can answer.

From Jean-Jacques Rousseau, *The Social Contract,* trans. Maurice Cranston (Harmondsworth: Penguin Books, 1968). Reprinted by permission of A.D. Peters & Co. Ltd.

If I were to consider only force and the effects of force, I should say: "So long as a people is constrained to obey, and obeys, it does well; but as soon as it can shake off the yoke, and shakes it off, it does better; for since it regains its freedom by the same right as that which removed it, a people is either justified in taking back its freedom, or there is no justifying those who took it away." But the social order is a sacred right which serves as a basis for all other rights. And as it is not a natural right, it must be one founded on covenants. The problem is to determine what those covenants are. . . .

CHAPTER 3
THE RIGHT OF THE STRONGEST

The strongest man is never strong enough to be master all the time, unless he transforms force into right and obedience into duty. Hence "the right of the strongest"—a "right" that sounds like something intended ironically, but is actually laid down as a principle. But shall we never have this phrase explained? Force is a physical power; I do not see how its effects could produce morality. To yield to force is an act of necessity, not of will; it is at best an act of prudence. In what sense can it be a moral duty?

Let us grant, for a moment, that this so-called right exists. I suggest it can only produce a tissue of bewildering nonsense; for once might is made to be right, cause and effect are reversed, and every force which overcomes another force inherits the right which belonged to the vanquished. As soon as man can disobey with impunity, his disobedience becomes legitimate; and as the strongest is always right, the only problem is how to become the strongest. But what can be the validity of a right which perishes with the force on which it rests? If force compels obedience, there is no need to invoke a duty to obey, and if force ceases to compel obedience, there is no longer any obligation. Thus the word "right" adds nothing to what is said by "force"; it is meaningless.

"Obey those in power." If this means "yield to force" the precept is sound, but superfluous; it has never, I suggest, been violated. All power comes from God, I agree; but so does every disease, and no one forbids us to summon a physician. If I am held up by a robber at the edge of a wood, force compels me to hand over my purse. But if I could somehow contrive to keep the purse from him, would I still be obliged in conscience to surrender it? After all, the pistol in the robber's hand is undoubtedly a *power*.

Surely it must be admitted, then, that might does not make right, and that the duty of obedience is owed only to legitimate powers. . . .

CHAPTER 4
SLAVERY

Since no man has any natural authority over his fellows, and since force alone bestows no right, all legitimate authority among men must be based on covenants. . . .

CHAPTER 5
THAT WE MUST ALWAYS GO BACK TO AN ORIGINAL COVENANT

Even if I were to concede all that I have so far refuted, the champions of despotism would be no better off. There will always be a great difference between subduing a multitude and ruling a society. If one man successively enslaved many separate individuals, no matter how numerous, he and they would never bear the aspect of anything but a master and his slaves, not at all that of a people and their ruler; an aggregation, perhaps, but certainly not an association, for they would neither have a common good nor be a body politic. Even if such a man were to enslave half the world, he would remain a private individual, and his interest, always at variance with that of the others, would never be more than a personal interest. When he died, the empire he left would be scattered for lack of any bond of union, even as an oak crumbles and falls into a heap of ashes when fire has consumed it.

"A people," says Grotius, "may give itself to a king." Therefore, according to Grotius a people is *a people* even before the gift to the king is made. The gift itself is a civil act; it presupposes public deliberation. Hence, before considering the act by which a people submits to a king, we ought to scrutinize the act by which people become *a* people, for that act, being necessarily antecedent to the other, is the real foundation of society.

Indeed, if there were no earlier agreement, then how, unless the election were unanimous, could there be any obligation on the minority to accept the decision of the majority? What right have the hundred who want to have a master to vote on behalf of the ten who do not? The law of majority-voting itself rests on a covenant, and implies that there has been on at least one occasion unanimity.

CHAPTER 6
THE SOCIAL PACT

I assume that men reach a point where the obstacles to their preservation in a state of nature prove greater than the strength that each man has to preserve himself in that state. Beyond this point, the primitive condition cannot endure, for then the human race will perish if it does not change its mode of existence.

Since men cannot create new forces, but merely combine and control those which already exist, the only way in which they can preserve themselves is by uniting their separate powers in a combination strong enough to overcome any resistance, uniting them so that their powers are directed by a single motive and act in concert.

Such a sum of forces can be produced only by the union of separate men, but as each man's own strength and liberty are the chief instruments of his preservation, how can he merge his with others' without putting himself in peril and neglecting the care he owes to himself? This difficulty, which brings me back to my present subject, may be expressed in these words:

"How to find a form of association which will defend the person and goods of each member with the collective force of all, and under which each individual, while uniting himself with the others, obeys no one but himself, and remains as free as before." This is the fundamental problem to which the social contract holds the solution.

The articles of this contract are so precisely determined by the nature of the act, that the slightest modification must render them null and void; they are such that, though perhaps never formally stated, they are everywhere tacitly admitted and recognized; and if ever the social pact is violated, every man regains his original rights and, recovering his natural freedom, loses that social freedom for which he exchanged it.

These articles of association, rightly understood, are reducible to a single one, namely the total alienation by each associate of himself and all his rights to the whole community. Thus, in the first place, as every individual gives himself absolutely, the conditions are the same for all, and precisely because they are the same for all, it is in no one's interest to make the conditions onerous for others.

Secondly, since the alienation is unconditional, the union is as perfect as it could be, and no individual associate has any longer any rights to claim; for if rights were left to individuals, in the absence of any higher authority to judge between them and the public, each individual, being his own judge in some causes, would soon demand to be his own judge in all; and in this way the state of nature would be kept in being, and the association inevitably become either tyrannical or void.

Finally, since each man gives himself to all, he gives himself to no one; and since there is no associate over whom he does not gain the same rights as others gain over him, each man recovers the equivalent of everything he loses, and in the bargain he acquires more power to preserve what he has.

If, then, we eliminate from the social pact everything that is not essential to it, we find it comes down to this: "Each one of us puts into the community his person and all his powers under the supreme direction of the general will; and as body, we incorporate every member as an indivisible part of the whole."

Immediately, in place of the individual person of each contracting party, this act of association creates an artificial and collective body composed of as many members as there are voters in the assembly, and by this same act that body acquires its unity, its common *ego,* its life and its will. The public person thus formed by the union of all other persons was once called the *city,* and is now known as the *republic* or the *body politic. . . .*

CHAPTER 7
THE SOVEREIGN

This formula shows that the act of association consists of a reciprocal commitment between society and the individual, so that each person, in making a contract, as it were, with himself, finds himself doubly committed, first, as a member of the sovereign body in relation to individuals, and secondly as a member of the state in relation to the sovereign. Here there can be no invoking the principle of civil law which says that no man is bound by a contract with himself, for there is a great difference between having an obligation to oneself and having an obligation to something of which one is a member.

We must add that a public decision can impose an obligation on all the subjects towards the sovereign, by reason of the two aspects under which each can be seen, while, contrariwise, such decisions cannot impose an obligation on the sovereign towards itself; and hence it would be against the very nature of a political body for the sovereign to set over itself a law which it could not infringe. The sovereign, bearing only one single and identical aspect, is in the position of a private person making a contract with himself, which shows that there neither is, nor can be, any kind of fundamental law binding on the people as a body, not even the social contract itself. This does not mean that the whole body cannot incur obligations to other nations, so long as those obligations do not infringe the contract; for in relation to foreign powers, the body politic is a simple entity, an individual.

However, since the body politic, or sovereign, owes its being to the sanctity of the contract alone, it cannot commit itself, even in treaties with foreign powers, to anything that would derogate from the original act of association; it could not, for example, alienate a part of itself or submit to another sovereign. To violate the act which has given it existence would be to annihilate itself; and what is nothing can produce nothing.

As soon as the multitude is united thus in a single body, no one can injure any one of the members without attacking the whole, still less injure the whole without each member feeling it. Duty and self-interest thus equally oblige the two contracting parties to give each other mutual aid; and the same men should seek to bring together in this dual relationship, all the advantages that flow from it.

Now, as the sovereign is formed entirely of the individuals who compose it, it has not, nor could it have, any interest contrary to theirs; and so the sovereign has no need to give guarantees to the subjects, because it is impossible for a body to wish to hurt all of its members, and, as we shall see, it cannot hurt any particular member. The sovereign by the mere fact that it is, is always all that it ought to be.

But this is not true of the relation of subject to sovereign. Despite their common interest, subjects will not be bound by their commitment unless means are found to guarantee their fidelity.

For every individual as a man may have a private will contrary to, or different from, the general will that he has as a citizen. His private interest may speak with a very different voice from that of the public interest; his absolute and naturally independent existence may make him regard what he owes to the common cause as a gratuitous contribution, the loss of which would be less painful for others than the payment is onerous for him; and fancying that the artificial person which constitutes the state is a mere rational entity (since it is not a man), he might seek to enjoy the rights of a citizen without doing the duties of a subject. The growth of this kind of injustice would bring about the ruin of the body politic.

Hence, in order that the social pact shall not be an empty formula, it is tacitly implied in that commitment—which alone can give force to all others—that whoever refuses to obey the general will shall be constrained to do so by the whole body, which means nothing other than that he shall be forced to be free; for this is the condition which, by giving each citizen to the nation, secures him against all personal dependence, it is the condition which shapes both the design and the working of the political machine, and which alone bestows justice on civil contracts —without it, such contracts would be absurd, tyrannical and liable to the grossest abuse.

CHAPTER 8
CIVIL SOCIETY

The passing from the state of nature to the civil society produces a remarkable change in man; it puts justice as a rule of conduct in the place of instinct, and gives his actions the moral quality they previously lacked. It is only then, when the voice of duty has taken the place of physical impulse, and right that of desire, that man, who has hitherto thought only of himself, finds himself compelled to act on other principles, and to consult his reason rather than study his inclinations. And although in civil society man surrenders some of the advantages that belong to the state of nature, he gains in return far greater ones; his faculties are so exercised and developed, his mind is so enlarged, his sentiments so ennobled, and his whole spirit so elevated that, if the abuse of his new condition did not in many cases lower him to something worse than what he had left, he should constantly bless the happy hour that lifted him for ever from the state of nature and from a narrow, stupid animal made a creature of intelligence and a man.

Suppose we draw up a balance sheet, so that the losses and gains may be readily compared. What man loses by the social contract is his natural liberty and the absolute right to anything that tempts him and that he can take; what he gains by the social contract is civil liberty and the legal right of property in what he possesses. If we are to avoid mistakes in weighing the one side against the other, we must clearly distinguish between *natural* liberty, which has no limit but the physical power of the individual concerned, and *civil* liberty, which is limited by the general will; and we must distinguish also between *possession,* which is based only on force or "the right of the first occupant," and *property,* which must rest on a legal title.

We might also add that man acquires with civil society, moral freedom, which alone makes man the master of himself; for to be governed by appetite alone is slavery, while obedience to a law one prescribes to oneself is freedom. However, I have already said more than enough on this subject, and the philosophical meaning of the word "freedom" is no part of my subject here. . . .

Book II

CHAPTER 6
ON LAW

We have given life and existence to the body politic by the social pact; now it is a matter of giving it movement and will by legislation. For the primitive act by which the body politic is formed and united does not determine what it shall do to preserve itself.

What is good and in conformity with order is such by the very nature of things and independently of human agreements. All justice comes from God, who alone is its source; and if only we knew how to receive it from that exalted fountain, we should need neither governments nor laws. There is undoubtedly a universal justice which springs from reason alone, but if that justice is to be admitted among men it must be reciprocal. Humanly speaking, the laws of natural justice, lacking any natural sanction, are unavailing among men. In fact, such laws merely benefit the wicked and injure the just, since the just respect them while others do not do so in return. So there must be covenants and positive laws to unite rights with duties and to direct justice to its object. In the state of nature, where everything is common, I owe nothing to those to whom I have promised nothing, and I recognize as belonging to others only those things that are of no use to me. But this is no longer the case in civil society, where all rights are determined by law.

Yet what, in the last analysis, is law? If we simply try to define it in terms of metaphysical ideas, we shall go on talking without reaching any understanding; and when we have said what natural law is, we shall still not know what the law of the state is.

I have already said that the general will cannot relate to any particular object. For such a particular object is either within the state or outside the state. If it is outside, then a will which is alien to it is not general with regard to it: if the object is within the state, it forms a part of the state. Then there comes into being a relationship between the whole and the part which involves two separate entities, the part being one, and the whole, less that particular part, being the other. But a whole less a particular part is no longer a whole; and so as long as this relationship exists there is no whole but only two unequal parts, from which it follows that the will of the one is no longer general with respect to the other.

But when the people as a whole makes rules for the people as a whole, it is dealing only with itself; and if any relationship emerges, it is between the entire body seen from one perspective and the same entire body seen from another, without any division whatever. Here the matter concerning which a rule is made is as general as the will which makes it. And *this* is the kind of act which I call a law.

When I say that the province of the law is always general, I mean that the law considers all subjects collectively and all actions in the abstract; it does not consider any individual man or any specific action. Thus the law may well lay down that there shall be privileges, but it may not nominate the persons who shall have those privileges; the law may establish several classes of citizen, and even specify the qualifications which shall give access to those several classes, but it may not say that this man or that shall be admitted; the law may set up a royal government and a hereditary succession, but it may not elect a king or choose a royal family—in a word, no function which deals with the individual falls within the province of the legislative power.

On this analysis, it is immediately clear that we can no longer ask *who* is to make laws, because laws are acts of the general will; no longer ask if the prince is above the law, because he is a part of the state; no longer ask if the law can be unjust, because no one is unjust to himself; and no longer ask how we can be both free and subject to laws, for the laws are but registers of what we ourselves desire.

It is also clear that since the law unites universality of will with universality of the field of legislation, anything that any man, no matter who, commands on his own authority is not a law; even what the sovereign itself commands with respect to a particular object is not a law but a decree, not an act of sovereignty but an act of government.

Any state which is ruled by law I call a "republic," whatever the form of its constitution; for then, and then alone, does the public interest govern and then alone is the "public thing"—the *res publica*—a reality. All legitimate government is "republican."* . . .

Laws are really nothing other than the conditions on which civil society exists. A people, since it is subject to laws, ought to be the author of them. The right of laying down the rules of society belongs only to those who form the society; but how can they exercise it? Is it to be by common agreement, by a sudden inspiration? Has the body politic an organ to declare its will? Who is to give it the foresight necessary to formulate enactments and proclaim them in advance, and how is it to announce them in the hour of need? How can a blind multitude, which often does not know what it wants, because it seldom knows what is good for it, undertake by itself an enterprise as vast and difficult as a system of legislation? By themselves the people always will what is good, but by themselves they do not always discern it. The general will is always rightful, but the judgment which guides it is not always enlightened. It must be made to see things as they are, and sometimes as they should be seen; it must be shown the good path which it is seeking, and secured against seduction by the desires of individuals; it must be given a sense of situation and season, so as to weigh immediate and tangible advantages against distant and hidden evils. Individuals see the good and reject it; the public desires the good but does not see it. Both equally need guidance. Individuals must be obliged to subordinate their will to their reason; the public must be taught to recognize what it desires. Such public enlightenment would produce a union of understanding and will in the social body, bring the parts into perfect harmony and lift the whole to its fullest strength. Hence the necessity of a lawgiver.

*By this word I understand not only an aristocracy or democracy, but generally any government directed by the general will, which is law. If it is to be legitimate, the government must not be united with the sovereign, but must serve it as its ministry. So even a monarchy can be a republic. . . .

Immanuel Kant

Groundwork of the Metaphysic of Morals

CHAPTER I
PASSAGE FROM ORDINARY RATIONAL KNOWLEDGE OF MORALITY TO PHILOSOPHICAL

It is impossible to conceive anything at all in the world, or even out of it, which can be taken as good without qualification, except a *good will*. Intelligence, wit, judgment, and any other *talents* of the mind we may care to name, or courage, resolution, and constancy of purpose, as qualities of *temperament,* are without doubt good and desirable in many respects; but they can also be extremely bad and hurtful when the will is not good which has to make use of these gifts of nature, and which for this reason has the term *"character"* applied to its peculiar quality. It is exactly the same with *gifts of fortune*. Power, wealth, honor, even health and that complete well-being and contentment with one's state which goes by the name of *"happiness,"* produce boldness, and as a consequence often over-boldness as well, unless a good will is present by which their influence on the mind—and so too the whole principle of action—may be corrected and adjusted to universal ends; not to mention that a rational and impartial spectator can never feel approval in contemplating the uninterrupted prosperity of a being graced by no touch of a pure and good will, and that consequently a good will seems to constitute the indispensable condition of our very worthiness to be happy.

Some qualities are even helpful to this good will itself and can make its task very much easier. They have none the less no inner unconditioned worth, but rather presuppose a good will which sets a limit to the esteem in which they are rightly held and does not permit us to regard them as absolutely good. Moderation in affections and passions, self-control, and sober reflection are not only good in many respects: they may even seem to constitute part of the *inner* worth of a person. Yet they are far from being properly described as good without qualification (however unconditionally they have been commended by the ancients). For without the principles of a good will they may become exceedingly bad; and the very coolness of a scoundrel makes him, not merely more dangerous, but also immediately more abominable in our eyes than we should have taken him to be without it.

A good will is not good because of what it effects or accomplishes—because of its fitness for attaining some proposed end: it is good through its willing alone—that is, good in itself. Considered in itself it is to be esteemed beyond comparison as far higher than anything it could ever bring about merely in order to favor some inclination or, if you like, the sum total of inclinations. Even if, by some special disfavor of destiny or by the niggardly endowment of step-motherly

Immanuel Kant, *Groundwork of the Metaphysic of Morals,* trans. H. J. Paton (London: Hutchinson, an imprint of Century Hutchinson). Reprinted by permission.

nature, this will is entirely lacking in power to carry out its intentions; if by its utmost effort it still accomplishes nothing, and only good will is left (not, admittedly, as a mere wish, but as the straining of every means so far as they are in our control); even then it would still shine like a jewel for its own sake as something which has its full value in itself. Its usefulness or fruitlessness can neither add to, nor subtract from, this value. Its usefulness would be merely, as it were, the setting which enables us to handle it better in our ordinary dealings or to attract the attention of those not yet sufficiently expert, but not to commend it to experts or to determine its value.

Yet in this Idea of the absolute value of a mere will, all useful results being left out of account in its assessment, there is something so strange that, in spite of all the agreement it receives even from ordinary reason, there must arise the suspicion that perhaps its secret basis is merely some high-flown fantasticality, and that we may have misunderstood the purpose of nature in attaching reason to our will as its governor. We will therefore submit our Idea to an examination from this point of view.

In the natural constitution of an organic being—that is, of one contrived for the purpose of life—let us take it as a principle that in it no organ is to be found for any end unless it is also the most appropriate to that end and the best fitted for it. Suppose now that for a being possessed of reason and a will the real purpose of nature were his *preservation*, his *welfare*, or in a word his *happiness*. In that case nature would have hit on a very bad arrangement by choosing reason in the creature to carry out this purpose. For all the actions he has to perform with this end in view, and the whole rule of his behavior, would have been mapped out for him far more accurately by instinct; and the end in question could have been maintained far more surely by instinct than it ever can be by reason. If reason should have been imparted to this favored creature as well, it would have had to serve him only for contemplating the happy disposition of his nature, for admiring it, for enjoying it, and for being grateful to its beneficent Cause—not for subjecting his power of appetition to such feeble and defective guidance or for meddling incompetently with the purposes of nature. In a word, nature would have prevented reason from striking out into a *practical use* and from presuming, with its feeble vision, to think out for itself a plan for happiness and for the means to its attainment. Nature would herself have taken over the choice, not only of ends, but also of means, and would with wise precaution have entrusted both to instinct alone....

For since reason is not sufficiently serviceable for guiding the will safely as regards its objects and the satisfaction of all our needs (which it in part even multiplies)—a purpose for which an implanted natural instinct would have led us much more surely; and since none the less reason has been imparted to us as a practical power—that is, as one which is to have influence on the *will;* its true function must be to produce a *will* which is *good*, not as a *means* to some further end, but *in itself;* and for this function reason was absolutely necessary in a world where nature, in distributing her aptitudes, has everywhere else gone to work in a purposive manner. Such a will need not on this account be the sole and complete good, but it must be the highest good and the condition of all the rest, even of all our demands for happiness. In that case we can easily reconcile with the wisdom of nature our observation that the cultivation of reason which is required for the first and unconditioned purpose may in many ways, at least in this life, restrict the attainment of the second purpose—namely, happiness—which is always conditioned; and indeed that it can even reduce happiness to less than zero without nature proceeding contrary to its purpose; for reason, which recognizes as its highest practical function the establishment of a good will, in attaining this end is capable only of its own peculiar kind of contentment—contentment in fulfilling a purpose which in turn is determined by reason alone, even if this fulfillment should often involve interference with the purposes of inclination.

We have now to elucidate the concept of a will estimable in itself and good apart from any further end. This concept, which is already present in a sound natural understanding and requires not so much to be taught as merely to be clarified, always holds the highest place in estimating the total worth of our actions and constitutes the condition of all the rest. We will therefore take up the concept of *duty*, which includes that of a good will, exposed, however, to certain subjective limitations and obstacles. These, so far from hiding a good will or disguising it, rather bring it out by contrast and make it shine forth more brightly.

I will here pass over all actions already recognized as contrary to duty, however useful they may be with a view to this or that end; for about these the question does not even arise whether they could have been done *for the sake of duty* inasmuch as they are directly opposed to it. I will also set aside actions which in fact accord with duty, yet for which men have *no immediate inclination*, but perform them because impelled to do so by some other inclination. For there it is easy to decide whether the action which accords with duty has been done *from duty* or from some purpose of self-interest. This distinction is far more difficult to perceive when the action accords with duty and the subject has in addition an *immediate* inclination to the action. For example, it certainly accords with duty that a grocer should not overcharge his inexperienced customer; and where there is much competition a sensible shopkeeper refrains from so doing and keeps to a fixed and general price for everybody so that a child can buy from him just as well as anyone else. Thus people are served *honestly;* but this is not nearly enough to justify us in believing that the shopkeeper has acted in this way from duty or from principles of fair dealing; his interests required him to do so. We cannot assume him to have in addition an immediate inclination toward his customers, leading him, as it were out of love, to give no man preference over another in the matter of price. Thus the action was done neither from duty nor from immediate inclination, but solely from purposes of self-interest.

On the other hand, to preserve one's life is a duty, and besides this every one has also an immediate inclination to do so. But on account of this the often anxious precautions taken by the greater part of mankind for this purpose have no inner worth, and the maxim of their action is without moral content. They do protect their lives *in conformity with duty,* but not *from the motive of duty.* When on the contrary, disappointments and hopeless misery have quite taken away the taste for life; when a wretched man, strong in soul and more angered at his fate than faint-hearted or cast down, longs for death and still preserves his life without loving it—not from inclination or fear but from duty; then indeed his maxim has a moral content.

To help others where one can is a duty, and besides this there are many spirits of so sympathetic a temper that, without any further motive of vanity or self-interest, they find an inner pleasure in spreading happiness around them and can take delight in the contentment of others as their own work. Yet I maintain that in such a case an action of this kind, however right and however amiable it may be, has still no genuinely moral worth. It stands on the same footing as other inclinations—for example, the inclination for honor, which if fortunate enough to hit on something beneficial and right and consequently honorable, deserves praise and encouragement, but not esteem; for its maxim lacks moral content, namely, the performance of such actions, not from inclination, but *from duty.* Suppose then that the mind of this friend of man were overclouded by sorrows of his own which extinguished all sympathy with the fate of others, but that he still had power to help those in distress, though no longer stirred by the need of others because sufficiently occupied with his own; and suppose that, when no longer moved by any inclination, he tears himself out of this deadly insensibility and does the action without any inclination for the sake of duty alone; then for the first time his action has its genuine moral worth. Still further: if nature had implanted little sympathy in this or that man's heart; if (being in other respects an honest fellow) he were cold in temperament, and indifferent to the sufferings of others—perhaps because, being endowed with the special gift of patience and robust endurance in his own sufferings, he assumed the like in others or even demanded it; if such a man (who would in truth not be the worst product of nature) were not exactly fashioned by her to be a philanthropist, would he not still find in himself a source from which he might draw a worth far higher than any that a good-natured temperament can have? Assuredly he would. It is precisely in this that the worth of character begins to show—a moral worth and beyond all comparison the highest—namely, that he does good, not from inclination, but from duty.

To assure one's own happiness is a duty (at least indirectly); for discontent with one's state, in a press of cares and amidst unsatisfied wants, might easily become a great *temptation to the transgression of duty.* But here also, apart from regard to duty, all men have already of themselves the strongest and deepest inclination toward happiness, because precisely in this Idea of happiness all inclinations are combined into a sum total. The prescription for happiness is, however, often so constituted as greatly to interfere with some inclinations, and yet men cannot form under the name of "happiness" any determinate and assured conception of the satisfaction of all inclinations as a sum. Hence it is not to be wondered at that a single inclination which is determinate as to what it promises and as to the time of its satisfaction may outweigh a wavering Idea; and that a man, for example, a sufferer from gout, may choose to enjoy what he fancies and put up with what he can—on the ground that on balance he has here at least not killed the enjoyment of the present moment because of some possibly groundless expectations of the good fortune supposed to attach to soundness of health. But in this case also, when the universal inclination toward happiness has failed to determine his will, when good health, at least for him, has not entered into his calculations as so necessary, what remains over, here as in other cases, is a law—the law of furthering his happiness, not from inclination, but from duty; and in this for the first time his conduct has a real moral worth.

It is doubtless in this sense that we should understand too the passages from Scripture in which we are commanded to love our neighbor and even our enemy. For love out of inclination cannot be commanded; but kindness done from duty—although no inclination impels us, and even although natural and unconquerable disinclination stands in our way—is *practical,* and not *pathological,* love, residing in the will and not in the propensions of feeling, in principles of action and not of melting compassion; and it is this practical love alone which can be an object of command.

Our second proposition is this: An action done from duty has its moral worth, *not in the purpose* to be attained by it, but in the maxim in accordance with which it is decided upon; it depends therefore, not on the realization of the object of the action, but solely on the *principle* of *volition* in accordance with which, irrespective of all objects of the faculty of desire, the action has been performed. That the purposes we may have in our actions, and also their effects considered as ends and motives of the will, can give to actions no unconditioned and moral worth is clear from what has gone before. Where then can this worth be found if we are not to find it in the will's relation to the effect hoped for from the action? It can be found nowhere but *in the principle of the will,* irrespective of the ends which can be brought about by such an action; for between its *a priori* principle, which is formal, and its *a posteriori* motive, which is material, the will stands, so to speak, at a parting of the ways; and since it must be determined by some principle, it will have to be determined by the formal principle of volition when an action is done from duty, where, as we have seen, every material principle is taken away from it.

Our third proposition, as an inference from the two preceding, I would express thus: *Duty is the necessity to act out of reverence for the law.* For an object as the effect of my proposed action I can have an *inclination,* but *never reverence,* precisely because it is merely the effect, and not the activity, of a will. Similarly for inclination as such, whether my own or that of another, I cannot have reverence: I can at most in the first case approve, and in the second case sometimes even love—that is, regard it as favorable to my own advantage. Only something which is conjoined with my will solely as a ground and never as an effect—something which does not serve my inclination, but outweighs it or at least leaves it entirely out of account in my choice—and therefore only bare law for its own sake, can be an object of reverence and therewith a command. Now an action done from duty has to set aside altogether the influence of inclination, and along with inclination every object of the will; so there is nothing left able to determine the will except objectively the *law* and subjectively *pure reverence* for this practical law, and therefore the maxim* of obeying this law even to the detriment of all my inclinations.

Thus the moral worth of an action does not depend on the result expected from it, and so too does not depend on any principle of action that needs to borrow its motive from this expected result. For all these results (agreeable states and even the promotion of happiness in others) could have been brought about by other

---

*A *maxim* is the subjective principle of a volition: an objective principle (that is, one which would also serve subjectively as a practical principle for all rational beings if reason had full control over the faculty of desire) is a practical *law.*

causes as well, and consequently their production did not require the will of a rational being, in which, however, the highest and unconditioned good can alone be found. Therefore nothing but the *idea of the law* in itself, *which admittedly is present only in a rational being*—so far as it, and not an expected result, is the ground determining the will—can constitute that pre-eminent good which we call moral, a good which is already present in the person acting on this idea and has not to be awaited merely from the result.

But what kind of law can this be the thought of which, even without regard to the results expected from it, has to determine the will if this is to be called good absolutely and without qualification? Since I have robbed the will of every inducement that might arise for it as a consequence of obeying any particular law, nothing is left but the conformity of actions to universal law as such, and this alone must serve the will as its principle. That is to say, I ought never to act except in such a way *that I can also will that my maxim should become a universal law.* Here bare conformity to universal law as such (without having as its base any law prescribing particular actions) is what serves the will as its principle, and must so serve it if duty is not to be everywhere an empty delusion and a chimerical concept. The ordinary reason of mankind also agrees with this completely in its practical judgments and always has the aforesaid principle before its eyes.

Take this question, for example. May I not, when I am hard pressed, make a promise with the intention of not keeping it? Here I readily distinguish the two senses which the question can have—Is it prudent, or is it right, to make a false promise? The first no doubt can often be the case. I do indeed see that it is not enough for me to extricate myself from present embarrassment by this subterfuge: I have to consider whether from this lie there may not subsequently accrue to me much greater inconvenience than that from which I now escape, and also—since, with all my supposed *astuteness,* to foresee the consequences is not so easy that I can be sure there is no chance, once confidence in me is lost, of this proving far more disadvantageous than all the ills I now think to avoid—whether it may not be a *more prudent* action to proceed here on a general maxim and make it my habit not to give a promise except with the intention of keeping it. Yet it becomes clear to me at once that such a maxim is always founded solely on fear of consequences. To tell the truth for the sake of duty is something entirely different from doing so out of concern for inconvenient results; for in the first case the concept of the action already contains in itself a law for me, while in the second case I have first of all to look around elsewhere in order to see what effects may be bound up with it for me. When I deviate from the principle of duty, this is quite certainly bad; but if I desert my prudential maxim, this can often be greatly to my advantage, though it is admittedly safer to stick to it. Suppose I seek, however, to learn in the quickest way and yet unerringly how to solve the problem "Does a lying promise accord with duty?" I have then to ask myself "Should I really be content that my maxim (the maxim of getting out of a difficulty by a false promise) should hold as a universal law (one valid both for myself and others)? And could I really say to myself that every one may make a false promise if he finds himself in a difficulty from which he can extricate himself in no other way?" I then become aware at once that I can indeed will to lie, but I can by no means will a universal law of lying; for by such a law there could properly be no promises at all, since it would be futile to profess a will for future action to others who would not believe my profession or who, if they did so over-hastily, would pay me back in like coin; and consequently my maxim, as soon as it was made a universal law, would be bound to annul itself.

Thus I need no far-reaching ingenuity to find out what I have to do in order to possess a good will. Inexperienced in the course of world affairs and incapable of being prepared for all the chances that happen in it, I ask myself only "Can you also will that your maxim should become a universal law?" Where you cannot, it is to be rejected, and that not because of a prospective loss to you or even to others, but because it cannot fit as a principle into a possible enactment of universal law. For such an enactment reason compels my immediate reverence, into whose grounds (which the philosopher may investigate) I have as yet no *insight,* although I do at least understand this much: reverence is the assessment of a worth which far outweighs all the worth of what is commended by inclination, and the necessity for me to act out of *pure* reverence for the practical law is what constitutes duty, to which every other motive must give way because it is the condition of a will good *in itself,* whose value is above all else. . . .

CHAPTER II
PASSAGE FROM POPULAR MORAL PHILOSOPHY TO A METAPHYSIC OF MORALS

. . . Everything in nature works in accordance with laws. Only a rational being has the power to act *in accordance with his idea* of laws—that is, in accordance with principles—and only so has he a *will.* Since *reason* is required in order to derive actions from laws, the will is nothing but practical reason. If reason infallibly determines the will, then in a being of this kind the actions which are recognized to be objectively necessary are also subjectively necessary—that is to say, the will is then a power to choose *only that* which reason independently of inclination recognizes to be practically necessary, that is, to be good. But if reason solely by itself is not sufficient to determine the will; if the will is exposed also to subjective conditions (certain impulsions) which do not always harmonize with the objective ones; if, in a word, the will is not *in itself* completely in accord with reason (as actually happens in the case of men); then actions which are recognized to be objectively necessary are subjectively contingent, and the determining of such a will in accordance with objective laws is *necessitation.* That is to say, the relation of objective laws to a will not good through and through is conceived as one in which the will of a rational being, although it is determined by principles of reason, does not necessarily follow these principles in virtue of its own nature.

The conception of an objective principle so far as this principle is necessitating for a will is called a command (of reason), and the formula of this command is called an *Imperative.*

All imperatives are expressed by an *"ought" (Sollen).* By this they mark the relation of an objective law of reason to a will which is not necessarily determined by this law in virtue of its subjective constitution (the relation of necessitation). They say that something would be good to do or to leave undone; only they say it to a will which does not always do a thing because it has been informed that this is a good thing to do. The practically *good* is that which determines the will by concepts of reason, and therefore not by subjective causes, but objectively—that is, on grounds valid for every rational being as such. It is distinguished from the *pleasant* as that which influences the will, not as a principle of reason valid for every one, but solely through the medium of sensation by purely subjective causes valid only for the senses of this person or that.

A perfectly good will would thus stand quite as much under objective laws (laws of the good), but it could not on this account be conceived as *necessitated* to act in conformity with law, since of itself, in accordance with its subjective constitution, it can be determined only by the concept of the good. Hence for the *divine* will, and in general for a *holy* will, there are no imperatives: *"I ought"* is here out of place, because *"I will"* is already of itself necessarily in harmony with the law. Imperatives are in consequence only formulae for expressing the relation of objective laws of willing to the subjective imperfection of the will of this or that rational being— for example, of the human will.

All *imperatives* command either *hypothetically* or *categorically*. Hypothetical imperatives declare a possible action to be practically necessary as a means to the attainment of something else that one wills (or that one may will). A categorical imperative would be one which represented an action as objectively necessary in itself apart from its relation to a further end.

Every practical law represents a possible action as good and therefore as necessary for a subject whose actions are determined by reason. Hence all imperatives are formulae for determining an action which is necessary in accordance with the principle of a will in some sense good. If the action would be good solely as a means *to something else,* the imperative is *hypothetical;* if the action is represented as good *in itself* and therefore as necessary, in virtue of its principle, for a will which of itself accords with reason, then the imperative is *categorical.*

An imperative therefore tells me which of my possible actions would be good; and it formulates a practical rule for a will that does not perform an action straight away because the action is good—whether because the subject does not always know that it is good or because, even if he did know this, he might still act on maxims contrary to the objective principles of practical reason.

A hypothetical imperative thus says only that an action is good for some purpose or other, either *possible* or *actual.* In the first case it is a *problematic* practical principle; in the second case an *assertoric* practical principle. A categorical imperative, which declares an action to be objectively necessary in itself without reference to some purpose—that is, even without any further end—ranks as an *apodeictic* practical principle.

Everything that is possible only through the efforts of some rational being can be conceived as a possible purpose of some will; and consequently there are in fact innumerable principles of action so far as action is thought necessary in order to achieve some possible purpose which can be effected by it. All sciences have a practical part consisting of problems which suppose that some end is possible for us and of imperatives which tell us how it is to be attained. Hence the latter can in general be called imperatives of *skill.* Here there is absolutely no question about the rationality or goodness of the end, but only about what must be done to attain it. A prescription required by a doctor in order to cure his man completely and one required by a poisoner in order to make sure of killing him are of equal value so far as each serves to effect its purpose perfectly. Since in early youth we do not know what ends may present themselves to us in the course of life, parents seek above all to make their children learn things *of many kinds;* they provide carefully for *skill* in the use of means to all sorts of arbitrary ends, of none of which can they be certain that it could not in the future become an actual purpose of their ward, while it is always *possible* that he might adopt it. Their care in this matter is so great that they commonly neglect on this account to form and correct the judgment of their children about the worth of the things which they might possibly adopt as ends.

There is, however, *one* end that can be presupposed as actual in all rational beings (so far as they are dependent beings to whom imperatives apply); and thus there is one purpose which they not only *can* have, but which we can assume with certainty that they all *do* have by a natural necessity—the purpose, namely, of *happiness.* A hypothetical imperative which affirms the practical necessity of an action as a means to the furtherance of happiness is *assertoric.* We may represent it, not simply as necessary to an uncertain, merely possible purpose, but as necessary to a purpose which we can presuppose *a priori* and with certainty to be present in every man because it belongs to his very being. Now skill in the choice of means to one's own greatest well-being can be called *prudence** in the narrowest sense. Thus an imperative concerned with the choice of means to one's own happiness—that is, a precept of prudence—still remains *hypothetical:* an action is commanded, not absolutely, but only as a means to a further purpose.

Finally, there is an imperative which, without being based on, and conditioned by, any further purpose to be attained by a certain line of conduct, enjoins this conduct immediately. This imperative is *categorical.* It is concerned, not with the matter of the action and its presumed results, but with its form and with the principle from which it follows; and what is essentially good in the action consists in the mental disposition, let the consequences be what they may. This imperative may be called the imperative of *morality.*

Willing in accordance with these three kinds of principle is also sharply distinguished by a *dissimilarity* in the necessitation of the will. To make this dissimilarity obvious we should, I think, name these kinds of principle most appropriately in their order if we said they were either *rules* of skill or *counsels* of prudence or *commands (laws)* of morality. For only *law* carries with it the concept of an *unconditioned,* and yet objective and so universally valid, *necessity;* and commands are laws which must be obeyed—that is, must be followed even against inclination. *Counsel* does indeed involve necessity, but necessity valid only under a subjective and contingent condition—namely, if this or that man counts this or that as belonging to his happiness. As against this, a categorical imperative is limited by no condition and can quite precisely be called a command, as being absolutely,

---

*The word "prudence" (*Klugheit*) is used in a double sense: in one sense it can have the name of "worldly wisdom" (*Weltklugheit*); in a second sense that of "personal wisdom" *(Privatklugheit)*. The first is the skill of a man in influencing others in order to use them for his own ends. The second is sagacity in combining all these ends to his own lasting advantage. The latter is properly that to which the value of the former can itself be traced; and of him who is prudent in the first sense, but not in the second, we might better say that he is clever and astute, but on the whole imprudent.

although practically, necessary. We could also call imperatives of the first kind *technical* (concerned with art); of the second kind *pragmatic* (concerned with well-being); of the third kind *moral* (concerned with free conduct as such—that is, with morals).

The question now arises "How are all these imperatives possible?" This question does not ask how we can conceive the execution of an action commanded by the imperative, but merely how we can conceive the necessitation of the will expressed by the imperative in setting us a task. How an imperative of skill is possible requires no special discussion. Who wills the end, wills (so far as reason has decisive influence on his actions) also the means which are indispensably necessary and in his power. So far as willing is concerned, this proposition is analytic: for in my willing of an object as an effect there is already conceived the causality of myself as an acting cause—that is, the use of means; and from the concept of willing an end the imperative merely extracts the concept of actions necessary to this end. (Synthetic propositions are required in order to determine the means to a proposed end, but these are concerned, not with the reason for performing the act of will, but with the cause which produces the object.) That in order to divide a line into two equal parts on a sure principle I must from its ends describe two intersecting arcs—this is admittedly taught by mathematics only in synthetic propositions; but when I know that the aforesaid effect can be produced only by such an action, the proposition "If I fully will the effect, I also will the action required for it" is analytic; for it is one and the same thing to conceive something as an effect possible in a certain way through me and to conceive myself as acting in the same way with respect to it.

If it were only as easy to find a determinate concept of happiness, the imperatives of prudence would agree entirely with those of skill and would be equally analytic. For here as there it could alike be said "Who wills the end, wills also (necessarily, if he accords with reason) the sole means which are in his power." Unfortunately, however, the concept of happiness is so indeterminate a concept that although every man wants to attain happiness, he can never say definitely and in unison with himself what it really is that he wants and wills. The reason for this is that all the elements which belong to the concept of happiness are without exception empirical—that is, they must be borrowed from experience; but that none the less there is required for the Idea of happiness an absolute whole, a maximum of well-being in my present, and in every future, state. Now it is impossible for the most intelligent, and at the same time most powerful, but nevertheless finite, being to form here a determinate concept of what he really wills. Is it riches that he wants? How much anxiety, envy, and pestering might he not bring in this way on his own head! Is it knowledge and insight? This might perhaps merely give him an eye so sharp that it would make evils at present hidden from him and yet unavoidable seem all the more frightful, or would add a load of still further needs to the desires which already give him trouble enough. Is it long life? Who will guarantee that it would not be a long misery? Is it at least health? How often has infirmity of body kept a man from excesses into which perfect health would have let him fall!—and so on. In short, he has no principle by which he is able to decide with complete certainty what will make him truly happy, since for this he would require omniscience. Thus we cannot act on determinate principles in order to be happy, but only on empirical counsels, for example, of diet, frugality, politeness, reserve, and so on—things which experience shows contribute most to well-being on the average. From this it follows that imperatives of prudence, speaking strictly, do not command at all—that is, cannot exhibit actions objectively as practically *necessary;* that they are rather to be taken as recommendations *(consilia),* than as commands *(praecepta),* of reason; that the problem of determining certainly and universally what action will promote the happiness of a rational being is completely insoluble; and consequently that in regard to this there is no imperative possible which in the strictest sense could command us to do what will make us happy, since happiness is an Ideal, not of reason, but of imagination— an Ideal resting merely on empirical grounds, of which it is vain to expect that they should determine an action by which we could attain the totality of a series of consequences which is in fact infinite. Nevertheless, if we assume that the means to happiness could be discovered with certainty, this imperative of prudence would be an analytic practical proposition; for it differs from the imperative of skill only in this—that in the latter the end is merely possible, while in the former the end is given. In spite of this difference, since both command solely the means to something assumed to be willed as an end, the imperative which commands him who wills the end to will the means is in both cases analytic. Thus there is likewise no difficulty in regard to the possibility of an imperative of prudence.

Beyond all doubt, the question "How is the imperative of *morality* possible?" is the only one in need of a solution; for it is in no way hypothetical, and consequently we cannot base the objective necessity which it affirms on any presupposition, as we can with hypothetical imperatives. Only we must never forget here that it is impossible to settle *by an example,* and so empirically, whether there is any imperative of this kind at all: we must rather suspect that all imperatives which seem to be categorical may none the less be covertly hypothetical. Take, for example, the saying "Thou shalt make no false promises." Let us assume that the necessity for this abstention is no mere advice for the avoidance of some further evil —as it might be said "You ought not to make a lying promise lest, when this comes to light, you destroy your credit." Let us hold, on the contrary, that an action of this kind must be considered as bad in itself, and that the imperative of prohibition is therefore categorical. Even so, we cannot with any certainty show by an example that the will is determined here solely by the law without any further motive, although it may appear to be so; for it is always possible that fear of disgrace, perhaps also hidden dread of other risks, may unconsciously influence the will. Who can prove by experience that a cause is not present? Experience shows only that it is not perceived. In such a case, however, the so-called moral imperative, which as such appears to be categorical and unconditioned, would in fact be only a pragmatic prescription calling attention to our advantage and merely bidding us take this into account.

We shall thus have to investigate the possibility of a *categorical* imperative entirely *a priori,* since here we do not enjoy the advantage of having its reality given in experience and so of being obliged merely to explain, and not to establish, its possibility. So much, however, can be seen provisionally—that the categorical imperative alone purports to be a practical *law,* while all the rest may be called *principles* of the will but not laws; for an action necessary merely in order to achieve an arbitrary purpose can be considered as in itself contingent, and we can always escape from the precept if we abandon the purpose; whereas an unconditioned command does not leave it open to the will to do the opposite at its discretion and therefore alone carries with it that necessity which we demand from a law. . . .

In this task we wish first to inquire whether perhaps the mere concept of a categorical imperative may not also provide us with the formula containing the only proposition that can be a categorical imperative; for even when we know the purport of such an absolute command, the question of its possibility will still require a special and troublesome effort, which we postpone to the final chapter.

When I conceive a *hypothetical* imperative in general, I do not know beforehand what it will contain—until its condition is given. But if I conceive a *categorical* imperative, I know at once what it contains. For since besides the law this imperative contains only the necessity that our maxim* should conform to this law, while the law, as we have seen, contains no condition to limit it, there remains nothing over to which the maxim has to conform except the universality of a law as such; and it is this conformity alone that the imperative properly asserts to be necessary.

There is therefore only a single categorical imperative and it is this: *"Act only on that maxim through which you can at the same time will that it should become a universal law."*

. . . [T]he universal imperative of duty may also run as follows: *"Act as if the maxim of your action were to become through your will a universal law of nature."*

We will now enumerate a few duties, following their customary division into duties toward self and duties toward others and into perfect and imperfect duties.†

1. A man feels sick of life as the result of a series of misfortunes that has mounted to the point of despair, but he is still so far in possession of his reason as to ask himself whether taking his own life may not be contrary to his duty to himself. He now applies the test "Can the maxim of my action really become a universal law of nature?" His maxim is "From self-love I make it my principle to shorten my life if its continuance threatens more evil than it promises pleasure." The only further question to ask is whether this principle of self-love can become a universal law of nature. It is then seen at once that a system of nature by whose law the very same feeling whose function *(Bestimmung)* is to stimulate the furtherance of life should actually destroy life would contradict itself and consequently could not subsist as a system of nature. Hence this maxim cannot possibly hold as a universal law of nature and is therefore entirely opposed to the supreme principle of all duty.

2. Another finds himself driven to borrowing money because of need. He well knows that he will not be able to pay it back; but he sees too that he will get no loan unless he gives a firm promise to pay it back within a fixed time. He is inclined to

---

*A *maxim* is a subjective principle of action and must be distinguished from an *objective principle*—namely, a practical law. The former contains a practical rule determined by reason in accordance with the conditions of the subject (often his ignorance or again his inclinations): it is thus a principle on which the subject *acts*. A law, on the other hand, is an objective principle valid for every rational being; and it is a principle on which he *ought to act*—that is, an imperative

†. . . I understand here by a perfect duty one which allows no exception in the interests of inclination, and so I recognize among *perfect duties,* not only outer ones, but also inner.

make such a promise; but he has still enough conscience to ask "Is it not unlawful and contrary to duty to get out of difficulties in this way?" Supposing, however, he did resolve to do so, the maxim of his action would run thus: "Whenever I believe myself short of money, I will borrow money and promise to pay it back, though I know that this will never be done." Now this principle of self-love or personal advantage is perhaps quite compatible with my own entire future welfare; only there remains the question "Is it right?" I therefore transform the demand of self-love into a universal law and frame my question thus: "How would things stand if my maxim became a universal law?" I then see straight away that this maxim can never rank as a universal law of nature and be self-consistent, but must necessarily contradict itself. For the universality of a law that every one believing himself to be in need can make any promise he pleases with the intention not to keep it would make promising, and the very purpose of promising, itself impossible, since no one would believe he was being promised anything, but would laugh at utterances of this kind as empty shams.

3. A third finds in himself a talent whose cultivation would make him a useful man for all sorts of purposes. But he sees himself in comfortable circumstances, and he prefers to give himself up to pleasure rather than to bother about increasing and improving his fortunate natural aptitudes. Yet he asks himself further "Does my maxim of neglecting my natural gifts, besides agreeing in itself with my tendency to indulgence, agree also with what is called duty?" He then sees that a system of nature could indeed always subsist under such a universal law, although (like the South Sea Islanders) every man should let his talents rust and should be bent on devoting his life solely to idleness, indulgence, procreation, and, in a word, to enjoyment. Only he cannot possibly *will* that this should become a universal law of nature or should be implanted in us as such a law by a natural instinct. For as a rational being he necessarily wills that all his powers should be developed, since they serve him, and are given him, for all sorts of possible ends.

4. Yet *a fourth* is himself flourishing, but he sees others who have to struggle with great hardships (and whom he could easily help); and he thinks "What does it matter to me? Let every one be as happy as Heaven wills or as he can make himself; I won't deprive him of anything; I won't even envy him; only I have no wish to contribute anything to his well-being or to his support in distress." Now admittedly if such an attitude were a universal law of nature, mankind could get on perfectly well—better no doubt than if everybody prates about sympathy and goodwill, and even takes pains, on occasion, to practice them, but on the other hand cheats where he can, traffics in human rights, or violates them in other ways. But although it is possible that a universal law of nature could subsist in harmony with this maxim, yet it is impossible to *will* that such a principle should hold everywhere as a law of nature. For a will which decided in this way would be in conflict with itself, since many a situation might arise in which the man needed love and sympathy from others, and in which, by such a law of nature sprung from his own will, he would rob himself of all hope of the help he wants for himself.

These are some of the many actual duties—or at least of what we take to be such—whose derivation from the single principle cited above leaps to the eye. We must *be able to will* that a maxim of our action should become a universal law—this is the general canon for all moral judgment of action. Some actions are so constituted that their maxim cannot even be *conceived* as a universal law of nature without contradiction, let alone be *willed* as what *ought* to become one. In the case of others we do not find this inner impossibility, but it is still impossible to *will* that their maxim should be raised to the universality of a law of nature, because such a will would contradict itself. It is easily seen that the first kind of action is opposed to strict or narrow (rigorous) duty, the second only to wider (meritorious) duty; and thus that by these examples all duties—so far as the type of obligation is concerned (not the object of dutiful action)—are fully set out in their dependence on our single principle.

If we now attend to ourselves whenever we transgress a duty, we find that we in fact do not will that our maxim should become a universal law—since this is impossible for us—but rather that its opposite should remain a law universally: we only take the liberty of making an *exception* to it for ourselves (or even just for this once) to the advantage of our inclination. Consequently if we weighed it all up from one and the same point of view—that of reason—we should find a contradiction in our own will, the contradiction that a certain principle should be objectively necessary as a universal law and yet subjectively should not hold universally but should admit of exceptions. Since, however, we first consider our action from the point of view of a will wholly in accord with reason, and then consider precisely the same action from the point of view of a will affected by inclination, there is here actually no contradiction, but rather an opposition of inclination to the precept of reason *(antagonismus)*, whereby the universality of the principle *(universalitas)* is turned into a mere generality *(generalitas)* so that the practical principle of reason may meet our maxim half-way. This procedure, though in our own impartial judgment it cannot be justified, proves none the less that we in fact recognize the validity of the categorical imperative and (with all respect for it) merely permit ourselves a few exceptions which are, as we pretend, inconsiderable and apparently forced upon us. . . .

The will is conceived as a power of determining oneself to action *in accordance with the idea of certain laws*. And such a power can be found only in rational beings. Now what serves the will as a subjective ground of its self-determination is an *end;* and this, if it is given by reason alone, must be equally valid for all rational beings. What, on the other hand, contains merely the ground of the possibility of an action whose effect is an end is called a *means.* The subjective ground of a desire is an *impulsion* . . . ; the objective ground of a volition is a *motive.* . . . Hence the difference between subjective ends, which are based on impulsions, and objective ends, which depend on motives valid for every rational being. Practical principles are *formal* if they abstract from all subjective ends; they are *material,* on the other hand, if they are based on such ends and consequently on certain impulsions. Ends that a rational being adopts arbitrarily as *effects* of his action (material ends) are in every case only relative; for it is solely their relation to special characteristics in the subject's power of appetition which gives them their value. Hence this value can provide no universal principles, no principles valid and necessary for all rational beings and also for every volition—that is, no practical laws. Consequently all these relative ends can be the ground only of hypothetical imperatives.

Suppose, however, there were something *whose existence* has *in itself* an absolute value, something which as *an end in itself* could be a ground of determinate laws; then in it, and in it alone, would there be the ground of a possible categorical imperative—that is, of a practical law.

Now I say that man, and in general every rational being, *exists* as an end in himself, *not merely as a means* for arbitrary use by this or that will: he must in all his actions, whether they are directed to himself or to other rational beings, always be viewed *at the same time as an end.* All the objects of inclination have only a conditioned value; for if there were not these inclinations and the needs grounded on them, their object would be valueless. Inclinations themselves, as sources of needs, are so far from having an absolute value to make them desirable for their own sake that it must rather be the universal wish of every rational being to be wholly free from them. Thus the value of all objects that can *be produced* by our action is always conditioned. Beings whose existence depends, not on our will, but on nature, have none the less, if they are non-rational beings, only a relative value as means and are consequently called *things.* Rational beings, on the other hand, are called *persons* because their nature already marks them out as ends in themselves—that is, as something which ought not to be used merely as a means—and consequently imposes to that extent a limit on all arbitrary treatment of them (and is an object of reverence). Persons, therefore, are not merely subjective ends whose existence as an object of our actions has a value *for us:* they are *objective ends*—that is, things whose existence is in itself an end, and indeed an end such that in its place we can put no other end to which they should serve *simply* as means; for unless this is so, nothing at all of *absolute* value would be found anywhere. But if all value were conditioned—that is, contingent—then no supreme principle could be found for reason at all.

If then there is to be a supreme practical principle and—so far as the human will is concerned—a categorical imperative, it must be such that from the idea of something which is necessarily an end for every one because it is an *end in itself* it forms an *objective* principle of the will and consequently can serve as a practical law. The ground of this principle is: *Rational nature exists as an end in itself.* This is the way in which a man necessarily conceives his own existence: it is therefore so far a *subjective* principle of human actions. But it is also the way in which every other rational being conceives his existence on the same rational ground which is valid also for me; hence it is at the same time an *objective* principle, from which, as a supreme practical ground, it must be possible to derive all laws for the will. The practical imperative will therefore be as follows: *Act in such a way that you always treat humanity, whether in your own person or in the person of any other, never simply as a means, but always at the same time as an end. . . .*

This principle of humanity, and in general of every rational agent, *as an end in itself* (a principle which is the supreme limiting condition of every man's freedom of action) is not borrowed from experience; firstly, because it is universal, applying as it does to all rational beings as such, and no experience is adequate to determine universality; secondly, because in it humanity is conceived, not as an end of man (subjectively)—that is, as an object which, as a matter of fact, happens to be made an end—but as an objective end—one which, be our ends what they may, must, as a law, constitute the supreme limiting condition of all subjective ends and so must spring from pure reason. That is to say, the ground for every enactment of practical law lies *objectively in the rule* and in the form of universality which (according to our first principle) makes the rule capable of being a law (and indeed a law of nature); *subjectively,* however, it lies in the *end;* but (according to our second principle) the subject of all ends is to be found in every rational being as an end in himself. From this there now follows our third practical principle for the will—as the supreme condition of the will's conformity with universal practical reason—namely, the Idea *of the will of every rational being as a will which makes universal law.*

By this principle all maxims are repudiated which cannot accord with the will's own enactment of universal law. The will is therefore not merely subject to the law, but is so subject that it must be considered as also *making the law* for itself and precisely on this account as first of all subject to the law (of which it can regard itself as the author). . . .

. . . [A] will *which is subject to law* may be bound to this law by some interest, nevertheless a will which is itself a supreme lawgiver cannot possibly as such depend on any interest; for a will which is dependent in this way would itself require yet a further law in order to restrict the interest of self-love to the condition that this interest should itself be valid as a universal law.

Thus the *principle* that every human will is *a will which by all its maxims enacts universal law*—provided only that it were right in other ways—would be *well suited* to be a categorical imperative in this respect: that precisely because of the Idea of making universal law it is *based on no interest* and consequently can alone among all possible imperatives be *unconditioned.* Or better still—to convert the proposition—if there is a categorical imperative (that is, a law for the will of every rational being), it can command us only to act always on the maxim of such a will in us as can at the same time look upon itself as making universal law; for only then is the practical principle and the imperative which we obey unconditioned, since it is wholly impossible for it to be based on any interest.

We need not now wonder, when we look back upon all the previous efforts that have been made to discover the principle of morality, why they have been made to discover the principle of morality, why they have one and all been bound to fail. Their authors saw man as tied to laws by his duty, but it never occurred to them that he is subject only to *laws which are made by himself* and yet are *universal,* and that he is bound only to act in conformity with a will which is his own but has as nature's purpose for it the function of making universal law. For when they thought of man merely as subject to a law (whatever it might be), the law had to carry with it some interest in order to attract or compel, because it did not spring as a law from *his own* will: in order to conform with the law his will had to be necessitated by *something else* to act in a certain way. This absolutely inevitable conclusion meant that all the labor spent in trying to find a supreme principle of duty was lost beyond recall; for what they discovered was never duty, but only the necessity of acting from a certain interest. This interest might be one's own or another's; but on such a view the imperative was bound to be always a conditioned one and could not possibly serve as a moral law. I will therefore call my principle the principle of the *Autonomy* of the will in contrast with all others, which I consequently class under *Heteronomy.*

The concept of every rational being as one who must regard himself as making universal law by all the maxims of his will, and must seek to judge himself and his actions from this point of view, leads to a closely connected and very fruitful concept—namely, that of *a kingdom of ends.*

I understand by a *"kingdom"* a systematic union of different rational beings under common laws. Now since laws determine ends as regards their universal validity, we shall be able—if we abstract from the personal differences between rational beings, and also from all the content of their private ends—to conceive a whole of all ends in systematic conjunction (a whole both of rational beings as ends in themselves and also of the personal ends which each may set before himself); that is, we shall be able to conceive a kingdom of ends which is possible in accordance with the above principles.

For rational beings all stand under the *law* that each of them should treat himself and all others, *never merely as a means,* but always *at the same time as an end in himself.* But by so doing there arises a systematic union of rational beings under common objective laws—that is, a kingdom. Since these laws are directed precisely to the relation of such beings to one another as ends and means, this kingdom can be called a kingdom of ends (which is admittedly only an Ideal).

A rational being belongs to the kingdom of ends as a *member,* when, although he makes its universal laws, he is also himself subject to these laws. He belongs to it as its *head,* when as the maker of laws he is himself subject to the will of no other.

A rational being must always regard himself as making laws in a kingdom of ends which is possible through freedom of the will—whether it be as member or as head. The position of the latter he can maintain, not in virtue of the maxim of his will alone, but only if he is a completely independent being, without needs and with an unlimited power adequate to his will.

Thus morality consists in the relation of all action to the making of laws whereby alone a kingdom of ends is possible. This making of laws must be found in every rational being himself and must be able to spring from his will. The principle of his will is therefore never to perform an action except on a maxim such as can also be a universal law, and consequently such *that the will can regard itself as at the same time making universal law by means of its maxim.* Where maxims are not already by their very nature in harmony with this objective principle of rational beings as makers of universal law, the necessity of acting on this principle is practical necessitation—that is, *duty.* Duty does not apply to the head in a kingdom of ends, but it does apply to every member and to all members in equal measure.

The practical necessity of acting on this principle—that is, duty—is in no way based on feelings, impulses, and inclinations, but only on the relation of rational beings to one another, a relation in which the will of a rational being must always be regarded as *making universal law,* because otherwise he could not be conceived as *an end in himself.* Reason thus relates every maxim of the will, considered as making universal law, to every other will and also to every action toward oneself: it does so, not because of any further motive or future advantage, but from the Idea of the *dignity* of a rational being who obeys no law other than that which he at the same time enacts himself. . . .

What is it then that entitles a morally good attitude of mind—or virtue—to make claims so high? It is nothing less than the *share* which it affords to a rational being *in the making of universal law,* and which therefore fits him to be a member in a possible kingdom of ends. For this he was already marked out in virtue of his own proper nature as an end in himself and consequently as a maker of laws in the kingdom of ends—as free in respect of all laws of nature, obeying only those laws which he makes himself and in virtue of which his maxims can have their part in the making of universal law (to which he at the same time subjects himself). For nothing can have a value other than that determined for it by the law. But the law-making which determines all value must for this reason have a dignity—that is, an unconditioned and incomparable worth—for the appreciation of which, as necessarily given by a rational being, the word *"reverence"* is the only becoming expression. *Autonomy* is therefore the ground of the dignity of human nature and of every rational nature. . . .

From what was said a little time ago we can now easily explain how it comes about that, although in the concept of duty we think of subjection to the law, yet we also at the same time attribute to the person who fulfills all his duties a certain sublimity and *dignity.* For it is not in so far as he is *subject* to the law that he has sublimity, but rather in so far as, in regard to this very same law, he is at the same time its *author* and is subordinated to it only on this ground. We have also shown above how neither fear nor inclination, but solely reverence for the law, is the motive which can give an action moral worth. Our own will, provided it were to act only under the condition of being able to make universal law by means of its maxims—this ideal will which can be ours is the proper object of reverence; and the dignity of man consists precisely in his capacity to make universal law, although only on condition of being himself also subject to the law he makes.

Autonomy of the Will
as the supreme principle of morality.

Autonomy of the will is the property the will has of being a law to itself (independently of every property belonging to the objects of volition). Hence the principle of autonomy is "Never to choose except in such a way that in the same volition the maxims of your choice are also present as universal law." . . . [B]y mere analysis of the concepts of morality we can quite well show that the above principle of autonomy is the sole principle of ethics. For analysis finds that the principle of morality must be a categorical imperative, and that this in turn commands nothing more nor less than precisely this autonomy.

Heteronomy of the Will
as the source of all spurious principles of morality.

If the will seeks the law that is to determine it *anywhere else* than in the fitness of its maxims for its own making of universal law—if therefore in going beyond itself it seeks this law in the character of any of its objects—the result is always *heteronomy.* In that case the will does not give itself the law, but the object does so in virtue of its relation to the will. This relation, whether based on inclination or on rational ideas, can give rise only to hypothetical imperatives: "I ought to do something *because I will something else*." As against this, the moral, and therefore categorical, imperative, says: "I ought to will thus or thus, although I have not willed something else." For example, the first says: "I ought not to lie if I want to maintain my reputation"; while the second says: "I ought not to lie even if so doing were to bring me not the slightest disgrace." The second imperative must therefore abstract from all objects to this extent—they should be without any *influence* at all on the will so that practical reason (the will) may not merely administer an alien interest but may simply manifest its own sovereign authority as the supreme maker of law. Thus, for example, the reason why I ought to promote the happiness of others is not because the realization of their happiness is of consequence to myself (whether on account of immediate inclination or on account of some satisfaction gained indirectly through reason), but solely because a maxim which excludes this cannot also be present in one and the same volition as a universal law.

SUGGESTIONS FOR DISCUSSION

1. What are the basic differences between Rousseau's conception of the social contract and Hobbes's? Do these differences have implications for social policy?

2. Does Rousseau's conception of the "general will" establish a basis for deciding what ought properly to be done in respect to such social questions as affirmative action (see Part II, Chapter 8) and censorship (Chapter 9)?

3. John Stuart Mill argues that Kant's practical application of the categorical imperative does not show that immoral rules of conduct rest on contradictions. It shows rather, Mill claims, that no rational person would be prepared to accept the *consequences* of universal adoption of immoral rules. Why does Mill's point amount to a criticism of Kant's theory of morality? Can Kant's view be defended against Mill's attack?

4. How would Kant's fundamental moral principle oblige us to act when applied to capital punishment (see Part II, Chapter 13) or euthanasia (Chapter 12) or sexual relations (Chapter 10)?

FURTHER READING

ROUSSEAU

Cassirer, E. *The Question of Jean-Jacques Rousseau*. Trans. P. W. Gay. Bloomington: Indiana University Press, 1963. (Interpretation, critical analysis; intermediate)

Cohen, J. "Reflections on Rousseau: Autonomy and Democracy." *Philosophy and Public Affairs* 15,3 (Summer 1986): 275–97. (Interpretation, critical analysis; advanced)

Gildin, H. *Rousseau's Social Contract*. Chicago: University of Chicago Press, 1983. (Interpretation; intermediate)

Miller, J. *Rousseau: Dreamer of Democracy*. New Haven: Yale University Press, 1984. (Interpretation, critical analysis; advanced)

Rousseau, Jean-Jacques *The Social Contract*. Trans. M. Cranston. London: Penguin Classics, 1968.

————. *The 1st and 2nd Discourses*. Trans. R. and J. Masters. New York: St. Martin's Press, 1978.

Shklar, J. *Men and Citizens: A Study in Rousseau's Social Theory*. 2nd ed. Cambridge: Cambridge University Press, 1985. (Interpretation, critical analysis; advanced)

Aune, B. *Kant's Theory of Morals*. Princeton: Princeton University Press, 1979. (Interpretation, critical analysis; advanced)

Auxter, T. *Kant's Moral Teleology*. Macon, Ga.: Mercer University Press, 1982. (Interpretation, critical analysis; intermediate)

Bernstein, J. A. *Shaftesbury, Rousseau, and Kant*. London: Associated University Presses, 1980. (Interpretation; intermediate)

Donagan, A. *The Theory of Morality*. Chicago: University of Chicago Press, 1977. (Interpretation, critical analysis; advanced)

Herman, B. "The Practice of Moral Judgment." *Journal of Philosophy* 82 (August 1985): 414–35. (Interpretation, critical analysis; advanced)

———. "Mutual Aid and Respect for Persons." *Ethics* 94 (July 1984): 577–602. (Interpretation, critical analysis; advanced)

Hill, Thomas E., Jr. "Humanity as an End in Itself." *Ethics* 91 (October 1980): 81–99. (Interpretation, critical analysis; intermediate)

Kant, Immanuel. *Critique of Practical Reason*. Trans. L. W. Beck. Indianapolis: Bobbs-Merrill, 1956.

———. *The Metaphysical Elements of Justice*. Trans. J. Ladd. Indianapolis: Bobbs-Merrill, 1965.

———. *The Doctrine of Virtue*. Trans. M. Gregor. Philadelphia: University of Pennsylvania Press, 1971.

———. *Lectures on Ethics*. Trans. L. Infield. Indianapolis: Hackett Publishing, 1980.

Körner, S. *Kant*. New Haven: Yale University Press, 1982. (Interpretation; introductory)

Murphy, J. *Kant: The Philosophy of Right*. London: St. Martin's Press, 1970. (Survey, critical analysis; introductory)

Nell, O. *Acting on Principle: An Essay on Kantian Ethics*. New York: Columbia University Press, 1975. (Interpretation, critical analysis; advanced)

Paton, H. J. *The Categorical Imperative: A Study in Kant's Moral Philosophy*. Philadelphia: University of Pennsylvania Press, 1971. (Interpretation, critical analysis; intermediate)

Schneewind, J., and Hoy, D., eds. *Kantian Ethical Thought*. Tallahassee: Council of Philosophical Studies, 1984. (Bibliography; intermediate, advanced)

Scruton, R. *Kant*. Oxford: Oxford University Press, 1982. (Interpretation, critical analysis; introductory)

Wolff, R. P., ed. *Kant: A Collection of Critical Essays*. South Bend: University of Notre Dame Press, 1968. (Interpretation, critical analysis; advanced)

4

□

Bentham and Mill

Utilitarianism Utilitarianism defines the moral rightness or wrongness of an act, rule, principle, or policy in terms of the balance in each case of good or bad consequences. The value assigned by utilitarianism to an act in producing these consequences is termed its *utility* or *disutility*. The various utilitarian theories may be distinguished in two ways: according to the interpretation each assigns to the concept of "utility"; and according to whether it is consequences of individual acts or types of acts that are to be assessed.

JEREMY BENTHAM (1748–1832): CLASSICAL UTILITARIANISM

Bentham's Principle of Utility David Hume and others had used the term utility in their moral writings. Nevertheless, Jeremy Bentham was the first to formulate an explicitly utilitarian moral theory, although it seems to have been his student John Stuart Mill who actually coined the term *utilitarianism* to refer to this account of morality. Bentham's primary interests lay in instituting legal, political, and social reforms. He wanted to provide a rational basis for identifying and justifying widespread reforms, and to remove the hold that the clerics exercised on moral justification, by offering a way of analyzing morality in secular terms. He developed a simple *moral calculus* for specifying the right action to be done in any act-context an agent might face. Bentham's science of ethics consisted in formulating a simple but universal basic moral rule, and in demonstrating its application in widely varying contexts. Bentham called this single moral standard the *principle of utility*.

The principle of utility claims that any act or institution is good if and only if it tends to produce the greatest amount of happiness. In particular, an act will be good if and only if it tends to increase the happiness of the agent and those likely to be affected by it more than any other act; or failing this, if it tends to diminish unhappiness more than any other act. Bentham interpreted happiness (or utility) strictly as pleasure, and unhappiness as pain. In terms of this moral calculus, each individual is considered to be equal, and no act is deemed superior in kind to any other. The sole consideration in what he called the *hedonic* or *felicific calculus* is the balance in *quantity* of pleasure and pain (to be) experienced. As Bentham so eloquently concluded, "Quantity of pleasure being equal, pushpin is as good as poetry." (Pushpin is a simple children's game). Bentham assumed that pleasure and pain are the sole direct causes of human action, and claimed in this way to provide a common explanation both for how agents *do* act and how they *ought* to act.

Measuring Pleasure and Pain The rightness or wrongness of any act or type of act is determined by the balance of immediate and distant pleasure or pain this act or type of act tends to produce for all the agents it affects. Pleasures and pains are to be measured quantitatively in terms of their intensity, the span of time they last, their certainty of occurrence, and their immediacy or remoteness. Bentham perhaps thought that the more immediate the pleasure or pain, the more assured one is that it will occur, and that this should be reflected in the calculus. To these criteria must be added the tendency of the act or type of act to bring about further pleasurable or painful acts. Consider an act of promise-breaking: Measured in these terms, we must sum up the utilities or disutilities for all persons that a broken promise might create. If the total pleasure outweighs the total pain, and tends to outweigh the pleasures that would be produced by any other appropriate act (or type) in the circumstances, then it is right: the agent would thus have *a duty* to break the promise. Where, on balance, as much pleasure would be produced by breaking the promise as by some other appropriate act, it will be *permissible*— though not required—to act in this way. Where more pain is produced, on balance, the act or type will be *im*permissible.

Criticism Bentham's theory has been criticized in various ways. On his view, agents could be required to institute slavery if it turned out that the pleasure produced by it really outweighed the sum of individual pains and the social disutilities it caused. Yet there are reasons having nothing to do with the hedonic calculus that commit us to rejecting slavery, even if the pleasure from it proved to be greater than the painful consequences. Bentham's contemporary critics raised a related difficulty for the hedonic calculus concerning its requirement that the measure of pleasure and pain be strictly quantitative. It was argued that because some pleasures are inherently better than others (getting an education, say, is better than getting drunk), they are intrinsically more worthy of human pursuit. If we accept the claim that some acts or goals have inherent worth that makes them desirable, it throws in question the very possibility of a hedonic calculus: It would mean that pleasure and pain are no longer considered the basic units in terms of which the worth of all acts or goals are to be measured. These considerations prompted John Stuart Mill to reformulate the theory of utilitarianism.

JOHN STUART MILL (1806–1873):
REVISED UTILITARIANISM

Bentham and Mill Bentham perceived in the principle of utility a universal criterion for distinguishing good government from bad. Mill found in this principle a foundation for his philosophical arguments in support of maximizing individual and social freedoms. Good government, for Mill, is one that would guarantee the fullest range of individual liberties for all citizens. Mill set about his defense of utilitarianism by conceiving the principle of utility as Bentham had: Happiness alone is desirable as an end, and it consists in pleasure and freedom from pain. Acts are right insofar as they tend to promote pleasure, and wrong in tending to prompt pain. From the social point of view, acts are right in tending to add to the sum of happiness or, failing this, to diminish pain. Thus pleasure is the only thing that is inherently good, pain the only thing inherently bad.

Higher and Lower Pleasures   However, Mill considered it self-evident that pushpin, foolishness, or selfishness are inferior to poetry, intelligence, or generosity. Mill admitted that some goods (generally, the intellectual) are by their nature more valuable, and so more worthy of human pursuit, than others (generally, the bodily). The way Mill put this is that pleasures and pains are to be measured not only in terms of their *quantities* but also in terms of their *qualities*, though he never makes clear how. But if the "higher" and "lower" pleasures are distinguished in this way, it appears to undermine Bentham's claim that the utility principle is at basis empirical in its appeal to what people actually find pleasurable. Mill took two steps to save this empirical or factual appeal underlying the utility principle. He argued, first, that human beings in fact mostly prefer the higher pleasures. And he urged, second, that what counts as a higher or lower pleasure is to be decided by the majority decision of those having experience of *both* sorts of pleasure. Mill thought that almost all with such common experience would agree with his famous summary: "It is better to be a human being dissatisfied than a pig satisfied: better to be Socrates dissatisfied than a fool satisfied."

Mill's Revisions   Bentham held that the principle of utility is incapable of proof: the standard of proof itself cannot be proved. He suggested, nevertheless, that the principle of utility could be denied only be experiencing personal displeasure caused by its misapplication, and so by actually appealing to the principle denied. Similarly, Mill argued that any attempt, like Kant's, to avoid consequences by deriving moral rules strictly from the commands of reason must inevitably appeal to the benevolent consequences of those rules in order to justify their rightness (see Kant, Part I, Chapter 3). Mill added that each person desires his or her own happiness. So, by aggregation, happiness must be generally desirable as a good for all. Mill acknowledged that intrinsically good ends like virtue are desirable for their own sakes, and not for the happiness they effect. He insisted, though, that in being desired as ends in themselves and not merely as means to happiness, these intrinsic goods are desired as *parts* or representatives of happiness. Mill countered in like manner the criticism that the principle of utility is unable to account for our common intuition, that acts such as promise-breaking or slavery are intrinsically immoral. Acts of some kinds, he argued, are commonly experienced as *tending* to create more pain than pleasure. A particular act of the kind can be presumed wrong because of this general tendency. For example, breaking a promise tends overwhelmingly to undermine trust, and so as a rule it is unacceptable. Yet the utility generated by breaking a promise under some specific conditions may be sufficiently great that it would be morally required in the exceptional circumstance.

Act- and Rule-utilitarianism Considerations of this sort have encouraged philosophers more recently to distinguish between two kinds of utilitarianism. *Act-utilitarianism* holds that what is morally right in any situation is established by assessing which of the available acts would maximize the general sum of good over bad. Act-utilitarians are not concerned to assess the utility of *kinds* of acts (such as truth-telling or stealing), nor are they concerned with the effects on utility of everyone acting in a given way. Whether the balance of good over bad is maximized must be directly assessed for each of the *particular acts* under consideration. If a given act of lying or stealing maximizes the good, act-utilitarianism will consider it to be obligatory. It may be that among the alternatives, no act produces positive utility; here the act that produces the least disutility or evil will be required.

Rule-utilitarianism holds that moral right is to be determined by assessing what applicable principle or social practice would maximize the sum of the general good. Here the question is not whether one's individual act would maximize goodness, but whether goodness would be maximized if everyone did the act. The principle of utility applies in establishing what the rules, principles, or practices should be. Social rules or practices are chosen or changed solely on the grounds of their utility. Whether an act is required in a given situation would depend upon whether it is obliged by a rule or practice whose application in the context is considered to maximize the good. Rule-utilitarianism seeks to justify the intuition that what as a rule or practice is considered moral may sometimes override a particular act that would maximize utility. The general good of the rule or practice that promises should not be broken, say, would require rule-utilitarians always to keep their promises, even though breaking a promise in a given circumstance may maximize the general utility. Act-utilitarians, by contrast, may use rules of thumb as a general guide to acts that tend to maximize utility. But if it is found that a particular act, like one of promise-breaking, would create greater good than an act required by a rule like promise-keeping, then an act-utilitarian would be obliged to break the promise.

Ideal Rule-utilitarianism We can distinguish also between two types of rule-utilitarianism. The first assesses the utility of the actual rules, principles, or practices of a given society; the second sets out to establish those *ideal* rules that would maximize goodness. Richard Brandt develops a form of the latter, which he calls "ideal moral code rule-utilitarianism." Here an act is right if and only if the ideal moral code for the society does not prohibit it. A moral code is ideal for a society if its acceptance by the vast majority of the society's members (at least 90 percent, say) would produce more good per person than any competing moral code. The moral code is made up of general rules, such as "Keep promises" or "Do not harm," rather than particular institutional principles, such as those concerning repayment of loans from the government or police brutality. Thus the moral acceptability of particular institutional rules may be judged on the basis of the ideal moral code. An institutional principle allowing politicians to renege on repaying campaign loans may be deemed immoral if the ideal code commands keeping promises (a loan involves a promise to repay); and a law enforcement principle that permitted police generally "to shoot first and ask questions later" may entail violation of a moral rule not to harm.

Aggregate and Average Utilitarianism   It remains open to interpretation whether Bentham and Mill were act- or rule-utilitarians. Nevertheless, both clearly emphasized that what is to be maximized is happiness or pleasure. But here, too, there may be an ambiguity. On Bentham's classical utilitarianism, the mark of morality is the sum total or *aggregate* utility that might be produced. Mill and contemporary utilitarians have suggested that the criterion should not be the greatest aggregate happiness produced for all, but the maximizing of *average* utility, the total *per person*, resulting from the act or rule (Brandt endorses such an interpretation). This requires that it is not simply total utility which must be maximized, but the number of people for whom utility is maximized. Attempts to combine the criteria of aggregate and average utility may cause conflict: Cases may arise where an act or rule that maximizes utility by greatly satisfying a few people clashes with one that maximizes the number of those experiencing some modest or small amount of satisfaction. For example, it must be decided whether a tax increase that greatly benefits 10 percent of the population but has minimal benefits for the rest is preferable to one that benefits all members of the population equally but in modest ways. Cases of this sort require utilitarians to indicate which criterion they take to be primary.

The appeal of utilitarianism has been a function of its simplicity, egalitarianism, and comprehensiveness, as well as the fact that we do value the good or happiness or pleasure. Utilitarianism has held out the promise of a single, simple, and general quantitative calculus for ethics, government, economics, and the law. Historically, hedonic utilitarianism encountered difficulties in establishing an acceptable unit of quantitative measurement for the calculus: specific weights are not assignable to pleasures and pains in every—some might argue, in any— occurrence. Despite this, utilitarianism has continued to offer a method for determining efficient rules for law, politics, and economic distributions. Contemporary utilitarians no longer interpret "utility" simply as pleasure or happiness. The calculus is conducted more technically now in terms of preferences, interests, benefits, or welfare. Instead of evaluating the consequences of acts or rules in terms of maximizing pleasure and pain, *preference utilitarianism* seeks to evaluate their acceptability in terms of maximizing the satisfaction of desires and preferences. Yet it remains an open question whether the notion of utilitarian efficiency furnishes the fundamental criterion of morality.

Jeremy Bentham

An Introduction to the Principles of Morals and Legislation

CHAP. I—OF THE PRINCIPLE OF UTILITY

I. Nature has placed mankind under the governance of two sovereign masters, *pain* and *pleasure*. It is for them alone to point out what we ought to do, as well as to determine what we shall do. On the one hand the standard of right and wrong, on the other the chain of causes and effects, are fastened to their throne. They govern us in all we do, in all we say, in all we think: every effort we can make to throw off our subjection, will serve but to demonstrate and confirm it. In words a man may pretend to abjure their empire: but in reality he will remain subject to it all the while. The *principle of utility** recognizes this subjection, and assumes it for the foundation of that system, the object of which is to rear the fabric of felicity by the hands of reason and of law. . . .

II. The principle of utility is the foundation of the present work: it will be proper therefore at the outset to give an explicit and determinate account of what is meant by it. By the principle† of utility is meant that principle which approves or disapproves of every action whatsoever, according to the tendency which it appears to have to augment or diminish the happiness of the party whose interest is in question: or, what is the same thing in other words, to promote or to oppose that happiness. I say of every action whatsover; and therefore not only of every action of a private individual, but of every measure of government.

From Jeremy Bentham, *An Introduction to the Principles of Morals and Legislation*, revised edition (1823).

* Note by the Author, July 1822.

To this denomination has of late been added, or substituted, the *greatest happiness* or *greatest felicity* principle: this for shortness, instead of saying at length *that principle* which states the greatest happiness of all those whose interest is in question, as being the right and proper and only right and proper and universally desirable, end of human action: of human action in every situation, and in particular in that of a functionary or set of functionaries exercising the powers of Government. The word *utility* does not so clearly point to the ideas of *pleasure* and *pain* as the words *happiness* and *felicity* do: nor does it lead us to the consideration of the *number*, of the interests affected; to the *number*, as being the circumstance, which contributes, in the largest proportion, to the formation of the standard here in question; the *standard of right and wrong*, by which alone the propriety of human conduct, in every situation, can with propriety be tried. This want of a sufficiently manifest connection between the ideas of *happiness* and *pleasure* on the one hand, and the idea of *utility* on the other, I have every now and then found operating, and with but too much efficiency, as a bar to the acceptance, that might otherwise have been given, to this principle.

† [Principle] . . . The principle here in question may be taken for an act of the mind; a sentiment; a sentiment of approbation; a sentiment which, when applied to an action, approves of its utility, as that quality of it by which the measure of approbation or disapprobation bestowed upon it ought to be governed.

III.   By utility is meant that property in any object, whereby it tends to produce benefit, advantage, pleasure, good, or happiness, (all this in the present case comes to the same thing) or (what comes again to the same thing) to prevent the happening of mischief, pain, evil, or unhappiness to the party whose interest is considered: if that party be the community in general, then the happiness of the community: if a particular individual, then the happiness of that individual.

IV.   ... The community is a fictitious *body*, composed of the individual persons who are considered as constituting as it were its *members*. The interest of the community then is, what?—the sum of the interests of the several members who compose it.

V.   ... A thing is said to promote the interest, or to be *for* the interest, of an individual, when it tends to add to the sum total of his pleasures: or, what comes to the same thing, to diminish the sum total of his pains.

VI.   An action then may be said to be conformable to the principle of utility, or, for shortness sake, to utility (meaning with respect to the community at large), when the tendency it has to augment the happiness of the community is greater than any it has to diminish it.

VII.   A measure of government (which is but a particular kind of action, performed by a particular person or persons) may be said to be conformable to or dictated by the principle of utility, when in like manner the tendency which it has to augment the happiness of the community is greater than any which it has to diminish it.

VIII.   When an action, or in particular a measure of government, is supposed by a man to be conformable to the principle of utility, it may be convenient, for the purposes of discourse, to imagine a kind of law or dictate, called a law or dictate of utility: and to speak of the action in question, as being conformable to such law or dictate.

IX.   A man may be said to be a partisan of the principle of utility, when the approbation or disapprobation he annexes to any action, or to any measure, is determined by, and proportioned to the tendency which he conceives it to have to augment or to diminish the happiness of the community: or in other words, to its conformity or unconformity to the laws or dictates of utility.

X.   Of an action that is conformable to the principle of utility, one may always say either that it is one that ought to be done, or at least that it is not one that ought not to be done. One may say also, that it is right it should be done; at least that it is not wrong it should be done: that it is a right action; at least that it is not a wrong action. When thus interpreted, the words *ought*, and *right* and *wrong*, and others of that stamp, have a meaning: when otherwise, they have none.

XI.   Has the rectitude of this principle been ever formally contested? It should seem that it had, by those who have not known what they have been meaning. Is it susceptible of any direct proof? It should seem not: for that which is used to prove every thing else, cannot itself be proved: a chain of proofs must have their commencement somewhere. To give such proof is as impossible as it is needless. ...

XIII. When a man attempts to combat the principle of utility, it is with reasons drawn, without his being aware of it, from that very principle itself.* His arguments, if they prove any thing, prove not that the principle is *wrong*, but that, according to the applications he supposes to be made of it, it is *misapplied*. . . .

XIV. To disprove the propriety of it by arguments is impossible; but, from the causes that have been mentioned, or from some confused or partial view of it, a man may happen to be disposed not to relish it. Where this is the case, if he thinks the settling of his opinions on such a subject worth the trouble, let him take the following steps, and at length, perhaps, he may come to reconcile himself to it.

1. Let him settle with himself, whether he would wish to discard this principle altogether; if so, let him consider what it is that all his reasonings (in matters of politics especially) can amount to?

2. If he would, let him settle with himself, whether he would judge and act without any principle, or whether there is any other he would judge and act by?

3. If there be, let him examine and satisfy himself whether the principle he thinks he has found is really any separate intelligible principle; or whether it be not a mere principle in words, a kind of phrase, which at bottom expresses neither more nor less than the mere averment of his own unfounded sentiments; that is, what in another person he might be apt to call caprice?

4. If he is inclined to think that his own approbation or disapprobation, annexed to the idea of an act, without any regard to its consequences, is a sufficient foundation for him to judge and act upon, let him ask himself whether his sentiment is to be a standard of right and wrong, with respect to every other man, or whether every man's sentiment has the same privilege of being a standard to itself?

5. In the first case, let him ask himself whether his principle is not despotical, and hostile to all the rest of human race?

6. In the second case, whether it is not anarchical, and whether at this rate there are not as many different standards of right and wrong as there are men? and whether even to the same man, the same thing, which is right to-day, may not (without the least change in its nature) be wrong to-morrow? and whether the same thing is not right and wrong in the same place at the same time? and in either case, whether all argument is not at an end? and whether, when two men have said, "I like this," and "I don't like it," they can (upon such a principle) have any thing more to say?

7. If he should have said to himself, No: for that sentiment which he proposes as a standard must be grounded on reflection, let him say on what particulars the reflection is to turn? if on particulars having relation to the utility of the act, then let him say whether this is not deserting his own principle, and borrowing assistance from that very one in opposition to which he sets it up: or if not on those particulars, on what other particulars?

8. If he should be for compounding the matter, and adopting his own principle in part, and the principle of utility in part, let him say how far he will adopt it?

---

* "The principle of utility (I have heard it said) is a dangerous principle: it is dangerous on certain occasions to consult it." This is as much as to say, what? that it is not consonant to utility, to consult utility: in short, that it is *not* consulting it, to consult it.

9.   When he has settled with himself where he will stop, then let him ask himself how he justifies to himself the adopting it so far? and why he will not adopt it any farther?

10.   Admitting any other principle than the principle of utility to be a right principle, a principle that it is right for a man to pursue; admitting (what is not true) that the word *right* can have a meaning without reference to utility, let him say whether there is any such thing as a *motive* that a man can have to pursue the dictates of it: if there is, let him say what that motive is, and how it is to be distinguished from those which enforce the dictates of utility: if not, then lastly let him say what it is this other principle can be good for?

CHAP. II—OF PRINCIPLES ADVERSE TO THAT OF UTILITY

I.   If the principle of utility be a right principle to be governed by, and that in all cases, it follows from what has been just observed, that whatever principle differs from it in any case must necessarily be a wrong one. To prove any other principle, therefore, to be a wrong one, there needs no more than just to show it to be what it is, a principle of which the dictates are in some point or other different from those of the principle of utility: to state it is to confute it.

II.   A principle may be different from that of utility in two ways: 1. By being constantly opposed to it: this is the case with a principle which may be termed the principle of *asceticism*. 2. By being sometimes opposed to it, and sometimes not, as it may happen: this is the case with another, which may be termed the principle of *sympathy* and *antipathy*.

III.   By the principle of asceticism I mean that principle, which, like the principle of utility, approves or disapproves of any action, according to the tendency which it appears to have to augment or diminish the happiness of the party whose interest is in question; but in an inverse manner: approving of actions in as far as they tend to diminish his happiness; disapproving of them in as far as they tend to augment it. . . . .

IX.   The principle of asceticism seems originally to have been the reverie of certain hasty speculators, who having perceived, or fancied, that certain pleasures, when reaped in certain circumstances, have, at the long run, been attended with pains more than equivalent to them, took occasion to quarrel with every thing that offered itself under the name of pleasure. Having then got thus far, and having forgot the point which they set out from, they pushed on, and went so much further as to think it meritorious to fall in love with pain. Even this, we see, is at bottom but the principle of utility misapplied.

X.   The principle of utility is capable of being consistently pursued; and it is but tautology to say, that the more consistently it is pursued, the better it must ever be for human-kind. The principle of asceticism never was, nor ever can be, consistently pursued by any living creature. Let but one tenth part of the inhabitants of this earth pursue it consistently, and in a day's time they will have turned it into a hell.

XI.   Among principles adverse to that of utility, that which at this day seems to have most influence in matters of government, is what may be called the principle of sympathy and antipathy. By the principle of sympathy and antipathy, I mean that principle which approves or disapproves of certain actions, not on account of their tending to augment the happiness, nor yet on account of their tending to diminish the happiness of the party whose interest is in question, but merely because a man finds himself disposed to approve or disapprove of them: holding up that approbation or disapprobation as a sufficient reason for itself, and disclaiming the necessity of looking out for any extrinsic ground.

XII.   It is manifest, that this is rather a principle in name than in reality: it is not a positive principle of itself, so much as a term employed to signify the negation of all principle. What one expects to find in a principle is something that points out some external consideration, as a means of warranting and guiding the internal sentiments of approbation and disapprobation: this expectation is but ill fulfilled by a proposition, which does neither more nor less than hold up each of those sentiments as a ground and standard for itself. . . .

XIV.   The various systems that have been formed concerning the standard of right and wrong, may all be reduced to the principle of sympathy and antipathy. One account may serve for all of them. They consist all of them in so many contrivances for avoiding the obligation of appealing to any external standard, and for prevailing upon the reader to accept of the author's sentiment or opinion as a reason for itself. The phrases different, but the principle the same.* . . .

XVIII.   It may be wondered, perhaps, that in all this while no mention has been made of the *theological* principle; meaning that principle which professes to recur for the standard of right and wrong to the will of God. But the case is, this is not in fact a distinct principle. It is never any thing more or less than one or other of the three before-mentioned principles presenting itself under another shape. The *will* of God here meant cannot be his revealed will, as contained in the sacred writings: for that is a system which nobody ever thinks of recurring to at this time of day, for the details of political administration: and even before it can be applied to the details of private conduct, it is universally allowed, by the most eminent divines of all persuasions, to stand in need of pretty ample interpretations; else to what use are the works of those divines? And for the guidance of these interpretations, it is also allowed, that some other standard must be assumed. The will then which is meant on this occasion, is that which may be called the *presumptive* will; that is to say, that which is presumed to be his will on account of the conformity of its dictates to those of some other principle. What then may be this other principle? It must be one or other of the three mentioned above: for there cannot, as we have seen, be any more. It is plain, therefore, that, setting revelation out of the question, no light can ever be thrown upon the standard of right and wrong, by any thing that

---

* A great multitude of people are continually talking of the Law of Nature; and then they go on giving you their sentiments about what is right and what is wrong: and these sentiments, you are to understand, are so many chapters and sections of the Law of Nature.

Instead of the phrase, Law of Nature, you have sometimes, Law of Reason, Right Reason, Natural Justice, Natural Equity, Good Order. Any of them will do equally well. This latter is most used in politics. The three last are much more tolerable than the others, because they do not very explicitly claim to be any thing more than phrases: they insist but feebly upon the being looked upon as so many positive standards of themselves, and seem content to be taken, upon occasion, for phrases expressive of the conformity of the thing in question to the proper standard, whatever that may be. On most occasions, however, it will be better to say *utility: utility* is clearer, as referring more explicitly to pain and pleasure.

can be said upon the question, what is God's will. We may be perfectly sure, indeed, that whatever is right is conformable to the will of God: but so far is that from answering the purpose of showing us what is right, that it is necessary to know first whether a thing is right, in order to know from thence whether it be conformable to the will of God.*

XIX.   There are two things which are very apt to be confounded, but which it imports us carefully to distinguish:—the motive or cause, which, by operating on the mind of an individual, is productive of any act: and the ground or reason which warrants a legislator, or other by-stander, in regarding that act with an eye of approbation. When the act happens, in the particular instance in question, to be productive of effects which we approve of, much more if we happen to observe that the same motive may frequently be productive, in other instances, of the like effects, we are apt to transfer our approbation to the motive itself, and to assume, as the just ground for the approbation we bestow on the act, the circumstance of its originating from that motive. It is in this way that the sentiment of antipathy has often been considered as a just ground of action. Antipathy, for instance, in such or such a case, is the cause of an action which is attended with good effects: but this does not make it a right ground of action in that case, any more than in any other. Still farther. Not only the effects are good, but the agent sees beforehand that they will be so. This may make the action indeed a perfectly right action: but it does not make antipathy a right ground of action. For the same sentiment of antipathy, if implicitly deferred to, may be, and very frequently is, productive of the very worst effects. Antipathy, therefore, can never be a right ground of action. No more, therefore, can resentment, which . . . is but a modification of antipathy. The only right ground of action, that can possibly subsist, is, after all, the consideration of utility, which, if it is a right principle of action, and of approbation, in any one case, is so in every other. Other principles in abundance, that is, other motives, may be the reasons why such and such an act *has* been done: that is, the reasons or causes of its being done: but it is this alone that can be the reason why it might or ought to have been done. Antipathy or resentment requires always to be regulated, to prevent its doing mischief: to be regulated by what? always by the principle of utility. The principle of utility neither requires nor admits of any other regulator than itself. . . .

* The principle of theology refers every thing to God's pleasure. But what is God's pleasure? God does not, he confessedly does not now, either speak or write to us. How then are we to know what is his pleasure? By observing what is our own pleasure, and pronouncing it to be his. Accordingly, what is called the pleasure of God, is and must necessarily be (revelation apart) neither more nor less than the good pleasure of the person, whoever he be, who is pronouncing what he believes, or pretends, to be God's pleasure. How know you it to be God's pleasure that such or such an act should be abstained from? whence come you even to suppose as much? "Because the engaging in it would, I imagine, be prejudicial upon the whole to the happiness of mankind"; says the partisan of the principle of utility; "Because the commission of it is attended with a gross and sensual, or at least with a trifling and transient satisfaction"; says the partisan of the principle of asceticism: "Because I detest the thoughts of it; and I cannot, neither ought I to be called upon to tell why"; says he who proceeds upon the principle of antipathy. In the words of one or other of these must that person necessarily answer (revelation apart) who professes to take for his standard the will of God.

CHAP. IV—VALUE OF A LOT OF PLEASURE OR PAIN, HOW TO BE MEASURED

I. Pleasures then, and the avoidance of pains, are the *ends* which the legislator has in view: it behoves him therefore to understand their *value*. Pleasures and pains are the *instruments* he has to work with: it behoves him therefore to understand their force, which is again, in other words, their value.

II. To a person considered *by himself*, the value of a pleasure or pain considered *by itself*, will be greater or less, according to the four following circumstances:

1. Its *intensity*.
2. Its *duration*.
3. Its *certainty* or *uncertainty*.
4. Its *propinquity* or *remoteness*.

III. These are the circumstances which are to be considered in estimating a pleasure or a pain considered each of them by itself. But when the value of any pleasure or pain is considered for the purpose of estimating the tendency of any *act* by which it is produced, there are two other circumstances to be taken into the account; these are,

5. Its *fecundity*, or the chance it has of being followed by sensations of the *same* kind; that is, pleasures, if it be a pleasure: pains, if it be a pain.

6. Its *purity*, or the chance it has of *not* being followed by sensations of the *opposite* kind: that is, pains, if it be a pleasure: pleasures, if it be a pain.

These two last, however, are in strictness scarcely to be deemed properties of the pleasure or the pain itself; they are not, therefore, in strictness to be taken into the account of the value of that pleasure or that pain. They are in strictness to be deemed properties only of the act, or other event, by which such pleasure or pain has been produced; and accordingly are only to be taken into the account of the tendency of such act or such event.

IV. To a *number* of persons, with reference to each of whom the value of a pleasure or a pain is considered, it will be greater or less, according to seven circumstances: to wit, the six preceding ones; viz.

1. Its *intensity*.
2. Its *direction*.
3. Its *certainty* or *uncertainty*.
4. Its *propinquity* or *remoteness*.
5. Its *fecundity*.
6. Its *purity*.

And one other; to wit:

7. Its *extent;* that is, the number of persons to whom it *extends;* or (in other words) who are affected by it.

V. To take an exact account then of the general tendency of any act, by which the interests of a community are affected, proceed as follows. Begin with any one person of those whose interests seem most immediately to be affected by it: and take an account,

1. Of the value of each distinguishable *pleasure* which appears to be produced by it in the *first* instance.

2. Of the value of each *pain* which appears to be produced by it in the *first* instance.

3. Of the value of each pleasure which appears to be produced by it *after* the first. This constitutes the *fecundity* of the first *pleasure* and the *impurity* of the first *pain*.

4. Of the value of each *pain* which appears to be produced by it after the first. This constitutes the *fecundity* of the first *pain*, and the *impurity* of the first pleasure.

5. Sum up all the values of all of the *pleasures* on the one side, and those of all the pains on the other. The balance, if it be on the side of pleasure, will give the *good* tendency of the act upon the whole, with respect to the interests of that *individual* person; if on the side of pain, the *bad* tendency of it upon the whole.

6. Take an account of the *number* of persons whose interests appear to be concerned; and repeat the above process with respect to each. *Sum up* the numbers expressive of the degrees of *good* tendency, which the act has, with respect to each individual, in regard to whom the tendency of it is *good* upon the whole: do this again with respect to each individual, in regard to whom the tendency of it is *bad* upon the whole. Take the *balance;* which, if on the side of *pleasure*, will give the general *good tendency* of the act, with respect to the total number or community of individuals concerned; if on the side of pain, the general *evil tendency*, with respect to the same community.

VI. It is not to be expected that this process should be strictly pursued previously to every moral judgment, or to every legislative or judicial operation. It may, however, be always kept in view: and as near as the process actually pursued on these occasions approaches to it, so near will such process approach to the character of an exact one.

VII. The same process is alike applicable to pleasure and pain, in whatever shape they appear: and by whatever denomination they are distinguished: to pleasure, whether it be called *good* (which is properly the cause or instrument of pleasure) or *profit* (which is distant pleasure, or the cause or instrument of distant pleasure,) or *convenience*, or *advantage, benefit, emolument, happiness,* and so forth: to pain, whether it be called *evil,* (which corresponds to *good*) or *mischief,* or *inconvenience*, or *disadvantage*, or *loss*, or *unhappiness*, and so forth.

VIII. Nor is this a novel and unwarranted, any more than it is a useless theory. In all this there is nothing but what the practice of mankind, wheresoever they have a clear view of their own interest, is perfectly conformable to. An article of property, an estate in land, for instance, is valuable, on what account? On account of the pleasures of all kinds which it enables a man to produce, and, what comes to the same thing, the pains of all kinds which it enables him to avert. But the value of such an article of property is universally understood to rise or fall according to the length or shortness of the time which a man has in it: the certainty or uncertainty of its coming into possession: and the nearness or remoteness of the time at which, if at all, it is to come into possession. As to the *intensity* of the pleasures which a man may derive from it, this is never thought of, because it depends upon the use which each particular person may come to make of it; which cannot be estimated till the particular pleasures he may come to derive from it, or the particular pains he may come to exclude by means of it, are brought to view. For the same reason, neither does he think of the *fecundity* or *purity* of those pleasures.

John Stuart Mill

Utilitarianism

CHAPTER I
GENERAL REMARKS

To inquire . . . to what extent the moral beliefs of mankind have been vitiated or made uncertain by the absence of any distinct recognition of an ultimate standard, would imply a complete survey and criticism of past and present ethical doctrine. It would, however, be easy to show that whatever steadiness or consistency these moral beliefs have attained, has been mainly due to the tacit influence of a standard not recognized. Although the non-existence of an acknowledged first principle has made ethics not so much a guide as a consecration of men's actual sentiments, still, as men's sentiments, both of favor and of aversion, are greatly influenced by what they suppose to be the effects of things upon their happiness, the principle of utility, or as Bentham latterly called it, the greatest happiness principle, has had a large share in forming the moral doctrines even of those who most scornfully reject its authority. Nor is there any school of thought which refuses to admit that the influence of actions on happiness is a most material and even predominant consideration in many of the details of morals, however unwilling to acknowledge it as the fundamental principle of morality, and the source of moral obligation. I might go much further, and say that to all those *à priori* moralists who deem it necessary to argue at all, utilitarian arguments are indispensable. It is not my present purpose to criticize these thinkers; but I cannot help referring, for illustration, to a systematic treatise by one of the most illustrious of them, the *Metaphysics of Ethics*, by Kant. This remarkable man, whose system of thought will long remain one of the landmarks in the history of philosophical speculation, does, in the treatise in question, lay down a universal first principle as the origin and ground of moral obligation; it is this:—"So act, that the rule on which thou actest would admit of being adopted as a law by all rational beings." But when he begins to deduce from this precept any of the actual duties of morality, he fails, almost grotesquely, to show that there would be any contradiction, any logical (not to say physical) impossibility, in the adoption by all rational beings of the most outrageously immoral rules of conduct. All he shows is that the *consequences* of their universal adoption would be such as no one would choose to incur.

From John Stuart Mill, *Utilitarianism* (1863).

On the present occasion, I shall, without further discussion of the other theories, attempt to contribute something toward the understanding and appreciation of the Utilitarian or Happiness theory, and toward such proof as it is susceptible of. It is evident that this cannot be proof in the ordinary and popular meaning of the term. Questions of ultimate ends are not amenable to direct proof. Whatever can be proved to be good, must be so by being shown to be a means to something admitted to be good without proof. The medical art is proved to be good, by its conducing to health; but how is it possible to prove that health is good? The art of music is good, for the reason, among others, that it produces pleasure; but what proof is it possible to give that pleasure is good? If, then, it is asserted that there is a comprehensive formula, including all things which are in themselves good, and that what ever else is good, is not so as an end, but as a mean, the formula may be accepted or rejected, but is not a subject of what is commonly understood by proof. We are not, however, to infer that its acceptance or rejection must depend on blind impulse, or arbitrary choice. There is a larger meaning of the word proof, in which this question is as amenable to it as any other of the disputed questions of philosophy. The subject is within the cognizance of the rational faculty; and neither does that faculty deal with it solely in the way of intuition. Considerations may be presented capable of determining the intellect either to give or withhold its assent to the doctrine; and this is equivalent to proof. . . .

CHAPTER II
WHAT UTILITARIANISM IS

. . . The creed which accepts as the foundation of morals, Utility, or the Greatest Happiness Principle, holds that actions are right in proportion as they tend to promote happiness, wrong as they tend to produce the reverse of happiness. By happiness is intended pleasure, and the absence of pain; by unhappiness, pain, and the privation of pleasure. To give a clear view of the moral standard set up by the theory, much more requires to be said; in particular, what things it includes in the ideas of pain and pleasure; and to what extent this is left an open question. But these supplementary explanations do not affect the theory of life on which this theory of morality is grounded—namely, that pleasure, and freedom from pain, are the only things desirable as ends; and that all desirable things (which are as numerous in the utilitarian as in any other scheme) are desirable either for the pleasure inherent in themselves, or as means to the promotion of pleasure and the prevention of pain.

Now, such a theory of life excites in many minds, and among them in some of the most estimable in feeling and purpose, inveterate dislike. To suppose that life has (as they express it) no higher end than pleasure—no better and nobler object of desire and pursuit—they designate as utterly mean and grovelling; as a doctrine worthy only of swine, to whom the followers of Epicurus were, at a very early period, contemptuously likened. . . . The comparison of the Epicurean life to that of beasts is felt as degrading, precisely because a beast's pleasures do not satisfy a human being's conceptions of happiness. Human beings have faculties more elevated than the animal appetites, and when once made conscious of them, do not regard anything as happiness which does not include their gratification. I do not, indeed, consider the Epicureans to have been by any means faultless in drawing out their scheme of consequences from the utilitarian principle. To do this in any sufficient manner, many Stoic, as well as Christian elements require to be included. But there is no known Epicurean theory of life which does not assign to the pleasures of the intellect, of the feelings and imagination, and of the moral sentiments, a much higher value as pleasures than to those of mere sensation. It must be admitted, however, that utilitarian writers in general have placed the superiority of mental over bodily pleasures chiefly in the greater permanency, safety, uncostliness, &c., of the former—that is, in their circumstantial advantages rather than in their intrinsic nature. And on all these points utilitarians have fully proved their case; but they might have taken the other, and, as it may be called, higher ground, with entire consistency. It is quite compatible with the principle of utility to recognize the fact, that some *kinds* of pleasure are more desirable and more valuable than others. It would be absurd that while, in estimating all other things, quality is considered as well as quantity, the estimation of pleasures should be supposed to depend on quantity alone.

If I am asked, what I mean by difference of quality in pleasures, or what makes one pleasure more valuable than another, merely as a pleasure, except its being greater in amount, there is but one possible answer. Of two pleasures, if there be one to which all or almost all who have experience of both give a decided preference, irrespective of any feeling of moral obligation to prefer it, that is the more desirable pleasure. If one of the two is, by those who are competently acquainted with both, placed so far above the other that they prefer it, even though knowing it to be attended with a greater amount of discontent, and would not resign it for any quantity of the other pleasure which their nature is capable of, we are justified in ascribing to the preferred enjoyment a superiority in quality, so far outweighing quantity as to render it, in comparison, of small account.

Now it is an unquestionable fact that those who are equally acquainted with, and equally capable of appreciating and enjoying, both, do give a most marked preference to the manner of existence which employs their higher faculties. Few human creatures would consent to be changed into any of the lower animals, for a promise of the fullest allowance of a beast's pleasures; no intelligent human being would consent to be a fool, no instructed person would be an ignoramus, no person of feeling and conscience would be selfish and base, even though they should be persuaded that the fool, the dunce, or the rascal is better satisfied with his lot than they are with theirs. They would not resign what they possess more than he, for the most complete satisfaction of all the desires which they have in common with him. If they ever fancy they would, it is only in cases of unhappiness so extreme, that to escape from it they would exchange their lot for almost any other, however undesirable in their own eyes. A being of higher faculties requires more to make him happy, is capable probably of more acute suffering, and is certainly accessible to it at more points, than one of an inferior type; but in spite of these liabilities, he can never really wish to sink into what he feels to be a lower grade of existence. We may give what explanation we please of this unwillingness; ... but its most appropriate appellation is a sense of dignity, which all human beings possess in one form or other, and in some, though by no means in exact, proportion to their higher faculties, and which is so essential a part of the happiness of those in whom it is strong, that nothing which conflicts with it could be, otherwise than momentarily, an object of desire to them. Whoever supposes that this preference takes place at a sacrifice of happiness—that the superior being, in anything like equal circumstances, is not happier than the inferior—confounds the two very different ideas, of happiness, and content. It is indisputable that the being whose capacities of enjoyment are low, has the greatest chance of having them fully satisfied, and a highly-endowed being will always feel that any happiness which he can look for, as the world is constituted, is imperfect. But he can learn to bear its imperfections, if they are at all bearable; and they will not make him envy the being who is indeed unconscious of the imperfections, but only because he feels not at all the good which those imperfections qualify. It is better to be a human being dissatisfied than a pig satisfied; better to be Socrates dissatisfied than a fool satisfied. And if the fool, or the pig, is of a different opinion, it is because they only know their own side of the question. The other party to the comparison knows both sides.

It may be objected, that many who are capable of the higher pleasures, occasionally, under the influence of temptation, postpone them to the lower. But this is quite compatible with a full appreciation of the intrinsic superiority of the higher. Men often, from infirmity of character, make their election for the nearer good, though they know it to be the less valuable; and this no less when the choice is between two bodily pleasures, than when it is between bodily and mental. They pursue sensual indulgences to the injury of health, though perfectly aware that health is the greater good. It may be further objected, that many who begin with youthful enthusiasm for everything noble, as they advance in years sink into indolence and selfishness. But I do not believe that those who undergo this very common change, voluntarily choose the lower description of pleasures in preference to the higher. I believe that before they devote themselves exclusively to the one, they have already become incapable of the other. Capacity for the nobler feelings is in most natures a very tender plant, easily killed, not only by hostile influences, but by mere want of sustenance; and in the majority of young persons it speedily dies away if the occupations to which their position in life has devoted them, and society into which it has thrown them, are not favorable to keeping that higher capacity in exercise. Men lose their high aspirations as they lose their intellectual tastes, because they have not time or opportunity for indulging them; and they addict themselves to inferior pleasures, not because they deliberately prefer them, but because they are either the only ones to which they have access, or the only ones which they are any longer capable of enjoying. It may be questioned whether any one who has remained equally susceptible to both classes of pleasures, ever knowingly and calmly preferred the lower; though many, in all ages, have broken down in an ineffectual attempt to combine both.

From this verdict of the only competent judges, I apprehend there can be no appeal. On a question which is the best worth having of two pleasures, or which of two modes of existence is the most grateful to the feelings, apart from its moral attributes and from its consequences, the judgment of those who are qualified by knowledge of both, or, if they differ, that of the majority among them, must be admitted as final. And there needs be the less hesitation to accept this judgment respecting the quality of pleasures, since there is no other tribunal to be referred to even on the question of quantity. What means are there of determining which is the acutest of two pains, or the intensest of two pleasurable sensations, except the general suffrage of those who are familiar with both? Neither pains nor pleasures are homogeneous, and pain is always heterogeneous with pleasure. What is there to decide whether a particular pleasure is worth purchasing at the cost of a particular pain, except the feelings and judgment of the experienced? When, therefore, those feelings and judgment declare the pleasures derived from the higher faculties to be preferable *in kind*, apart from the question of intensity, to those of which the animal nature, disjoined from the higher faculties, is susceptible, they are entitled on this subject to the same regard.

I have dwelt on this point, as being a necessary part of a perfectly just conception of Utility or Happiness, considered as the directive role of human conduct. But it is by no means an indispensable condition to the acceptance of the utilitarian standard; for that standard is not the agent's own greatest happiness, but the greatest amount of happiness altogether; and if it may possibly be doubted whether a noble character is always the happier for its nobleness, there can be no doubt that it makes other people happier, and that the world in general is immensely a gainer by it. Utilitarianism, therefore, could only attain its end by the general cultivation of nobleness of character, even if each individual were only benefited by the nobleness of others, and his own, so far as happiness is concerned, were a sheer deduction from the benefit. But the bare enunciation of such an absurdity as this last, renders refutation superfluous.

According to the Greatest Happiness Principle, as above explained, the ultimate end, with reference to and for the sake of which all other things are desirable (whether we are considering our own good or that of other people), is an existence exempt as far as possible from pain, and as rich as possible in enjoyments, both in point of quantity and quality; the test of quality, and the rule for measuring it against quantity, being the preference felt by those who, in their opportunities of experience, to which must be added their habits of self-consciousness and self-observation, are best furnished with the means of comparison. This, being, according to the utilitarian opinion, the end of human action, is necessarily also the standard of morality; which may accordingly be defined, the rules and precepts for human conduct, by the observance of which an existence such as has been described might be, to the greatest extent possible, secured to all mankind; and not to them only, but, so far as the nature of things admits, to the whole sentient creation. . . .

. . . [T]he assailants of utilitarianism seldom have the justice to acknowledge, that the happiness which forms the utilitarian standard of what is right in conduct, is not the agent's own happiness, but that of all concerned. As between his own happiness and that of others, utilitarianism requires him to be as strictly impartial as a disinterested and benevolent spectator. In the golden rule of Jesus of Nazareth, we read the complete spirit of the ethics of utility. To do as one would be done by, and to love one's neighbor as oneself, constitute the ideal perfection of utilitarian morality. As the means of making the nearest approach to this ideal, utility would enjoin, first, that laws and social arrangements should place the happiness, or (as speaking practically it may be called) the interest, of every individual, as nearly as possible in harmony with the interest of the whole; and secondly, that education and opinion, which have so vast a power over human character, should so use that power as to establish in the mind of every individual an indissoluble association between his own happiness and the good of the whole; especially between his own happiness and the practice of such modes of conduct, negative and positive, as regard for the universal happiness prescribes: so that not only he may be unable to conceive the possibility of happiness to himself, consistently with conduct opposed to the general good, but also that a direct impulse to promote the general good may be in every individual one of the habitual motives of action, and the sentiments connected therewith may fill a large and prominent place in every human being's sentient existence. If the impugners of the utilitarian morality represented it to their own minds in this its true character, I know not what recommendation possessed by any other morality they could possibly affirm to be wanting to it: what more beautiful or more exalted developments of human nature any other ethical system can be supposed to foster, or what springs of action, not accessible to the utilitarian, such systems rely on for giving effect to their mandates.

The objectors to utilitarianism . . . who entertain anything like a just idea of its disinterested character, sometimes find fault with its standard as being too high for humanity. They say it is exacting too much to require that people shall always act from the inducement of promoting the general interests of society. But this is to mistake the very meaning of a standard of morals, and to confound the rule of action with the motive of it. It is the business of ethics to tell us what are our duties, or by what test we may know them; but no system of ethics requires that the sole motive of all we do shall be a feeling of duty; on the contrary, ninety-nine hundredths of all our actions are done from other motives, and rightly so done, if the rule of duty does not condemn them. It is the more unjust to utilitarianism that this particular misapprehension should be made a ground of objection to it, inasmuch as utilitarian moralists have gone beyond almost all others in affirming that the motive has nothing to do with the morality of the action, though much with the worth of the agent. He who saves a fellow creature from drowning does what is morally right, whether his motive be duty, or the hope of being paid for his trouble: he who betrays the friend that trusts him, is guilty of a crime, even if his object be to serve another friend to whom he is under greater obligations.*

---

* An opponent, whose intellectual and moral fairness it is a pleasure to acknowledge (the Rev. J. Llewellyn Davies), has objected to this passage, saying, "Surely the rightness or wrongness of saving a man from drowning does depend very much upon the motive with which it is done. Suppose that a tyrant, when his enemy jumped into the sea to escape from him, saved him from drowning simply in order that he might inflict upon him more exquisite tortures, would it tend to clearness to speak of that rescue as 'a morally right action?' Or suppose again, according to one of the stock illustrations of ethical inquiries, that a man betrayed a trust received from a friend, because the discharge of it would fatally injure that friend himself or some one belonging to him, would utilitarianism compel one to call the betrayal 'a crime' as much as if it had been done from the meanest motive?"

I submit, that he who saves another from drowning in order to kill him by torture afterwards, does not differ only in motive from him who does the same thing from duty or benevolence; the act itself is different. The rescue of the man is, in the case supposed, only the necessary first step of an act far more atrocious than leaving him to drown would have been. Had Mr. Davies said, "The rightness or wrongness of saving a man from drowning does depend very much"—not upon the motive, but—"upon the *intention*," no utilitarian would have differed from him. Mr. Davies, by an oversight too common not to be quite venial, has in this case confounded the very different ideas of Motive and Intention. There is no

But to speak only of actions done from the motive of duty, and in direct obedience to principle: it is a misapprehension of the utilitarian mode of thought, to conceive it as implying that people should fix their minds upon so wide a generality as the world, or society at large. The great majority of good actions are intended, not for the benefit of the world, but for that of individuals, of which the good of the world is made up; and the thoughts of the most virtuous man need not on these occasions travel beyond the particular persons concerned, except so far as is necessary to assure himself that in benefiting them he is not violating the rights—that is, the legitimate and authorized expectations—of any one else. The multiplication of happiness is, according to the utilitarian ethics, the object of virtue: the occasions on which any person (except one in a thousand) has it in his power to do this on an extended scale, in other words, to be a public benefactor, are but exceptional; and on these occasions alone is he called on to consider public utility; in every other case, private utility, the interest or happiness of some few persons, is all he has to attend to. Those alone the influence of whose actions extends to society in general, need concern themselves habitually about so large an object. In the case of abstinences indeed—of things which people forbear to do, from moral considerations, though the consequences in the particular case might be beneficial—it would be unworthy of an intelligent agent not to be consciously aware that the action is of a class which, if practiced generally, would be generally injurious, and that this is the ground of the obligation to abstain from it. The amount of regard for the public interest implied in this recognition, is no greater than is demanded by every system of morals; for they all enjoin to abstain from whatever is manifestly pernicious to society.

The same considerations dispose of another reproach against the doctrine of utility, founded on a still grosser misconception of the purpose of a standard of morality, and of the very meaning of the words right and wrong. It is often affirmed that utilitarianism renders men cold and unsympathizing; that it chills their moral feelings toward individuals; that it makes them regard only the dry and hard consideration of the consequences of actions, not taking into their moral estimate the qualities from which those actions emanate. If the assertion means that they do not allow their judgment respecting the rightness or wrongness of an action to be influenced by their opinion of the qualities of the person who does it, this is a complaint not against utilitarianism, but against having any standard of morality at all; for certainly no known ethical standard decides an action to be good or bad because it is done by a good or a bad man, still less because done by an amiable, a brave, or a benevolent man, or the contrary. These considerations are relevant, not to the estimation of actions, but of persons; and there is nothing in the utilitarian theory inconsistent with the fact that there are other things which interest us in persons besides the rightness and wrongness of their actions. The Stoics, indeed, with the paradoxical misuse of language which was part of their system, and by

point which utilitarian thinkers (and Bentham pre-eminently) have taken more pains to illustrate than this. The morality of the action depends entirely upon the intention—that is, upon what the agent *wills to do.* But the motive, that is, the feeling which makes him will so to do, when it makes no difference in the act, makes none in the morality: though it makes a great difference in our moral estimation of the agent, especially if it indicates a good or a bad habitual *disposition*—a bent of character from which useful, or from which hurtful actions are likely to arise.

which they strove to raise themselves above all concern about anything but virtue, were fond of saying that he who has that has everything; that he, and only he, is rich, is beautiful, is a king. But no claim of this description is made for the virtuous man by the utilitarian doctrine. Utilitarians are quite aware that there are other desirable possessions and qualities besides virtue, and are perfectly willing to allow to all of them their full worth. They are also aware that a right action does not necessarily indicate a virtuous character, and that actions which are blameable often proceed from qualities entitled to praise. When this is apparent in any particular case, it modifies their estimation, not certainly of the act, but of the agent. I grant that they are, notwithstanding, of opinion, that in the long run the best proof of a good character is good actions; and resolutely refuse to consider any mental disposition as good, of which the predominant tendency is to produce bad conduct. This makes them unpopular with many people; but it is an unpopularity which they must share with every one who regards the distinction between right and wrong in a serious light; and the reproach is not one which a conscientious utilitarian need be anxious to repel.

If no more be meant by the objection than that many utilitarians look on the morality of actions, as measured by the utilitarian standard, with too exclusive a regard, and do not lay sufficient stress upon the other beauties of character which go toward making a human being lovable or admirable, this may be admitted. Utilitarians who have cultivated their moral feelings, but not their sympathies nor their artistic perceptions, do fall into this mistake; and so do all other moralists under the same conditions. What can be said in excuse for other moralists is equally available for them, namely, that if there is to be any error, it is better that it should be on that side. As a matter of fact, we may affirm that among utilitarians as among adherents of other systems, there is every imaginable degree of rigidity and of laxity in the application of their standard: some are even puritanically rigorous, while others are as indulgent as can possibly be desired by sinner or by sentimentalist. But on the whole, a doctrine which brings prominently forward the interest that mankind have in the repression and prevention of conduct which violates the moral law, is likely to be inferior to no other in turning the sanctions of opinion against such violations. It is true, the question, What does violate the moral law? is one on which those who recognize different standards of morality are likely now and then to differ. But difference of opinion on moral questions was not first introduced into the world by utilitarianism, while the doctrine does supply, if not always an easy, at all events a tangible and intelligible mode of deciding such differences. . . .

Again, Utility is often summarily stigmatized as an immoral doctrine by giving it the name of Expediency, and taking advantage of the popular use of that term to contrast it with Principle. But the Expedient, in the sense in which it is opposed to the Right, generally means that which is expedient for the particular interest of the agent himself; as when a minister sacrifices the interest of his country to keep himself in place. When it means anything better than this, it means that which is expedient for some immediate object, some temporary purpose, but which violates a rule whose observance is expedient in a much higher degree. The Expedient, in this sense, instead of being the same thing with the useful, is a branch of the hurtful. Thus, it would often be expedient, for the purpose of getting over some momentary embarrassment, or attaining some object immediately useful to ourselves or others, to tell a lie. But inasmuch as the cultivation in ourselves of a sensitive feeling on the subject of veracity, is one of the most useful, and the enfeeblement of that feeling one of the most hurtful, things to which our conduct can be instrumental; and inasmuch as any, even unintentional, deviation from truth, does that much toward weakening the trustworthiness of human assertion, which is not only the principal support of all present social well-being, but the insufficiency of which does more than any one thing that can be named to keep back civilization, virtue, everything on which human happiness on the largest scale depends; we feel that the violation, for a present advantage, of a rule of such transcendant expediency, is not expedient, and that he who, for the sake of a convenience to himself or to some other individual, does what depends on him to deprive mankind of the good, and inflict upon them the evil, involved in the greater or less reliance which they can place in each other's word, acts the part of one of their worst enemies. Yet that even this rule, sacred as it is, admits of possible exceptions, is acknowledged by all moralists; the chief of which is when the withholding of some fact (as of information from a malefactor, or of bad news from a person dangerously ill) would preserve some one (especially a person other than oneself) from great and unmerited evil, and when the withholding can only be effected by denial. But in order that the exception may not extend itself beyond the need, and may have the least possible effect in weakening reliance on veracity, it ought to be recognized, and, if possible, its limits defined; and if the principle of utility is good for anything, it must be good for weighing these conflicting utilities against one another, and marking out the region within which one or the other preponderates.

Again, defenders of utility often find themselves called upon to reply to such objections as this—that there is not time, previous to action, for calculating and weighing the effects of any line of conduct on the general happiness. This is exactly as if any one were to say that it is impossible to guide our conduct by Christianity, because there is not time, on every occasion on which anything has to be done, to read through the Old and New Testaments. The answer to the objection is, that there has been ample time, namely, the whole past duration of the human species. During all that time mankind have been learning by experience the tendencies of actions; on which experience all the prudence, as well as all the morality of life, is dependent. People talk as if the commencement of this course of experience had hitherto been put off, and as if, at the moment when some man feels tempted to meddle with the property or life of another, he had to begin considering for the first time whether murder and theft are injurious to human happiness. Even then I do not think that he would find the question very puzzling; but, at all events, the matter is now done to his hand. It is truly a whimsical supposition that if mankind were agreed in considering utility to be the test of morality, they would remain without any agreement as to what *is* useful, and would take no measures for having their notions on the subject taught to the young, and enforced by law and opinion. There is no difficulty in proving any ethical standard whatever to work ill, if we suppose universal idiocy to be conjoined with it; but on any hypothesis short of that, mankind must by this time have acquired positive beliefs as to the effects of some actions on their happiness; and the beliefs which have thus come down are the rules of morality for the multitude, and for the philosopher until he has succeeded in finding better. That philosophers might easily do this, even now, on many subjects; that the received code of ethics is by no means of divine right; and that mankind have still much to learn as to the effects of actions on the general happiness, I admit, or rather, earnestly maintain. The corollaries from the principle of utility, like the precepts of every practical art, admit of indefinite improvement, and, in a progressive state of the human mind, their improvement is perpetually going on. But to consider the rules of morality as improvable, is one thing; to pass over the intermediate generalizations entirely, and endeavor to test each individual action directly by the first principle, is another. It is a strange notion that the acknowledgment of a first principle is inconsistent with the admission of secondary ones. . . . Whatever we adopt as the fundamental principle of morality, we require subordinate principles to apply it by: the impossibility of doing without them, being common to all systems, can afford no argument against any one in particular: but gravely to argue as if no such secondary principles could be had, and as if mankind had remained till now, and always must remain, without drawing any general conclusions from the experience of human life, is as high a pitch, I think, as absurdity has ever reached in philosophical controversy.

The remainder of the stock arguments against utilitarianism mostly consist in laying to its charge the common infirmities of human nature, and the general difficulties which embarrass conscientious persons in shaping their course through life. We are told that a utilitarian will be apt to make his own particular case an exception to moral rules, and, when under temptation, will see a utility in the breach of rule, greater than he will see in its observance. But is utility the only creed which is able to furnish us with excuses for evil doing, and means of cheating our own conscience? They are afforded in abundance by all doctrines which recognize as a fact in morals the existence of conflicting considerations; which all doctrines do, that have been believed by sane persons. It is not the fault of any creed, but of the complicated nature of human affairs, that rules of conduct cannot be so framed as to require no exceptions, and that hardly any kind of action can safely be laid down as either always obligatory or always condemnable. There is no ethical creed which does not temper the rigidity of its laws, by giving a certain latitude, under the moral responsibility of the agent, for accommodation to peculiarities of circumstances; and under every creed, at the opening thus made, self-deception and dishonest casuistry get in. There exists no moral system under which there do not arise unequivocal cases of conflicting obligation. These are the real difficulties, the knotty points both in the theory of ethics, and in the conscientious guidance of personal conduct. They are overcome practically with greater or with less success according to the intellect and virtue of the individual; but it can hardly be pretended that any one will be the less qualified for dealing with them, from possessing an ultimate standard to which conflicting rights and duties can be referred. If utility is the ultimate source of moral obligations, utility may be invoked to decide between them when their demands are incompatible. Though the application of the standard may be difficult, it is better than none at all: while in other systems, the moral laws all claiming independent authority, there is no common umpire entitled to interfere between them; their claims to precedence one over another rest on little better than sophistry, and unless determined, as they generally are, by the unacknowledged influence of considerations of utility, afford a free scope for the action of personal desires and partialities. We must remember that only in these cases of conflict between secondary principles is it requisite that first principles should be appealed to. There is no case of moral obligation in which some secondary principle is not involved; and if only one, there can seldom be any real doubt which one it is, in the mind of any person by whom the principle itself is recognized.

CHAPTER IV
OF WHAT SORT OF PROOF THE PRINCIPLE OF UTILITY IS SUSCEPTIBLE

It has already been remarked, that questions of ultimate ends do not admit of proof, in the ordinary acceptation of the term. To be incapable of proof by reasoning is common to all first principles; to the first premises of our knowledge, as well as to those of our conduct. But the former, being matters of fact, may be the subject of a direct appeal to the faculties which judge of fact—namely, our senses, and our internal consciousness. Can an appeal be made to the same faculties on questions of practical ends? Or by what other faculty is cognizance taken of them?

Questions about ends are, in other words, questions about what things are desirable. The utilitarian doctrine is, that happiness is desirable, and the only thing desirable, as an end; all other things being only desirable as means to that end. What ought to be required of this doctrine—what conditions is it requisite that the doctrine should fulfill—to make good its claim to be believed?

The only proof capable of being given that an object is visible, is that people actually see it. The only proof that a sound is audible, is that people hear it: and so of the other sources of our experience. In like manner, I apprehend, the sole evidence it is possible to produce that anything is desirable, is that people do actually desire it. If the end which the utilitarian doctrine proposes to itself were not, in theory and in practice, acknowledged to be an end, nothing could ever convince any person that it was so. No reason can be given why the general happiness is desirable, except that each person, so far as he believes it to be attainable, desires his own happiness. This, however, being a fact, we have not only all the proof which the case admits of, but all which it is possible to require, that happiness is a good: that each person's happiness is a good to that person, and the general happiness, therefore, a good to the aggregate of all persons. Happiness has made out its title as *one* of the ends of conduct, and consequently one of the criteria of morality.

But it has not, by this alone, proved itself to be the sole criterion. To do that, it would seem, by the same rule, necessary to show, not only that people desire happiness, but that they never desire anything else. . . .

. . . The ingredients of happiness are very various, and each of them is desirable in itself, and not merely when considered as swelling an aggregate. The principle of utility does not mean that any given pleasure, as music, for instance, or any given exemption from pain, as for example health, are to be looked upon as means to a collective something termed happiness, and to be desired on that account. They are desired and desirable in and for themselves; besides being means, they are a part of the end. Virtue, according to the utilitarian doctrine, is not naturally and originally part of the end, but it is capable of becoming so; and in those who love it disinterestedly it has become so, and is desired and cherished, not as a means to happiness, but as a part of their happiness. . . .

We have now, then, an answer to the question, of what sort of proof the principle of utility is susceptible. If the opinion which I have now stated is psychologically true—if human nature is so constituted as to desire nothing which is not either a part of happiness or a means of happiness, we can have no other proof, and we require no other, that these are the only things desirable. If so, happiness is the sole end of human action, and the promotion of it the test by which to judge of all human conduct; from whence it necessarily follows that it must be the criterion of morality, since a part is included in the whole.

And now to decide whether this is really so; whether mankind do desire nothing for itself but that which is a pleasure to them, or of which the absence is a pain; we have evidently arrived at a question of fact and experience, dependent, like all similar questions, upon evidence. It can only be determined by practiced self-consciousness and self-observation, assisted by observation of others. I believe that these sources of evidence, impartially consulted, will declare that desiring a thing and finding it pleasant, aversion to it and thinking of it as painful, are phenomena entirely inseparable, or rather two parts of the same phenomenon, in strictness of language, two different modes of naming the same psychological fact: that to think of an object as desirable (unless for the sake of its consequences), and to think of it as pleasant, are one and the same thing; and that to desire anything, except in proportion as the idea of it is pleasant, is a physical and metaphysical impossibility.

So obvious does this appear to me, that I expect it will hardly be disputed: and the objection made will be, not that desire can possibly be directed to anything ultimately except pleasure and exemption from pain, but that the will is a different thing from desire; that a person of confirmed virtue, or any other person whose purposes are fixed, carries out his purposes without any thought of the pleasure he has in contemplating them, or expects to derive from their fulfillment; and persists in acting on them, even though these pleasures are much diminished, by changes in his character or decay of his passive sensibilities, or are outweighed by the pains which the pursuit of the purposes may bring upon him. All this I fully admit, and have stated it elsewhere, as positively and emphatically as any one. Will, the active phenomenon, is a different thing from desire, the state of passive sensibility, and though originally an offshoot from it, may in time take root and detach itself from the parent stock; so much so, that in the case of an habitual purpose, instead of willing the thing because we desire it, we often desire it only because we will it. This, however, is but an instance of that familiar fact, the power of habit, and is nowise confined to the case of virtuous actions. Many indifferent things, which men originally did from a motive of some sort, they continue to do from habit. Sometimes this is done unconsciously, the consciousness coming only after the action: at other times with conscious volition, but violition which has become habitual, and is put into operation by the force of habit, in opposition perhaps to the deliberate preference, as often happens with those who have contracted habits of vicious or hurtful indulgence. Third and last comes the case in which the habitual act of will in the individual instance is not in contradiction to the general intention prevailing at other times, but in fulfillment of it; as in the case of the person of confirmed virtue, and of all who pursue deliberately and consistently any determinate end. The distinction between will and desire thus understood, is an authentic and highly important psychological fact; but the fact consists solely in this—that will, like all other parts of our constitution, is amenable to habit, and that we may will from habit what we no longer desire for itself, or desire only because we will it. It is not the less true that will, in the beginning, is entirely produced by desire; including in that term the repelling influence of pain as well as the attractive one of pleasure. Let us take into consideration, no longer the person who has a confirmed will to do right, but him in whom that virtuous will is still feeble, conquerable by temptation, and not to be fully relied on; by what means can it be strengthened? How can the will be virtuous, where it does not exist in sufficient force, be implanted or awakened? Only by making the person *desire* virtue—by making him think of it in a pleasurable light, or of its absence in a painful one. It is by associating the doing right with pleasure, or the doing wrong with pain, or by eliciting and impressing and bringing home to the person's experience the pleasure naturally involved in the one or the pain in the other, that it is possible to call forth that will to be virtuous, which, when confirmed, acts without any thought of either pleasure or pain. Will is the child of desire, and passes out of the dominion of its parent only to come under that of habit. That which is the result of habit affords no presumption of being intrinsically good; and there would be no reason for wishing that the purpose of virtue should become independent of pleasure and pain, were it not that the influence of the pleasurable and painful associations which prompt to virtue is not sufficiently to be depended on for unerring constancy of action until it has acquired the support of habit. Both in feeling and in conduct, habit is the only thing which imparts certainty; and it is because of the importance to others of being able to rely absolutely on one's feelings and conduct, and to oneself of being able to rely on one's own, that the will to do right ought to be cultivated into this habitual independence. In other words, this state of the will is a means to good, not intrinsically a good; and does not contradict the doctrine that nothing is a good to human beings but in so far as it is either itself pleasurable, or a means of attaining pleasure or averting pain.

But if this doctrine be true, the principle of utility is proved. Whether it is so or not, must now be left to the consideration of the thoughtful reader.

On Liberty

The object of this Essay is to assert one very simple principle, as entitled to govern absolutely the dealings of society with the individual in the way of compulsion and

From John Stuart Mill, *On Liberty* (1859).

control, whether the means used be physical force in the form of legal penalties, or the moral coercion of public opinion. That principle is, that the sole end for which mankind are warranted, individually or collectively, in interfering with the liberty of action of any of their number, is self-protection. That the only purpose for which power can be rightfully exercised over any member of a civilized community, against his will, is to prevent harm to others. His own good, either physical or moral, is not a sufficient warrant. He cannot rightfully be compelled to do or forbear because it will be better for him to do so, because it will make him happier, because, in the opinions of others, to do so would be wise, or even right. These are good reasons for remonstrating with him, or reasoning with him, or persuading him, or entreating him, but not for compelling him, or visiting him with any evil in case he do otherwise. To justify that, the conduct from which it is desired to deter him, must be calculated to produce evil to some one else. The only part of the conduct of any one, for which he is amenable to society, is that which concerns others. In the part which merely concerns himself, his independence is, of right, absolute. Over himself, over his own body and mind, the individual is sovereign.

It is, perhaps, hardly necessary to say that this doctrine is meant to apply only to human beings in the maturity of their faculties. We are not speaking of children, or of young persons below the age which the law may fix as that of manhood and womanhood. Those who are still in a state to require being taken care of by others, must be protected against their own actions as well as against external injury. . . .

There is a sphere of action in which society, as distinguished from the individual, has, if any, only an indirect interest, comprehending all that portion of a person's life and conduct which affects only himself, or if it also affects others, only with their free, voluntary, and undeceived consent and participation. When I say only himself, I mean directly, and in the first instance: for whatever affects himself, may affect others *through* himself; and the objection which may be grounded on this contingency, will receive consideration in the sequel. This, then, is the appropriate region of human liberty. It comprises, first, the inward domain of consciousness; demanding liberty of conscience, in the most comprehensive sense; liberty of thought and feeling; absolute freedom of opinion and sentiment on all subjects, practical or speculative, scientific, moral, or theological. The liberty of expressing and publishing opinions may seem to fall under a different principle, since it belongs to that part of the conduct of an individual which concerns other people; but, being almost of as much importance as the liberty of thought itself, and resting in great part on the same reasons, is practically inseparable from it. Secondly, the principle requires liberty of tastes and pursuits; of framing the plan of our life to suit our own character; of doing as we like, subject to such consequences as may follow; without impediment from our fellow-creatures, so long as what we do does not harm them, even though they should think our conduct foolish, perverse, or wrong. Thirdly, from this liberty of each individual, follows the liberty, within the same limits, of combination among individuals; freedom to unite, for any purpose not involving harm to others: the persons combining being supposed to be of full age, and not forced or deceived.

No society in which these liberties are not, on the whole, respected, is free, whatever may be its form of government; and none is completely free in which they do not exist absolute and unqualified. The only freedom which deserves the name, is that of pursuing our own good in our own way, so long as we do not attempt to deprive others of theirs, or impede their efforts to obtain it. Each is the proper guardian of his own health, whether bodily, or mental and spiritual. Mankind are greater gainers by suffering each other to live as seems good to themselves, than by compelling each to live as seems good to the rest. . . .

Again, there are many acts which, being directly injurious only to the agents themselves, ought not to be legally interdicted, but which, if done publicly, are a violation of good manners, and coming thus within the category of offenses against others, may rightfully be prohibited. Of this kind are offenses against decency; on which it is unnecessary to dwell, the rather as they are only connected indirectly with our subject, the objection to publicity being equally strong in the case of many actions not in themselves condemnable, nor supposed to be so.

SUGGESTIONS FOR DISCUSSION

1. Should utilitarianism be concerned to bring about the greatest amount of happiness, or to maximize the number of people who are happy?

2. Should the decision by a doctor to agree to remove a terminal patient's life-support system (see Part II, Chapter 12), or to abort a fetus (See Chapter 11), be decided on the basis of whether the act will maximize pleasure or minimize pain?

3. Justices Stewart, Powell, and Stevens argued that the majority of Americans support capital punishment. Justice Marshall countered that if the American people were fully informed about all the considerations concerning capital punishment, they would not support it (See Part II, Chapter 13). Are each of these contesting views utilitarian at basis? Should utilitarian considerations determine whether capital punishment is socially and morally acceptable or not?

4. Compare an act-utilitarian argument for affirmative action (see Part II, Chapter 8), or against mandatory AIDS testing (see Chapter 10), with a non-utilitarian one. Which of the arguments are more compelling?

FURTHER READING

Utilitarianism

Bayles, M., ed. *Contemporary Utilitarianism.* New York: Doubleday, 1962. (Interpretation, critical analysis; advanced)

Bentham, Jeremy. *An Introduction to the Principles of Morals and Legislation.* Oxford: Clarendon Press, 1948.

Brandt, R. B. *Ethical Theory.* Englewood Cliffs, N.J.: Prentice-Hall, 1959. (Interpretation, critical analysis; advanced)

———. *A Theory of the Good and the Right.* Oxford: Oxford University Press, 1979. (Interpretation, critical analysis; advanced)

———. "Some Merits of One Form of Rule-Utilitarianism." *University of Colorado Studies,* Series in Philosophy, no. 3 (January 1967): 39–65. (Interpretation, critical analysis; advanced)

Frey, R., ed. *Utility and Rights.* Minneapolis: University of Minnesota Press, 1984. (Interpretation, critical analysis; advanced)

Griffin, J. *Well-Being: Its Meaning, Measurement and Social Importance.* Oxford: Clarendon Press, 1987. (Interpretation, critical analysis; advanced)

Hare, R. M. *Freedom and Reason.* London: Oxford University Press, 1963. (Interpretation, critical analysis; intermediate)

————. *Applications of Moral Philosophy.* London: Macmillan, 1972. (Interpretation, critical analysis; intermediate)

————. *Essays on the Moral Concepts.* London: Macmillan, 1972. (Interpretation, critical analysis; intermediate)

Lyons, D. *Forms and Limits of Utilitarianism.* Oxford: Oxford University Press, 1965. (Interpretation, critical analysis; intermediate)

Rawls, J. "Two Concepts of Rules," *Philosophical Review* 64 (1955): 3–32. (Interpretation, critical analysis; advanced)

Sen, A., and Williams B., eds. *Utilitarianism and Beyond.* Cambridge: Cambridge University Press, 1982. (Interpretation, critical analysis; advanced)

Sidgwick, H. *Methods of Ethics.* 7th ed. London: Macmillan, 1962. (Interpretation, critical analysis; advanced)

Singer, M. G. *Generalization in Ethics.* New York: Knopf, 1961. (Interpretation, critical analysis; intermediate)

Smart, J. J. C., and Williams, B. *Utilitarianism: For and Against.* Cambridge: Cambridge University Press, 1973. (Interpretation, critical analysis; intermediate)

Warnock, M., ed. *Utilitarianism, by J. S. Mill.* London: Fontana, 1962.

5

□

Marx and Nietzsche

Marx, Nietzsche, and Moral Criticism Neither Karl Marx nor Friedrich Nietzsche was a moral philosopher in any standard sense. Though trained as a philosopher, Marx is better known for defining the scope of political economy and social theory than as a moral theorist. Nietzsche's legacy, by contrast, lies not in his professional field of philology, but in his social and philosophical critiques. Nevertheless, the views on morality of both reflect the ambivalence toward moral matters that marked the late nineteenth century. On one hand, Marx and Nietzsche critically attacked the prevailing conception of morality that each considered constitutive of European capitalism. First, each criticized accepted social practices prevalent at the time; and second, each condemned the history of philosophical representations that was found to rationalize such social practices. On the other hand, both Marx and Nietzsche had underlying views, though never fully formulated, about what moral relations and practices should properly be. They will be treated here primarily as critics of traditional moral theory.

KARL MARX (1818–1883): MORALITY AND IDEOLOGY

Morality and Material Production Marx considered moral codes to be ideological representations of socioeconomic class relations. He defined these class relations in terms of the class positions relative to the mode of economic (material) production at a given stage of history. Broadly, Marx (and his long-standing collaborator, Friedrich Engels) specified five stages of economic production: primitive communism, slavery, feudalism, capitalism, and socialism (leading ultimately to comprehensive communism). Marx formulated lawlike generalizations relating "mental production"—ideas of morality, religion, metaphysics, but also politics and law—to material economic intercourse. These generalizations were supposed to relate ideological beliefs (including morality), as effects, to the material conditions of production and class structures of society, as their underlying causes.

Alienation For Marx, contemporary capitalism may be represented essentially in terms of the economic relations between the capitalist class, or owners of the means of production, and workers (the proletariat), who own nothing save their labor power. The laws of political economy require workers to sell their labor to capitalists at rates sufficient only to enable workers to continue working. The capitalist *appropriates* from the worker the *surplus value* the latter produces; that is, the productive value over and above that which represents the worker's wage. In producing commodities, wage-labor reproduces itself as a commodity. Accordingly, the social relations of capitalism, primarily those between worker and capitalist, are objectified: they are fixed as unchangeable givens of the production process. This objectification is the basis of what Marx called *alienation* or *estrangement.* The social manifestation of capitalism assumes four forms, which Marx analyzed closely. First, workers are alienated from their product. Appropriated from them, the product that workers produce represents a power hostile and alien to them. Second, workers suffer self-estrangement and emiseration (or general impoverishment and suffering). It follows that workers feel free only in their animal functions; at work—and work, on Marx's view, is the definitive human function— they are made to feel no better than animals. Estranged in this way from what defines them as human, workers are alienated from their nature as a species. In social terms, this entailed for Marx, finally, that humans are alienated from each other: workers are alienated from other workers and from capitalists. Marx condemned the unequal distribution inherent in capitalist appropriation of surplus value and the unjustifiable social alienation that accompanies it; this is what he called *exploitation.*

Marx was also critical of the moral conceptions encouraged by these and earlier economic formations. He argued that an ethics of duty (see Kant, Part I, Chapter 3) or natural law (see Aquinas, Chapter 1), or Mill's brand of utilitarianism (see Chapter 4), served to fix as given the alienated social relations of capitalism. Marx was especially critical of juridical concepts such as "justice" and "rights," which he took to be bourgeois ideological fictions. The notion of "equal rights" was rejected for failing inevitably to recognize the diversity of individual human needs. It is likely that Marx would have rejected any social policy—such as affirmative action (see Part II, Chapter 8)—based upon appeal to such rights. He would have considered affirmative action policies to be simply rationalizations for continued exploitation, and so inherently inadequate to the task of ending exploitation of large social groups.

Liberation and Morality Marx contrasted with his account of the sources of oppression a vision of human emancipation from the material conditions of wage slavery. Some commentators insist that Marx rejected all notions of morality. Yet his critique of capitalism and theory of revolution make sense only against a background conception of nonexploitative social conditions in a future communist society. Marx considered the evils of exploitation to be basic to capitalism, inherent in its forms of production and social relations. He thought that they could be ended only by revolutionary transformation to a new communist society; material liberation was supposed to alter the moral codes radically. Embedded in Marx's schematic comments about the transformation to communist society, then, is an implicit conception of distributive justice; that is, of how the product of society ought to be distributed among its members (see Part II, Chapter 7). This conception is summarized oversimplistically in the famous line from *The Communist Manifesto:* "From each according to his abilities; to each according to his needs."

The positive conception of morality and justice that Marx suggested to replace dominant morality is broadly teleological or goal-directed (see Part I, Chapter 1). The fundamental feature is the set of moral relations that in the long term would enable the fullest development of human expressive and productive powers. Marx thought that revolutionary violence would most likely be necessary in transforming the dominant capitalist order. He never made clear, though, how far the use of violence in social transformation and liberation is morally justifiable (on political violence, see Part II, Chapter 14).

FRIEDRICH NIETZSCHE (1844–1900): BEYOND GOOD AND EVIL

Critique of Moral Objectivity   Similarly, it is against a background perspective of self-realization of powers that Nietzsche criticized the prevailing moral values of Christianity and democracy. Christianity advocates pity for the suffering of victims; and democracy, equality for all. Christianity and democracy, he argued, both claim moral objectivity or truth for their respective principles of pity and equality; and both justify their principles by appealing to one of the historically dominant moral systems, such as the theory of moral sentiments or conscience, the utility principle, or the universalizability rule of the categorical imperative. In turn, once these moral systems become entrenched, they exclude as immoral those same principles and practices without which their doctrines could not have prevailed.

Thus Nietzsche attacked these traditional appeals to moral objectivity as smokescreens for philosophers' unsubstantiated and subjective assertions. He condemned each principle of modern moral expression as furnishing a moral façade for some philosopher's favored practice. Nietzsche denied that there are moral *facts:* Moral values are interpretations from a standpoint concerned always with "preservation of the community." There is no natural order, and so no natural moral order. Philosophers' claims to moral discovery refer not to the world, but simply to their own values.

Unlike Marx, though, Nietzsche was no social revolutionary: He called not for abandoning the moral beliefs themselves, only for undermining the dominant mode of *justifying* those beliefs. On Nietzsche's view, to call for new moral beliefs serves to perpetuate the myth that (some) moral beliefs are capable of justification. Morality, in short, was regarded as a distortion, though one that Nietzsche thought humans find necessary.

Master and Slave Morality   In contrast to moralities defined in terms of objective good and evil, for Nietzsche there are only two kinds of morality: *slave morality* and *master morality*. Slave morality is the moral conception of the violated, oppressed, unfree, and those uncertain of themselves. Its characteristic "virtues" were taken to include pity, deference and submissiveness, patience, industry, humility, and a longing for freedom and happiness. By contrast, the "virtues" of master morality were supposed to include assertiveness, authority, aristocratic dignity, fearlessness, and a strong will, indeed, an overriding will to power. No appeal was made to a notion of objective good: each kind of morality considers itself good, the other evil. These forms of morality are idealizations: Nietzsche found most practical moral systems, and nearly all human beings, to be characterized by a mixture of both.

So Nietzsche argued that rational justifications of morality fail. They are simply rationalizations in each case of parochial moral conceptions circumscribed by class, church, or social force dominant at a given time and place. They are rationalizations, in other words, of subjects' lack of self-assertive power. What Nietzsche found most objectionable about morality is its claim to be universal, unconditional, and equally applicable to all. His critique took aim, accordingly, at any set of moral principles or rules requiring unconditional acceptance and adherence.

Will-to-Power Nietzsche considered only power, not happiness or pleasure, to be desirable in itself: all else is desired and done for the sake of asserting power. It is this basic condition of pursuing any and all things that he called the *Will-to-Power*. For the enslaved, the Will-to-Power is the drive to overpower those who are more powerful and free; for the master, it is represented as the desire to be saintly. Moralities—for there is no single morality—must therefore consist simply in subjective expressions of the will. Subjects would become moral by exerting their wills in "aristocratic" self-assertion. There is no rational principle that sets a moral standard; subjects present the principles of morality to themselves by asserting them in action. This self-assertive free creation of value is what, on Nietzsche's view, amounts to going "beyond good and evil." Nietzsche sustained the critical thrust in his positive view by referring occasionally to this antirational subjectivism as "immoral." He encouraged moralizing only to challenge, to find moral situations questionable and problematic, rather than safe and boring.

Karl Marx

Economic and Philosophical Manuscripts

ESTRANGED LABOR

We have started out from the premises of political economy. We have accepted its language and its laws. We presupposed private property; the separation of labor,

From Karl Marx, *Early Writings,* trans. Gregor Benton and Rodney Livingstone, edited by Quintin Hoare. Copyright © 1975 by New Left Review. Reprinted by permission of Random House, Inc.

capital and land, and likewise of wages, profit and capital; the division of labor; competition; the concept of exchange value, etc. From political economy itself, using its own words, we have shown that the worker sinks to the level of a commodity, and moreover the most wretched commodity of all; that the misery of the worker is in inverse proportion to the power and volume of his production; that the necessary consequence of competition is the accumulation of capital in a few hands and hence the restoration of monopoly in a more terrible form; and that finally the distinction between capitalist and landlord, between agricultural worker and industrial worker, disappears and the whole of society must split into the two classes of *property owners* and propertyless *workers*.

Political economy proceeds from the fact of private property. It does not explain it. It grasps the *material* process of private property, the process through which it actually passes, in general and abstract formulae which it then takes as *laws*. It does not *comprehend* these laws, i.e., it does not show how they arise from the nature of private property. Political economy fails to explain the reason for the division between labor and capital, between capital and land. For example, when it defines the relation of wages to profit it takes the interests of the capitalists as the basis of its analysis; i.e., it assumes what it is supposed to explain. Similarly, competition is frequently brought into the argument and explained in terms of external circumstances. Political economy teaches us nothing about the extent to which these external and apparently accidental circumstances are only the expression of a necessary development. We have seen how exchange itself appears to political economy as an accidental fact. The only wheels which political economy sets in motion are *greed* and the *war of the avaricious—competition*.

Precisely because political economy fails to grasp the interconnections within the movement, it was possible to oppose, for example, the doctrine of competition to the doctrine of monopoly, the doctrine of craft freedom to the doctrine of the guild and the doctrine of the division of landed property to the doctrine of the great estate; for competition, craft freedom, and division of landed property were developed and conceived only as accidental, deliberate, violent consequences of monopoly, of the guilds and of feudal property and not as their necessary, inevitable and natural consequences.

We now have to grasp the essential connection between private property, greed, the separation of labor, capital and landed property, exchange and competition, value and the devaluation of man, monopoly and competition, etc.—the connection between this entire system of estrangement and the *money* system.

We must avoid repeating the mistake of the political economist, who bases his explanations on some imaginary primordial condition. Such a primordial condition explains nothing. It simply pushes the question into the gray and nebulous distance. It assumes as facts and events what it is supposed to deduce, namely the necessary relationship between two things, between, for example, the division of labor and exchange. Similarly, theology explains the origin of evil by the fall of man, i.e., it assumes as a fact in the form of history what it should explain.

We shall start out from a *present-day* economic fact.

The worker becomes poorer the more wealth he produces, the more his production increases in power and extent. The worker becomes an ever cheaper commodity the more commodities he produces. The *devaluation* of the human world grows in direct proportion to the *increase in value* of the world of things. Labor not only produces commodities; it also produces itself and the workers as a *commodity* and it does so in the same proportion in which it produces commodities in general.

This fact simply means that the object that labor produces, its product, stands opposed to it as *something alien,* as a *power independent* of the producer. The product of labor is labor embodied and made material in an object, it is the *objectification of labor. The realization of labor is its objectification. In the sphere of political economy this realization of labor appears as a loss of reality* for the worker, objectification as *loss of and bondage to the object,* and appropriation as *estrangement,* as *alienation.*

So much does the realization of labor appear as loss of reality that the worker loses his reality to the point of dying of starvation. So much does objectification appear as loss of the object that the worker is robbed of the objects he needs most not only for life but also for work. Work itself becomes an object which he can only obtain through an enormous effort and with spasmodic interruptions. So much does the appropriation of the object appear as estrangement that the more objects the worker produces the fewer can he possess and the more he falls under the domination of his product, of capital.

All these consequences are contained in this characteristic, that the worker is related to the *product of his labor* as to an *alien* object. For it is clear that, according to this premise, the more the worker exerts himself in his work, the more powerful the alien, objective world becomes which he brings into being over against himself, the poorer he and his inner world become, and the less they belong to him. It is the same in religion. The more man puts into God, the less he retains within himself. The worker places his life in the object; but now it no longer belongs to him, but to the object. The greater his activity, therefore, the fewer objects the worker possesses. What the product of his labor is, he is not. Therefore, the greater this product, the less is he himself. The externalization of the worker in his product means not only that his labor becomes an object, an *external* existence, but that it exists *outside him,* independently of him and alien to him, and begins to confront him as an autonomous power; that the life which he has bestowed on the object confronts him as hostile and alien.

Let us now take a closer look at *objectification,* at the production of the worker, and the *estrangement,* the *loss* of the object, of his product, that this entails.

The worker can create nothing without *nature,* without the *sensuous external world.* It is the material in which his labor realizes iself, in which it is active and from which and by means of which it produces.

But just as nature provides labor with the *means of life* in the sense that labor cannot *live* without objects on which to exercise itself, so also it provides the *means of life* in the narrower sense, namely the means of physical subsistence of the *worker.*

The more the worker *appropriates* the external world, sensuous nature, through his labor, the more he deprives himself of the *means of life* in two respects: firstly, the sensuous external world becomes less and less an object belonging to his labor, a *means of life* of his labor; and secondly, it becomes less and less a *means of life* in the immediate sense, a means for the physical subsistence of the worker.

In these two respects, then, the worker becomes a slave of his object; firstly in that he receives an *object of labor,* i.e., he receives work, and secondly in that he receives *means of subsistence.* Firstly, then, so that he can exist as a *worker,* and secondly as a *physical subject.* The culmination of this slavery is that it is only as a *worker* that he can maintain himself as a *physical subject* and only as a *physical subject* that he is a worker.

(The estrangement of the worker in his object is expressed according to the laws of political economy in the following way: the more the worker produces, the less he has to consume; the more values he creates, the more worthless he becomes; the more his product is shaped, the more misshapen the worker; the more civilized his object, the more barbarous the worker; the more powerful the work, the more powerless the worker; the more intelligent the work, the duller the worker and the more he becomes a slave of nature.)

Political economy conceals the estrangement in the nature of labor by ignoring the direct relationship between the worker (labor) *and production.* It is true that labor produces marvels for the rich, but it produces privation for the worker. It produces palaces, but hovels for the worker. It produces beauty, but deformity for the worker. It replaces labor by machines, but it casts some of the workers back into barbarous forms of labor and turns others into machines. It produces intelligence, but it produces idiocy and cretinism for the worker.

The direct relationship of labor to its products is the relationship of the worker to the objects of his production. The relationship of the rich man to the objects of production and to production itself is only a *consequence* of this first relationship, and confirms it. . . .

Up to now we have considered the estrangement, the alienation of the worker only from one aspect, i.e., his *relationship to the products of his labor.* But estrangement manifests itself not only in the result, but also in the *act of production,* within the *activity of production* itself. How could the product of the worker's activity confront him as something alien if it were not for the fact that in the act of production he was estranging himself from himself? After all, the product is simply the résumé of the activity, of the production. So if the product of labor is alienation, production itself must be active alienation, the alienation of activity, the activity of alienation. The estrangement of the object of labor merely summarizes the estrangement, the alienation in the activity of labor itself.

What constitutes the alienation of labor?

Firstly, the fact that labor is *external* to the worker, i.e., does not belong to his essential being; that he therefore does not confirm himself in his work, but denies himself, feels miserable and not happy, does not develop free mental and physical energy, but mortifies his flesh and ruins his mind. Hence the worker feels himself only when he is not working; when he is working he does not feel himself. He is at home when he is not working, and not at home when he is working. His labor is therefore not voluntary but forced, it is *forced labor.* It is therefore not the satisfaction of a need but a mere *means* to satisfy needs outside itself. Its alien character is clearly demonstrated by the fact that as soon as no physical or other compulsion exists it is shunned like the plague. External labor, labor in which man alienates himself, is a labor of self-sacrifice, of mortification. Finally, the external character of labor for the worker is demonstrated by the fact that it belongs not to him but to another, and that in it he belongs not to himself but to another. Just as in religion the spontaneous activity of the human imagination, the human brain and the human heart detaches itself from the individual and reappears as the alien activity of a god or of a devil, so the activity of the worker is not his own spontaneous activity. It belongs to another, it is a loss of his self.

The result is that man (the worker) feels that he is acting freely only in his animal functions—eating, drinking, and procreating, or at most in his dwelling and adornment—while in his human functions he is nothing more than an animal.

It is true that eating, drinking, and procreating, etc., are also genuine human functions. However, when abstracted from other aspects of human activity and turned into final and exclusive ends, they are animal.

We have considered the act of estrangement of practical human activity, of labor, from two aspects: (1) the relationship of the worker to the *product of labor* as an alien object that has power over him. This relationship is at the same time the relationship to the sensuous external world, to natural objects, as an alien world confronting him in hostile opposition. (2) The relationship of labor to the *act of production* within *labor*. This relationship is the relationship of the worker to his own activity as something which is alien and does not belong to him, activity as passivity, power as impotence, procreation as emasculation, the worker's *own* physical and mental energy, his personal life—for what is life but activity?—as an activity directed against himself which is independent of him and does not belong to him. *Self-estrangement,* as compared with the estrangement of the *object* mentioned above.

We now have to derive a third feature of *estranged labor* from the two we have already looked at.

Man is a species-being, not only because he practically and theoretically makes the species—both his own and those of other things—his object, but also—and this is simply another way of saying the same thing—because he looks upon himself as the present, living species, because he looks upon himself as a *universal* and therefore free being. . . .

Estranged labor not only (1) estranges nature from man and (2) estranges man from himself, from his own active function, from his vital activity; because of this it also estranges man from his *species.* It turns his *species-life* into a means for his individual life. Firstly it estranges species-life and individual life, and secondly it turns the latter, in its abstract form, into the purpose of the former, also in its abstract and estranged form.

For in the first place labor, *life activity, productive life* itself appears to man only as a *means* for the satisfaction of a need, the need to preserve physical existence. But productive life is species-life. It is life-producing life. The whole character of a species, its species-character, resides in the nature of its life activity, and free conscious activity constitutes the species-character of man. Life itself appears only as a *means of life.*

The animal is immediately one with its life activity. It is not distinct from that activity; it *is* that activity. Man makes his life activity itself an object of his will and consciousness. He has conscious life activity. It is not a determination with which he directly merges. Conscious life activity directly distinguishes man from animal life activity. Only because of that is he a species-being. Or rather, he is a conscious being, i.e., his own life is an object for him, only because he is a species-being. Only because of that is his activity free activity. Estranged labor reverses the relationship so that man, just because he is a conscious being, makes his life activity, his *being,* a mere means for his *existence.*

The practical creation of an *objective world,* the *fashioning* of inorganic nature, is proof that man is a conscious species-being, i.e., a being which treats the species as its own essential being or itself as a species-being. It is true that animals also produce. They build nests and dwellings, like the bee, the beaver, and ant, etc. But they produce only their own immediate needs or those of their young; they produce one-sidedly, while man produces universally; they produce only when immediate physical need compels them to do so, while man produces even when he is free from physical need and truly produces only in freedom from such need; they produce only themselves, while man reproduces the whole of nature; their products belong immediately to their physical bodies, while man freely confronts his own product. Animals produce only according to the standards and needs of the species to which they belong, while man is capable of producing according to the standards of every species and of applying to each object its inherent standard; hence man also produces in accordance with the laws of beauty....

In the same way as estranged labor reduces spontaneous and free activity to a means, it makes man's species-life a means of his physical existence.

Consciousness, which man has from his species, is transformed through estrangement so that species-life becomes a means for him.

(3) Estranged labor therefore turns *man's species-being*—both nature and his intellectual species-powers—into a being *alien* to him and a *means* of his *individual existence.* It estranges man from his own body, from nature as it exists outside him, from his spiritual essence, his *human* essence.

(4) An immediate consequence of man's estrangement from the product of his labor, his life activity, his species-being, is the *estrangement of man from man.* When man confronts himself, he also confronts *other* men. What is true of man's relationship to his labor, to the product of his labor and to himself, is also true of his relationship to other men, and to the labor and the object of the labor of other men.

In general, the proposition that man is estranged from his species-being means that each man is estranged from the others and that all are estranged from man's essence.

Man's estrangement, like all relationships of man to himself, is realized and expressed only in man's relationship to other men.

In the relationship of estranged labor each man therefore regards the other in accordance with the standard and the situation in which he as a worker finds himself.

We started out from an economic fact, the estrangement of the worker and of his production. We gave this fact conceptual form: *estranged, alienated* labor. We have analyzed this concept, and in so doing merely analyzed an economic fact.

Let us now go on to see how the concept of estranged, alienated labor must express and present itself in reality.

If the product of labor is alien to me and confronts me as an alien power, to whom does it then belong?

To a being *other* than me.

Who is this being? . . .

The *alien* being to whom labor and the product of labor belong, in whose service labor is performed and for whose enjoyment the product of labor is created, can be none other than *man* himself.

If the product of labor does not belong to the worker, and if it confronts him as an alien power, this is only possible because it belongs to *a man other than the worker.* If his activity is a torment for him, it must provide *pleasure* and enjoyment for someone else. Not the gods, not nature, but only man himself can be this alien power over men.

Consider the above proposition that the relationship of man to himself becomes *objective* and *real* for him only through his relationship to other men. If therefore he regards the product of his labor, his objectified labor, as an *alien, hostile* and powerful object which is independent of him, then his relationship to that object is such that another man—alien, hostile, powerful, and independent of him—is its master. If he relates to his own activity as unfree activity, then he relates to it as activity in the service, under the rule, coercion, and yoke of another man.

Every self-estrangement of man from himself and nature is manifested in the relationship he sets up between other men and himself and nature. Thus religious self-estrangement is necessarily manifested in the relationship between layman and priest, or, since we are here dealing with the spiritual world, between layman and mediator, etc. In the practical, real world, self-estrangement can manifest itself only in the practical, real relationship to other men. The medium through which estrangement progresses is itself a *practical* one. So through estranged labor man not only produces his relationship to the object and to the act of production as to alien and hostile powers; he also produces the relationship in which other men stand to his production and product, and the relationship in which he stands to these other men. Just as he creates his own production as a loss of reality, a punishment, and his own product as a loss, a product which does not belong to him, so he creates the domination of the non-producer over production and its product. Just as he estranges from himself his own activity, so he confers upon the stranger an activity which does not belong to him.

Karl Marx and Friedrich Engels

The German Ideology

FIRST PREMISES OF MATERIALIST METHOD

The premises from which we begin are not arbitrary ones, not dogmas, but real premises from which abstraction can only be made in the imagination. They are the

From Karl Marx and Friedrich Engels, *The German Ideology* (New York: International Publishers, 1947). Reprinted by permission of International Publishers, New York.

real individuals, their activity and the material conditions under which they live, both those which they find already existing and those produced by their activity. These premises can thus be verified in a purely empirical way.

The first premise of all human history is, of course, the existence of living human individuals. Thus the first fact to be established is the physical organization of these individuals and their consequent relation to the rest of nature. Of course, we cannot here go either into the actual physical nature of man, or into the natural conditions in which man finds himself—geological, oreohydrographical, climatic and so on. The writing of history must always set out from these natural bases and their modification in the course of history through the action of men.

Men can be distinguished from animals by consciousness, by religion or anything else you like. They themselves begin to distinguish themselves from animals as soon as they begin to *produce* their means of subsistence, a step which is conditioned by their physical organization. By producing their means of subsistence men are indirectly producing their actual material life.

The way in which men produce their means of subsistence depends first of all on the nature of the actual means of subsistence they find in existence and have to reproduce. This mode of production must not be considered simply as being the production of the physical existence of the individuals. Rather it is a definite form of activity of these individuals, a definite form of expressing their life, a definite *mode of life* on their part. As individuals express their life, so they are. What they are, therefore, coincides with their production, both with *what* they produce and with *how* they produce. The nature of individuals thus depends on the material conditions determining their production. . . .

The fact is, therefore, that definite individuals who are productively active in a definite way enter into these definite social and political relations. Empirical observation must in each separate instance bring out empirically, and without any mystification and speculation, the connection of the social and political structure with production. The social structure and the State are continually evolving out of the life-process of definite individuals, but of individuals, not as they may appear in their own or other people's imaginations, but as they *really* are; i.e., as they operate, produce materially, and hence as they work under definite material limits, presuppositions, and conditions independent of their will.

The production of ideas, of conceptions, of consciousness, is at first directly interwoven with the material activity and the material intercourse of men, the language of real life. Conceiving, thinking, the mental intercourse of men, appear at this stage as the direct efflux of their material behavior. The same applies to mental production as expressed in the language of politics, laws, morality, religion, metaphysics, etc. of a people. Men are the producers of their conceptions, ideas, etc.—real, active men, as they are conditioned by a definite development of their productive forces and of the intercourse corresponding to these, up to its furthest forms. Consciousness can never be anything else than conscious existence, and the existence of men is their actual life-process. If in all ideology men and their circumstances appear upside-down as in a *camera obscura,* this phenomenon arises just as much from their historical life-process as the inversion of objects on the retina does from their physical life-process.

In direct contrast to German philosophy which descends from heaven to earth, here we ascend from earth to heaven. That is to say, we do not set out from what men say, imagine, conceive, nor from men as narrated, thought of, managed, conceived, in order to arrive at men in the flesh. We set out from real, active men, and on the basis of their real life-process we demonstrate the development of the ideological reflexes and echoes of this life-process. The phantoms formed in the human brain are also, necessarily, sublimates of their material life-process, which is empirically verifiable and bound to material premises. Morality, religion, metaphysics, all the rest of ideology and their corresponding forms of consciousness, thus no longer retain the semblance of independence. They have no history, no development; but men, developing their material production and their material intercourse, alter, along with this their real existence, their thinking and the products of their thinking. Life is not determined by consciousness, but consciousness by life. In the first method of approach the starting-point is consciousness taken as the living individual; in the second method, which conforms to real life, it is the real living individuals themselves, and consciousness is considered solely as *their* consciousness. . . .

. . . Here, as everywhere, the identity of nature and man appears in such a way that the restricted relation of men to nature determines their restricted relation to one another, and their restricted relation to one another determines men's restricted relation to nature. On the other hand, man's consciousness of the necessity of associating with the individuals around him is the beginning of the consciousness that he is living in society at all. This beginning is as animal as social life itself at this stage. It is mere herd-consciousness, and at this point man is only distinguished from sheep by the fact that with him consciousness takes the place of instinct or that his instinct is a conscious one. This sheep-like or tribal consciousness receives its further development and extension through increased productivity, the increase of needs, and, what is fundamental to both of these, the increase of population. With these there develops the division of labor, which was originally nothing but the division of labor in the sexual act, then that division of labor which develops spontaneously or "naturally" by virtue of natural predisposition (e.g., physical strength), needs, accidents, etc. etc. Division of labor only becomes truly such from the moment when a division of material and mental labor appears. (The first form of ideologists, *priests,* is concurrent.) From this moment onwards consciousness *can* really flatter itself that it is something other than consciousness of existing practice, that it *really* represents something without representing something real; from now on consciousness is in a position to emancipate itself from the world and to proceed to the formation of "pure" theory, theology, philosophy, ethics, etc. But even if this theory, theology, philosophy, ethics, etc. comes into contradiction with the existing relations, this can only occur because existing social relations have come into contradiction with existing forces of production; this, moreover, can also occur in a particular national sphere of relations through the appearance of the contradiction, not within the national orbit, but between this national consciousness and the practice of other nations, i.e., between the national and the general consciousness of a nation (as we see it now in Germany).

Moreover, it is quite immaterial what consciousness starts to do on its own: out of all such muck we get only the one inference that these three moments, the forces of production, the state of society, and consciousness, can and must come into contradiction with one another, because the *division of labor* implies the possibility, nay the fact that intellectual and material activity—enjoyment and labor, production and consumption—devolve on different individuals, and that the only possibility of their not coming into contradiction lies in the negation in its turn of the division of labor. It is self-evident, moreover, that "spectres," "bonds," "the higher being," "concept," "scruple," are merely the idealistic, spiritual expression, the conception apparently of the isolated individual, the image of very empirical fetters and limitations, within which the mode of production of life and the form of intercourse coupled with it move.

Friedrich Nietzsche

Beyond Good and Evil

31   When one is young, one venerates and despises without that art of nuances which constitutes the best gain of life, and it is only fair that one has to pay dearly for having assaulted men and things in this manner with Yes and No. Everything is arranged so that the worst of tastes, the taste for the unconditional, should be cruelly fooled and abused until a man learns to put a little art into his feelings and rather to risk trying even what is artificial—as the real artists of life do.

The wrathful and reverent attitudes characteristic of youth do not seem to permit themselves any rest until they have forged men and things in such a way that these attitudes may be vented on them—after all, youth in itself has something of forgery and deception. Later, when the young soul, tortured by all kinds of disappointments, finally turns suspiciously against itself, still hot and wild, even in its suspicion and pangs of conscience—how wroth it is with itself now! how it tears itself to pieces, impatiently! how it takes revenge for its long self-delusion, just as if it had been a deliberate blindness! In this transition one punishes oneself with mistrust against one's own feelings; one tortures one's own enthusiasm with doubts; indeed, one experiences even a good conscience as a danger, as if it were a way of wrapping oneself in veils and the exhaustion of subtler honesty—and above all one takes sides, takes sides on principle, *against* "youth."—Ten years later one comprehends that all this, too—was still youth.

32   During the longest part of human history—so-called prehistorical times— the value or disvalue of an action was derived from its consequences. The action

    From Friedrich Nietzsche, *Beyond Good and Evil*, trans. Walter Kaufmann (New York: Vintage Books, 1966). Copyright © 1966 by Random House. Reprinted by permission of the publisher.

itself was considered as little as its origin. It was rather the way a distinction or disgrace still reaches back today from a child to its parents, in China: it was the retroactive force of success or failure that led men to think well or ill of an action. Let us call this period the *pre-moral* period of mankind: the imperative "know thyself!" was as yet unknown.

In the last ten thousand years, however, one has reached the point, step by step, in a few large regions on the earth, where it is no longer the consequences but the origin of an action that one allows to decide its value. On the whole this is a great event which involves a considerable refinement of vision and standards; it is the unconscious aftereffect of the rule of aristocratic values and the faith in "descent" —the sign of a period that one may call *moral* in the narrower sense. It involves the first attempt at self-knowledge. Instead of the consequences, the origin: indeed a reversal of perspective! Surely, a reversal achieved only after long struggles and vacillations. To be sure, a calamitous new superstition, an odd narrowness of interpretation, thus became dominant: the origin of an action was interpreted in the most definite sense as origin in an *intention;* one came to agree that the value of an action lay in the value of the intention. The intention as the whole origin and prehistory of an action—almost to the present day this prejudice dominated moral praise, blame, judgment, and philosophy on earth.

But today—shouldn't we have reached the necessity of once more resolving on a reversal and fundamental shift in values, owing to another self-examination of man, another growth in profundity? Don't we stand at the threshold of a period which should be designated negatively, to begin with, as *extra-moral?* After all, today at least we immoralists have the suspicion that the decisive value of an action lies precisely in what is *unintentional* in it, while everything about it that is intentional, everything about it that can be seen, known, "conscious," still belongs to its surface and skin—which, like every skin, betrays something but *conceals* even more. In short, we believe that the intention is merely a sign and symptom that still requires interpretation—moreover, a sign that means too much and therefore, taken by itself alone, almost nothing. We believe that morality in the traditional sense, the morality of intentions, was a prejudice, precipitate and perhaps provisional— something on the order of astrology and alchemy—but in any case something that must be overcome. The overcoming of morality, in a certain sense even the self-overcoming of morality—let this be the same for that long secret work which has been saved up for the finest and most honest, also the most malicious, consciences of today, as living touchstones of the soul.

108   There are no moral phenomena at all, but only a moral interpretation of phenomena—

186   . . . With a stiff seriousness that inspires laughter, all our philosophers demanded something far more exalted, presumptuous, and solemn from themselves as soon as they approached the study of morality: they wanted to supply a *rational foundation* for morality—and every philosopher so far has believed that he has provided such a foundation. Morality itself, however, was accepted as "given." How remote from their clumsy pride was that task which they considered insignificant and left in dust and must—the task of description—although the subtlest fingers and senses can scarcely be subtle enough for it.

Just because our moral philosophers knew the facts of morality only very approximately in arbitrary extracts or in accidental epitomes—for example, as the morality of their environment, their class, their church, the spirit of their time, their climate and part of the world—just because they were poorly informed and not even very curious about different peoples, times, and past ages—they never laid eyes on the real problems of morality; for these emerge only when we compare *many* moralities. In all "science of morals" so far one thing was *lacking,* strange as it may sound: the problem of morality itself; what was lacking was any suspicion that there was something problematic here. What the philosophers called "a rational foundation for morality" and tried to supply was, seen in the right light, merely a scholarly variation of the common *faith* in the prevalent morality; a new means of *expression* for this faith; and thus just another fact within a particular morality; indeed, in the last analysis a kind of denial that this morality might ever be considered problematic—certainly the very opposite of an examination, analysis, questioning, and vivisection of this very faith.

Listen, for example, with what almost venerable innocence Schopenhauer still described his task, and then draw your conclusions about the scientific standing of a "science" whose ultimate masters still talk like children and little old women: "The principle," he says (p. 136 of *Grundprobleme der Moral*), "the fundamental proposition on whose contents all moral philosophers are really agreed—*neminem laede, immo omnes, quantum potes, juva*[1] —that is *really* the proposition for which all moralists endeavor to find the rational foundation . . .the *real* basis of ethics for which one has been looking for thousands of years as for the philosopher's stone." . . .

187   Even apart from the value of such claims as "there is a categorical imperative in us," one can still always ask: what does such a claim tell us about the man who makes it? There are moralities which are meant to justify their creator before others. Other moralities are meant to claim him and lead him to be satisfied with himself. With yet others he wants to crucify himself and humiliate himself. With others he wants to wreak revenge, with others conceal himself, with others transfigure himself and place himself way up, at a distance. This morality is used by its creator to forget, that one to have others forget him or something about him. Some moralists want to vent their power and creative whims on humanity; some others, perhaps including Kant, suggest with their morality: "What deserves respect in me is that I can obey—and you *ought* not to be different from me."—In short, moralities are also merely a *sign language of the affects.*

228   May I be forgiven the discovery that all moral philosophy so far has been boring and was a soporific and that "virtue" has been impaired more for me by its *boring* advocates than by anything else, though I am not denying their general utility. It is important that as few people as possible should think about morality; hence it is *very* important that morality should not one day become interesting. But there is no reason for worry. Things still stand today as they have always stood: I see nobody in Europe who has (let alone, *promotes*) any awareness that thinking

[1]Hurt no one; rather, help all as much as you can.

about morality could become dangerous, captive, seductive—that there might be any *calamity* involved.

Consider, for example, the indefatigable, inevitable British utilitarians, how they walk clumsily and honorably in Bentham's footsteps, walking along (a Homeric simile says it more plainly), even as he himself had already walked in the footsteps of the honorable Helvetius. . . .Not a new idea, no trace of a subtler version or twist of an old idea, not even a real history of what had been thought before: altogether an *impossible* literature, unless one knows how to flavor it with some malice.

For into these moralists, too (one simply has to read them with ulterior thoughts, if one *has* to read them), that old English vice has crept which is called *cant* and consists in *moral Tartuffery;* only this time it hides in a new, scientific, form. A secret fight against a bad conscience is not lacking either, as it is only fair that a race of former Puritans will have a bad conscience whenever it tries to deal with morality scientifically. (Isn't a moral philosopher the opposite of a Puritan? Namely, insofar as he is a thinker who considers morality questionable, as calling for question marks, in short as a problem? Should moralizing not be—immoral?)

Ultimately they all want *English* morality to be proved right—because this serves humanity best, or "the general utility," or "the happiness of the greatest number"—no, the happiness of *England.* With all their powers they want to prove to themselves that the striving for *English* happiness—I mean for comfort and fashion (and at best a seat in Parliament)—is at the same time also the right way to virtue; indeed that whatever virtue has existed in the world so far must have consisted in such striving.

None of these ponderous herd animals with their unquiet consciences (who undertake to advocate the cause of egoism as the cause of the general welfare) wants to know or even sense that "the general welfare" is no ideal, no goal, no remotely intelligible concept, but only an emetic—that what is fair for one *cannot* by any means for that reason alone also be fair for others; that the demand of one morality for all is detrimental for the higher men; in short, that there is an order of rank between man and man, hence also between morality and morality. They are a modest and thoroughly mediocre type of man, these utilitarian Englishmen, and, as said above, insofar as they are boring one cannot think highly enough of their utility. They should even be *encouraged:* the following rhymes represent an effort in this direction.

> Hail, dear drudge and patient fretter!
> "More drawn out is always better,"
> Stiffness grows in head and knee,
> No enthusiast and no joker,
> Indestructibly mediocre,
> *Sans génie et sans esprit!*

260   Wandering through the many subtler and coarser moralities which have so far been prevalent on earth, or still are prevalent, I found that certain features recurred regularly together and were closely associated—until I finally discovered two basic types and one basic difference.

There are *master morality* and *slave morality*—I add immediately that in all the higher and more mixed cultures there also appear attempts at mediation between these two moralities, and yet more often the interpenetration and mutual misunderstanding of both, and at times they occur directly alongside each other—even in the same human being, within a *single* soul. The moral discrimination of values has originated either among a ruling group whose consciousness of its difference from the ruled group was accompanied by delight—or among the ruled, the slaves and dependents of every degree.

In the first case, when the ruling group determines what is "good," the exalted, proud states of the soul are experienced as conferring distinction and determining the order of rank. The noble human being separates from himself those in whom the opposite of such exalted, proud states finds expression: he despises them. It should be noted immediately that in this first type of morality the opposition of "good" and "*bad*" means approximately the same as "noble" and "contemptible." (The opposition of "good" and "*evil*" has a different origin.) One feels contempt for the cowardly, the anxious, the petty, those intent on narrow utility; also for the suspicious with their unfree glances, those who humble themselves, the doglike people who allow themselves to be maltreated, the begging flatterers, above all the liars: it is part of the fundamental faith of all aristocrats that the common people lie. "We truthful ones"—thus the nobility of ancient Greece referred to itself.

It is obvious that moral designations were everywhere first applied to *human beings* and only later, derivatively, to actions. Therefore it is a gross mistake when historians of morality start from such questions as: why was the compassionate act praised? The noble type of man experiences *itself* as determining values; it does not need approval; it judges, "what is harmful to me is harmful in itself"; it knows itself to be that which first accords honor to things; it is *value-creating*. Everything it knows as part of itself it honors: such a morality is self-glorification. In the foreground there is the feeling of fullness, of power that seeks to overflow, the happiness of high tension, the consciousness of wealth that would give and bestow: the noble human being, too, helps the unfortunate, but not, or almost not, from pity, but prompted more by an urge begotten by excess of power. The noble human being honors himself as one who is powerful, also as one who has power over himself, who knows how to speak and be silent, who delights in being severe and hard with himself and respects all severity and hardness. "A hard heart Wotan put into my breast," says an old Scandinavian saga: a fitting poetic expression, seeing that it comes from the soul of a proud Viking. Such a type of man is actually proud of the fact that he is *not* made for pity, and the hero of the saga therefore adds as a warning: "If the heart is not hard in youth it will never harden." Noble and courageous human beings who think that way are furthest removed from that morality which finds the distinction of morality precisely in pity, or in acting for others, or in *désintéressement;* faith in oneself, pride in oneself, a fundamental hostility and irony against "selflessness" belong just as definitely to noble morality as does a slight disdain and caution regarding compassionate feelings and a "warm heart."

It is the powerful who *understand* how to honor; this is their art, their realm of invention. The profound reverence for age and tradition—all law rests on this double reverence—the faith and prejudice in favor of ancestors and disfavor of those yet to come are typical of the morality of the powerful; and when the men of "modern ideas," conversely, believe almost instinctively in "progress" and "the future" and more and more lack respect for age, this in itself would sufficiently betray the ignoble origin of these "ideas."

A morality of the ruling group, however, is most alien and embarrassing to the present taste in the severity of its principle that one has duties only to one's peers; that against beings of a lower rank, against everything alien, one may behave as one pleases or "as the heart desires," and in any case "beyond good and evil"—here pity and like feelings may find their place. The capacity for, and the duty of, long gratitude and long revenge—both only among one's peers—refinement in repaying, the sophisticated concept of friendship, a certain necessity for having enemies (as it were, as drainage ditches for the affects of envy, quarrelsomeness, exuberance—at bottom, in order to be capable of being good *friends*): all these are typical characteristics of noble morality which, as suggested, is not the morality of "modern ideas" and therefore is hard to empathize with today, also hard to dig up and uncover.

It is different with the second type of morality, *slave morality*. Suppose the violated, oppressed, suffering, unfree, who are uncertain of themselves and weary, moralize: what will their moral valuations have in common? Probably, a pessimistic suspicion about the whole condition of man will find expression, perhaps a condemnation of man along with his condition. The slave's eye is not favorable to the virtues of the powerful: he is skeptical and suspicious, *subtly* suspicious, of all the "good" that is honored there—he would like to persuade himself that even their happiness is not genuine. Conversely, those qualities are brought out and flooded with light which serve to ease existence for those who suffer: here pity, the complaisant and obliging hand, the warm heart, patience, industry, humility, and friendliness are honored—for here these are the most useful qualities and almost the only means for enduring the pressure of existence. Slave morality is essentially a morality of utility.

Here is the place for the origin of that famous opposition of "good" and "evil"; into evil one's feelings project power and dangerousness, a certain terribleness, subtlety, and strength that does not permit contempt to develop. According to slave morality, those who are "evil" thus inspire fear; according to master morality it is precisely those who are "good" that inspire, and wish to inspire, fear, while the "bad" are felt to be contemptible.

The opposition reaches its climax when, as a logical consequence of slave morality, a touch of disdain is associated also with the "good" of this morality—this may be slight and benevolent—because the good human being has to be *undangerous* in the slaves' way of thinking: he is good-natured, easy to deceive, a little stupid perhaps, *un bonhomme*. Whenever slave morality becomes preponderant, language tends to bring the words "good" and "stupid" closer together.

One last fundamental difference: the longing for *freedom,* the instinct for happiness and the subtleties of the feeling of freedom belong just as necessarily to slave morality and morals as artful and enthusiastic reverence and devotion are the regular symptom of an aristocratic way of thinking and evaluating.

SUGGESTIONS FOR DISCUSSION

1. Are any of the theories of distributive justice offered in Part II, Chapter 7 compatible with Marx's views on justice?

2. Is there a distinction to be drawn between revolutionary violence and terrorism? How might Marx have justified his view that revolutionary violence may be necessary under certain sociohistorical conditions? Would the same argument(s) justify some, if not all, forms of terrorism?

3. What are Nietzsche's criticisms of Kantian morality and utilitarianism? Can either be reasonably defended against Nietzsche's attack?

4. What implications might Nietzsche's attack on traditional moral theory have for addressing social issues such as those in Part II? On Nietzsche's view, can one expect to arrive at the "moral truth" for any one of these issues?

FURTHER READING

MARX

Anderson, P. *Considerations on Western Marxism*. London: Verso, 1979. (Survey, critical analysis; introductory)

————. *Arguments Within English Marxism*. London: Verso, 1983. (Interpretation, critical analysis; intermediate)

Brenkert, G. *Marx's Ethics of Freedom*. London: Routledge and Kegan Paul, 1983. (Interpretation, critical analysis; intermediate)

Buchanan, A.E. *Marx and Justice: The Radical Critique of Liberalism*. London: Methuen, 1982. (Interpretation, critical analysis; advanced)

————. "Marx, Morality and History: Assessment of Recent Analytic Work." *Ethics* 98, 1 (October 1987): 104–36. (Interpretation, critical analysis; advanced)

Cohen, M., Nagel, T., and Scanlon, M., eds. *Marx, Justice and History*. Princeton: Princeton University Press, 1980. (Interpretation, critical analysis; advanced)

Kamenka, E. *Marxism and Ethics*. New York: St. Martin's Press, 1969. (Survey, critical analysis; introductory)

Lukes, S. *Marxism and Morality*. Oxford: Clarendon Press, 1985. (Interpretation, critical analysis; advanced)

Marx, K., and Engels, F. *The Collected Works of Marx and Engels*. London: Lawrence and Wishart, 1975.

Miller, R., *Analyzing Marx*. Princeton: Princeton University Press, 1984. (Interpretation, critical analysis; advanced)

Nielsen, K., and Patten, S. C., eds. *Marx and Morality*. Ontario: Canadian Association for Publishing in Philosophy, 1982. (Interpretation, critical analysis; advanced)

Roemer, J., ed. *Analytical Marxism*. Cambridge: Cambridge University Press, 1986. (Interpretation, critical analysis; advanced)

Wood, A. *Karl Marx*. London: Routledge and Kegan Paul, 1981. (Interpretation, critical analysis; advanced)

NIETZSCHE

Allison, D., ed. *The New Nietzsche Reader*. New York: Dell, 1977. (Interpretation, critical analysis; advanced)

Danto, A. *Nietzsche as Philosopher*. New York: Macmillan, 1985. (Interpretation, critical analysis; intermediate)

Hollingdale, R. J. *Nietzsche: The Man and His Philosophy*. Baton Rouge: Louisiana State University Press, 1965. (Interpretation; intermediate)

Kaufmann, W. *Nietzsche: Philosopher, Psychologist, Anti-Christ*. Princeton: Princeton University Press, 1950. (Interpretation, critical analysis; intermediate)

Nehemas, A. *Nietzsche: Life as Literature*. Cambridge, Mass.: Harvard University Press, 1985. (Interpretation, critical analysis; advanced)

Nietzsche, Friedrich. *The Genealogy of Morals*. New York: Doubleday, 1965.

———. *Beyond Good and Evil*. New York: Vintage Books, 1966.

———. *Daybreak*. New York: Cambridge University Press, 1982.

6

□

Ross, Mackie, Gauthier, and MacIntyre

Contemporary Ethical Theory Twentieth-century ethical theory has been rich and varied. A concern with metaethics prevailed in the first half of this century: theoretical analysis focused overwhelmingly upon the meanings of moral terms and on the logical form of ethical reasoning and justification. More recently, ethical theory has largely consisted in recasting the major ethical traditions in new and more acceptable terms; or in drawing out their normative implications for establishing right conduct in different act-contexts. The formative debate in contemporary theory has taken place for the most part between revised interpretations of utilitarianism and reconstructions of Kantianism. The former construes the rightness or wrongness of acts or rules no longer simply in terms of pleasure and pain, but in terms of preferences (see Part I, Chapter 4); while the latter rejects the claim that the rightness or wrongness of acts is a function of their good or bad consequences (see Chapter 3). Much of contemporary ethics may be interpreted either as alternatives to classical utilitarianism or as critical rejections of both classical utilitarianism and reformulations of the utilitarian framework. The four views included in this chapter represent major trends in ethical theory of this century. Though they are at basis different, they share a critical rejection of utilitarianism.

W. D. ROSS (1877–1971): MORAL INTUITIONISM

Intuitionism and Moral Conflict W. D. Ross, the eminent Aristotle scholar, found utilitarianism inconsistent with the moral beliefs of ordinary persons. He considered it self-evident that there are circumstances in which agents ought morally to act from duty regardless of the consequences. The moral duty in each instance is to be apprehended by *moral intuition,* an insight that was supposed to recognize objectively the truth or falsity of any moral claim. If moral terms, such as "good" or "right," are not simply different names for sense-perceivable natural (or nonmoral) properties, such as pleasure, then they must designate moral properties recognizable only by intuition.

Ross emphasized that moral conflict is basic to ordinary moral experience. A person is often confronted by conflicting moral claims only one of which circumstances enable her to fulfill. By fulfilling one of the claims made upon her, the agent would be disabled at that time from fulfilling any other. Ross admitted, first, that each of these initial claims on the agent may be genuine; and second, that only one of the conflicting claims is the actual duty. Each act-context must require that only one claim be fulfilled. The difficulty for intuitionism is to show how to determine one's actual duty from among the genuine initial claims.

Prima Facie Duties   Ross proposed to resolve this problem by introducing the concept of "*prima facie* duty." A *prima facie* duty is a duty that *tends* to make a claim on a person in virtue of some relation she may have; it is, in that respect, an action-type or a conditional duty, and not an actual one. In a specific act-situation, a person may have various relations and so tend to be bound by conflicting *prima facie* duties, only one of which she will actually be able to fulfill. According to Ross, *prima facie* duties are self-evident. For example, an employer apprehends the *prima facie* rightness of one act that fulfills a duty in instituting equal opportunity, of another in maintaining equal opportunity, and so on, until she intuits that equality of opportunity in general is *prima facie* right. Ross believed that almost every act-type is in some respects *prima facie* right, and in some other(s) *prima facie* wrong. In the former respect(s), agents would have a *prima facie* duty to do an act of that type; in the latter, to refrain. Thus a moral rule or principle that is considered to be absolute or universal may have exceptions. The agent's *actual* duty in the specific situation, the act she is obliged to do, is determined by her considered opinion as to which possible act has the greatest balance of *prima facie* rightness over *prima facie* wrongness. Nevertheless, Ross insisted that in affirming one *prima facie* duty as the actual one, agents do not cease to acknowledge the remaining *prima facie* duties. The employer who hires a black woman candidate over a white male applicant for the sake only of instituting greater social equality, other things like qualifications being equal, ought to recognize also the ongoing duty all have not to discriminate against persons on the basis of their race or gender (see Part II, Chapter 8).

One problem facing intuitionism is its apparent inability to furnish an objective criterion for determining which of different agents' conflicting claims about moral rightness or wrongness is correct. If, for a given issue, two morally mature persons claim to intuit the truth of conflicting judgments, no other grounds seem available to intuitionism for settling the dispute. Despite the difficulty with intuitionism, Ross's concept of "*prima facie* duty" has become standard usage in ethical theory and its applications in resolving social problems.

J. L. MACKIE (1917–1982): RIGHT-BASED ETHICS

Rights, Duties, and Goals   J. L. Mackie noted that ethical theories can be classified into three basic kinds: goal-based, duty-based, and right-based. Each kind has claimed to account for items of the other two kinds, by showing how the other items are derivable from the one taken as basic. So utilitarianism derives duties and rights from their utility or consequential good. Kant, by contrast, attempted to show that goals and rights are derivable from one fundamental duty. Mackie argued that the appeal of right-discourse and the difficulties with duty- and goal-based theories encourage the formulation of a right-based view. Rights are basic to legal language and to political relations: they are legislated, enacted by government executives, ruled upon judicially, and demanded politically. Rights are more popular than duties: People want rights for their own sake, whereas duties are impositions tolerated to secure morality and freedom. Like Ross, Mackie rejected utilitarianism, the leading goal-based theory, for being committed in some cases to morally unacceptable judgments.

The Basic Right   Mackie argued that any adequate goal-based morality must assume the basic goal to be an activity. This implies that there is not simply one but indefinitely many diverse goals, as many as there are valued activities. These goals cannot be an object of a single conclusive choice; they involve a range of successive choices. Thus, on a goal-based theory, what must be considered central are "the *rights* of persons progressively to choose how they shall live." Goal-based theories invariably have this fundamental right as their basis. Mackie concluded that the only acceptable moral theories must be right-based.

A person's right to do x is understood, minimally, as the conjunction of the freedom to do x, if she so chooses, and a claim in so doing to protection from interference by others. Duties and goals are both derivable from this right. If the agent has a right to do x, others have a duty to refrain from interfering. Moreover, if she really has the right, circumstances must be such as to enable her to fulfill it. Mackie concluded that goals may be interpreted as necessary conditions for the fulfillment of rights, and so derivative from these rights. Rights may be derived also from other rights. If an agent has a right to do x, and x causally requires doing y, then there is a right to y in the absence of other mitigating circumstances. For example, if a person has a right to defend himself when under harmful attack, and in a given circumstance this necessitates injuring the assailant, then the defendant has the right here to cause injury. Mackie insisted that the fundamental right to choose how to lead one's life is universal: All persons are to have it, and to have it equally. Thus, unlike utilitarianism, no individual's or group's rights to life, liberty, and the pursuit of happiness can be sacrificed for the advantage of others.

Conflicts and *Prima Facie* Rights   Clearly the major difficulty facing this view is that specific rights of different individuals derived in historically determinate contexts may conflict. Mackie aimed to resolve this by interpreting conflicting rights as no more than "*prima facie* rights." The "final rights" that people in practice actually end up with are the results of compromises worked out by the parties whose *prima facie* rights conflict. These historically determinate agreements are always subject to the condition of equality of the fundamental right. It follows that the basic procedure by which we are to arrive at the terms of morality— whether rights, duties, or goals—may involve some form of (hypothetical) contract.

DAVID GAUTHIER (B. 1932): CONTRACTARIANISM

Morals by Agreement   The central claim of the doctrine of contractarianism is that the principles of morality are just those that would be agreed to by rational agents. The contractual agreement is reached by agents deciding what moral principles it is in their rational self-interest to have rule their social institutions. Each social agent as party to the contract must be subject to the same impartial constraints or limitations on his or her rational decision-making as all others.

John Rawls and the Limits on Information   In the most influential version of the theory of contractarianism, John Rawls limits the relevant information that rational parties to the agreement know about themselves and others. In particular, Rawls places constraints upon agents' information about characteristics or abilities that might advantage themselves in choosing principles of justice, or disadvantage others. This limit on information includes knowledge of one's own and others' sex, age, race, class, nationality, and religion, but also of such characteristics as health status, height, and talents. In deciding originally what institutional principles should rationally order their lives, agents know only general information about the world. Rawls's underlying moral assumption here is that agents' should not be advantaged by their natural talents or social position, nor suffer their lack of talent or social condition; these are features of life for which agents are not themselves responsible. It follows that any rational agent would agree to impartial principles of justice, for given the constraints on information, they are principles self-interested rationality demands each agent choose. Nobody would agree to a distributive principle that is race- or sex-biased, for when the constraints on information about one's own race or sex are lifted, it may turn out that one has chosen a principle that disadvantages oneself, and to do so would be irrational.

The Universalistic Conception of Rationality   On Rawls's view, contractual agreement is ensured by a *universalistic* conception of rationality. Not only do agents use the same formal procedures to make rational decisions, but the informational input is also identical. Differences between agents are eliminated by restricting information all have about themselves. Rational choice is universal: The choice of any agent would be the same as every agent's, given identity of information. Rawls is interested in establishing what principles of justice would be agreed to, rather than in deriving moral rules from nonmoral premises. Moral presuppositions are thus built by Rawls into the universalistic conception of rationality. (For a fuller account of Rawls's view, see Part II, Chapter 7.) David Gauthier emphasizes a difficulty faced by Rawls concerning compliance with the principles so chosen. What rational motivation would there be for an agent to comply with a principle chosen under Rawlsian constraints on information, if upon lifting these constraints it were found that the principle failed to serve his or her interests? Some contractors may not be willing to sacrifice a given advantage they currently enjoy in wealth or especially power, as commanded by principles of justice.

The Maximizing Conception of Rationality   Gauthier argues that the version of contractarianism he calls "morals by agreement" avoids this difficulty. He rejects the universalistic conception of practical rationality in favor of a *maximizing* conception. The task of rationality is defined as maximizing the satisfaction of individual self-interests. In choosing principles of justice, the position of each self-interested agent is addressed in turn; every principle requires agreement by each agent looking to maximize his or her own utility. Thus Gauthier undertakes to generate the impartial constraints morality imposes upon self-interest, not by building moral constraints into a universalist conception of reason, but from non-moral presuppositions of rationality. The fundamental challenge facing Gauthier is to show that, though moral duty overrides advantage, acceptance of duty is maximally advantageous in that it maximizes rational self-interest.

Moral Bargaining   Gauthier starts from the assumption of a perfectly competitive economy governed solely by the laws of the market. Rational agents aim only to maximize satisfaction of their individual interests; they are unconstrained by moral requirements. Rational agents would not agree to moral constraints unless they were mutually advantageous. Contractual agreement to establish mutually beneficial moral principles can be reached solely by following the procedure of *moral bargaining*. Gauthier formulates rational principles for bargaining. The initial position of parties to the bargaining is subject to a *proviso:* no party should be worse off at the outset than if no bargaining had commenced between the parties. This prevents any bargainer bettering her or his initial position by worsening that of another. The assumption that bargainers are equally rational implies two procedural principles. First, each must concede as little as possible ("minimax relative concession"); and second, each must benefit as much as possible ("maximin relative benefit"). These principles embody constraints of fairness and impartiality, for every party to the agreement is treated alike in giving up as little as circumstances allow, and each benefits to the fullest extent.

The Prisoner's Dilemma   Given these procedural principles, Gauthier suggests that rational agents would maximize satisfaction of self-interest by mutually agreeing to constrain individual interest. The advantages of cooperating in a joint social venture generally outweigh those that could proceed from pursuing simple self-interest. The concept of rationality at work here is illustrated by the *Prisoner's Dilemma*. Consider two prisoners, suspected of criminal complicity, who are confined in separate cells. The prosecutor confronts each individually with the following proposal: "Confess to the more serious charge and you will be treated leniently. Your partner in crime will be jailed for ten years, you for one. If you fail to confess but your partner does, the sentences will be reversed. Should both of you confess, each will be sentenced to five years. Yet should neither of you confess, evidence now suffices to convict both only on a lesser charge drawing three-year sentences each." If both prisoners are rational and committed to minimizing their own sentences, each will reason thus: "I don't want to confess, but the other person might. If he confesses and I do not, I get ten years and he one. So, I should confess. For then, if he fails to confess, I get one year; and if we both confess, we each get five." So, if rational, both will confess.

Justice by Contract   Gauthier concludes that rational, self-interested agents, like the prisoners, would not be best served by blindly pursuing their own individual utility-maximization. Benefits would be maximized for all if each subjected his or her choices to moral constraints established cooperatively. A utilitarian society would enable unconstrained realization of the greatest sum of individual goods. By contrast, the just society that follows from Gauthier's contractarian agreement allows each individual interactively to maximize his or her own good, on terms acceptable to all.

ALASDAIR MACINTYRE (B. 1929): THE DOCTRINE OF THE VIRTUES

Alasdair MacIntyre embraces a sweeping Nietzschean indictment of modern moral philosophy. He attacks as illusion the supposition of universality central to moral thinking, especially in the Kantian and utilitarian accounts. MacIntyre argues that this ahistorical, traditionless conception of universality replaced the Aristotelian doctrine of the virtues that had been rejected by post-medieval philosophers. He suggests that Nietzsche alone comprehended the consequences for modern moral theory of this rejection of Aristotle's view. MacIntyre offers a revised Aristotelianism as an alternative. He accepts Aristotle's doctrine of virtue, and the conceptual structure upon which it rests, as the basis of morality.

Virtue-based theories reject duties or rights as the fundamental moral concepts. The basic concern of virtue-based theories is not with how we ought or have a right to act but with establishing what sort of moral character persons should develop.

The Structure of Virtues   Central to MacIntyre's analysis is the attempt to show that the differing historical accounts of the virtues presuppose a unified conceptual structure. A virtue consists of three conceptual elements: a practice, a narrative order of a single life, and a moral tradition. A *practice* is the most basic. MacIntyre defines this as a complex form of cooperative social activity specified by standards of excellence. These standards establish *goods internal* rather than *goods external* to a practice. Internal goods are those that can be specified only in terms of, and achieved by participating in, the practice. External goods are those that are identifiable independent of the practice, only contingently related to it, and achievable by a range of alternative means. The game of basketball is a practice; money earned by playing it is an external good; and graceful proficiency at scoring field goals is an internal good. A practice involves historically defined standards of excellence, obedience to rules, and achievement of goals. The standards for the practice set the criteria in terms of which the participants' performances will be judged. External goods are always possessed by someone, thereby limiting the quantity available to others; achieving internal goods, by contrast, benefits all participants in the practice.

Virtues and Practices   MacIntyre defines virtue in terms of practices. A *virtue* is a human quality acquired in practices. Virtues make possible bringing about goods internal to practices; their lack bars such accomplishment (see Aristotle, Part I,

Chapter 1). Thus virtues are historically specific, altering relative to social complex. MacIntyre argues that a small set of virtues are nevertheless necessary qualities of any practice. These include the Aristotelian virtues of justice, courage, and honesty. They are qualities required for achieving excellence in all social relations. Justice and honesty are conditions for the principled equality with which all participants in the practice are to be treated. Courage is the capacity to risk harm to oneself for the sake of others; it reveals care and concern. These, then, are standards of excellence characteristic of human activity, irrespective of private moral standpoints. Lack of these virtues simply reveals that a character has failed in some way or another. It indicates that the entire character is defective.

MacIntyre stresses that these core virtues, and the standards of human excellence they represent, are open to interpretations relative to time and place. He insists also that virtuous activity by a person in some respect does not preclude vicious activity in another. However, the success of vicious activity depends upon the virtues of others. So MacIntyre offers a complex historical conception of morality, relativized to time and place, as an alternative to the major traditions of contemporary ethical theorizing.

W. D. Ross

What Makes Right Acts Right?

In fact the theory of "ideal utilitarianism," if I may for brevity refer so to the theory of Professor Moore, seems to simplify unduly our relations to our fellows. It says, in effect, that the only morally significant relation in which my neighbors stand to me is that of being possible beneficiaries by my action. They do stand in this relation to me, and this relation is morally significant. But they may also stand to me in the relation of promisee to promiser, of creditor to debtor, of wife to husband, of child to parent, of friend to friend, of fellow countryman to fellow countryman, and the like; and each of these relations is the foundation of a *prima facie* duty, which is more or less incumbent on me according to the circumstances of the case. When I am in a situation, as perhaps I always am, in which more than one of these *prima facie* duties is incumbent on me, what I have to do is to study the situation as fully as I can until I form the considered opinion (it is never more) that in the circumstances one of them is more incumbent than any other; then I am bound to think that to do this *prima facie* duty is my duty *sans phrase* in the situation.

I suggest "*prima facie* duty" or "conditional duty" as a brief way of referring to the characteristic (quite distinct from that of being a duty proper) which an act

From W. D. Ross, *The Right and the Good* (Oxford: Oxford University Press, 1930). Reprinted by permission of Oxford University Press.

has, in virtue of being of a certain kind (e.g., the keeping of a promise), of being an act which would be a duty proper if it were not at the same time of another kind which is morally significant. Whether an act is a duty proper or actual duty depends on *all* the morally significant kinds it is an instance of. The phrase "*prima facie* duty" must be apologized for, since (1) it suggests that what we are speaking of is a certain kind of duty, whereas it is in fact not a duty, but something related in a special way to duty. Strictly speaking, we want not a phrase in which duty is qualified by an adjective, but a separate noun. (2) "*Prima*" *facie* suggests that one is speaking only of an appearance which a moral situation presents at first sight, and which may turn out to be illusory; whereas what I am speaking of is an objective fact involved in the nature of the situation, or more strictly in an element of its nature, though not, as duty proper does, arising from its *whole* nature. I can, however, think of no term which fully meets the case. "Claim" has been suggested by Professor Prichard. The word "claim" has the advantage of being quite a familiar one in this connection, and it seems to cover much of the ground. It would be quite natural to say, "a person to whom I have made a promise has a claim on me," and also, "a person whose distress I could relieve (at the cost of breaking the promise) has a claim on me." But (1) while "claim" is appropriate from *their* point of view, we want a word to express the corresponding fact from the agent's point of view—the fact of his being subject to claims that can be made against him; and ordinary language provides us with no such correlative to "claim." And (2) (what is more important) "claim" seems inevitably to suggest two persons, one of whom might make a claim on the other; and while this covers the ground of social duty, it is inappropriate in the case of that important part of duty which is the duty of cultivating a certain kind of character in oneself. It would be artificial, I think, and at any rate metaphorical, to say that one's character has a claim on oneself.

There is nothing arbitrary about these *prima facie* duties. Each rests on a definite circumstance which cannot seriously be held to be without moral significance. Of *prima facie* duties I suggest, without claiming completeness or finality for it, the following division.[1]

(1) Some duties rest on previous acts of my own. These duties seem to include two kinds, (*a*) those resting on a promise of what may fairly be called an implicit promise, such as the implicit undertaking not to tell lies which seems to be implied in the act of entering into conversation (at any rate by civilized men), or of writing books that purport to be history and not fiction. These may be called the duties of fidelity. (*b*) Those resting on a previous wrongful act. These may be called the duties of reparation. (2) Some rest on previous acts of other men, i.e., services done by them to me. These may be loosely described as the duties of gratitude. (3)

---

[1] I should make it plain at this stage that I am *assuming* the correctness of some of our main convictions to *prima facie* duties, or, more strictly, am claiming that we *know* them to be true. To me it seems as self-evident as anything could be, that to make a promise, for instance, is to create a moral claim on us in someone else. Many readers will perhaps say that they do *not* know this to be true. If so, I certainly cannot prove it to them; I can only ask them to reflect again, in the hope that they will ultimately agree that they also know it to be true. The main moral convictions of the plain man seem to me to be, not opinions which it is for philosophy to prove or disprove, but knowledge from the start; and in my own case I seem to find little difficulty in distinguishing these essential convictions from other moral convictions which I also have, which are merely fallible opinions based on an imperfect study of the working for good or evil of certain institutions or types of action.

Some rest on the fact or possibility of a distribution of pleasure or happiness (or of the means thereto) which is not in accordance with the merit of the persons concerned; in such cases there arises a duty to upset or prevent such a distribution. These are the duties of justice. (4) Some rest on the mere fact that there are other beings in the world whose condition we can make better in respect of virtue, or of intelligence, or of pleasure. These are the duties of beneficence. (5) Some rest on the fact that we can improve our own condition in respect of virtue or of intelligence. These are the duties of self-improvement. (6) I think that we should distinguish from (4) the duties that may be summed up under the title of "not injuring others." No doubt to injure others is incidentally to fail to do them good; but it seems to me clear that non-maleficence is apprehended as a duty distinct from that of beneficence, and as a duty of a more stringent character. It will be noticed that this alone among the types of duty has been stated in a negative way. An attempt might no doubt be made to state this duty, like the others, in a positive way. It might be said that it is really the duty to prevent ourselves from acting either from an inclination to harm others or from an inclination to seek our own pleasure, in doing which we should incidentally harm them. But on reflection it seems clear that the primary duty here is the duty not to harm others, this being a duty whether or not we have an inclination that if followed would lead to our harming them; and that when we have such an inclination the primary duty not to harm others gives rise to a consequential duty to resist the inclination. The recognition of this duty of non-maleficence is the first step on the way to the recognition of the duty of beneficence; and that accounts for the prominence of the commands "thou shalt not kill," "thou shalt not commit adultery," "thou shalt not steal," "thou shalt not bear false witness," in so early a code as the Decalogue. But even when we have come to recognize the duty of beneficence, it appears to me that the duty of non-maleficence is recognized as a distinct one, and as *prima facie* more binding. We should not in general consider it justifiable to kill one person in order to keep another alive, or to steal from one in order to give alms to another.

The essential defect of the "ideal utilitarian" theory is that it ignores, or at least does not do full justice to, the highly personal character of duty. If the only duty is to produce the maximum of good, the question who is to have the good—whether it is myself, or my benefactor, or a person to whom I have made a promise to confer that good on him, or a mere fellow man to whom I stand in no such special relation —should make no difference to my having a duty to produce that good. But we are all in fact sure that it makes a vast difference. . . .

It is necessary to say something by way of clearing up the relation between *prima facie* duties and the actual or absolute duty to do one particular act in particular circumstances. If, as almost all moralists except Kant are agreed, and as most plain men think, it is sometimes right to tell a lie or to break a promise, it must be maintained that there is a difference between *prima facie* duty and actual or absolute duty. When we think ourselves justified in breaking, and indeed morally obliged to break, a promise in order to relieve some one's distress, we do not for a moment cease to recognize a *prima facie* duty to keep our promise, and this leads us to feel, not indeed shame or repentance, but certainly compunction, for behaving as we do; we recognize, further, that it is our duty to make up somehow to the promisee for the breaking of the promise. We have to distinguish from the characteristic of being our duty that of tending to be our duty. Any act that we do contains various elements in virtue of which it falls under various categories. In virtue of being the breaking of a promise, for instance, it tends to be wrong; in virtue of being an instance of relieving distress it tends to be right. Tendency to be one's duty may be called a parti-resultant attribute, i.e., one which belongs to an act in virtue of some one component in its nature. *Being* one's duty is a toti-resultant attribute, one which belongs to an act in virtue of its whole nature and of nothing less than this. . . .

Our judgments about our actual duty in concrete situations have none of the certainty that attaches to our recognition of the general principles of duty. A statement is certain, i.e. is an expression of knowledge, only in one or other of two cases; when it is either self-evident, or a valid conclusion from self-evident premises. And our judgments about our particular duties have neither of these characters. (1) They are not self-evident. Where a possible act is seen to have two characteristics, in virtue of one of which it is *prima facie* right, and in virtue of the other *prima facie* wrong, we are (I think) well aware that we are not certain whether we ought or ought not to do it; that whether we do it or not, we are taking a moral risk. We come in the long run, after consideration, to think one duty more pressing than the other, but we do not feel certain that it is so. And though we do not always recognize that a possible act has two such characteristics, and though there *may* be cases in which it has not, we are never certain that any particular possible act has not, and therefore never certain that it is right, nor certain that it is wrong. For, to go no further in the analysis, it is enough to point out that any particular act will in all probability in the course of time contribute to the bringing about of good or of evil for many human beings, and thus have a *prima facie* rightness or wrongness of which we know nothing. (2) Again, our judgments about our particular duties are not logical conclusions from self-evident premises. The only possible premises would be the general principles stating their *prima facie* rightness or wrongness *qua* having the different characteristics they do have; and even if we could (as we cannot) apprehend the extent to which an act will tend on the one hand, for example, to bring about advantages for our benefactors, and on the other hand to bring about disadvantages for fellow men who are not our benefactors, there is no principle by which we can draw the conclusion that it is on the whole right or on the whole wrong. In this respect the judgment as to the rightness of a particular act is just like the judgment as to the beauty of a particular natural object or work of art. A poem is, for instance, in respect of certain qualities beautiful and in respect of certain others not beautiful; and our judgment as to the degree of beauty it possesses on the whole is never reached by logical reasoning from the apprehension of its particular beauties or particular defects. Both in this and in the moral case we have more or less probable opinions which are not logically justified conclusions from the general principles that are recognized as self-evident.

There is therefore much truth in the description of the right act as a fortunate act. If we cannot be certain that it is right, it is our good fortune if the act we do is the right act. This consideration does not, however, make the doing of our duty a mere matter of chance. There is a parallel here between the doing of duty and the doing of what will be to our personal advantage. We never *know* what act will in the long run be to our advantage. Yet it is certain that we are more likely in general to secure our advantage if we estimate to the best of our ability the probable tendencies of our actions in this respect, than if we act on caprice. And similarly we are more likely to do our duty if we reflect to the best of our ability on the *prima facie* rightness or wrongness of various possible acts in virtue of the characteristics we perceive them to have, than if we act without reflection. With this greater likelihood we must be content. . . .

The general principles of duty are obviously not self-evident from the beginning of our lives. How do they come to be so? The answer is that they come to be self-evident to us just as mathematical axioms do. We find by experience that this couple of matches and that couple make four matches, that this couple of balls on a wire and that couple make four balls: and by reflection on these and similar discoveries we come to see that it is of the nature of two and two to make four. In a precisely similar way, we see the *prima facie* rightness of an act which would be the fulfillment of a particular promise, and of another which would be the fulfillment of another promise, and when we have reached sufficient maturity to think in general terms, we apprehend *prima facie* rightness to belong to the nature of any fulfillment of promise. What comes first in time is the apprehension of the self-evident *prima facie* rightness of an individual act of a particular type. From this we come by reflection to apprehend the self-evident general principle of *prima facie* duty. From this, too, perhaps along with the apprehension of the self-evident *prima facie* rightness of the same act in virtue of its having another characteristic as well, and perhaps in spite of the apprehension of its *prima facie* wrongness in virtue of its having some third characteristic, we come to believe something not self-evident at all, but an object of probable opinion, viz., that this particular act is (not *prima facie* but) actually right. . . .

It is worth while to try to state more definitely the nature of the acts that are right. We may try to state first what (if anything) is the universal nature of *all* acts that are right. It is obvious that any of the acts that we do has countless effects, directly or indirectly, on countless people, and the probability is that any act, however right it be, will have adverse effects (though these may be very trivial) on some innocent people. Similarly, any wrong act will probably have beneficial effects on some deserving people. Every act therefore, viewed in some aspects, will be *prima facie* right, and viewed in others, *prima facie* wrong, and right acts can be distinguished from wrong acts only as being those which, of all those possible for the agent in the circumstances, have the greatest balance of *prima facie* rightness, in those respects in which they are *prima facie* right, over their *prima facie* wrongness, in those respects in which they are *prima facie* wrong—*prima facie* rightness and wrongness being understood in the sense previously explained. For the estimation of the comparative stringency of these *prima facie* obligations no general rules can, so far as I can see, be laid down. We can only say that a great deal of stringency belongs to the duties of "perfect obligation"—the duties of keeping our promises, of repairing wrongs we have done, and of returning the equivalent of services we have received. For the rest, ἐν τῇ αἰσθήσει ἡ κρίσις.* This sense of our particular duty in particular circumstances, preceded and informed by the fullest reflection we can bestow on the act in all its bearings, is highly fallible, but it is the only guide we have to our duty.

... [W]e turn to consider the nature of the individual right acts. ... my act is right *qua* being an ensuring of one of the particular states of affairs of which it is an ensuring, viz., in the case we have taken, of my friend's receiving the book I have promised to return to him. But this answer requires some correction; for it refers only to the *prima facie* rightness of my act. If to be a fulfillment of promise were a sufficient ground of the rightness of an act, all fulfillments of promises would be right, whereas it seems clear that there are cases in which some other *prima facie* duty overrides the *prima facie* duty of fulfilling a promise. The more correct answer would be that the ground of the actual rightness of the act is that, of all acts possible for the agent in the circumstances, it is that whose *prima facie* rightness in the respects in which it is *prima facie* right most outweighs its *prima facie* wrongness in any respects in which it is *prima facie* wrong. But since its *prima facie* rightness is mainly due to its being a fulfillment of promise, we may call its being so the salient element in the ground of its rightness.

Subject to this qualification, then, it is as being the production (or if we prefer the word, the securing or ensuring) of the reception by my friend of what I have promised him (or in other words as the fulfillment of my promise) that my act is right. It is not right as a packing and posting of a book. The packing and posting of the book is only incidentally right, right only because it is a fulfillment of promise, which is what is directly or essentially right.

Our duty, then, is not to do certain things which will produce certain results. Our acts, at any rate our acts of special obligation, are not right because they will produce certain results—which is the view common to all forms of utilitarianism. To say that is to say that in the case in question what is essentially right is to pack and post a book, whereas what is essentially right is to secure the possession by my friend of what I have promised to return to him. An act is not right because it, being one thing, produces good results different from itself; it is right because it is itself the production of a certain state of affairs. Such production is right in itself, apart from any consequence.

But, it might be said, this analysis applies only to acts of special obligation; the utilitarian account still holds good for the acts in which we are not under a special obligation to any person or set of persons but only under that of augmenting the general good. Now merely to have established that there *are* special obligations to do certain things irrespective of their consequences would be already to have made a considerable breach in the utilitarian walls; for according to utilitarianism there is no such thing, there is only the single obligation to promote the general good. But, further, on reflection it is clear that just as (in the case we have taken) my act is not only the packing and posting of a book but the fulfilling of a promise, and just as it is in the latter capacity and not in the former that it is my duty, so an act whereby I augment the general good is not only, let us say, the writing of a begging

---

* "The decision rests with perception." Arist. *Nic. Eth.* 1109 b 23, 1126 b 4.

letter on behalf of a hospital, but the producing (or ensuring) of whatever good ensues therefrom, and it is in the latter capacity and not in the former that it is right, if it *is* right. That which is right is right not because it is an act, one thing, which will produce another thing, an increase of the general welfare, but because it is itself the producing of an increase in the general welfare. Or, to qualify this in the necessary way, its being the production of an increase in the general welfare is the salient element in the ground of its rightness. Just as before we were led to recognize the *prima facie* rightness of the fulfillment of promises, we are now led to recognize the *prima facie* rightness of promoting the general welfare. In both cases we have to recognize the *intrinsic* rightness of a certain type of act, not depending on its consequences but on its own nature.

J. L. Mackie

Can There Be a Right-Based Moral Theory?

In the course of a discussion of Rawls's theory of justice, Ronald Dworkin suggests a "tentative initial classification" of political theories into goal-based, right-based, and duty-based theories.[1] Though he describes this, too modestly, as superficial and trivial ideological sociology, it in fact raises interesting questions. In particular, does some such classification hold for moral as well as for political theories? We are familiar with goal-based or consequentialist moral views and with duty-based or deontological ones; but it is not so easy to find right-based examples, and in discussions of consequentialism and deontology this third possibility is commonly ignored. Dworkin's own example of a right-based theory is Tom Paine's theory of revolution; another, recent, example might be Robert Nozick's theory of the minimal state.[2] But each of these is a political theory; the scope of each is restricted to the criticism of some political structures and policies and the support of others; neither is a fully developed general moral theory. If Rawls's view is, as Dworkin argues, fundamentally right-based, it may be the only member of this class. Moreover, it is only for Rawls's "deep theory" that Dworkin can propose this identification: as explicitly formulated, Rawls's moral philosophy is not right-based. The lack of any convincing and decisive example leaves us free to ask the abstract

From *Midwest Studies in Philosophy*, edited by Peter French, Theodore Uehling and Howard Wettstein (Minneapolis: The University of Minnesota Press, 1978). Reprinted by kind permission of the editors, The University of Minnesota Press, and Mrs. Joan Mackie. Copyright © 1980 by The University of Minnesota Press.

question, "Could there be a right-based general moral theory, and, if there were one, what would it be like?"

It is obvious that most ordinary moral theories include theses about items of all three kinds, goals, duties, and rights, or, equivalently, about what is good as an end, about what is obligatory or about what ought or ought not to be done or must or must not be done, and about what people are entitled to have or receive or do. But it is also obvious that moral theories commonly try to derive items of some of these sorts from items of another of them. It is easy to see how a consequentialist, say a utilitarian, may derive duties and rights from his basic goal. There are certain things that people must or must not do if the general happiness is to be maximized. Equally, the securing for people of certain entitlements and protections, and therefore of areas of freedom in which they can act as they choose, is, as Mill says, something which concerns the essentials of human well-being more nearly, and is therefore of more absolute obligation, than any other rules for the guidance of life.[3]

Again, it is possible to derive both goals and rights from duties. Trivially, there could just be a duty to pursue a certain end or to respect and defend a certain right. More interestingly, though more obscurely, it is conceivable that sets of goals and rights should follow from a single fundamental duty. Kant, for example, attempts to derive the principle of treating humanity as an end from the categorical imperative, "Act only on that maxim through which you can at the same time will that it should become a universal law."[4] Taken as literally as it can be taken, the principle of treating humanity—that is, persons, or more generally rational beings—as an end would seem to set up a goal. But it could well be interpreted as assigning rights to persons. Alternatively it could be argued that some general assignment of rights would follow directly from the choice of maxims which one could will to be universal. In either of these ways rights might be derived from duties.

But is it possible similarly to derive goals and duties from rights? And, if we are seeking a systematic moral theory, is it possible to derive a multiplicity of rights from a single fundamental one or from some small number of basic rights?

A right, in the most important sense, is the conjunction of a freedom and a claim-right. That is, if someone, A, has the moral right to do X, not only is he entitled to do X if he chooses—he is not morally required not to do X—but he is also protected in his doing of X—others are morally required not to interfere or prevent him. This way of putting it suggests that duties are at least logically prior to rights: this sort of right is built up out of two facts about duties, that A does not have a duty not to do X and that others have a duty not to interfere with A of X. But we could look at it the other way round: what is primary is A's having this right in a sense indicated by the prescription "Let A be able to do X if he chooses," and the duty of others not to interfere follows from this (as does the absence of a duty for A not to do X). Here we have one way, at least, in which duties (and negations of duties) may be derived from rights.

I cannot see any way in which the mere fact of someone's having a certain right would in itself entail that anyone should take something as a goal. Nor does someone's having a right in itself require the achievement or realization of any goal. But the achievement of certain things as goals, or of things that may be taken as goals, may well be a necessary condition for the exercise of a right. Things must be thus and so if A is really to be able to do X; his merely having the right is not in itself sufficient. In this way a goal may be derived from a right, as a necessary condition of its exercise.

Rights can be derived from other rights in fairly obvious logical ways. For example, if I have a right to walk from my home to my place of work by the most direct route, and the most direct route is across Farmer Jones's potato field, then I have a right to walk across Farmer Jones's potato field. Again, there may be a right to create rights—in Hohfeld's terminology, a power. If someone has a certain power, and exercises it appropriately, then it follows that there will be the rights he has thus created. But what may be of more interest is a causal derivation of rights from rights. Suppose that A has a right to do X, but it is causally impossible for him to do X unless he does Y. It does not follow from this alone that he has a right to do Y, and in many cases we may have other grounds for denying him the right to do Y. But at least a *prima facie* case for his having the right to do Y could be based on the fact that doing Y is causally necessary for doing X, which he already has the right to do.

It seems, then, to be at least formally possible to have a system of moral ideas in which some rights are fundamental and other rights, and also goals and duties, are derived from these. But is it substantially possible? Are rights really the sort of thing that could be fundamental?

It is true that rights are not plausible candidates for objective existence. But neither are goods or intrinsic goals, conceived as things whose nature in itself requires that they should be pursued, or duties taken as intrinsic requirements, as constituting something like commands for which there need be, and is, no commander, which issue from no source. A belief in objective prescriptivity has flourished within the tradition of moral thinking, but it cannot in the end be defended.[5] So we are not looking for objective truth or reality in a moral system. Moral entities—values or standards or whatever they may be—belong within human thinking and practice: they are either explicitly or implicitly posited, adopted, or laid down. And the positing of rights is no more obscure or questionable than the positing of goals or obligations.

We might, then, go on to consider what rights to posit as fundamental. But it will be better, before we do this, to consider the comparative merits of right-based, goal-based, and duty-based theories. When we know what advantages a right-based theory might secure, we shall be better able to specify the rights that would secure them.

Rights have obvious advantages over duties as the basis and ground of morality. Rights are something that we may well want to have; duties are irksome. We may be glad that duties are imposed on others, but only (unless we are thoroughly bloody-minded) for the sake of the freedom, protection, or other advantages that other people's duties secure for us and our friends. The point of there being duties must lie elsewhere. Duty for duty's sake is absurd, but rights for their own sake are not. Duty is, as Wordsworth says, the stern daughter of the voice of God, and if we deny that there is a god, her parentage becomes highly dubious. Even if we accepted a god, we should expect his commands to have some further point, though possibly one not known to us; pointless commands, even from a god, would be gratuitous tyranny. Morality so far as we understand it might conceivably be thus based on divine commands, and therefore have, for us, a duty-based form; but if we reject this mythology and see morality as a human product we cannot intelligibly take duties as its starting point. Despite Kant, giving laws to oneself is not in itself a rational procedure. For a group to give laws to its members may be, but not for the sake of the restrictions they impose, or even for the sake of the similarity of those restrictions, but only for the sake of the correlative rights they create or the products of the cooperation they maintain.

However, such points as these can be and commonly are made against duty-based theories on behalf of goal-based ones. When duties have been eliminated from the contest, is there anything to be said for rights as against goals?

A central embarrassment for the best-known goal-based theories, the various forms of utilitarianism, is that they not merely allow but positively require, in certain circumstances, that the well-being of one individual should be sacrificed, without limits, for the well-being of others. It is not that these theories are collectivist in principle; it is not that the claims of individual welfare are overridden by those of some unitary communal welfare. They can and usually do take utility to be purely a resultant of individual satisfactions and frustrations. It is, quite literally, to other individuals that they allow one individual to be sacrificed. If some procedure produces a greater sum of happiness made up of the enjoyments experienced separately by B and C and D and so on than the happiness that this procedure takes away from A—or a sum greater than that needed to balance the misery that this procedure imposes on A—then, at least on a simple utilitarian view, that procedure is to be followed. And of course this holds whether the quantity to be maximized is total or average utility.

I have called this an embarrassment for utilitarianism, and it is no more than this. There are at least three well known possible reactions to it. The tough-minded act utilitarian simply accepts this consequence of his principles, and is prepared to dismiss any contrary "intuitions." Indirect utilitarianism, of which rule utilitarianism is only one variety, distinguishes two levels of moral thinking.[6] At the level of ordinary practical day-to-day thinking, actions and choices are to be guided by rules, principles, dispositions (virtues), and so on, which will indeed protect the welfare of each individual against the claims of the greater happiness of others: rights, in fact, will be recognized at this level. But at a higher level of critical or philosophical thinking these various provisions are to be called in question, tested, explained, justified, amended, or rejected by considering how well practical thinking that is guided by them is likely to promote the general happiness. Such intermediate devices, interposed between practical choices and the utilitarian goal, may for various reasons do more for that goal than the direct application of utility calculations to everyday choices. But in this goal itself, the general happiness which constitutes the ultimate moral aim and the final test in critical moral thought, the well-being of all individuals is simply aggregated, and the happiness of some can indeed compensate for the misery (even the undeserved misery) of others. This, then, is the second possible reaction. The third says that the difficulty or embarrassment results, not because utilitarianism is a goal-based theory, but because it is a purely aggregative one, and that what is required is the addition to it of a distributive principle that prescribes fairness in the distribution of happiness. It is not fair to sacrifice one individual to others.

Of these three reactions, the first would be attractive only if there were some strong *prima facie* case for adopting a simple utilitarian morality; but there is not.[7] The indirect view also has to assume that there are good general grounds for taking a sheer aggregate of happiness as the ultimate moral aim. But its great difficulty lies in maintaining the two levels of thinking while keeping them insulated from one another. There is, I admit, no difficulty in distinguishing them. The problem is rather the practical difficulty, for someone who is for part of the time a critical moral philosopher in this utilitarian style, to keep this from infecting his everyday moral thought and conduct. It cannot be easy for him to retain practical dispositions of honesty, justice, and loyalty if in his heart of hearts he feels that these don't really matter, and sees them merely as devices to compensate for the inability of everyone, himself included, to calculate reliably and without bias in terms of aggregate utility. And a thinker who does achieve this is still exposed to the converse danger that his practical morality may weaken his critical thinking. He will be tempted to believe that the virtues built into his own character, the principles to which he automatically appeals in practice, are the very ones that will best promote the general happiness, not because he has reached this conclusion by cogent reasoning, but just because this belief reconciles his theory with his practice. He may come to cultivate a quite artificial distrust of his own ability to work out the consequences of actions for the general happiness. And what happens if the two levels cannot be kept apart? If the critical thinkers let their higher level thinking modify their own day-to-day conduct, the division will cease to be between two levels of thinking for at least some people, and become a division between two classes of people, those who follow a practical morality devised for them by others, and those who devise this but themselves follow a different, more directly utilitarian, morality. If, alternatively, the critical thinkers let their practical morality dominate their criticism, there can indeed be the same moral system for everyone, but it will have ceased to be a goal-based one. The derivation of the working principles from utility will have become a mere rationalization. Altogether, then, indirect utilitarianism is a rather unhappy compromise. And it is inadequately motivated. Why should it not be a *fundamental* moral principle that the well-being of one person cannot be simply replaced by that of another? There is no cogent proof of purely aggregative consequentialism at any level.[8]

Is the remedy, then, to add a distributive principle? This is still not quite what we need. If one individual is sacrificed for advantages accruing to others, what is deplorable is the ill-treatment of this individual, the invasion of his rights, rather than the relational matter of the unfairness of his treatment in comparison with others. Again, how are we to understand fairness itself? Within a purely goal-based theory it would have to be taken as an end or good, presumably a collective good, a feature of multiperson distributions which it is good to have in a group, or perhaps good for the group, though not good for any one member. And this would be rather mysterious. Further, within a goal-based theory it would be natural to take fairness, if it were recognized, as one additional constituent of utility, and then, unless it were given an infinite utility value, it in turn could be outweighed by a sufficient aggregate of individual satisfactions. There could still be a moral case for sacrificing not only A's welfare but also fairness along with it to the greater utility summed up in the welfare of B and C and so on.

Fairness as a distributive principle, added to an otherwise aggregative theory, would prescribe some distribution of utility. But what distribution? Presumably an equal one would be the ideal, to which distributions in practice would be expected to approximate as closely as was reasonably possible. But though extreme inequalities of satisfaction are deplorable, it is not clear that simple equality of satisfaction is the ideal. We surely want to leave it open to people to make what they can of their lives. But then it is inevitable that some will do better for themselves than others. This same point can be made about groups rather than individuals. Consider a society containing two groups, A and B, where the members of each group are in contact mainly with co-members of their own group. Suppose that the members of A are more cooperative, less quarrelsome, and so more successful in coordinating various activities than the members of B. Then the members of A are likely to do better, achieve more satisfaction, than the members of B. And why shouldn't they? Would there be any good reason for requiring an equal distribution of welfare in such circumstances? There is, of course, no need to adopt the extravagances and the myths of sturdy individualism, above all no ground for supposing that all actual inequalities of satisfaction result from some kind of merit and are therefore justified. All I am suggesting is that inequalities may be justified, and in particular that we should think of protecting each individual in an opportunity to do things rather than of distributing satisfactions.

Perhaps when fairness is added to an otherwise goal-based theory it should be thought of as a duty-based element. But then the arguments against duty-based systems apply to this element. What merit has even the duty to be fair for its own sake? It would be easier to endorse something like fairness as a right-based element, giving us a partly goal-based and partly right-based system.

But even this is not enough. A plausible goal, or good for man, would have to be something like Aristotle's *eudaimonia*: it would be in the category of activity. It could not be just an end, a possession, a termination of pursuit. The absurdity of taking satisfaction in the sense in which it is such a termination as the moral goal is brought out by the science-fictional pleasure machine described by Smart.[9] But Aristotle went wrong in thinking that moral philosophy could determine that a particular sort of activity constitutes the good for man in general, and is objectively and intrinsically the best way of life. People differ radically about the kinds of life that they choose to pursue. Even this way of putting it is misleading: in general people do not and cannot make an overall choice of a total plan of life. They choose successively to pursue various activities from time to time, not once and for all. And while there is room for other sorts of evaluation of human activities, morality as a source of constraints on conduct cannot be based on such comparative evaluations.[10] I suggest that if we set out to formulate a goal-based moral theory, but in identifying the goal to try to take adequate account of these three factors, namely that the "goal" must belong to the category of activity, that there is not one goal but indefinitely many diverse goals, and that they are the objects of progressive (not once-for-all or conclusive) choices, then our theory will change insensibly into a right-based one. We shall have to take as central the right of persons progressively to choose how they shall live.

This suggestion is dramatically illustrated by some of the writings of the best known of utilitarian moralists, John Stuart Mill. When he reiterates, in *On Liberty*, that he regards utility "as the ultimate appeal on all ethical questions," he hastens to add that "it must be utility in the largest sense, grounded on the permanent interests of a man as a progressive being." Not, as it is sometimes misquoted, "of man as a progressive being": that would imply a collectivist view, but here the stress is on the claims of each individual. "These interests, I contend, authorize the subjection of individual spontaneity to external control, only in respect to those actions of each, which concern the interest of other people." And the next few lines make it clear that he is thinking not of *any* interests of other people, but particularly of their rights and the defense of their rights. It is at least as plausible to say that the deep theory of *On Liberty* is right-based as that this holds of Rawls's *A Theory of Justice.*[11] The same point emerges from a close examination of the last chapter of *Utilitarianism,* "On the Connection between Justice and Utility." There Mill argues that what is morally required or obligatory is included in but not coextensive with what is expedient or worthy, and that what is just (or rather, what is required for justice) is similarly a proper sub-class of what is obligatory. By "justice" he makes it clear that he means the body of rules which protect rights which "reside in persons." They are "The moral rules which forbid mankind to hurt one another (in which we must never forget to include wrongful interference with each other's freedom)" and "are more vital to human well-being than any maxims, however important, which only point out the best way of managing some department of human affairs." And though he still says that general utility is the reason why society ought to defend me in the possession of these rights, he explains that it is an "extraordinarily important and impressive kind of utility which is concerned." "Our notion, therefore, of the claim we have on our fellow-creatures to join in making safe for us the very groundwork of our existence, gathers feelings around it so much more intense than those concerned in any of the more common cases of utility, that the difference in degree . . . becomes a real difference in kind." In such passages as these we can see Mill, while still working within the framework of a goal-based theory, moving toward a right-based treatment of at least the central part of morality.

When we think it out, therefore, we see that not only can there be a right-based moral theory, there cannot be an acceptable moral theory that is not right-based. Also, in learning why this approach is superior to those based either on duties or on goals, we have at least roughly identified what we may take as the fundamental right. If we assume that, from the point of view of the morality we are constructing, what matters in human life is activity, but diverse activities determined by successive choices, we shall, as I have said, take as central the right of persons progressively to choose how they shall live. But this is only a rough specification, and at once raises problems. Who is to have this right? Let us make what is admittedly a further decision and say that all persons are to have it, and all equally. It is true that this leaves in a twilight zone sentient and even human beings that are not and never will be persons; let us simply admit that there are problems here, but postpone them to another occasion.[12] Other problems are more pressing. The rights we have assigned to all persons will in practice come into conflict with one another. One person's choice of how to live will constantly be interfering with the choices of others. We have come close to Jefferson's formulation of fundamental rights to life, liberty, and the pursuit of happiness. But one person's pursuit of happiness will obstruct another's, and diverse liberties, and even the similar liberties of different people, are notoriously incompatible. Liberty is an all-purpose slogan: in all wars and all revolutions both sides have been fighting for freedom. This means that the rights we have called fundamental can be no more than *prima face* rights: the rights that in the end people have, their final rights, must result from compromises between their initially conflicting rights. These compromises will have to be worked out in practice, but will be morally defensible only insofar as they reflect the equality of the *prima facie* rights. This will not allow the vital interests of any to be sacrificed for the advantage of others, to be outweighed by an aggregate of less vital interests. Rather we might think in terms of a model in which each person is represented by a point-center of force, and the forces (representing *prima facie* rights) obey an inverse square law, so that a right decreases in weight with the remoteness of the matter on which it bears from the person whose right it is. There will be some matters so close to each person that, with respect to them, his rights will nearly always outweigh any aggregate of other rights, though admittedly it will sometimes happen that issues arise in which the equally vital interests of two or more people clash. . . .

Any right-based moral or political theory has to face the issue whether the rights it endorses are "natural" or "human" rights, universally valid and determinable *a priori* by some kind of reason, or are historically determined in and by the concrete institutions of a particular society, to be found out by analysis of its actual laws and practices. However, the view I am suggesting straddles this division. The fundamental right is put forward as universal. On the other hand I am not claiming that it is objectively valid, or that its validity can be found out by reason: I am merely adopting it and recommending it for general adoption as a moral principle. Also, I have argued that this fundamental right has to be formulated only as a *prima facie* right. Derived specific rights (which can be final, not merely *prima facie*) will be historically determined and contingent upon concrete circumstances and upon the interplay of the actual interests and preferences that people have. But the fact that something is an institutional right, recognized and defended by the laws and practices of a particular society, does not necessarily establish it as a moral right. It can be criticized from the moral point of view by considering how far the social interactions which have generated and maintain this institutional right express the fundamental right of persons progressively to choose how they shall live, interpreted along the lines of our model of centers of force, and to what extent they violate it. Our theory could have conservative implications in some contexts, but equally it could have reforming or revolutionary implications in others.

It may be asked whether this theory is individualist, perhaps too individualist. It is indeed individualist in that individual persons are the primary bearers of rights, and the sole bearers of fundamental rights, and one of its chief merits is that, unlike aggregate goal-based theories, it offers a persistent defense of some interests of each individual. It is, however, in no way committed to seeing individuals as spontaneous originators of their thoughts and desires. It can recognize that the inheritance of cultural traditions and being caught up in movements help to make each individual what he is, and that even the most independent individuals constitute their distinctive characters not by isolating themselves or by making "existential" choices but by working with and through inherited traditions. Nor need it be opposed to cooperation or collective action. I believe that Rousseau's description of a community with a general will, general "both in its object and in its essence," that is, bearing in its expression upon all members alike and located in every member of the community, provides a model of a conceivable form of association, and there is nothing in our theory that would be hostile to such genuine cooperation. But I do not believe that there could actually be a community with a genuine, not fictitious, general will of this sort of the size of an independent political unit, a sovereign state. The fundamental individual rights could, however, be expressed in joint activity or communal life on a smaller scale, and organizations of all sorts can have derived, though not fundamental, moral rights. Our theory, therefore, is not anti-collectivist; but it will discriminate among collectivities, between those which express and realize the rights of their members and those which sacrifice some or even most of their members to a supposed collective interest, or to the real interest of some members, or even to some maximized aggregate of interests.

I hope I have not given the impression that I think it an easy matter to resolve conflicts of rights and to determine, in concrete cases, what the implications of our theory will be. What I have offered is not an algorithm or decision procedure, but only, as I said, a model, an indication of a framework of ideas within which the discussion of actual specific issues might go on. And in general this paper is no more than a tentative initial sketch of a right-based moral theory. I hope that others will think it worth further investigation.

NOTES

1. R. Dworkin, *Taking Rights Seriously* (London, 1977), ch. 6 "Justice and Rights," esp. 171–172. This chapter appeared first as an article, "The Original Position," *University of Chicago Law Review* 40 (1973), reprinted as ch. 2 in N. Daniels, ed., *Reading Rawls* (Oxford, 1975).

2. R. Nozick, *Anarchy, State and Utopia* (New York and Oxford, 1974).

3. J. S. Mill, *Utilitarianism,* ch. 5.

4. I. Kant, *Groundwork of the Metaphysic of Morals,* sect. 2.

5. This is argued at length in ch. 1 of my *Ethics, Inventing Right and Wrong* (Harmondsworth, 1977).

6. For example, R. M. Hare, "Ethical Theory and Utilitarianism," in *Contemporary British Philosophy—Personal Statements,* ed. H. D. Lewis (London, 1976).

7. I have tried to show this in ch. 6 of *Ethics, Inventing Right and Wrong,* appealing to radical weaknesses in anything like Mill's proof of utility.

8. The discussion referred to in note 7 applies here also.

9. J. J. C. Smart and B. Williams, *Utilitarianism, For and Against* (Cambridge, 1973), 18–21.

10. I am speaking here of what I call morality in the narrow sense in *Ethics, Inventing Right and Wrong,* ch. 5.

11. Dworkin makes this point, at least implicitly, in ch. 11, "Liberty and Liberalism," of *Taking Rights Seriously.*

12. I have touched on it in ch. 8, sect. 8, of *Ethics, Inventing Right and Wrong.*

David Gauthier

Morals By Agreement

1.   What theory of morals can ever serve any useful purpose, unless it can show that all the duties it recommends are also the true interest of each individual?[1] David Hume, who asked this question, seems mistaken; such a theory would be too useful. Were duty no more than interest, morals would be superfluous. Why appeal to right or wrong, to good or evil, to obligation or to duty, if instead we may appeal to desire or aversion, to benefit or cost, to interest or to advantage? An appeal to morals takes its point from the failure of these latter considerations as sufficient guides to what we ought to do. . . . We may lament duty's stern visage but we may not deny it. For it is only as we believe that some appeals do, alas, override interest or advantage that morality becomes our concern.

But if the language of morals is not that of interest, it is surely that of reason. What theory of morals, we might better ask, can ever serve any useful purpose, unless it can show that all the duties it recommends are also truly endorsed in each individual's reason? If moral appeals are entitled to some practical effect, some influence on our behavior, it is not because they whisper invitingly to our desires, but because they convince our intellect. Suppose we should find, as Hume himself believes, that reason is impotent in the sphere of action apart from its role in deciding matters of fact?[2] Or suppose we should find that reason is no more than the handmaiden of interest, so that in overriding advantage a moral appeal must also contradict reason. In either case we should conclude that the moral enterprise, as traditionally conceived, is impossible.

To say that our moral language assumes a connection with reason is not to argue for the rationality of our moral views, or of any alternative to them. Moral language may rest on a false assumption.[3] If moral duties are rationally grounded, then the emotivists, who suppose that moral appeals are no more than persuasive, and the egoists, who suppose that rational appeals are limited by self-interest, are mistaken.[4]   But are moral duties rationally grounded? This we shall seek to prove, showing that reason has a practical role related to but transcending individual interest, so that principles of action that prescribe duties overriding advantage may be rationally justified. We shall defend the traditional conception of morality as a rational constraint on the pursuit of individual interest.

Yet Hume's mistake in insisting that moral duties must be the true interest of each individual conceals a fundamental insight. Practical reason is linked to interest, or, as we shall come to say, to individual utility, and rational constraints on the pursuit of interest have themselves a foundation in the interest they constrain. Duty overrides advantage, but the acceptance of duty is truly advantageous. We shall find this seeming paradox embedded in the very structure of interaction. As

From David Gauthier, *Morals by Agreement* (Oxford: Oxford University Press, 1986). Reprinted by permission of Oxford University Press. Copyright © 1986 by David Gauthier.

we come to understand this structure, we shall recognize the need for restraining each person's pursuit of her own utility, and we shall examine its implications for both our principles of action and our conception of practical rationality. Our inquiry will lead us to the rational basis for a morality, not of absolute standards, but of agreed constraints. . . .

2.2 Rational choice provides an exemplar of normative theory. One might suppose that moral theory and choice theory are related only in possessing similar structures. But as we have said, we shall develop moral theory as part of choice theory. Those acquainted with recent work in moral philosophy may find this a familiar enterprise; John Rawls has insisted that the theory of justice is "perhaps the most significant part, of the theory of rational choice," and John Harsanyi explicitly treats ethics as part of the theory of rational behavior.[5] But these claims are stronger than their results warrant. Neither Rawls nor Harsanyi develops the deep connection between morals and rational choice that we shall defend. A brief comparison will bring our enterprise into sharper focus.

Our claim is that in certain situations involving interaction with others, an individual chooses rationally only in so far as he constrains his pursuit of his own interest or advantage to conform to principles expressing the impartiality character-istic of morality. To choose rationally, one must choose morally. This is a strong claim. Morality, we shall argue, can be generated as a rational constraint from the non-moral premises of rational choice. Neither Rawls nor Harsanyi makes such a claim. Neither Rawls nor Harsanyi treats moral principles as a subset of rational principles for choice.

Rawls argues that the principles of justice are the objects of a rational choice— the choice that any person would make, were he called upon to select the basic principles of his society from behind a "veil of ignorance" concealing any knowledge of his own identity.[6] The principles so chosen are not directly related to the making of individual choices.[7] Derivatively, acceptance of them must have implications for individual behavior, but Rawls never claims that these include rational constraints on individual choices. They may be, in Rawls's terminology, reasonable constraints, but what is reasonable is itself a morally substantive matter beyond the bounds of rational choice.[8]

Rawls's idea, that principles of justice are the objects of a rational choice, is indeed one that we shall incorporate into our own theory, although we shall represent the choice as a bargain, or agreement, among persons who need not be unaware of their identities. But this parallel between our theory and Rawls's must not obscure the basic difference; we claim to generate morality as a set of rational principles for choice. We are committed to showing why an individual, reasoning from non-moral premises, would accept the constraints of morality on his choices.

Harsanyi's theory may seem to differ from Rawls's only in its account of the principles that a person would choose from behind a veil of ignorance; Rawls supposes that persons would choose the well-known two principles of justice, whereas Harsanyi supposes that persons would choose principles of average rule-utilitarianism.[9] But Harsanyi's argument is in some respects closer to our own; he is concerned with principles for moral choice, and with the rational way of arriving at such principles. However, Harsanyi's principles are strictly hypothetical; they govern rational choice from an impartial standpoint or given impartial preferences, and so they are principles only for someone who wants to choose morally or impartially.[10] But Harsanyi does not claim, as we do, that there are situations in which an individual must choose morally in order to choose rationally. For Harsanyi there is a rational way of choosing morally but no rational requirement to choose morally. And so again there is a basic difference between our theory and his.

Putting now to one side the views of Rawls and Harsanyi . . . we may summarize the import of the differences we have sketched. Our theory must generate, strictly as rational principles for choice, and so without introducing prior moral assumptions, constraints on the pursuit of individual interest or advantage that, being impartial, satisfy the traditional understanding of morality. We do not assume that there must be such impartial and rational constraints. We do not even assume that there must be rational constraints, whether impartial or not. We claim to demonstrate that there are rational constraints, and that these constraints are impartial. We then identify morality with these demonstrated constraints, but whether their content corresponds to that of conventional moral principles is a further question, which we shall not examine in detail. No doubt there will be differences, perhaps significant, between the impartial and rational constraints supported by our argument, and the morality learned from parents and peers, priests and teachers. But our concern is to validate the conception of morality as a set of rational, impartial constraints on the pursuit of individual interest, not to defend any particular moral code. And our concern, once again, is to do this without incorporating into the premises of our argument any of the moral conceptions that emerge in our conclusions.

2.3 To seek to establish the rationality of moral constraints is not in itself a novel enterprise, and its antecedents are more venerable than the endeavor to develop moral theory as part of the theory of rational choice. But those who have engaged in it have typically appealed to a conception of practical rationality, deriving from Kant, quite different from ours.[11] In effect, their understanding of reason already includes the dimension of impartiality that we seek to generate.

Let us suppose it agreed that there is a connection between reason and interest —or advantage, benefit, preference, satisfaction, or individual utility, since the differences among these, important in other contexts, do not affect the present discussion. Let it further be agreed that in so far as the interests of others are not affected, a person acts rationally if and only if she seeks her greatest interest or benefit. This might be denied by some, but we wish here to isolate the essential difference between the opposed conceptions of practical rationality. And this appears when we consider rational action in which the interests of others are involved. Proponents of the *maximizing* conception of rationality, which we endorse, insist that essentially nothing is changed; the rational person still seeks the greatest satisfaction of her own interests. On the other hand, proponents of what we shall call the *universalistic* conception of rationality insist that what makes it rational to satisfy an interest does not depend on whose interest it is. Thus the rational person seeks to satisfy all interests. Whether she is a utilitarian, aiming at the greatest happiness of the greatest number, or whether she takes into independent consideration the fair distribution of benefit among persons, is of no importance to the present discussion.

To avoid possible misunderstandings, note that neither conception of rationality requires that practical reasons be self-interested. On the maximizing conception it is not interests in the self, that take oneself as object, but interests of the self, held by oneself as subject, that provide the basis for rational choice and action. On the universalistic conception it is not interests in anyone, that take any person as object, but interests of anyone, held by some person as subject, that provide the basis for rational choice and action. If I have a direct interest in your welfare, then on either conception I have reason to promote your welfare. But your interest in your welfare affords me such reason only given the universalistic conception.

Morality, we have insisted, is traditionally understood to involve an impartial constraint on the pursuit of individual interest. The justification of such a constraint poses no problem to the proponents of universalistic rationality. The rational requirement that all interests be satisfied to the fullest extent possible directly constrains each person in the pursuit of her own interests. The precise formulation of the constraint will of course depend on the way in which interests are to be satisfied, but the basic rationale is sufficiently clear.

The main task of our moral theory—the generation of moral constraints as rational—is thus easily accomplished by proponents of the universalistic conception of practical reason. For them the relation between reason and morals is clear. Their task is to defend their conception of rationality, since the maximizing and universalistic conceptions do not rest on equal footings. The maximizing conception possesses the virtue, among conceptions, of weakness. Any consideration affording one a reason for acting on the maximizing conception, also affords one such a reason on the universalistic conception. But the converse does not hold. On the universalistic conception all persons have in effect the same basis for rational choice—the interests of all—and this assumption, of the impersonality or impartiality of reason, demands defense....

In developing moral theory within rational choice we thus embrace the weaker and more widely accepted of the two conceptions of rationality that we have distinguished. Of course, we must not suppose that the moral principles we generate will be identical with those that would be derived on the universalistic conception. Its proponents may insist that their account of the connection between reason and morals is correct, even if they come to agree that a form of morality may be grounded in maximizing rationality. But we may suggest, without here defending our suggestion, that few persons would embrace the universalistic conception of practical reason did they not think it necessary to the defense of any form of rational morality. Hence the most effective rebuttal of their position may be not to seek to undermine their elaborate and ingenious arguments, but to construct an alternative account of a rational morality grounded in the weaker assumptions of the theory of rational choice.

3.1 Morals by agreement begin from an initial presumption against morality, as a constraint on each person's pursuit of his own interest. A person is conceived as an independent center of activity, endeavoring to direct his capacities and resources to the fulfillment of his interests. He considers what he can do, but initially draws no distinction between what he may and may not do. How then does he come to acknowledge the distinction? How does a person come to recognize a moral dimension to choice, if morality is not initially present?

Morals by agreement offer a contractarian rationale for distinguishing what one may and may not do. Moral principles are introduced as the objects of fully voluntary *ex ante* agreement among rational persons. Such agreement is hypothetical, in supposing a pre-moral context for the adoption of moral rules and practices. But the parties to agreement are real, determinate individuals, distinguished by their capacities, situations, and concerns. In so far as they would agree to constraints on their choices, restraining their pursuit of their own interests, they acknowledge a distinction between what they may and may not do. As rational persons understanding the structure of their interaction, they recognize a place for mutual constraint, and so for a moral dimension in their affairs.

That there is a contractarian rationale for morality must of course be shown. That is the task of our theory. Here our immediate concern is to relate the idea of such a rationale to the introduction of fundamental moral distinctions. This is not a magical process. Morality does not emerge as the rabbit from the empty hat. Rather, as we shall argue, it emerges quite simply from the application of the maximizing conception of rationality to certain structures of interaction. Agreed mutual constraint is the rational response to these structures. Reason overrides the presumption against morality.

The genuinely problematic element in a contractarian theory is not the introduction of the idea of morality, but the step from hypothetical agreement to actual moral constraint. Suppose that each person recognizes himself as one of the parties to agreement. The principles forming the object of agreement are those that he would have accepted *ex ante* in bargaining with his fellows, had he found himself among them in a context initially devoid of moral constraint. Why need he accept, *ex post* in his actual situation, these principles as constraining his choices? A theory of morals by agreement must answer this question. . . .

To the conceptual underpinning that may be found in Hobbes, . . . we seek to add the rigor of rational choice. . . . [T]he appeal to rational choice enables us to state, with new clarity and precision, why rational persons would agree *ex ante* to constraining principles, what general characteristics these principles must have as objects of rational agreement, and why rational persons would comply *ex post* with the agreed constraints.

3.2   A useful vantage point for appreciating the rationale of constraint results from juxtaposing two ideas formulated by John Rawls. A contractarian views society as "a cooperative venture for mutual advantage" among persons "conceived as not taking an interest in one another's interests."[12] The contractarian does not claim that all actual societies are cooperative ventures; he need not claim that all afford the expectation of mutual advantage. Rather, he supposes that it is in general possible for a society, analyzed as a set of institutions, practices, and relationships, to afford each person greater benefit than she could expect in a non-social "state of nature," and that only such a society could command the willing allegiance of every rational individual. The contractarian need not claim that actual persons take no interest in their fellows; indeed, we suppose that some degree of sociability is characteristic of human beings. But the contractarian sees sociability as enriching human life; for him, it becomes a source of exploitation if it induces persons to acquiesce in institutions and practices that but for their fellow-feelings would be costly to them. Feminist thought has surely made this, perhaps the core form of human exploitation, clear to us. Thus the contractarian insists that a society could not command the willing allegiance of a rational person if, without appealing to her feelings for others, it afforded her no expectation of net benefit.

If social institutions and practices can benefit all, then some set of social arrangements should be acceptable to all as a cooperative venture. Each person's concern to fulfill her own interests should ensure her willingness to join her fellows in a venture assuring her an expectation of increased fulfillment. She may of course reject some proposed venture as insufficiently advantageous to her when she considers both the distribution of benefits that it affords, and the availability of alternatives. Affording mutual advantage is a necessary condition for the acceptability of a set of social arrangements as a cooperative venture, not a sufficient condition. But we suppose that some set affording mutual advantage will also be mutually acceptable; a contractarian theory must set out conditions for sufficiency.

The rationale for agreement on society as a cooperative venture may seem unproblematic. The step from hypothetical agreement *ex ante* on a set of social arrangements to *ex post* adherence to those arrangements may seem straightforward. If one would willingly have joined the venture, why would one now continue with it? Why is there need for constraint?

The institutions and practices of society play a coordinative role. Let us say, without attempting a precise definition, that a practice is coordinative if each person prefers to conform to it provided (most) others do, but prefers not to conform to it provided (most) others do not.[13] And let us say that a practice is beneficially coordinative if each person prefers that others conform to it rather than conform to no practice, and does not (strongly) prefer that others conform to some alternative practice. Hume's example, of two persons rowing a boat that neither can row alone, is a very simple example of a beneficially coordinative practice.[14] Each prefers to row if the other rows, and not to row if the other does not. And each prefers the other to row than to act in some alternative way.

It is worth noting that a coordinative practice need not be beneficial. Among peaceable persons, who regard weapons only as instruments of defense, each may prefer to be armed provided (most) others are, and not armed provided (most) others are not. Being armed is a coordinative practice but not a beneficial one; each prefers others not to be armed.

The coordinative advantages of society are not to be underestimated. But not all beneficial social practices are coordinative. Let us say that a practice is beneficial if each person prefers that (almost) everyone conform to it rather than that (most) persons conform to no practice, and does not (strongly) prefer that (almost) everyone conform to some alternative practice. Yet it may be the case that each person prefers not to conform to the practice if (most) others do. In a community in which tax funds are spent reasonably wisely, each person may prefer that almost everyone pay taxes rather than not, and yet may prefer not to pay taxes herself whatever others do. For the payments each person makes contribute negligibly to the benefits she receives. In such a community persons will pay taxes voluntarily only if each accepts some constraint on her pursuit of individual interest; otherwise, each will pay taxes only if coerced, whether by public opinion or by public authority.

The rationale for agreement on society as a cooperative venture may still seem unproblematic. But the step from hypothetical agreement *ex ante* on a set of social arrangements to *ex post* adherence may no longer seem straightforward. We see why one might willingly join the venture, yet not willingly continue with it. Each joins in the hope of benefiting from the adherence of others, but fails to adhere in the hope of benefiting from her own defection. . . .

3.3   Although a successful contractarian theory defeats the presumption against morality arising from its conception of rational, independent individuals, yet it should take the presumption seriously. The first conception central to our theory is therefore that of a morally free zone, a context within which the constraints of morality would have no place. The free zone proves to be that habitat familiar to economists, the perfectly competitive market. Such a market is of course an idealization; how far it can be realized in human society is an empirical question beyond the scope of our inquiry. Our argument is that in a perfectly competitive market, mutual advantage is assured by the unconstrained activity of each individual in pursuit of her own greatest satisfaction, so that there is no place, rationally, for constraint. Futhermore, since in the market each person enjoys the same freedom in her choices and actions that she would have in isolation from her fellows, and since the market outcome reflects the exercise of each person's freedom, there is no basis for finding any partiality in the market's operations. Thus there is also no place, morally, for constraint. The market exemplifies an ideal of interaction among persons who, taking no interest in each other's interests, need only follow the dictates of their own individual interests to participate effectively in a venture for mutual advantage. We do not speak of a *cooperative* venture, reserving that label for enterprises that lack the natural harmony of each with all assured by the structure of market interaction.

The perfectly competitive market is thus a foil against which morality appears more clearly. Were the world such a market, morals would be unneccessary. But this is not to denigrate the value of morality, which makes possible an artificial harmony where natural harmony is not to be had. Market and morals share the non-coercive reconciliation of individual interest with mutual benefit.

Where mutual benefit requires individual constraint, this reconciliation is achieved through rational agreement. As we have noted, a necessary condition of such agreement is that its outcome be mutually advantageous; our task is to provide a sufficient condition. This problem is addressed in a part of the theory of games, the theory of rational bargaining, and divides into two issues. The first is the bargaining problem proper, which in its general form is to select a specific outcome, given a range of mutually advantageous possibilities, and an initial bargaining position. The second is then to determine the initial bargaining position. Treatment of these issues has yet to reach consensus, so that we shall develop our own theory of bargaining.

Solving the bargaining problem yields a principle that governs both the process and the content of rational agreement. We . . . introduce a measure of each person's stake in a bargain—the difference between the least he might accept in place of no agreement, and the most he might receive in place of being excluded by others from agreement. And we . . . argue that the equal rationality of the bargainers leads to the requirement that the greatest concession, measured as a proportion of the conceder's stake, be as small as possible. We formulate this as the principle of minimax relative concession. And this is equivalent to the requirement that the least relative benefit, measured again as a proportion of one's stake, be as great as possible. So we formulate an equivalent principle of maximin relative benefit, which we claim captures the ideas of fairness and impartiality in a bargaining situation, and so serves as the basis of justice. Minimax relative concession, or maximin relative benefit, is thus the second conception central to our theory.

If society is to be a cooperative venture for mutual advantage, then its institutions and practices must satisfy, or nearly satisfy, this principle. For if our theory of bargaining is correct, then minimax relative concession governs the *ex ante* agreement that underlies a fair and rational cooperative venture. But in so far as the social arrangements constrain our actual *ex post* choices, the question of compliance demands attention. Let it be ever so rational to agree to practices that ensure maximin relative benefit; yet is it not also rational to ignore these practices should it serve one's interest to do so? Is it rational to internalize moral principles in one's choices, or only to acquiesce in them in so far as one's interests are held in check by external, coercive constraints? The weakness of traditional contractarian theory has been its inability to show the rationality of compliance.

Here we introduce the third conception central to our theory, constrained maximization. We distinguish the person who is disposed straightforwardly to maximize her satisfaction, or fulfill her interest, in the particular choices she makes, from the person who is disposed to comply with mutually advantageous moral constraints, provided he expects similar compliance from others. The latter is a constrained maximizer. And constrained maximizers, interacting one with another, enjoy opportunities for cooperation which others lack. Of course, constrained maximizers sometimes lose by being disposed to compliance, for they may act cooperatively in the mistaken expectation of reciprocity from others who instead benefit at their expense. Nevertheless, . . . under plausible conditions, the net advantage that constrained maximizers reap from cooperation exceeds the exploitative benefits that others may expect. From this we conclude that it is rational to be disposed to constrain maximizing behavior by internalizing moral principles to govern one's choices. The contractarian is able to show that it is irrational to admit appeals to interest against compliance with those duties founded on mutual advantage.

But compliance is rationally grounded only within the framework of a fully cooperative venture, in which each participant willingly interacts with her fellows. And this leads us back to the second issue addressed in bargaining theory—the initial bargaining position. If persons are willingly to comply with the agreement that determines what each takes from the bargaining table, then they must find initially acceptable what each brings to the table. And if what some bring to the table includes the fruits of prior interaction forced on their fellows, then this initial acceptability will be lacking. If you seize the products of my labor and then say "Let's make a deal," I may be compelled to accept, but I will not voluntarily comply.

We are therefore led to constrain the initial bargaining position, through a proviso that prohibits bettering one's position through interaction worsening the position of another. No person should be worse off in the initial bargaining position than she would be in a non-social context of no interaction. The proviso thus constrains the base from which each person's stake in agreement, and so her relative concession and benefit, are measured. . . .

The proviso is the fourth of the core conceptions of our theory. Although a part of morals by agreement, it is not the product of rational agreement. Rather, it is a condition that must be accepted by each person for such agreement to be possible. Among beings, however rational, who may not hope to engage one another in a cooperative venture for mutual advantage, the proviso would have no force. Our theory denies any place to rational constraint, and so to morality, outside the context of mutual benefit. A contractarian account of morals has no place for duties that are strictly redistributive in their effects, transferring but not increasing benefits, or duties that do not assume reciprocity from other persons. Such duties would be neither rationally based, nor supported by considerations of impartiality. . . .

4 A contractarian theory of morals, developed as part of the theory of rational choice, has evident strengths. It enables us to demonstrate the rationality of impartial constraints on the pursuit of individual interest to persons who may take no interest in others' interests. Morality is thus given a sure grounding in a weak and widely accepted conception of practical rationality. No alternative account of morality accomplishes this. Those who claim that moral principles are objects of rational choice in special circumstances fail to establish the rationality of actual compliance with these principles. Those who claim to establish the rationality of such compliance appeal to a strong and controversial conception of reason that seems to incorporate prior moral suppositions. No alternative account generates morals, as a rational constraint on choice and action, from a non-moral, or morally neutral, base.

But the strengths of a contractarian theory may seem to be accompanied by grave weaknesses. We have already noted that for a contractarian, morality requires a context of mutual benefit. John Locke held that "an Hobbist . . . will not easily admit a great many plain duties of morality." And this may seem equally to apply to the Hobbist's modern-day successor. Our theory does not assume any fundamental concern with impartiality, but only a concern derivative from the benefits of agreement, and those benefits are determined by the effects that each person can have on the interests of her fellows. Only beings whose physical and mental capacities are either roughly equal or mutually complementary can expect to find cooperation beneficial to all. Humans benefit from their interaction with horses, but they do not cooperate with horses and may not benefit them. Among unequals, one party may benefit most by coercing the other, and on our theory would have no reason to refrain. We may condemn all coercive relationships, but only within the context of mutual benefit can our condemnation appeal to a rationally grounded morality.

Cooperation may then seem a second-best form of interaction, not because it runs counter to our desires, but because each person would prefer a natural harmony in which she could fulfill herself without constraint. But a natural harmony could exist only if our preferences and capabilities dovetailed in ways that would preclude their free development. Natural harmony would require a higher level of artifice, a shaping of our natures in ways that, at least until genetic engineering is perfected, are not possible, and were they possible, would surely not be desirable. If human individuality is to bloom, then we must expect some degree of conflict among the aims and interests of persons rather than natural harmony. Market and morals tame this conflict, reconciling individuality with mutual benefit. . . .

. . . We seek to forge a link between the rationality of individual maximization and the morality of impartial constraint. Suppose that we have indeed found such a link. How shall we interpret this finding? Are our conceptions of rationality and morality, and so of the contractarian link between them, as we should like them to be, fixed points in the development of the conceptual framework that enables us to formulate permanent practical truths? Or are we contributing to the history of ideas of a particular society, in which peculiar circumstances have fostered an ideology of individuality and interaction that coheres with morals by agreement? Are we telling a story about ideas that will seem as strange to our descendants, as the Form of the Good and the Unmoved Mover do to us?

NOTES

1. See David Hume, *An Enquiry Concerning the Principles of Morals*, sect. ix, pt. ii, in L.A. Selby-Bigge, ed., *Enquiries Concerning Human Understanding and Concerning the Principles of Morals,* 3rd ed. (Oxford, 1975), 280.

2. See David Hume, *A Treatise of Human Nature*, bk. ii, pt. iii, sect. iii, ed. L.A. Selby-Bigge (Oxford, 1888). 413–18.

3. Thus one might propose an error theory of moral language; for the idea of an error theory, see J. L. Mackie, *Ethics: Inventing Right and Wrong* (Harmondsworth, 1977), ch. 1, esp. 35, 48–9.

4. The idea that moral appeals are persuasive is developed by C. L. Stevenson; see *Ethics and Language* (New Haven, 1944), esp. chs. vi, ix.

5. J. Rawls, *A Theory of Justice* (Cambridge, Mass., 1971), 16; J. Harsanyi, "Morality and the Theory of Rational Behavior," *Social Research*, (Winter 1977) 44, 4:42

6. See Rawls, 12.

7. See ibid., 11; "The principles . . . are to assign basic rights and duties and to determine the division of social benefits." Principles for individuals are distinguished from the principles of justice; see 108.

8. See Rawls's distinction of "the Reasonable" and "the Rational," in "Kantian Constructivism in Moral Theory," *Journal of Philosophy* 77 (1980), 528–30.

9. See Rawls, *A Theory of Justice*, 14–15, and Harsanyi, "Morality and the Theory of Rational Behavior," 44–6, 56–60.

10. See Harsanyi, "Morality and the Theory of Rational Behavior," 62.

11. This conception of practical rationality appears with particular clarity in T. Nagel, *The Possibility of Altruism* (Oxford, 1970), esp. ch. x. It can also be found in the moral theory of R. M. Hare; see *Moral Thinking* (Oxford, 1981), esp. chs. 5 and 6.

12. Rawls, *A Theory of Justice*, 4, 13.

13. The discussion here is related to my characterization of a convention in "David Hume, Contractarian," *Philosophical Review* 88 (1979); 5–8.

14. See Hume, *Treatise*, iii, ii, ii, 490

Alasdair MacIntyre

The Virtues, the Unity of a Human Life, and the Concept of a Tradition

... We thus have at least three very different conceptions of a virtue to confront: a virtue is a quality which enables an individual to discharge his or her social role (Homer); a virtue is a quality which enables an individual to move toward the achievement of the specifically human *telos*, whether natural or supernatural (Aristotle, the New Testament, and Aquinas); a virtue is a quality which has utility in achieving earthly and heavenly success (Franklin). Are we to take these as three different things? Perhaps the moral structures in archaic Greece, in fourth-century Greece, and in eighteenth-century Pennsylvania were so different from each other that we should treat them as embodying quite different concepts, whose difference is initially disguised from us by the historical accident of an inherited vocabulary which misleads us by linguistic resemblance long after conceptual identity and similarity have failed. Our initial question has come back to us with redoubled force. . . .

The question can therefore now be posed directly: are we or are we not able to disentangle from these rival and various claims a unitary core concept of the virtues of which we can give a more compelling account than any of the other accounts so far? I am going to argue that we can in fact discover such a core concept and that it turns out to provide the tradition of which I have written the history with its conceptual unity. It will indeed enable us to distinguish in a clear way those beliefs about the virtues which genuinely belong to the tradition from those which do not. Unsurprisingly perhaps it is a complex concept, different parts of which derive from different stages in the development of the tradition. Thus the concept itself in some sense embodies the history of which it is the outcome.

One of the features of the concept of a virtue which has emerged with some clarity from the argument so far is that it always requires for its application the acceptance for some prior account of certain features of social and moral life in terms of which it has to be defined and explained. So in the Homeric account the concept of a virtue is secondary to that of a *social role*, in Aristotle's account it is secondary to that of *the good life for man* conceived as the *telos* of human action, and in Franklin's much later account it is secondary to that of utility. What is it in the account which I am about to give which provides in a similar way the necessary background against which the concept of a virtue has to be made intelligible? It is in answering this question that the complex, historical, multi-layered character of

From Alasdair MacIntyre, *After Virtue: A Study in Moral Theory* (South Bend: University of Notre Dame Press, 1984). Reprinted by permission of University of Notre Dame Press. Copyright © 1981, 1984 by Alasdair MacIntyre.

the core concept of virtue becomes clear. For there are no less than three stages in the logical development of the concept which have to be identified in order, if the core conception of a virtue is to be understood, and each of these stages has its own conceptual background. The first stage requires a background account of what I shall call a practice, the second an account of what I have already characterized as the narrative order of a single human life, and the third an account a good deal fuller than I have given up to now of what constitutes a moral tradition. Each later stage presupposes the earlier, but not *vice versa*. Each earlier stage is both modified by and reinterpreted in the light of, but also provides an essential constituent of each later stage. The progress in the development of the concept is closely related to, although it does not recapitulate in any straightforward way, the history of the tradition of which it forms the core.

In the Homeric account of the virtues—and in heroic societies more generally—the exercise of a virtue exhibits qualities which are required for sustaining a social role and for exhibiting excellence in some well-marked area of social practice: to excel is to excel at war or in the games, as Achilles does, in sustaining a household, as Penelope does, in giving counsel in the assembly, as Nestor does, in the telling of a tale, as Homer himself does. When Aristotle speaks of excellence in human activity, he sometimes though not always, refers to some well-defined type of human practice: flute-playing, or war, or geometry. I am going to suggest that this notion of a particular type of practice as providing the arena in which the virtues are exhibited and in terms of which they are to receive their primary, if incomplete, definition is crucial to the whole enterprise of identifying a core concept of the virtues. . . .

By a "practice" I am going to mean any coherent and complex form of socially established cooperative human activity through which goods internal to that form of activity are realized in the course of trying to achieve those standards of excellence which are appropriate to, and partially definitive of, that form of activity, with the result that human powers to achieve excellence, and human conceptions of the ends and goods involved, are systematically extended. Tic-tac-toe is not an example of a practice in this sense, nor is throwing a football with skill; but the game of football is, and so is chess. Bricklaying is not a practice; architecture is. Planting turnips is not a practice; farming is. So are the inquiries of physics, chemistry, and biology, and so is the work of the historian, and so are painting and music. In the ancient and medieval worlds the creation and sustaining of human communities—of households, cities, nations—is generally taken to be a practice in the sense in which I have defined it. Thus the range of practices is wide: arts, sciences, games, politics in the Aristotelian sense, the making and sustaining of family life, all fall under the concept. But the question of the precise range of practices is not at this stage of the first importance. Instead let me explain some of the key terms involved in my definition, beginning with the notion of goods internal to a practice.

Consider the example of a highly intelligent seven-year-old child whom I wish to teach to play chess, although the child has no particular desire to learn the game. The child does however have a very strong desire for candy and little chance of obtaining it. I therefore tell the child that if the child will play chess with me once a week I will give the child 50 cents worth of candy; moreover I tell the child that I will always play in such a way that it will be difficult, but not impossible, for the child to win and that, if the child wins, the child will receive an extra 50 cents worth of candy. Thus motivated the child plays and plays to win. Notice however that, so long as it is the candy alone which provides the child with a good reason for playing chess, the child has no reason not to cheat and every reason to cheat, provided he or she can do so successfully. But, so we may hope, there will come a time when the child will find in those goods specific to chess, in the achievement of a certain highly particular kind of analytical skill, strategic imagination and competitive intensity, a new set of reasons, reasons not just for winning on a particular occasion, but for trying to excel in whatever way the game of chess demands. Now if the child cheats, he or she will be defeating not me, but himself or herself.

There are thus two kinds of good possibly to be gained by playing chess. On the one hand there are those goods externally and contingently attached to chess-playing and to other practices by the accidents of social circumstance—in the case of the imaginary child candy, in the case of real adults such goods as prestige, status, and money. There are always alternative ways for achieving such goods, and their achievement is never to be had *only* by engaging in some particular kind of practice. On the other hand there are the goods internal to the practice of chess which cannot be had in any way but by playing chess or some other game of that specific kind. We call them internal for two reasons: first, as I have already suggested, because we can only specify them in terms of chess or some other game of that specific kind and by means of examples from such games. . . . ; and secondly because they can only be identified and recognized by the experience of partici-pating in the practice in question. Those who lack the relevant experience are incompetent thereby as judges of internal goods.

A practice involves standards of excellence and obedience to rules as well as the achievement of goods. To enter into a practice is to accept the authority of those standards and the inadequacy of my own performance as judged by them. It is to subject my own attitudes, choices, preferences, and tastes to the standards which currently and partially define the practice. Practices of course, as I have just noticed, have a history: games, sciences, and arts all have histories. Thus the standards are not themselves immune from criticism, but nonetheless we cannot be initiated into a practice without accepting the authority of the best standards realized so far. . . .

We are now in a position to notice an important difference between what I have called internal and what I have called external goods. It is characteristic of what I have called external goods that when achieved they are always some individual's property and possession. Moreover characteristically they are such that the more someone has of them, the less there is for other people. This is sometimes necessarily the case, as with power and fame, and sometimes the case by reason of contingent circumstance as with money. External goods are therefore characteristi-cally objects of competition in which there must be losers as well as winners. Internal goods are indeed the outcome of competition to excel, but it is character-istic of them that their achievement is a good for the whole community who participate in the practice. . . .

But what does all or any of this have to do with the concept of the virtues? It turns out that we are now in a position to formulate a first, even if partial and tentative definition of a virtue: *A virtue is an acquired human quality the possession and exercise of which tends to enable us to achieve those goods which are internal to practices and the lack of which effectively prevents us from achieving any such goods.* Later this definition will need amplification and amendment. But as a first approximation to an adequate definition it already illuminates the place of the virtues in human life. For it is not difficult to show for a whole range of key virtues that without them the goods internal to practices are barred to us, but not just barred to us generally, barred in a very particular way.

It belongs to the concept of a practice as I have outlined it—and as we are all familiar with it already in our actual lives, whether we are painters or physicists or quarterbacks or indeed just lovers of good painting or first-rate experiments or a well-thrown pass—that its goods can only be achieved by subordinating ourselves within the practice in our relationship to other practitioners. We have to learn to recognize what is due to whom; we have to be prepared to take whatever self-endangering risks are demanded along the way; and we have to listen carefully to what we are told about our own inadequacies and to reply with the same carefulness for the facts. In other words we have to accept as necessary components of any practice with internal goods and standards of excellence the virtues of justice, courage, and honesty. For not to accept these, to be willing to cheat as our imagined child was willing to cheat in his or her early days at chess, so far bars us from achieving the standards of excellence or the goods internal to the practice that it renders the practice pointless except as a device for achieving external goods.

We can put the same point in another way. Every practice requires a certain kind of relationship between those who participate in it. Now the virtues are those goods by reference to which, whether we like it or not, we define our relationships to those other people with whom we share the kind of purposes and standards which inform practices. . . .

I take it then that from the standpoint of those types of relationship without which practices cannot be sustained truthfulness, justice, and courage—and perhaps some others—are genuine excellences, are virtues in the light of which we have to characterize ourselves and others, whatever our private moral standpoint or our society's particular codes may be. For this recognition that we cannot escape the definition of our relationships in terms of such goods is perfectly compatible with the acknowledgment that different societies have and have had different codes of truthfulness, justice, and courage. Lutheran pietists brought up their children to believe that one ought to tell the truth to everybody at all times, whatever the circumstances or consequences, and Kant was one of their children. Traditional Bantu parents brought up their children not to tell the truth to unknown strangers, since they believed that this could render the family vulnerable to witchcraft. In our culture many of us have been brought up not to tell the truth to elderly great-aunts who invite us to admire their new hats. But each of these codes embodies an acknowledgment of the virtue of truthfulness. So it is also with varying codes of justice and of courage.

Practices then might flourish in societies with very different codes; what they could not do is flourish in societies in which the virtues were not valued, although institutions and technical skills serving unified purposes might well continue to flourish. . . .

... It is no part of my thesis that great violinists cannot be vicious or great chess-players mean-spirited. Where the virtues are required, the vices also may flourish. It is just that the vicious and mean-spirited necessarily rely on the virtues of others for the practices in which they engage to flourish and also deny themselves the experience of achieving those internal goods which may reward even not very good chess-players and violinists.

To situate the virtues any further within practices it is necessary now to clarify a little further the nature of a practice by drawing two important contrasts. The discussion so far I hope makes it clear that a practice, in the sense intended, is never just a set of technical skills, even when directed toward some unified purpose and even if the exercise of those skills can on occasion be valued or enjoyed for their own sake. What is distinctive in a practice is in part the way in which conceptions of the relevant goods and ends which the technical skills serve—and every practice does require the exercise of technical skills—are transformed and enriched by these extensions of human powers and by that regard for its own internal goods which are partially definitive of each particular practice or type of practice. Practices never have a goal or goals fixed for all time—painting has no such goal nor has physics—but the goals themselves are transmuted by the history of the activity. It therefore turns out not to be accidental that every practice has its own history and a history which is more and other than that of the improvement of the relevant technical skills. This historical dimension is crucial in relation to the virtues.

To enter into a practice is to enter into a relationship not only with its contemporary practitioners, but also with those who have preceded us in the practice, particularly those whose achievements extended the reach of the practice to its present point. It is thus the achievement, and *a fortiori* the authority, of a tradition which I then confront and from which I have to learn. And for this learning and the relationship to the past which it embodies the virtues of justice, courage, and truthfulness are prerequisite in precisely the same way and for precisely the same reasons as they are in sustaining present relationships within practices.

It is not only of course with sets of technical skills that practices ought to be contrasted. Practices must not be confused with institutions. Chess, physics and medicine are practices; chess clubs, laboratories, universities, and hospitals are institutions. Institutions are characteristically and necessarily concerned with what I have called external goods. They are involved in acquiring money and other material goods; they are structured in terms of power and status, and they distribute money, power, and status as rewards. Nor could they do otherwise if they are to sustain not only themselves, but also the practices of which they are the bearers. For no practices can survive for any length of time unsustained by institutions. Indeed so intimate is the relationship of practices to institutions—and consequently of the goods external to the goods internal to the practices in question—that institutions and practices characteristically form a single causal order in which the ideals and the creativity of the practice are always vulnerable to the acquisitiveness of the institution, in which the cooperative care for common goods of the practice is always vulnerable to the competitiveness of the institution. In this context the essential function of the virtues is clear. Without them, without justice, courage, and truthfulness, practices could not resist the corrupting power of institutions.

Yet if institutions do have corrupting power, the making and sustaining of forms of human community—and therefore of institutions—itself has all the characteristics of a practice, and moreover of a practice which stands in a peculiarly close relationship to the exercise of the virtues in two important ways. The exercise of the virtues is itself apt to require a highly determinate attitude to social and political issues; and it is always within some particular community with its own specific institutional forms that we learn or fail to learn to exercise the virtues. . . . If my account of the complex relationship of virtues to practices and to institutions is correct, it follows that we shall be unable to write a true history of practices and institutions unless that history is also one of the virtues and vices. For the ability of a practice to retain its integrity will depend on the way in which the virtues can be and are exercised in sustaining the institutional forms which are the social bearers of the practice. The integrity of a practice causally requires the exercise of the virtues by at least some of the individuals who embody it in their activities; and conversely the corruption of institutions is always in part at least an effect of the vices. . . .

The time has come to ask the question of how far this partial account of a core conception of the virtues—and I need to emphasize that all that I have offered so far is the first stage of such an account—is faithful to the tradition which I delineated. How far, for example, and in what ways is it Aristotelian? It is—happily —not Aristotelian in two ways in which a good deal of the rest of the tradition also dissents from Aristotle. First, although this account of the virtues is teleological, it does not require any allegiance to Aristotle's metaphysical biology. And secondly, just because of the multiplicity of human practices and the consequent multiplicity of goods in the pursuit of which the virtues may be exercised—goods which will often be contingently incompatible and which will therefore make rival claims upon our allegiance—conflict will not spring solely from flaws in individual character. But it was just on these two matters that Aristotle's account of the virtues seemed most vulnerable; hence if it turns out to be the case that this socially teleological account can support Aristotle's general account of the virtues as well as does his own biologically teleological account, these differences from Aristotle himself may well be regarded as strengthening rather than weakening the case for a generally Aristotelian standpoint.

There are at least three ways in which the account that I have given *is* clearly Aristotelian. First it requires for its completion a cogent elaboration of just those distinctions and concepts which Aristotle's account requires: voluntariness, the distinction between the intellectual virtues and the virtues of character, the relationship of both to natural abilities and to the passions and the structure of practical reasoning. On every one of these topics something very like Aristotle's view has to be defended, if my own account is to be plausible.

Secondly my account can accommodate an Aristotelian view of pleasure and enjoyment, whereas it is interestingly irreconcilable with any utilitarian view and more particularly with Franklin's account of the virtues.

. . . Utilitarianism cannot accommodate the distinction between goods internal to and goods external to a practice. Not only is that distinction marked by none of the classical utilitarians—it cannot be found in Bentham's writings nor in those of either of the Mills or of Sidgwick—but internal goods and external goods are not commensurable with each other. Hence the notion of summing goods—and *a fortiori* in the light of what I have said about kinds of pleasure and enjoyment the notion of summing happiness—in terms of one single formula or conception of utility, whether it is Franklin's or Bentham's or Mill's, makes no sense. Nonetheless we ought to note that although *this* distinction is alien to J. S. Mill's thought, it is plausible and in no way patronizing to suppose that something like this is the distinction which he was trying to make in *Utilitarianism* when he distinguished between "higher" and "lower" pleasures. . . .

Thirdly my account is Aristotelian in that it links evaluation and explanation in a characteristically Aristotelian way. From an Aristotelian standpoint to identify certain actions as manifesting or failing to manifest a virtue or virtues is never only to evaluate; it is also to take the first step toward explaining why those actions rather than some others were performed. Hence for an Aristotelian quite as much as for a Platonist the fate of a city or an individual can be explained by citing the injustice of a tyrant or the courage of its defenders. Indeed without allusion to the place that justice and injustice, courage and cowardice play in human life very little will be genuinely explicable. . . .

I stressed earlier that any account of the virtues in terms of practices could only be a partial and first account. What is required to complement it? The most notable difference so far between my account and any account that could be called Aristotelian is that although I have in no way restricted the exercise of the virtues to the context of practices, it is in terms of practices that I have located their point and function. Whereas Aristotle locates that point and function in terms of the notion of a type of whole human life which can be called good. And it does seem that the question "What would a human being lack who lacked the virtues?" must be given a kind of answer which goes beyond anything which I have said so far. For such an individual would not merely fail *in a variety of particular ways* in respect of the kind of excellence which can be achieved through participation in practices and in respect of the kind of relationship required to sustain such excellence. His own life *viewed as a whole* would perhaps be defective; it would not be the kind of life which someone would describe in trying to answer the question "What is the best kind of life for this kind of man or woman to live?" And that question cannot be answered without at least raising Aristotle's own question, "What is the good life for man?" Consider three ways in which human life informed only by the conception of the virtues sketched so far would be defective.

It would be pervaded, first of all, by *too many* conflicts and *too much* arbitrariness. . . .

Secondly without an overriding conception of the *telos* of a whole human life, conceived as a unity, our conception of certain individual virtues has to remain partial and incomplete. . . .

I have suggested so far that unless there is a *telos* which transcends the limited goods of practices by constituting the good of a whole human life, the good of a human life conceived as a unity, it will *both* be the case that a certain subversive arbitrariness will invade the moral life *and* that we shall be unable to specify the context of certain virtues adequately. These two considerations are reinforced by a third: that there is at least one virtue recognized by the tradition which cannot be specified at all except with reference to the wholeness of a human life—the virtue of integrity or constancy. "Purity of heart," said Kierkegaard, "is to will one thing." This notion of singleness of purpose in a whole life can have no application unless that of a whole life does.

It is clear therefore that my preliminary account of the virtues in terms of practices captures much, but very far from all, of what the Aristotelian tradition taught about the virtues. It is also clear that to give an account that is at once more fully adequate to the tradition and rationally defensible, it is necessary to raise a question to which the Aristotelian tradition presupposed an answer, an answer so widely shared in the pre-modern world that it never had to be formulated explicitly in any detailed way. This question is: is it rationally justifiable to conceive of each human life as a unity, so that we may try to specify each such life as having its good and so that we may understand the virtues as having their function in enabling an individual to make of his or her life one kind of unity rather than another?

SUGGESTIONS FOR DISCUSSION

1. A prosecutor has an intuition that a judge is morally obliged to impose the death penalty for some cases; a defense lawyer has an intuition that the legislature is similarly obliged to outlaw capital punishment. How, on Ross's theory of intuitionism, is this conflict to be resolved? Is there any difference between our ordinary pretheoretical intuitions on moral matters and Ross's notion of "intuition"?

2. Mackie suggests that we have *prima facie* rights. Does having a *prima facie* right—of a terminally ill patient to euthanasia, say—entail that someone has a correlative *prima facie* duty? In the case of euthanasia, what might such a duty be (see Part II, Chapter 12)? How would a *prima facie* right or duty become an actual one?

3. Both pro- and anti-abortion arguments are often based on appeals to rights—for example, the right of the woman to choose, or the right to life of the fetus (see Part II, Chapter 11). Would Mackie consider these conflicting claims to be *prima facie* rights? How, on Mackie's view, would one of these become the actual right? Is this how rights are actualized?

4. Marx attacks rights as bourgeois fictions (see Part I, Chapter 5). What might be Mackie's defense against such an attack?

5. How does Gauthier's "morals by agreement" differ from and how is it similar to Rawls's contractarian theory of morality? How, on each view, do we determine what social policy ought to be for any one of the social issues discussed in Part II?

6. What does the Prisoner's Dilemma show about the *rationality* of collective decision-making? What does Gauthier claim that it shows about *morality*? Is whatever we rationally agree to, for that reason alone, always moral?

7. In what ways are MacIntyre's criticisms of the modern moral tradition influenced by Nietzsche? If effective, do MacIntyre's criticisms preclude morally informed decisions about censoring pornography (see Part II, Chapter 9) or about abortion (see Chapter 11) or about sexual practices (see Chapter 10)?

8. In what ways is MacIntyre's view of the virtues influenced by Aristotle (see Part I, Chapter 1)? How does MacIntyre's view differ from the account of the virtues offered by Philippa Foot in her article on euthanasia (See Part II, Chapter 12)? Would MacIntyre's view commit him to an account of the permissibility of euthanasia that is different from Foot's?

FURTHER READING

Baier, K. *The Moral Point of View*. Ithaca: Cornell University Press, 1958. (Critical analysis; advanced)

Brandt, R. J. *Ethical Theory*. Englewood Cliffs, N.J.: Prentice-Hall, 1959. (Critical analysis; advanced)

————. *A Theory of the Right and the Good*. Oxford: Oxford University Press, 1979. (Interpretation, critical analysis; advanced)

Dworkin, R. *Taking Rights Seriously*. Cambridge, Mass.: Harvard University Press, 1977. (Critical analysis; advanced)

Elster, J. *Sour Grapes: Studies in the Subversion of Rationality*. Cambridge: Cambridge University Press, 1985. (Critical analysis; advanced)

Foot, P. *Virtues and Vices*. Oxford: Oxford University Press, 1977. (Critical analysis; advanced)

Frey, R. G., ed. *Utility and Rights*. Minneapolis: University of Minnesota Press, 1984. (Critical analysis; advanced)

Gauthier, D. *Morals by Agreement*. New York: Oxford University Press, 1986.

"Gauthier's *Morals by Agreement*." *Ethics* 97,3 (April 1987). (Interpretation, critical analysis; advanced)

Hare, R. M. *Essays on the Moral Concepts*. London: Macmillan, 1972. (Critical analysis; intermediate)

Harsanyi, J. C. *Rational Behavior and Bargaining Equilibrium in Games and Social Institutions*. Cambridge: Cambridge University Press, 1977. (Interpretation, critical analysis; advanced)

MacIntyre, A. *After Virtue*. South Bend: University of Notre Dame Press, 1981.

Mackie, J. *Ethics: Inventing Right and Wrong*. Harmondsworth: Penguin Books, 1977.

Moore, G. E. *Principia Ethica*. Cambridge: Cambridge University Press, 1903.

Nagel, T. *Mortal Questions*. Cambridge: Cambridge University Press, 1979. (Critical analysis, advanced)

Parfit, D. *Reasons and Persons*. Oxford: Oxford University Press, 1984. (Critical analysis; advanced)

Ross, W. D. *The Right and the Good*. Oxford: Oxford University Press, 1930.

Sen, A., and Williams, B., eds. *Utilitarianism and Beyond*. Cambridge: Cambridge University Press, 1984. (Critical analysis; advanced)

Shue, H. *Basic Rights*. Princeton: Princeton University Press, 1980. (Critical analysis; intermediate)

Williams, B. *Moral Luck*. Cambridge: Cambridge University Press, 1981. (Critical analysis; advanced)

————. *Ethics and the Limits of Philosophy*. Cambridge, Mass.: Harvard University Press, 1984. (Critical analysis; advanced)

Part
II
□
SOCIAL ISSUES:
CONTEMPORARY READINGS

Social Issues: Introduction

Moral Theory and Scientific Theory   The application of principles theoretically elaborated in Part I to pressing social issues will serve as a testing ground for moral theory. It may prove instructive to draw a parallel here between moral and scientific theory. Like scientific theories, moral theories must be assessed against empirical data. The data for morality are generally the set of common, firmly held, and reasoned convictions and principles concerning permissible social behavior and relationships. If a moral theory, directly or by implication, is inconsistent with some widely held, cherished, and reasoned conviction, such as the wrongness of taking innocent life, it may be sufficient grounds to reject the theory.

There is a further sense in which moral theory can be likened to scientific theory. An acceptable moral theory must not simply rationalize given beliefs and practices. A revolution in scientific theory will usually lead to new discoveries, to viewing the world in a new way, and to new knowledge. Similarly, a moral theory may lead us to acknowledge that some beliefs or social practices are morally unacceptable. We may discover something morally pertinent about ourselves, about our relations to others and to our world. If taken seriously, this should lead us to change our social convictions and behavior in the relevant way.

A recent example of this is the widespread appeal to rights in social, political, and moral analysis. The concept of rights can be traced back in moral theory at least to Hobbes (Part I, Chapter 2). Nevertheless, the contemporary theoretical currency of rights-analysis was prompted in large part by the civil rights and nationalist movements of the 1960s. The theoretical refinement of the concept that followed has established more clearly the kinds of social practices we are now prepared to accept. Many of the arguments concerning the social issues discussed in Part II turn on basic appeals to rights. Application of this concept to actual social contexts and problems may lead in turn to further refinement, or to acknowledging the limits of the concept's applicability.

Basic and Intermediate Principles   In applying moral theory to decide on ethical practice, some ethicists have assumed the model of *deduction*. Moral policies or acts are supposed to be logically derivable directly from basic ethical principles and the relevant facts. Like principles from which they are deduced, the policy- or act-conclusion is considered unchangeable, no matter that it may be inconsistent with firmly held moral intuitions about the issue at hand (see Hare, Part II, Chapter 11). However, most agree that the application of theoretical ethics to genuine ethical problems requires sensitivity to a variety of issues. The choice of intermediate principles linking ethical theory to act- or policy-decisions for some concrete issue is crucially important. (Philosophers sometimes call these "bridging principles.") Choosing one intermediate or bridging principle rather than another as relevant to the case at hand is important, for it may critically alter how a proposed act or policy will be judged. For example, two agents may agree on the basic importance of the Principle of Liberty (that is, that people should be free to do with their lives as they choose), yet disagree on which intermediate principles may limit liberty in a given context. So one agent may accept the Offense Principle as justifying a legitimate limitation of the liberty of pornographic consumption; while another may argue that only actual harm (the Harm Principle), and not mere subjective offense, supports morally acceptable restrictions on freedoms or rights (see Chapter 9). Moreover, different moral theories may weigh the same basic principle differently. Kantianism and utilitarianism may agree that respect for persons is an important value. Yet a Kantian must reject any attempt to qualify or override the Principle of Respect, while a utilitarian must be willing to sacrifice it if this would maximize utility.

In their concern to resolve a genuine moral dilemma posed by a given social issue, many ethicists reject the constraints of deductive purism. Instead, there is a call to clarify the appropriate moral concepts and to present the moral facts properly. The various basic and intermediate principles offered by each of the competing theories must be compared, their strengths assessed against the moral data and refined accordingly. For example, the morality of abortion will involve knowing the facts about fetal development and pertinent socioeconomic data; analyzing the concept of personhood; and weighing the relative importance of various basic principles, such as respect and autonomy, and intermediate principles, such as the right to life and the right to choose. In the final analysis, then, the moral decision must rest with informed and reasoned judgment.

Theory and Practice Ethical theories, as Aristotle noted, are fundamentally theories of right action and virtuous character. One of the ultimate tests of a moral theory is whether it is capable of guiding action and public policy in a reasoned manner. Part II of this book provides contending philosophical analyses of important contemporary social and legal issues. These contending positions on such issues as the permissibility of euthanasia or capital punishment may be grounded in different, often competing ethical theories. Understanding the underlying theoretical terrain will serve to clarify the respective arguments and to reveal the seriousness of competing viewpoints. It will help to direct criticism where it is due; and most importantly, it should encourage tolerance for those whose reasoned views conflict with one's own. Attempting to resolve conflicts over social issues in this way will commit persons to trying to convince by reasoned means those holding opposing views, for rational deliberation and critical exchange are surely preferable to the unpredictability of irrational aggression.

7

□

Distributive Justice

The application of ethical principles to social practices inevitably raises concerns of a social and political sort. Similarly, normative social or political analysis prompts ethical questions. Plato and Aristotle, and many philosophers since, recognized that questions about ethics are in the final analysis social or political questions. For both Plato and Aristotle and others, this intersection of ethical, social, and political concerns is reflected in their efforts to elaborate theories of justice.

Distributive and Rectificatory Justice   For Aristotle, the political virtue of justice includes the principles in terms of which social institutions ought to be arranged (see Aristotle, *Nicomachean Ethics,* Book V, Part I, Chapter 1). Aristotle divided these particular principles into two kinds. On one hand, he focused upon principles for distributing social goods (*distributive justice*). On the other, he emphasized the need for principles to rectify wrongs (*rectificatory justice*). This chapter concentrates upon the application of moral analysis to questions of distributive justice. (Rectificatory justice includes questions about justifying punishment; see Part II, Chapter 14).

Principles of Distribution   Questions concerning distributive justice are generally of two sorts. Primary questions involve the principles according to which social resources—goods such as wealth, income, or power—are distributed among members of the society. Secondary questions concern the socioeconomic system (or political economy) best able to institute these principles of distribution. Principles of distribution may differ widely, and include strict equality; equality relative to need; freedom of choice; effort, merit, or achievement; and actual individual output. The controversy about principles of distributive justice involves the conflict between the respective demands of liberty and equality.

Liberty and Equality   Some (called libertarians) argue that the only acceptable ground for distributing or accumulating resources is individual liberty of choice. Others (called egalitarians) insist that income, wealth, and power should be distributed equally, although they usually recognize that it is unreasonable for a family of two, say, to receive a quantity of goods equal to that of a family of five.

Thus the standard of equality requires qualification according to relevant need. Nevertheless, it is clear that liberty and equality may conflict: increasing either in some cases militates against the other. Moreover, liberties of one individual often conflict with another's, and one kind of liberty with some other kind. For example, one's liberty to accumulate the only available food may conflict with another's, and one's liberty to enjoy one's wealth as one pleases may conflict with another's liberty not to be harmed by what one does with one's wealth. Accordingly, there are those who argue for a principle of distributive justice that combines liberty and equality in some integrated form. Here the optimal set of distributions would be endorsed that would maximize correlative individual liberties and equality in given socio-historical circumstances.

Each of these three views tends to be correlated with an idealized socioeconomic system generally considered to encourage institution of the distributive principle endorsed. The *libertarian* view usually sanctions free market or *laissez faire* capitalism with minimal state interference. The *liberal* view, which attempts to integrate liberty and equality, tends to support welfare state capitalism. Strict *egalitarians* tend to esteem socialism. The readings in this chapter reflect each of these positions. They throw in sharp relief the question concerning which type of socioeconomic system best institutes principles of distributive justice.

Readings: Nozick's Entitlement Theory   Justice, on Robert Nozick's libertarian conception, does not necessitate any preordained "pattern" or structure of distribution. Economic arrangements would be just if they were consented to freely and involved no fraud or coercion. In contrast to a *patterned* conception of just distribution, Nozick holds that any person's "holdings" at some given time would be just, provided that neither the original historical acquisition of goods held nor any subsequent transfer involved coercion. If acquisition of goods is just in the sense given, the title-holder is *entitled* to the goods held, no matter the quantity. A patterned approach specifying some *end-state* or predefined arrangement that the distribution is to achieve is likely on Nozick's view to be unjust. It will tend to deny people goods to which Nozick thinks they are "historically" entitled. Nozick's principle of distributive justice holds a distribution D to be just if and only if all people are *entitled* to their possessions, and D renders none worse off than they would have been without it. The libertarian is concerned to maximize liberty, negatively conceived as freedom *from* constraint, and in particular from the coercive power of government.

Rawls's Contract Theory   For John Rawls, a just or fair social arrangement of the basic socioeconomic institutions for a modern constititional democracy is one all social members would agree to, though they are ignorant of any personal effects the chosen arrangement would have for themselves. Rawls reconstructs the idea of a social contract as formulated by Hobbes, Locke, and Rousseau. In the social contract theories of the seventeenth and eighteenth centuries, isolated individuals were considered to live originally in a "state of nature" lacking all social institutions. The poverty of life here encouraged them to contract with each other to form a structured society (see Hobbes, Part I, Chapter 2, and Rousseau, Chapter 3). Rawls reinterprets the "state of nature" as an *original position* from which individuals are to choose the basic institutional structure of their society.

People are to agree in the original position to the fundamental principles of justice that will order their cooperative social relations with each other. Every individual is conceived as rational and self-interested: the principles each chooses will be those that would most probably maximize his or her individual self-interest. Yet the original choice or agreement is governed by a *veil of ignorance*: Individuals choosing the basic principles are not to have any information about themselves or others that is likely to advantage themselves or disadvantage others in respect to the principles agreed to. Any accidental advantages or past influences—including those of race, sex, class, and talent—are to be discounted in the initial institutional choices. So in choosing basic institutions that would maximize self-interest, any agent is actually choosing a basic structure of society that is most likely to maximize benefits for all.

Persons, on Rawls's view, are to choose ideal principles of institutional justice against a background of *primary goods*. These are goods every rational self-interested agent would desire, if she or he desired anything. Primary goods include basic rights and liberties, powers and opportunities, income and wealth, and self-respect. Rawls argues that, from the standpoint of equality, agents would agree to two basic principles. They would agree, first, to maximum liberty for themselves, compatible with a like liberty for all. Second, they would accept the *difference principle*. This justifies differential distributions in favor of some if and only if such inequality benefits most the least advantaged in the social arrangement. Injustices, then, are inequalities that fail to benefit all. Satisfaction of the difference principle presupposes satisfying the equal liberty principle. Unlike utilitarianism (see Part I, Chapter 4), it will never be permissible to sacrifice liberty—by giving up power, say —for some economic benefit. Yet, in contrast to Nozick, it would not be permissible for any person to have greater liberty than any other.

It has been suggested that Rawls's principles are consistent with socialism. Benefits relevant to the difference principle involve increases in all the primary goods, including self-respect. Self-respect may be interpreted as requiring worker self-determination for its fulfillment. However, Rawls's contractarianism has been widely considered to offer a defense of welfare state capitalism in a constitutional democracy. (Rawls himself has argued that his theory supports any just constitutional structure, not only a liberal one.) Rawls's principles are ideals for directing only new distributions; they presuppose, by applying to, currently given inequalities.

Nielsen's Radical Egalitarianism   Kai Nielsen takes issue with this last point. Nielsen argues that it is unjust for, and unfair to ask, anyone to begin life from a position of inequality. Such inequality—in class position, function, power, and control—determines the life prospects facing the individual. All unjustified inequalities should be eliminated by a pervasive equitable redistribution of wealth, income, power, and control. This would transform liberal capitalism effectively into socialism.

Capitalism is characterized as the social system in which the proportionately small class of capitalists privately own and control disproportionately large shares of social resources. Wealth is produced by exploiting workers' labor power to produce surplus value (profit). At best, capitalist society could be a *political* democracy. Socialism, by contrast, is supposed to involve worker ownership and control of the means of production. In pure form, socialist society would be an economic and industrial democracy. Workers' councils would decide cooperatively what and how much would be produced, and how the goods would be distributed. In addition, these cooperative councils would determine conditions of work and of social and political life. Nielsen suggests that socialism increases liberty for all. He admits, nevertheless, that in actual state socialisms increased equality is often attained at the expense of individual liberties (see Marx, Part I, Chapter 5.). This places in sharp relief the two general questions at issue here: First, to what extent must we sacrifice liberties in order to meet the demands of equality; and second, what socioeconomic system are we thus committed to accept?

Robert Nozick

Equality

THE ENTITLEMENT THEORY

The subject of justice in holdings consists of three major topics. The first is the *original acquisition of holdings,* the appropriation of unheld things. This includes the issues of how unheld things may come to be held, the process, or processes, by which unheld things may come to be held, the things that may come to be held by these processes, the extent of what comes to be held by a particular process, and so on. We shall refer to the complicated truth about this topic, which we shall not formulate here, as the principle of justice in acquisition. The second topic concerns the *transfer of holdings* from one person to another. By what processes may a person transfer holdings to another? How may a person acquire a holding from another who holds it? Under this topic come general descriptions of voluntary exchange, and gift and (on the other hand) fraud, as well as reference to particular conventional details fixed upon in a given society. The complicated truth about this subject (with placeholders for conventional details) we shall call the principle of justice in transfer. (And we shall suppose it also includes principles governing how a person may divest himself of a holding, passing it into an unheld state.)

If the world were wholly just, the following inductive definition would exhaustively cover the subject of justice in holdings.

1. A person who acquires a holding in accordance with the principle of justice in acquisition is entitled to that holding.

From Robert Nozick, *Anarchy, State and Utopia* (New York: Basic Books, 1974). Reprinted by permission of the publisher. Copyright © 1974 by Basic Books, Inc.

2. A person who acquires a holding in accordance with the principle of justice in transfer, from someone else entitled to the holding, is entitled to the holding.

3. No one is entitled to a holding except by (repeated) applications of 1 and 2.

The complete principle of distributive justice would say simply that a distribution is just if everyone is entitled to the holdings they possess under the distribution.

A distribution is just if it arises from another just distribution by legitimate means. The legitimate means of moving from one distribution to another are specified by the principle of justice in transfer. The legitimate first "moves" are specified by the principle of justice in acquisition. Whatever arises from a just situation by just steps is itself just. The means of change specified by the principle of justice in transfer preserve justice. . . .

HISTORICAL PRINCIPLES
AND END-RESULT PRINCIPLES

The general outlines of the entitlement theory illuminate the nature and defects of other conceptions of distributive justice. The entitlement theory of justice in distribution is *historical;* whether a distribution is just depends upon how it came about. In contrast, *current time-slice principles* of justice hold that the justice of a distribution is determined by how things are distributed (who has what) as judged by some *structural* principle(s) of just distribution. A utilitarian who judges between any two distributions by seeing which has the greater sum of utility and, if the sums tie, applies some fixed equality criterion to choose the more equal distribution, would hold a current time-slice principle of justice. As would someone who had a fixed schedule of trade-offs between the sum of happiness and equality. According to a current time-slice principle, all that needs to be looked at, in judging the justice of a distribution, is who ends up with what; in comparing any two distributions one need look only at the matrix presenting the distributions. No further information need be fed into a principle of justice. It is a consequence of such principles of justice that any two structurally identical distributions are equally just. (Two distributions are structurally identical if they present the same profile, but perhaps have different persons occupying the particular slots. My having ten and your having five, and my having five and your having ten, are structurally identical distributions.) Welfare economics is the theory of current time-slice principles of justice. . . .

We construe the position we discuss too narrowly by speaking of *current* time-slice principles. Nothing is changed if structural principles operate upon a time sequence of current time-slice profiles and, for example, give someone more now to counterbalance the less he has had earlier. A utilitarian or an egalitarian or any mixture of the two over time will inherit the difficulties of his more myopic comrades. He is not helped by the fact that *some* of the information others consider relevant in assessing a distribution is reflected, unrecoverably, in past matrices. Henceforth, we shall refer to such unhistorical principles of distributive justice, including the current time-slice principles, as *end-result principles* or *end-state principles.*

In contrast to end-result principles of justice, *historical principles* of justice hold that past circumstances or actions of people can create differential entitlements or differential deserts to things. An injustice can be worked by moving from one distribution to another structurally identical one, for the second, in profile the same, may violate people's entitlements or deserts; it may not fit the actual history.

PATTERNING

The entitlement principles of justice in holdings that we have sketched are historical principles of justice. To better understand their precise character, we shall distinguish them from another subclass of the historical principles.... Let us call a principle of distribution *patterned* if it specifies that a distribution is to vary along with some natural dimension, weighted sum of natural dimensions, or lexicographic ordering of natural dimensions. And let us say a distribution is patterned if it accords with some patterned principle.... The principle of distribution in accordance with moral merit is a patterned historical principle, which specifies a patterned distribution. "Distribute according to I.Q." is a patterned principle that looks to information not contained in distributional matrices. It is not historical, however, in that it does not look to any past actions creating differential entitlements to evaluate a distribution; it requires only distributional matrices whose columns are labeled by I.Q. scores. The distribution in a society, however, may be composed of such simple patterned distributions, without itself being simply patterned. Different sectors may operate different patterns, or some combination of patterns may operate in different proportions across a society. A distribution composed in this manner, from a small number of patterned distributions, we also shall term "patterned." And we extend the use of "pattern" to include the overall designs put forth by combinations of end-state principles.

Almost every suggested principle of distributive justice is patterned: to each according to his moral merit, or needs, or marginal product, or how hard he tries, or the weighted sum of the foregoing, and so on. The principle of entitlement we have sketched is *not* patterned. There is no one natural dimension or weighted sum or combination of a small number of natural dimensions that yields the distributions generated in accordance with the principle of entitlement. The set of holdings that results when some persons receive their marginal products, others win at gambling, others receive a share of their mate's income, others receive gifts from foundations, others receive interest on loans, others receive gifts from admirers, others receive returns on investment, others make for themselves much of what they have, others find things, and so on, will not be patterned. Heavy strands of patterns will run through it; significant portions of the variance in holdings will be accounted for by pattern-variables. If most people most of the time choose to transfer some of their entitlements to others only in exchange for something from them, then a large part of what many people hold will vary with what they held that others wanted. More details are provided by the theory of marginal productivity. But gifts to relatives, charitable donations, bequests to children, and the like, are not best conceived, in the first instance, in this manner. Ignoring the strands of pattern, let us suppose for the moment that a distribution actually arrived at by the operation of the principle of entitlement is random with respect to any pattern. Though the resulting set of holdings will be unpatterned, it will not be incomprehensible, for it can be seen as arising from the operation of a small number of principles. These principles specify how an initial distribution may arise (the principle of acquisition of holdings) and how distributions may be transformed into others (the principle of transfer of holdings). The process whereby the set of holdings is generated will be intelligible, though the set of holdings itself that results from this process will be unpatterned. . . .

EQUALITY

The legitimacy of altering social institutions to achieve greater equality of material condition is, though often assumed, rarely *argued* for. Writers note that in a given country the wealthiest *n* percent of the population holds more than that percentage of the wealth, and the poorest *n* percent holds less; that to get to the wealth of the top *n* percent from the poorest, one must look at the bottom *p* percent (where *p* is vastly greater than *n*), and so forth. They then proceed immediately to discuss how this might be altered. On the entitlement conception of justice in holdings, one *cannot* decide whether the state must do something to alter the situation merely by looking at a distributional profile or at facts such as these. It depends upon how the distribution came about. Some processes yielding these results would be legitimate, and the various parties would be entitled to their respective holdings. If these distributional facts *did* arise by a legitimate process, then they themselves are legitimate. This is, of course, *not* to say that they may not be changed, provided this can be done without violating people's entitlements. Any persons who favor a particular end-state pattern may choose to transfer some or all of their own holdings so as (at least temporarily) more nearly to realize their desired pattern.

The entitlement conception of justice in holdings makes no presumption in favor of equality, or any other overall end state or patterning. It cannot merely be *assumed* that equality must be built into any theory of justice. There is a surprising dearth of arguments for equality capable of coming to grips with the considerations that underlie a nonglobal and nonpatterned conception of justice in holdings. (However, there is no lack of unsupported statements of a presumption in favor of equality.) I shall consider the argument which has received the most attention from philosophers in recent years; that offered by Bernard Williams in his influential essay "The Idea of Equality." (No doubt many readers will feel that all hangs on some other argument; I would like to see *that* argument precisely set out, in detail.)

Leaving aside preventive medicine, the proper ground of distribution of medical care is ill health: this is a necessary truth. Now in very many societies, while ill health may work as a necessary condition of receiving treatment, it does not work as a sufficient condition, since such treatment costs money, and not all who are ill have the money; hence the possession of sufficient money becomes in fact an additional necessary condition of actually receiving treatment. . . . When we have the situation in which, for instance, wealth is a further necessary condition of the receipt of medical treatment, we can once more apply the notions of equality and inequality: not now in connection with the inequality between the well and the ill, but in connection with the inequality between the rich ill and the poor ill, since we have straightforwardly the situation of those whose needs are the same not receiving the same treatment, though the needs are the ground of the treatment. This is an irrational state of affairs . . . it is a situation in which reasons are insufficiently operative; it is a situation insufficiently controlled by reasons—and hence by reason itself.

Williams seems to be arguing that if among the different descriptions applying to an activity, there is one that contains an "internal goal" of the activity, then (it is a necessary truth that) the only proper grounds for the performance of the activity, or its allocation if it is scarce, are connected with the effective achievement of the internal goal. If the activity is done upon others, the only proper criterion for distributing the activity is their need for it, if any. Thus it is that Williams says (it is a necessary truth that) the only proper criterion for the distribution of medical care is medical need. Presumably, then, the only proper criterion for the distribution of barbering services is barbering need. But why must the internal goal of the activity take precedence over, for example, the person's particular purpose in performing the activity? (We ignore the question of whether one activity can fall under two different descriptions involving different internal goals.) If someone becomes a barber because he likes talking to a variety of different people, and so on, is it unjust of him to allocate his services to those he most likes to talk to? Or if he works as a barber in order to earn money to pay tuition at school, may he cut the hair of only those who pay or tip well? Why may not a barber use exactly the same criteria in allocating his services as someone else whose activities have no internal goal involving others? Need a gardener allocate his services to those lawns which need him most?

In what way does the situation of a doctor differ? Why must his activities be allocated via the internal goal of medical care? (If there was no "shortage," could some *then* be allocated using other criteria as well?) It seems clear that *he* needn't do that; just because he has this skill, why should *he* bear the costs of the desired allocation, why is he less entitled to pursue his own goals, within the special circumstances of practicing medicine, than everyone else? So it is *society* that, somehow, is to arrange things so that the doctor, in pursuing his own goals, allocates according to need; for example, the society pays him to do this. But why must the society do this? (Should they do it for barbering as well?) Presumably, because medical care is important, people need it very much. This is true of food as well, though farming does *not* have an internal goal that refers to other people in the way doctoring does. When the layers of Williams' argument are peeled away, what we arrive at is the claim that society (that is, each of us acting together in some organized fashion) should make provision for the important needs of all its members. This claim, of course, has been stated many times before. Despite appearances, Williams presents no argument for it.* Like others, Williams looks

---

*We have discussed Williams' position without introducing an essentialist view that some activities necessarily involve certain goals. Instead we have tied the goals to *descriptions* of the activities. For essentialist issues only becloud the discussion, and they still leave open the question of why the only proper ground for allocating the activity is its essentialist goal. The motive for making such an essentialist claim would be to avoid someone's saying: let "schmoctoring" be an activity just like doctoring except that *its* goal is to earn money for the practitioner; has Williams presented any reason why *schmoctoring* services should be allocated according to need?

only to questions of allocation. He ignores the question of where the things or actions to be allocated and distributed come from. Consequently, he does not consider whether they come already tied to people who have entitlements over them (surely the case for service activities, which are people's *actions*), people who therefore may decide for themselves to whom they will give the thing and on what grounds.

EQUALITY OF OPPORTUNITY

Equality of opportunity has seemed to many writers to be the minimal egalitarian goal, questionable (if at all) only for being too weak. (Many writers also have seen how the existence of the family prevents fully achieving this goal.) There are two ways to attempt to provide such equality: by directly worsening the situations of those more favored with opportunity, or by improving the situation of those less well-favored. The latter requires the use of resources, and so it too involves worsening the situation of some: those from whom holdings are taken in order to improve the situation of others. But holdings to which these people are entitled may not be seized, even to provide equality of opportunity for others. In the absence of magic wands, the remaining means toward equality of opportunity is convincing persons each to choose to devote some of their holdings to achieving it.

The model of a race for a prize is often used in discussions of equality of opportunity. A race where some started closer to the finish line than others would be unfair, as would a race where some were forced to carry heavy weights, or run with pebbles in their sneakers. But life is not a race in which we all compete for a prize which someone has established; there is no unified race, with some person judging swiftness. Instead, there are different persons separately giving other persons different things. Those who do the giving (each of us, at times) usually do not care about desert or about the handicaps labored under; they care simply about what they actually get. No centralized process judges people's use of the opportunities they had; that is not what the processes of social cooperation and exchange are *for*.

There is a reason why some inequality of opportunity might seem *unfair*, rather than merely unfortunate in that some do not have every opportunity (which would be true even if no one else had greater advantage). Often the person entitled to transfer a holding has no special desire to transfer it to a particular person; this contrasts with a bequest to a child or a gift to a particular person. He chooses to transfer to someone who satisfies a certain condition (for example, who can provide him with a certain good or service in exchange, who can do a certain job, who can pay a certain salary), and he would be equally willing to transfer to anyone else who satisfied that condition. Isn't it unfair for one party to receive the transfer, rather than another who had less opportunity to satisfy the condition the transferrer used? Since the giver doesn't care to whom he transfers, provided the recipient satisfies a certain general condition, equality of opportunity to be a recipient in such circumstances would violate no entitlement of the giver. Nor would it violate any entitlement of the person with the greater opportunity; while entitled to what he has, he has no entitlement that it be more than another has. Wouldn't it be *better* if the person with less opportunity had an equal opportunity? If one so could equip him without violating anyone else's entitlements (the magic wand?) shouldn't one do so? Wouldn't it be fairer? If it *would* be fairer, can such fairness also justify overriding some people's entitlements in order to acquire the resources to boost those having poorer opportunities into a more equal competitive position?

The process is competitive in the following way. If the person with greater opportunity didn't exist, the transferrer might deal with some person having lesser opportunity who then would be, under those circumstances, the best person available to deal with. This differs from a situation in which unconnected but similar beings living on different planets confront different difficulties and have different opportunities to realize various of their goals. There, the situation of one does *not* affect that of another; though it would be better if the worse planet were better endowed than it is (it also would be better if the better planet were better endowed than *it* is), it wouldn't be *fairer*. It also differs from a situation in which a person does not, though he could, choose to *improve* the situation of another. In the particular circumstances under discussion, a person having lesser opportunities would be better off if some particular person having better opportunities didn't exist. The person having better opportunities can be viewed not merely as someone better off, or as someone not choosing to aid, but as someone *blocking* or *impeding* the person having lesser opportunities from becoming better off. Impeding another by being a more alluring alternative partner in exchange is not to be compared to directly *worsening* the situation of another, as by stealing from him. But still, cannot the person with lesser opportunity justifiably complain at being so impeded by another who does not *deserve* his better opportunity to satisfy certain conditions? (Let us ignore any similar complaints another might make about *him*.)

While feeling the power of the questions of the previous two paragraphs (it is *I* who ask them), I do not believe they overturn a thoroughgoing entitlement conception. If the woman who later became my wife rejected another suitor (whom she otherwise would have married) for me, partially because (I leave aside my lovable nature) of my keen intelligence and good looks, neither of which did I earn, would the rejected less intelligent and less handsome suitor have a legitimate complaint about unfairness? Would my thus impeding the other suitor's winning the hand of fair lady justify taking some resources from others to pay for cosmetic surgery for him and special intellectual training, or to pay to develop in him some sterling trait that I lack in order to equalize our chances of being chosen? (I here take for granted the impermissibility of worsening the situation of the person having better opportunities so as to equalize opportunity; in this sort of case by disfiguring him or injecting drugs or playing noises which prevent him from fully using his intelligence.) *No such consequences follow.* (Against whom would the rejected suitor have a legitimate complaint? Against what?) Nor are things different if the differential opportunities arise from the accumulated effects of people's acting or transferring their entitlement as they choose. The case is even easier for consumption goods which cannot plausibly be claimed to have any such triadic impeding effect. *Is* it unfair that a child be raised in a home with a swimming pool, using it daily even though he is no more *deserving* than another child whose home is without one? Should such a situation be prohibited? Why then should there be objection to the transfer of the swimming pool to an adult by bequest?

The major objection to speaking of everyone's having a right to various things such as equality of opportunity, life, and so on, and enforcing this right, is that these "rights" require a substructure of things and materials and actions; and *other* people may have rights and entitlements over these. No one has a right to something whose realization requires certain uses of things and activities that other people have rights and entitlements over. Other people's rights and entitlements to *particular things (that* pencil, *their* body, and so on) and how they choose to exercise these rights and entitlements fix the external environment of any given individual and the means that will be available to him. If his goal requires the use of means which others have rights over, he must enlist their voluntary cooperation. Even to *exercise* his right to determine how something he owns is to be used may require other means he must acquire a right to, for example, food to keep him alive; he must put together, with the cooperation of others, a feasible package.

There are particular rights over particular things held by particular persons, and particular rights to reach agreements with others, *if* you and they together can acquire the means to reach an agreement. (No one has to supply you with a telephone so that you may reach an agreement with another.) No rights exist in conflict with this substructure of particular rights. Since no neatly contoured right to achieve a goal will avoid incompatibility with this substructure, no such rights exist. The particular rights over things fill the space of rights, leaving no room for general rights to be in a certain material condition. The reverse theory would place only such universally held general "rights to" achieve goals or to be in a certain material condition into its substructure so as to determine all else; to my knowledge no serious attempt has been made to state this "reverse" theory.

John Rawls

A Theory of Justice

THE MAIN IDEA OF THE THEORY OF JUSTICE

My aim is to present a conception of justice which generalizes and carries to a higher level of abstraction the familiar theory of the social contract as found, say, in Locke, Rousseau, and Kant.[1] In order to do this we are not to think of the original

From John Rawls, *A Theory of Justice* (Cambridge, Mass.: The Belknap Press, 1971). Excerpted by permission of Harvard University Press. Copyright © 1971 by The President and Fellows of Harvard College.

[1]As the text suggests, I shall regard Locke's *Second Treatise of Government,* Rousseau's *The Social Contract,* and Kant's ethical works beginning with *The Foundations of the Metaphysics of Morals* as definitive of the contract tradition. For all of its greatness, Hobbes's *Leviathan* raises special problems. A general historical survey is provided by J. W. Gough, *The Social Contract,* 2d ed. (Oxford: Clarendon Press, 1957), and Otto Gierke, *Natural Law and the Theory of Society,* trans. with an introduction by

contract as one to enter a particular society or to set up a particular form of government. Rather, the guiding idea is that the principles of justice for the basic structure of society are the object of the original agreement. They are the principles that free and rational persons concerned to further their own interests would accept in an initial position of equality as defining the fundamental terms of their association. These principles are to regulate all further agreements; they specify the kinds of social cooperation that can be entered into and the forms of government that can be established. This way of regarding the principles of justice I shall call justice as fairness.

Thus we are to imagine that those who engage in social cooperation choose together, in one joint act, the principles which are to assign basic rights and duties and to determine the division of social benefits. Men are to decide in advance how they are to regulate their claims against one another and what is to be the foundation charter of their society. Just as each person must decide by rational reflection what constitutes his good, that is, the system of ends which it is rational for him to pursue, so a group of persons must decide once and for all what is to count among them as just and unjust. The choice which rational men would make in this hypothetical situation of equal liberty, assuming for the present that this choice problem has a solution, determines the principles of justice.

In justice as fairness the original position of equality corresponds to the state of nature in the traditional theory of the social contract. This original position is not, of course, thought of as an actual historical state of affairs, much less as a primitive condition of culture. It is understood as a purely hypothetical situation character-ized so as to lead to a certain conception of justice. Among the essential features of this situation is that no one knows his place in society, his class position or social status, nor does any one know his fortune in the distribution of natural assets and abilities, his intelligence, strength, and the like. I shall even assume that the parties do not know their conceptions of the good or their special psychological propensi-ties. The principles of justice are chosen behind a veil of ignorance. This ensures that no one is advantaged or disadvantaged in the choice of principles by the outcome of natural chance or the contingency of social circumstances. Since all are similarly situated and no one is able to design principles to favor his particular condition, the principles of justice are the result of a fair agreement or bargain. For given the circumstances of the original position, the symmetry of everyone's relations to each other, this initial situation is fair between individuals as moral persons, that is, as rational beings with their own ends and capable, I shall assume, of a sense of justice. The original position is, one might say, the appropriate initial status quo, and thus the fundamental agreements reached in it are fair. This explains the propriety of the name "justice as fairness": it conveys the idea that the principles of justice are agreed to in an initial situation that is fair. The name does not mean that the concepts of justice and fairness are the same, any more than the phrase "poetry as metaphor" means that the concepts of poetry and metaphor are the same.

Ernest Barker (Cambridge: University Press, 1934). A presentation of the contract view as primarily an ethical theory is to be found in G. R. Grice, *The Grounds of Moral Judgment* (Cambridge: University Press, 1967). John Rawls, *A Theory of Justice* (Cambridge, Mass.: The Belknap Press, 1971). §19, note 30.

Justice as fairness begins, as I have said, with one of the most general of all choices which persons might make together, namely, with the choice of the first principles of a conception of justice which is to regulate all subsequent criticism and reform of institutions. Then, having chosen a conception of justice, we can suppose that they are to choose a constitution and a legislature to enact laws, and so on, all in accordance with the principles of justice initially agreed upon. Our social situation is just if it is such that by this sequence of hypothetical agreements we would have contracted into the general system of rules which defines it. Moreover, assuming that the original position does determine a set of principles (that is, that a particular conception of justice would be chosen), it will then be true that whenever social institutions satisfy these principles those engaged in them can say to one another that they are cooperating on terms to which they would agree if they were free and equal persons whose relations with respect to one another were fair. They could all view their arrangements as meeting the stipulations which they would acknowledge in an initial situation that embodies widely accepted and reasonable constraints on the choice of principles. The general recognition of this fact would provide the basis for a public acceptance of the corresponding principles of justice. No society can, of course, be a scheme of cooperation which men enter voluntarily in a literal sense; each person finds himself placed at birth in some particular position in some particular society, and the nature of this position materially affects his life prospects. Yet a society satisfying the principles of justice as fairness comes as close as a society can to being a voluntary scheme, for it meets the principles which free and equal persons would assent to under circumstances that are fair. In this sense its members are autonomous and the obligations they recognize self-imposed.

One feature of justice as fairness is to think of the parties in the initial situation as rational and mutually disinterested. This does not mean that the parties are egoists, that is, individuals with only certain kinds of interests, say in wealth, prestige, and domination. But they are conceived as not taking an interest in one another's interests. They are to presume that even their spiritual aims may be opposed, in the way that the aims of those of different religions may be opposed. Moreover, the concept of rationality must be interpreted as far as possible in the narrow sense, standard in economic theory, of taking the most effective means to given ends. I shall modify this concept to some extent, . . . but one must try to avoid introducing into it any controversial ethical elements. The initial situation must be characterized by stipulations that are widely accepted.

In working out the conception of justice as fairness one main task clearly is to determine which principles of justice would be chosen in the original position. To do this we must describe this situation in some detail and formulate with care the problem of choice which it presents. . . . It may be observed, however, that once the principles of justice are thought of as arising from an original agreement in a situation of equality, it is an open question whether the principle of utility would be acknowledged. Offhand it hardly seems likely that persons who view themselves as equals, entitled to press their claims upon one another, would agree to a principle which may require lesser life prospects for some simply for the sake of a greater sum of advantages enjoyed by others. Since each desires to protect his interests, his capacity to advance his conception of the good, no one has a reason to acquiesce in an enduring loss for himself in order to bring about a greater net balance of satisfaction. In the absence of strong and lasting benevolent impulses, a rational man would not accept a basic structure merely because it maximized the algebraic sum of advantages irrespective of its permanent effects on his own basic rights and interests. Thus it seems that the principle of utility is incompatible with the conception of social cooperation among equals for mutual advantage. It appears to be inconsistent with the idea of reciprocity implicit in the notion of a well-ordered society. . . .

I shall maintain instead that the persons in the initial situation would choose two rather different principles: the first requires equality in the assignment of basic rights and duties, while the second holds that social and economic inequalities, for example inequalities of wealth and authority, are just only if they result in compensating benefits for everyone, and in particular for the least advantaged members of society. These principles rule out justifying institutions on the grounds that the hardships of some are offset by a greater good in the aggregate. It may be expedient but it is not just that some should have less in order that others may prosper. But there is no injustice in the greater benefits earned by a few provided that the situation of persons not so fortunate is thereby improved. The intuitive idea is that since everyone's well-being depends upon a scheme of cooperation without which no one could have a satisfactory life, the division of advantages should be such as to draw forth the willing cooperation of everyone taking part in it, including those less well situated. Yet this can be expected only if reasonable terms are proposed. The two principles mentioned seem to be a fair agreement on the basis of which those better endowed, or more fortunate in their social position, neither of which we can be said to deserve, could expect the willing cooperation of others when some workable scheme is a necessary condition of the welfare of all. Once we decide to look for a conception of justice that nullifies the accidents of natural endowment and the contingencies of social circumstance as counters in quest for political and economic advantage, we are led to these principles. They express the result of leaving aside those aspects of the social world that seem arbitrary from a moral point of view. . . .

TWO PRINCIPLES OF JUSTICE

I shall now state in a provisional form the two principles of justice that I believe would be chosen in the original position. In this section I wish to make only the most general comments, and therefore the first formulation of these principles is tentative. . . .

The first statement of the two principles reads as follows:

First: each person is to have an equal right to the most extensive basic liberty compatible with a similar liberty for others.

Second: social and economic inequalities are to be arranged so that they are both (a) reasonably expected to be to everyone's advantage, and (b) attached to positions and offices open to all. . . .

By way of general comment, these principles primarily apply, as I have said, to the basic structure of society. They are to govern the assignment of rights and duties and to regulate the distribution of social and economic advantages. As their formulation suggests, these principles presuppose that the social structure can be divided into two more or less distinct parts, the first principle applying to the one, and the second to the other. They distinguish between those aspects of the social system that define and secure the equal liberties of citizenship and those that specify and establish social and economic inequalities. The basic liberties of citizens are, roughly speaking, political liberty (the right to vote and to be eligible for public office) together with freedom of speech and assembly; liberty of conscience and freedom of thought; freedom of the person along with the right to hold (personal) property; and freedom from arbitrary arrest and seizure as defined by the concept of the rule of law. These liberties are all required to be equal by the first principle, since citizens of a just society are to have the same basic rights.

The second principle applies, in the first approximation, to the distribution of income and wealth and to the design of organizations that make use of differences in authority and responsibility, or chains of command. While the distribution of wealth and income need not be equal, it must be to everyone's advantage, and at the same time, positions of authority and offices of command must be accessible to all. One applies the second principle by holding positions open, and then, subject to this constraint, arranges social and economic inequalities so that everyone benefits.

These principles are to be arranged in a serial order with the first principle prior to the second. This ordering means that a departure from the institutions of equal liberty required by the first principle cannot be justified, or compensated for, by greater social and economic advantages. The distribution of wealth and income, and the hierarchies of authority, must be consistent with both the liberties of equal citizenship and equality of opportunity.

It is clear that these principles are rather specific in their content, and their acceptance rests on certain assumptions that I must eventually try to explain and justify. A theory of justice depends upon a theory of society in ways that will become evident as we proceed. For the present, it should be observed that the two principles (and this holds for all formulations) are a special case of a more general conception of justice that can be expressed as follows.

All social values—liberty and opportunity, income and wealth, and the bases of self-respect—are to be distributed equally unless an unequal distribution of any, or all, of these values is to everyone's advantage.

Injustice, then, is simply inequalities that are not to the benefit of all. Of course, this conception is extremely vague and requires interpretation.

As a first step, suppose that the basic structure of society distributes certain primary goods, that is, things that every rational man is presumed to want. These goods normally have a use whatever a person's rational plan of life. For simplicity, assume that the chief primary goods at the disposition of society are rights and liberties, powers and opportunities, income and wealth. . . . These are the social primary goods. Other primary goods such as health and vigor, intelligence and imagination, are natural goods; although their possession is influenced by the basic structure, they are not so directly under its control. Imagine, then, a hypothetical initial arrangement in which all the social primary goods are equally distributed: everyone has similar rights and duties, and income and wealth are evenly shared. This state of affairs provides a benchmark for judging improvements. If certain inequalities of wealth and organizational powers would make everyone better off than in this hypothetical starting situation, then they accord with the general conception.

Now it is possible, at least theoretically, that by giving up some of their fundamental liberties men are sufficiently compensated by the resulting social and economic gains. The general conception of justice imposes no restrictions on what sort of inequalities are permissible; it only requires that everyone's position be improved. We need not suppose anything so drastic as consenting to a condition of slavery. Imagine instead that men forego certain political rights when the economic returns are significant and their capacity to influence the course of policy by the exercise of these rights would be marginal in any case. It is this kind of exchange which the two principles as stated rule out; being arranged in serial order they do not permit exchanges between basic liberties and economic and social gains. The serial ordering of principles expresses an underlying preference among primary social goods. When this preference is rational so likewise is the choice of these principles in this order.

In developing justice as fairness I shall, for the most part, leave aside the general conception of justice and examine instead the special case of the two principles in serial order. The advantage of this procedure is that from the first the matter of priorities is recognized and an effort made to find principles to deal with it. One is led to attend throughout to the conditions under which the acknowledgment of the absolute weight of liberty with respect to social and economic advantages, as defined by the lexical order of the two principles, would be reasonable. Offhand, this ranking appears extreme and too special a case to be of much interest; but there is more justification for it than would appear at first sight.... Furthermore, the distinction between fundamental rights and liberties and economic and social benefits marks a difference among primary social goods that one should try to exploit. It suggests an important division in the social system. Of course, the distinctions drawn and the ordering proposed are bound to be at best only approximations. There are surely circumstances in which they fail. But it is essential to depict clearly the main lines of a reasonable conception of justice; and under many conditions anyway, the two principles in serial order may serve well enough. When necessary we can fall back on the more general conception.

The fact that the two principles apply to institutions has certain consequences. Several points illustrate this. First of all, the rights and liberties referred to by these principles are those which are defined by the public rules of the basic structure. Whether men are free is determined by the rights and duties established by the major institutions of society. Liberty is a certain pattern of social forms. The first principle simply requires that certain sorts of rules, those defining basic liberties, apply to everyone equally and that they allow the most extensive liberty compatible with a like liberty for all. The only reason for circumscribing the rights defining liberty and making men's freedom less extensive than it might otherwise be is that these equal rights as institutionally defined would interfere with one another.

Another thing to bear in mind is that when principles mention persons, or require that everyone gain from an inequality, the reference is to representative persons holding the various social positions, or offices, or whatever, established by the basic structure. Thus in applying the second principle I assume that it is possible to assign an expectation of well-being to representative individuals holding these positions. This expectation indicates their life prospects as viewed from their social station. In general, the expectations of representative persons depend upon the distribution of rights and duties throughout the basic structure. When this changes, expectations change. I assume, then, that expectations are connected: by raising the prospects of the representative man in one position we presumably increase or decrease the prospects of representative men in other positions. Since it applies to institutional forms, the second principle (or rather the first part of it) refers to the expectations of representative individuals.... [N]either principle applies to distributions of particular goods to particular individuals who may be identified by their proper names. The situation where someone is considering how to allocate certain commodities to needy persons who are known to him is not within the scope of the principles. They are meant to regulate basic institutional arrangements. We must not assume that there is much similarity from the standpoint of justice between an administrative allotment of goods to specific persons and the appropriate design of society. Our common sense intuitions for the former may be a poor guide to the latter.

Now the second principle insists that each person benefit from permissible inequalities in the basic structure. This means that it must be reasonable for each relevant representative man defined by this structure, when he views it as a going concern, to prefer his prospects with the inequality to his prospects without it. One is not allowed to justify differences in income or organizational powers on the ground that the disadvantages of those in one position are outweighed by the greater advantages of those in another. Much less can infringements of liberty be counterbalanced in this way. Applied to the basic structure, the principle of utility would have us maximize the sum of expectations of representative men (weighted by the number of persons they represent, on the classical view); and this would permit us to compensate for the losses of some by the gains of others. Instead, the two principles require that everyone benefit from economic and social inequalities. It is obvious, however, that there are indefinitely many ways in which all may be advantaged when the initial arrangement of equality is taken as a benchmark. How then are we to choose among these possibilities? The principles must be specified so that they yield a determinate conclusion.

Kai Nielsen

Capitalism, Socialism, and Justice

I

There is, understandably, a not inconsiderable amount of argument about justice under capitalism and socialism as well as much argument about what principles of

From Kai Nielsen, "Capitalism and Social Justice," in *And Justice for All*, edited by Tom Regan and Donald Vanderveer (Totowa, N.J.: Rowman and Littlefield, 1981.) Reprinted by permission of author and publisher.

justice, if any, would characterize these socio-economic systems. When we reflect on capitalist and socialist societies, when we think about fundamental alternatives in our social world, we want to gain, if we can, a sense of which societies, particularly under optimal conditions, would be the juster societies and which would answer most fully to the needs and legitimate aspirations of human beings. However, before we can even begin to approach these questions, we should say something about what capitalism and socialism are....

A common view of the difference between capitalism and socialism simply equates capitalism with the private ownership of capital and socialism with the public or State ownership of capital. The basic distinction is drawn in terms of the legal ownership of the means or instruments of production. It is, however, a mistake to characterize either capitalism or socialism solely in terms of legal relations of ownership. We also need to take note of forms of effective control and power, as well as different class formations and different conceptions of democracy. Capitalism is a system in which a class of owners (the capitalists), typically a numerically very small class, owns and controls most of the means of production and buys the labor power—where that labor power is a commodity—of workers. These workers (the proletariat) typically are the greater majority of the people in the society. The capitalists use the proletariat's labor power to produce wealth, i.e., to produce profits and accumulate capital, which in turn is owned and controlled by the capitalist. Capitalism is thus a system of wage labor with private ownership and control of the means of production, and, as a consequence, a capitalist society is a class society divided into two principal classes—classes that Marxists regard as antagonistic classes—the capitalist class, which owns and controls the major means of production and buys labor power, and the working class (the proletariat), which either owns no means of production or very little and sells its labor power to the capitalist for wages.

A socialist society by contrast is a society in which all able-bodied people are, except during periods of childhood and retirement, workers. In its pure form it is, no more than capitalism, a state ownership and control of the means of production. It is rather a form of social ownership and control of the means of production. This means that the workers collectively have effective control of their own workplaces. This further requires that a socialist society be a worker's democracy which in turn means that it will, unlike a capitalist society, which is at best a political democracy, also be an economic and industrial democracy, with workers, in the form of worker's councils and the like, owning and controlling their own means of production and workplace and deciding, in consultation and cooperation with other workers, who similarly own and control their means of production and workplace, what is to be produced, how much is to be produced, what is to be done with what is to be produced and what the working hours and conditions are to be.

Such a society will be decentralized with participatory controls for the individuals, though the various working units will also be centrally coordinated by democratically elected and recallable worker's representatives from the various working units. The inequalities of wealth, power, and control characteristic of all capitalist societies (pure and impure) could not obtain in a socialist society of the pure and paradigmatic form I have just described. In a socialist society the needs of everyone are considered alike and the ultimate community unit is all of human-kind.

A socialist society would be a society in which every able-bodied adult person would be required to work—he who does not work does not eat—and labor contribution would be according to ability. But the wage relation would be abolished—no one would or could sell their labor power as a commodity, for there would be no one to buy it—and the workers would be in cooperative control of their own instruments of production in a society in which the cleavage between physical and mental labor would gradually be overcome, through the all-around develop-ment of human beings....

Even in their impure forms, there are still important differences between State capitalism and State socialism. Unlike State capitalist societies, in State socialist societies there is no way to inherit ownership and control of the means of production. Moreover, "state socialist societies have gone much further toward equalizing the distribution of essential goods and services such as food, housing, medical care, and transportation."[1] The underlying rationale of socialist production is the satisfaction of the needs of everyone in the community, with an interest in capital accumulation only being instrumental to that end.... *In this respect* a State's socialist society is no different from any other socialist society. But crucial differences remain. In particular, Non-Statist socialist societies are participatory and democratic forms of socialism in which State bureaucracies and social and economic hierarchies managing the society have been eliminated. We have in a socialist society of the pure form a society of self-governing and self-managing workers with directly chosen representatives subject to recall and replacement. Socialism should not be confused with State ownership, as perhaps it is in the Soviet Union, or with the labor reformism and welfare policies of even the most progressive social democracies (Sweden, Iceland, and Denmark), as some in capitalist countries have a tendency to do. What is central to socialism is the common or social ownership and control of the means of production in a society in which everyone is a worker. The ownership and control is vested in these workers, working together fraternally and cooperatively.

II

The four socio-economic systems previously discussed (1) capitalism (*laissez-faire,* competitive capitalism), (2) State capitalism, (3) State socialism, and (4) socialism may be viewed as models both for how industrial societies *can* be organized and for how they *ought* to be organized. State capitalism and State socialism—both in various forms and degrees—are not only models: they are also social realities. *Laissez-faire* capitalism and socialism (participatory socialism if you will) remain at present only ideals: conceptions of what some people think a just or a truly human society would be like.

What I would like to do now is to articulate, particularly where they have strong philosophical representation, what some of those alternative conceptions and accounts of justice are when they are matched with these four distinct systems for organizing society, beginning with *laissez-faire* capitalism, especially as this view is defended by this century's leading philosophical spokesman for libertarianism, Robert Nozick.

For libertarians individual liberty is the cardinal moral conception. It can never be sacrificed or traded off or even be diminished to attain a greater equality or even to attain a more extensive overall system of secure basic liberties. It is, for libertarians, the highest value in the firmament of values.

Liberty for libertarians is negative liberty. They would indeed be happy, as an initial rough characterization, with J. S. Mill's conception of liberty as that of a person having the right, free from interference, to pursue what that person takes to be her own good in her own way as long as her actions do not interfere with the similar liberties of others. In a free society, we must not be interfered with in the doing of what we want to do as long as we do not violate the rights of others. To be free is to be able to choose your own life plans according to your own lights and to be free from governmental and other institutional interference or regulation.

The conception of justice that goes with that libertarian stress on freedom—a conception defended most elaborately by Robert Nozick—claims that justice exists to protect an individual's liberty. Given this conception, it is taken by libertarians to be an evident corollary that whatever economic arrangements we freely consent to are thereby just, if they do not involve fraud, deceit, or the appropriation of something already justly appropriated or acquired.[2] Contrary to orthodox liberal assumptions—Welfare State capitalist assumptions—there is no particular *pattern of distribution* that justice requires. And since there is no pattern of distribution that justice requires, it cannot be the case, unless it can be shown that extensive rectifications of past injustices are in order, that justice demands extensive economic redistribution.

Not only do libertarians conceive of liberty negatively as the right to choose as one will, free from interference, they also, in stressing, as they do, individual rights, stress negative rights. Indeed it is very likely that "negative rights" for a libertarian is redundant. They are the only kind of genuine rights except for those contractually acquired. There are things we have a right to do and have, if we can do them or get them, where we, in these activities, are not to be interfered with by others. There are boundaries between people that just *must* not be crossed....

The central thing to see is that there are negative rights that all human beings have that can never, according to such an account, justly or rightly be overridden. But no one is obliged or in anyway morally required to do anything for anyone, unless they have agreed to do so or they have already harmed that person and must rectify a past violation of rights. Even when the society has the industrial and technical capacity to do so, there is no obligation at all to provide people with material goods they might urgently need or with health care or with education or with meaningful, satisfying or even gainful work. There is no obligation in any circumstances (where there has been no violation of rights) to meet even the most basic subsistence needs of other persons, even when it is not difficult for the agent to whom a plea for aid is directed to do so. The appropriate way to view human beings, on a libertarian account, is as autonomous and responsible individuals capable of fending for themselves. We must, of course, not harm them but we need not help them no matter how dire their straits unless we are responsible for their being in such straits. What is to be done, according to libertarians, is to create a social environment in which human beings are left to fashion their own lives free from the interference of others. We neither need a big daddy nor a big brother and we have a right to be free from any such paternalistic interference with our lives. It is evident enough that libertarianism is a radical individualism.

It is a deeply embedded libertarian belief that *only* by an acknowledgment of this near absolute right to negative liberty, to choose without interference how one is to live one's life, and what social arrangements one will make, can the distinctiveness or separateness of individuals as persons be respected. Such a conception, when translated into a social theory, involves a rejection of anything like the Welfare State and involves either a rejection of state authority altogether, and the acceptance of *individualistic* anarchism, or the commitment to the accepting as legitimate a minimal, night watchman state. It involves endorsing the minimal state and rejecting the legitimacy of any more extensive state control or state functions. The State, for example, has no right to tax us and to take that money—money in reality stolen from us—and use it for its redistributive schemes, no matter how benevolent they may be. This remains the case even when the redistributive schemes are enlightened and humane and would relieve considerable misery. The State's legitimate functions are limited to protecting the negative rights of its citizens. That is to say, it is to protect them from theft, fraud, violence, coercion, and the like. But it has no right to get into the redistribution business. It can and should play a night watchman role but it is not to play a paternalistic role.

It is called the minimal state because its authority is so severely restricted and it is called the night watchman state because of the minimal legitimate functions it has.

Libertarians are also committed to a parallel economic doctrine, namely *laissez-faire* capitalism. Just as they reject the Welfare State and defend a minimal State, they reject contemporary corporate or State capitalism and defend *laissez-faire* (free market, competitive) capitalism. To disturb the free market, on their view, is to tread on liberty and to redistribute wealth through taxation is to engage in coercive practices which in effect utilize forced labor. It is, on the libertarian view, quite incompatible with justice to do anything like that....

III

Robert Nozick...develops, as a further specification of this libertarian social theory, a distinctive *entitlement* theory of justice. What this means can be explained as follows.

Justice, for Nozick, as for libertarians generally, is a backward looking virtue concerned with who, because of his past acts, is entitled to what. It is not, for him, a forward-looking virtue concerned with what distributive or redistributive patterns to achieve or to maintain.[3] Instead, an entitlement theory is concerned most fundamentally with (1) justice in original acquisition, (2) justice in transfer, as in a voluntary exchange from a just original acquisition, and (3), where some injustice in acquisition or transfer has already taken place, justice in rectification. In determining what is just, it is almost always crucial to ascertain what happened in the past: how some state of affairs came about. This is why Nozick calls the entitlement theory a historical theory. Whether a certain distribution of benefits and burdens is just does not depend *at all* on what the actual pattern of distribution is but on how the pattern came about. *Any* pattern of holdings is just, if the distributive pattern results from just original acquisitions and just transfers, or, where in the past some violation in the justice of original acquisition has occurred or something like fraud in transfer has occurred, rectification is required and the pattern meets those requirements.

Our common talk—at least common in roughly liberal circles—of "distributive justice" is not, on Nozick's view, ideologically neutral. It gives us a skewed picture of what justice is. If we are held captive by that theory, we will, when we think of what is just or unjust, operate with a picture something like that of an adult in a position of authority seeking to make a fair division of a pie to children. But in our social life there is no authority, no central distribution center, which is "entitled to control all the resources" and decide "how they are to be doled out" in what this authority takes to be a fair way. We should reject such paternalistic political images. The morally appropriate picture is one of a society in which each person gets what he gets from his own efforts or from others who give to him these things in exchange or as a gift. . . . There is no overall governing principle here. *Justice just is these various entitlements.* It is not some preferred distributive pattern, either egalitarian or otherwise. "The complete principle of distributive justice would say simply that a distribution is just if everyone is entitled to the holdings they possess under the distribution."[4]

For such an account one plain and very central question is *how do we,* if indeed we can at all, *identify a just original acquisition? . . .*

This Lockean account of justice in initial acquisition gives us an account of when we came to have a property right in some unowned object. *We gain a property right in such an object, we are entitled to such an object, when (a) we mix our labor with it and (b) when there is "enough and as good left in common for others"* (b is called *Locke's proviso*). If (a) and (b) obtain we have justly acquired it. We are now entitled to it; it is now a holding of ours and, as something which is ours, we are entitled to do with it what we like as long as we do not harm others in doing so. Thus, if I find a stick in an unowned forest and I fashion it into a spear (thus mixing my labor with it), it is thereby mine, if there are enough other sticks of similar quality lying around for others to use. I now own it and can do with it what I will, short of harming others with it by, for example, running them through.

Mixing one's labor with something previously unowned is a *necessary* but not a *sufficient* condition for coming to own such an object in an original just acquisition. We do not automatically get full ownership over something if "the stock of unowned objects that might be improved is limited. When this condition obtains, it is crucial to ask whether the appropriation of the unowned object worsens the situation of others."[5] The Lockean proviso that there be "enough and as good left in common for others" is "meant to ensure that the situation of others is not worsened."[6] . . . [A] "medical researcher who synthesizes a new substance that effectively treats a certain disease and who refuses to sell except on his terms does not worsen the situation of others by depriving them of whatever he has appropriated."[7] He has a right, not to be overridden, to refuse to sell it.

Nozick believes that a competitive capitalist socio-economic system will not sanction actions which violate the Lockean proviso. "The free operation of a market system will not actually run afoul of the Lockean proviso. . . ."[8] This being so, there will be no justification for state action in the acquisition of property and the like. We do not need a State with powers greater than the minimal state.

IV

Nozick's conception of how we determine whether original acquisitions are just is subject to an array of criticisms, criticisms which reflect back on his entitlement theory generally and on the very foundations of libertarianism.

For Nozick an acquisition is a just acquisition of an unowned object only if it doesn't make people worse off than they were before the acquisition. Suppose we have a system of property relations that bring about a state of affairs S in which many people remain miserable and are worked very hard at very low wages, but still are not worse off, everything considered, than they were prior to the institution of those property relations. However, the situation is one in which another state of affairs S' could be brought about in which there is generally much less misery and exploitation. But to bring about S' requires some overriding of that system of private property, i.e., those just initial acquisitions. It requires, that is, the end of a system of private property rights in the *means of production* and the institution of a social ownership and control of the means of production. Even if this new situation S' would provide better work at a better pay scale and be a situation in which there was far less misery than in S, still, on Nozick's account, we should stick with S and take property rights as inalienable and absolute as long as the Lockean proviso is met. Such a judgment conflicts in a radical way with my considered judgments. It seems to me just wrong, indeed evil, to stick with inalienable *property* rights in such a situation: a situation where by sanctioning them we ensure far more misery than would otherwise obtain. Nozick, no doubt, would reply that here I am simply invoking an "end-state principle" of a roughly utilitarian sort. I would reply that whatever we should say *in general* about utilitarian reasoning it is morally arbitrary not to so reason here. We have a duty to prevent misery where we reasonably can. To treat some *property* rights, particularly property rights in the means of production, as inalienable when by overriding them great suffering for many people can be alleviated is, morally speaking, monstrous.[9]. . .

To see what is involved in such a judgment consider the case of the medical researcher who effectively synthesizes a new substance which will effectively cure cancer. Nozick rightly remarks that if he refuses to sell it except on his own terms, he does not violate the Lockean proviso, even if he does sell it at such a high price that few can purchase it and many will die from cancer who otherwise would not if they had had the drug. Nozick says that if the researcher so acts he has done nothing wrong. He can do what he likes with his property as long as he doesn't use it in such a way that he harms others. By so acting, he doesn't harm others, though he admittedly doesn't help them, for without the new drug they would have died anyway. They are no worse off than they otherwise would be if he hadn't made the invention. So by making the invention, by acquiring that particular bit of property, he hasn't done them any harm. I say such behavior on the part of the researcher is morally monstrous. To have a drug that will save lives and prevent extensive misery and yet to withhold it from those who need it is simply vile. In such a situation there are moral obligations to provide *mutual aid* and to relieve suffering: if the researcher is not willing to make the drug available, property which he owns or not, he should be forced to do so by the State or by social pressure.

Nozick would respond that such state intervention would be too destructive of human freedom to be morally acceptable. But why should this be so if we interfere with freedom in *such cases*? Why should we think this would start a slippery slope that would lead to our interfering with freedom all over the place? There are no good grounds for believing that that will be the upshot of overriding property rights in such a circumstance.

There is also a distinct lack of realism in Nozick's account. He gives us what in effect is an inapplicable model. For any of the property relations that now actually obtain, we do not know, or even have any reasonable grounds for believing, that they were acquired by an original just acquisition meeting anything like the Lockean proviso. What we do know is that, if we go back far enough, there were plenty of unowned objects around that could have been initially acquired under conditions that would meet the Lockean proviso. At one time there must have been more than enough to go around and as good in kind or nearly so. But what the original transfers were like we do not know. It is, of course, *logically* possible that they could have been just transfers but it is far more likely that plunder, the use of violence, force, and deceit were there from the very beginning. In many cases it surely must be the case that we hardly properly speak of anything like a contractual transfer, but just of marauders seizing other people's holdings. We do not know what these human transactions were like; there are no reasonable grounds for believing that the present holdings of people are on Nozick's criteria just and legitimate holdings. He frankly throws up his hands at this problem, but this shows that his model is inapplicable to the real world. It is a model which is utterly useless in determining what our actual entitlements are. In an important sense his "historical theory" is very unhistorical.

V

... Nozick is surely right in stressing the deep moral import of individuals being able to shape their own lives, in being free to carve out a meaningful life for themselves. But in a capitalist system—or at least in a system of unrestricted capitalism—it is only a very privileged or lucky few who can do so. The rights and liberties that Nozick takes to be morally required are a very restrictive list. We have an inviolable right not to be interfered with in certain determinate ways. That is, others must abstain from murdering us, assaulting us, stealing from us, breaching contracts with us and the like. These rights are what have been called *negative* rights and they require abstention from certain things on the part of others. But to limit rights to negative rights is an arbitrary move. Why should people not have a right to have their basic needs met (health needs, needs for security and decent housing, needs for meaningful work and for education) where these needs can be met? It is simply morally arbitrary (to put it minimally) to claim that a person has an absolute, permanent, exclusive, inheritable and uncodifiable right to own and control productive property (say, a factory) and to deny, in a society of reasonable affluence, that a person has any right at all to an education, to health care, and to be protected from starvation. It is meaningless to talk of the protection of an individual's right to a meaningful life which he shapes himself while denying him the right to the necessary means to live such a life. Under the system of unrestricted capitalism Nozick favors, most people, through no fault of their own, would find it quite impossible to live the meaningful life that Nozick takes to be essential to human life. To will such a life is to will the necessary means to it. Among these necessary means are certain material and social conditions and opportunities that libertarians claim that society—that is individuals acting collectively—is under no moral constraint to provide. This turns the familiar libertarian description of a "free society" into a cruel joke. To think of a system of unrestricted capitalism as a "free society" is to have a very impoverished conception of a free society.

VI

Nozick is a trenchant critic of egalitarianism of both a Welfare State sort and a socialist sort. To press home his point, and make it vividly concrete, he develops his Wilt Chamberlain parable, a parable many, on first reading at least, find quite compelling.

Nozick asks us to suppose we are living in an egalitarian society operating under an egalitarian principle of justice—a principle which specifies that a certain patterned end-result is to obtain. Suppose Wilt Chamberlain lives in that society as well as many avid basketball fans who are very keen on seeing Wilt play. Suppose further he signs the following contract with a professional basketball team. In each home game twenty-five cents added to the price of each ticket will go to him. The season starts and the home fans cheerfully attend the games quite willing to pay the extra twenty-five cents to see Wilt play basketball. During the course of the season Wilt gains a very considerable additional income—say, 250,000 dollars—upsetting the previously egalitarian income patterns in our egalitarian society. But isn't he plainly entitled to the extra income? He freely contracted for it, he worked for it, and the fans freely and happily paid the extra twenty-five cents to see him play. It was their money, on a previously equal distribution, to do with what they wanted to as long as they did not so use it as to harm others. In this instance, they simply disposed of their resources as they wanted to and people who didn't go to the games cannot complain that any injustice has been done to them, for they still have what they were entitled to (their rightful "shares") under the egalitarian distributional pattern. To keep an egalitarian pattern would, Nozick claims, be too destructive of individual liberty. We must, in the name of liberty and a respect for people's rights and moral integrity, reject patterned end-state principles of justice. (An end-state distributional principle is a principle which maintains that the justice of a distribution depends on certain structural features of the situation it depicts, such as its utility or the degree of equality which results from acting in accordance with it. Where a principle of justice is an end-state principle which specifies that holdings are to vary along with some natural dimension or some combination of natural dimensions, it is also called a patterned principle by Nozick.)

This argument of Nozick's has been, I believe, refuted by G. A. Cohen and in the course of his refutation Cohen also makes plain how a socialist society would not undermine liberty in the way Nozick fears.[10]

I shall set out and examine some of the core portions of Cohen's argument. He first points out that the Chamberlain parable, as Nozick presents it, seems morally innocuous. What could be wrong, we ask ourselves, with the fans so financially compensating Chamberlain? They get to see him play, which is what they want, and he gets some more money, which is what he wants. And he doesn't get it by stealing from them or by defrauding them or coercing them or exploiting them, for they voluntarily transfer some of their holdings to him to get what they want. This respects both their freedom and his freedom. If the initial situation is just, which *ex hypothesis* it is, the resulting situation of just transfers must also be just. If we have respect for liberty and believe that justice requires liberty, we will not view it as morally right to require (by some deliberate social policy) a redistribution so as to return to the *initial status quo* before Chamberlain made his wad. It seems morally arbitrary to require such a redistribution.

Cohen argues that actually it is not and that there is a rationale for such a redistribution that respecters of liberty should acknowledge. The reason why we should limit the amount that Wilt Chamberlain, or any individual should have a right to hold, is to prevent them or their heirs from acquiring through such holdings an unacceptable amount of power and control over others. Through their enhanced wealth, which will tend to go on accumulating (the rich tend to get richer), they will gain power, in a previously egalitarian society, the possession of which tends to undermine the liberty of others. Because of this accrual of power to the rich, the non-rich have rather less control over their lives than they otherwise would have.[11] Even if, as in this case, the Wilt Chamberlain types come to hold what they hold in a morally innocuous way, the effects of their coming to have these holdings, whatever their intentions, are going to be anything but innocuous. It is slightly hysterical to get worried about Wilt Chamberlain *per se* but the effect of a number of people so acquiring holdings in that way is to create a situation in which there will be a large power differential between this class of people and others. And this will translate into a differential in their respective liberty, one which is plainly harmful to democracy. If we prize moral autonomy we will not favor such situations. In short, what Cohen shows is that the Chamberlain transaction is not, as Nozick presents it, beneficial or even harmless to everyone with an interest in it. Quite to the contrary, "it threatens to generate a situation in which some have unacceptable amounts of power over others."[12] Indeed it is very likely to worsen the situation of many people.

Once Chamberlain has received the "payments he is in a very special position of power in what was previously an egalitarian society."[13] Socialists will be wary of such transactions because they can see the potentially destructive effects of them on both liberty and equality in an egalitarian society. The socialist's reluctance here is not grounded in envy of Wilt Chamberlain's getting such a wad. The socialist's worry is about the potential for undermining an egalitarian society (a republic of equals), where people are genuinely equals and can control their own political and social destinies, free from the coercive control of power hierarchies who gain control of the society. In an egalitarian society, at last free from class division and domination, the socialist sees a wedge being entered, which, if allowed to widen, will once more set the society on the road to class division and domination. The resistance of socialists to *such* freedoms flows from their commitment to a society where, for all of us, there will be no master above us or servants under us, a society where we will be free and equal moral persons living together in fraternity and solidarity. Seeing the Chamberlain case as morally innocuous fails to take into consideration the corrupting effects of such precedents on such a society....

Nozick seems to take as absolute, or nearly so, the fans' entitlement to dispose of their resources (in this instance their money) as they deem fit, as long as they do not harm others. But why should this right be so absolute? Their rights would be violated only if they are taken to be absolute. But why not take all rights as *prima facie* and as defeasible? They can be overridden without being violated, if certain conditions obtain. Nozick has not shown that any restrictions which would forbid the Chamberlain transaction must be unjustified. Although it might turn out that sanctioning *that* transaction will not be particularly harmful, if we do so in that case, we must sanction such transactions in relevantly similar cases. But if we do allow such arrangements it is likely that they will generate an inordinate power and consequent control in the hands of a few. With that power we have at least the very real possibility of the control of the many by the few with the big holdings. This is something that is repeatedly neglected in bourgeois apologetics.[14] And Nozick indeed utterly neglects it. But it is a potent source of harm to many human beings....

Nozick has not *justified* an appeal to certain rights as being absolute. Given that Nozick has failed in that task, socialists plainly "need not apologize for being willing to restrict freedom in order to expand it."[15] Generally, libertarians wish to take their stand here and argue that they are the protectors of individual rights and liberty with a conception of society which, if it were to be exemplified in modern industrial societies, would have to be exemplified in competitive capitalist societies.

I have been concerned to show that this is not true. We cannot equate such a capitalist society with a free society. It would further some freedoms and severely restrict others.[16] It would maximize the freedom of the market place for those who are the great owners of capital. It would further strengthen the control the big capitalists have on society and further undermine the freedom of most people.[17] It would give economic freedom to the privileged few while weakening generally the structures of freedom in the society. It legitimizes selfishness and makes a virtue of callousness in human relations.[18]

VIII

State Capitalism, particularly the Welfare State Capitalism defended by contemporary liberals and social democrats, has a different conception of the just society, as we have seen and as we shall see more fully in what follows. Our next question is whether, as Welfare State liberals believe, but socialist critics deny, a Welfare State capitalist society would be as just or juster than a non-Statist socialist system. We shall explore this question by concentrating on *A Theory of Justice,* the seminal work by Nozick's colleague at Harvard, John Rawls.

IX

I shall begin by examining some of the core arguments between Rawls and his socialist critics in an attempt to see if we can get a grip on whether, under conditions of material abundance, ideal but still achievable forms of socialism are, or are not, juster social systems than ideal but still achievable forms of Welfare State capitalism.

I shall first simply state fundamental liberal principles of justice and fundamental socialist principles of justice—and then turn to commentary on them. The liberal principles are in Rawls's formulation and the socialist principles are my own.

Liberal Principles of Justice: Justice as Fairness

1. Each person is to have an equal right to the most extensive total system of equal basic liberties compatible with a similar system of liberty for all.

2. Social and economic inequalities are to be arranged so that they are both:

   a. to the greatest benefit of the least advantaged consistent with the just savings principle, and

   b. attached to offices and positions open to all under conditions of fair equality of opportunity.

Socialist Principles of Justice: Justice as Equality

1. Each person is to have an equal right to the most extensive total system of equal basic liberties and opportunities (including equal opportunities for meaningful work, for self-determination and political and economic participation) compatible with a like treatment of all. (This principle gives expression to a commitment to attain and/or sustain equal moral autonomy and equal self-respect.)

2. After provisions are made for common social (community) values, for capital overhead to preserve the society's productive capacity, allowances are made for differing unmanipulated needs and preferences, and due weight is given to the just entitlements of individuals, the income and wealth (the common stock of means) is to be so divided that each person will have a right to an equal share. The necessary burdens requisite to enhance human well-being are also to be equally shared, subject, of course, to limitations by differing abilities and differing situations (natural environment not class position).[19]...

Someone arguing for the Socialist Principles could very well begin their critique of the Liberal Principles by starting with the *difference* principle, namely with the claim that inequalities are just, or at least are justified, only if they maximally benefit the worst off under the constraints articulated by Rawls. For it could be the case, as Rawls allows, that the Liberal Principles are in force, that they are actually being correctly applied, and that we would, if we reasoned in accordance with them, still be committed to accepting as *just* a not inconsiderable disparity in total life prospects between children of entrepreneurs and the professional class, on the one hand, and children of unskilled laborers or people on welfare, on the other, even when those children are equally talented, equally energetic and the like.

This seems manifestly unjust. It is unfair that one child's life prospects are such that, when he starts out in life, it is close to inevitable that he will end up working (if he has any work at all) all his life in a factory, a mine or the like, while another child's life prospects are such that it makes it almost inevitable that he will enter the professional or entrepreneurial strata of society. Such disparities in life prospects are basically unfair or unjust, unless they are unalterable or the costs of their cure are worse than the grave ills they perpetuate. Given that such disparities in total life prospects are such plain ills *and* that they do not appear to be unalterable, the burden of proof is surely on the defender of the capitalist order to show that they cannot be altered or that the costs of breaking down these disparities are too high.

The liberal Rawlsian response is that they are necessary evils that we have to live with, even in affluent societies, to avoid still greater evils. It is, such liberals would plausibly argue, bad enough that such inequalities in total life prospects must exist, but it is still worse, by narrowing them, to make the children of unskilled workers still worse off. It is, everything considered, juster and more decent, to accept these not inconsiderable disparities in life and apply the *difference* principle, accepting only such reductions in these disparities as are sanctioned by the *difference* principle.

If we start, as defenders of both the Liberal Principles and the Socialist Principles insist, with the deep underlying commitment that in the design of institutions all people are to have *a right to equal concern and respect,* and if we believe that liberation from class society is possible, we will not be satisfied with the *difference* principle, even when it is surrounded by Rawls's safeguards, for, where such differences in whole life prospects obtain, there will be differences in power and control in society riding with these differences in life prospects. Differences, recall, sanctioned by the *difference* principle. These in turn will make it impossible for the most disadvantaged effectively to exercise anything like fully equal citizenship and this in turn will undermine their standing on a footing of equal liberty with the more advantaged, e.g., the capitalists and the professional elite. Moreover, much work in capitalist society is degrading and undermining of human autonomy, and, where the worker sees her condition with any clarity, undermining of self-respect. This could be lessened in capitalist society but not obliterated, for in the capitalist production process workers are simply told to carry out certain tasks. In that very important area of their lives, they lack autonomy. They work for a salary and do what they are told: they, generally, have no alternative, except the even more degrading alternative of going on the dole.

Where this is seen by people subjected to alienated labor, there is a tendency to suffer a loss of self-respect, a loss not certain to be made good by abiding by Rawls's *difference* principle. Contrary to Rawls, then, it is arguable that in a society of material abundance the most disadvantaged would, where fully informed and rational, choose the second Socialist Principle rather than the *difference* principle, if they prize the good of self-respect and autonomy as much as Rawls believes they would and should. They would prefer, under these circumstances, a somewhat lesser income (lesser material wealth) if this would enable them to have a greater control over their own lives—a fuller realization of liberty and the good of self-respect. They would not and should not accept the differences in power and control acceptable under the *difference* principle.

A socialist belief is that this cannot be attained in class society with its inevitable differences in power and control in society. State capitalist societies, committed to Liberal Principles, can ameliorate this condition and they are an advance over *laissez-faire* capitalism with its commitment to libertarianism. But in class society —any class society—equal citizenship, equal liberty, and equal opportunity cannot be attained. Thus, if they are otherwise obtainable, a capitalist society (even a Social Democratically oriented Liberal Welfare State Capitalism) cannot be a fully just society. It is the claim of socialism that there are such alternatives: that there is a liberation, or at least the reasonable hope of liberation, from class society.

X

(1) In comparing the Liberal Principles and the Socialist Principles, I have argued that the socialist second principle ought to be accepted rather than the *difference* principle, but I have said nothing in favor of the first principle, either to distinguish it from the first liberal principle or to show why, as both the liberal formulation and the socialist formulation do, such stress should be placed on the attainment and protection of equal liberty and moral autonomy.

... the liberal first principle and the socialist first principle are very alike in that they call for the widest possible system of equal liberty, though the socialist principle makes more explicit what is involved. It is not basic differences over whether to accept something like an equal liberty principle that divide liberals and socialists.

However, there are people (some utilitarians among them) who would not accept the equal liberty principle. Why, they would ask, even in situations of abundance, give such weight to liberty, to self-determination, and to something as obscure and airy-fairy as the good of self-respect? Why care so much about equal citizenship, equal autonomy, and the good of self-respect? The answer, I believe, lies in recognizing that the value of moral autonomy and the good of self-respect are rooted in deeply felt considered judgments and beliefs about what it is to live a human life. It is tied up, I believe, with our deepest hopes about ourselves and about what it would be to live a life with integrity.

The need to have some control over one's own existence, to be able to direct and orient one's own life according to a conception chosen by oneself from alternatives that seem meaningful to one, is a very powerful and persistent need indeed and becomes more powerful the more securely one's basic subsistence needs are met and the more leisured one is from endless backbreaking toil. That in barest outline is why the attainment and protection of equal liberty and autonomy are so important.

(2) I have argued for socialism over *laissez-faire* capitalism. But suppose I am wrong and socialism is not a reasonable non-fanciful possibility and our actual choices are only between State capitalism and State socialism. Then is it not reasonable to believe that, not State capitalism *sans phrase,* but Liberal Welfare

State capitalism is a juster and better social system than *any form* of State socialism? Isn't Sweden clearly a better society to live in than Cuba?

It is not unreasonable to be skeptical about whether the aims of socialism are attainable. If it is not reasonable to believe that they are, should we opt for the reformist aims of social democracy or State socialism?

Now, in view of the Liberal Principles and Socialist Principles of justice I have articulated, we readily can see that even the best forms of State capitalism and State socialism are flawed in terms of liberty, the good of self-respect, equal citizenship, equality and industrial democracy, and that they both are hierarchical, bureaucratic societies with elites and with paternalistic control.

However, unlike some actual State capitalist and State socialist societies, there is no reason at all why possible forms of each could not be political democracies, have respect for rights and civil liberties and be societies of plenty. Assuming this much, what grounds, if any, in terms of justice and morality, do we have for choosing one of these social systems over the other? Three reasons can be given for choosing State socialism. First, State socialism is committed to maximally, and equally, satisfy needs and to foster capital accumulations as instrumental only to that. State capitalism, by contrast, has no such underlying rationale. Second, State capitalism rests on its class structure. State socialism will indeed produce elites, but a) its belief system cannot justify their existence, except as temporary expedients, and b) the elites lack the clear structural means of the capitalist class for intragenerationally passing on their privileges. Third, since socialists are committed to attaining classlessness and to taking the standpoint of labor, there are strong grounds, in terms of social legitimization in the socialist belief system, to push for a greater equality and for the expansion of liberty.

NOTES

1. Richard C. Edwards, Michael Reich, and Thomas E. Weisskopf, eds., *The Capitalist System,* 2nd ed. (Englewood Cliffs, N.J.: Prentice Hall, 1978), xiii.

2. That this economic doctrine is actually such a corollary of liberty is powerfully challenged by G.A. Cohen in his "Capitalism, Freedom and the Proletariat" in *The Idea of Freedom,* ed. Alan Ryan (Oxford: Oxford University Press, 1979), 9–25, and by John Exdell, "Liberty, Equality and Capitalism," *Canadian Journal of Philosophy* (1981).

3. Robert Nozick argues this in the middle section of *Anarchy, State and Utopia* (New York: Basic Books, 1974) and it has been argued by Antony Flew in "Equality *or* Justice," *Midwest Studies in Philosophy,* III (1978), 176–194 and "A Theory of Social Justice," in *Contemporary British Philosophy,* ed. H. D. Lewis (New York: Humanities Press, 1976), 69–85. I have criticized such accounts in my "Impediments to Radical Egalitarianism," *American Philosophical Quarterly* (1981) and my "A Rationale for Egalitarianism," *Social Research* (1981).

4. Nozick, op. cit., 152–53.

5. Ibid., 175–76.

6. Ibid.

7. Ibid.

8. Ibid.

9. George Kateb, "The Night Watchman State," *The American Scholar* (1977), 816–25.

10. G. A. Cohen, "Robert Nozick and Wilt Chamberlain: How Patterns Preserve Liberty" in *Justice and Economic Distribution,* eds. J. Arthur and W. H. Shaw (Englewood Cliffs, N.J.: Prentice-Hall, 1978), 246–62. See also his essay cited in footnote 2.

11. Cohen, "Robert Nozick and Wilt Chamberlain: How Patterns Preserve Liberty," 251.

12. Ibid.

13. Ibid.

14. Ibid, 253.

15. Ibid, 257.

16. Cohen, "Capitalism, Freedom and the Proletariat."

17. Martin J. Sklar, "Liberty and Equality and Socialism," *Socialist Revolution* 7, no. 4 (July–Aug., 1977): 92–104.

18. Boris Frankel, "Review Symposium of Anarchy, State and Utopia," *Theory and Society,* 3 (1976): 443–49.

19. It might be thought that there is a qualifying element in my second principle of socialist justice that gives everything away to the libertarian. Things are to be divided equally *only after due weight is given to the just entitlements of individuals.* What more could Nozick ask for? But the catch here is on the reading to be given to "due weight." As my discussion of the principle makes clear, as well as my discussion of Nozick's principles of justice, entitlements cannot be legitimately insisted on in situations where insisting on them would cause great harm and suffering or in an undermining of human liberty, e.g., one cannot rightly hold on to one's patent rights and let thousands die as a result of hanging on to them, and one cannot hold on to productive property where having that property gives one power over the lives of others such that whole life prospects of people are radically unequal. Thus, "due weight" is accorded one's entitlements by recognizing that to have an entitlement to something is to have a *prima facie* right to it and that we have a *prima facie* obligation not to interfere with the exercising of that right. Such a recognition is giving "due weight." However, in order to maintain patterns which preserve liberty, we will occasionally be required to override a particular entitlement, just as we will also disallow some entitlements (e.g., no one is allowed privately to own productive property) in order to maintain patterns which preserve liberty. This is consistent with insisting that we can never rightly ignore the claims of entitlement.

SUGGESTIONS FOR DISCUSSION

1. Are the principles of distributive justice to be established by way of a social contract? In what ways would distributive principles established by a social contract (Gauthier, Rawls, or Nielsen) differ from Aristotelian principles of distribution (see Part I, Chapter 1).

2. Should the liberty to accumulate holdings be regarded as a social value more fundamental than the principle of equality, or should egalitarianism be regarded as a "liberty-limiting principle"?

3. Political economies may be judged morally on economic and political grounds. Does free market capitalism or liberal welfare state capitalism or socialism best meet the joint constraint of distributive justice and guaranteeing rights?

FURTHER READING

Arthur, J., and Shaw, W., eds. *Justice and Economic Distribution.* Englewood Cliffs, N.J.: Prentice-Hall, 1978. (Interpretation, critical analysis; advanced)

Braverman, H. *Labor and Monopoly Capital*. New York: Monthly Review Press, 1974. (Critical analysis; advanced)

Brown, P., Johnson, C., and Vernier, P., eds. *Income Support: Conceptual and Policy Issues*. Totowa, N.J.: Rowman and Littlefield, 1981. (Interpretation, critical analysis; advanced)

Feinberg, J. *Social Philosophy*. Englewood Cliffs, N.J.: Prentice-Hall, 1973. (Interpretation, critical analysis; intermediate)

Fisk, M. *Ethics and Society*. Brighton: Harvester Press, 1980. (Interpretation, critical analysis; advanced)

Friedman, M. *Capitalism and Freedom*. Chicago: University of Chicago Press, 1958. (Critical analysis; introductory)

Gray, J. *Liberalism*. Minneapolis: University of Minnesota Press, 1986. (Interpretation, critical analysis; introductory)

Harrington, M. *Socialism*. New York: Bantam Books, 1973. (Interpretation, critical analysis; introductory)

Hayek, F. A. *The Constitution of Liberty*. Chicago: University of Chicago Press, 1960. (Interpretation, critical analysis; intermediate)

Held, V., ed. *Property, Profits and Economic Justice*. Belmont, Calif.: Wadsworth, 1980. (Interpretation, critical analysis; advanced)

Lucash, F., ed. *Justice and Equality Here and Now*. Ithaca: Cornell University Press, 1986. (Interpretation, critical analysis; advanced)

McMurrin, S., ed. *Liberty, Equality and the Law*. Salt Lake City: University of Utah Press, 1987. (Critical analysis; advanced)

Nielsen, K. *Equality and Liberty: A Defense of Radical Egalitarianism*. Totowa, N.J.: Rowman and Littlefield, 1984.

Nozick, R. *Anarchy, State, and Utopia*. New York: Basic Books, 1974.

Rawls, J. *A Theory of Justice*. Cambridge, Mass.: Harvard University Press, 1971.

———. "Justice as Fairness: Political Not Metaphysical." *Philosophy and Public Affairs* 14 (Summer 1985): 223–51.

Reiman, J. "The Fallacy of Libertarian Capitalism." *Ethics* (October 1981): 85–95. (Critical analysis; advanced)

Sterba, J., ed. *Justice: Alternative Political Perspectives*. Belmont, Calif.: Wadsworth, 1980. (Interpretation, critical analysis; intermediate)

Williams, B. "The Idea of Equality." In *Philosophy, Politics and Society 2,* edited by P. Laslett and W. Runciman. Oxford: Basil Blackwell, 1962. (Interpretation, critical analysis; advanced)

8

□

Affirmative Action
(Race and Sex)

Discrimination Discrimination against members of minority racial groups or against women in virtue of their sex has been a persistent feature of social history. It was widely held in the past that blacks and women are irrational or intellectually inferior, and so incapable of performing intellectually demanding functions. Where evidence was cited to support such derogatory and injurious claims, it turned out to involve biased samples; the testing was inadequate and culturally skewed; and the test results were overgeneralized or manipulated to "substantiate" prejudiced hypotheses. We generally agree now that it is wrong for both persons and social institutions to discriminate against others on grounds of their race or sex. There is no natural or biological relation between racial membership or gender, on one hand, and ability, task performance, or moral desert, on the other. Social institutions play a formative role in our lives; so institutional discrimination on the basis of race or sex is especially unjust, for it excludes persons from social goods, services, and opportunities that ought to be available to all. In short, racial membership or gender is irrelevant to just social distributions, and any form of racial or sexual discrimination violates the moral principle that people be treated equally (see Part II, Chapter 7).

Minorities, especially blacks, and women have suffered the injustices of being denied social goods readily available to others (especially white males). Minorities and women have been handicapped in realizing available opportunities, and in many cases completely excluded from the competition for social resources. This has served to militate against the self-respect of minority group members and women, and to undermine their sense of self-worth.

Affirmative Remedies Pressing questions arise concerning social justice. Given the long history and deep legacy of discrimination, would justice be best served simply by outlawing these unfair discriminatory practices, as some hold? If no affirmative programs are instituted to complement the declaration that such practices are illegal, would it not leave in place current control of social institutions and economic inequities that favor white males? Affirmative remedies may be introduced, accordingly, either to compensate for past wrongs and inequities or to institute a more just social arrangement.

258

Compensation and Equality   Remedies for discrimination generally tend to be of two kinds. Retrospective remedies set out to rectify past harms by instituting compensatory programs. These remedies appeal to the *principle of compensation,* which claims that anyone harmed in violation of his or her rights should be (in legal language) "made whole again" by the injuring party; that is, reinstated to the position that would have been occupied had the harm not taken place. So these remedies are mainly consequentialist in aiming to remove the harms of extensive discrimination. By contrast, prospective remedies tend to be deontological, and appeal to the *principle of equality.* This principle maintains that the interests of each individual must carry the same weight as those of any other. Remedies appealing to the principle are concerned with the moral quality of future society and aim to bring about a racial and sexual blend in institutions, which is considered to be just independent of any good consequences that may follow from it. These retrospective-consequentialist and prospective-deontological patterns are trends, not hard and fast rules. Some have argued that a backward-looking duty of reparation is deontological; and some prospective arguments directed at achieving a good society are consequentialist.

Affirmative Action and Preferential Treatment   *Affirmative action* programs tend more to be prospective than retrospective. While they may aim at compensating for past wrongs, they tend mostly to establish equal opportunity (if not equal distributions) for minorities and women. Now there is much that the principle of equality might require in this respect: that every effort be made to find minority and women candidates in job hiring, promotions, and university and other admissions; that availability of positions be openly advertised and characterized in nondiscriminatory ways; and that hiring or admissions committees employ nondiscriminatory categories and criteria in their decisions. One prominent form that affirmative action programs have assumed is *preferential treatment;* that is, hiring or admitting minorities or women primarily because of their group membership. Some have objected that preferential treatment of groups whose members have been excluded from access to social resources amounts to unacceptable forms of *reverse discrimination* against those formerly favored (usually white males). Preferential treatment programs favoring minorities and women are taken to exclude or discriminate against others unfairly on the basis of their race or sex. The moral question facing us here, then, is whether preferential treatment programs by nature discriminate in reverse and so are morally impermissible, or whether to conceive of them in this way is to misunderstand their nature.

Supreme Court Rulings   This issue can be illustrated in terms of recent Supreme Court decisions concerning remedies for racial discrimination. In *Brown v. Board of Education* (1954), the "separate but equal" principle was declared unconstitutional. This principle had afforded southern states a convenient justification for maintaining segregated schooling, despite the Fourteenth Amendment (1868). Over the ensuing two decades, the Court moved considerably beyond the race-neutral spirit of the Fourteenth Amendment and the Civil Rights Act (1964). Preferential treatment of minorities and women in job hiring and college admissions was considered permissible: minority and women candidates could be hired or admitted to positions reserved for them even when white or male candidates might be at least as well qualified. For institutions where the effects of racial discrimination were found to be deep-seated, the Court has permitted employment, promotion, or admissions *quotas* to be used. Quotas guarantee set proportions of available positions for minority or women candidates.

This progressive trend was restricted in a landmark ruling, *University of California v. Bakke* (1978). The University of California, Davis Medical School had reserved 16 of 100 first-year slots for minority students (blacks, Hispanics, and Filipinos) whose entrance qualifications might be lower than those of white candidates. Alan Bakke, a white applicant, was twice rejected by Davis despite better test scores than those of some minority candidates who were accepted. The Court ruled that Bakke had been the victim of reverse racial discrimination. Use of racial quotas in hiring or admissions could not be justified simply on the basis of their beneficial social effects. The Court nevertheless upheld that colleges and universities may use "race" as *one* of their criteria for admission. Since *Bakke,* the Court has granted limited sanction to the temporary use of quotas. Quotas have been considered an exceptional institutional remedy for deep-seated intentional discrimination (as in the Alabama state police which has continued to exclude blacks from promotions to senior positions). Use of quotas or goals becomes impermissible once it is evident that the discriminatory trend at issue has been reversed.

Readings   Michael E. Levin claims that a policy of preferential treatment rewards blacks or women regardless of whether *they* have been wronged and that it tends to do so at the expense of innocent whites or men. Levin admits that racial discrimination is wrong. He contends, however, that it is not the worst of wrongs one might face. Acts of murder or theft, for example, are worse. If victims of discrimination or their ancestors deserve special compensation for past wrongs, then victims of murder and *their* ancestors deserve redress first. Levin thinks that as the latter is absurd, the former must be also. Moreover, if compensation is justifiable at all in the former case, Levin insists that it should not take the form of employment, for this replaces "merit" with "race" as the standard of hiring. The proper redress would be the monetary equivalent of jobs. Levin concludes that there is nothing special about the wrongness of racial discrimination: lynching is wrong not because it discriminates against blacks, but because it is an act of murder. He concludes that racial discrimination fails to warrant the special compensation of reverse discrimination.

Levin fails to address the argument that pervasive racism and sexism have encouraged the dominant stereotype that blacks and women are inferior and that this dehumanization perpetuates the status quo, leaving group members persistently exposed to being objects of abusive behavior. This abusive behavior may include rape, murder, assaults, and discriminatory hiring practices. Louis Katzner develops a form of this argument. He acknowledges the criticism that preferential compensation may discriminate in reverse against white males without benefiting the actual victims of the original discrimination. This would be the case where a preferential treatment program is designed to benefit a *group,* though some group members have not suffered discrimination. Accordingly, Katzner formulates four individually necessary and jointly sufficient conditions for *justified* reverse discrimination: The compensation must redress an initial act of discrimination; it must benefit either the person(s) directly handicapped or those indirectly inheriting the handicap arising from the discrimination; the victim of the proposed reverse discrimination must have benefited from some discriminatory act; and without reverse discrimination, future generations would continue to suffer the effects of past discrimination. Katzner suggests that blacks but not women typically meet all four criteria. (Katzner may be wrong about women here.) He adds that if it is to be justifiable to treat blacks (or women) preferentially as a *group,* two additional arguments would have to be made: first, that it is unfeasible to treat racial (or sex) discrimination on a case-by-case basis; and second, that almost all blacks (or women) continue to suffer discrimination directly.

Howard McGary, Jr., argues that virtually all blacks, and many women, have suffered severe discrimination, including those who have overcome the burdens of injustice and are now advantaged. Discrimination has constituted a devastating attack on blacks' self-respect and sense of self-worth. Those wronged are entitled to have these injustices acknowledged and redressed, thereby restoring the primary social good of self-respect. The appropriate form of redress, in addition to properly targeted preferential treatment programs, is a carefully administered reparations policy. Reparations would remove illegitimate advantages of the discriminating group and "make the victims whole." McGary's defense of the "reparations theory of social justice" is not consequentialist but right-based (see Mackie, Part I, Chapter 6). Persons have a fundamental right to self-respect: Victims of discrimination are entitled to the restoration of self-respect by way of reparations.

Justice Lewis F. Powell, Jr.

Majority Opinion in *University of California v. Bakke*

I

Over the past 30 years, this Court has embarked upon the crucial mission of interpreting the Equal Protection Clause with the view of assuring to all persons "the protection of equal laws," in a Nation confronting a legacy of slavery and racial discrimination. Because the landmark decisions in this area arose in response to the continued exclusion of Negroes from the mainstream of American society, they could be characterized as involving discrimination by the "majority" white race against the Negro minority. But they need not be read as depending upon that

United States Supreme Court, 438 U.S. 265 (1978).

characterization for their results. It suffices to say that "[o]ver the years, this Court has consistently repudiated '[d]istinctions between citizens solely because of their ancestry' as being 'odious to a free people whose institutions are founded upon the doctrine of equality.' "

Petitioner urges us to adopt for the first time a more restrictive view of the Equal Protection Clause and hold that discrimination against members of the white "majority" cannot be suspect if its purpose can be characterized as "benign." The clock of our liberties, however, cannot be turned back to 1868. It is far too late to argue that the guarantee of equal protection to *all* persons permits the recognition of special wards entitled to a degree of protection greater than that accorded others. "The Fourteenth Amendment is not directed solely against discrimination due to a 'two-class theory'—that is, based upon differences between 'white' and Negro." ...

II

We have held that in "order to justify the use of a suspect classification, a State must show that its purpose or interest is both constitutionally permissible and substantial, and that its use of the classification is 'necessary . . . to the accomplishment' of its purpose or the safeguarding of its interest." The special admissions program purports to serve the purposes of: (i) "reducing the historic deficit of traditionally disfavored minorities in medical schools and in the medical profession"; (ii) countering the effects of societal discrimination; (iii) increasing the number of physicians who will practice in communities currently underserved; and (iv) obtaining the educational benefits that flow from an ethnically diverse student body. It is necessary to decide which, if any, of these purposes is substantial enough to support the use of a suspect classification. ...

III

A

It may be assumed that the reservation of a specified number of seats in each class for individuals from the preferred ethnic groups would contribute to the attainment of considerable ethnic diversity in the student body. But petitioner's argument that this is the only effective means of serving the interest of diversity is seriously flawed. In a most fundamental sense the argument misconceives the nature of the state interest that would justify consideration of race or ethnic background. It is not an interest in simple ethnic diversity, in which a specified percentage of the student body is in effect guaranteed to be members of selected ethnic groups, with the remaining percentage an undifferentiated aggregation of students. The diversity that furthers a compelling state interest encompasses a far broader array of qualifications and characteristics of which racial or ethnic origin is but a single though important element. Petitioner's special admissions program, focused *solely* on ethnic diversity, would hinder rather than further attainment of genuine diversity.

Nor would the state interest in genuine diversity be served by expanding petitioner's two-track system into a multitrack program with a prescribed number of seats set aside for each identifiable category of applicants. Indeed, it is inconceivable that a university would thus pursue the logic of petitioner's two-track program to the illogical end of insulating each category of applicants with certain desired qualifications from competition with all other applicants. . . .

. . . [A]n admissions program which considers race only as one factor is simply a subtle and more sophisticated—but no less effective—means of according racial preference than the Davis program. A facial intent to discriminate, however, is evident in petitioner's preference program and not denied in this case. No such facial infirmity exists in an admissions program where race or ethnic background is simply one element—to be weighed fairly against other elements—in the selection process. "A boundary line," as Mr. Justice Frankfurter remarked in another connection, "is none the worse for being narrow." And a court would not assume that a university, professing to employ a facially nondiscriminatory admissions policy, would operate it as a cover for the functional equivalent of a quota system. In short, good faith would be presumed in the absence of a showing to the contrary in the manner permitted by our cases.

B

In summary, it is evident that the Davis special admissions program involves the use of an explicit racial classification never before countenanced by this Court. It tells applicants who are not Negro, Asian, or Chicano that they are totally excluded from a specific percentage of the seats in an entering class. No matter how strong their qualifications, quantitative and extracurricular, including their own potential for contribution to educational diversity, they are never afforded the chance to compete with applicants from the preferred groups for the special admissions seats. At the same time, the preferred applicants have the opportunity to compete for every seat in the class.

The fatal flaw in petitioner's preferential program is its disregard of individual rights as guaranteed by the Fourteenth Amendment. Such rights are not absolute. But when a State's distribution of benefits or imposition of burdens hinges on ancestry or the color of a person's skin or ancestry, that individual is entitled to a demonstration that the challenged classification is necessary to promote a substantial state interest. Petitioner has failed to carry this burden. For this reason, that portion of the California court's judgment holding petitioner's special admissions program invalid under the Fourteenth Amendment must be affirmed.

C

In enjoining petitioner from ever considering the race of any applicant, however, the courts below failed to recognize that the State has a substantial interest that legitimately may be served by a properly devised admissions program involving the competitive consideration of race and ethnic origin. For this reason, so much of the California court's judgment as enjoins petitioner from any consideration of the race of any applicant must be reversed.

Michael E. Levin

Is Racial Discrimination Special?

I take "reverse discrimination" to be the policy of favoring members of certain groups (usually racial), in situations in which merit has been at least ideally the criterion, on the grounds that *past* members of these groups have suffered discrimination. I do not include giving someone a job he was denied because *he* was discriminated against, since such redress is justified by ordinary canons of justice, in particular that of giving someone what he is owed. I am referring, rather, to the practice of hiring or admitting a preset number of (e.g.) blacks regardless of whether the blacks so hired have been wronged, and regardless of the qualifications of competing whites. The difference between the two policies is that between restoring a robbery victim's property to him, and hunting up the descendants of robbery victims and giving them goods at the expense of people who themselves robbed no one. I have no quarrel with the former, many quarrels with the latter: I believe reverse discrimination is as ill-advised a course of action as any undertaken by this country in at least a century. It cannot be justified by its social benefits, since experience suggests that the consequences of this policy are proving disastrous.[1] It cannot be justified as giving particular members of the chosen group what they would have gotten if they had not been discriminated against, since by stipulation "affirmative action" goes beyond such an appeal to ordinary ideas of justice and compensation.[2] It penalizes a group of present-day whites—those who are at least as well qualified but passed over—without proof that they have discriminated or directly benefited from discrimination; whites no more responsible for past discrimination than anyone else.

But such frontal assaults on reverse discrimination (or "affirmative action," in bureaucratese) usually accomplish nothing, so I will not attempt one here. I will try instead to focus on a clear-cut issue which is central to the debate but which has, surprisingly, been almost completely ignored. It is this: what is so special about racial discrimination? Let me put the question more exactly. I will be arguing shortly that the only possible defense of reverse discrimination represents it as an attempt to rectify the consequences of past racial discrimination. But why has society selected one kind of wrong—discrimination—as particularly deserving or demanding rectification? Other past wrongs have left their traces—acts of theft, despoliation, fraud, anti-Semitism—yet society has no organized policy of rectifying those wrongs. It surely seems that if the consequences of one kind of wrong should not be allowed to unfold, neither should those of any other. And this is what I want to convince you of: acts of racial discrimination have no morally special status. Important consequences flow from this. For reasons I will propose, it seems to me clear that society—and in particular the employer—has no general standing

From *The Journal of Value Inquiry* 15, 3 (1981): 225–34. Reprinted by permission of the Executive Editor and author.

obligation to block the consequences of past wrongs. So if discriminatory acts are no more deserving of rectification than wrong acts generally, no one is under any obligation at all to rectify them, or to be deprived so that these acts may be rectified.

With these preliminary points as background, let us look at the issue again. I noted that reverse discrimination discriminates against whites in a way which cannot be justified by ordinary notions of justice. Thus, if it is justifiable at all, it must be because we owe something to present-day blacks in some extraordinary sense. And the standard reason offered is that the blacks to be hired today bear the burdens of past discrimination. Had there been no racial discrimination, they would have been able to get those jobs; their qualifications would have been as good as those of the better-qualified whites they are displacing. (It is sometimes added that all whites benefit in some way from past discrimination, so all whites owe blacks something, namely a more advantageous position.) Affirmative action is supposed to rectify the consequences of past discrimination, to draw the string from acts so bad that their consequences cannot be permitted to unfold.[3]

But if our aim is to undo the consequences of past discrimination, the issue I raised becomes very pressing. If there is nothing morally special about discrimination, nothing which makes it especially deserving of rectification, any policy which treats discrimination as if it were morally special is arbitrary and irrational. Consider: Mr. X, a black of today, is supposedly owed special treatment. But surely if you owe Mr. X special treatment because his ancestors were the target of one wrong—discrimination—it would seem you owe Mr. Y special treatment if his ancestors were the target of some other wrong—theft, say. Racial discrimination is not the *only* wrong that can be committed against someone, and indeed it is far from the worst. I would rather be denied a job because I am Jewish than be murdered. My murderer violates my rights and handicaps my children much more seriously than someone who keeps me out of medical school. So the question is: if I owe Mr. X a job because his ancestors were discriminated against, don't I owe Mr. Y the same if his ancestors were defrauded? I believe the answer must be yes: there is nothing special about acts of discrimination. And even if you think I have misrepresented affirmative action or its rationale, the question and its answer are important. Other justifications for reverse discrimination also tend to treat racial discrimination as somehow special. Indeed, a quarter-century's preoccupation with race has created a sense that racial prejudice is not just a wrong but a sin, an inexpungeable blot on the soul. Whether this atttude is rational is an issue worth considering.

Let me start with a truism. Discrimination deserves to be halted where it exists, and redressed where it can be, because it is *wrong*. Discrimination is worth doing something about because *wrongs* are worth doing something about and discrimination is wrong. Once we grant this, we start to see that there is nothing *sui generis* about discrimination. It competes with other wrongs for righting. And I take it as obvious that some wrongs demand righting more urgently than others. If I pass a negative comment on Jones's tie in private but defame Robinson's ancestry on national television, I had better apologize to Robinson before I do so to Jones. And if I have embezzled the funds of an orphanage, top priority goes to seeing that I give the money back. Finally, if Smith is destitute because I defrauded Smith's father, I had better make amends before I worry about the sons of men I insulted. So: denying a man a job on grounds of color is evidently just one among many ways of wronging him. It is far less egregious than assault or murder.

It is frequently but mistakenly claimed that racial discrimination is special because it involves a group. Certainly, an act of racial discrimination involves a whole group in the sense that it involves treating an individual not in his own right but insofar as he belongs to a group. But racial discrimination is not the only kind of act that is thus group-related. Many wrongs having nothing to do with race are discriminatory in the precise sense that they base the treatment of an individual on membership in a morally irrelevant group. Nepotism is discrimination against nonrelatives. When I make my lazy nephew district manager, I am disqualifying more able competitors because they belong to a group—nonfamily—membership in which should not count in the matter at hand. Discrimination need not be racial: any time you make a moral distinction on morally irrelevant grounds, you discriminate invidiously. In a society in which racial discrimination was unknown but capricious nepotism was the norm, denial of due process on grounds of family would provoke as much indignation as racial discrimination does now.

It would be sheer confusion to argue that acts of racial discrimination are special because they insult a whole race as well as wrong an individual. When I assault you, I assault no one else—and when I discriminate against you, I discriminate against no one else. True, my discrimination may indicate a readiness to discriminate against others and may create widespread anxiety—but my assaulting you may indicate a readiness to assault others and create even greater general anxiety. If I bypass Mr. X because he is black, only Mr. X and his dependents suffer thereby. Perhaps because color is so salient a trait, we tend in uncritical moments to think of the black race as an entity existing in and of itself, above and beyond the particular blacks who make it up. Philosophers call this "reification". We then think that an insult to this reified race is particularly malign, either in itself or because this entity somehow transmits to all blacks the harm done by single acts of discrimination. Some such reasoning must underlie the oft-heard ideas that the harm done to a single black man "hurts blacks everywhere" and that the appointment of a black to the Supreme Court is "a victory for blacks everywhere," remarks which make no literal sense. This tendency to reify is especially pernicious in the context of compensation. Why are we willing to contemplate special treatment for blacks now, when we would not contemplate special treatment for someone whose ancestors were defrauded by a man who left no descendants? Because, I suspect, we think that by benefiting today's black we will apologize for the long-ago insult to the race, and that this apology and benefit will somehow be transmitted back to the blacks who endured the original discrimination. Were this picture accurate, it might justify supposing that past discriminatory acts cast longer shadows than other wrongs. But it is just a myth. A racial grouping no more deserves reification than does the class of people whose ancestors were defrauded. We resist the impulse in the latter case only because the trait in question is not visually salient and has no especially coherent history.

(Some slight sense can be made of "injury to a group," as when we say that a traitor endangers the security of a nation. But even here the harm done is to individuals, the particular citizens. The traitor deserves punishment because of the harm he has done to each citizen, not to "the nation" as a thing apart.)

Perhaps the main reason for thinking of acts of racial discrimination as morally distinctive is that each is an instance of a pattern. My discriminating against Mr. X is part of a self-sustaining pattern of wrongs. And, indeed, we do find wrong acts that together form a pattern more disturbing than each wrong act taken singly: Jack the Ripper's legacy is more appalling than eleven isolated murders. Wrongs seem to be like notes, which have different musical values when part of a melody than when heard in isolation. But this intuition must be carefully assessed. A single wrong act cannot be made *more wrong* because there is some other wrong act which it resembles. If I discriminate against you, my act has a certain amount of wrongness. If I then discriminate against someone else, my previous act against you does not take on more wrongness. This is so even with Jack the Ripper. His murder of the first prostitute did not become *more wrong* when he murdered the second. If he had died before committing his second murder, his first murder would still have been as bad as it actually was. If, say, he owed the family of the first prostitute some compensation for his action, he did not suddenly owe them more after his second. So the fact that acts of discrimination come in groups does not show that a single act of discrimination is any worse, any more deserving of rectification, than it would have been had it occurred alone.

Two factors account for our feeling that patterned wrongs are worse than isolated ones. The first is that the *perpetrator* of a patterned wrong is worse. Jack the Ripper is worse than a man who kills once from passion. But this does not mean that what he did, in each case, is worse than a single act of murder. Similarly, the most we can say of bigotry is that a habitual bigot is worse than a one-shot bigot, not that an act of bigotry is in itself worse than an act of caprice. The second reason patterned wrongs seem especially malign is that they create anxiety through their promise of repetition. Jack the Ripper's actions create more anxiety than eleven unconnected murders because we believe he will strike again. But this shows only that it is especially important to *halt patterns*, be they of murder or discrimination. It does not mean that a particular act in a discriminatory pattern is worse than it would have been in isolation. And it is worth repeating that antidiscrimination laws without benefit of affirmative action suffice to halt patterns of discrimination.

Granted, racial wrongs have gone beyond discrimination in hiring or the use of public facilities, extending all the way to lynching. But to acknowledge this is to bring racial wrongs under independent headings—denial of due process, assault, murder. Lynching Emmet Till was wrong not because Emmet Till was black, but because lynching is murder. So if blacks deserve special treatment because of (say) this country's history of lynching, it is because descendants of murder victims deserve special treatment. But this concedes my point: what was wrong about especially egregious acts of racial discrimination is what is wrong about parallel nonracial acts; and if we treat the former as special, we must treat the latter as special as well. I also deny that past discriminations were special because they were state-approved and in some case state-mandated. State sanction in itself can make no difference. Even if "the state" is an entity over and above its citizens and their legal relations, the wrongness of an act (although not the blameworthiness of an agent) is independent of who performs it. So if discriminating is wrong, it is wrong, and to the same extent, no matter who performs it. Therefore, state-sanctioned past discrimination is no stronger a candidate for rectification than any other discrimination. In any case, even if we did consider state sanction to be morally significant, to be consistent we would have to apply this to all other state-sanctioned wrongs. We would have to say, for example, that we ought to give special treatment now to descendants of people who were harmed under the terms of a statute repealed decades ago. But I take it that no one would support affirmative action for the grandchildren of brewmasters bankrupted by the Volstead Act.

Finally, it has been suggested that grave discriminatory wrongs, such as the lynching of Negroes, were special because done with intention of intimidating the other members of the terrorized group. Quite so: but again this makes my very point. To call an act of lynching wrong for this reason is to bring it under the umbrella of *intimidation*: a precisely parallel nonracial act of intimidation is just as wrong (although we might have reason to think the perpetrator is not as vicious). Many years ago, unions were in the habit of wrecking restaurants that refused to be unionized as a warning to other restaurants. Even today, Mob enforcers will kill an informer, or a retailer who refuses to pay protection, in order to intimidate other potential informers or defaulters. So if we treat blacks as special because they belong to a class other members of which were terrorized, so must we treat restaurateurs as special, and indeed all small businessmen in businesses once victimized by the protection racket. And I take it that no one would suggest affirmative action for restaurateurs. Nor will it do to say that this is because today no restaurateur is in danger from union or Mob goons. In fact, a restaurateur is in considerably more danger than a black. The last lynching occurred in 1954, while union vandalism and criminal extortion are the stuff of today's sensational press.

A subsidiary point. I have so far let pass one peculiarity of affirmative action programs: they award jobs (or placement) to rectify past wrongs. Yet normally when we compensate someone for wrongful deprivation, we give him the equivalent of what he lost, giving him the thing itself only when feasible. If a pianist loses his hands through your negligence, you are not obliged to hire him to do a concert. The whole thrust of his complaint, after all, is that he is no longer competent to undertake such an enterprise. You owe him the money he would have made from concertizing, plus some monetary equivalent of the satisfaction your negligence has cost him. So *even if* past racial discrimination has wrongfully cost Mr. X a job, it does not follow that proper compensation is a job. What he is owed is the job or the monetary equivalent thereof. If the job is unavailable—where this normally includes Mr. X's not being the best-qualified applicant—all he is owed is its monetary equivalent. Why, then, is it assumed without question in so many quarters that if past discrimination has cost present-day blacks jobs, they deserve *jobs* rather than the monetary equivalent of the jobs they would have gotten? Only, I believe, because we think there is something *special* about discrimination, that its consequences deserve amelioration in a way that the consequences of other wrongs do not. Discrimination is so bad that not only must we compensate for it, we must so change the world that things will become as if the wrong had never been. Only by attributing such reasoning can I make sense of the special form "affirmative action" programs invariably take. And if indeed racial discrimination is not especially wrong, such special compensation starts to appear morally arbitrary and even bizarre.

It is obvious that no employer has a general obligation to rectify wrongful acts, to offer extraordinary compensation. I am not speaking, again, of righting wrongs he perpetrates or directly benefits from. I mean that if, as a result of some wrong once done—not necessarily to an ancestor—I am worse off than I would have been, you, an arbitrarily chosen employer, have no obligation whatever to neutralize the consequences of that wrong. No one has any obligation to make me as well off as I would have been had that wrong not been committed. Why? Basically because it is *impossible* to rectify the consequences of all past wrongs. Consider how we might decide on compensatory payments. We trace the world back to the moment at which the wrong was done, suppose the wrong not done, and hypothetically trace forward the history of the world. Where I end up under this hypothetical reconstruction is where I deserve to be. I am owed the net difference between where I am now and where I would have been had the wrong not been done.[4] But for most wrongs, it would take omniscience to say how the world would have turned out had the wrong not been done. If you wanted to make up to me for the theft of my grandfather's watch in 1900, how on Earth do you propose to reckon the position I would have been in had my grandfather's watch not been stolen? I might have been richer by a watch. I might have been poorer—since, being in fact deprived of a watch, I have worked harder than I otherwise would have. I might not have existed—if my grandfather met my grandmother while hunting for his stolen watch. Indeed, if you suppose yourself under a general ameliorative obligation, you will have to calculate simultaneously how well off each and every one of us would have been had all past wrongs not occurred. There is more: I am supposedly owed a certain something, but who owes it to me? Surely not you—you don't owe me *all* of it. Do all employers owe me an equal proportion? Or is their proportion dependent on how much they have benefited from the initial theft? If the latter, how is one to calculate their debt, if the theft was in another country and another century?

Suppose I take it on myself to yield to Mr. X if I am better off than he is because of some past wrong—not to him, necessarily, since I am offering extraordinary compensation. Now surely there is some *other* past wrong which has made *me* worse off than I would otherwise have been, worse off than (say) Mr. Y. So I must drop myself down to make way for Mr. X, but I also deserve a push up beyond Mr. Y. If each of us tried to put himself just where he would be if there had been no past wrongs, we would all be caught in a mad whirl of exchanging positions and privileges with one another. If a full reckoning were in, those who now seem as if they would end up in a better position might end up in a worse one. Take Mr. X, an American black, who we think is worse off than he would have been had there been no slavery. Yet he may now be better off than he would have been had his African ancestors not conquered a neighboring tribe that was then raided by slave traders; had his ancestors respected territorial boundaries, Mr. X might now be a sickly native of Uganda. So unless we quite arbitrarily decide to rectify only some wrongs, we are undertaking a quite impossible task. What about limiting ourselves to rectifying wrongs we know about? But then we should surely try as hard as possible to find out about other wrongs, and trace their consequences. Once again, if we set out on that path, we will find ourselves with obligations that cannot be discharged. And an undischargeable obligation is no obligation at all. Indeed, it is far from obvious that the consequences of discrimination are easier to trace than those of other wrongs. I know victims of theft who have nothing to show for it. Why not benefit them? It is clearer that they are worse off from a past wrong than that an arbitrarily chosen black is.

We must remember that we are all where we are in the competitive and distributional scheme of things because of past wrongs. It may be that we got something in a wrongful way, but those from whom we got it may have gotten it wrongfully in turn. Who knows but that all of us are in this room because of some dirty Hellenic trick on the plains of Marathon. Perhaps we should award Western Civilization to the descendants of Xerxes, or give them its dollar equivalent! Each of us lies on a "competition curve," which graphs jobs against our chances of getting them. These curves are connected: I can't move to a better one without bumping someone else down to a worse. If we try to put each person on the curve he would have occupied had there been no relevant wrongdoing, we will be raising and lowering everybody, sometimes at the same time, with no end in sight. Perhaps God is sufficiently powerful, well-intentioned, and well-informed to put each of us on his proper curve. But no lesser power—not ITT and not HEW—can undertake the task without absurdity.

Since, then, no one has any general rectificatory obligation, and since—as I argued earlier—past discrimination does not stand out from other wrongs as especially demanding righting, I can see no justification at all for reverse discrimination.

I have embedded my main point in a somewhat complex argumentative context. Let me end by highlighting it. While racial discrimination is wrong, it is only one wrong among many and has no special claim on our moral attention. Past discrimination no more deserves extraordinary compensation than many other wrongs. And any employment policy which does treat racial discrimination as special is arbitrary and irrational.[5]

NOTES

1. David Kahn's *Hitler's Spies* (New York: Macmillan, 1978) provides a good account of what happens when a society replaces merit standards by racial ones. The primary qualification for the SD (the Nazi party intelligence organ) was "German or similar blood." Kahn notes acidly, "Never mentioned was objectivity in evaluating information" (254). Data in this country are rare, since concerned parties, such as the Medical School of the University of California at Davis, have kept no records of the performance of its affirmative action admittees. So, apart from the interesting but incomplete work of the sociologists Nathan Glazer, Thomas Sowell, and Pierre Vandenberg, one must rely on personal impressions. And the question remains—would you fly in an airplane whose pilot was admitted to an affirmative action training program?

2. I have encountered the argument that reverse discrimination is necessary to prevent future discrimination. So construed, it has all the disadvantages of preventive detention with none of the advantages, such as the elimination of clear and present danger to life and limb.

3. "Rectification" is the best word I can think of for what proponents of affirmative action see themselves as advocating. It is better than "annulment," which carries no implication that an annulled act is wrong *in se*. "Extraordinary compensation" is not only

prolix, it would not sit well with the many defenders of affirmative action I have met who disavow any compensatory aims. I would prefer "visiting the sins of the fathers on the sons," but this might be viewed as tendentious. Statements of particular affirmative action programs —that such-and-such a percentage of so-and-so's be taken on—generally do not carry any statement of justification, and government officials may settle for arguments *ad baculum*. For instance when, on *60 Minutes*, Eleanor Holmes Norton, the head of the Office of Economic Opportunity, was asked about the fairness issue, she replied: "White males will just have to bite the bullet." I suspect that no English word quite captures what reverse discrimination is supposed to do—a fact which says something about the deep confusion underlying this policy and its rationales.

4. This account of compensation is given quite casually in Robert Nozick's *Anarchy, State and Utopia* (New York: Basic Books, 1974). Astonishingly, it has drawn criticism in the literature—astonishingly, because it is not a *theory* of compensation, but a rather uncontroversial description of what compensation is. It is the reasoning juries run through whenever they award an accident victim on the basis of what he would have done had he not suffered the accident. David Lyons ("Rights Against Humanity," *The Philosophical Review* [1976]: 208–15) complains that Nozick ignores "the enormous debt due blacks and Native Americans in our own country" (214). This remark and the passage in which it appears exhibit a disproportionate number of the fallacies I am discussing. Lawrence Davis ("Comments on Nozick's Entitlement Theory," *Journal of Philosophy* [1976]: 836–44) recognizes that on the present sort of account "full-scale rectification of the injustices in our society [in the] past . . . 200 years" is impossible (842), and concludes that this is a weakness of the account. But surely (see below) common sense does not require that an account of rectification guide us through the Sisyphean task of righting 200 years of wrong!

5. I have nowhere discussed the claims of women, among the chief beneficiaries of affirmative action. I find the claim that women have been discriminated against, so discriminated against that women today deserve special treatment, too absurd to merit extensive discussion. The only argument feminists cite in support of the claim that past discrimination has left its mark is the low proportion of managers in the female work force. But not only does this argument itself use equality of result as its criterion for equality of opportunity, the datum itself is quite consistent with the hypothesis that men rise higher in hierarchies because of greater innate aggressiveness: see Steven Goldberg, *The Inevitability of Patriarchy*, 2d ed. (London: Temple Smith, 1977). What I say elsewhere about halting present discrimination and "preventive discrimination" of course applies in the case of women as well.

Louis Katzner

Is the Favoring of Women and Blacks in Employment and Educational Opportunities Justified?

There is presently a call to favor blacks and women in employment and educational opportunities because in the past many of them have been discriminated against in these areas. The basic concern of this paper is whether or not reverse discrimination in this sense is justified. Given that, as will be shown, all acts of reverse discrimination involve prejudgment, it is appropriate to scrutinize first the notion of discrimination itself. Next, the idea of reverse discrimination will be explicated by distinguishing among several different forms that it may take; and from this explication the set of conditions under which a bias of redress is justified will emerge. Finally, the situation of blacks and women in the United States will be examined to see what conclusions can be drawn concerning the justification of reverse discrimination for these two classes.

I. DISCRIMINATION

There are certain things that are relevant to the way people should be treated and certain things that are not. The size of one's chest is relevant to the size shirt he should have, but it has nothing to do with the size his shoes should be. The rate of one's metabolism is pertinent to the amount of food she should be served, but not to the color of the napkin she is given. People should be treated on the basis of their attributes and merits that are relevant to the circumstances. When they are, those who are similar are treated similarly and those who are dissimilar are treated differently. Although these distinctions do involve treating people differently (those with large chests get larger shirts than those with smaller chests), it does not involve discrimination. For discrimination means treating people differently when they are similar in the relevant respects or treating them similarly when they are different in the relevant respects.

It follows that to determine what constitutes discrimination in vocational and educational opportunities, we must first determine what qualities are relevant to a career and the capacity to learn. People today generally seem to accept the principle of meritocracy—that is, that an individual's potential for success, which is a combination of his native and/or developed ability and the amount of effort he can be expected to put forth, is the sole criterion that should be used in hiring and college admissions practices. It may be that until recently many people did not

From *Philosophy of Law,* edited by Joel Feinberg and Hyman Gross (Belmont, Calif.: Dickinson Publishing Co., 1975). Reprinted by permission of the author.

accept this view, and it may be that there are some even today who do not accept it. Nevertheless, this is one of the basic principles of the "American Dream"; it is the foundation of the civil service system; it is a principle to which even the most ardent racists and sexists at least give lip service; and it is the principle that most people seem to have in mind when they speak of the problem of discrimination in hiring and college admissions practices. And because it is generally agreed that people with the same potential should be treated similarly in employment and college admissions, and that those with more potential should receive preference over those with less, the discussion begins with this assumption.

II. REVERSE DISCRIMINATION

With the notion of discrimination clarified, it is now possible to see what is involved in the idea of reverse discrimination. Reverse discrimination is much more than a call to eliminate bias; it is a call to offset the effects of past acts of bias by skewing opportunity in the opposite direction. This paper will consider only the claims that blacks, women, et cetera, have been discriminated against in the past (that is, they have been treated as if they have less potential than they actually do); and that the only way to offset their subsequent disadvantages is to discriminate now in their favor (that is, to treat them as if they have more potential than they actually do).

It follows that those who are currently calling for the revision of admission standards at our colleges because they do not accurately reflect a student's chances of success there are not calling for reverse discrimination. They are merely saying that we should find a way of determining precisely who is qualified (that is, who has the potential) to go to college, and then admit the most qualified. On the other hand, those who are calling for us to admit students whom they allow are less qualified than others who are denied admission, and to provide these less qualified students with special tutorial help, are calling for reverse discrimination.

This example clearly illustrates the basic problem that any justification of reverse discrimination must come to grips with—viz., that every act of reverse discrimination is itself discriminatory. For every less qualified person who is admitted to a college, or hired for a job, there is a more qualified person who is being discriminated against, and who has a right to complain. Hence the justification of reverse discrimination must involve not only a justification of *discriminating for* those who are benefiting from it, it must also involve a justification of discriminating *against* those at whose expense the reverse discrimination is being practiced.

III. JUSTIFICATION OF REVERSE DISCRIMINATION: DIRECT

There are at least two significantly different kinds of situations in which reverse discrimination can be called for. On the one hand, a person might argue that he should be favored because he was arbitrarily passed over at some time in the past. Thus, for example, a Chicano might maintain that since he was denied a job for which he was the most qualified candidate simply because of his race, he should now be given one for which he is not the most qualified candidate, simply because he was discriminated against in the past. On the other hand, one might argue that he should be given preference because his ancestors (parents, grandparents, great-grandparents, et cetera) were discriminated against. In this case, the Chicano would claim that he should be given a job for which he is not the most qualified applicant because his ancestors were denied jobs for which they were the most qualified.

In the former case, that of rectifying bias against an individual by unduly favoring him, there are several interesting points that can be made. First of all, the case for reverse discrimination of this type is strongest when the person to be passed over in the reverse discrimination is the same one who benefited from the initial discriminatory act. Suppose, for example, that when it comes time to appoint the vice-president of a company, the best qualified applicant (that is, the one who has the most potential) is passed over because of his race, and a less qualified applicant is given the job. Suppose that the following year the job of president in the same firm becomes open. At this point, the vice-president, because of the training he had as second in command, is the most qualified applicant for the job. It could be argued, however, that the presidency should go to the person who was passed over for the vice-presidency. For he should have been the vice-president, and if he had been he would probably now be the best-equipped applicant for the top post; it is only because he was passed over that the current vice-president is now the most qualified candidate. In other words, since the current vice-president got ahead at his expense, it is warranted for him to move up at the vice-president's expense. In this way the wrong that was done him will be righted.

There are two main problems with this argument. First of all, certainly to be considered is how well the individual who benefited from the initial act of discrimination exploited his break. If he used this opportunity to work up to his capacity, this would seem to be a good reason for not passing him over for the presidency. If, on the other hand, although performing very adequately as vice-president, he was not working up to the limits of his capacity, then perhaps the job of president should be given to the man who was passed over in the first place—even though the vice-president's experience in his job leads one to think that he is the one most qualified to handle the difficult tasks of the presidency. In other words, how much a person has made of the benefit he has received from an act of discrimination seems to be relevant to the question of whether or not he should be discriminated against so that the victim of that discrimination may now be benefited.

Secondly, there are so few cases of this kind that even if reverse discrimination is justified in such cases, this would not show very much. In most instances of reverse discrimination, the redress is at the expense of someone who did not benefit from the initial act of discrimination rather than someone who did.

One species of this form of reverse discrimination is that in which the victim of the proposed act of reverse discrimination has not benefited from *any* acts of discrimination. In such a case, what is in effect happening is that the burden of discrimination is being transferred from one individual who does not deserve it to another individual who does not deserve it. There is no sense in which "the score is being evened," as in the case above. Because there is no reason for saying that one of the individuals deserves to be penalized by prejudice while the other one does not, it is difficult to see how this kind of reverse discrimination can be justified.

The only argument that comes to mind as a justification for this species of reverse discrimination is the following: The burdens of discrimination should be shared rather than placed on a few. It is better that the liabilities of discrimination be passed from person to person than that they remain the handicap only of those who have been disfavored. It follows that if we find someone who has been discriminated against, we are warranted in rectifying that injustice by an act of reverse discrimination, as long as the victim of the reverse discrimination has not himself been discriminated against in the past.

But this is not a very persuasive argument. For one thing, the claim that discrimination should be shared does not seem a very compelling reason for discriminating against a totally innocent bystander. Secondly, even if this is viewed as a forceful reason, the image of society that emerges is a horrifying one. The moment someone is discriminated against, he seeks out someone who has not been unfairly barred, and asks for reverse discrimination against this person to rectify the wrong he has suffered. Such a procedure would seem to entrench rather than eliminate discrimination, and would produce an incredibly unstable society.

Another species of this form of reverse discrimination is that in which the victim of the proposed reverse bias has benefited from a previous unfair decision, although it is not the particular act that is being rectified. In other words, he did not get ahead at the expense of the individual to whom we are trying to "make things up" by reverse discrimination, but he has benefited from bias against other individuals. In such a case, there is a sense, admittedly extended, in which a score is being evened.

Now it appears that such cases are more like those in which the victim of the proposed act of reverse discrimination benefited from the initial instance of discrimination than those in which he is a completely innocent bystander, and hence in such cases reverse discrimination can be justified. Of course it would be preferable if we could find the beneficiary of the original act of discrimination—but very often this just is not possible. And we must make sure that the reverse discrimination is proportionate to both the liability suffered by the proposed · beneficiary and the advantage previously gained by the proposed victim—a very difficult task indeed. But there does not seem to be any reason for saying that reverse discrimination can only be visited upon those who benefited from the particular discriminatory act that is being rectified. It seems more reasonable to say that reverse discrimination can be visited upon those who benefited from either the particular instance of discrimination being rectified or from roughly similar acts.

Although the conclusions drawn from this discussion of the various species of one form of reverse discrimination do not seem conclusive, this discussion has brought to light three conditions which are necessary for the justification of reverse discrimination: First, there must have been an act of discrimination that is being rectified. Second, the initial act of discrimination must have in some way handicapped its victim, for if he has not been handicapped or set back in some way, then there is nothing to "make up to him" through reverse discrimination. And third, the victim of the proposed reverse discrimination must have benefited from an act of discrimination (either the one that is being rectified or a similar one); otherwise it is unacceptable to say that he should now be disfavored.

IV. JUSTIFICATION OF REVERSE DISCRIMINATION: INDIRECT

Not all of the claims that are made for reverse discrimination, however, assume that the individual involved has himself been the victim of bias. In many cases what is being claimed is that an individual is entitled to benefit from a rectifying bias because his ancestors (parents, grandparents, great-grandparents, et cetera) were unfairly denied opportunity. Keeping in mind the three conditions necessary for reverse discrimination that we have just developed, this form of reverse discrimination will be examined.

In a society in which wealth could not be accumulated, or, even if it could, it did not give one access to a better education and/or job, and a good education did not give one access to a better job and/or greater wealth, it would be hard to see how educational and/or economic discrimination against one's ancestors could be a handicap. That is, if education was not a key to economic success, then the educational discrimination one's ancestors suffered could not handicap one in the search for a job. If wealth did not buy better teachers and better schools, then the fact that one's ancestors have been handicapped economically could not be a reason for his being educationally disadvantaged. If wealth could not start a business, buy into a business, or give one direct access to a good job, then the economic shackling one's ancestors endured could in no way handicap her in the economic realm. But if wealth and education do these things, as in our society they clearly do, and if because of discrimination some people were not allowed to accumulate the wealth that their talents normally would bring, then it is quite clear that their offspring are handicapped by the discrimination they have suffered.

It is important to note that this point in no way turns on the controversy that is currently raging over the relationship between IQ and race. For it is not being claimed that unless there is complete equality there is discrimination. The members of a suppressed group may be above, below, or equal to the other members of society with regard to potential. All that is being claimed is that to the extent that the members of a group have been denied a fair chance to do work commensurate with their capacities, and to the extent that this has handicapped subsequent members of that group, reverse discrimination may be justified to offset this handicap.

But, as we have already seen, for reverse discrimination to be justified, not only must the victims of discrimination be handicapped by the discrimination, those who will suffer from its reversal must have benefited from the original injustice. In this particular case, it may be that they are the children of the beneficiaries of discrimination who have passed these advantages on to them. Or it may be that they benefit in facing reduced competition for schooling and jobs, and hence they are able to get into a better school and land a better job than they would if those suffering the effects of discrimination were not handicapped. Or they may have benefited from discrimination in some other way. But the proposed victims of reverse discrimination must be the beneficiaries of previous discrimination.

In addition to all of this, however, it seems that there is one more condition that must be met for reverse discrimination to be justified. Assuming that if we eliminated all discrimination immediately, the people who have suffered from it could compete on an equal basis with all other members of society, then reverse discrimination would not be justified. This of course is trivially true if it is only being claimed that if the elimination of all discrimination entails the eradication of all the handicaps it creates, then only the elimination of discrimination (and not reverse discrimination) is justified. But the claim involves much more than this. What is being argued is that even if the immediate elimination of all discrimination does not allow all suppressed people to compete equally with other members of society, as long as it allows equal opportunity to all children born subsequent to the end of discrimination, then reverse discrimination is not justified—*not even for those who have been handicapped by discrimination.* In other words, reverse discrimination will not prevent its debilitating effects from being passed on to generations yet unborn.

The justification of this claim is a straightforward utilitarian one (it cannot be a justification in terms of justice since what is being countenanced is blatant injustice). The social cost of implementing a policy of reverse discrimination is very high. The problems in determining who are the victims of discrimination and how great their handicaps, and who are the beneficiaries of discrimination and how great their benefits, as well as the problems in both developing and administering policies that will lead to a proper rectification of discrimination, are not merely enormously complex, they are enormously costly to solve. Moreover, the benefits of ending all discrimination are very great. Not only will many people be hired for jobs and admitted to colleges otherwise barred to them because of discrimination, but many people who have themselves been handicapped by discrimination will take great satisfaction in the knowledge that their offspring will not be held back as they have. This, of course, in no way eliminates the injustice involved in allowing acts of reverse discrimination to go unrectified. All it shows is that given the tremendous cost of implementing a comprehensive program of reverse discrimination, and given the tremendous benefits that would accrue simply from the elimination of all discrimination, it is reasonable to claim that reverse discrimination is justified only if the elimination of discrimination will not prevent its debilitating effects from being passed on to generations yet unborn.

Thus there is a fourth condition that must be added to the list of conditions that are necessary for the justification of reverse discrimination. Moreover, the addition of this condition renders the list jointly sufficient for the justification of reverse discrimination. Thus, reverse discrimination is justified if, and only if, the following conditions are met:

1. There must have been an initial act of discrimination that the reverse discrimination is going to rectify.

2. The beneficiary of the proposed act of reverse discrimination must have been handicapped by the initial act—either directly, if he was the victim of the initial discrimination, or indirectly, if he is the offspring of a victim (and inherited the handicap).

3. The victim of the proposed act of reverse discrimination must have benefited from an act of discrimination—the one that is being rectified or a similar one—and either directly, if he was the beneficiary of an initial act of discrimination or indirectly, if he is the offspring of a beneficiary (and inherited the benefit).

4. It must be the case that even if all discrimination were ended immediately, the debilitating effects of discrimination would be passed on to generations yet unborn.

V. REVERSE DISCRIMINATION FAVORING WOMEN AND BLACKS

A partial answer, at least, to the question of whether or not reverse discrimination is justified in the case of women and blacks is now possible. Let us begin with blacks.

It seems clear that the situation of many blacks in this country meets the four conditions shown to be individually necessary and jointly sufficient for the justification of reverse discrimination. First, there can be no doubt that many blacks have been the victims of educational and vocational discrimination. Second, given the relationships existing between wealth, education, and vocation, there can be no doubt that the discrimination that blacks have met with has handicapped both themselves and their offspring. Third, it also seems clear that within our economic framework, if blacks had not been discriminated against, there are many whites (those who got an education or a job at the expense of a more qualified black or in competition with the handicapped offspring of disadvantaged blacks) who would be in far less advantageous educational and vocational situations than they currently are—that is, there are people who have benefited from discrimination. And finally, again given the relationships existing among wealth, education, and vocation, even if all discrimination against blacks were to cease immediately, many black children born subsequent to this time would not be able to compete for educational and vocational opportunities on the same basis that they would had there been no bias against their ancestors.

Of course this in no way shows that reverse discrimination for all blacks is justified. After all, there are some blacks who have not let themselves be handicapped by discrimination. There are also undoubtedly some whites who have not benefited from the discrimination against blacks. And finally, there are many whites who have endured discrimination in the same way blacks have. In other words, so far it has only been shown that all those who have been discriminated against in a way that meets the conditions established are entitled to reverse discrimination and that some blacks have been discriminated against in this way.

To move from this claim to the conclusion that blacks as a class are entitled to reverse discrimination, several additional things must be shown. First, it must be demonstrated that it is unfeasible to handle reverse discrimination on a case by case basis (for example, it might be argued that such a procedure would be far too costly). Second, it must be proven that the overwhelming percentage of blacks have been victimized by discrimination—that is, the number of blacks who would benefit from reverse discrimination, but who do not deserve to, must be very small. And finally, it must be shown that the overwhelming majority of the potential victims of bias of redress have benefited from the acts of discrimination (or similar acts) that are being rectified—that is, it must be that the number of whites who will suffer the effects of reverse discrimination, without deserving to, must also be very small. If these conditions are met, then although there will be some unwarranted discrimination resulting from the reverse discrimination in favor of blacks (that is, some blacks benefiting who were not victimized and some whites suffering who were not benefited), such cases will be kept to a bare minimum, and hence the basic result will be the offsetting of the handicaps with which blacks have unwarrantedly been saddled.

When it comes to the case of (white) women, however, the situation is quite different. There is little doubt that many women have been denied opportunity, and thus handicapped while many men have benefited from this discrimination (although I believe that discrimination has been far less pervasive in the case of women that it has been for blacks). But women generally do not constitute the kind of class in which the handicaps of discrimination are passed on to one's offspring. This is because, unlike blacks, they are not an isolated social group. Most women are reared in families in which the gains a father makes, even if the mother is limited by society's prejudice, work to the advantage of *all* offspring. (White) women have attended white schools and colleges and, even if they have been discriminated against, their children have attended these same schools and colleges. If all discrimination were ended tomorrow, there would be no external problem at all for most women in competing, commensurate with their potential, with the male population.

Two important things follow from this. First, it is illegitimate for most women to claim that they should be favored because their mothers were disfavored. Second, and most importantly, if all discrimination against women were ended immediately, in most cases none of its debilitating effects would be transmitted to the generations of women yet unborn; hence, for most women, the fourth condition necessary for the justification of reverse discrimination is not satisfied. Thus, reverse discrimination for women as a class cannot be justified, although there are undoubtedly some cases in which, for a particular woman, it can.

One must be careful, however, not to interpret this judgment too broadly. For one thing, the conclusion that reverse discrimination is not warranted for women as a class is contingent upon the immediate elimination of all discrimination. Hence it does not apply if discrimination against women continues. In other words, the conclusion does not show that reverse discrimination for women as a class is unjustified in the face of continuing bias against them. Under these circumstances, reverse discrimination may or may not be justified.

Secondly, as reverse discrimination has been described here, it involves offsetting the impact of a particular kind of discrimination (that is, in educational and job opportunities) by another instance of the same kind of discrimination (that is, preferential treatment in education and job opportunities). All our argument shows is that this is unwarranted for women as a class. One might, however, want to argue in favor of discriminating for women as a class in the area of education and jobs, not to offset previous discrimination in this area, but rather to counter the debilitating effects that institutionalized sexism has had on the female psyche. That is, one might argue that because our society has conditioned women to desire subservient roles (for example, that of a nurse rather than a doctor, secretary rather than executive, housewife rather than breadwinner, and so on), even if all forms of discrimination were eliminated tomorrow, very few (or at least not enough) women would take advantage of the opportunities open to them. Hence we need (reverse) discrimination as a means of placing women in visible positions of success, so that other women will have models to emulate and will strive for success in these areas.

Now although it is not clear whether or not such a program can legitimately be labeled "reverse discrimination," the important point is that this paper has not been addressed to this kind of problem, and hence has not shown that it is illegitimate to give preferential treatment to women (or blacks) for this reason.

Howard McGary, Jr.

Reparations, Self-Respect, and Public Policy

When we reflect on what should be the appropriate societal response to individuals and groups who have been the victims of unjust practices, a variety of considerations come to mind. For instance, we believe that any appropriate response should be in line with the constraints of justice, whatever they might be. We also believe that we should be concerned about things like the "public good." But it is difficult to determine what the appropriate constraints of justice are and whether a particular response is in accordance with these constraints. With regard to the "public good," there is a vast body of literature that attests to the fact that defining the "public good" and deciding when some policy or program is in the public interest is formidable.[1] But even with these difficulties noted, policy makers must still construct policies that serve as the society's response to the problems created by injustice.

Responses to injustice can be attitudinal or behavioral. By attitudinal I mean emotional responses like regret, remorse, resentment, and shame. When I say that they can be behavioral, I mean they may involve ceasing the unjust actions in question or they may involve the awarding of goods and services to: a) make amends for the injustices inflicted or b) to promote things like the "public good." Policy makers have given great weight to considerations like "the greatest good for the greatest number," but such a consideration is ambiguous. They might mean the greatest total aggregate good or the greatest average good. But with either interpretation critics have argued that giving great weight to this consideration can lead to morally unacceptable arrangements.

Although I do not wish to discuss the general validity of the principle of utility, I do want to point out what I take to be major problems with any teleological justification of policies that are viewed as a response to or remedy for injustice.[2] The principle of utility, for example, is not a desert-based principle. As Joel

From *The Journal of the Society for the Study of Black Philosophy* 1, 1 (1984): 15–26. Reprinted by permission of the author. Copyright © 1984 by The Society for the Study of Black Philosophy and MBPI, Inc.

Feinberg has argued, to say that S deserves X because giving it to him would promote the public good is to misuse the term "deserve."[3] He notes "that responsive attitudes are the things that people deserve and that 'modes of treatment' are deserved only in a derivative way, insofar perhaps as they are the natural or conventional means of expressing the morally fitting attitudes."[4] He warns that utilitarians are naive when they contend that utilitarian considerations can capture our responsive attitudes to injustice. Utilitarian considerations can only capture the public or conventional expression of these responsive attitudes.

I will argue that there are compelling reasons for appealing to rights-based arguments in a justification of policies that favor certain previously oppressed groups.[5] In my opinion, if we do not take into account these arguments, we will be unable to give all citizens what they are entitled to; namely, being full-fledged members of society. This entails that people not face "social institutions" that act as an affront to their self-respect simply because of such things as their race, religion, or sex.[6]

In the first section of this paper I note that it is important that the framers of public policies concentrate on material concerns like personal incomes or the reduction of poverty but I argue that it is important for them to focus on the psychological response to injustice as a crucial aspect of social justice. I argue that because of past and present unjust institutional design, a deeply biased and harmful stereotypical attitude about certain groups persists in all aspects of society today, and that this negative stereotypical attitude toward these groups causes them to feel deep resentment and this resentment acts as an affront to the self-respect of these group members.

In Section II I illustrate the difficulties by focusing on Ronald Dworkin's[7] ingenious teleological defense of affirmative action as preferential treatment for minorities and women. In the final section I argue that even a mixed account of justice like John Rawls's[8] will be teleological rather than rights-based; therefore, it is subject to the criticisms that I advanced against teleological accounts of this issue. This conclusion will be surprising to some because one would not suspect that a Rawlsian and a utilitarian would be in the same camp on this issue. For our purposes here, I adopt the position that there is a type of self-respect for persons that does not depend upon one's achievements or abilities, but on the recognition that as a person one is an authentic rights-holder worthy of all the rights that our moral law accords to persons.

I

One way to show how faulty institutional design has led to an affront to the self-concepts of *all* members of a group is through the following illustration. In a book entitled *Black Power,* Carmichael and Hamilton give the following definition of institutional white racism:

> Racism is both overt and covert. It takes two, closely related forms: individual whites acting against individual blacks, and acts by the total white community against the black community. We call these individual and institutional racism. The first consists of overt acts by individuals, which cause death, injury or the violent destruction of

property. This type can be reached by television cameras; it can frequently be observed in the process of commission. The second type is less overt, far more subtle, less identifiable in terms of specific individuals committing the acts. But it is no less destructive of human life. The second type originates in the operation of established and respected forces in the society, and thus receives far less condemnation than the first type.[9]

Individual and institutional racism both are morally repugnant; however, both can occur without bigotry. The toy store owner who feels that black children are in his store to steal and that white children are there to purchase, and treats them accordingly, demonstrates individual racism. The toy store owner may not conceive of himself as being prejudiced and, in fact, may not be a bigot. The police department that uses a test that reflects a cultural bias may not intend their test to be racist, but the police department is pursuing a course which creates and supports institutional racism. When very few black candidates pass the test, the response by the department is that there is something wrong with the black candidates rather than the test. In the case of the store owner and the police officials, by a statistical inference we are warranted in concluding that their actions are shaped by negative racial stereotyping.

Institutions are stable social arrangements and practices through which collective actions are taken. Institutions in our society that foster racism or sexism in a significant way can be found in the areas of economic life, education, and the administration of justice.[10] These institutions in some cases overtly discriminate, but in other cases the discrimination is covert. Knowles and Prewitt, in their important work on institutional racism, describe how covert institutional racism works:

> Maintenance of the basic racial controls is now less dependent upon specific discriminatory decisions. Such behavior has become so well institutionalized that the individual generally does not have to exercise a choice to operate in a racist manner. The rules and procedures of the large organizations have already prestructured the choice.[11]

In a covert manner those who are in control of American institutions display a negative stereotypical attitude toward racial minorities and women. They assume that members of these groups in general are like irresponsible children who cannot be trusted with power and responsibility. Since institutions have the power to reward and penalize, institutions that embody these stereotypes place members of certain groups in a most unfortunate position. These group members either must reject these institutions and the benefits that they bestow because they act as an offense to them as self-respecting persons, or accept them and have them act as an affront to their self-respect.

My critics might retort that this analysis may apply to some, but certainly not to those group members who hold prestigious positions in society, which serves to prove that they are responsible, intelligent, and industrious individuals. They believe that this falsifies my claim that every group member is harmed because of the existence of things like institutional racism or sexism. One possible reply to this criticism would be to say that those group members who hold prestigious positions are harmed because fellow group members are harmed, but I will not adopt this defense because I suspect that the degree of solidarity necessary to substantiate something like vicarious harm in these cases does not exist.

A more realistic response to my critics would be one that does not depend upon vicarious harm, but a reply that shows how even those who hold prestigious positions *actually* are harmed because of biased institutional design. I take the following to be such a reply. Those group members who hold prestigious positions may be able to have high self-esteem because of the jobs or offices they hold in society, but yet they still experience an affront to their self-respect because they are still confronted by social institutions that have negative consequences in regard to their rights as persons, irrespective of their socioeconomic status. They have been forced to develop a thick skin so to speak. But because they have been able to do this, we should not conclude that they should and that this institutional design is acceptable. Although they are able to cope with this affront to human dignity,[12] they should rightly resent it.

Injustice can take a variety of forms and it can cause emotional as well as physical harm. However, we should not bunch all unjust acts together. Some unjust acts are due to such things as greed and temptation and do not necessarily involve an invidious denial of the equality and worth of the persons who are treated unjustly. On the other hand, there is a class of unjust acts that are motivated by a serious lack of respect for the equality and worth of the victims. Racist and sexist acts fall into this category. The victims of this type of injustice experience various feelings and emotions which range from anger to self-doubt. But one important emotion that should be present is resentment.

Resentment plays the crucial role of alerting us to the fact that we have been treated in a manner that we do not believe is appropriate or just.[13] We should be careful and not confuse resentment with envy. A person can be envious even though she does not believe that she has been treated unjustly or in an inappropriate manner. A just society need not be concerned with designing social institutions such that people are not envious of each other.

Now the depth of the resentment that people feel when they have been treated unjustly will vary depending upon such factors as their maturity and their psychological and moral stability. It will also depend upon the nature of the injustice. If the injustice deprives them of their just deserts in terms of goods and services, then they certainly will and should resent it. But if the injustice cuts at their very right to be treated as bona fide members of the moral and legal communities, then this creates even a deeper resentment. When this resentment is allowed to fester it can lead to psychopathology or to a disrespect for the institutions and persons that caused or fail to prevent the injustice which led to the resentment.

Individuals who have been systematically denied full membership within our moral and legal communities for long periods of time because of characteristics like their race or sex will feel this deep resentment. All too often when we focus on the victims of this type of unjust discrimination we tend to focus only on the material consequences of being treated unjustly. When we do this we fail to address the emotional damage that results from a prolonged systematic denial of basic moral and legal rights. To merely halt the unjust practice and to enhance the economic well-being of the victims is not enough to remove this rightful feeling of resentment. We should be careful here and note that there is certainly virtue in being able to forgive and forget; but as I have claimed, unjust practices that deny basic moral and legal rights on the ground that some members of society are less worthy than other members because of their race or sex are extremely difficult to forgive and forget because of the deep resentment that such wrongs foster.

An important first step in forgiving and forgetting is putting the injustice behind one and getting on with one's life. However, in cases where one's moral status as a bona fide member of the community has been denied, an acknowledgment by the transgressors that they have wronged you when they treated you in this way is necessary as an affirmation that one has full moral and legal status. Orlando Patterson, in this connection, notes that when the slave stole from the slavemaster, this was an assertion on the part of the slave of his moral worth; and when the slavemaster punished the slave for stealing he implicitly admits that the slave is a moral being.[14] We can distinguish two views with regard to the claim that certain people are not full-fledged members of the moral community. On one view, those in question are believed to lack those attributes or characteristics that are necessary for membership in the community due to factors that are not beyond their control. In other words, they are constitutionally capable of being members, but for whatever reason, fail to meet the requirements for full membership. The other view presupposes that those who are denied membership are constitutionally ineligible. Both views have been used as the basis for the denial of basic rights to certain individuals and groups; but the latter view was usually employed as the rationale to justify the unjust discrimination against the members of racial groups.

Providing the victims only goods and services when basic rights have been violated will not remove a deep-seated feeling of resentment. Perhaps the following example will help to make this idea explicit. Suppose person X borrows a sum of money S from person Y and promises to pay him back at time t, and when t arrives X claims that he does not owe S to Y, but that he will give S to Y anyway in order to promote harmony or good social consequences. I believe that Y will still feel resentful even though X is willing to give S to Y. Y feels resentful because there is the tacit implication or intimation that Y is getting something he does not deserve and that X's actions, although in some sense commendable, are done for the wrong reasons. By X not having to acknowledge his debt to Y his actions leave the door open for his behavior to be interpreted as charity or a gift.

When we put this phenomenon in the larger societal context we find that the resentment experienced by those who have been and still are the victims of systematic unjust discrimination is very deep. The psychological scars due to a systematic denial of basic moral rights are not so deep that they prevent most of the victims from functioning, but functioning with this resentment is not as healthy as ridding one's self of it. In order to remove this resentment in a rational person, one must provide the person with good reasons for believing that there is no longer adequate evidence to support the belief that he is not being treated as a full-fledged member of the moral community. If we fail to acknowledge that the person was treated in this terribly unjust way, and that the reason for the special treatment that this person now receives is to rectify this wrongdoing, we fail to provide the person with adequate evidence that he is a moral equal. Like our example involving the forgetful debtor, if the treatment accorded to this individual can be seen as flowing from motives such as kindness or sympathy, then such treatment does not serve as adequate evidence that the persons offering such treatment believe that the beneficiaries are their moral equals. People can show kindness and sympathy for animals and plants, yet most people do not believe that these living things are equal members of the moral community.

Policy makers must understand that from the point of view of justice, we must eliminate wrongful institutional design for the right reasons. This should not be done simply to maximize the average utility in society or to produce an equal distribution of the benefits that flow from these institutions, but to give people what they are entitled to as a matter of *right* as persons and citizens. In my opinion, respecting the dignity and worth of those who were victimized by dehumanizing institutional design requires that our moral outlook be rights-based. However, because I characterize my approach to injustice as rights-based, it should not be assumed that I believe that social consequences are irrelevant.[15]

II

One of the most eloquent defenses of affirmative action as preferential treatment for minorities and women is advanced by Ronald Dworkin. He supports the position that the greatest average utility and a noble social ideal will be brought about by adopting policies that favor minorities and women.[16] According to Dworkin we have a right to be treated as equal under the law; but this does not entail that we have a legal or moral right to equal treatment in every instance. In other words, he believes that there are cases where unequal treatment of citizens is justified providing that doing so promotes the greatest average utility for society as a whole and that it promotes a worthy social ideal.

Given Dworkin's argument in favor of preferential treatment, any group can be deserving of such treatment. Even if a group fell from the sky and had no history of discrimination and oppression but, for whatever reason, found themselves incapable of obtaining the desired social positions, preferential treatment for the members of this group would be warranted. What Dworkin fails to see is that if he is committed to preferential policies to eliminate disadvantage irrespective to the nature of the actions that led to this state of affairs, he will fail to address the important emotional attitudes that are associated with a certain class of unjust acts.

Teleologists who argue that things should be changed by concentrating on the future rather than past injustices fail to consider the rightful resentment of those who are down and out, and those who have overcome poverty and lack of education, but continue to feel rightly that they are being wronged because they live in a society with a historical legacy that assigns an inferior stereotype to a person simply because he or she is a member of a certain group. A utilitarian could certainly argue that steps should be taken to eliminate this infectious resentment, but only if doing so brought about greater utility than not doing so. On the utilitarian account it is conceivable that economically secure members of wronged groups would be asked to endure this debasing injustice for the good of society as a whole.

Here again we encounter the old deontological criticism that utilitarianism sacrifices or uses some people in society as means rather than ends in themselves. The teleologist who is a utilitarian could argue that if these stereotypes and feelings of resentment were so destructive, then removing them would have to raise the utility value in society. This may be overly optimistic. As I stated above, eliminating injustice that has been in the making for hundreds of years, no matter if it is destructive, may decrease the total amount of utility in society. In any case, we have no guarantee that it will not. Simply proposing that we include these considerations in our utility calculations will not do. Since the utilitarian must give everyone's preferences equal weight, he cannot guarantee that people in a utilitarian society will not prefer social institutions that act as an affront to some minority group. The utilitarian must accept people's biased and prejudiced preferences unless he has some principled way of ruling them out. Dworkin's proposal of discounting external preferences and striving for some noble social ideal will not work unless we accept egalitarian, perfectionist, or welfarist goals.[17] Dworkin has not given us a convincing argument for accepting such goals. Hence, his argument for discounting external preferences either is ad hoc or it begs the question.

Let us now turn to a Rawlsian account. Remember Rawls claims to have captured the virtues of utilitarianism without falling prey to the frequent deontological criticism that utilitarianism forces us to unfairly use some members of society as means rather than ends. In the next section I will explain why retreating to a Rawlsian position will not silence the rights-based critics who favor reparation arguments.

III

Rawls provides us with a powerful theory with which we are supposed to be able to decide questions of social justice. Rawls's theory has been praised because it includes what many take to be the virtue of utilitarianism, namely promoting the public good, while not falling prey to Kant's criticism of utilitarianism: that it unfairly uses some people as means. However, my major criticism will be that Rawls does not go far enough in his deontological thinking. I employ Rawls's theory here for two reasons: first, it is a very well wrought account of social justice and, second, it appears that he might be sympathetic to both of the approaches that I described above.

Rawls's conception of justice can be characterized properly as a form of welfarism, but not obviously in the pejorative sense of a handout. One might expect that any supporter of reparations as a concept of social justice would find Rawls's conception of justice appealing. Historically, those who have been victimized usually find themselves occupying the least advantaged positions in society. However, this is a contingent truth; it is not necessarily this way. We can think of cases where individuals have overcome the burdens of oppression to occupy positions of advantage in society. In a society where people have become the advantaged members of society in spite of oppression, these people would be ignored by Rawls's theory, yet I feel that they would be entitled, on grounds of justice, to reparation.

Rawls believes that some wrongs are not rectifiable. He feels that the best we can do in some cases is to cease the unjust actions and ensure against injustices of this sort in the future. We might have to forget trying to redistribute land or wealth in these cases. Can we always forget gross injustices and still maintain that we have an adequate account of justice? Is there justice when more advantaged members in society are owed a debt of justice by members of society who are less fortunate? I believe that the answer to both of these questions is negative. Rawls would disagree. According to Rawls, in a just society benefits should be distributed so that they are to the benefit of the least-advantaged members of society. This is his difference principle.[18] Because of his difference principle, Rawls would be hard pressed to justify many of the nonegalitarian measures that would be required to eliminate the destructive racial stereotyping in our society. I am sure that an egalitarian would not adopt measures that did not reduce the disparities between the haves and the have-nots. Especially if those who benefit from the measures are not among the have-nots.

Above I said that a Rawlsian can justify, to a limited extent, certain kinds of reparation programs, but that he would reject programs that would upset the (just) basic institutions of our society. He would oppose returning all land taken unjustly from American Indians provided that we make present institutions just in terms of distribution of goods and services and that we take steps to ensure fair equality of opportunity. To do so would violate his difference principle. Remember, I said that Rawls would not allow rectification policies that create further injustice. Will policies that favor members of oppressed groups, on grounds of reparation, create further injustices? I think not. They may take away another group's illegitimate advantages and create difficulties for some but, properly administered, they need not create further injustices.

In stressing the importance of reparations as a concept of social justice, I recognize that the problem of converting emotional injury to money or something material is very challenging. It would be very difficult to calculate the aggregate amount that might be awarded if the nation undertook to compensate people for damages to their self-concepts. We cannot totally repay members of oppressed groups for all the injuries done to them. However, it is wrong to ignore the historical debt of justice owed to them because they are not economically disadvantaged. Remember, it is not so much that being economically disadvantaged is an affront to a person's self-respect as it is that they are not being given what is owed to them. In my account, self-respect is a very important good that is theoretically prior to a right to reparation. The failure to rectify a wrong does not always result in an affront to a person's self-respect; but in cases where there have been prolonged wrongs against a group and the assignment of an unjust inferior status, demanding reparation is crucial to one's self-respect and thus one's psychological well-being.

I should stress that I am not claiming that a person has self-respect only if he always demands that he be treated fairly. Whether a person's toleration of unfair treatment signals a lack of self-respect depends upon what his reasons are for tolerating such treatment. For example, a slave who did not insist upon his right as a person to be treated fairly out of fear for his life could not be said to lack self-respect.[19]

Rawlsians and other teleologists want to eliminate the injustice faced by members of oppressed groups, but I am afraid that a purely teleological approach to remedying these injustices will not succeed. All people have the right to live in a society where they will not be wronged by social institutions simply because of things like their race or sex. In order to achieve this end we must take note of past injustices to eliminate the legacy of racial and sexual injustice.

Purely teleological justifications of policies that favor certain oppressed groups are inadequate. A heavy moral and psychological cost is attached to letting one's right to have wrongs against one acknowledged and rectified be over-ridden by utilitarian, egalitarian, or Rawlsian considerations. In my view this right is a fundamental moral commodity that should be taken seriously.[20]

NOTES

1. For a good discussion of this issue see Brian Barry, "The Public Interest," *Proceedings of the Aristotelian Society,* supp. vol. 38 (1964): 1–18.

2. The teleological approach says that an act is right if and only if it produces or will probably produce the greatest balance of good over evil. For examples of this approach involving preferential treatment of racial minorities and women, see Richard Wasserstrom's "Racism, Sexism and Preferential Treatment: An Approach to the Topics," *U.C.L.A. Law Review* 24:581 (1977): 581–622; Thomas Nagel's "Equal Treatment and Compensatory Discrimination," *Philosophy and Public Affairs* 2 (1973): 348–63; Ronald Dworkin's *Taking Rights Seriously* (Cambridge: Harvard University Press, 1977), ch. 9; and Irving Thalberg's "Reverse Discrimination and the Future," in *Women and Philosophy,* ed. Carol Gould and Marx Wartofsky (New York: G. P. Putnam's Sons, 1976): 294–308.

3. Joel Feinberg, *Doing and Deserving* (Princeton: Princeton University Press, 1970), 81.

4. Ibid., 82.

5. The demand for reparation by the victims of injustice is rights-based. By reparation I mean the acknowledgement and redress of wrongdoing when it is known who is at fault. For examples of the reparation approach, see Judith Jarvis Thompson's "Preferential Hiring," *Philosophy and Public Affairs* 2 (1973): 364–84; Graham Hughes in "Reparations for Blacks," *The New York University Law Review* 43 (1968): 1063–74; Bernard Boxill, "The Morality of Reparation," *Social Theory and Practice* 2 (1972): 113–22, and Howard McGary, Jr., "Justice and Reparations," *The Philosophical Forum* 9, nos. 2–3 (1977–78): 250–63.

6. A "social institution" acts as an affront to a person's self-respect if the members of a group (e.g., racial, religious, sexual) are forced to view themselves in accordance with "social institutions" that define and treat members of their group as inferior or subhuman. I want to be careful to point out that I am only making the minimal claim that people have a right not to face "social institutions" that have embodied negative stereotypical attitudes about them. They do not have a right to force people in their private lives not to hold racist or sexist views. In my view, people have the right to dislike people for whatever reason they choose. However, a person's biased dislikes for certain groups should not be a part of "social institutions." Here I basically follow Rawls in defining "social institutions." Social institutions are:

A public system of rules which defines offices and positions with their rights and duties, powers and immunities, and the like. These rules specify certain forms of action as permissible, others as forbidden; and they provide for certain penalties and defenses, and so on, when violations occur. (*A Theory of Justice,* 55)

7. Ronald Dworkin's *Taking Rights Seriously* (Cambridge: Harvard University Press, 1977), ch. 9. All references to Dworkin will be to this work.

8. See John Rawls, *A Theory of Justice* (Cambridge: Belknap Press, 1971). All references to Rawls will be to this work.

9. Stokeley Carmichael and Charles Hamilton, *Black Power: The Politics of Liberation in America* (New York: Vintage Books, 1967), 4.

10. See L. J. Barker and J. J. McCorry, Jr., *Black Americans in the Political System* (Cambridge: Winthrop Publishers, Inc. 1976); John F. Kain, *Race and Poverty* (Englewood Cliffs, N.J.: Prentice-Hall, 1969); Marvin J. Levine, *The Urban Negro and Employment Equality* (Morristown, N.J.: General Learning Corporation, 1972); *Report of the National Advisory Commission on Civil Disorders* (New York: Bantam Books, 1968); Lois B. Moreland, *White Racism and the Law* (Columbus: Charles E. Merrill Publishing Co., 1970).

11. Louis L. Knowles and Kenneth Prewitt, *Institutional Racism in America* (Englewood Cliffs, N.J.: Prentice-Hall, 1969), 142–43.

12. For a good discussion of the relationship between human dignity, self-respect, and human emotions, see Herbert Spiegelberg, "Human Dignity: A Challenge to Contemporary Philosophy," *Philosophy Forum* 9 (1971): 39–64; Michael S. Pritchard, "Human Dignity and Justice," *Ethics* 82 (1971–72): 299–313; and I. A. Menkiti, "The Resentment of Injustice: Some Consequences of Institutional Racism," *The Philosophical Forum* 9 (1977–78): 227–49.

13. Rawls, op. cit., 533.

14. Orlando Patterson, "Towards a Future That Has No Past—Reflections on the Fate of Blacks in the Americas," *The Public Interest* 27 (Spring 1972): 43.

15. For a good defense of certain rights within a consequentialist theory of ethics see T. M. Scanlon, "Rights, Goals and Fairness," in Stuart Hampshire, ed., *Public and Private Morality* (Cambridge: Cambridge University Press, 1978).

16. Dworkin, op. cit., 239.

17. For Dworkin's discussion of discounting external preferences see Ibid., 234–35.

18. Rawls, op. cit., 75–78.

19. For a complete discussion of this point, see Bernard Boxill's "Self-respect and Protest," *Philosophy and Public Affairs* 6 (1976): 58–69; Thomas Hill's "Servility and Self-Respect," *The Monist* 57 (1973): 87–104; and Larry Thomas' "Morality and Our Self-concept," *The Journal of Value Inquiry* 12 (1978): 258–68.

20. I read earlier versions of this paper at Rutgers University and the University of the District of Columbia. In addition to my colleagues Martha Bolton and Peter Klein, a number of other people were kind enough to offer comments. I thank the Rutgers University Research Council for support for this project.

SUGGESTIONS FOR DISCUSSION

1. Why are racial discrimination and gender discrimination respectively wrong? Are the wrongs of racial discrimination considerably worse than Levin is willing to admit? Does the severity of racial discrimination require preferential treatment programs as compensation or to institute equality; or is any form of preferential treatment tantamount to reverse discrimination? Would the same *kinds* of argument require or mitigate against preferential treatment in behalf of women?

2. Should hiring, promotions, and admissions be determined strictly on the basis of merit?

3. McGary bases his claim for reparations on an appeal to rights. What are the rights to which he appeals? Are such rights morally basic (see Mackie, Part I, Chapter 6)? Would appeal to these rights also justify affirmative action in hiring, promotions, and admissions?

FURTHER READING

Bittker, B. *The Case for Black Reparations.* New York: Random House, 1973. (Introduction, critical analysis; intermediate)

Bishop, S., and Weinzweig, M., eds. *Philosophy and Women.* Belmont, Calif.: Wadsworth, 1979. (Interpretation, critical analysis; intermediate)

Blackstone, W. T., and Heslep, R., eds. *Social Justice and Preferential Treatment.* Athens: University of Georgia Press, 1976. (Interpretation, critical analysis; intermediate)

Boxill, B. *Blacks and Social Justice.* Totowa, N.J.: Rowman and Littlefield, 1984. (Interpretation, critical analysis; advanced)

Cohen, M., Nagel, T., and Scanlon, T., eds. *Equality and Preferential Treatment.* Princeton: Princeton University Press, 1977. (Interpretation, critical analysis; advanced)

English, J., ed. *Sex Equality.* Englewood Cliffs, N.J.: Prentice-Hall, 1977. (Interpretation, critical analysis; intermediate)

Fullinwider, R. *The Reverse Discrimination Controversy.* Totowa, N.J.: Rowman and Littlefield, 1980. (Interpretation, critical analysis; intermediate)

Glazer, N. *Affirmative Discrimination.* New York: Basic Books, 1975. (Critical analysis; intermediate)

Goldberg, D. T., ed. *Anatomy of Racism.* Minneapolis: University of Minnesota Press, 1988. (Critical analysis; advanced)

Goldman, A. *Justice and Reverse Discrimination.* Princeton: Princeton University Press, 1979. (Interpretation, critical analysis; advanced)

Gossett, T. *Race: The History of an Idea in America.* New York: Schocken Books, 1968. (Survey; intermediate)

Gould, S. J. *The Mismeasure of Man.* New York: W. W. Norton, 1981. (Interpretation, critical analysis; intermediate)

Gross, B., ed. *Reverse Discrimination.* Buffalo: Prometheus Books, 1976. (Interpretation, critical analysis; intermediate)

Jencks, C. et al. *Inequality.* New York: Basic Books, 1972. (Critical analysis; intermediate)

Sowell, T. *Black Education: Myths and Tragedies.* New York: D. McKay, 1972. (Critical analysis; intermediate)

Vetterling-Braggin, M., Elliston, F., and English, J., eds. *Feminism and Philosophy.* Totowa, N.J.: Littlefield Adams, 1977. (Critical analysis; intermediate)

Wartofsky, M., McDade, J., and Lesnor, C., eds. "Philosophy and the Black Experience." *The Philosophical Forum* IX, 2–3, 1977–78: 113–382. (Critical analysis; intermediate)

Wasserstrom, R. *Philosophy and Social Issues: Five Studies.* Notre Dame: University of Notre Dame Press, 1980. (Critical analysis; intermediate)

9

□

Censorship and Pornography

Morals Offenses   The issue of *morals offenses* is central to a general conception of justice. A morals offense involves behavior considered by the law to go beyond the bounds of moral decency and propriety. It is unlike criminal acts such as murder, which are also morally unacceptable. Obscene and lewd behavior or representations are offensive not because of serious harm they may cause, but because they tend largely to produce discomfort, shame, and embarrassment. A good deal of pornographic literature may also represent or encourage violence, and this may be restricted due to the harm caused or encouraged rather than because it is offensive. There are two related questions here: First, what (if any) are acceptable restrictions that may be imposed upon the freedom of expression? And second, should lewd behavior or representations that are considered by many in the moral community to be repugnant, though they are not necessarily harmful, nevertheless be proscribed by law?

   We would do well to distinguish between an offensive act, its representation, and how the representation is viewed. Though perhaps related, the conditions of wrongfulness for each will clearly differ. Harms caused by an offensive act tend to differ from those that generally arise (if at all) in viewing representations of such acts. Moreover, an unseen depiction or representation—on a bookshelf, say—fails to harm at all. The kind of offensive behavior most obviously at issue concerns socially unacceptable forms of sexuality and their depiction. Pornography will be taken, then, as representations of sexual organs or sexual behavior that transgress social propriety and are intended to arouse. (Again, violent pornography is always objectionable, at the very least because of the harm or degradation it encourages.) In confronting us with a basic dilemma about whether pornographic representations should be allowed free expression, pornography provides a crucial case for formulating general principles concerning morals offenses.

Freedom and Offense   The basic dilemma is this: Freedom is a fundamental value; it is a general condition for developing the particular things each individual may value. Joel Feinberg suggests that there is a presumption always in freedom's favor. Should we face a choice between leaving people free to do something and coercing them to act in some way, we should *prima facie* favor leaving them free. As John Rawls argues (see Part II, Chapter 7), we ought to endorse the widest available liberties compatible with like liberties for all. These would include freedom of expression and—so it seems to follow—of pornographic expression and consumption. Read in this light, the First Amendment appears to protect pornography. Nevertheless, some have found it unfair, if not immoral, to guarantee free expression and consumption of pornographic material to a small minority at the expense of offending the sensibilities of most. Free speech, it is argued, should not extend to morally offensive expression; pornography is not covered by the First Amendment. In light of the presumption favoring liberty, are there principles that may serve to justify limiting liberty? In particular, what grounds could there be for restricting freedom of expression?

Liberty-limiting Principles Feinberg identifies six principles that have been advanced as justifications for restricting liberty. These principles provide reasons generally relevant, though perhaps not always conclusive, for coerced restriction of liberty. The most prominent is the *Harm Principle*, applied so eloquently by John Stuart Mill in "On Liberty" (see Part I, Chapter 4). This principle may be interpreted either "privately" or "publicly." The *Private Harm Principle* justifies limitations on liberty to prevent injury to individual persons. Those who claim a causal connection between pornography and violent behavior against individuals advance the Private Harm Principle to support their proposed restrictions of free expression. The *Public Harm Principle* justifies restrictions on liberty to prevent impairment of institutional practices considered to be in the public interest. Pro-censorship arguments that criticize pornographic obsession with impersonal sex, because it leads to lack of restraint and to tyranny, appeal to the Public Harm Principle. (Mill is interpreted usually—and mistakenly—as defending *only* the Private Harm Principle).

Second, the *Offense Principle* would limit liberty so as to prevent offense to others. Third, the principles of *Legal Paternalism* would justify legislation to prevent self-inflicted harms. Fourth, the principle of *Legal Moralism* undertakes to justify legal enforcement of morality for its own sake. Feinberg's fifth and sixth principles, *Extreme Paternalism* and *Welfare*, are not considered relevant to the pornography issue.

Legal Paternalism and Legal Moralism have been rejected as inadequate justifications of liberty-limiting censorship. In the former case, the harms to oneself that obscenity and pornography are supposed to produce seem illusory. Though paternalistic laws are not uncommon (e.g., the requirement to wear seat belts), they do not apply to restricting freedom of pornographic expression and consumption. Many have claimed, by contrast, that widespread moral condemnation of pornography justifies making morality law. Legal Moralism requires restrictions on access of consenting adults to pornographic material. The limitation of liberties supported by Legal Moralism presupposes a noncoerced moral consensus among very nearly all members of the community. However, there may be significant numbers of consenting adults wanting access to pornographic material, and this would challenge the premise that community agreement about pornography's unacceptability is pervasive. So it is doubtful that such a consensus could be established in cases where no harms are involved (and where harms are involved, the liberties that prompt them may be restricted under the Harm Principle).

Supreme Court Rulings It follows that justifications for censoring pornography and obscenity hinge upon the viability of the Harm and Offense Principles. In *Paris Adult Theatres v. Slaton* (1973), one of the leading censorship cases, the Supreme Court ruled narrowly that pornographic materials (here films) may be restricted by state legislatures. In writing the majority opinion, Chief Justice Warren Burger appealed to the Public Harm Principle. He argued that though no proof may exist of a causal connection between viewing pornography and antisocial behavior, states would not be unreasonable in assuming such a connection. Thus states might reasonably judge that the distribution and consumption of obscene material tend to injure the entire population, to endanger public safety, and to undermine the states' charge to maintain a decent society. Consequently, obscene material cannot be protected under the First Amendment, nor can its *commerce* be protected under any constitutional right to privacy. Public exhibition of obscene material (as in movie theaters), even for consenting adults, may be restricted. Writing the dissenting opinion, Justice William Brennan countered that there is great difficulty in defining obscenity, and a lack of substantive evidence connecting obscenity with antisocial behavior. He concludes that restricting access of consenting adults to obscene materials violates their First Amendment rights. He adds, however, that states may prohibit distribution to juveniles, and they may regulate distribution so as to avoid exposure of unconsenting adults.

Readings Lorenne M. G. Clark develops a feminist argument for censorship that appeals to revised versions of the Offense and Harm Principles. Clark begins from the assumption that pornography is a species of hate literature against women. She views pornography as functioning to socialize women into maintaining traditional male advantages and power. Pornography, whether violent or not, is taken to offend and to harm women directly, as well as society at large. It is considered an affront to women's dignity, enforcing women's disadvantaged position and inhibiting desirable social progress. Censorship is found necessary to promote gender equality in both the public and private realms. Thus the Offense and Harm Principles are considered by Clark to justify restrictions on freedom of obscene expressions.

Upon careful analysis of the concept of "harm" as violation of interest, Joel Feinberg concludes that sufficiently severe harms caused by pornography (for minors, say) justify restrictions upon its free expression. Where pornography harms unconsenting adults, the harms basically result from its public occurrence. Such harms can be regulated simply by restrictions on public exhibition. So if the pornographic material is to be more widely restricted, it must be on the basis of the Offense Principle alone. Feinberg argues that this principle justifies limitations on liberties only if two conditions are cojointly satisfied. The material must be found offensive almost universally by adult members of the community regardless of sex, race, age, or religion; and it must be avoidable only with unreasonable effort or inconvenience. Feinberg contends that neither condition is generally satisfied. He concludes that both the Harm Principle and the Offense Principle fail to justify violations of the First Amendment caused by restricting access of consenting adults to obscene material. Children's consumption of pornographic material may be considered harmful to them in ways analogous to their consumption of alcohol and tobacco. So children's access to pornography may be restricted in the same way that alcohol or tobacco are restricted.

Against pro-censorship arguments, Fred R. Berger argues that pornography is by nature an unlikely source of social harm. He admits that male violence and aggression toward women may be reflected in some pornography and as such is objectionable. He denies that it is a necessary feature of pornographic depiction. Berger suggests that violence in pornography is a reflection of social and political attitudes generated by other social conditions. Valuing liberty and self-determination presupposes assuming risks for freedom's sake. In addition, Berger argues more assertively that pornography undermines sexual inhibitions. He considers it to encourage and sustain autonomous development of persons. Thus censorship of nonviolent pornographic material would constitute an unjustified interference with freedom.

Chief Justice Warren Burger

Majority Opinion in *Paris Adult Theatre I v. Slaton*

We categorically disapprove the theory, apparently adopted by the trial judge, that obscene, pornographic films acquire constitutional immunity from state regulation simply because they are exhibited for consenting adults only. This holding was properly rejected by the Georgia Supreme Court. Although we have often pointedly recognized the high importance of the state interest in regulating the exposure of obscene materials to juveniles and unconsenting adults, this Court has never declared these to be the only legitimate state interests permitting regulation of obscene material. The States have a long-recognized legitimate interest in regulating the use of obscene material in local commerce and in all places of public accommodation, as long as these regulations do not run afoul of specific constitutional prohibitions. "In an unbroken series of cases extending over a long stretch of this Court's history, it has been accepted as a postulate that 'the primary requirements of decency may be enforced against obscene publications.'"

In particular, we hold that there are legitimate state interests at stake in stemming the tide of commercialized obscenity, even assuming it is feasible to enforce effective safeguards against exposure to juveniles and to the passerby. Rights and interests "other than those of the advocates are involved." These include the interest of the public in the quality of life and the total community

United States Supreme Court, 413 U.S. 49 (1973).

environment, the tone of commerce in the great city centers, and, possibly, the public safety itself. . . .

But, it is argued, there is no scientific data which conclusively demonstrates that exposure to obscene materials adversely affects men and women or their society. It is urged on behalf of the petitioner that, absent such a demonstration, any kind of state regulation is "impermissible." We reject this argument. It is not for us to resolve empirical uncertainties underlying state legislation, save in the exceptional case where that legislation plainly impinges upon rights protected by the Constitution itself. Mr. Justice Brennan, speaking for the Court in *Ginsberg v. New York* (1968), said "We do not demand of legislatures 'scientifically certain criteria of legislation.' " Although there is no conclusive proof of a connection between antisocial behavior and obscene material, the legislature of Georgia could quite reasonably determine that such a connection does or might exist. . . .

If we accept the unprovable assumption that a complete education requires the reading of certain books, and the well nigh universal belief that good books, plays, and art lift the spirit, improve the mind, enrich the human personality and develop character, can we then say that a state legislature may not act on the corollary assumption that commerce in obscene books, or public exhibitions focused on obscene conduct, have a tendency to exert a corrupting and debasing impact leading to antisocial behavior? "Many of these effects may be intangible and indistinct, but they are nonetheless real." Mr. Justice Cardozo said that all laws in Western civilization are "guided by a robust common sense. . . ." The sum of experience, including that of the past two decades, affords an ample basis for legislatures to conclude that a sensitive, key relationship of human existence, central to family life, community welfare, and the development of human personality, can be debased and distorted by crass commercial exploitation of sex. Nothing in the Constitution prohibits a State from reaching such a conclusion and acting on it legislatively simply because there is no conclusive evidence or empirical data.

It is argued that individual "free will" must govern, even in activities beyond the protection of the First Amendment and other constitutional guarantees of privacy, and that Government cannot legitimately impede an individual's desire to see or acquire obscene plays, movies, and books. We do indeed base our society on certain assumptions that people have the capacity for free choice. Most exercises of individual free choice—those in politics, religion, and expression of ideas—are explicitly protected by the Constitution. Totally unlimited play for free will, however, is not allowed in ours or any other society. We have just noted, for example, that neither the First Amendment nor "free will" precludes States from having "blue sky" laws to regulate what sellers of securities may write or publish about their wares. Such laws are to protect the weak, the uninformed, the unsuspecting, and the gullible from the exercise of their own volition. Nor do modern societies leave disposal of garbage and sewage up to the individual "free will," but impose regulation to protect both public health and the appearance of public places. States are told by some that they must await a "laissez faire" market solution to the obscenity-pornography problem, paradoxically "by people who have never otherwise had a kind word to say for laissez-faire," particularly in solving urban, commercial, and environmental pollution problems.

The States, of course, may follow such a "laissez faire" policy and drop all controls on commercialized obscenity, if that is what they prefer, just as they can ignore consumer protection in the market place, but nothing in the Constitution *compels* the States to do so with regard to matters falling within state jurisdiction. . . .

Our prior decisions recognizing a right to privacy guaranteed by the Fourteenth Amendment included "only those personal rights that can be deemed 'fundamental' or 'implicit in the concept of ordered liberty.'" This privacy right encompasses and protects the personal intimacies of the home, the family, marriage, motherhood, procreation, and child rearing. Nothing, however, in this Court's decisions intimates that there is any "fundamental" privacy right "implicit in the concept of ordered liberty" to watch obscene movies in places of public accommodation. . . .

. . . The idea of a "privacy" right and a place of public accommodation are, in this context, mutually exclusive. Conduct or depictions of conduct that the state police power can prohibit on a public street does not become automatically protected by the Constitution merely because the conduct is moved to a bar or a "live" theatre stage, any more than a "live" performance of a man and woman locked in a sexual embrace at high noon in Times Square is protected by the Constitution because they simultaneously engage in a valid political dialogue. . . .

Finally, petitioners argue that conduct which directly involves "consenting adults" only has, for that sole reason, a special claim to constitutional protection. Our Constitution establishes a broad range of conditions on the exercise of power by the states, but for us to say that our Constitution incorporates the proposition that conduct involving consenting adults only is always beyond state regulation, that is a step we are unable to take. Commercial exploitation of depictions, descriptions, or exhibitions of obscene conduct on commercial premises open to the adult public falls within a State's broad power to regulate commerce and protect the public environment. The issue in this context goes beyond whether someone, or even the majority, considers the conduct depicted as "wrong" or "sinful." The States have the power to make a morally neutral judgment that public exhibition of obscene material, or commerce in such material, has a tendency to injure the community as a whole, to endanger the public safety, or to jeopardize in Chief Justice Warren's words, the States' "right . . . to maintain a decent society."

Justice William Brennan

Dissenting Opinion in *Paris Adult Theatre I v. Slaton*

Our experience since *Roth v. United States* (1957) requires us not only to abandon the effort to pick out obscene materials on a case-by-case basis, but also to reconsider a fundamental postulate of *Roth:* that there exists a definable class of sexually oriented expression that may be totally suppressed by the Federal and State Governments. Assuming that such a class of expression does in fact exist, I am forced to conclude that the concept of "obscenity" cannot be defined with sufficient specificity and clarity to provide fair notice to persons who create and distribute sexually oriented materials, to prevent substantial erosion of protected speech as a by-product of the attempt to suppress unprotected speech, and to avoid very costly institutional harms. Given these inevitable side-effects of state efforts to suppress what is assumed to be *unprotected* speech, we must scrutinize with care the state interest that is asserted to justify the suppression. For in the absence of some very substantial interest in suppressing such speech, we can hardly condone the ill-effects that seem to flow inevitably from the effort. . . .

Because we assumed—incorrectly, as experience has proven—that obscenity could be separated from other sexually oriented expression without significant costs either to the First Amendment or to the judicial machinery charged with the task of safeguarding First Amendment freedoms, we had no occasion in *Roth* to probe the asserted state interest in curtailing unprotected, sexually oriented speech. Yet as we have increasingly come to appreciate the vagueness of the concept of obscenity, we have begun to recognize and articulate the state interests at stake. . . .

In *Stanley v. Georgia* we pointed out that "[t]here appears to be little empirical basis for" the assertion that "exposure to obscene materials may lead to deviant sexual behavior or crimes of sexual violence." In any event, we added that "if the State is only concerned about printed or filmed materials inducing antisocial conduct, we believe that in the context of private consumption of ideas and information we should adhere to the view that '[a]mong free men, the deterrents ordinarily to be applied to prevent crime are education and punishment for violations of the law. . . .' "

Moreover, in *Stanley* we rejected as "wholly inconsistent with the philosophy of the First Amendment," the notion that there is a legitimate state concern in the "control [of] the moral content of a person's thoughts," and we held that a State "cannot constitutionally premise legislation on the desirability of controlling a person's private thoughts." That is not to say, of course, that a State must remain utterly indifferent to—and take no action bearing on—the morality of the community. The traditional description of state police power does embrace the regulation

United States Supreme Court, 413 U.S. 49 (1973).

of morals as well as the health, safety, and general welfare of the citizenry. And much legislation—compulsory public education laws, civil rights laws, even the abolition of capital punishment—are grounded at least in part on a concern with the morality of the community. But the State's interest in regulating morality by suppressing obscenity, while often asserted, remains essentially unfocused and ill-defined. And, since the attempt to curtail unprotected speech necessarily spills over into the area of protected speech, the effort to serve this speculative interest through the suppression of obscene material must tread heavily on rights protected by the First Amendment.

In *Roe v. Wade* (1973), we held constitutionally invalid a state abortion law, even though we were aware of

> the sensitive and emotional nature of the abortion controversy, of the vigorous opposing views, even among physicians, and of the deep and seemingly absolute convictions that the subject inspires. One's philosophy, one's experiences, one's exposure to the raw edges of human existence, one's religious training, one's attitudes toward life and family and their values, and the moral standards one establishes and seeks to observe, are all likely to influence and to color one's thinking and conclusions about abortion.

Like the proscription of abortions, the effort to suppress obscenity is predicated on unprovable, although strongly held, assumptions about human behavior, morality, sex, and religion. The existence of these assumptions cannot validate a statute that substantially undermines the guarantees of the First Amendment, any more than the existence of similar assumptions on the issue of abortion can validate a statute that infringes the constitutionally protected privacy interests of a pregnant woman.

If, as the Court today assumes, "a state legislature may . . . act on the . . . assumption that . . . commerce in obscene books, or public exhibitions focused on obscene conduct, have a tendency to exert a corrupting and debasing impact leading to antisocial behavior," then it is hard to see how state-ordered regimentation of our minds can ever be forestalled. For if a State may, in an effort to maintain or create a particular moral tone, prescribe what its citizens cannot read or cannot see, then it would seem to follow that in pursuit of that same objective a State could decree that its citizens must read certain books or must view certain films. However laudable its goal—and that is obviously a question on which reasonable minds may differ—the State cannot proceed by means that violate the Constitution. . .

. . . Even a legitimate, sharply focused state concern for the morality of the community cannot, in other words, justify an assault on the protections of the First Amendment. Where the state interest in regulation of morality is vague and ill-defined, interference with the guarantees of the First Amendment is even more difficult to justify.

In short, while I cannot say that the interests of the State—apart from the question of juveniles and unconsenting adults—are trivial or nonexistent, I am compelled to conclude that these interests cannot justify the substantial damage to constitutional rights and to this Nation's judicial machinery that inevitably results from state efforts to bar the distribution even of unprotected material to consenting adults. I would hold, therefore, that at least in the absence of distribution to juveniles or obtrusive exposure to unconsenting adults, the First and Fourteenth Amendments prohibit the state and federal governments from attempting wholly to suppress sexually oriented materials on the basis of their allegedly "obscene" contents. Nothing in this approach precludes those governments from taking action to serve what may be strong and legitimate interests through regulation of the manner of distribution of sexually oriented material.

Lorenne M. G. Clark

Liberalism and Pornography

Since at least the mid-nineteenth century, the fight for women's rights has largely been fought under the banner of liberalism. The ethical principles of people like John Stuart Mill formed the moral justification for these struggles, and many of these individuals were themselves committed to the cause of women's equality.[1] Thus, the cause of women's liberation has much thanks to give both to the theory and to its proponents. But it is, I believe, time to take another look at the moral underpinnings we have until now accepted, though I am by no means suggesting that utilitarianism, or more popular versions of liberal, or libertarian ethics, have been the only moral touchstones upon which the demand for sexual equality has rested. . . .

The reason for this is clear. The central value of liberalism is the freedom, or liberty, of the individual. Thus, demands by women for greater participation in public life were straightforward demands for greater liberty. The demands made in the name of sexual equality were, first, to establish that women ought to be entitled to the same rights as men, and, second, to ensure that these rights could be practically and effectively exercised. But there is a central difficulty with liberalism in this respect. The central value of liberalism is freedom, or what has been termed more specifically "negative liberty."[2] "Negative" liberty or freedom is the freedom to do or get what you want unimpeded by interference from others. It is contrasted with "positive" liberty, which entails not only that other persons refrain from interference, but that the person with the freedom in fact has the means or ability to get what he or she wants. Thus one is free in the negative sense when one is not prohibited or prevented from entering a restaurant to obtain a meal even if one lacks the money to pay for it. One is free in the positive sense only if one has both the means to get what is wanted and is not prevented from using those means to get

First published under the title "Sexual Equality and the Problem of an Adequate Moral Theory: The Poverty of Liberalism," *Resources for Feminist Research,* Special Publication 5, Ontario Institute for Studies in Education, Toronto, 1979; published under current title in *Pornography and Censorship,* edited by D. Copp and S. Wendell (Buffalo: Prometheus Books, 1983). Reprinted by permission of the author.

what he or she wants. Negative freedom can be seen therefore to consist merely in the *absence of restraint.*

Since a central tenet of liberalism is that one can be said to be free, or to have a right to something merely from the fact that there is no statute or other legal limitation which prohibits the doing of the thing in question, the absence of a prohibition is itself enough to generate the idea that one has a right. Legally speaking, the right that one has is what is properly termed a "privilege" or "liberty" right,[3] and does not entail that anything or anyone has a correlative duty to do anything, or provide anything, which would facilitate one in actually getting that to which the right entitled one. A "privilege" or "liberty" right is a right which arises from the absence of restraint, like one's right to use a public park or to vote. It entails simply that one has no duty to refrain from doing the thing in question. But it also entails that no one else is under a duty to see that we do or get the thing we are not duty-bound to refrain from. Thus, if the right we have is a privilege right, we can do it if we want to, since we are under no duty not to do it; but if we lack the means to do it, no one has an obligation to see that we can do it, our lack of resources notwithstanding. Rights of this sort are contrasted with "claim" rights, rights which arise out of the fact that others have a duty to see that we get that to which we are said to have the right, things such as the right to an education up to at least a certain minimum age or standard. Claim rights do not therefore depend for their effective exercise on our having the means to utilize them. They are things to which we are entitled regardless of our other resources. Thus, if a right is a claim, this entails that someone or something necessarily has a duty with respect to providing us with the thing, or the means to the thing, in question, whereas if the right is a privilege, no such correlative obligation exists on others.

... The history of social reform is largely the history of first establishing that some previously disenfranchised group ought to have rights that have already been accorded to others, then removing legal or other social and institutional impediments to their getting what they want, and then fighting further to have these privileges converted into claims. But this involves liberalism in a fundamental contradiction, because it means that, during the third stage, the libertarian has to argue for the *limitation* of the freedom of some in the name of promoting greater equality among all those nominally said to be in possession of the right....

The fundamental question we have to ask is: Is the moral theory of liberalism consistent with equality? If it is, then we must be able to show how the mistakes it has made can be explained without throwing out the theory, and hence, how it must be revised in order to prevent similar errors from occurring in future. And if it isn't, then it is time we turned our attention to looking for or developing moral alternatives which are.

One of the fundamental principles endorsed by a liberal ethic is that there must be some areas of one's life in which one has the freedom to do what one wants, free from interference by others. It has been argued that there simply are some areas of life which are none of the law's business.... The right to use pornography ... has been justified both because it is personal, related solely to one's individual private sexual proclivities and preferences, and because it has to do with freedom of the press, or more broadly speaking, freedom of information, the right to read and to see what one wants and with the need to promote a wide divergence in the range of available materials.

There is virtually no one who would want to say that we should have no negative liberty or no privacy, but the debate still rages as to which areas of one's life should be guaranteed as areas of negative liberty through the creation of a legal right to privacy. The difficulty is that no one has found a satisfactory method of drawing the boundaries between the private and other areas of life. In the past, the boundary was thought to be a *natural* one, based on the traditional distinction between the public and the private. The private just *was* "the private," and, as such, should be guaranteed as an area of negative liberty and fully protected by means of a legally enforceable right to privacy. . . . The best defense of this liberal tenet is the view developed by Mill that the law is justified in prohibiting actions if and only if doing them results in the inability of others to exercise rights of a similar kind. The underlying view is that rights should be distributed equally, which entails that no one can have rights the exercise of which would prevent others from exercising similar rights. The difficulty is that liberals have all too often assumed that the area of life traditionally thought to be "private," and hence immune from regulation and control, conforms to the rules Mill laid down as to what should be left as an area of negative freedom.

But as is now abundantly clear, it is indefensible to draw the legal boundary between public and private on the basis of the historical division between these spheres of human activity. Privacy functioned historically to protect those who were privileged to begin with. Privacy was a consequence of the ownership of private property and, hence, a commodity purchased with property. It has been a privilege accorded those of wealth and high social status. More important from a feminist perspective, it protected not only the dominant economic class in the Marxist sense, but the dominant sex-class as well. The traditionally "private" was the sphere of the personal, home and hearth. And that area was the area within which women and children were forms of private property under the exclusive ownership and control of males. As the person in whom the absolute personality of the family vested, male heads of households had virtually absolute rights over their wives and children. The family, clearly, was not and is not a partnership of equals. There is no mutuality in the marital relation, and the rights and duties are decidedly one-sided. . . .

Why, then, has the demand for privacy centered so exclusively on preserving the traditional domain of male privilege? And why do the staunchest defenders of that view fail to see that in invoking these principles within a domain characterized by fundamental sexual inequality they are in fact both reinforcing that inequality and sanctioning its worst abuses? At the very least, adherents of the liberal ethic must acknowledge that there is no *natural* basis for deciding on what is private and what public for the purpose of entrenching a legal right to privacy, and that the traditional area of the private is the area most in need of loss of privacy in the name of promoting greater positive liberty and greater equality. How this fares on a purely utilitarian principle is of course problematic, for since men and women each make up roughly half the population, we cannot be sure that the benefits to women will in fact outweigh the losses to men.

Equality cannot flourish without limiting the privileges some already have in both the private and the public spheres, because the inequalities of the present system were a product of the unequal attribution of rights in the first instance; thus greater equality and liberty for those least advantaged under the present system necessitates placing restrictions on the privilege rights of those who are presently most advantaged. And since this must be done by creating obligations either to do or to forbear actions previously permitted, it can be accomplished only at the expense of negative liberty. While the principles of the liberal ethic itself do not require the historical division between public and private, it has certainly been presupposed in liberal thinking about these issues. Recognition of the extent to which this has played a role must lead to a reappraisal of what it is that people should be at liberty to do, and it must find a basis for this which does not rest on traditional views of the different spheres of life, and the different roles of the sexes.

What is needed, at base, is a reappraisal of what is *harmful*. That, too, has historically been defined in terms of what the dominant sex and the dominant economic class find "harmful."

... [I]t is clear from a consideration of the issue of pornography that so far at least the ethic of liberalism has been unable to rethink its concept of harm in a way which is consistent with sexual equality. Feminists and civil libertarians are now at complete loggerheads over this issue. The trend among feminists is clear. More and more of them are coming to see pornography as a species of hate literature.[4] Hate literature seeks to make one dislike and despise the people depicted, to make those persons seem inferior and unworthy of our respect. It seeks to set them apart and to show them as relevantly different from "us" in a way which justifies "us" in treating them differently, or it shows them as deserving to be treated badly because they have no respect for "us" or "our" values. What it must do to succeed is enforce a radical sense of their difference, their non-identity, with "us," a difference which is either utterly distasteful to "us," or one utterly opposed to "our" shared goals and values. It may also revel in their misery in an attempt to encourage feelings of wishing to contribute to that misery by doing things to them we would not think of doing to those we perceive to be relevantly similar to ourselves. So too with pornography. To achieve its impact, it relies on depicting women in humiliating, degrading, and violently abusive situations. To make matters worse, it frequently depicts them willingly, even avidly, suffering and inviting such treatment. As is obvious to even the naivest of eyes, such re-creations of heterosexual behavior and relationships feed traditional male phantasies about both themselves and women, and glorify the traditional advantages men have enjoyed in relation to exploitation of female sexuality.

Pornography is a method of socialization; it is the tangible, palpable embodiment of the imposition of the dominant sexual system which is a part of the dominant sex-class system. It is a vivid depiction of how to deploy male sexuality in just the way that will achieve maximum effect in maintaining the *status quo*. Pornography would be neither desired nor tolerated within any system other than one which sprang from the differential attribution of rights of ownership in which women and children are forms of sexual property, and in which they must either like it or quite literally lump it. It is a morality which stresses female passivity and submissiveness, and it encourages the actualization of such states through active aggression and violence. Pornography has very little to do with sex, certainly with any conception of egalitarian sexual relations between the sexes, but it has everything to do with showing how to use sexuality as an instrument of active oppression, and that is why it is wrong. Some allege that it also feeds female phantasies about themselves and men, but that is certainly being questioned, at least in so far as it can be said that there is any hard empirical data to support it.

That there should be no laws prohibiting the manufacture, sale, and distribution of pornography has traditionally and increasingly been defended as a freedom of speech, and freedom of press, issue. It is alleged that the reading or viewing of such material does not cause any harm, or that if it does, it is harm only to those who willingly consent to it. The premise that it doesn't cause harm is defended by arguing that it relates only to the phantasy level and does not translate itself into interpersonal behavior. And it goes further than this to argue that, indeed, it provides a healthy outlet, a cathartic effect, for those who might otherwise be tempted to act out their phantasies. Those who oppose pornography, particularly those who advocate its prohibition, are treated as Victorian prudes with sexual hangups. Women who object to it are seen as up-tight, unliberated, and just not "with it," sexually speaking.

The general principle underlying the liberal view is of course that expressed by Mill in "On Liberty," who argued against any form of censorship on the ground that it was only through the free flow of information that the true and the false could be separated. Prohibitions against the dissemination of any form of information function to preserve the *status quo* and to prevent the development of a critically reflective morality which is itself necessary to pave the way for needed social change. The principle has much to be said for it. But that cannot change the fact that when it is uncritically made to apply within a domain characterized by inequality and by frankly abusive behavior, a domain which is fundamentally shaped by a framework of social relations and institutions which makes all sexual relationships between men and women fundamentally coercive in nature,[5] it is bound to produce results which will be unacceptable because harmful to those who are in the preexisting inferior position and who stand to be most affected by the attitudes and beliefs, as well as the practices, of those who use it.

The liberal argument has been that such material isn't harmful at all, and certainly cannot be seen as harmful because it functions merely to inflame male sexual desire. What is the harm if all it does is give a guy a bit of a rush? And it is right here that we must begin our critique. Surely we must acknowledge at least two things. First, it is not "normal" to get one's rushes from just anything. Secondly, if one gets desirable reactions from things which create a clear and substantial risk to others, then one can justifiably be prohibited from getting them that way. Persons who get their sexual stimulation from watching the atrocities perpetrated against the Jews during the holocaust are not regarded as "normal," and rightly so. Furthermore, we do not feel that we are infringing any legitimate rights of others in preventing them access to material designed to provide sexual stimulation by this means. And the reasons for that are at least two-fold. First, as history has made all too clear, actions of this particular species do not remain at the level of mere phantasy. They have been acted out on the grand scale, so grand as to make any rational and reflective person aware that the possibility of a correlation between thought and action is at least strong enough to justify the imposition of prohibitions against material of this sort. Second, it stems from recognizing that even if the actual actions themselves are not acted out, the attitudes and beliefs of the persons enjoying it reflect attitudes toward the objects of the actions which are bad in themselves and which are bound to produce practical effects in real life, if only to be expressed in bigoted and racist attitudes. All of the same arguments apply to material which depicts black people in degrading, humiliating, and abusive circumstances. Such material is, in itself, an affront to the dignity of the objects depicted, not least because they *are* being depicted purely as objects, dehumanized and depersonalized instruments for the satisfaction of someone else's perverted tastes.

The same case can be made with respect to heterosexual pornography.[6] As Camille Le Grand puts it, "pornography teaches society to view women as less than human. It is this view which keeps women as victims."[7] The typical way in which women are depicted in pornography certainly reflects a view of them as inferior to men, as inherently masochistic, and as primarily of value as instruments for the satisfaction of male lust. That is, in itself, offensive to women, and is a straightforward objective affront to their dignity as equal persons. So on that ground alone, pornography ought to be prohibited, just as we prohibit material depicting other social groups in such a fashion.

. . . *[I]t is not a mark of personal depravity or immorality to be aroused by such material.* Given the cultural pattern of which it is a manifestation, that is not at all surprising. Indeed, it is just what we would expect. But what must be recognized is that it *is* a socialized response, and that it is a response about which men as well as women should be both concerned and angry. And certainly, once its cultural roots are exposed, it is a response which should not be seen as needing or justifying the sale and distribution of the material which elicited it. Women must object to pornography because it both reflects and reinforces the patterns of socialization appropriate to a system based on the unequal status of the sexes, in which women are consistently regarded and treated as the inferiors, and the sexual property, of men. The socialization it brings about is *in itself* a limitation of the autonomy of women. Men ought to object to it for the same reason, and they ought to recognize that the socialization it brings about in terms of their self-images and internalized standards of conduct is also undesirable, given any commitment to the notion of sexual equality.

To the extent that men are able to internalize the conviction that women and men are equal persons, and that men are not justified in using physical coercion to force women into sexual servitude, they must recognize that the pleasurable responses they get from pornography are inappropriate to that conviction and are destructive to their ability to form self-images consistent with it. But that does not entail that they are in any sense to blame for those responses: they had as little choice about that as they did about their names. But we have, then, given strong arguments in support of the view that the eliciting of a pleasurable response is not in itself any reason to condone the sale and distribution of pornography, and that a proper understanding of the nature and causes of that response gives men as well as women solid grounds for objecting to the material which occasioned it. I believe that many more men would be able to understand and accept the feminist perspective on pornography if they could come to realize that they are not responsible for their sexual responses to it given the pattern of socialization which exists to mold us all into a set of social relations which institutionalizes male aggression and female passivity.

Thus, pornography is harmful, both to women and to men, because it encourages men to combat feelings of inadequacy and low self-esteem by being aggressive and sadistic and women to feel shamed and humiliated just for being women. It encourages just that radical difference between men and women which allows men to see women as deserving of treatment they would refrain from subjecting someone to whom they perceived to be like themselves. To the extent that it also encourages women to combat insecurity and low self-esteem by becoming passive and masochistic, it presents even clearer dangers to them than it does to men, since it creates the conditions for their own victimization, but the damage it does to men who do not identify themselves as aggressive and superior to women cannot be underestimated either. However, that does not end the argument with defenders of liberalism, because their argument then moves on to the assertion that the harm to women is not direct enough to justify the legal prohibition of pornography. Frankly, I think that the argument that pornography is intrinsically offensive to the dignity of women ought to carry the day, but in the interests of completeness I want to go on to consider the other arguments that are brought to pornography's defense.

Apart from this notion of being intrinsically offensive and an infringement of the rights of women, it will be argued that even if pornography is harmful to the user, it does not lead to direct harm to women, because the phantasies it supports remain phantasies, and it in fact prevents direct harm to women through its cathartic effect. I may say at the outset that I'm not at all impressed with either of these arguments. So far as the first is concerned, there is plenty of hard evidence available which supports the contention that role modeling has a powerful effect on human behavior. Studies of wife and child abuse consistently attest to the fact that there is a strong correlation between those who are abusers and those who come from family situations which were themselves abusive. The battered child becomes the battering parent; the son who witnessed his father battering his mother, and who was himself battered, becomes a battering husband.[8] Also, the evidence about the effect of violence depicted on television on the behavior of children also points strongly in this direction.[9] People tend to act out and operationalize the behavior that they see typically acted out around them. And surely that is hardly surprising. It is what has kept civilization going. If we weren't able to perpetuate the patterns of behavior developed through cultural organization we wouldn't have come very far. So far as I know, however, there is no hard data to support the catharsis theory. It is a theory espoused by those who are looking for a rationale, though doubtless it has its roots in their awareness that they read pornography but don't rape and brutalize women. But raping and brutalizing women isn't the only harm that can be perpetrated against women. But so far there is little empirical support offered for the view that pornography feeds only the phantasy. Most psychiatric literature dealing with the "perversions" asserts that some people remain content with the phantasy while others do not.[10] But no one knows what differentiates the one who does actualize it from the one who doesn't. If this argument is going to be effective, it must be empirically demonstrated that this is so, and surely we cannot predict until the data is in that those who don't so outnumber those who do that we should, in the interests of an open society, tolerate the risk that some will. And since we are all imprisoned by the cultural stereotypes and the patterns of socialization appropriate to a society based on the sexual coercion of one sex by the other, how can those who do read it assert with certainty that they do not cause harm to women? They are hardly the best judges. As rape makes clear again, there is nowhere greater difference in perception than there is in the confusion surrounding rape and seduction. The men believe they are merely seducing, but the women perceive it as rape. And who is to judge? Certainly it is unfair to permit only those who are the perpetrators of such behavior to have a say in its interpretation.

While the liberal principle behind opposition to censorship is based on a recognition that desirable social change requires public access to information which challenges the beliefs and practices of the *status quo*, what it does not acknowledge is that information which supports the *status quo* through providing role models which advocate the use or threat of coercion as a technique of social control directed at a clearly identifiable group depicted as inferior, subordinate, and subhuman, works against the interest both of desirable social change and of the members of the subgroup so identified. This has been clearly acknowledged in the case of violently anti-semitic and other forms of racist literature. The same principles apply with respect to violently anti-female literature, and the same conclusion should follow. But this cannot come about until it is recognized and acknowledged that the dissemination of such material is itself a harm to the members of the group involved. It remains to be seem whether liberalism can accomplish this, but until it does, we cannot hope for its support on this issue.

In refusing to count as "harms" actions and practices which serve the interest of the dominant sex by reinforcing the patterns and effects of modes of socialization which support a sexist system, it renders itself incapable of changing that system and of promoting greater equality and positive liberty for women. Liberalism serves the interest of the dominant sex and the dominant class, though it contains within itself the potential for promoting greater equality and greater positive liberty for all. It can realize this potential, however, only by reconceptualizing harm in a way consistent with sex and class equality, and by recognizing that negative liberty must take second place to the promotion of equality, at least until we have achieved a framework of enforceable rules which guarantees equality within both the public and the private spheres.

NOTES

1. This is, of course, true of John Stuart Mill himself, as is clear from his essay, "The Subjection of Women," written in 1860 and first published in 1869.

2. After the distinction between "negative" and "positive" liberty made current by Isaiah Berlin in "Two Concepts of Liberty," in *Four Essays on Liberty* (London: O.U.P., 1969).

3. I am relying here on the distinctions first made by W. N. Hohfeld, *Fundamental Legal Conceptions* (New Haven: Yale U.P., 1932).

4. Among the articles that spring readily to mind are Robin Morgan, "Theory and Practice: Pornography and Rape," *Going Too Far* (New York: Random House, 1977), ch. IV, 163–69; Diana Russell, "Pornography: A Feminist Perspective," unpublished paper;

Susan Brownmiller, *Against Our Will* (New York: Simon and Schuster, 1975), 394–96; and Marie Shear, "Free Meat Talks Back," *J. of Communication,* 26, no. 1 (Winter 1976): 38–39.

5. Clark and Lewis, *Rape: The Price of Coercive Sexuality* (Toronto: Canadian Women's Educational Press, 1977), chs. 7 and 8 in particular.

6. Indeed, it is true of male homosexual pornography as well. But in the interest of not legislating in the interest of others, I am not advocating that we should prohibit these species of pornography. If men object to it, as in my view they should, whether homo- or heterosexual, it is up to them to express their opposition. Certainly I do not wish to infringe the rights homosexuals have to look at what they like, even though I cannot say with certainty that I am not adversely affected by it.

7. Quoted in Diana Russell, "Pornography: A Feminist Perspective," op. cit., 7, no reference given.

8. See, for example, Del Martin, *Battered Wives* (San Francisco: Glide Publications, 1976), 22–23; Erin Pizzey, *Scream Quietly or the Neighbours Will Hear* (London: Penguin Books, 1974), ch. 4; Mary Van Stolk, *The Battered Child in Canada* (Toronto: McClelland & Stewart, 1972), 23–27.

9. A. Bandura, D. Ross, and S.A. Ross, "Transmission of Aggression Through Imitation of Aggressive Models," *J. Abnormal and Social Psychology* 63, no. 3: 575–82.

10. Richard von Kraft-Ebbing, *Psychopathia Sexualis,* 11th ed., rev. and enlarged (Stuttgard, 1901), 94–95; S. Freud, *Introductory Lectures on Psycho-Analysis,* standard ed., 16:306.

Joel Feinberg

Grounds for Coercion

Whatever else we believe about freedom, most of us believe it is something to be praised, or so luminously a Thing of Value that it is beyond praise. What is it that makes freedom a good thing? . . .

. . . When a free man violates his neighbor's interests, then his freedom, having been put to bad use, was, on balance, a bad thing, but . . . it was not an unalloyed evil. Whatever the harmful consequences of freedom in a given case, there is always a direct effect on the person of its possessor which must be counted a positive good. Coercion may prevent great evils, and be wholly justified on that account, but it always has its price. Coercion may be on balance a great gain, but its direct effects always, or nearly always, constitute a definite loss. If this is true, there is always a *presumption* in favor of freedom, even though it can in some cases be overridden by more powerful reasons on the other side.

From Joel Feinberg, *Social Philosophy* (Englewood Cliffs, N.J.: Prentice-Hall, 1973), pp. 20–22, 27–29, 33, 34, 36–37, 42–45. Adapted by permission of Prentice Hall, Inc. Copyright © 1973 Prentice-Hall, Inc.

The presumption in favor of freedom is usually said to rest on freedom's essential role in the development of traits of intellect and character which constitute the good of individuals and are centrally important means to the progress of societies. One consensus argument, attributable with minor variations to Von Humboldt, Mill, Hobhouse, and many others, goes roughly as follows. The highest good for man is neither enjoyment nor passive contentment, but rather a dynamic process of growth and self-realization. This can be called "happiness" if we mean by that term what the Greeks did, namely, "The exercise of vital powers along lines of excellence in a life affording them scope."[1] The highest social good is then the greatest possible amount of individual self-realization and (assuming that different persons are inclined by their natures in different ways) the resultant diversity and fullness of life. Self-realization consists in the actualization of certain uniquely human potentialities, the bringing to full development of certain powers and abilities. This in turn requires constant practice in making difficult choices among alternative hypotheses, policies, and actions—and the more difficult the better. John Stuart Mill explained why:

> The human faculties of perception, judgment, discriminative feeling, mental activity, and even moral preference are exercised only in making a choice. He who does anything because it is the custom makes no choice. He gains no practice either in discerning or in desiring what is best. The mental and moral, like the muscular, powers are improved only by being used.[2]

In short, one does not realize what is best in oneself when social pressures to conform to custom lead one mindlessly along. Even more clearly, one's growth will be stunted when one is given no choice in the first place, either because of being kept in ignorance or because one is terrorized by the wielders of bayonets.

Freedom to decide on one's own while fully informed of the facts thus tends to promote the good of the person who exercises it, even if it permits him to make foolish or dangerous mistakes. Mill added to this argument the citation of numerous social benefits that redound indirectly but uniformly to those who grant freedom as well as those who exercise it. We all profit from the fruits of genius, he maintained, and genius, since it often involves doggedness and eccentricity, is likely to flourish only where coercive pressures toward conformity are absent. Moreover, social progress is more likely to occur where there is free criticism of prevailing ways and adventurous experiments in living. Finally, true understanding of human nature requires freedom, since without liberty there will be little diversity, and without diversity all aspects of the human condition will be ascribed to fixed nature rather than to the workings of a particular culture.

Such are the grounds for holding that there is always a presumption in favor of freedom, that whenever we are faced with an option between forcing a person to do something and letting him decide on his own whether or not to do it, other things being equal, we should always opt for the latter. If a strong general presumption for freedom has been established, the burden of proof rests on the shoulders of the advocate of coercion, and the philosopher's task will be to state the conditions under which the presumption can be overridden....

HARM VS. HURT: THE ROLE OF KNOWLEDGE

Is it true that "what a person doesn't know can't *harm* him"? For most cases, this maxim certainly does *not* apply, and it is one of the merits of the "interest" analysis of harm that it explains why. Typically, having one's interests violated is one thing, and knowing that one's interests have been violated is another. The rich man is harmed at the time his home is burgled, even though he may not discover the harm for months; similarly, a soldier is harmed the moment he is wounded, though in the heat of the battle he may not discover even his serious wounds for some time. The law does not permit a burglar to plead "He will never miss it" even when that plea is true, for the crime of burglary consists in inflicting a forbidden harm, whether or not it will be discovered or will hurt. It is true that not all harms *hurt*, partly because not all harms ever come to be noticed. There may well be a relatively narrow and precise sense of "harm" in ordinary usage such that "being harmed" can be contrasted with being hurt (as well as with "being shocked" and "being offended"). However, if harm is understood as the violation of an interest, and all men have an interest in not being hurt, it follows that hurt is one species of harm. Hence, even though not all harms hurt, all hurts do harm (or more accurately, are themselves harm), and the harm principle could conceivably be used to justify coercion when it is necessary to prevent hurts, even when the hurts do not lead to any *further* harm.

There are some special cases where the maxim "What a person doesn't know can't *hurt* him" seems quite sound. In these cases, knowledge of some fact, such as the adulterous infidelities of one's spouse, is itself hurtful; indeed, the whole hurt consists in the knowledge and is inseparable from it. Here knowledge is both a necessary and sufficient condition of a hurt. What the cuckolded husband doesn't know "can't hurt him." That is not to say that he cannot be *harmed* unless he is hurt. An undetected adultery damages one of the victim's "interests in domestic relations," just as an unknown libelous publication can damage his interest in a good reputation, or an undetected trespass on his land can damage his interest in "the exclusive enjoyment and control" of that land. In all these cases, violation of the interest in question is itself a harm even though no *further* harm may result to any other interests.

The distinction between hurt and (generic) harm raises one additional question. We must include in the category of "hurts" not only physical pains but also forms of mental distress. Our question is whether, in applying the harm principle, we should permit coercion designed to prevent mental distress when the distress is not likely to be followed by hurt or harm of any other kind. Some forms of mental distress (e.g., "hurt feelings") can be ruled out simply on the ground that they are too minor or trivial to warrant interference. Others are so severe that they can lead to mental breakdowns. In such cases, however, it is the consequential harm to mental health and not the mere fact of distress that clearly warrants interference on the ground of harmfulness. Thus, a convenient criterion for determining whether a hurt is sufficiently harmful to justify preventive coercion on that ground suggests itself: the hurt is serious enough if and only if it is either a symptom of a prior or concurrent harm of another order (as a pain in an arm may be the result and sign of a broken bone), or is in itself the cause of a consequential harm (e.g., mental breakdown) of another order.

HARM VS. OFFENSE

The relation of offensiveness to harmfulness can be treated in much the same way as that of hurtfulness to harmfulness. The following points can be made of both:

1. Some harms do not offend (as some do not hurt).
2. All offenses (like all hurts) are harms, inasmuch as all men have an interest in not being offended or hurt.
3. Some offenses (like some hurts) are symptoms or consequences of prior or concurrent harms.
4. Some offenses (like some hurts) are causes of subsequent harms: in the case of extreme hurt, harm to health; in the case of extreme offense, harm from provoked ill will or violence. These subsequent harms are harms of a different order, i.e., violations of interests other than the interest in not being hurt or offended.
5. Some offenses, like some hurts, are "harmless," i.e., do not lead to any *further* harm (violations of any interests other than the interest in not being hurt or offended).
6. Although offense and hurt are in themselves harms, they are harms of a relatively trivial kind (unless they are of sufficient magnitude to violate interests in health and peace).

... For clarity and convenience only, I shall stipulate then that "offensiveness as such" is a proposed ground for coercion distinct from harm of the sort required by the harm principle (narrowly interpreted), so that "the offense principle" can be treated as an independent principle in its own right.

Offensive behavior is such in virtue of its capacity to induce in others any of a large miscellany of mental states that have little in common except that they are unpleasant, uncomfortable, or disliked. These states do not necessarily "hurt," as do sorrow and distress. Rather the relation between them and hurt is analogous to that between physical unpleasantness and pain, for there is also a great miscellany of unpleasant but not painful bodily states—itches, shocks, and discomforts—that have little in common except that they don't hurt but are nevertheless universally disliked. Among the main sorts of "harmless but disliked" *mental* states are irritating sensations (e.g., bad smells, cacophony, clashing colors), disgust, shocked moral sensibilities, and shameful embarrassment. . . .

OTHER PROPOSED GROUNDS FOR COERCION

. . . One might hold that restriction of one person's liberty can be justified:

1. To prevent harm to others, either
   a. injury to individual persons *(The Private Harm Principle)*, or

b. impairment of institutional practices that are in the public interest *(The Public Harm Principle)*;
2. To prevent offense to others *(The Offense Principle)*;
3. To prevent harm to self *(Legal Paternalism)*;
4. To prevent or punish sin, i.e., to "enforce morality as such" *(Legal Moralism)*;
5. To benefit the self *(Extreme Paternalism)*;
6. To benefit others *(The Welfare Principle)*.

The liberty-limiting principles on this list are best understood as stating neither necessary nor sufficient conditions for justified coercion, but rather specifications of the *kinds* of reasons that are always relevant or acceptable in support of proposed coercion, even though in a given case they may not be conclusive. Each principle states that interference might be permissible *if* (but not *only if*) a certain condition is satisfied. Hence the principles are not mutually exclusive; it is possible to hold two or more of them at once, even all of them together, and it is possible to deny all of them. Moreover, the principles cannot be construed as stating sufficient conditions for legitimate interference with liberty, for even though the principle is satisfied in a given case, the general presumption against coercion might not be outweighed. The harm principle, for example, does not justify state interference to prevent a tiny bit of inconsequential harm. Prevention of minor harm always counts in favor of proposals (as in a legislature) to restrict liberty, but in a given instance it might not count *enough* to outweigh the general presumption against interference, or it might be outweighed by the prospect of practical difficulties in enforcing the law, excessive costs, and forfeitures of privacy. A liberty-limiting principle states considerations that are always good reasons for coercion, though neither exclusively nor, in every case, decisively good reasons. . . .

Immoral conduct is no trivial thing, and we should hardly expect societies to tolerate it; yet if men are *forced* to refrain from immorality, their own choices will play very little role in what they do, so that they can hardly develop critical judgment and moral traits of a genuinely praiseworthy kind. Thus legal enforcement of morality seems to pose a dilemma. The problem does not arise if we assume that all immoral conduct is socially harmful, for immoral conduct will then be prohibited by law not just to punish sin or to "force men to be moral," but rather to prevent harm to others. If, however, there are forms of immorality that do not necessarily cause harm, "the problem of the enforcement of morality" becomes especially acute.

The central problem cases are those criminal actions generally called "morals offenses." Offenses against morality and decency have long constituted a category of crimes (as distinct from offenses against the person, offenses against property, and so on). These have included mainly sex offenses, such as adultery, fornication, sodomy, incest, and prostitution, but also a miscellany of nonsexual offenses, including cruelty to animals, desecration of the flag or other venerated symbols, and mistreatment of corpses. In a useful article,[3] Louis B. Schwartz maintains that what sets these crimes off as a class is not their special relation to morality (murder is also an offense against morality, but it is not a "morals offense") but the lack of an essential connection between them and social harm. In particular, their suppression is not required by the public security. Some morals offenses may harm the perpetrators themselves, but the risk of harm of this sort has usually been consented to in advance by the actors. Offense to other parties, when it occurs, is usually a consequence of perpetration of the offenses *in public,* and can be prevented by statutes against "open lewdness," or "solicitation" in public places. That still leaves "morals offenses" committed by consenting adults in private. Should they really be crimes? . . .

. . . Obscene literature and pornographic displays . . . are materials deliberately published for the eyes of others, and their existence can bring partisans of the unsupplemented harm principle into direct conflict with those who endorse *both* the harm and offense principles.

In its untechnical, prelegal sense, the word "obscenity" refers to material dealing with nudity, sex, or excretion in an offensive manner. Such material becomes obscene in the legal sense when, because of its offensiveness or for some other reason [this question had best be left open in the definition], it is or ought to be without legal protection. The legal definition then incorporates the everyday sense, and essential to both is the requirement that the material be *offensive.* An item may offend one person and not another. "Obscenity," if it is to avoid this subjective relativity, must involve an interpersonal objective sense of "offensive." Material must be offensive by prevailing community standards that are public and well known, or be such that it is apt to offend virtually everyone.

Not all material that is generally offensive need also be harmful in any sense recognized by the harm principle. It is partly an empirical question whether reading or witnessing obscene material causes social harm; reliable evidence, even of a statistical kind, of causal connections between obscenity and antisocial behavior is extremely hard to find.[4] In the absence of clear and decisive evidence of harmfulness, the American Civil Liberties Union insists that the offensiveness of obscene material cannot be a sufficient ground for its repression:

> . . . the question in a case involving obscenity, just as in every case involving an attempted restriction upon free speech, is whether the words or pictures are used in such circumstances and are of such a nature as to create a clear and present danger that they will bring about a substantial evil that the state has a right to prevent. . . . We believe that under the current state of knowledge, there is grossly insufficient evidence to show that obscenity brings about *any* substantive evil.[5]

The A.C.L.U. argument employs *only* the harm principle among liberty-limiting principles, and treats literature, drama, and painting as forms of expression subject to the same rules as expressions of opinion. In respect to both types of expression, "every act of deciding what should be barred carries with it a danger to the community."[6] The suppression itself is an evil to the author who is squelched. The power to censor and punish involves risks that socially valuable material will be repressed along with the "filth." The overall effect of suppression, the A.C.L.U. concludes, is almost certainly to discourage nonconformist and eccentric expression generally. In order to override these serious risks, there must be in a given case an even more clear and present danger that the obscene material, if not squelched, will cause even greater harm; such countervailing evidence is never forthcoming. (If such evidence were to accumulate, the A.C.L.U. would be perfectly willing to change its position on obscenity.)

The A.C.L.U. stand on obscenity seems clearly to be the position dictated by the unsupplemented harm principle and its corollary, the clear and present danger test. Is there any reason at this point to introduce the offense principle into the discussion? Unhappily, we may be forced to if we are to do justice to all of our particular intuitions in the most harmonious way. Consider an example suggested by Professor Schwartz. By the provisions of the new Model Penal Code, he writes, "a rich homosexual may not use a billboard on Times Square to promulgate to the general populace the techniques and pleasures of sodomy."[7] If the notion of "harm" is restricted to its narrow sense, that is, contrasted with "offense," it will be hard to reconstruct a rationale for this prohibition based on the harm principle. There is unlikely to be evidence that a lurid and obscene public poster in Times Square would create a clear and present danger of injury to those who fail to avert their eyes in time as they come blinking out of the subway stations. Yet it will be surpassingly difficult for even the most dedicated liberal to advocate freedom of expression in a case of this kind. Hence, if we are to justify coercion in this case, we will likely be driven, however reluctantly, to the offense principle.

There is good reason to be "reluctant" to embrace the offense principle until driven to it by an example like the above. People take perfectly genuine offense at many socially useful or harmless activities, from commercial advertisements to inane chatter. Moreover, widespread irrational prejudices can lead people to be disgusted, shocked, even morally repelled by perfectly innocent activities, and we should be loath to permit their groundless repugnance to override the innocence. The offense principle, therefore, must be formulated very precisely and applied in accordance with carefully formulated standards so as not to open the door to wholesale and intuitively unwarranted repression. At the very least we should require that the prohibited conduct or material be of the sort apt to offend almost everybody, and not just some shifting majority or special interest group.

It is instructive to note that a strictly drawn offense principle would not only justify prohibition of conduct and pictured conduct that is in its inherent character repellent, but also conduct and pictured conduct that is inoffensive in itself but offensive in inappropriate circumstances. I have in mind so-called indecencies such as public nudity. One can imagine an advocate of the unsupplemented harm principle arguing against the public nudity prohibition on the grounds that the sight of a naked body does no one any harm, and the state has no right to impose standards of dress or undress on private citizens. How one chooses to dress, after all, is a form of self-expression. If we do not permit the state to bar clashing colors or bizarre hair styles, by what right does it prohibit total undress? Perhaps the sight of naked people could at first lead to riots or other forms of antisocial behavior, but that is precisely the sort of contingency for which we have police. If we don't take away a person's right of free speech for the reason that its exercise may lead others to misbehave, we cannot in consistency deny his right to dress or undress as he chooses for the same reason.

There may be no answering this challenge on its own ground, but the offense principle provides a ready rationale for the nudity prohibition. The sight of nude bodies in public places is for almost everyone acutely *embarrassing*. Part of the explanation no doubt rests on the fact that nudity has an irresistible power to draw the eye and focus the thoughts on matters that are normally repressed. The conflict between these attracting and repressing forces is exciting, upsetting, and anxiety-producing. In some persons it will create at best a kind of painful turmoil, and at worst that experience of exposure to oneself of "peculiarly sensitive, intimate, vulnerable aspects of the self"[8] which is called *shame*. "One's feeling is involuntarily exposed openly in one's face; one is uncovered . . . taken by surprise . . . made a fool of."[9] The result is not mere "offense," but a kind of psychic jolt that in many normal people can be a painful wound. Even those of us who are better able to control our feelings might well resent the *nuisance* of having to do so.

If we are to accept the offense principle as a supplement to the harm principle, we must accept two corollaries which stand in relation to it similarly to the way in which the clear and present danger test stands to the harm principle. The first, the *standard of universality,* has already been touched upon. For the offensiveness (disgust, embarrassment, outraged sensibilities, or shame) to be sufficient to warrant coercion, it should be the reaction that could be expected from almost any person chosen at random from the nation as a whole, regardless of sect, faction, race, age, or sex. The second is the *standard of reasonable avoidability.* No one has a right to protection from the state against offensive experiences if he can effectively avoid those experiences with no unreasonable effort or inconvenience. If a nude person enters a public bus and takes a seat near the front, there may be no effective way for other patrons to avoid intensely shameful embarrassment (or other insupportable feelings) short of leaving the bus, which would be an unreasonable inconvenience. Similarly, obscene remarks over a loudspeaker, homosexual billboards in Times Square, and pornographic handbills thrust into the hands of passing pedestrians all fail to be reasonably avoidable.

On the other hand, the offense principle, properly qualified, can give no warrant to the suppression of *books* on the grounds of obscenity. When printed words hide decorously behind covers of books sitting passively on bookstore shelves, their offensiveness is easily avoided. The contrary view is no doubt encouraged by the common comparison of obscenity with "smut," "filth," or "dirt." This in turn suggests an analogy to nuisance law, which governs cases where certain activities create loud noises or terrible odors offensive to neighbors, and "the courts must weigh the gravity of the nuisance [substitute "offense"] to the neighbors against the social utility [substitute "redeeming social value"] of the defendant's conduct."[10] There is, however, one vitiating disanalogy in this comparison. In the case of "dirty books" the offense is easily avoidable. There is nothing like the evil smell of rancid garbage oozing right out through the covers of a book. When an "obscene" book sits on a shelf, who is there to be offended? Those who want to read it for the sake of erotic stimulation presumably will not be offended (or else they wouldn't read it), and those who choose not to read it will have no experience by which to be offended. If its covers are too decorous, some innocents may browse through it by mistake and be offended by what they find, but they need only close the book to escape the offense. Even this offense, minimal as it is, could be completely avoided by prior consultation of trusted book reviewers. I conclude that there are no sufficient grounds derived either from the harm or offense principles for suppressing obscene literature, unless that ground be the protection of children; but I can think of no reason why restrictions on sales to children cannot work as well for printed materials as they do for cigarettes and whiskey.

NOTES

1. Edith Hamilton, *The Greek Way* (New York: W. W. Norton, 1942), 35ff.
2. John Stuart Mill, *On Liberty* (New York: Liberal Arts Press, 1956), 71.
3. Louis B. Schwartz, "Morals Offenses and the Model Penal Code," *Columbia Law Review* LXIII (1963): 669ff.
4. There have been some studies made, but the results have been inconclusive. See the *Report of the Federal Commission on Obscenity and Pornography* (New York: Bantam Books, 1970), 169–308.
5. *Obscenity and Censorship,* pamphlet published by the American Civil Liberties Union, New York (March 1963), 7.
6. *Obscenity and Censorship,* 4.
7. Schwartz, "Morals Offenses and the Penal Code," 680.
8. Helen Merrill Lynd, *On Shame and the Search for Identity* (New York: Science Editions, 1961), 33.
9. Lynd, *On Shame and the Search for Identity,* 32.
10. William L. Prosser, *Handbook of the Law of Torts* (St. Paul: West Publishing, 1955), p. 411.

Fred R. Berger

Pornography, Sex, and Censorship

. . . In this paper, I want to put aside the First Amendment to ask if there are any justifiable grounds for rejecting the arguments offered for the censorship of pornography independent of First Amendment considerations. Moreover, I shall be concerned with the *censorship* of pornography, not its *regulation*. The regulation of speech often has the same effect as censorship, and that is an important danger; nevertheless, censorship and regulation differ radically in intention, and that is an important difference.[1] I should also indicate that I shall suppose that those who favor censorship (I shall refer to them as "the censors") are not *generally* in favor of censorship, and would not prohibit what they regard as "true" art or literature.

Moreover, to lend further clarity to my discussion I shall propose a definition which is useful for the purposes of this paper, and which picks out most of what is usually regarded as pornographic, and that is all I claim for it. I define pornography as art or literature which explicitly depicts sexual activity or arousal in a manner

From *Social Theory and Practice* 4, 2 (1977). Reprinted by permission.

having little or no artistic or literary value.[2] (I am assuming that scientific and medical texts are a kind of literature, with appropriate criteria of acceptability.)

The definition does, I believe, make pornography a relatively objective classification, insofar as there are clear cases on both sides of the divide, and there are relatively standard literary and artistic criteria by which to judge disputed cases.[3] In this respect, I am somewhat sympathetic to the conservatives who chide those liberals who claim they are not able to recognize standard cases of pornography as such.[4]

1. OBJECTIONS TO PORNOGRAPHY

Generally speaking, there are three forms of argument employed by the conservatives in favor of censorship. First, they simply hold that pornography itself is immoral or evil, irrespective of ill-consequences which may flow from it. Second, they sometimes assert that, irrespective of its morality, a practice which most people in a community find abhorrent and disgusting may be rightfully suppressed. Finally, they sometimes contend that pornography promotes or leads to certain kinds of socially harmful attitudes and/or behavior.

In this paper, I wish to concentrate on this last form of argument. . . .

The traditional form of the claim can be labeled the "incitement to rape" theory. It holds that pornography arouses sexual desire, which seeks an outlet, often in antisocial forms such as rape. It is this version of the claim we are most familiar with, and the evidence which is available tends to refute it.[5] I shall have more to say about it later.

The conservative views I want to take up hold that the harms from pornography are somewhat long-range. These commentators maintain that the modes of sex depicted in pornography, and the manner of depiction, will result in altering our basic attitudes towards sex and to one another, so that in the end a climate of antisocial behavior will result. . . .

2. THE RESPONSE TO CONSERVATIVE OBJECTIONS

I want to consider first the argument concerning privacy. It was Steiner's claim that pornography takes the "words of the night," and "by shouting them over the rooftops," robs us of the ability to use them or find them in private—sex becomes a matter in the public domain. Moreover, by dehumanizing the individual, people are treated as in concentration camps. As Steiner expressed it, subsequent to the original publication of his essay: "Both pornography and totalitarianism seem to me to set up power relations which must necessarily violate privacy."[6]

If there is any plausibility to the first part of these claims, it must derive entirely from the metaphor of shouting the sacred night words over the rooftops. Were anyone to do such a thing with night words, day words, winter words, and so on, we would have a legitimate gripe concerning our privacy. But in what *way* is the voluntary perusal or viewing of pornography an invasion of privacy? His point *seems* to be that the constant consumption by the public of explicit sexual materials will come to make sex something "pre-packaged" for us, so that we will not discover how to do it ourselves, in our own ways. This is extraordinarily implausible, and if it were true, would constitute a reason for banning all literature dealing with human feelings and emotions, and ways of relating to one another. The evidence is that greater sexual explicitness is utilized as a means for people to have greater awareness of their sexuality and its possibilities, and to assimilate the experiences of others into their own lifestyles. The capacity to do this is *part* of what is involved in our being the unique individuals we are. At any rate, people who *want* the stimulation of erotic materials, who feel freer in expressing themselves through the influence of sexy art, who do not *want* an environment in which sex cannot be appreciated through explicit literature and art, will hardly be impressed with the manner in which the censor protects *their* privacy.

I want now to turn to Kristol's view that pornography is autoerotic, hence, infantile, and thus promotes a sexual regression which is a danger to civilization itself. The danger which this supposed form of infantilism poses is that it would destroy the capacity for an integral feature of mature relations (and ultimately civilized relations) if "not controlled or sublimated in some way."[7]

Now the ultimate ground for censorship which the argument poses really has only secondary connections with the charges of autoeroticism and infantilism. Lots of things are "self-pleasuring" without being thought infantile or dangerous on that account. Consider the pleasures of the gourmet, or wine aficionado, or devotees of Turkish baths.

Kristol believes that masturbation, and pornography which is its mental form, has an appeal to us as adults, and this is dangerous. Because it *is so* attractive, it is liable to draw us away from real love, and this is why it must be headed off at the pass. The charge of infantilism, then, is only Kristol's way of making us feel bad about masturbating. By virtue of his claiming to know the rationale underlying "all the codes of sexual conduct ever devised by the human race," we are made to feel beyond the pale of civilized adult society. The argument turns, really, on the supposed dangers of an *overly* autoeroticized society, which he thinks the legalization of pornography will help produce.

In criticizing pornography on these grounds, Kristol has surely overshot his mark; for, there is nothing more masturbatory than masturbation itself. If Kristol is right, then his concern with pornography is too tepid a treatment of the danger. What the argument would show is that we must stamp out masturbation itself!

Moreover, Kristol is mistaken if he thinks that censorship of pornography will make one whit of difference to the incidence of masturbation. This is because the masturbatory imagination is perfectly limitless; it does not *need* explicit sexual stimuli. Deprived of that, it can make do with virtually anything—the impassioned kisses of film lovers, a well-filled female's sweater, or a male's crotch,[8] even, we are told, a neatly displayed ankle or bare shoulder. The enormity of the problem Kristol faces is shown in the revelation of the *Playboy* survey that: "a large majority of men and women in every age group say that while they masturbate, they fantasize about having intercourse with persons they love."[9] The implications for the censor are staggering!

There are two further reasons why reasonable people will not take Kristol's view seriously. First, he underestimates the human capacity to assimilate varieties of sexual experience. People can enjoy pornography and intercourse without giving up one or the other. Second, his entire argument grossly undervalues the appeal and attraction to us of the very thing he wants to preserve—mature sexual love which is fulfilling, rewarding, and integrated into the course of a loving relationship. Pornography may be in some sense autoerotic; it can be pleasant to be sexually stimulated. But it is rarely its own source of ultimate satisfaction; it usually stimulates to acquire further satisfactions. Indeed, this is presupposed by some of the conservative arguments. But there is no reason to assume that such satisfaction will be sought exclusively through masturbation, when a healthy sex relation is available with a loved one. I have *never* heard anyone, male or female, complain that their love life had been ruined by their partner's turn to masturbation as a result of an excess of pornography. On the other hand, I have heard couples rave about sex had after viewing pornographic films.

Still, there does seem to be a lingering problem which the conservatives will regard as not adequately dealt with in anything said thus far. They think that literature and art *can* influence people's attitudes and beliefs, and also their behavior, and they cannot understand why the liberal, who believes this to be true in other cases, is unwilling to admit this with respect to pornography. Now, I believe the liberal *can* admit the possibility of a causal role for pornography with respect to people's attitudes and behavior. Such an admission does not, however, establish a case for censorship.

It would be quite extraordinary if literary and visual materials which are capable of arousing normal men and women did not also have some tendency to arouse people already predisposed to harmful conduct, and especially people with an unstable psychological makeup. It is believable, even apart from any evidence, that such people might act from the fantasies such stimuli generate.

When the conservative is reasonable, however, he recognizes that the stimulation and consequent influence of pornography is a function not merely of the nature of the stimulus, but also of the person's background, upbringing, cultural environment, and his own genetic and personality structure and predisposition. Put *this* way, the conservative has a somewhat plausible claim that pornography can sometimes be implicated as having some causal role in the etiology of social harms.

Put in its most reasonable form, however, the claim makes quite *un*reasonable the censorship of pornography. There are two primary reasons for this: (1) Pornography is not distinguishable from other materials in producing *direct* harms of this kind; it may, in fact, exert a counter-influence to other materials which are more likely to have these effects. (2) The *indirect* harms—those produced through the influence of altered attitudes and beliefs, are highly unlikely, and not of a kind a society which values freedom will allow to become the basis of suppression without strong evidence of probable causal connections. It will seek to counter such remote influences with noncoercive means.

Let us turn to the first point—that other materials which no one would dream of suppressing are as likely to produce harms. . . .

. . . Studies [by Michael J. Goldstein and Harold S. Kant] seem to yield the conclusion that pornography itself does not tend to produce antisocial behavior, and that, at least in the case of rapists, other materials are more likely to do so:

> We must consider that sex offenders are highly receptive to suggestions of sexual behavior congruent with their previously formed desires and will interpret the material at hand to fit their needs. It is true, however, that while few, if any, sex offenders

suggest that erotica played a role in the commission of sex crimes, stimuli expressing brutality, with or without concomitant sexual behavior, were often mentioned as disturbing, by rapists in particular. This raises the question of whether the stimulus most likely to release sexual behavior is one representing sexuality, or one representing aggression.[10]

In summarizing the evidence they gathered, and which is supported by other studies, they conclude that pornography does not seem to be a significant factor in the behavior of sex offenders. Moreover, there is some evidence that "for rapists, exposure to erotica portraying 'normal' heterosexual relations can serve to ward off antisocial impulses."[11]

The point is that if we take the conservative's "harm" claim in its most plausible form, we must conclude that while pornography *can* play a causal role of this type, the evidence is that many other ordinary visual and literary depictions are more likely to do so. If we take seriously the claim that having this kind of causal role is sufficient for a case for censorship, then we must do a much greater housecleaning of our media offerings than we had imagined. The problem is that while we know where to begin—with unalloyed portrayals of violence, we can hardly know where to end.

A further serious difficulty for the conservative "harm" argument arises when we ask just what *kinds* of backgrounds and attitudes *do* predispose to the unwanted behavior. The studies of Kant and Goldstein are of help here, especially with respect to rapists:

... "It appears that all our noncontrol groups, no matter what their ages, education, or occupations, share one common characteristic: they had little exposure to erotica when they were adolescents."[12]

These results at the very least carry the suggestion that the very attitudes toward sex which motivate the censor are part of the background and psychological formation of the personality patterns of sex offenders—backgrounds which include the repression of sexual feelings, repression of exposure to explicit sexual stimuli, an overly developed sense of shame and guilt related to sex. As we have seen, some of the censors advocate *just* this sort of model for all of society, wherein suppression of pornography is just *one* way of safeguarding society. It may well be that they are in the paradoxical position of isolating a possible evil of great extent, and then recommending and fostering a response which will help produce that very evil.[13]

There is, however, a more profound reason why the admission of a possible causal role for pornography in affecting attitudes and behavior need not support the conservative view, and why the traditional liberal may well have been right in not taking pornography seriously.

To begin with, I believe we have granted the conservatives too much in admitting that pornography depersonalizes sex. While there is a measure of truth in this claim, it is not literally true. By concentrating on physical aspects of sex, pornography does, somewhat, abstract from the web of feelings, emotions, and needs which are usually attendant on sexual experience in ordinary life. Nonetheless, people are not depicted as mere machines or animals. Indeed, where there is explicit pornographic purpose—the arousal of the reader or viewer—the end could not be accomplished were it not real fleshy people depicted. In addition, pornography almost always does have *some* human context within which sex takes place —a meeting in a bar, the bridegroom carrying his bride over the threshold, the window washer observing the inhabitant of an apartment. A study of pornography will reveal certain set patterns of such contexts; there is, indeed, a sort of orthodoxy among pornographers. And, there is an obvious reason: pornography springs from and caters to sexual fantasies. This also explains why so little context is needed; the observer quickly identifies with the scene, and is able to elaborate it in his or her own mind to whatever extent he or she wishes or feels the need. That pornography is intimately tied to fantasy—*peopled* fantasy—also accounts for one of its worst features—its tendency to treat women in conventional male chauvinist ways. Pornography, as a matter of sociological fact, has been produced by and for men with such sexual attitudes.

There are further grounds for holding that pornography does not, by its nature, dehumanize sex in the feared ways. It usually depicts people as enjoying physical activity, that is, as mutually experiencing *pleasure*. Typical pornography displays sex as something people take fun in and enjoy. There is usually little doubt the persons involved are *liking* it. All of the censors we have discussed treat *Fanny Hill* as pornographic, but it is obvious to anyone who has read the book that it absolutely resists the claim that the characters are not portrayed as real people with the usual hopes and fears, who desire not to be harmed, and desire a measure of respect as persons. The book concentrates on sex and sexual enjoyment, and *that* is why it is taken as pornographic. Even sadistic pornography, it should be noted, depicts people as having enjoyment; and, it is usually sado-*masochistic* pleasures which are portrayed, with a resultant equalizing of the distribution of pleasure (if not of pain). In this respect, most pornography does not portray humans as *mere* instruments of whatever ends we have. And, in this respect, pornography does not express or evoke the genuinely immoral attitudes which a great deal of our movie, television, and literary materials cater to and reinforce.[14]

Indeed, much of what is found in the media *is* immoral in that it is expressive of, caters to, and fosters attitudes which *are* morally objectionable. People are treated as expendable units by international spies for whom *anything* is permitted in the name of national security; the typical laundry soap commercial treats women as idiotic house slaves; situation comedy typically portrays fathers as moronic bunglers who, nonetheless, rightfully rule their homes as dictators (albeit, benevolent ones); the various detective programs cater to the aggressive, dominating, *macho* image of male sexuality which is endemic within large portions of American society. Pornography cannot get off the hook merely by pointing out that it depicts *people*. On the other hand, most of it does not reflect or cater to attitudes as objectionable as one now finds dominating the output of television alone. And, where it does, it is not a result of the fact it is pornographic, but, rather, that it reflects conventional views widely expressed in other forms.

There remains a final point to be made about the influence of pornography on attitudes. Pornography, when it does attract us, affect us, appeal to us, has a limited, narrowly focused appeal—to our sexual appetite. Such appeal tends toward short-lived enjoyments, rather than any far-reaching effects on the personality. This is why pornography has essentially entertainment and recreational use and attraction; it is taken seriously by almost no one but the censors. It shows us people having sex, and that is it; we must do the rest. Serious literature and art, however, appeal to the whole person—to the entire range of his sensibilities, desires, needs, attitude patterns and beliefs and is thus far more likely to affect our ultimate behavior patterns. Even the limited reaction of sexual arousal is often better achieved through artistic technique. The conservatives deny this, but it is difficult to see on what grounds. . . . [I]t is hardly plausible that artistic technique should enhance and further every *other* objective of an artist, and *not* be an accessory to the end of evoking sexual arousal. Real artistic value is unobtrusive in this respect.

Of course, television pap may well influence attitudes without having significant artistic value, merely by its sheer preponderance on the airwaves. But it is not *this* sort of role we need envisage for pornography liberated from censorship. Moreover, it is not clear its influence would be worse than that of other materials which now hog the channels.

It seems to me, however, that we have yet to make the most important response to the conservative's claims. For, up to now, we have treated the issue as if it were merely a matter of weighing up possible harms from pornography against possible benefits, and the likelihood of the occurrence of the harms. Unfortunately, this is the form the debate usually takes, when it is not strictly concerned with the First Amendment. But, something important is lost if we think the issue resolves into these questions. The more important issue turns on the fact that a great many people *like* and *enjoy* pornography, and *want* it as part of their lives, either for its enjoyment, or for more serious psychological purposes. This fact means that censorship is an interference with the freedom and self-determination of a great many people, and it is on this ground that the conservative harm argument must ultimately be rejected. For a society which accepts freedom and self-determination as centrally significant values cannot allow interferences with freedom on such grounds as these.

To give a satisfactory argument for these claims would require another paper. Moreover, I believe (with certain reservations) this has been adequately done in Mill's *On Liberty*. As the conservatives do not regard *that* as enunciating a clear, defensible body of doctrine,[15] I cannot hope to present an entirely convincing argument here. I want at the very least, however, to outline a minimal set of claims which I think bear on the issue, and which can provide ground for further debate.

The idea of a self-determining individual involves a person developing his or her own mode of life according to the person's own needs, desires, personality, and perceptions of reality. This conception has at least three features: (1) the person's desires are (so far as possible) expressions of his or her own nature—not imposed from without; (2) the manner of the development of his or her character and the pattern of the person's life, are, in large measure, a resultant of his or her own judgment, choice, and personal experience; and (3) the person's unique capacities and potentialities have been developed, or at least tried out.[16] Now, *if* one regards this as a valuable manner of living, and freedom as of value, *both* because it is intrinsic to treating others *as* self-determining agents, *and* because it is requisite for the realization of self-determination, then I think one will accept the following propositions concerning freedom:

1. The burden of producing convincing reasons and evidence is always on the person who would interfere with people's freedom and life-styles.

2. The person who would interfere with freedom must show that the activity interfered with is likely to harm others or interfere with their rights as individuals.[17]

3. Those who would deny freedom must show that the harm or interference threatened is one from which others have a superior right to protection.

Though these propositions are subject to considerable interpretation, it seems to me that one who accepts them will, at the least, recognize that the burden of proof is not symmetric either in structure or degree. The person who would deny freedom shoulders the burden, and, moreover, he or she does not succeed merely by showing *some* harms are likely to result. Accepting freedom and self-determination as central values entails accepting some risks, in order to *be* free. We do *not* presuppose that freedom will always produce good. And, insofar as the alleged harms are indirect and remote, we are committed to employing noncoercive means to combat them. Of course, we need not interpret this in a suicidal way—allowing interference only when the harm is inevitably upon us. But, at the least, we should require a strong showing of likely harms which are far from remote, and this is a burden which the censors of pornography *cannot* meet. Indeed, on this score, the conservative arguments are *many* times *weaker* than ones which can be made concerning many other kinds of communications, and such activities as hunting for sport, automobile racing, boxing and so on.[18] If anyone wants a display of the extent to which our society allows recreation to instigate socially harmful attitudes and feelings, all he or she need do is sit in the stands during a hotly contested high school football or basketball game. And, of course these feelings quite often spill over into antisocial behavior.

Though I have defended pornography from criticism based on its content or nature, I have certainly not shown that it is always unobjectionable. Insofar as it arises in a social context entirely infused with male sexism, much of it reflects the worst aspects of our society's approved conceptions of sexual relations. Too often, the scenes depicted involve male violence and aggression toward women, male dominance over women, and females as sexual servants. Moreover, there are aspects of the commercial institutions which purvey it in the market which are quite objectionable. My argument has been that this is not necessary to pornography as such; where it is true, this reflects social and sexual attitudes already fostered by other social forces. Moreover, I have maintained that by virtue of a feature which does seem to characterize pornography—its break with certain inhibiting conceptions of sexuality, pornography may well play a role in people determining for themselves the life-style which most suits them. A society which values self-determination will interfere with it only under circumstances which the censors of pornography cannot show to hold.

Of course, I have said almost nothing about the nature of the specific freedoms we incorporate in our notion of freedom of speech. It may well be that that set of rights imposes even stricter obligations on those who would suppress forms of its exercise.

NOTES

1. Regulation of speech is one of the most pressing problems for free speech in our contemporary, mass society, in which the control of the media is in relatively few hands, primarily concerned with the use of that media to produce profits. Moreover, the spectre of nonlegal controls, which Mill feared, is very much with us. It is surprising that so little attention has been given to the issue of the principles properly governing regulation. An indication of various forms of control utilized by government for the suppression of pornography is found by studying the development of censorship in the United States. See James C. N. Paul and Murray L. Schwartz, *Federal Censorship: Obscenity in the Mail* (New York: Free Press, 1961).

2. I regard it as a serious drawback of the definition that it rules out by *fiat,* the claim that pornography *can* be, in and of itself, significant literature. This claim is convincingly argued for by Susan Sontag in her essay "The Pornographic Imagination," reprinted in *Perspectives on Pornography,* ed. Douglas A. Hughes (New York: St. Martin's Press, 1970), 131–69; also in her book *Styles of Radical Will* (New York: Farrar, Straus & Giroux, 1966). The argument for a broader, more inclusive definition is made convincingly by Morse Peckham in *Art and Pornography* (New York: Basic Books, 1969), ch. 1. Anyone with a serious interest in the subject of pornography will find this a most important work.

3. It is clear that the definition would be a disaster in the legal context, since there is so great an area of *disagreement.* Moreover, there is a tremendous danger of a secondary form of censorship, in which literary critics come to watch closely how they criticize a work lest the critique be used by the censors. That this in fact has happened is testified to in an eye-opening note by the English critic Horace Judson, in *Encounter* 30 (March 1968): 57–60. To his dismay, a critical review he wrote of Selby's *Last Exit to Brooklyn* was read into the record and used in banning that book in England.

4. See, for example, Ernest van den Haag, writing in *Censorship: For and Against,* 158. Also, in "Is Pornography a Cause of Crime?" *Encounter* 29 (Dec. 1967): 54.

5. *The Report of the Commission on Obscenity and Pornography* (New York: Bantam, 1970), 26–32, in which the effects are summarized. Also, Michael J. Goldstein and Howard S. Kant, *Pornography and Sexual Deviance* (Berkeley: University of California Press, 1973), 139–53.

6. George Steiner, "Night Words: High Pornography and Human Privacy," in *Perspectives on Pornography,* ed. Douglas A. Hughes (New York: St. Martin's Press, 1970), 96–108.

7. Irving Kristol, "Pornography, Obscenity and the Case for Censorship," *New York Times* Magazine, March 28, 1972.

8. That women look at, and are excited by, the bulges in men's trousers is given ample testimony in Nancy Friday's book on women's sexual fantasies. See *My Secret Garden* (New York: Pocket Books, 1974), the section entitled "Women Do Look," 214–22.

9. *Playboy* 20 (October 1973): 202.

10. Goldstein and Kant, *Pornography and Sexual Deviance,* 108–9.

11. Ibid., 152.

12. Ibid., 147.

13. To compound the paradox, if being a remote cause of harms is a prima facie ground for censoring literature, then we have some evidence that the conservative arguments ought to be censored. This is *not* a view I advocate.

14. Professor Van den Haag holds that pornography "nearly always leads to sadistic pornography." It is not clear what this means; moreover, his argument is that this results *because* pornography dehumanizes sex. Since we have grounds for doubting this, we have grounds for doubting the alleged result. Also, since I am denying that pornography

significantly dehumanizes sex, I am implicitly rejecting a further conservative argument I have not taken up, namely, that pornography is itself expressive of immoral attitudes irrespective of any further harmful effects. Since some liberals seem to be willing to silence Nazis or racists on such grounds, some conservatives think this argument will appeal to such liberals. I believe that both Kristol and Van den Haag maintain this view. See also Richard Kuh, *Foolish Figleaves?* (New York: Macmillan, 1967), 280ff. A position of this sort is maintained by Susan Brownmiller in her book *Against Our Will: Men, Women and Rape* (New York: Simon and Schuster, 1975), 201. Brownmiller regards pornography as an invention designed to humiliate women. I have not responded to her arguments as she gives none. Moreover, she employs a curious "double standard." She gives great weight to law enforcement officials' opinions about pornography, but would hardly be willing to take these same persons' views on rape at face value.

15. See, for example, Gertrude Himmelfarb's recent critical account of Mill, *On Liberty and Liberalism: The Case of John Stuart Mill* (New York: Knopf, 1974). It appears to me that she has not really understood Mill. Ronald Dworkin has picked out some of the most glaring of her errors in his review in *New York Review of Books* 21 (Oct. 31, 1974): 21.

16. I believe this is Mill's conception. See also Sharon Hill's essay, "Self-Determination and Autonomy," in *Today's Moral Problems,* ed. Richard Wasserstrom (New York: Macmillan, 1975), 171–86.

17. I want to note three points here. First, this view of freedom permits interferences for *moral* reasons; it does *not* insist on the moral neutrality of the law. It does, however, focus on the *kinds* of moral reasons allowed to count as grounds for the denial of freedom. Second, it does not rule out special legal recognition of modes of living which are central to the culture, for example, monogamous marriage. This will have indirect effects on freedom which a liberal theory would have to recognize and deal with, but it need not rule out such recognition out of hand. In addition, the notion of "harm" could be taken to include conduct or practices which are both intrusive on public consciousness, and offensive. This could provide a basis for *regulating* the sale and distribution of pornography, even if *prohibition* is not justified. Important discussion of the principles underlying the treatment of offensiveness in the law is to be found in an article by Joel Feinberg, "Harmless Immoralities and Offensive Nuisances," in *Issues in Law and Morality,* ed. Norman Care and Thomas Trelogan (Cleveland: Case Western Reserve University, 1973).Michael Bayles's commentary on that paper, also found in the same volume, is very useful. Third, valuing self-determination may entail a limited paternalism in circumstances where noninterference cannot possibly further autonomy. That it is at least possible for noninterference to promote self-determination seems to have been conceived by Mill as a presupposition for applications of his principle of liberty. This helps explain some of his "applications" at the end of the essay. Just how to incorporate limited paternalism in a liberal theory is a thorny issue. The pornography issue, however, does not appear to significantly involve that issue. A useful treatment of paternalism is in Gerald Dworkin, "Paternalism," in *Morality and the Law,* ed. Richard Wasserstrom (Belmont, Calif.: Wadsworth, 1971), 107–26.

18. So far as I can judge, the most telling "evidence" the conservatives have thus far come up with is: (a) *some* reasonable criticisms of the studies which have been done, and the interpretations which have been given them; and (b) a few, isolated, contrary studies (which are, coincidentally, open to similar or stronger objections). See especially the criticism of Victor B. Cline in the minority report of the Presidential Commission on Obscenity and Pornography, 463–89. While I do not think the conservatives need produce ironclad scientific data demonstrating their claims, we surely cannot allow the suppression of freedom when the reasons offered are poor, and the weight of available evidence is heavily *against* those claims. The minority report (it may be Dr. Cline writing in this instance—it is unclear) asserts that the "burden of proof" is on the one who would change current law. This

is an indefensible imprimatur of existing law as such; and it is absolutely inconsistent with the recognition of freedom and self-determination as important moral values. The mere *existence* of law cannot be allowed as a ground for its continued existence, if freedom is to have anything but secondary importance.

SUGGESTIONS FOR DISCUSSION

1. Define pornography (without assuming that it is immoral). Is pornography comparable in nature and effect to racist propaganda?

2. Are any of the liberty-limiting principles sufficiently strong to restrict the right to consume pornographic material in private? Would John Stuart Mill contest your arguments (see Part I, Chapter 4)?

3. Is nonviolent pornography inherently disrespectful of the class of persons depicted, or could it serve to enhance better ("healthy") sexual relations and practices?

FURTHER READING

Berger, F. *Freedom of Expression*. Belmont, Calif.: Wadsworth, 1980. (Interpretation, critical analysis; advanced)

Care, N., and Trelogan, T., eds. *Issues in Law and Morality*. Cleveland: Case Western Reserve University Press, 1973. (Interpretation, critical analysis; intermediate)

Clor, H. M. *Obscenity and Public Morality: Censorship in a Liberal Society*. Chicago: University of Chicago Press, 1969. (Interpretation, critical analysis; intermediate)

Copp, D., and Wendell, S., eds. *Pornography and Censorship*. Buffalo: Prometheus Books, 1983. (Interpretation, critical analysis; advanced)

Devlin, P. *The Enforcement of Morals*. Oxford: Oxford University Press, 1965. (Critical analysis; advanced)

Feinberg, J. *Social Philosophy*. Englewood Cliffs, N.J.: Prentice-Hall, 1973. (Interpretation, critical analysis; intermediate)

———. *Harm to Others*. Oxford: Oxford University Press, 1984. (Interpretation, critical analysis; advanced)

———. *Harm to Self*. Oxford: Oxford University Press, 1987. (Interpretation, critical analysis; advanced)

———. *Offense to Others*. Oxford: Oxford University Press, 1988. (Interpretation, critical analysis; advanced)

———. *Harmless Wrongdoings*. Oxford: Oxford University Press, 1988. (Interpretation, critical analysis; advanced)

Hart, H. H., ed. *Censorship: For and Against*. New York: Hart Publishing, 1971. (Interpretation, critical analysis; intermediate)

Holbrook, D. *The Case Against Pornography*. LaSalle, Ill.: Library Press, 1974. (Interpretation, critical analysis; intermediate)

Hughes, D. A., ed. *Perspectives on Pornography*. New York: St. Martin's Press, 1970. (Interpretation, critical analysis; intermediate)

Kappeler, S. *The Pornography of Representation*. Minneapolis: University of Minnesota Press, 1986. (Critical analysis; intermediate)

Lederer, L. ed. *Take Back the Night: Women on Pornography*. New York: Morrow, 1980. (Critical analysis; intermediate)

LeMoncheck, L. *Dehumanizing Women: Treating Persons as Sex Objects*. Totowa, N.J.: Rowman and Littlefield, 1984. (Critical analysis; intermediate)

MacKinnon, C. *Feminism Unmodified: Discourses on Life and Law.* Cambridge, Mass.: Harvard University Press, 1987. (Critical analysis; advanced)

Report of the Meese Commission on Obscenity and Pornography. Washington D.C.: U.S. Government Printing Office, 1986.

Report of the Commission on Obscenity and Pornography. New York: Bantam Books, 1970.

Richards, D. A. J. *The Moral Criticism of Law.* Encino, Calif.: Dickinson Publishing, 1977. (Interpretation, critical analysis; advanced)

Soble, A. *Pornography: Marxism, Feminism and the Future of Sexuality.* New Haven: Yale University Press, 1986. (Interpretation, critical analysis; advanced)

Wasserstrom, R., ed. *Morality and the Law.* Belmont, Calif.: Wadsworth, 1971. (Interpretation, critical analysis; advanced)

Williams, B. *Report of the Committee on Obscenity and Pornography.* London: Her Majesty's Stationery Office, 1979.

10

□

Sexual Morality and AIDS

Sex for the most part is fun. This suggests two general ways in which sexual desires play a central role in human life. The first is the fundamental requirement of procreation. The fulfillment of at least some sexual drives is necessary for perpetuating the human species. This "natural" imperative can be contrasted with the "cultural" role of sexual desires and responses. Sexuality plays a part in the cultural expression of human character. Of course there may be many ways in which natural drives and cultural expressions are intertwined. Nevertheless, it is important to keep the two conceptually distinct.

Clearly, some sexual acts are morally impermissible because they involve practices or outcomes the wrongs of which are independent of the *sexual* nature of the act. Rape is wrong because it is inevitably violent, involving severe physical and psychological harm; it is also abusive, for it violates respect for the autonomy of the victim. Adultery will be wrong if it trades upon deceit, causes distrust and hurt, and is likely to promote destruction of the marriage. Yet it remains an open question whether any sexual acts are immoral because of their inherently *sexual* nature. Are there rules governing sexual acts other than the general moral prohibitions on violence, harm, deception, promise-breaking, and so on? Any response to this question will turn on whether the "natural" or "cultural" sense of sexuality is stressed.

The Traditional View In formulating a sexual morality, the traditional Judeo-Christian ethic emphasizes the reproductive function of sexual acts. Judeo-Christian morality is rooted in Natural Law theory. Accordingly, acts are right if they are consistent with rational or human nature or promote the proper ends of its faculties, and wrong if they are inconsistent with this nature or undermine its ends (see Aquinas, Part I, Chapter 1). The proper end of the human sexual faculty, on this view, is procreative or the production of children. So permissible sex is restricted to occasions for reproduction. The family is considered the natural community, for it is supposed to provide the stability that enables the moral upbringing of children. Thus no sexual acts are permissible other than those between marriage partners for the purpose of procreation. (Sexual intercourse with a sterile spouse is the only exception; this is discussed below.)

The strict Judeo-Christian view rules out as immoral a large range of sexual acts and relations. First, any sexual intercourse outside the marriage relation will be impermissible: such acts are called *fornication*. It follows that premarital and adulterous sexual relations are considered immoral; so, also, are promiscuous or multiple sexual relations, whether simultaneous or successive. Second, all forms of *perversity* are ruled out, where perversity is given a narrow technical definition as any sexual act (save "normal" sex with a sterile spouse) that is incapable of ending in reproduction. Oral copulation and masturbation, even mutually among marriage partners, are impermissible; any use of contraception is unacceptable; and homosexuality is obviously disallowed.

Many of these restrictions may also be supported by a general welfare argument. Stable families are considered a necessary condition for the maintenance of general social welfare: children will receive a moral upbringing only in the context of stable family life. Thus, extramarital sex will be impermissible because it undermines family stability and so general social welfare. If sex is restricted to marriage, couples will want to get and stay married.

Note that while the Natural Law argument is *a priori* at basis, the welfare argument makes utilitarian appeals. The grounds for assessing the Natural Law argument, then, are conceptual: the basic concepts employed must be analyzed. For example, the concept of "unnatural sexual acts" is ambiguous: On one hand, it may mean sexual acts that are contrary to the laws of nature, in the sense either that they are likely to bring about the end of the human species or that they are contrary to the natural goal of sexuality. On the other hand, it may be interpreted less technically to mean abnormal or uncommon sexual acts. Here further argument would be needed to show that abnormal or uncommon sexual acts are by that token immoral and impermissible. By contrast, the grounds for assessing the welfare argument are empirical: it is a matter of fact whether family life alone guarantees social utility, or whether extramarital sex promotes disutility.

The Liberal View   The "cultural" view of sexuality presupposes the widely held assumption that liberty is a fundamental value. The freedom to express oneself without harming others is taken to encourage the development of unrepressed, creative, and sensitive persons. Sexuality is a major component of character. So the freedom of unharmful sexual expression for the sake of (mutual) pleasure is supposed to foster nonmechanistic, warm friendships grounded in respect for persons, rather than relations that simply treat sexual partners as means to reproductive ends (see Berger, Part II, Chapter 9). The only moral prohibitions on sexual practices will be extrasexual ones: ordinary moral restrictions on violence, harm, disrespect, lying, and so on. If some sexual act generally and genuinely harms social welfare, it may be restricted. So extramarital sex will not be restricted, unless it involves harm or deceit.

Homosexuality   The differences between these two views of sexuality are highlighted in terms of the moral rules each entails for homosexuality. The Judeo-Christian tradition treats homosexuality as a perversion, because it is considered unnatural. This is sometimes taken to mean that it is contrary to reproductive nature. However, it is unreasonable to think that homosexuality will end the human species. Its wrongness is more often taken to lie in its abnormality. If this merely means that the majority does not practice homosexuality, it is insufficient to make it immoral. That a minority among a population practices a given religion does not render it wrong. Thus the impermissibility must be taken to lie elsewhere. There are two possibilities. It may be claimed that the majority finds it offensive; or it may be thought to be inherently linked to unacceptable social practices, such as child abuse or promiscuity.

Critics of these views point out that because we value freedom of expression, it is unacceptable (if not dangerous) to restrict what even a majority consider to be personally offensive (on censorship, see Part II, Chapter 9). Further, it is simply prejudicial to link male homosexuality to child abuse: statistics show that the overwhelming incidence of child abuse is by male heterosexuals. Finally, it is suggested that the highly publicized promiscuity among homosexuals is not a function of sexual preference, but of social stigma and its accompanying emotional strain. This discourages the development of stable, long-term relationships. Those defending the permissibility of homosexuality support condemnation of any abusive or disrespectful act, including homosexual ones. They claim only that the wrongfulness is not tied to the specifically homosexual nature of the act. As such, homosexuals should be accorded the rights of heterosexuals, for free expression of sexual preference subject to the Harm Principle (see Chapter 9) is necessary for the development of fully rounded, stable members of the moral community.

A social welfare argument for the impermissibility of homosexual practices has recently been suggested. In the age of AIDS, a person engaging in homosexual sex with an infected partner (indeed, promiscuous sex in general) runs the very high risk of contracting and spreading the deadly HIV virus. Thus those tending to engage in homosexual (or promiscuous) sex have a duty to themselves and others to restrict their activities, and society has a right to require them to do so. This argument presupposes that homosexuality is necessarily linked to the AIDS virus. But although homosexuals are a high incidence group, many will not acquire the virus; and heterosexuals have also been stricken. Further, while promiscuity does increase the probability that the disease will spread, homosexuals are neither necessarily nor singularly promiscuous. Current proposals to restrict homosexuals, whether afflicted by the disease or not, tend to be both pragmatically and morally questionable. For example, restrictions that have been suggested include isolation and quarantine. *Isolation* involves setting apart, until cured, all those who are infected by the disease. *Quarantine* is the setting apart of those at risk, to determine whether they develop the virus. Both suggestions are fiscally prohibitive. However, it is more important to recognize that, given the lack of a cure and the limited means of transmission, both isolation and quarantine would involve impermissible limitations on the liberty of homosexuals. Moreover, both isolation and quarantine presuppose mandatory testing, which may violate individuals' rights. (Similar arguments may be formulated in respect of intravenous drug use.)

Supreme Court Rulings The Supreme Court has consistently ruled against the right to engage in homosexual sodomy. *Bowers v. Hardwick* (1986) is the most recent ruling in which this issue is addressed. The case concerns whether Georgia has to demonstrate that a compelling state interest is promoted by its antisodomy statute. The Georgia statute defines "sodomy" as "any sexual act involving the sex organs of one person and the mouth or anus of another." Though sodomy is defined independently of sexual preference, the issue of the right to engage in homosexual sodomy is explicitly addressed in the extract from *Bowers* included here. Justice White ruled that this claimed right has no support in the constitutional language of the due process clauses of the Fifth and Fourteenth Amendments. The claimed right has no roots in American legal history: Formerly outlawed in every state, sodomy is still illegal in twenty-four. Justice White invoked the principle of Legal Moralism in support of his ruling: that a majority among a state's population considers homosexual sodomy immoral is found to support a state's compelling interest in maintaining the illegality of homosexual practices. (On Legal Moralism, see Chapter 9.) Further, the right to engage in homosexual sodomy is not protected by the right to privacy. Sodomy is taken to be like drug consumption or incest, not like the consumption of obscene material. Thus it is unprotected by any First Amendment rights.

In a dissenting opinion, Justice Blackmun stressed that the real right at issue in this case is the right to be let alone. He rejected Legal Moralism as an acceptable principle of legality. He argued that because ways of life and sexuality in the United States are so varied, it is impermissible to outlaw even the most extraordinary simply because it is different. Sexual intimacy is a key feature of individual well-being; it cannot be lightly sanctioned. Justice Blackmun also rejected the claim that quietly engaging in acts violating the private norms of the majority entails a willingness to abandon public moral rules against murder, cruelty, lying, and so forth. The right to be let alone is taken to safeguard the right to privacy, as well as the right to engage privately in homosexual sodomy.

Readings The Vatican Declaration represents the traditional Roman Catholic view, and by extension Judeo-Christian orthodoxy, on issues central to sexual morality. Based on a Natural Law foundation, the declaration insists that only reproductive sexual acts between a married couple are permissible. Premarital sex, homosexuality, and masturbation are deemed immoral. This traditional view is subject to one qualification. Where natural sterility of one or both partners in a married couple prevents satisfaction of the primary end of reproduction, the couple may engage in coition (or "normal" intercourse) as an expression of affection.

Sara Ruddick attacks the claim that perverse sexual acts are inherently immoral. Here *perversion* is interpreted more widely to mean those sexual acts that deviate from the norm of ordinary sexual practices. Ruddick points out that perversity need be no less pleasurable than normal (or "natural") sex, and evil need not result from such sex. Ruddick denies that perversity has any special moral significance and that there is any reason to believe heterosexual relations produce greater benefits than homosexual ones. She outlines an ideal of "complete sex acts." These consist, minimally, of mutually embodied, mutually active, and responsive desires in relation to one's sexual partner. Embodiment, activity, and responsiveness give rise to the virtue of psychological well-being. But "complete sex acts," whether perverse or not, are also intrinsically moral. They resolve moral tensions; they promote the virtue of loving; and their completeness turns on reflecting the primary moral virtue of respect for persons. That some sexual acts may be inherently moral means that genuine moral dilemmas may arise when such acts conflict with other moral obligations. In a postscript, Ruddick warns that the language we use to talk about the sexual preferences of others may cause harm, and she hints at the relation between complete (moral) sex and, in general, better (moral) lives.

Dan E. Beauchamp challenges current policy concerning homosexuality and AIDS. Beauchamp argues that Legal Moralism (or legislating the morality of the majority) often collides with the social good of public health. The latter incorporates the principle of Legal Paternalism (or restriction on others' liberty to promote their and the public good). Discrimination against homosexuals in the law—for example, in state sodomy statutes—discourages AIDS victims from seeking prompt medical attention for fear of social ostracism. This threatens the health of homosexuals and others. Legal Moralism opposes public sex education and so it impedes changes in gay sexual practices, thereby slowing the fight against AIDS. Beauchamp suggests that we replace the exclusivist view of current health policy with an inclusive ideal combining principles of equality and community. Respecting the right to be different must be combined with mutual trust and a willingness to accept the burdens common to citizenship in the body politic. Legal Paternalism encourages regulation of sexual practices that genuinely threaten the health of all. Such restrictions are distinguished from those promoting an official sexual ethic. So homosexuality is not to be prohibited, only practices like anonymous sexual encounters that recklessly endanger public health. Further, a rigorous educational campaign aimed at discouraging high-risk sex is preferable to regulation of sexual practices, because it is less likely to involve conflicts of rights. Finally, Beauchamp urges homosexuals to recognize their duty, in face of a deadly disease and the common interest, to assume more conservative and restrictive standards of sexual behavior.

Justice Byron White

Majority Opinion in *Bowers v. Hardwick*

... [R]espondent would have us announce, as the Court of Appeals did, a fundamental right to engage in homosexual sodomy. This we are quite unwilling to do. It is true that despite the language of the Due Process Clauses of the Fifth and Fourteenth Amendments, which appears to focus only on the processes by which life, liberty, or property is taken, the cases are legion in which those Clauses have been interpreted to have substantive content, subsuming rights that to a great extent are immune from federal or state regulation or proscription. Among such

United States Supreme Court, 478 U.S. 92 L Ed 2d 140 (1986).

cases are those recognizing rights that have little or no textual support in the constitutional language. . . .

. . . Sodomy was a criminal offense at common law and was forbidden by the laws of the original thirteen States when they ratified the Bill of Rights. In 1868, when the Fourteenth Amendment was ratified, all but 5 of the 37 States in the Union had criminal sodomy laws. In fact, until 1961, all 50 States outlawed sodomy, and today, 24 States and the District of Columbia continue to provide criminal penalties for sodomy performed in private and between consenting adults. . . . Against this background, to claim that a right to engage in such conduct is "deeply rooted in this Nation's history and tradition" or "implicit in the concept of ordered liberty" is, at best, facetious.

Nor are we inclined to take a more expansive view of our authority to discover new fundamental rights imbedded in the Due Process Clause. The Court is most vulnerable and comes nearest to illegitimacy when it deals with judge-made constitutional law having little or no cognizable roots in the language or design of the Constitution. . . . There should be, therefore, great resistance to expand the substantive reach of those Clauses, particularly if it requires redefining the category of rights deemed to be fundamental. Otherwise, the Judiciary necessarily takes to itself further authority to govern the country without express constitutional authority. The claimed right pressed on us today falls far short of overcoming this resistance.

Respondent, however, asserts that the result should be different where the homosexual conduct occurs in the privacy of the home. He relies on *Stanley v Georgia,* . . . where the Court held that the First Amendment prevents conviction for possessing and reading obscene material in the privacy of his home. . . .

Stanley did protect conduct that would not have been protected outside the home, and it partially prevented the enforcement of state obscenity laws; but the decision was firmly grounded in the First Amendment. The right pressed upon us here has no similar support in the text of the Constitution, and it does not qualify for recognition under the prevailing principles for construing the Fourteenth Amendment. Its limits are also difficult to discern. Plainly enough, otherwise illegal conduct is not always immunized whenever it occurs in the home. Victimless crimes, such as the possession and use of illegal drugs do not escape the law where they are committed at home. *Stanley* itself recognized that its holding offered no protection for the possession in the home of drugs, firearms, or stolen goods. . . . And if respondent's submission is limited to the voluntary sexual conduct between consenting adults, it would be difficult, except by fiat, to limit the claimed right to homosexual conduct while leaving exposed to prosecution adultery, incest, and other sexual crimes even though they are committed in the home. We are unwilling to start down that road.

Even if the conduct at issue here is not a fundamental right, respondent asserts that there must be a rational basis for the law and that there is none in this case other than the presumed belief of a majority of the electorate in Georgia that homosexual sodomy is immoral and unacceptable. This is said to be an inadequate rationale to support the law. The law, however, is constantly based on notions of morality, and if all laws representing essentially moral choices are to be invalidated under the Due Process Clause, the courts will be very busy indeed. Even respondent makes no such claim, but insists that majority sentiments about the morality of homosexuality should be declared inadequate. We do not agree, and are unpersuaded that the sodomy laws of some 25 States should be invalidated on this basis.

Justice Harry Blackmun

Dissenting Opinion in *Bowers v. Hardwick*

Justice Blackmun, with whom Justice Brennan, Justice Marshall, and Justice Stevens, join, dissenting.

This case is [not] about "a fundamental right to engage in homosexual sodomy," as the Court purports to declare. . . . Rather, this case is about "the most comprehensive of rights and the right most valued by civilized men," namely, "the right to be let alone." . . .

Only the most willful blindness could obscure the fact that sexual intimacy is "a sensitive, key relationship of human existence, central to family life, community welfare, and the development of human personality," *Paris Adult Theatre I v Slaton.* . . . The fact that individuals define themselves in a significant way through their intimate sexual relationships with others suggests, in a Nation as diverse as ours, that there may be many "right" ways of conducting those relationships, and that much of the richness of a relationship will come from the freedom an individual has to *choose* the form and nature of these intensely personal bonds. . . .

. . . A way of life that is odd or even erratic but interferes with no rights or interests of others is not to be condemned because it is different." . . . The Court claims that its decision today merely refuses to recognize a fundamental right to engage in homosexual sodomy; what the Court really has refused to recognize is the fundamental interest all individuals have in controlling the nature of their intimate associations with others. . . .

The assertion that "traditional Judeo-Christian values proscribe" the conduct involved, Brief for Petitioner 20, cannot provide an adequate justification for § 16-6-2.* That certain, but by no means all, religious groups condemn the behavior at issue gives the State no license to impose their judgments on the entire citizenry. The legitimacy of secular legislation depends instead on whether the State can advance some justification for its law beyond its conformity to religious doctrine. . . . Thus, far from buttressing his case, petitioner's invocation of Levit-

United States Supreme Court, 478 U.S. 92 L Ed 2d 140 (1986).

*Editor's note: § 16-6-2 refers to the Georgia state law criminalizing sodomy, which is at issue in *Bowers v. Hardwick.*

icus, Romans, St. Thomas Aquinas, and sodomy's heretical status during the Middle Ages undermines his suggestion that § 16-6-2 represents a legitimate use of secular coercive power. A State can no more punish private behavior because of religious intolerance than it can punish such behavior because of racial animus. "The Constitution cannot control such prejudices, but neither can it tolerate them. Private biases may be outside the reach of the law, but the law cannot, directly or indirectly give them effect."... No matter how uncomfortable a certain group may make the majority of this Court, we have held that "[m]ere public intolerance or animosity cannot constitutionally justify the deprivation of a person's physical liberty."...

Nor can § 16-6-2 be justified as a "morally neutral" exercise of Georgia's power to "protect the public environment."... Certainly, some private behavior can affect the fabric of society as a whole. Reasonable people may differ about whether particular sexual acts are moral or immoral, but "we have ample evidence for believing that people will not abandon morality, will not think any better of murder, cruelty and dishonesty, merely because some private sexual practice which they abominate is not punished by the law."... Petitioner and the Court fail to see the difference between laws that protect public sensibilities and those that enforce private morality. Statutes banning public sexual activity are entirely consistent with protecting the individual's liberty interest in decisions concerning sexual relations: the same recognition that those decisions are intensely private which justifies protecting them from governmental interference can justify protecting individuals from unwilling exposure to the sexual activities of others. But the mere fact that intimate behavior may be punished when it takes place in public cannot dictate how States can regulate intimate behavior that occurs in intimate places....

This case involves no real interference with the rights of others, for the mere knowledge that other individuals do not adhere to one's value system cannot be a legally cognizable interest,... let alone an interest that can justify invading the houses, hearts, and minds of citizens who choose to live their lives differently.

Vatican Declaration on Some Questions of Sexual Ethics

I GENERAL CONSIDERATIONS

THE SOURCES OF MORAL KNOWLEDGE

3. The men of our day are increasingly persuaded that their dignity and calling as human beings requires them to use their minds to discover the values and powers

From *The Pope Speaks* 21, 1 (1976): 60–68. Copyright © Publications Office, United States Catholic Conference.

inherent in their nature, to develop these without ceasing and to translate them into action, so that they may make daily greater progress.

When it comes to judgments on moral matters, however, man may not proceed simply as he thinks fit. "Deep within, man detects the law of conscience—a law which is not self-imposed but which holds him to obedience. . . . For man has in his heart a law written by God. To obey it is the very dignity of man; according to it he will be judged."

To us Christians, moreover, God has revealed his plan of salvation and has given us Christ, the Savior and sanctifier, as the supreme and immutable norm of life through his teaching and example. Christ himself has said: "I am the light of the world. No follower of mine shall ever walk in darkness; no, he shall possess the light of life."

The authentic dignity of man cannot be promoted, therefore, except through adherence to the order which is essential to his nature. There is no denying, of course, that in the history of civilization many of the concrete conditions and relationships of human life have changed and will change again in the future but every moral evolution and every manner of life must respect the limits set by the immutable principles which are grounded in the constitutive elements and essential relations proper to the human person. These elements and relations are not subject to historical contingency.

The basic principles in question can be grasped by man's reason. They are contained in "the divine law—eternal, objective and universal—whereby God orders, directs and governs the entire universe and all the ways of the human community by a plan conceived in wisdom and love. God has made man a participant in this law, with the result that, under the gentle disposition of divine Providence, he can come to perceive ever more fully the truth that is unchanging." This divine law is something we can know.

THE PRINCIPLES OF MORALITY ARE PERENNIAL

4. Wrongly, therefore, do many today deny that either human nature or revealed law furnishes any absolute and changeless norm for particular actions except the general law of love and respect for human dignity. To justify this position, they argue that both the so-called norms of the natural law and the precepts of Sacred Scripture are simply products of a particular human culture and its expressions at a certain point in history.

But divine revelation and, in its own order, natural human wisdom show us genuine exigencies of human nature and, as a direct and necessary consequence, immutable laws which are grounded in the constitutive elements of human nature and show themselves the same in all rational beings.

Furthermore, the Church was established by Christ to be "the pillar and bulwark of truth." With the help of the Holy Spirit she keeps a sleepless watch over the truths of morality and transmits them without falsification. She provides the authentic interpretation not only of the revealed positive law but also of "those principles of the moral order which have their origin in human nature itself" and which relate to man's full development and sanctification. Throughout her history the Church has constantly maintained that certain precepts of the natural law bind immutably and without qualification, and that the violation of them contradicts the spirit and teaching of the Gospel.

THE FUNDAMENTAL PRINCIPLES OF SEXUAL MORALITY

5. Since sexual morality has to do with values which are basic to human and Christian life, the general doctrine we have been presenting applies to it. In this area there are principles and norms which the Church has always unhesitatingly transmitted as part of her teaching, however opposed they might be to the mentality and ways of the world. These principles and norms have their origin, not in a particular culture, but in knowledge of the divine law and human nature. Consequently, it is impossible for them to lose their binding force or to be called into doubt on the grounds of cultural change.

These principles guided Vatican Council II when it provided advice and directives for the establishment of the kind of social life in which the equal dignity of man and woman will be respected, even while the differences between them also are preserved.

In speaking of the sexual nature of the human being and of the human generative powers, the Council observes that these are "remarkably superior to those found in lower grades of life." Then it deals in detail with the principles and norms which apply to human sexuality in the married state and are based on the finality of the function proper to marriage.

In this context the Council asserts that the moral goodness of the actions proper to married life, when ordered as man's true dignity requires, "does not depend only on a sincere intention and the evaluating of motives, but must be judged by objective standards. These are drawn from the nature of the human person and of his acts, and have regard for the whole meaning of mutual self-giving and human procreation in the context of true love."

These last words are a brief summation of the Council's teaching (previously set forth at length in the same document) on the finality of the sexual act and on the chief norm governing its morality. It is respect for this finality which guarantees the moral goodness of the act.

The same principle, which the Church derives from divine revelation and from her authentic interpretation of the natural law, is also the source of her traditional teaching that the exercise of the sexual function has its true meaning and is morally good only in legitimate marriage.[1]

LIMITS OF THIS DECLARATION

6. It is not the intention of this declaration to treat all abuses of the sexual powers nor to deal with all that is involved in the practice of chastity but rather to recall the Church's norms on certain specific points, since there is a crying need of opposing certain serious errors and deviant forms of behavior.

1. The present declaration does not review all the moral norms for the use of sex, since they have already been set forth in the encyclicals *Casti Connubi* and *Humanae Vitae*.

II. SPECIFIC APPLICATIONS

PREMARITAL RELATIONS

7. Many individuals at the present time are claiming the right to sexual union before marriage, at least when there is a firm intention of marrying and when a love which both partners think of as already conjugal demands this further step which seems to them connatural. They consider this further step justified especially when external circumstances prevent the formal entry into marriage or when intimate union seems necessary if love is to be kept alive.

This view is opposed to the Christian teaching that any human genital act whatsoever may be placed only within the framework of marriage. For, however firm the intention of those who pledge themselves to each other in such premature unions, these unions cannot guarantee the sincerity and fidelity of the relationship between man and woman, and, above all, cannot protect the relationship against the changeableness of desire and determination.

Yet, Christ the Lord willed that the union be a stable one and he restored it to its original condition as founded in the difference between the sexes. "Have you not read that at the beginning the Creator made them male and female and declared, 'For this reason a man shall leave his father and mother and cling to his wife and the two shall become as one'? Thus they are no longer two but one flesh. Therefore, let no man separate what God has joined."

St. Paul is even more explicit when he teaches that if unmarried people or widows cannot be continent, they have no alternative but to enter into a stable marital union: "It is better to marry than to be on fire." For, through marriage the love of the spouses is taken up into the irrevocable love of Christ for his Church, whereas unchaste bodily union defiles the temple of the Holy Spirit which the Christian has become. Fleshly union is illicit, therefore, unless a permanent community of life has been established between man and woman.

Such has always been the Church's understanding of and teaching on the exercise of the sexual function. She finds, moreover, that natural human wisdom and the lessons of history are in profound agreement with her.

Experience teaches that if sexual union is truly to satisfy the requirements of its own finality and of human dignity, love must be safeguarded by the stability marriage gives. These requirements necessitate a contract which is sanctioned and protected by society; the contract gives rise to a new state of life and is of exceptional importance for the exclusive union of man and woman as well as for the good of their family and the whole of human society. Premarital relations, on the other hand, most often exclude any prospect of children. Such love claims in vain to be conjugal since it cannot, as it certainly should, grow into a maternal and paternal love; or, if the pair do become parents, it will be to the detriment of the children, who are deprived of a stable environment in which they can grow up in a proper fashion and find the way and means of entering into the larger society of men.

Therefore, the consent of those entering into marriage must be externally manifested, and this in such a way as to render it binding in the eyes of society. The faithful, for their part, must follow the laws of the Church in declaring their marital consent; it is this consent that makes their marriage a sacrament of Christ.

HOMOSEXUALITY

8. Contrary to the perennial teaching of the Church and the moral sense of the Christian people, some individuals today have, on psychological grounds, begun to judge indulgently or even simply to excuse homosexual relations for certain people.

They make a distinction which has indeed some foundation: between homosexuals whose bent derives from improper education or a failure of sexual maturation or habit or bad example or some similar cause and is only temporary or at least is not incurable; and homosexuals who are permanently such because of some innate drive or a pathological condition which is considered incurable.

The propensity of those in the latter class is—it is argued—so natural that it should be regarded as justifying homosexual relations within a sincere and loving communion of life which is comparable to marriage inasmuch as those involved in it deem it impossible for them to live a solitary life.

OBJECTIVE EVIL OF SUCH ACTS

As far as pastoral care is concerned, such homosexuals are certainly to be treated with understanding and encouraged to hope that they can some day overcome their difficulties and their inability to fit into society in a normal fashion. Prudence, too, must be exercised in judging their guilt. However, no pastoral approach may be taken which would consider these individuals morally justified on the grounds that such acts are in accordance with their nature. For, according to the objective moral order homosexual relations are acts deprived of the essential ordination they ought to have.

In Sacred Scripture such acts are condemned as serious deviations and are even considered to be the lamentable effect of rejecting God. This judgment on the part of the divinely inspired Scriptures does not justify us in saying that all who suffer from this anomaly are guilty of personal sin but it does show that homosexual acts are disordered by their very nature and can never be approved.

MASTURBATION

9. Frequently today we find doubt or open rejection of the traditional Catholic teaching that masturbation is a serious moral disorder. Psychology and sociology (it is claimed) show that masturbation, especially in adolescents, is a normal phase in the process of sexual maturation and is, therefore, not gravely sinful unless the individual deliberately cultivates a solitary pleasure that is turned in upon itself ("ipsation"). In this last case, the act would be radically opposed to that loving communion between persons of different sexes which (according to some) is the principal goal to be sought in the use of the sexual powers.

This opinion is contrary to the teaching and pastoral practice of the Catholic Church. Whatever be the validity of certain arguments of a biological and philosophical kind which theologians sometimes use, both the magisterium of the Church (following a constant tradition) and the moral sense of the faithful have unhesitatingly asserted that masturbation is an intrinsically and seriously disordered act. The chief reason for this stand is that, whatever the motive, the deliberate use of the sexual faculty outside of normal conjugal relations essentially contradicts its finality. In such an act there is lacking the sexual relationship which the moral order requires, the kind of relationship in which "the whole meaning of mutual self-giving and human procreation" is made concretely real "in the context of true love." Only within such a relationship may the sexual powers be deliberately exercised.

Even if it cannot be established that Sacred Scripture condemns this sin under a specific name, the Church's tradition rightly understands it to be condemned in the New Testament when the latter speaks of "uncleanness" or "unchasteness" or the other vices contrary to chastity and continence.

Sociological research can show the relative frequency of this disorder according to places, types of people and various circumstances which may be taken into account. It thus provides an array of facts. But facts provide no norm for judging the morality of human acts. The frequency of the act here in question is connected with innate human weakness deriving from original sin, but also with the loss of the sense of God, with the moral corruption fostered by the commercialization of vice, with the unbridled license to be found in so many books and forms of public entertainment and with the forgetfulness of modesty, which is the safeguard of chastity.

In dealing with masturbation, modern psychology provides a number of valid and useful insights which enable us to judge more equitably of moral responsibility. They can also help us understand how adolescent immaturity (sometimes pro-longed beyond the adolescent years) or a lack of psychological balance or habits can affect behavior, since they may make an action less deliberate and not always a subjectively serious sin. But the lack of serious responsibility should not be generally presumed; if it is, there is simply a failure to recognize man's ability to act in a moral way.

In the pastoral ministry, in order to reach a balanced judgment in individual cases account must be taken of the overall habitual manner in which the person acts, not only in regard to charity and justice, but also in regard to the care with which he observes the precept of chastity in particular. Special heed must be paid to whether he uses the necessary natural and supernatural helps which Christian asceticism recommends, in the light of long experience, for mastering the passions and attaining virtue.

Sara L. Ruddick

Better Sex

THE MORAL SIGNIFICANCE OF PERVERSION

What is the moral significance of the perversity of the sexual act? Next to none, so far as I can see. Though perverted sex may be "unnatural" both from an evolutionary and developmental perspective, there is no connection, inverse or correlative, between what is natural and what is good. Perverted sex is sometimes said to be less pleasurable than natural sex. We have little reason to believe that this claim is true and no clear idea of the kind of evidence on which it would be based. In any case, to condemn perverse acts for lack of pleasure is to recognize the worth of pleasure, not of naturalness.

There are many other claims about the nature and consequences of perversion. Some merely restate "scientific" facts in morally tinged terminology. Perverse acts are, by definition and according to psychiatric theory, "immature" and "abnormal," since natural sex acts are selected by criteria of "normal" sexual function and "normal" and "mature" psychological development. But there is no greater connection of virtue with maturity and normality than there is of virtue with nature. The elimination of a village by an invading army would be no less evil if it were the expression of controlled, normal, natural, and mature aggression.

Nagel claims that many perverted sex acts are incomplete, and in making his point, gives the most specific arguments that I have read for the inferiority of perverted sex. But as he points out, there is no reason to think an act consisting solely of oral-genital intercourse is incomplete; it is doubtful whether homosexual acts and acts of buggery are especially liable to be incomplete; and the incompleteness of sexual intercourse with animals is a relative matter depending upon their limited consciousness. And again, the alleged inferiority is not a consequence of perversion but of incompleteness, which can afflict natural sex as well.

Perverted acts might be thought to be inferior because they cannot result in children. Whatever the benefits and moral significance of the procreation and care of children (and I believe they are extensive and complicated), the virtue of proper care for children neither requires nor follows from biological parenthood. Even if it did, only a sexual life consisting solely of perverse acts rules out conception.

If perverted sex acts did rule out normal sex acts, if one were *either* perverted *or* natural, then certain kinds of sexual relations would be denied some perverts—relations that are benefits to those who enjoy them. It seems that sexual relations with the living and the human would be of greater benefit than those with the dead or with animals. But there is no reason to think that heterosexual relations are of greater benefit than homosexual ones. It might be thought that children can only

From Sara Ruddick, "Better Sex," in *Philosophy and Sex*, edited by Robert Baker and Frederick Elliston (Buffalo: Prometheus Books, 1984). Copyright © 1975 Sara L. Ruddick. "Postscript" from *Today's Moral Problems*, edited by Richard Wasserstrom (New York: Macmillan, 1975). Reprinted by permission of the author.

be raised by heterosexual couples who perform an abundance of natural sex acts. If true (though truth seems highly unlikely), perverts will be denied the happiness of parenthood. This deprivation would be an *indirect* consequence of perverted sex and might yield a moral dilemma: How is one to choose between the benefits of children and the benefits of more pleasurable, more complex sex acts?

Some perversions are immoral on independent grounds. Sadism is the obvious example, though sadism practiced with a consenting masochist is far less evil than other, more familiar forms of aggression. Voyeurism may seem immoral because, since it must be secret to be satisfying, it violates others' rights to privacy. Various kinds of rape can constitute perversion if rape, rather than genital intercourse, is the aim of desire. Rape is always seriously immoral, a vivid violation of respect for persons. Sometimes doubly perverse rape is doubly evil (the rape of a child), but in other cases (the rape of a pig) its evil is halved. In any case, though rape is always *wrong*, it is only perverse when raping becomes the aim and not the means of desire.

Someone can be dissuaded from acting on her/his perverse desires either from moral qualms or from social fears. Although there may be ample basis for the latter, I can find none for the former except the possible indirect loss of the benefits of child care. I am puzzled about this since reflective people who do not usually attempt to legislate the preferences of others think differently. There is no doubt that beliefs in these matters involve deep emotions that should be respected. But for those who do in fact have perverted desires, the first concern will be to satisfy them, not to divert or to understand them. For sexual pleasure is intrinsically a benefit, and complete sex acts, which depend upon expressing the desires one in fact has, are both beneficial and conducive to virtue. Therefore, barring extrinsic moral or social considerations, perverted sex acts are preferable to natural ones if the latter are less pleasurable or less complete.

THE MORAL SIGNIFICANCE OF COMPLETENESS

Complete sex consists in mutually embodied, mutually active, responsive desire. Embodiment, activity, and mutual responsiveness are instrumentally beneficial because they are conducive to our psychological well-being, which is an intrinsic benefit. The alleged pathological consequences of disembodiment are more specific and better documented than those of perversity. To dissociate oneself from one's actual body, either by creating a delusory body or by rejecting the bodily, is to court a variety of ill effects, ranging from self-disgust to diseases of the will, to faulty mental development, to the destruction of a recognizable "self," and finally to madness. It is difficult to assess psychiatric claims outside their theoretical contexts, but in this case I believe that they are justified. Relative embodiment is a stable, *normal* condition that is not confined to cases of complete embodiment. But psychiatrists tell us that exceptional physical occasions of embodiment seem to be required in order to balance tendencies to reject or to falsify the body. Sexual acts are not the only such occasions, but they do provide an immersion of consciousness in the bodily, which is pleasurable and especially conducive to correcting experiences of shame and disgust that work toward disembodiment.

The mutual responsiveness of complete sex is also instrumentally beneficial. It satisfies a general desire to be recognized as a particular "real" person and to make a difference to other particular "real" people. The satisfaction of this desire in sexual experience is especially rewarding, its thwarting especially cruel. Vulnerability is increased in complete sex by the active desiring of the partners. When betrayal, or for that matter, tenderness or ecstasy, ensues, one cannot dissociate oneself from the desire with which one identified and out of which one acted. . . .

In addition to being beneficial, complete sex acts are morally superior for three reasons. They tend to resolve tensions fundamental to moral life; they are conducive to emotions that, if they become stable and dominant, are in turn conducive to the virtue of living; and they involve a preeminently moral virtue—respect for persons.

In one of its aspects, morality is opposed to the private and untamed. Morality is "civilization," social and regulating; desire is "discontent," resisting the regulation. Obligation, rather than benefit, is the notion central to morality so conceived, and the virtues required of a moral person are directed to preserving right relations and social order. Both the insistence on natural sex and the encouragement of complete sex can be looked upon as attempts to make sexual desire more amenable to regulation. But whereas the regulation of perverted desires is extrinsic to them, those of completeness modify the desires themselves. The desiring sensual body that in our social lives we may laugh away or disown becomes our "self" and enters into a social relation. Narcissism and altruism are satisfied in complete sex acts in which one gives what one receives by receiving it. Social and private "selves" are unified in an act in which impersonal, spontaneous impulses govern an action that is responsive to a particular person. For this to be true we must surmount our social "roles" as well as our sexual "techniques," though we incorporate rather than surmount our social selves. We must also surmount regulations imposed in the name of naturalness if our desires are to be spontaneously expressed. Honestly spontaneous first love gives us back our private desiring selves while allowing us to see the desiring self of another. Mutually responding partners confirm each other's desires and declare them good. Such occasions, when we are "moral" without cost, help reconcile us to our moral being and to the usual mutual exclusion between our social and private lives.

The connection between sex and certain emotions—particularly love, jealousy, fear, and anger—is as evident as it is obscure. Complete sex acts seem more likely than incomplete pleasurable ones to lead toward affection and away from fear and anger, since any guilt and shame will be extrinsic to the act and meliorated by it. It is clear that we need not feel for someone any affection beyond that required (if any is) simply to participate with him/her in a complete sex act. However, it is equally clear that sexual pleasure, especially as experienced in complete sex acts, is conducive to many feelings—gratitude, tenderness, pride, appreciation, dependency, and others. These feelings magnify their object who occasioned them. When these magnifying feelings become stable and habitual they are conducive to love—not universal love, of course, but love of a particular sexual partner. However, even "selfish" love is a virtue, a disposition to care for someone as her/his interests and demands would dictate. Neither the best sex nor the best love require each other, but they go together more often than reason would expect—often enough to count the virtue of loving as one of the rewards of the capacity for sexual pleasure exercised in complete sex acts. . . .

Finally, as Sartre has suggested, complete sex acts preserve a respect for persons. Each person remains conscious and responsible, a "subject" rather than a depersonalized, will-less, or manipulated "object." Each actively desires that the other likewise remain a "subject." Respect for persons is a central virtue when matters of justice and obligation are at issue. Insofar as we can speak of respect for persons in complete sex acts, there are different, often contrary requirements of respect. Respect for persons, typically and in sex acts, requires that *actual present* partners participate, partners whose desires are recognized and endorsed. Respect for persons typically requires taking a distance from both one's own demands and those of others. But in sex acts the demands of desire take over, and equal distance is replaced by mutual responsiveness. Respect typically requires refusing to treat another person merely as a means to fulfilling demands. In sex acts, another person is so clearly a means to satisfaction that s/he is always on the verge of becoming merely a means ("intercourse counterfeits masturbation"). In complete sex acts, instrumentality vanishes only because it is mutual and mutually desired. Respect requires encouraging, or at least protecting, the autonomy of another. In complete sex, autonomy of will is recruited by desire, and freedom from others is replaced by frank dependence on another person's desire. Again the respect consists in the reciprocity of desiring dependence, which bypasses rather than violates autonomy.

Despite the radical differences between respect for persons in the usual moral contexts and respect for persons in sex acts, it is not, I think, a mere play on words to talk of respect in the latter case. When, in any sort of intercourse, persons are respected, their desires are not only, in fair measure, *fulfilled*. In addition, their desires are *active* and determine, in fair measure, the form of intercourse and the *manner* and *condition* of desire's satisfaction. These conditions are not only met in sexual intercourse when it is characterized by completeness; they come close to defining completeness.

Sartre is not alone in believing that just because the condition of completeness involves respect for persons, complete sex is impossible. Completeness is surely threatened by pervasive tendencies to fantasy, to possessiveness, and to varieties of a sadomasochistic desire. But a complete sex act, as I see it, does not involve an heroic restraint on our sexual interpulses. Rather, a complete sex act is a normal mode of sexual activity expressing the natural structure and impulses of sexual desire.

While complete sex is morally superior because it involves respect for persons, incomplete sex acts do not necessarily involve immoral disrespect for persons. Depending upon the desires and expectations of the partners, incompleteness may involve neither respect nor disrespect. Masturbation, for example, allows only the limited completeness of embodiment and often fails of that. But masturbation only rarely involves disrespect to anyone. Even the respect of Sartre's allegedly desirable sleeping woman may not be violated if she is unknowingly involved in a sex act. Disrespect, though probable, may in some cases be obviated by her sensibilities and expectations that she has previously expressed and her partner has understood. Sex acts provide one context in which respect for persons can be expressed. That context is important both because our sexual lives are of such importance to us and because they are so liable to injury because of the experience and the fear of the experience of disrespect. But many complete sex acts in which respect is maintained make other casual and incomplete sex acts unthreatening. In this case a goodly number of swallows can make a summer.

In sum, then, complete sex acts are superior to incomplete ones. First, they are, whatever their effects, better than various kinds of incomplete sex acts because they involve a kind of "respect for persons" in acts that are otherwise prone to violation of respect for, and often to violence to, persons. Second, complete sex acts are good because they are good for us. They are conducive to some fairly clearly defined kinds of psychological well-being that are beneficial. They are conducive to moral well-being because they relieve tensions that arise in our attempts to be moral and because they encourage the development of particular virtues.

To say that complete sex acts are preferable to incomplete ones is not to court a new puritanism. There are many kinds and degrees of incompleteness. Incomplete sex acts may not involve a disrespect for persons. Complete sex acts only *tend* to be good for us, and the realization of these tendencies depends upon individual lives and circumstances of sexual activity. The proper object of sexual desire is sexual pleasure. It would be a foolish ambition indeed to limit one's sexual acts to those in which completeness was likely. Any sexual act that is pleasurable is prima facie good, though the more incomplete it is—the more private, essentially autoerotic, unresponsive, unembodied, passive, or imposed—the more likely it is to be harmful to someone.

ON SEXUAL MORALITY: CONCLUDING REMARKS

. . . Some of the traditional sexual vices might be condemned on the ground that they are inimical to better sex. Obscenity, or repeated public exposure to sexual acts, might impair our capacity for pleasure or for response to desire. Promiscuity might undercut the tendency of complete sex acts to promote emotions that magnify their object. Other of the traditional sexual vices are neither inimical nor conducive to better sex, but are condemned because of conflicting nonsexual benefits and obligations. For example, infidelity qua infidelity neither secures nor prevents better sex. The obligations of fidelity have many sources, one of which may be a past history of shared complete sex acts, a history that included promises of exclusive intimacy. Such past promises are as apt to conflict with as to accord with a current demand for better sex. I have said nothing about how such a conflict would be settled. I hope I have shown that where the possibility for better sex conflicts with obligations and other benefits, we have a *moral dilemma*, not just an occasion for moral self-discipline.

The pursuit of more pleasurable and more complete sex acts is, among many moral activities, distinguished not for its exigencies but for its rewards. Since our sexual lives are so important to us, and since, whatever our history and our hopes, we are sexual beings, this pursuit rightly engages our moral reflection. It should not be relegated to the immoral, nor to the "merely" prudent.

I wrote this essay fourteen years ago. Since that time my ideas about thinking and writing, as well as about sexual morality, have been transformed by feminist and anti-militarist politics. The tone and language of the essay, as well as certain basic presuppositions of its arguments, now ring strangely in my ears. Nonetheless, what has been made public belongs to the public and I am pleased if this early paper still proves useful. In one respect, however, the essay seems seriously insensitive and limited. In 1970 I was largely unaware of the deep and extensive pain suffered by those whose sexuality is labeled "abnormal," "perverted," or "immature." On a more theoretical level, since 1970 we have learned to see the connection between misogyny, homophobia, militarism, and racism. I would like here to acknowledge my debt to the work of the feminist and gay liberation movements, which has made these theoretical connections while fighting ignorant and arrogant sexual politics. As a result many people now lead more complete and pleasurable sexual lives.

Dan E. Beauchamp

Morality and the Health of the Body Politic

The Acquired Immunodeficiency Syndrome (AIDS) is clearly a public health threat. The view that it is also a threat to the majority's values is a form of legal moralism.[1] Like public health, legal moralism relies on the use of law and regulation to promote community aims. But legal moralism restricts liberty as a defense against a moral rather than a physical harm. It uses law to protect the majority's morality from the deviant group....

Opposition to moralism is sometimes expressed as "Law has no business restricting private conduct." But it is using law to restrict private conduct in order to promote a private morality that is the crux of the problem.

The most powerful objections to moralism lie in disputing two claims often made on its behalf. According to the first thesis, if a common morality is shared by a majority, this alone is sufficient justification to include it in the criminal law.[2] The second thesis is that because a common morality holds a society together, legal moralism is justified on the grounds of self-preservation. But to opponents of legal moralism, serious restrictions on liberty cannot rest solely on appeals to tradition, even when backed by majority approval. Furthermore, there is no evidence that

From *The Hastings Center Report,* December 1986. Reprinted by permission of the Hastings Center and the author. Copyright © The Hastings Center.

violations of the majority's moral norms, like homosexuality, threaten the existence of society.

The most potent challenge to legal moralism is its frequent collision with a more widely shared value—public health. Restrictions on liberty to promote the public health—paternalism—are today more widely accepted than legal moralism. The trend seems to be, at least over the long run, toward rejecting tightly bounded moral codes in favor of loosely bounded restrictions that promote the public health as a common good. By permitting the majority the right to enforce legally its traditional prejudices, particularly in the sexual realm, the health and safety of the public can be directly threatened.

AIDS mainly strikes two groups—gay men and intravenous drug users—who under normal circumstances are shunned by the larger society. According to the Centers for Disease Control (CDC), the number of cases of heterosexual transmission is rising, but the percentage of all cases due to heterosexual transmission remains very low, roughly 1 percent, and shows no sign of change.

Our best weapon against AIDS would be a public health policy resting on the right to be different in fundamental choices and the democratic community as "one body" in matters of the common health. This new policy would mean the right of every individual to fundamental autonomy, as in abortion and sexual orientation, while viewing health and safety as a common good whose protection (through restrictions on liberty) promotes community and the common health. The public health policy would reject moralism as a threat to the right of each individual, including gays, to fundamental autonomy and also as a threat to the common health.

AIDS, at least in developed countries, does not seem to behave like a typical infectious disease, which spreads rapidly or easily. Until a vaccine is developed, AIDS will resemble drunk driving or cigarette smoking more than diphtheria or malaria; that is, mortality will rise to a high and stubborn level, which will prove very difficult to reduce. And, as in drunk driving, we will be strongly tempted to use the criminal law to punish the offender rather than to explore the roots of the disease, because the roots of the problem lie in American practices generally.

AIDS policy must begin with a realistic admission that, given the poor prospects for developing a vaccine in the immediate future, there is little hope for elimination of the disease. We can only hope to control the rate of increase among high-risk groups, and to prevent the spread into other groups. By how much we can't say for sure, but reducing the incidence of AIDS by one-half seems an almost utopian goal. Hence, neither quarantine nor isolation can be the principal path to conquering AIDS. Education is our only hope for prevention, and here we confront the barrier of social practices regarding homosexuality. . . .

Societal discrimination against gay people slows up the battle against AIDS in two ways. It threatens their health directly, and it impedes changes in gay sexual practices that heighten the risk of AIDS.

The laws against homosexuality in about half the states, as well as continuing social prejudice, prevent public health agencies from developing and aggressively carrying out frank and open sex education campaigns for safer homosexual sex, as well as frustrating prompt medical attention as a part of an overall prevention strategy. We already have ample evidence that this will occur. In the case of the federal government's recent solicitation for "Innovative Projects for AIDS Risk Reduction," the federal government requires that a program review panel, the majority of whom are not the members of at-risk groups, should review program materials to determine that the general public is not offended by sexually explicit material.[3] Federal officials obviously became jittery that successful applicants might draw the ire of opposed groups and even lawsuits, based on state sodomy statutes. . . .

The sodomy statutes also contribute to the poor health of many gays by discouraging their seeking prompt medical advice and treatment for many sexually transmitted diseases (STDs). The high rate of STDs among homosexual males may increase the risk that those who become infected will develop symptoms or become full-blown AIDS cases. The same might well be true for gay men using drugs of various kinds to increase sexual stimulation. Antisodomy statutes and fear of prosecution or exposure discourage prompt medical attention and limit opportunities for communicating clear advice about safer sexual practices. Indeed, the antisodomy statutes may encourage prejudice among the medical community toward homosexual patients.

The antisodomy statutes and other restrictions on gay men may also make it more likely that the sexual practices of some such individuals remain high-risk for venereal disease and AIDS. If the sexual practices of many gay men are to change, and if homosexual sex is to occur in the context of more stable relationships, the larger society will have to permit permanent forms of gay association and civil liberties that encourage such stable relationships. While societal discrimination is not the whole story behind gay liberation, gay sexual practices may have been shaped in part by societal pressures and laws forcing gay men to associate secretly in bars and bathhouses out of view of the majority community, while at the same time proscribing gay association by cohabitation and marriage. Gay people cannot now marry and are denied many other legal and social privileges of straights. The freedoms to live where one wants and with whom one wants; to make contracts; and to obtain employment in a normal manner are likely linked in subtle ways to encouraging enduring relationships, which lower the risk of exposure to STDs.

Success in the battle against AIDS depends on replacing old images of the tightly bound community based on sodomy statutes—"us" and "them"—with a more complex public health policy that combines the right to be different with the view that in matters of the common health and safety we are "one body" with a common good. This complex vision, combining equality and community, rests on a double movement; the health of the body politic depends on mutual trust and a willingness to accept the burdens of citizenship; these burdens are accepted because a narrow moralism is rejected and all are equal partners in the body politic, free to pursue their own ultimate ends.

Therefore, health education against AIDS should involve far more than disseminating explicit sex education materials. Health education means building and strengthening both equality and community, challenging traditional superstitions and defending the legitimate rights of homosexuals. Health officials should actively —albeit prudently—seek the repeal of state laws proscribing homosexuality as major barriers to this public education, laws whose continued existence threatens the public health. Public health groups should also support efforts to broaden the civil liberties of gay people and eliminate laws that permit employers, landlords, the military, or commercial establishments to discriminate in employment, housing, insurance, or military service.

While public health and the rights to citizenship are a cornerstone in any community, removing centuries of prejudice and discrimination dictates caution and political prudence. The prejudices against homosexuality are deep-seated and not likely to give way easily.

Of course, the moralist sees laws against homosexuality as ordained by God and tradition. In this view, laws forbidding sodomy among males and females or partners of the same sex are a vital bulwark against AIDS. If homosexuality were to decline sharply, the number of AIDS cases would fall in turn. Guidelines for safe sex are, accordingly, guidelines for safe sodomy and are, as such, patently repugnant.

There are many parallels between AIDS and abortion. In *Roe v. Wade,* legal abortion was justified not on grounds of privacy alone (equality) but also on public health grounds (the common good); Justice Blackmun justified his decision in significant part because legal abortions were much safer for the mother than pregnancy and illegal abortions.[4] Securing the right to abortion strengthened the public health by removing the barriers to safe abortions....

In the case of the Bible, John Boswell's exhaustive study of the issue of homosexuality suggests that Sodom was destroyed not because of the abomination of homosexuality, but because the Sodomites refused hospitality to strangers.[5] In fact, homosexuality is explicitly forbidden in only one place in the Old Testament and there for reasons of ritual impurity (like the eating of pork), and not as a fundamental sin.

In the New Testament, Jesus did not mention homosexuality at all; and his ministry to prostitutes, thieves, beggars, and the poor constituted a scandal to the moralists of his time. In fact, Jesus's reference to the story of Sodom's fall in Matthew 10:14 refers to the Sodomites' lack of hospitality: "Whosoever shall not receive you, nor hear your words, when ye depart out of that house or city, shake off the dust of your feet. Verily I say unto you, it shall be more tolerable for the land of Sodom and Gomorrah in the day of judgment, than for that city." Jesus's attack on religious moralism and his elevation of a gospel of love and community were the principal reasons for his being put to death.

Even Paul, who had some harsh things to say about homosexuality (references which John Boswell persuasively argues may refer more to male prostitution than to homosexuality per se) struggled mightily to rescue Christianity from a narrow religious moralism (witness his attack on religious superstitions surrounding circumcision), and to place it on the foundations of community and love for the neighbor....

...By a 5 to 4 vote in *Bowers v. Hardwick,*[6] the Court upheld the right of the majority to legislate against homosexual acts, committed even in private, on the grounds that repugnance for homosexuality is an ancient and deeply rooted community sentiment. In an earlier decision, the future Chief Justice compared these laws to public health legislation to prevent the spread of communicable diseases. Justice Rehnquist, in 1978, said that laws controlling homosexuals are constitutionally akin to "whether those suffering from measles have a constitutional right, in violation of quarantine regulations, to associate together and with others who do not presently have measles."[7] Rehnquist echoes James F. Stephen in the nineteenth century when he said, "Vice is as infectious as disease, and happily virtue is infectious, though health is not. Both vice and virtue are transmittable, and, to a considerable extent, hereditary."[8]

The decision of the Supreme Court is a threat to the entire advance of the privacy decisions of the past two decades. The work of the Court in trying to untangle the claims of moralism, and the claims of public health, by forging a new equality that combines the common good and the right to be left alone in new ways, has been left dangling. If the Court's ruling is to be reversed, the thesis that legal moralism threatens the public health as well as the rights of all citizens, including gays, must be pressed even more vigorously.

SEXUAL PRACTICES AND PATERNALISM

A sound public health policy depends on both loosening and tightening the bonds of community. Rejecting moral'sm does not mean that society can have nothing to say about sexual practices. Sex per se, and that includes homosexual sex, is not the business of the community. But sexual practices that threaten the common health are.

Sexual practices can have many consequences for the public health. Private conduct, even sexual conduct, which threatens compelling community interests like health and safety, is not beyond the reach of regulation, even if the individuals involved are consenting adults. Of course, there are overwhelming practical limits to this principle, but affirming it is important nonetheless.

Human sexuality is an imperative drive like hunger or safety, and sexual practices, at least in private, are likely very resistant to legal prohibition or regulation. Nevertheless, the public health official cannot ignore sexual practices that are unsafe, dangerous, and a threat to all. Public health information campaigns must not flinch from promoting a standard of sexual conduct that is safe and prudent from everyone's standpoint.

The sexual practices of male homosexuals have become a central controversy in the AIDS debate.

... [O]ne third of all male homosexuals surveyed nationally reported that they had more than 50 to 70 sexual partners in the previous year.[9] Gay men report that they participate in sexual contact with persons unknown to each other "very frequently" or "fairly frequently." Favorite cruising places for casual sex have included parks and public restrooms, as well as the back rooms of bars where the owners permit such liaisons. Another site for casual sex is the bathhouse, which many gay men prefer because so little effort is required to make contacts.

Another index to the sexual practices of male homosexuals is sexually transmitted diseases. Individuals who are exclusively homosexuals for a considerable part of their lives constitute 5 to 10 percent of the adult male population, according to Kinsey's estimate. If the statistics are reliable, this group accounts for a third of all cases of infectious syphilis, a high rate of gonorrhea, and an increasing rate of hepatitis A and B. Gay males are also at much greater risk for bacterial and enteric diseases like amebiasis and giardiasis. The risk of herpes and other dermatologic disorders is also much greater among gay males.[10]

In 1977, in New York City, 55 percent of all reported cases of syphilis occurred in homosexual males, even though syphilis, among heterosexuals nationwide, has been declining at a remarkable rate. Homosexual men are reported to be ten times more likely to contract syphilis than heterosexuals.

... If recent reports are borne out, exposure to the virus may bring the full-blown AIDS disease to as many as 25 to 40 percent of those infected, a much higher risk than originally thought. The spectre of as many as 250,000 to 400,000 cases (the current level of deaths is 15,000), will dramatically increase societal pressures to blame the victim.

As the toll of the disease among homosexuals mounts, the deadly risks associated with homosexual sex are likely to have the greatest impact in reshaping homosexual life. Words like "promiscuity" are regarded by gays with deep suspicion as covert attacks on homosexuality itself. To minimize suspicion we should observe the distinction between restrictions for sexual standards protecting the common life and restrictions promoting an official sexual morality. Frequent sexual activity is of no interest to the law and the community unless it escalates the risk of serious disease. When the disease is AIDS, the community interest becomes paramount, and official educational campaigns should discourage high-risk sex with strangers. Even if such practices as oral and anal sex are presently beyond the law, informed self-interest should help work to bring sharp declines in free-wheeling sex with strangers.

Should public officials go beyond education? Should, for instance, police monitor gay "cruising" for sexual liaisons where there is a high likelihood of contacts between strangers and where the risk of spreading infection is very high? Here the potential for abuse by the police is very great, and the boundaries between controlling homosexuality per se, versus protecting health and safety, are extremely blurred. The likely outcome will be only to make heterosexuals feel (falsely) reassured and the gay community discriminated against.

The major debate has concerned closing or regulating public places such as bathhouses where dangerous sex is practiced. San Francisco took such steps, but the New York City health authorities took a different position. While the state health officials ultimately overruled them, New York City officials argued that the impact of such closings would be minuscule in terms of the overall threat. Still, the public health official is not required to demonstrate that the closings or regulation will result in containing the epidemic. But at the same time, officials should take steps to assure all concerned that the aim is to regulate the public health, not homosexuality, tipping the scales toward regulation versus outright closing. It may well be that regulation, and in the worst cases outright closings, could be a potent symbol for community action.

On the other hand, some argue that these commercial establishments ought to be used to promote safer sex. This tactic has a familiar ring, something like getting the liquor industry to promote "responsible drinking." An industry that has an interest in promoting casual sex—whether bathhouses or bars—is unlikely to be seriously interested in a health education campaign. Realism should guide our regulatory policy. The goal is to restrict commercial establishments that have an interest in unsafe sex—places where sex between strangers is promoted as a commodity. The fact that some hotels, incidental to their doing business, have couples among their guests practicing high-risk sex, is not an adequate argument against closing bathhouses or bars where casual sex is a main feature.

The lead in any public discourse about gay sexual practices must come from the gay community itself. Such a change can only come from a full and extensive dialogue, which should be open, frank, and based on as much careful and dispassionate research as is possible. At all times the participants should remind themselves that the discussion is about public health, not moralism.

Gay people who object that the majority community ought not control the private behavior of consenting adults forget that membership in the community—which is the ground of public health protections against AIDS—carries obligations as well as benefits. Paternalism to defend the common life protects the health and safety of sexual partners and helps solidify the norms of the shared community. At the present time, frequent sexual activity among strangers promotes spread of a deadly disease. Until this disease is controlled we all share a common interest in a more conservative and restrictive standard for sexual morality.

For their side, homosexuals need to take the leadership and to call for self-imposed restrictions. This is already happening. Also, health statistics in San Francisco and New York City suggest that thousands of gays are altering their lifestyles. Many gay leaders have begun publicly to repudiate the fast-lane life. Political prudence suggests that if gay people want gains against discrimination in housing, employment, medical care, and insurance, then their leaders should speak out against dangerous sexual practices within their community.

Above all else . . . we should keep our eyes on the central issue—the many ways in which centuries of religious and social superstitions and prejudice stand in the way of improving the public health. Modern public health rests on a complex equality that replaces traditional restrictions with limits rooted in protection against actual harms. Equating the public health with simplistic restrictions on homosexuality per se will only result in fruitless debates over matters like quarantine and isolation, public health strategies that have little role in this epidemic. Hoping for a technological shortcut in the form of a vaccine is not realistic and can cost tens of thousands of lives, especially if this hope keeps us from facing the task of public education and reform of our laws against homosexuality. These reforms can help prepare the way for altering sexual lifestyles among the gay community. The public health community should take the lead and, state by state, demand the repeal of harmful statutes and restrictions on gay life. The health of the body politic depends on rejecting the communal disease of sexual prejudice.

NOTES

1. For a good discussion of "moralism," see Hugo Adam Bedau's discussion in Edwin M. Schur and Hugo Adam Bedau, *Victimless Crimes* (Englewood Cliffs, N.J.: Prentice-Hall, 1974). See also Joel Feinberg, *Social Philosophy* (Englewood Cliffs, N.J.: Prentice-Hall, 1973) and H. L. A. Hart, *Law, Liberty, and Morality* (New York: Vintage Books, 1963); Ronald Dworkin, *Taking Rights Seriously* (Cambridge: Harvard University Press, 1977), ch. 11; and A. D. Woozley, "Law and the Legislation of Morality," in *Ethics in Hard Times*, eds. Daniel Callahan and Arthur Caplan (New York: Plenum, 1981).

2. See H. L. A. Hart, "Social Solidarity and the Enforcement of Morality," *The University of Chicago Law Review* 35 (1967): 1–13, for one of the best critiques of the thesis that society is held together by a specific moral practice.

3. See Barry Adkins, "GMHC Accepts Grant from CDC for Sex Education Research," *The New York Native*, Feb. 10–16, 1986, p. 8. For a good discussion of the potential for an anti-AIDS campaign to serve as cover for a campaign to control homosexuality, see "AIDS—A New Reason to Regulate Homosexuality?" *Journal of Contemporary Law* 11 (1984): 315–43.

4. *Roe v. Wade*, 410 U.S. 113 (1973). [Editor's note: See chapter 11, p. 358.]

5. The source of this history of Roman and Christian attitudes toward homosexuality is John Boswell's *Christianity, Social Tolerance, and Homosexuality* (Chicago: The University of Chicago Press, 1980).

6. *Bowers v. Hardwick*, 478 U.S. 92 L Ed 2d 140 (1986). [Editor's note: See Chapter 10, p. 331.]

7. See David A. J. Richards, "Homosexual Acts and the Constitutional Right to Privacy," and "Public Manifestations of Personal Morality: Limitations on the Use of Solicitation Statutes to Control Homosexual Cruising," in *Homosexuality and the Law* (special double issue of *The Journal of Homosexuality*), 5 (1979–80), 43–66. The 1978 case is *Ratchford v. Gay Lib*, 434 U.S. 1080, 1082, reh'g denied, 435 U.S. 981 (1978).

8. James Fitzjames Stephen, *Liberty, Equality, Fraternity*, ed. R. J. White, (Cambridge: Cambridge University Press, 1967), 146.

9. Karla Jay and Allen Young, *The Gay Report* (New York: Summit Books, 1977).

10. Terry Alan Sandholzer, "Factors Affecting the Incidence and Management of Sexually Transmitted Diseases in Homosexual Men," in *Sexually Transmitted Diseases in Homosexual Men: Diagnosis, Treatment, and Research*, ed. David G. Ostrow, Terry Alan Sandholzer, and Yehudi M. Felman (New York: Plenum, Medicae, 1983), 3–12. The estimates of the numbers of gay males in the adult population are from *Sexual Behavior in the Human Male* by Alfred C. Kinsey, Wardell B. Pomeroy, and Clyde E. Martin (Philadelphia: W. B. Saunders Co., 1948) (The Kinsey Report).

SUGGESTIONS FOR DISCUSSION

1. Is promiscuity inherently disrespectful of persons, or inherently immoral in some other sense? Are all perverse acts immoral?

2. Are there any kinds of sexual acts that should be criminalized? Given the danger of AIDS, should homosexual practices be criminalized?

3. Is Beauchamp right in maintaining that current public health policy discriminates against homosexuals? Would mandatory testing for the AIDS virus violate the rights of those who are required to be tested?

FURTHER READING

AIDS. Special Supplement, Hastings Center Report, December 1986. (Interpretation, critical analysis; intermediate)

Anscombe, G.E.M. "You Can Have Sex Without Children: Christianity and the New Offer." In *Collected Papers*. Vol. II. Minneapolis: University of Minnesota Press, 1981. (Interpretation, critical analysis; intermediate)

Atkinson, R. *Sexual Morality*. New York: Harcourt Brace, 1966. (Interpretation, critical analysis; intermediate)

Baker, R., and Elliston, F., eds. *Philosophy and Sex*. Buffalo: Prometheus Books, 1984. (Interpretation, critical analysis; intermediate)

Feinberg, J. *Social Philosophy*. Englewood Cliffs, N.J.: Prentice-Hall, 1973. (Interpretation, critical analysis; intermediate)

———. *Harm to Others*. Oxford: Oxford University Press, 1984. (Interpretation, critical analysis; advanced)

———. *Harm to Self*. Oxford: Oxford University Press, 1987. (Interpretation, critical analysis; advanced)

———. *Offense to Others*. Oxford: Oxford University Press, 1988. (Interpretation, critical analysis; advanced)

———. *Harmless Wrongdoings*. Oxford: Oxford University Press, 1988. (Interpretation, critical analysis; advanced)

Freud, S. *Three Essays on the Theory of Sexuality*. New York: Basic Books, 1962. (Critical analysis; advanced)

Homosexuality and the Law. Special double issue. *Journal of Homosexuality* 5 (1979–80). (Critical analysis; intermediate)

Leiser, B. *Liberty, Justice and Morals*. 3rd ed. New York: Macmillan, 1986. (Interpretation, critical analysis; introductory)

Nagel, T. "Sexual Perversion." *Journal of Philosophy* 66 (1969): 5–17. (Interpretation, critical analysis; advanced)

Noonan, J. *Contraception*. Cambridge, Mass.: Harvard University Press, 1965. (Interpretation, critical analysis; intermediate)

Pierce, C., and VanDeVeer, D., eds. *AIDS: Ethics and Public Policy*. Belmont, Calif.: Wadsworth, 1987. (Interpretation, critical analysis; advanced)

Seckel, A., ed. *Bertrand Russell on Ethics, Sex and Marriage*. Buffalo: Prometheus, 1987. (Interpretation, critical analysis; introductory)

Soble, A., ed. *Philosophy of Sex*. Totowa, N.J.: Rowman and Littlefield, 1980. (Interpretation, critical analysis; intermediate)

Taylor, R. *Having Love Affairs*. Buffalo: Prometheus, 1982. (Interpretation, critical analysis; advanced)

Vannoy, R. *Sex Without Love: A Philosophical Explanation*. Buffalo: Prometheus, 1980. (Interpretation, critical analysis; intermediate)

Verene, D., ed. *Sexual Love and Western Morality: A Philosophical Anthology*. New York: Harper & Row, 1966. (Interpretation, critical analysis; advanced)

Wasserstrom, R., ed. *Morality and the Law*. Belmont, Calif.: Wadsworth, 1971. (Interpretation, critical analysis; advanced)

Watney, S. *Policing Desire: Pornography, AIDS and the Media*. Minneapolis: University of Minnesota Press, 1987. (Interpretation, critical analysis; introductory)

Wilson, J. *Logic and Sexual Morality*. Baltimore: Penguin, 1966. (Interpretation, critical analysis; advanced)

11
□
Abortion

As sexual attitudes and behavior in the second half of this century have become increasingly liberalized, views concerning abortion have also been debated more openly and heatedly. Although the moral issues of abortion have been addressed for many centuries by philosophers and theologians, increasing sexual tolerance has focused general social attention upon the pressing moral and legal questions that abortion raises.

Viability   Abortion may be defined as the termination of pregnancy either spontaneously or by artificial induction. *Viability* is the point at which the fetus is capable of development independent of its mother; removal of the fetus from the woman's body prior to viability involves its inevitable destruction. At present, the earliest viable point occurs at approximately twenty weeks. It is possible, nevertheless, that technological advance could reduce the time it takes for the fetus to become viable.

The point at which the fetus becomes viable is considered irrelevant to the morality of abortion by those holding either that abortion is always wrong or that it is generally permissible. The point of viability tends to make a difference only for those who hold that abortion will be permissible up to some point in fetal development, and impermissible after that point. Underlying these differences in moral attitude to abortion are different views about the fetus's moral status. The basic question here is the moral one of whether the fetus is a *person*.

Personhood and Rights   Intentional killing of an innocent person is *prima facie* wrong. If a fetus is an innocent person, abortion must be (*prima facie*) wrong also. Antiabortionists usually argue that conception is the only nonarbitrary point during pregnancy at which personhood can be established (see John T. Noonan). Accordingly, moral and legal protection from abortion must be provided for the full life of the fetus. This argument is often cast in terms of *rights*. (On right-based moral theories, see Mackie, Part I, Chapter 6.) If the fetus is a person, it has the full rights a person enjoys, and hence the right to life. Yet the appeal to rights suggests a qualification of the extreme antiabortion position. Some have argued that where a woman's life is endangered by pregnancy, her right to life would override the fetus's, for autonomous life is considered more worthy than dependent life. An abortion may be performed in such circumstances. (Note that this qualification does not represent the formal Roman Catholic position, which allows only "indirect" abortion resulting from necessary treatment that the fetus is highly unlikely to survive, but where there is no intention to terminate fetal life. An example is the removal of a cancerous uterus.)

A common objection to this line of analysis in terms of personhood is that the fetus clearly fails to possess characteristics definitive of a person (see Mary Anne Warren). Antiabortionists usually respond by emphasizing the *potentiality* of the fetus to acquire personhood rather than its possessing the actual characteristics of full personhood. Potentiality is thought to be a sufficient condition for possessing full human rights.

By contrast, the proabortion argument tends to deny that the fetus has personhood and hence that it has the human right to life. Personhood is taken usually to arise at birth rather than at conception. Proabortionists may admit that the fetus is human in the biological or genetic sense, yet insist that this differs from the morally relevant sense of being a person with human rights. The proabortionist can even admit that the fetus has some rights, while insisting that these rights are not (fully) human and hence that they can be easily overridden. While the antiabortionist holds that the fetus has the rights of a person, the proabortionist usually insists that the fetus has no (full) human rights. Fetal potentiality for personhood is taken by the proabortionist to be neither a necessary nor a sufficient condition for having rights. Accordingly, abortion is not murder, for no human is killed. The woman's right to choose what befalls her body is taken to be the only or at least the crucial right that counts here.

Many have tried to fashion a path between the antiabortion and pro-choice views. Intermediate positions are united in holding that abortion is permissible under some conditions, and impermissible under others (see R. M. Hare). Some (though not Hare) argue that the fetus has no rights at conception. It acquires rights later in its development—at viability, say, or at *quickening* (the point at which the woman begins to feel fetal movement, generally between the twelfth and sixteenth weeks). Accordingly, abortion may be performed until that point, but not after. One justification commonly cited for permitting abortion before but not after viability is that the likelihood of a woman's death in an abortion prior to viability is less than in childbirth, while it is greater after the fetus becomes viable. It follows that if technological developments make possible an earlier point of viability, the fetus on this view must acquire its rights at the earlier point. Moreover, potential conflicts between the woman's and the fetus's rights would be commonplace. Some mechanism must be provided for their resolution.

Supreme Court Rulings   Prior to the 1970s, most states had conservative criminal statutes outlawing abortions. In 1973, a pregnant woman (under the pseudonym of Jane Roe) challenged the Texas statute in the courts. In a landmark decision, *Roe v. Wade*, the Supreme Court ruled that the Constitution nowhere recognizes the unborn as legal persons and that state criminalization of abortion in the first *trimester* (or three months) of pregnancy violates women's rights to privacy. The Court concluded that the decision to abort during this period must be left to the woman and her physician. Nevertheless, the right to privacy, though a fundamental right, was found not to be absolute, for it could be overridden by "compelling" interests with which it competes at later stages of pregnancy. States were considered to have legitimate interests in protecting and preserving pregnant women's health and life. These interests were thought to become compelling or binding in the second trimester and to justify state regulation of abortion from that point. Regulation could range from administering abortion procedures to prohibiting abortion unless necessary to save the woman's life. It was ruled, finally, that states have an interest in protecting the potential human life of the fetus. This interest becomes compelling at the point of viability. It justifies legal prohibition of abortion from this point, save when it is necessary to preserve the woman's life or health.

The Court reaffirmed *Roe's* finding in numerous cases, most notably a decade later, in *Akron v. Akron Center for Reproductive Health* (1983). However, in the dissenting opinion to *Akron*, newly appointed Justice Sandra Day O'Connor criticized the ruling in *Roe*. O'Connor agreed that states have a legitimate interest in ensuring maternal safety from the second trimester, but she argued that this does not entail that there is no legitimate state interest in the first trimester. O'Connor admitted similarly that states have legitimate interests in protecting potential human life. She contended here also that state interests are compelling throughout pregnancy, and not only from the point of viability. O'Connor concluded that the Court's findings in both *Roe* and *Akron* should have been to prohibit abortion.

Readings Roman Catholic scholar John Noonan arrives at moral conclusions consistent with O'Connor's legal position. Representing the Natural Law tradition (see Aquinas, Part I, Chapter 1), Noonan critically rejects all attempts to establish the point at which humanity is acquired any later than at conception. He defines a human being as a being conceived by human parents, having a human genetic code, and so possessing at least the potentiality of "becoming a man." Noonan claims to derive the equal right to life of the fetus from the humanity of the fetus and the principle of "equality of human lives." From this follows the obligation "not to injure another without reason." Noonan contends that abortions violate both the principle of equality and the obligation not to harm. He concludes that the life of a fetus may not be taken, except in rare cases, to save the woman's life.

R. M. Hare thinks that the radically conflicting intuitions of antiabortionists, on one hand, and of those who endorse a woman's right to choose what happens to her own body, on the other, can be resolved only by appealing to a background moral theory. Hare rejects as arbitrary any appeal to the rights of the fetus or the woman, or to the personhood of the fetus. The basic moral principle Hare proposes is a reformulation of the Golden Rule: "Do to others what we are glad was done to us." Applied to abortion, this entails that if we are glad nobody terminated our birth, other things being equal we should not terminate another's. This requires, in turn, that we accept the *potentiality principle:* We should not prevent those with the potential for developing into adult human beings from doing so. Hare's reading of the Golden Rule establishes the *prima facie* wrongness of abortion (on *prima facie* wrongness, see Ross, Part I, Chapter 6). Nevertheless, Hare's basic moral principle requires that we respect also—and equally—the interests of potential adults who would be conceived if this fetus is aborted. It follows that circumstances might be such that a woman is required to abort her present fetus in favor of conceiving one in the near future. A woman's obligation to abort or not will be determined by a utilitarian calculus, weighing up the probability of a future fetus developing into a person living a happy as opposed to a harmful life against the probability of same for the present fetus (on utilitarianism, see Part I, Chapter 4). If there is more likelihood that the present fetus will enjoy a happy life than a future fetus will, the woman has the obligation not to abort; if the life faced by a future fetus will more probably be better, then she is obliged to abort in favor of getting pregnant later. Hare concludes that the *prima facie* wrongness of abortion consists in preventing a person coming into existence, not in any wrong done to the fetus as such. Yet this general wrongness of abortion may be overridden quite easily in given cases, if the satisfaction of interests that follows from terminating a pregnancy outweighs the sacrifice of other interests.

Mary Anne Warren attacks Noonan's argument against abortion. Noonan's view, claims Warren, plays upon an ambiguity in the concept of "human being." A being is human in the *genetic* sense simply if it is a member of the species *homo sapiens;* a being is human in the *moral* sense if it is a fully developed member of the moral community, with complete moral rights. Noonan defines humanity in the genetic sense. If he is to show that it is almost always impermissible to abort, he must demonstrate that the genetic and moral senses of humanity are equivalent. Warren argues that Noonan cannot demonstrate this, for the moral community consists of persons and not simply of biological entities. Persons are defined by characteristics that a fetus fails to possess, including consciousness, reasoning, communicability, self-motivation, and self-awareness. So a fetus, even at late stages of development, is not personlike. Warren thinks that a fetus's potential for becoming a person as grounds for its right to life provides insufficient reason to override a woman's right to health, happiness, and freedom. Hence, no laws may restrict a woman's right to terminate her pregnancy at any stage. (In a postscript, Warren argues that her defense of a woman's right to abort does not entail a justification of infanticide.)

It is evident, then, that competing moral considerations are invoked in the conflicting attempts to restrict abortion by law and to restrict laws limiting abortion. (On law and morality, see also Part II, Chapter 9.)

Justice Harry A. Blackmun

Majority Opinion in *Roe v. Wade*

This right of privacy, whether it be founded in the Fourteenth Amendment's concept of personal liberty and restrictions upon state action, as we feel it is, or, as the District Court determined, in the Ninth Amendment's reservation of rights to the people, is broad enough to encompass a woman's decision whether or not to terminate her pregnancy....

... [A]ppelants and some *amici* argue that the woman's right is absolute and that she is entitled to terminate her pregnancy at whatever time, in whatever way, and so for whatever reason she alone chooses. With this we do not agree. Appellants' arguments that Texas either has no valid interest at all in regulating the abortion decision, or no interest strong enough to support any limitation upon the woman's sole determination, is unpersuasive. The Court's decisions recognizing a right of privacy also acknowledge that some state regulation in areas protected by that right is appropriate. As noted above, a state may properly assert important interests in safe-guarding health, in maintaining medical standards, and in protecting potential life. At some point in pregnancy, these respective interests become sufficiently compelling to sustain regulation of the factors that govern the abortion decision. The privacy right involved, therefore, cannot be said to be absolute.

We therefore conclude that the right of personal privacy includes the abortion decision, but that this right is not unqualified and must be considered against important state interests in regulation....

With respect to the State's important and legitimate interest in the health of the mother, the "compelling" point, in the light of present medical knowledge, is at approximately the end of the first trimester. This is so because of the now established medical fact... that until the end of the first trimester mortality in abortion is less than mortality in normal childbirth. It follows that, from and after this point, a State may regulate the abortion procedure to the extent that the regulation reasonably relates to the preservation and protection of maternal health. Examples of permissible state regulation in this area are requirements as to the qualifications of the person who is to perform the abortion; as to the licensure of that person; as to the facility in which the procedure is to be performed, that is, whether it must be a hospital or may be a clinic or some other place of less-than-hospital status; as to the licensing of the facility; and the like.

... The decision leaves the State free to place increasing restrictions on abortion as the period of pregnancy lengthens, so long as those restrictions are tailored to the recognized state interests. The decision vindicates the right of the physician to administer medical treatment according to his professional judgment up to the points where important state interests provide compelling justifications for intervention. Up to those points the abortion decision in all its aspects is inherently, and

United States Supreme Court, 410 U.S. 113 (1973).

primarily, a medical decision, and basic responsibility for it must rest with the physician. If an individual practitioner abuses the privilege of exercising proper medical judgment, the usual remedies, judicial and intraprofessional, are available. . . .

Justice Sandra Day O'Connor

Dissenting Opinion in *Akron v. Akron Center for Reproductive Health*

The Court in *Roe* correctly realized that the State has important interests "in the areas of health and medical standards" and that "[t]he State has a legitimate interest in seeing to it that abortion, like any other medical procedure, is performed under circumstances that insure maximum safety for the patient." The Court also recognized that the State has "*another* important and legitimate interest in protecting the potentiality of human life." I agree completely that the State has these interests, but in my view, the point at which these interests become compelling does not depend on the trimester of pregnancy. Rather, these interests are present *throughout* pregnancy.

This Court has never failed to recognize that "a State may properly assert important interests in safeguarding health [and] in maintaining medical standards." *Roe*. It cannot be doubted that as long as a state statute is within "the bounds of reason and [does not] assume the character of a merely arbitrary fiat . . . [then] [t]he State . . . must decide upon measures that are needful for the protection of its people. . . ." "There is nothing in the United States Constitution which limits the State's power to require that medical procedures be done safely. . . ." "The mode and procedure of medical diagnostic procedures is not the business of judges." Under the *Roe* framework, however, the state interest in maternal health cannot become compelling until the onset of the second trimester of pregnancy because "until the end of the first trimester mortality in abortion may be less than mortality in normal childbirth." *Roe*. Before the second trimester, the decision to perform an abortion "must be left to the medical judgment of the pregnant woman's attending physician." *Roe*.

The fallacy inherent in the *Roe* framework is apparent: just because the State has a compelling interest in ensuring maternal safety once an abortion may be more dangerous than childbirth, it simply does not follow that the State has *no* interest before that point that justifies state regulation to ensure that first-trimester abortions are performed as safely as possible.

United States Supreme Court, 462 U.S. 416 (1983).

The state interest in potential human life is likewise extant throughout pregnancy. In *Roe*, the Court held that although the State had an important and legitimate interest in protecting potential life, that interest could not become compelling until the point at which the fetus was viable. The difficulty with this analysis is clear: *potential* life is no less potential in the first weeks of pregnancy than it is at viability or afterward. At any stage in pregnancy, there is the *potential* for human life. Although the Court refused to "resolve the difficult question of when life begins," the Court chose the point of viability—when the fetus is *capable* of life independent of its mother—to permit the complete proscription of abortion. The choice of viability as the point at which the state interest in *potential* life becomes compelling is not less arbitrary than choosing any point before viability or any point afterward. Accordingly, I believe that the State's interest in protecting potential human life exists throughout the pregnancy.

John T. Noonan, Jr.

An Almost Absolute Value in History

The most fundamental question involved in the long history of thought on abortion is: How do you determine the humanity of a being? To phrase the question that way is to put in comprehensive humanistic terms what the theologians either dealt with as an explicitly theological question under the heading of "ensoulment" or dealt with implicitly in their treatment of abortion. The Christian position as it originated did not depend on a narrow theological or philosophical concept. It had no relation to the theories of infant baptism. It appealed to no special theory of instantaneous ensoulment. It took the world's view on ensoulment as that view changed from Aristotle to Zacchia. There was, indeed, theological influence affecting the theory of ensoulment finally adopted, and, of course, ensoulment itself was a theological concept, so that the position was always explained in theological terms. But the theological notion of ensoulment could easily be translated into humanistic language by substituting "human" for "rational soul"; the problem of knowing when a man is a man is common to theology and humanism.

If one steps outside the specific categories used by the theologians, the answer they gave can be analyzed as a refusal to discriminate among human beings on the basis of their varying potentialities. Once conceived, the being was recognized as man because he had man's potential. The criterion for humanity, thus, was simple and all-embracing: if you are conceived by human parents, you are human.

From *The Morality of Abortion,* edited by John T. Noonan, Jr. (Cambridge, Mass.: Harvard University Press, 1970). Reprinted by permission of the publisher. Copyright © 1970 by The President and Fellows of Harvard College.

The strength of this position may be tested by a review of some of the other distinctions offered in the contemporary controversy over legalizing abortion. Perhaps the most popular distinction is in terms of viability. Before an age of so many months, the fetus is not viable, that is, it cannot be removed from the mother's womb and live apart from her. To that extent, the life of the fetus is absolutely dependent on the life of the mother. This dependence is made the basis of denying recognition to its humanity.

There are difficulties with this distinction. One is that the perfection of artificial incubation may make the fetus viable at any time: it may be removed and artificially sustained. Experiments with animals already show that such a procedure is possible. This hypothetical extreme case relates to an actual difficulty: there is considerable elasticity to the idea of viability. Mere length of life is not an exact measure. The viability of the fetus depends on the extent of its anatomical and functional development. The weight and length of the fetus are better guides to the state of its development than age, but weight and length vary. . . . If viability is the norm, the standard would vary with . . . many individual circumstances.

The most important objection to this approach is that dependence is not ended by viability. The fetus is still absolutely dependent on someone's care in order to continue existence; indeed a child of one or three or even five years of age is absolutely dependent on another's care for existence; uncared for, the older fetus or the younger child will die as surely as the early fetus detached from the mother. The unsubstantial lessening in dependence at viability does not seem to signify any special acquisition of humanity.

A second distinction has been attempted in terms of experience. A being who has had experience, has lived and suffered, who possesses memories, is more human than one who has not. Humanity depends on formation by experience. The fetus is thus "unformed" in the most basic human sense.

This distinction is not serviceable for the embryo which is already experiencing and reacting. The embryo is responsive to touch after eight weeks and at least at that point is experiencing. At an earlier stage the zygote is certainly alive and responding to its environment. The distinction may also be challenged by the rare case where aphasia has erased adult memory: has it erased humanity? More fundamentally, this distinction leaves even the older fetus or the younger child to be treated as an unformed inhuman thing. Finally, it is not clear why experience as such confers humanity. It could be argued that certain central experiences such as loving or learning are necessary to make a man human. But then human beings who have failed to love or to learn might be excluded from the class called man.

A third distinction is made by appeal to the sentiments of adults. If a fetus dies, the grief of the parents is not the grief they would have for a living child. The fetus is an unnamed "it" till birth, and is not perceived as personality until at least the fourth month of existence when movements in the womb manifest a vigorous presence demanding joyful recognition by the parents.

Yet feeling is notoriously an unsure guide to the humanity of others. Many groups of humans have had difficulty in feeling that persons of another tongue, color, religion, sex, are as human as they. Apart from reactions to alien groups, we mourn the loss of a ten-year-old boy more than the loss of his one-day-old brother or his 90-year-old grandfather. The difference felt and the grief expressed vary with the potentialities extinguished, or the experience wiped out; they do not seem to point to any substantial difference in the humanity of baby, boy, or grandfather.

Distinctions are also made in terms of sensation by the parents. The embryo is felt within the womb only after about the fourth month. The embryo is seen only at birth. What can be neither seen nor felt is different from what is tangible. If the fetus cannot be seen or touched at all, it cannot be perceived as man.

Yet experience shows that sight is even more untrustworthy than feeling in determining humanity. By sight, color became an appropriate index for saying who was a man, and the evil of racial discrimination was given foundations. Nor can touch provide the test; a being confined by sickness, "out of touch" with others, does not thereby seem to lose his humanity. To the extent that touch still has appeal as a criterion, it appears to be a survival of the old English idea of "quickening"—a possible mistranslation of the Latin *animatus* used in the canon law. To that extent touch as a criterion seems to be dependent on the Aristotelian notion of ensoulment, and to fall when this notion is discarded.

Finally, a distinction is sought in social visibility. The fetus is not socially perceived as human. It cannot communicate with others. Thus, both subjectively and objectively, it is not a member of society. As moral rules are rules for the behavior of members of society to each other, they cannot be made for behavior toward what is not yet a member. Excluded from the society of men, the fetus is excluded from the humanity of men.

By force of the argument from the consequences, this distinction is to be rejected. It is more subtle than that founded on an appeal to physical sensation, but it is equally dangerous in its implications. If humanity depends on social recognition, individuals or whole groups may be dehumanized by being denied any status in their society. Such a fate is fictionally portrayed in *1984* and has actually been the lot of many men in many societies. In the Roman empire, for example, condemnation to slavery meant the practical denial of most human rights; in the Chinese Communist world, landlords have been classified as enemies of the people and so treated as nonpersons by the state. Humanity does not depend on social recognition, though often the failure of society to recognize the prisoner, the alien, the heterodox as human has led to the destruction of human beings. Anyone conceived by a man and a woman is human. Recognition of this condition by society follows a real event in the objective order, however imperfect and halting the recognition. Any attempt to limit humanity to exclude some group runs the risk of furnishing authority and precedent for excluding other groups in the name of the consciousness or perception of the controlling group in the society.

A philosopher may reject the appeal to the humanity of the fetus because he views "humanity" as a secular view of the soul and because he doubts the existence of anything real and objective which can be identified as humanity. One answer to such a philosopher is to ask how he reasons about moral questions without supposing that there is a sense in which he and the others of whom he speaks are human. Whatever group is taken as the society which determines who may be killed is thereby taken as human. A second answer is to ask if he does not believe that there is a right and wrong way of deciding moral questions. If there is such a difference, experience may be appealed to: to decide who is human on the basis of the sentiment of a given society has led to consequences which rational men would characterize as monstrous.

The rejection of the attempted distinctions based on viability and visibility, experience and feeling, may be buttressed by the following considerations: Moral judgments often rest on distinctions, but if the distinctions are not to appear arbitrary fiat, they should relate to some real difference in probabilities. There is a kind of continuity in all life, but the earlier stages of the elements of human life possess tiny probabilities of development. Consider, for example, the spermatozoa in any normal ejaculate: There are about 200,000,000 in any single ejaculate, of which one has a chance of developing into a zygote. Consider the oocytes which may become ova: there are 100,000 to 1,000,000 oocytes in a female infant, of which a maximum of 390 are ovulated. But once spermatozoon and ovum meet and the conceptus is formed, such studies as have been made show that roughly in only 20 percent of the cases will spontaneous abortion occur. In other words, the chances are about 4 out of 5 that this new being will develop. At this stage in the life of the being there is a sharp shift in probabilities, an immense jump in potentialities. To make a distinction between the rights of spermatozoa and the rights of the fertilized ovum is to respond to an enormous shift in possibilities. For about twenty days after conception the egg may split to form twins or combine with another egg to form a chimera, but the probability of either event happening is very small.

It may be asked, What does a change in biological probabilities have to do with establishing humanity? The argument from probabilities is not aimed at establishing humanity but at establishing an objective discontinuity which may be taken into account in moral discourse. As life itself is a matter of probabilities, as most moral reasoning is an estimate of probabilities, so it seems in accord with the structure of reality and the nature of moral thought to found a moral judgment on the change in probabilities at conception. The appeal to probabilities is the most commensensical of arguments, to a greater or smaller degree all of us base our actions on probabilities, and in morals, as in law, prudence and negligence are often measured by the account one has taken of the probabilities. If the chance is 200,000,000 to 1 that the movement in the bushes into which you shoot is a man's, I doubt if many persons would hold you careless in shooting; but if the chances are 4 out of 5 that the movement is a human being's, few would acquit you of blame. Would the argument be different if only one out of ten children conceived came to term? Of course this argument would be different. This argument is an appeal to probabilities that actually exist, not to any and all states of affairs which may be imagined.

The probabilities as they do exist do not show the humanity of the embryo in the sense of a demonstration in logic any more than the probabilities of the movement in the bush being a man demonstrate beyond all doubt that the being is a man. The appeal is a "buttressing" consideration, showing the plausibility of the standard adopted. The argument focuses on the decisional factor in any moral judgment and assumes that part of the business of a moralist is drawing lines. One evidence of the nonarbitrary character of the line drawn is the difference of probabilities on either side of it. If a spermatozoon is destroyed, one destroys a being which had a chance of far less than 1 in 200 million of developing into a reasoning being, possessed of the genetic code, a heart and other organs, and capable of pain. If a fetus is destroyed, one destroys a being already possessed of the genetic code, organs, and sensitivity to pain, and one which had an 80 percent chance of developing further into a baby outside the womb who, in time, would reason.

The positive argument for conception as the decisive moment of humanization is that at conception the new being receives the genetic code. It is this genetic information which determines his characteristics, which is the biological carrier of the possibility of human wisdom, which makes him a self-evolving being. A being with a human genetic code is man.

This review of current controversy over the humanity of the fetus emphasizes what a fundamental question the theologians resolved in asserting the inviolability of the fetus. To regard the fetus as possessed of equal rights with other humans was not, however, to decide every case where abortion might be employed. It did decide the case where the argument was that the fetus should be aborted for its own good. To say a being was human was to say it had a destiny to decide for itself which could not be taken from it by another man's decision. But human beings with equal rights often come in conflict with each other, and some decision must be made as whose claims are to prevail. Cases of conflict involving the fetus are different only in two respects: the total inability of the fetus to speak for itself and the fact that the right of the fetus regularly at stake is the right to life itself.

The approach taken by the theologians to these conflicts was articulated in terms of "direct" and "indirect." Again, to look at what they were doing from outside their categories, they may be said to have been drawing lines or "balancing values." "Direct" and "indirect" are spatial metaphors; "line-drawing" is another. "To weigh" or "to balance" values is a metaphor of a more complicated mathematical sort hinting at the process which goes on in moral judgments. All the metaphors suggest that, in the moral judgments made, comparisons were necessary, that no value completely controlled. The principle of double effect was no doctrine fallen from heaven, but a method of analysis appropriate where two relative values were being compared. In Catholic moral theology, as it developed, life even of the innocent was not taken as an absolute. Judgments on acts affecting life issued from a process of weighing. In the weighing, the fetus was always given a value greater than zero, always a value separate and independent from its parents. This valuation was crucial and fundamental in all Christian thought on the subject and marked it off from any approach which considered that only the parents' interests needed to be considered.

Even with the fetus weighed as human, one interest could be weighed as equal or superior: that of the mother in her own life. The casuists between 1450 and 1895 were willing to weigh this interest as superior. Since 1895, that interest was given decisive weight only in the two special cases of the cancerous uterus and the ectopic pregnancy. In both of these cases the fetus itself had little chance of survival even if the abortion were not performed. As the balance was once struck in favor of the mother whenever her life was endangered, it could be so struck again. The balance reached between 1895 and 1930 attempted prudentially and pastorally to forestall a multitude of exceptions for interests less than life.

The perception of the humanity of the fetus and the weighing of fetal rights against other human rights constituted the work of the moral analysts. But what spirit animated their abstract judgments? For the Christian community it was the injunction of Scripture to love your neighbor as yourself. The fetus as human was a neighbor; his life had parity with one's own. The commandment gave life to what otherwise would have been only rational calculation.

The commandment could be put in humanistic as well as theological terms: Do not injure your fellow man without reason. In these terms, once the humanity of the fetus is perceived, abortion is never right except in self-defense. When life must be taken to save life, reason alone cannot say that a mother must prefer a child's life to her own. With this exception, now of great rarity, abortion violates the rational humanist tenet of the equality of human lives.

For Christians the commandment to love had received a special imprint in that the exemplar proposed of love was the love of the Lord for his disciples. In the light given by this example, self-sacrifice carried to the point of death seemed in the extreme situations not without meaning. In the less extreme cases, preference for one's own interests to the life of another seemed to express cruelty or selfishness irreconcilable with the demands of love.

R. M. Hare

Abortion and the Golden Rule

If philosophers are going to apply ethical theory successfully to practical issues, they must first have a theory. This may seem obvious; but they often proceed as if it were not so. A philosopher's chief contribution to a practical issue should be to show us which are good and which are bad arguments; and to do this he has to have some way of telling one from the other. Moral philosophy therefore needs a basis in philosophical logic—the logic of the moral concepts. But we find, for example, Professor Judith Jarvis Thomson, in an article on abortion which has been justly praised for the ingenuity and liveliness of her examples, proceeding as if this were not necessary at all.[1] She simply parades the examples before us and asks what we would say about them. But how do we know whether what we feel inclined to say has any secure ground? May we not feel inclined to say it just because of the way we were brought up to think? And was this necessarily the right way? It is highly diverting to watch the encounter in the same volume between her and Mr. John Finnis, who, being a devout Roman Catholic, has intuitions which differ from hers (and mine) in the wildest fashion.[2] I just do not know how to tell whether Mr. Finnis is on safe ground when he claims that suicide is "a paradigm case of an action that is always wrong"; nor Professor Thomson when she makes the no doubt

From *Philosophy and Public Affairs* 4, 3 (Spring 1975). Reprinted by permission of the author and Princeton University Press. Copyright © 1975 by R. M. Hare.

more popular claim that we have a right to decide what happens in and to our own bodies.[3] How would we choose between these potentially conflicting intuitions? Is it simply a contest in rhetoric?

In contrast, a philosopher who wishes to contribute to the solution of this and similar practical problems should be trying to develop, on the basis of a study of the moral concepts and their logical properties, a theory of moral reasoning that will determine which arguments we ought to accept. Professor Thomson might be surprised to see me saying this, because she thinks that I am an emotivist,[4] in spite of the fact that I devoted two of the very first papers I ever published to a refutation of emotivisim.[5] Her examples are entertaining, and help to show up our prejudices; but they will do no more than that until we have a way of telling which prejudices ought to be abandoned.

II

I shall abjure two approaches to the question of abortion which have proved quite unhelpful. The first puts the question in terms of the "rights" of the fetus or the mother; the second demands, as a necessary condition for solving the problem, an answer to the question, Is the fetus a person? The first is unhelpful at the moment, because nobody has yet proposed an even plausible account of how we might argue conclusively about rights. Rights are the stamping ground of intuitionists, and it would be difficult to find any claim confidently asserted to a right which could not be as confidently countered by a claim to another right, such that both rights cannot simultaneously be complied with. This is plainly true in the present controversy, as it is in the case of rights to property—one man has a right not to starve, another a right to hold on to the money that would buy him food. Professor Thomson evidently believes in property rights, because she curiously bases the right of a woman to decide what happens in and to her own body on her ownership of it. We might ask whether, if this is correct, the property is disposable; could it be held that by the marriage contract a wife and a husband yield up to each other some of their property rights in their own bodies? If so, might we find male chauvinists who were prepared to claim that, if the husband wants to have an heir, the wife cannot claim an absolute liberty to have an abortion? As a question of law, this could be determined by the courts and the legislature; but as a question of morals. . . ?

In the law, cash value can be given to statements about rights by translating them into statements about what it is or is not lawful to do. An analogous translation will have to be effected in morals, with "right" (adjective), "wrong," and "ought" taking the place of "lawful" and "unlawful," before the word "rights" can be a dependable prop for moral arguments. It may be that one day somebody will produce a theory of rights which links the concept firmly to those of "right," "wrong," and "ought"—concepts whose logic is even now a *little* better understood. The simplest such theory would be one which said that A has a right, in one sense of the word, to do X if and only if it is not wrong for A to do X; and that A has a right, in another sense, to do X if and only if it is wrong to prevent A from doing X; and that A has a right to do X in a third sense if and only if it is wrong not to assist A to do X (the extent of the assistance, and the persons from whom it is due, being unspecified and, on many occasions of the use of this ambiguous word "rights," unspecifiable). It is often unclear, when people claim that women have a right to do what they like with their own bodies, which of these senses is being used. (Does it, for example, mean that it is not wrong for them to terminate their own pregnancies, or that it is wrong to stop them from doing this, or that it is wrong not to assist them in doing this?) For our present purposes it is best to leave these difficulties on one side and say that *if* at some future time a reliable analysis of the various senses of "rights" in terms of "wrong" or "ought" is forthcoming, then arguments about rights will be restatable in terms of what it is wrong to do, or what we ought or ought not to do. Till that happy day comes, we shall get the issues in better focus if we discuss them directly in terms of what we ought or ought not to do, or what it would be right or wrong to do, to the fetus or the mother in specified circumstances.

III

The other unhelpful approach, that of asking whether the fetus is a person, has been so universally popular that in many of the writings it is assumed that this question is the key to the whole problem. The reason for this is easy to see; if there is a well-established moral principle that the intentional killing of other innocent persons is always murder, and therefore wrong, it looks as if an easy way to determine whether it is wrong to kill fetuses is to determine whether they are persons, and thus settle once for all whether they are subsumable under the principle. But this approach has run into well-known difficulties, the basic reason for which is the following. If a normative or evaluative principle is framed in terms of a predicate which has fuzzy edges (as nearly all predicates in practice have), then we are not going to be able to use the principle to decide cases on the borderline without doing some more normation or evaluation. If we make a law forbidding the use of wheeled vehicles in the park, and somebody thinks he can go in the park on roller skates, no amount of cerebration, and no amount of inspection of roller skates, is going to settle for us the question of whether roller skates are wheeled vehicles "within the meaning of the Act" if the Act has not specified whether they are; the judge has to decide whether they are *to be* counted as such. And this is a further determination of the law.[6] The judge may have very good reasons of public interest or morals for his decision; but he cannot make it by any physical or metaphysical investigation of roller skates to see whether they are *really* wheeled vehicles. If he had not led too sheltered a life, he knew all he needed to know about roller skates before the case ever came to court.

In the same way the decision to say that the fetus becomes a person at conception, or at quickening, or at birth, or whenever takes your fancy, and that thereafter, because it is a person, destruction of it is murder, is inescapably a moral decision, for which we have to have moral reasons. It is not necessary, in order to make this point, to insist that the word "person" is a moral word; though in many contexts there is much to be said for taking this line. It is necessary only to notice that "person," even if descriptive, is not a fully determinate concept; it is loose at the edges, as the abortion controversy only too clearly shows. Therefore, if we decide that, "within the meaning of" the principle about murder, a fetus becomes a person as soon at it is conceived, we are deciding a moral question, and ought to have a moral reason for our decision. It is no use looking more closely at the fetus to satisfy ourselves that it is *really* a person (as the people do who make so much of the fact that it has arms and legs); we already have all the information that we need about the fetus. What is needed is thought about the moral question, How ought a creature, about whose properties, circumstances, and probable future we are quite adequately informed, to be treated? If, in our desire to get out of addressing ourselves to this moral question—to get it settled for us without any moral thought on our part—we go first to the physicians for information about whether the fetus is really a person, and then, when they have told us all they can, to the metaphysicians, we are only indulging in the well-known vice of philosophers (which my fellow linguistic philosophers, at any rate, ought to be on their guard against because that is the mainstay of our training)—the vice of trying to settle substantial questions by verbal maneuvers.

I am not saying that physiological research on the fetus has no bearing on moral questions about abortion. If it brought to light, for example, that fetuses really do suffer on the same scale as adults do, then that would be a good moral reason for not causing them to suffer. It will not do to show that they wriggle when pricked, for so do earthworms; and I do not think that the upholders of the rights of unborn children wish to extend these rights to earthworms. Encephalograms are better; but there are enormous theoretical and practical difficulties in the argument from encephalograms to conscious experiences. In default of these latter, which would have to be of such a sort as to distinguish fetuses radically from other creatures which the antiabortionists would not lift a finger to protect, the main weight of the antiabortionist argument is likely to rest, not on the sufferings of the fetus, but on harms done to the interests of the person into whom the fetus would normally develop. These will be the subject of most of the rest of this paper.

Approaching our moral question in the most general way, let us ask whether there is *anything* about the fetus *or* about the person it may turn into that should make us say that we ought not to kill it. If, instead of asking this question, somebody wants to go on asking, indirectly, whether the fetus is a person, and whether, *therefore*, killing it is wrong, he is at liberty to do so; but I must point out that the reasons he will have to give for saying that it is a person, and that, therefore, killing it is wrong (or that it is not a person and, therefore, killing it is not wrong) will be the very same moral reasons as I shall be giving for the answer to my more direct question. Whichever way one takes it, one cannot avoid giving a reasoned answer to this moral question; so why not take it the simplest way? To say that the fetus is (or is not) a person gives *by itself* no moral reason for or against killing it; it merely encapsulates any reasons we may have for including the fetus within a certain category of creatures that it is, or is not, wrong to kill (that is, persons or nonpersons). The word "person" is doing no work here (other than that of bemusing us).

IV

Is there then anything about the fetus which raises moral problems about the legitimacy of killing it? At this point I must declare that I have no axe to grind—I am not a fervent abortionist nor a fervent antiabortionist—I just want fervently to get to the root of the matter. It will be seen, as the argument goes on, that the first move I shall make is one which will give cheer to the antiabortionists; but, before they have had time to celebrate, it will appear that this move brings with it, inescapably, another move which should encourage the other side. We shall end up somewhere in between, but perhaps with a clearer idea of how, in principle, to set about answering questions about particular abortions.

The single, or at least the main, thing about the fetus that raises the moral question is that, if not terminated, the pregnancy is highly likely to result in the birth and growth to maturity of a person just like the rest of us. The word "person" here reenters the argument, but in a context and with a meaning that does not give rise to the old troubles; for it is clear at least that we ordinary adults are persons. If we knew beyond a peradventure that a fetus was going to miscarry anyway, then little would remain of the moral problem beyond the probably minimal sufferings caused to the mother and just possibly the fetus by terminating the pregnancy now. If, on the other hand, we knew (to use Professor Tooley's science-fiction example[7]) that an embryo kitten would, if not aborted but given a wonder drug, turn into a being with a human mind like ours, then that too would raise a moral problem. Perhaps Tooley thinks not; but we shall see. It is, to use his useful expression, the "potentiality" that the fetus has of becoming a person in the full ordinary sense that creates the problem. It is because Tooley thinks that, once the "potentiality principle" (see below) is admitted, the conservatives or extreme antiabortionists will win the case hands down, that he seeks reasons for rejecting it; but, again, we shall see.

We can explain why the potentiality of the fetus for becoming a person raises a moral problem if we appeal to a type of argument which, in one guise or another, has been the formal basis of almost all theories of moral reasoning that have contributed much that is worthwhile to our understanding of it. I am alluding to the Christian (and indeed pre-Christian) "Golden Rule," the Kantian Categorical Imperative, the ideal-observer theory, the rational-contractor theory, various kinds of utilitarianism, and my own universal prescriptivism.[8] I would claim that the last of these gives the greatest promise of putting what is common to all these theories in a perspicuous way, and so revealing their justification in logic; but it is not the purpose of this paper to give this justification. Instead, since the problem of abortion is discussed as often as not from a Christian standpoint, and since I hope thereby to find a provisional starting point for the argument on which many would agree, I shall use that form of the argument which rests on the Golden Rule that we should do to others as we wish them to do to us.[9] It is a logical extension of this form of argument to say that we should do to others what *we are glad was* done to us. Two (surely readily admissible) changes are involved here. The first is a mere difference in the two tenses which cannot be morally relevant. Instead of saying that we should do to others as we wish them (in the future) to do to us, we say that we should do to others as we wish they had done to us (in the past). The second is a change from the hypothetical to the actual: instead of saying that we should do to others as we are glad that they did do to us. I cannot see that this could make any difference in the spirit of the injunction, and logical grounds could in any case be given, based on the universal prescriptivist thesis, for extending the Golden Rule in this way.

The application of this injunction to the problem of abortion is obvious. If we are glad that nobody terminated the pregnancy that resulted in *our* birth, then we are enjoined not, *ceteris paribus*, to terminate any pregnancy which will result in the birth of a person having a life like ours. Close attention obviously needs to be paid to the "*ceteris paribus*" clause, and also to the expression "like ours." The "universalizability" of moral judgments, which is one of the logical bases of the Golden Rule, requires us to make the same moral judgment about qualitatively identical cases, and about cases which are *relevantly* similar. Since no cases in this area are going to be qualitatively *identical*, we shall have to rely on relevant similarity. Without raising a very large topic in moral philosophy, we can perhaps avoid the difficulty by pointing out that the relevant respects here are going to be those things about our life which make us glad that we were born. These can be stated in a general enough way to cover all those persons who are, or who are going to be or would be, glad that they were born. Those who are not glad they were born will still have a reason for not aborting those who would be glad; for even the former wish that, if they had been going to be glad that they were born, nobody should have aborted them. So, although I have, for the sake of simplicity, put the injunction in a way that makes it apply only to the abortion of people who will have a life just like that of the aborter, it is generalizable to cover the abortion of any fetus which will, if not aborted, turn into someone who will be glad to be alive.

I now come back to Professor Tooley's wonder kitten. He says that if it became possible by administering a wonder drug to an embryo kitten to cause it to turn into a being with a human mind like ours, we should still not feel under any obligation either to administer the drug to kittens or to refrain from aborting kittens to whom the drug had been administered by others. He uses this as an argument against the "potentiality principle," which says that if there are any properties which are possessed by adult human beings and which endow any organisms possessing them with a serious right to life, then "at least one of those properties will be such that any organism *potentially* possessing that property has a serious right to life even now, simply by virtue of that potentiality, where an organism possesses a property potentially if it will come to have that property in the normal course of its development."[10] Putting this more briefly and in terms of "wrong" instead of "rights," the potentiality principle says that if it would be wrong to kill an adult human being because he has a certain property, it is wrong to kill an organism (for example, a fetus) which will come to have that property if it develops normally.

There is one minor objection to what Tooley says which we can pass over quickly. The administration of wonder drugs is not normal development; so Tooley ought not to have used the words "in the normal course of its development"; they spoil his "kitten" example. But let us amend our summary of his principle by omitting the words "if it develops normally" and substituting "if we do not kill it." I do not think that this substitution makes Tooley's argument any weaker than it is already.

Now suppose that I discovered that I myself was the result of the administration of the wonder drug to a kitten embryo. To make this extension of the example work, we have to suppose that the drug is even more wonderful and can make kitten embryos grow into beings with human bodies as well as minds; but it is hard to see how this could make any moral difference, especially for Tooley, who rests none of his argument on bodily shape. If this happened, it would not make my reasons for being glad that I was not aborted cease to apply. I certainly prescribe that they should not have aborted an embryo kitten which the wonder drug was going to turn into *me*. And so, by the Golden Rule, I must say that I should not abort an embryo kitten to whom the wonder drug had been administered and which therefore was going to turn into a creature just like me. And, for what it is worth, this is what I would say. The fact that I confidently assert this, whereas Tooley confidently asserts the opposite—so confidently, in fact, that he thinks that this single example is enough to establish his entire case against the potentiality principle, and produces no other—just shows how inadequate intuitions are as a guide to moral conclusions. The fantastic nature of his example (like that of some of Professor Thomson's) makes it even more difficult to be certain that we are saying what we *should* say about it. Our intuitions are the result of our upbringings, and we were not brought up on cases where kittens can be turned into beings with human minds, or where people get kidnapped and have distinguished violinists with kidney failure plugged into their bloodstreams, in Professor Thomson's example.

The problem becomes more difficult if we ask whether the same argument could be used to establish that it would be wrong, if this wonder drug were invented, not to administer it to all the embryo kittens one could get hold of. I shall postpone discussion of this problem until we have discussed the similar problem of whether the potentiality principle, once established, will not force upon us an extreme conservative position not only about abortion but also about contraception, and even forbid chastity. If we allow the potentiality of procreating human beings to place upon us obligations to procreate them, shall we not have a duty to procreate all the human beings that we can, and will not even monks and nuns have to obey King Lear's injunction to "let copulation thrive"?[11] To the general problem which this raises I shall return. We shall see that it is simply the familiar problem about the right population policy, which has to be faced whatever view we take of the present question.

V

I propose to take it as established that the potentiality principle is *not* refuted by Tooley's one example, and that it therefore holds the field until somebody produces a better argument against it—which I do not expect to happen, because the potentiality principle itself can be based on the Golden Rule, as the examples already considered show, and the Golden Rule has a secure logical foundation which I have already mentioned, though I have not had room to expound it.

Why does Tooley think that, if the potentiality principle is once granted, the extreme conservative position on abortion becomes impregnable? Obviously because he has neglected to consider some other potential beings. Take, to start with, the next child that this mother will have if this pregnancy is terminated but will not have if this pregnancy is allowed to continue. Why will she not have it? For a number of alternative reasons. The most knockdown reason would be that the mother would die or be rendered sterile if this pregnancy were allowed to continue. Another would be that the parents had simply decided, perhaps for morally adequate reasons, that their family would be large enough if and when this present fetus was born. I shall be discussing later the morality of family limitation; for the moment I shall assume for the sake of argument that it is morally all right for parents to decide, after they have had, say, fifteen children, not to have any more, and to achieve this modest limitation of their family by remaining completely chaste.

In all these cases there is, in effect, a choice between having this child now and having another child later. Most people who oppose abortion make a great deal of the wrongness of stopping the birth of this child but say nothing about the morality of stopping the birth of the later child. My own intuition (on which I am by no means going to rely) is that they are wrong to make so big a distinction. The basis of the distinction is supposed to be that the fetus already exists as a single living entity all in one place, whereas the possible future child is at the moment represented only by an unfertilized ovum and a sperm which may or may not yet exist in the father's testes. But will this basis support so weighty a distinction?

First, why is it supposed to make a difference that the genetic material which causes the production of the future child and adult is in two different places? If I have a duty to open a certain door, and two keys are required to unlock it, it does not seem to me to make any difference to my duty that one key is already in the lock and the other in my trousers. This, so far, is an intuition, and I place no reliance on it; I introduce the parallel only to remove some prejudices. The real argument is this: when I am glad that I was born (the basis, it will be remembered, of the argument that the Golden Rule therefore places upon me an obligation not to stop others being born) I do not confine this gladness to gladness that they did not abort me. I am glad, also, that my parents copulated in the first place, without contraception. So from my gladness, in conjunction with the extended Golden Rule, I derive not only a duty not to abort, but also a duty not to abstain from procreation. In the choice-situation that I have imagined, in which it is either this child or the next one but not both, I cannot perform both these duties. So, in the words of a wayside pulpit reported to me by Mr. Anthony Kenny, "if you have conflicting duties, one of them isn't your duty." But which?

I do not think that any general answer can be given to this question. If the present fetus is going to be miserably handicapped if it grows into an adult, perhaps because the mother had rubella, but there is every reason to suppose that the next child will be completely normal and as happy as most people, there would be reason to abort this fetus and proceed to bring to birth the next child, in that the next child will be much gladder to be alive than will this one. The Golden Rule does not directly guide us in cases where we cannot help failing to do to *some* others what we wish were done to us, because if we did it to some, we should thereby prevent ourselves from doing it to others. But it can guide us indirectly, if further extended by a simple maneuver, to cover what I have elsewhere called "multilateral" situations. We are to do to the others affected, taken together, what we wish were done to us if we had to be all of them by turns in random order.[12] In this case, by terminating this pregnancy, I get, on this scenario, no life at all in one of my incarnations and a happy life in the other; but by not terminating it, I get a miserable life in one and no life at all in the other. So I should choose to terminate. In order to reach this conclusion it is not necessary to assume, as we did, that the present fetus will turn into a person who will be positively miserable; only that that person's expectation of happiness is so much less than the expectation of the later possible person that the other factors (to be mentioned in a moment) are outweighed.

In most cases, the probability that there will be another child to replace this one is far lower than that this fetus will turn into a living child. The latter probability is said in normal cases to be about 80 percent; the probability of the next child being born may be much lower (the parents may separate; one of them may die or become sterile; or they may just change their minds about having children). If I do not terminate in such a normal case, I get, on the same scenario, an 80 percent chance of a normal happy life in one incarnation, and no chance at all of any life in the other; but if I do terminate, I get a much lower chance of a normal happy life in the second incarnation and no chance at all in the first. So in this case I should not terminate. By applying this kind of scenario to different cases, we get a way of dramatizing the application of the Golden Rule to them. The cases will all be different, but the relevance of the differences to the moral decision becomes clearer. It is these differences in probabilities of having a life, and of having a happy one, that justify, first of all the presumptive policy, which most people would follow, that abortions in general ought to be avoided, and secondly the exceptions to this policy that many people would now allow—though of course they will differ in their estimation of the probabilities.

I conclude, therefore, that the establishment of the potentiality principle by no means renders impregnable the extreme conservative position, as Tooley thinks it does. It merely creates a rebuttable or defeasible presumption against abortion, which is fairly easily rebutted if there are good indications. The interests of the mother may well, in many cases, provide such good indications, although, because hers is not the only interest, we have also to consider the others. Liberals can, however, get from the present form of argument all that they could reasonably demand, since in the kinds of cases in which they would approve of termination, the interests of the mother will usually be predominant enough to tip the balance between those of the others affected, including potential persons.

The effect of this argument is to bring the morality of contraception and that of abortion somewhat closer together. Important differences will remain, however. There is the fact that the fetus has a very good chance of turning into a normal adult if allowed to develop, whereas the chance that a single coitus will have that result is much lower. Further, if a general duty to produce children be recognized (as the view I have suggested requires), to kill a fetus means the nonfulfillment of this duty for a much longer period (the period from its begetting to the begetting of the next child, if any), whereas, if you do not beget a child now, you may five minutes later. Thirdly, parents become attached to the child in the womb (hence the argument, "We should all think differently if wombs were transparent"), and therefore an abortion may (whatever the compensating good) do some harm to them in addition to that (if any) done to the prospective child that is aborted; this is not so if they merely refrain from procreation. These differences are enough to account for the moral gap between contraception and abortion which will be found in the intuitions of most people; one has to be very extreme in one's views either to consider contraception as sinful as abortion or to think of abortion as *just* another alternative to contraception.

We must now consider some possible objections to this view. Some of these rest on supposed conflicts with received opinion. I shall not deal at great length with these, for a number of reasons. The first is that it would be hard at the moment to point to any at all generally received opinion about abortion. But even if we could, it is a difficult question in moral philosophy, which I have discussed at length elsewhere,[13] how much attention should be paid to received opinion on moral issues. I will sum up my view, without defending it. It is that there are two levels of moral thinking. The first (level 1) consists in the application of learnt principles, which, in order to be learnt, have to be *fairly* general and simple; the second (level 2) consists in the criticism, and possibly the modification, of these general principles in the light of their effect in particular cases, actual and imagined. The purpose of this second, reflective kind of thinking is to select those general principles for use in the first kind of thinking which will lead to the nearest approximation, if generally accepted and inculcated, to the results that would be achieved if we had the time and the information and the freedom from self-deception to make possible the practice of level-2 thinking in every single case. The intuitions which many moral philosophers regard as the final court of appeal are the result of their upbringing—that is, of the fact that just these level-1 principles were accepted by those who most influenced them. In discussing abortion, we ought to be doing some level-2 thinking; it is therefore quite futile to appeal to those level-1 intuitions that we happen to have acquired. It is a question, not of what our intuitions *are,* but of what they *ought to be*—a question which can usefully be dramatized by asking, What opinions about abortion ought we to be teaching to our children?

This may help to answer two objections which often crop up. The first claims that common opinion makes a larger moral distinction between failure to procreate and killing a fetus than the present view would warrant. Sometimes this distinction is said to be founded on the more general one between omissions and acts. There are strong arguments against the moral relevance of this last distinction;[14] and if we are always careful to compare like with like in our examples, and apply the Golden Rule to them, we shall not obtain any morally relevant difference between acts and omissions, provided that we are engaged in level-2 thinking. However, it may well be that the level-1 principles, which we selected as a result of this thinking, *would* use the distinction between acts and omissions. The reason for this is that, although this distinction is philosophically very puzzling and even suspect, it is operable by the ordinary man at the commonsense level; moreover, it serves to separate from each other classes of cases which a more refined thinking would also separate, but would do so only as a result of a very protracted investigation which did not itself make use of the act-omission distinction. So the act-omission distinction serves as a useful surrogate for distinctions which really are morally relevant, although it itself is not. Thus there may be no morally relevant distinction, so far as the Golden Rule goes, between killing and failing to keep alive *in otherwise identical cases;* but if people have ingrained in them the principle that it is wrong to kill innocent adults, but not always so wrong to fail to keep them alive, they are more likely in practice to do the right thing than if their ingrained principles made no such distinction. This is because most cases of killing differ from most cases of failing to keep alive in *other* crucial ways, such that the former are very much more likely to be wrong than the latter. And in the case of abortion and failure to procreate, it is *possible* (I do not say that it is so) that the best level-1 principles for practical use would make bigger distinctions at birth and at conception than a refined level-2 thinking could possibly support. The reason is that conception and birth are dividing lines that are easily discerned by the ordinary man and that therefore a level-1 principle which uses these dividing lines in order to draw the moral line (what moral line?) *may* lead in practice to the morally best results. But if we are arguing (as we are) whether or not this is so, appeals to the intuitions of the ordinary man are entirely beside the point.

Second, we have the "thin end of the wedge" or "slippery slope" objection. If we sanction contraception, why not abortion; and if abortion, why not infanticide; and if infanticide, why not the murder of adults? As an argument against the too ready abandonment of accepted general level-1 principles this argument has some force; for, psychologically speaking, if the ordinary man or the ordinary doctor has got hold of some general principles about killing, which serve well enough in the ordinary run, and then somebody tells him that these principles ought not to be followed universally, it may well be that he will come to disregard them in cases where he ought not. The argument can be overplayed—I do not think that many doctors who have come to accept abortion are thereby made any more prone to murder their wives) but at this level the argument has *some* force, especially if, in the upbringing of the ordinary man and the ordinary doctor, enormous stress has been laid on general principles of great rigidity—such principles are naturally susceptible to thin ends of wedges. But when we are disputing at level 2 about what our level-1 principles ought to be, the argument has little force. For it may be that we could devise other, equally simple principles which would be wedge-resistant and would draw lines in different places; it may be that we *ought* to do this, if the new places were more likely, if generally recognized, to lead most often to the right results in practice. Tooley recommends such a moral line very shortly *after* birth, and his arguments have a great attraction.[15] For the present, it is enough to say that if the line proved wedge-resistant and if it separated off, in a workable manner, nearly all the cases that would be pronounced wrong by level-2 thinking from nearly all those which would be pronounced permissible, then it would be no argument against this proposal that it conflicted with people's intuitions. These intuitions, like earlier ones which made a big distinction at quickening, are the results of attempts to simplify the issues for a laudable practical purpose; they cannot without circularity be used in an appraisal of themselves. As Tooley implies, we have to find real moral reasons for distinguishing cases. If, as is sure to happen, the distinctions that result are very complicated, we have to simplify them for ordinary use as best we can, and there is no reason to assume that the simplifications which will be best are those which have been current hitherto—certainly not in a context in which circumstances have changed as radically as they have with regard to abortion.

VII

It might be objected, as we have seen, that the view I have advocated would require unlimited procreation, on the ground that not to produce any single child whom one might have produced lays one open to the charge that one is not doing to that child as one is glad has been done to oneself (namely, causing him to be born). But there are, even on the present view, reasons for limiting the population. Let us suppose that fully grown adults were producible ad lib, not by gestation in human mothers or in the wombs of cats or in test tubes, but instantaneously by waving a wand. We should still have to formulate a population policy for the world as a whole, and for particular societies and families. There would be a point at which the additional member of each of these units imposed burdens on the other members great enough in sum to outweigh the advantage gained by the additional member. In utilitarian terms, the classical or total utility principle sets a limit to population which, although higher than the average utility principle, is nevertheless a limit.[16] In terms of the Golden Rule, which is the basis of my present argument, even if the "others" to whom we are to do what we wish, or what we are glad, to have done to us are to include potential people, good done to them may be outweighed by harm done to other actual or potential people. If we had to submit to all their lives or nonlives in turn, we should have a basis for choosing a population policy which would not differ from that yielded by the classical utility principle. How restrictive this policy would be would depend on assumptions about the threshold effects of certain increases in population size and density. I think myself that even if potential people are allowed to be the objects of duties, the policy will be fairly restrictive; but this is obviously not the place to argue for this view.

One big gap in the argument of this paper is my failure to deal with the question of whether, when we are balancing the interests of the potential person into whom this fetus will turn against the interests of other people who might be born, we ought to limit the second class to other members of the same family, or include in it *any* potential person who might in some sense "replace" the first-mentioned potential person. This major question would seem to depend for its answer on a further question: To what extent will the birth or non-birth of *this* person make more or less likely the birth or non-birth of the others? This is a demographic question which at the moment baffles me; but it would obviously have to be gone into in any exhaustive account of the morality of abortion. I have, however, written (possibly too hastily) as if only other potential members of the same family need to be considered. That was enough to illustrate the important principle that I was trying to explain.

VIII

Lastly, a logician might object that these potential people do not exist, and cannot be identified or individuated, and therefore cannot be the objects of duties. If I had put my own view in terms of rights or interests, the same objections could be expressed by saying that only actual people have these. Two points can be made against this objection at once. The first is a perhaps superficial one: it would be strange if there were an act whose very performance made it impossible for it to be wrong. But if the objection were correct, the act of aborting a possible person would be such an act; by preventing the existence of the object of the wrongdoing, it would remove its wrongness. This seems too easy a way of avoiding crime.

Second, there seems to be no objection in principle to condemning hypothetical acts: it would have been wrong for Nixon to stay on any longer in the presidency. And it seems a fairly safe principle that if it makes sense to make value judgments about an act that was done, it makes equal sense to make opposite judgments about the hypothetical omission to do that act. "Nixon did right to resign" makes sense; and so, therefore, does "Nixon would have done wrong not to resign." But we do commend actions which resulted in our own existence—every Sunday in thousands of churches we give thanks for our creation as well as for our preservation and all the blessings of this life; and Aristotle says that we ought to show the same gratitude to our earthly fathers as "causes for our being."[17] So it is at least meaningful to say of God or of our fathers that if they had not caused us to exist, they would not have been doing as well for us as they could. And this is all that my argument requires.

Coming now to the purely logical points, we notice that the nonactuality of the potential person (the supposed object of the duty to procreate or not abort) is a separate issue from his nonidentifiability. Unfortunately "identifiable" is an ambiguous word; in one sense I can identify the next man to occupy my carrel at the library by describing him thus, but in another sense I cannot identify him because I have no idea who he is. The person who will be born if these two people start their coitus in precisely five minutes is identified by that description; and so, therefore, is the person who would have been born if they had started it five minutes ago. Moreover (this is an additional point) if we had enough mechanical and other information, we could specify the hair color and all the other traits of that person, if we wished, with as much precision as we could the result of a lottery done on a computer whose randomizing mechanism we could minutely inspect. In this sense, therefore, the potential person is identifiable. We do not know who he will be, in the sense that we do not know what actually now existing person he will be, because he will not be identical with any actually now existing person. But it is hard to see how his inability to meet this logically unmeetable demand for identifiability with some already existing person affects the argument; he is identifiable in the sense that identifying reference can be made to him. So it cannot be nonidentifiability that is the trouble.

Is it then nonactuality? Certainly not *present* nonactuality. We can do harm to, and wrong, succeeding generations by using up all the world's resources or by releasing too much radioactive material. But suppose that this not merely made them miserable, but actually stopped them being born (for example, that the radioactive material made everybody sterile all at once). As before it seems that we can be thankful that our fathers did not do this, thereby stopping us coming into existence; why cannot we say, therefore, that if we behave as well as our fathers, we shall be doing well by our children or grandchildren, or that if we were to behave in this respect worse than our fathers, we would be doing worse by our children or grandchildren. It seems strange to say that if we behaved only a little worse, so that the next generation was half the size it would have been, we had done badly for that generation, but that if we behaved much worse, so that the succeeding generation was reduced to nil, we had not done badly for it at all.

This is obviously a very perplexing matter, and needs much more discussion. All I can hope to do here is to cast doubt on the assumption that some people accept without question, namely, that one cannot harm a person by preventing him coming into existence. True, he does not exist to be harmed; and he is not *deprived* of existence, in the sense of having it taken away from him, though he is *denied* it. But if it would have been a good for him to exist (because this made possible the good that, once he existed, he was able to enjoy), surely it was a harm to him not to exist, and so not to be able to enjoy these goods. He did not suffer; but there were enjoyments he could have had and did not.

IX

I conclude, then, that a systematic application of the Christian Golden Rule yields the following precepts about abortion. It is prima facie and in general wrong in default of sufficient countervailing reasons. But since the wrongness of it consists, in the main, of stopping a person coming into existence and not in any wrong done to the fetus as such, such countervailing reasons are not too hard to find in many cases. And if the termination of this pregnancy facilitates or renders possible or probable the beginning of another more propitious one, it really does not take much to justify it.

I have not discussed what the law on abortion ought to be; that question would have to be the subject of another paper. I have been speaking only about the morality of terminating individual pregnancies. I will end as I began by saying that my argument has been based on a developed ethical theory, though I have not had room to expound this theory (I have done it in my books). This theory provides the logical basis of the Golden Rule. Though not *founded on* a utilitarian principle, it also provides the basis for a certain sort of utilitiarianism that escapes the vices which have been decried in some other sorts.[18] But I shall not now try to defend these last assertions. If they are challenged, and if the view that I have advanced in this paper is challenged, the issue can only be fought out on the terrain of ethical theory itself. That is why it is such a pity that so many people—even philosophers —think that they can discuss abortion without making up their minds about the fundamental problems of moral philosophy.

NOTES

1. Judith Jarvis Thomson, "A Defense of Abortion," *Philosophy & Public Affairs* 1, no. 1 (Fall 1971). Reprinted in *The Rights and Wrongs of Abortion*, ed. Marshall Cohen, Thomas Nagel, and Thomas Scanlon (Princeton, N.J., 1974), hereafter cited as *RWA*; and reprinted herein, 201–17.

2. John Finnis, "The Rights and Wrongs of Abortion: A Reply to Judith Thomson," *Philosphy & Public Affairs* 2, (Winter 1973); reprinted in *RWA*.

3. Finnis, "Rights and Wrongs," 129; *RWA*, 97. Thomson, "Defense," herein, 310.

4. Judith Jarvis Thomson and Gerald Dworkin, *Ethics* (New York, 1968), 2. Cf. D. A. J. Richards, *Chicago Law Review* 41 (1973): 71, for a similar misunderstanding. I am most grateful to Professor Richards for clearing up this misunderstanding in his article "Free Speech and Obscenity Law," in *University of Pennsylvania Law Review* 123 (1974), n. 225.

5. "Imperative Sentences," *Mind* 58 (1949), reprinted in my *Practical Inferences* (London, 1971); "Freedom of the Will," *Aristotelian Society Supp.* 25 (1951), reprinted in my *Essays on the Moral Concepts* (London, 1972).

6. Cf. Aristotle, *Nicomachean Ethics* 5, 1137b20. I owe the roller-skate example to H. L. A. Hart.

7. "Abortion and Infanticide," *Philosophy & Public Affairs* 2, no. 1 (Fall 1972): 60; *RWA*, 75. It will be clear what a great debt I owe to this article.

8. See my "Rules of War and Moral Reasoning," *Philosophy & Public Affairs* 1, no. 2 (Winter 1972), n. 3; reprinted in *War and Moral Responsibility*, ed. Marshall Cohen, Thomas Nagel, and Thomas Scanlon (Princeton, N.J., 1974). See also my review of John Rawls, *A Theory of Justice*, in *Philosophical Quarterly* 23 (1973): 154f.; and my "Ethical Theory and Utilitarianism," in *Contemporary British Philosophy*, vol. 3, ed. H.D. Lewis (Atlantic Highlands, N.J.: Humanities Press, 1976).

9. Matthew 7:12. There have been many misunderstandings of the Golden Rule, some of which I discuss in my "Euthanasia: A Christian View," lecture at the State University College of New York at Brockport, *Philosophical Exchange* 2 (Summer 1975), 43–52.

10. Tooley, "Abortion and Infanticide," 55; *RWA*, 70–71 (my italics).

11. Act 4, sc. 6.

12. See C. I. Lewis, *An Analysis of Knowledge and Valuation* (La Salle, Ill., 1946), 547; D. Haslett, *Moral Rightness* (The Hague, 1974), ch. 3. Cf. my *Freedom and Reason* (Oxford, 1963), 123.

13. See "The Argument from Received Opinion," in my *Essays of Philosophical Method* (London, 1971); "Principles," *Aristotelian Society* 72 (1972–73); and my "Ethical Theory and Utilitarianism."

14. Tooley, "Abortion and Infanticide," 59; *RWA*, 74. See also J. C. B. Glover's *Causing Death and Saving Lives* (New York: Penguin Books, 1979)

15. Tooley, 64; *RWA*, 79. If the potentiality principle be granted, the number of permissible infanticides is greatly reduced, but not to nothing. See my "Survival of the Weakest," in *Documentation in Medical Ethics* 2 (1973); reprinted in *Moral Problems in Medicine*, ed. S. Gorovitz et al. (Englewood Cliffs, N.J.: Prentice-Hall, 1976).

16. See my review of Rawls, 224f.

17. *Nicomachean Ethics* 8, 1161a17, 1163a6, 1165a23.

18. See my "Ethical Theory and Utilitarianism."

Mary Anne Warren

On the Moral and Legal Status
of Abortion

The question which we must answer in order to produce a satisfactory solution to the problem of the moral status of abortion is this: How are we to define the moral community, the set of beings with full and equal moral rights, such that we can

From *The Monist* 57, 1 (January 1973). "Postscript on Infanticide" from *Today's Moral Problems* edited by Richard Wasserstrom (New York: Macmillan, 1975). Reprinted by permission of the author and publishers.

decide whether a human fetus is a member of this community or not? What sort of entity, exactly, has the inalienable rights to life, liberty, and the pursuit of happiness? Jefferson attributed these rights to all *men*, and it may or may not be fair to suggest that he intended to attribute them *only* to men. Perhaps he ought to have attributed them to all human beings. If so, then we arrive, first, at Noonan's problem of defining what makes a being human, and, second, at the equally vital question which Noonan does not consider, namely, What reason is there for identifying the moral community with the set of all human beings, in whatever way we have chosen to define that term.

1   ON THE DEFINITION OF "HUMAN"

One reason why this vital second question is so frequently overlooked in the debate over the moral status of abortion is that the term "human" has two distinct, but not often distinguished, senses. This fact results in a slide of meaning, which serves to conceal the fallaciousness of the traditional argument that since (1) it is wrong to kill innocent human beings, and (2) fetuses are innocent human beings, then (3) it is wrong to kill fetuses. For if "human" is used in the same sense in both (1) and (2) then, whichever of the two senses is meant, one of these premises is question-begging. And if it is used in two different senses then of course the conclusion doesn't follow.

Thus, (1) is a self-evident moral truth,[1] and avoids begging the question about abortion, only if "human being" is used to mean something like "a full-fledged member of the moral community." (It may or may not also be meant to refer exclusively to members of the species *Homo sapiens*.) We may call this the *moral* sense of "human." It is not to be confused with what we will call the *genetic* sense, i.e., the sense in which *any* member of the species is a human being, and no member of any other species could be. If (1) is acceptable only if the moral sense is intended, (2) is non-question-begging only if what is intended is the genetic sense.

In "Deciding Who Is Human," Noonan argues for the classification of fetuses with human beings by pointing to the presence of the full genetic code, and the potential capacity for rational thought.[2] It is clear that what he needs to show, for his version of the traditional argument to be valid, is that fetuses are human in the moral sense, the sense in which it is analytically true that all human beings have full moral rights. But, in the absence of any argument showing that whatever is genetically human is also morally human, and he gives none, nothing more than genetic humanity can be demonstrated by the presence of the human genetic code. And, as we will see, the *potential* capacity for rational thought can at most show that an entity has the potential for *becoming* human in the moral sense.

2   DEFINING THE MORAL COMMUNITY

Can it be established that genetic humanity is sufficient for moral humanity? I think that there are very good reasons for not defining the moral community in this way. I would like to suggest an alternative way of defining the moral community, which I will argue for only to the extent of explaining why it is, or should be, self-evident. The suggestion is simply that the moral community consists of all and only *people,* rather than all and only human beings;[3] and probably the best way of demonstrating its self-evidence is by considering the concept of personhood, to see what sorts of entity are and are not persons, and what the decision that a being is or is not a person implies about its moral rights.

What characteristics entitle an entity to be considered a person? This is obviously not the place to attempt a complete analysis of the concept of personhood, but we do not need such a fully adequate analysis just to determine whether and why a fetus is or isn't a person. All we need is a rough and approximate list of the most basic criteria of personhood, and some idea of which, or how many, of these an entity must satisfy in order to properly be considered a person.

In searching for such criteria, it is useful to look beyond the set of people with whom we are acquainted, and ask how we would decide whether a totally alien being was a person or not. (For we have no right to assume that genetic humanity is necessary for personhood.) Imagine a space traveler who lands on an unknown planet and encounters a race of beings utterly unlike any he has ever seen or heard of. If he wants to be sure of behaving morally toward these beings, he has to somehow decide whether they are people, and hence have full moral rights, or whether they are the sort of thing which he need not feel guilty about treating as, for example, a source of food.

How should he go about making this decision? If he has some anthropological background, he might look for such things as religion, art, and the manufacturing of tools, weapons, or shelters, since these factors have been used to distinguish our human from our prehuman ancestors, in what seems to be closer to the moral than the genetic sense of "human." And no doubt he would be right to consider the presence of such factors as good evidence that the alien beings were people, and morally human. It would, however, be overly anthropocentric of him to take the absence of these things as adequate evidence that they were not, since we can imagine people who have progressed beyond, or evolved without ever developing, these cultural characteristics.

I suggest that the traits which are most central to the concept of personhood, or humanity in the moral sense, are, very roughly, the following:

1. consciousness (of objects and events external and/or internal to the being), and in particular the capacity to feel pain;

2. reasoning (the *developed* capacity to solve new and relatively complex problems);

3. self-motivated activity (activity which is relatively independent of either genetic or direct external control);

4. the capacity to communicate, by whatever means, messages of an indefinite variety of types, that is, not just with an indefinite number of possible contents, but on indefinitely many possible topics;

5. the presence of self-concepts, and self-awareness, either individual or racial, or both.

Admittedly, there are apt to be a great many problems involved in formulating precise definitions of these criteria, let alone in developing universally valid behavioral criteria for deciding when they apply. But I will assume that both we and our explorer know approximately what (1)–(5) mean, and that he is also able to determine whether or not they apply. How, then, should he use his findings to decide whether or not the alien beings are people? We needn't suppose that an entity must have *all* of these attributes to be properly considered a person; (1) and (2) alone may well be sufficient for personhood, and quite probably (1)–(3) are sufficient. Neither do we need to insist that any one of these criteria is *necessary* for personhood, although once again (1) and (2) look like fairly good candidates for necessary conditions, as does (3), if "activity" is construed so as to include the activity of reasoning.

All we need to claim, to demonstrate that a fetus is not a person, is that any being which satisfies *none* of (1)–(5) is certainly not a person. I consider this claim to be so obvious that I think anyone who denied it, and claimed that a being which satisfied none of (1)–(5) was a person all the same, would thereby demonstrate that he had no notion at all of what a person is—perhaps because he had confused the concept of a person with that of genetic humanity. If the opponents of abortion were to deny the appropriateness of these five criteria, I do not know what further arguments would convince them. We would probably have to admit that our conceptual schemes were indeed irreconcilably different, and that our dispute could not be settled objectively.

I do not expect this to happen, however, since I think that the concept of a person is one which is very nearly universal (to people), and that it is common to both proabortionists and antiabortionists, even though neither group has fully realized the relevance of this concept to the resolution of their dispute. Futhermore, I think that on reflection even the antiabortionists ought to agree not only that (1)–(5) are central to the concept of personhood, but also that it is a part of this concept that all and only people have full moral rights. The concept of a person is in part a moral concept; once we have admitted that *x* is a person we have recognized, even if we have not agreed to respect, *x*'s right to be treated as a member of the moral community. It is true that the claim that *x* is a *human being* is more commonly voiced as part of an appeal to treat *x* decently than is the claim that *x* is a person, but this is either because "human being" is here used in the sense which implies personhood, or because the genetic and moral senses of "human" have been confused.

Now if (1)–(5) are indeed the primary criteria of personhood, then it is clear that genetic humanity is neither necessary nor sufficient for establishing that an entity is a person. Some human beings are not people, and there may well be people who are not human beings. A man or woman whose consciousness has been permanently obliterated but who remains alive is a human being which is no longer a person; defective human beings, with no appreciable mental capacity, are not and presumably never will be people; and a fetus is a human being which is not yet a person, and which therefore cannot coherently be said to have full moral rights. Citizens of the next century should be prepared to recognize highly advanced, self-aware robots or computers, should such be developed, and intelligent inhabitants of other worlds, should such be found, as people in the fullest sense, and to respect their moral rights. But to ascribe full moral rights to an entity which is not a person is as absurd as to ascribe moral obligations and responsibilities to such an entity.

3 FETAL DEVELOPMENT AND THE RIGHT TO LIFE

Two problems arise in the application of these suggestions for the definition of the moral community to the determination of the precise moral status of a human fetus. Given that the paradigm example of a person is a normal adult human being, then (1) How like this paradigm, in particular how far advanced since conception, does a human being need to be before it begins to have a right to life by virtue, not of being fully a person as of yet, but of being *like* a person? and (2) To what extent, if any, does the fact that a fetus has the *potential* for becoming a person endow it with some of the same rights? Each of these questions requires some comment.

In answering the first question, we need not attempt a detailed consideration of the moral rights of organisms which are not developed enough, aware enough, intelligent enough, etc., to be considered people, but which resemble people in some respects. It does seem reasonable to suggest that the more like a person, in the relevant respects, a being is, the stronger is the case for regarding it as having a right to life, and indeed the stronger its right to life is. Thus we ought to take seriously the suggestion that, insofar as "the human individual develops biologically in a continuous fashion . . . the rights of a human person might develop in the same way."[4] But we must keep in mind that the attributes which are relevant in determining whether or not an entity is enough like a person to be regarded as having some of the same moral rights are no different from those which are relevant to determining whether or not it is fully a person—i.e., are no different from (1)–(5)—and that being genetically human, or having recognizably human facial and other physical features, or detectable brain activity, or the capacity to survive outside the uterus, are simply not among these relevant attributes.

Thus it is clear that even though a seven- or eight-month fetus has features which make it apt to arouse in us almost the same powerful protective instinct as is commonly aroused by a small infant, nevertheless it is not significantly more personlike than is a very small embryo. It is *somewhat* more personlike; it can apparently feel and respond to pain, and it may even have a rudimentary form of consciousness, insofar as its brain is quite active. Nevertheless, it seems safe to say that it is not fully conscious, in the way that an infant of a few months is, and that it cannot reason, or communicate messages of indefinitely many sorts, does not engage in self-motivated activity, and has no self-awareness. Thus, in the *relevant* respects, a fetus, even a fully developed one, is considerably less personlike than is the average mature mammal, indeed the average fish. And I think that a rational person must conclude that if the right to life of a fetus is to be based upon its resemblance to a person, then it cannot be said to have any more right to life than, let us say, a newborn guppy (which also seems to be capable of feeling pain), and that a right of that magnitude could never override a woman's right to obtain an abortion, at any stage of her pregnancy.

There may, of course, be other arguments in favor of placing legal limits upon the stage of pregnancy in which an abortion may be performed. Given the relative safety of the new techniques of artificially inducing labor during the third trimester, the danger to the woman's life or health is no longer such an argument. Neither is the fact that people tend to respond to the thought of abortion in the later stages of pregnancy with emotional repulsion, since mere emotional responses cannot take the place of moral reasoning in determining what ought to be permitted. Nor, finally, is the frequently heard argument that legalizing abortion, especially late in the pregnancy, may erode the level of respect for human life, leading, perhaps, to an increase in unjustified euthanasia and other crimes. For this threat, if it is a threat, can be better met by educating people to the kinds of moral distinctions which we are making here than by limiting access to abortion (which limitation may, in its disregard for the rights of women, be just as damaging to the level of respect for human rights).

Thus, since the fact that even a fully developed fetus is not personlike enough to have any significant right to life on the basis of its personlikeness shows that no legal restrictions upon the stage of pregnancy in which an abortion may be performed can be justified on the grounds that we should protect the rights of the older fetus, and since there is no other apparent justification for such restrictions, we may conclude that they are entirely unjustified. Whether or not it would be *indecent* (whatever that means) for a woman in her seventh month to obtain an abortion just to avoid having to postpone a trip to Europe, it would not, in itself, be *immoral*, and therefore it ought to be permitted.

4 POTENTIAL PERSONHOOD AND THE RIGHT TO LIFE

We have seen that a fetus does not resemble a person in any way which can support the claim that it has even some of the same rights. But what about its *potential*, the fact that if nurtured and allowed to develop naturally it will very probably become a person? Doesn't that alone give it at least some right to life? It is hard to deny that the fact than an entity is a potential person is a strong prima facie reason for not destroying it; but we need not conclude from this that a potential person has a right to life, by virtue of that potential. It may be that our feeling that it is better, other things being equal, not to destroy a potential person is better explained by the fact that potential people are still (felt to be) an invaluable resource, not to be lightly squandered. Surely, if every speck of dust were a potential person, we would be much less apt to conclude that every potential person has a right to become actual.

Still, we do not need to insist that a potential person has no right to life whatever. There may well be something immoral, and not just imprudent, about wantonly destroying potential people, when doing so isn't necessary to protect anyone's rights. But even if a potential person does have some prima facie right to life, such a right could not possibly outweigh the right of a woman to obtain an abortion, since the rights of any actual person invariably outweigh those of any potential person, whenever the two conflict. Since this may not be immediately obvious in the case of a human fetus, let us look at another case.

Suppose that our space explorer falls into the hands of an alien culture, whose scientists decide to create a few hundred thousand or more human beings, by breaking his body into component cells, and using these to create fully developed human beings, with, of course, his genetic code. We may imagine that each of these newly created men will have all of the original man's abilities, skills, knowledge, and so on, and also have an individual self-concept, in short that each of them will be a bona fide (though hardly unique) person. Imagine that the whole project will take only seconds, and that its chances of success are extremely high, and that our explorer knows all of this, and also knows that these people will be treated fairly. I maintain that in such a situation he would have every right to escape if he could, and thus to deprive all of these potential people of their potential lives; for his right to life outweighs all of theirs together, in spite of the fact that they are all genetically human, all innocent, and all have a very high probability of becoming people very soon, if only he refrains from acting.

Indeed, I think he would have a right to escape even if it were not his life which the alien scientists planned to take, but only a year of his freedom, or, indeed, only a day. Nor would he be obligated to stay if he had gotten captured (thus bringing all these people-potentials into existence) because of his own carelessness, or even if he had done so deliberately, knowing the consequences. Regardless of how he got captured, he is not morally obligated to remain in captivity for *any* period of time for the sake of permitting any number of potential people to come into actuality, so great is the margin by which one actual person's right to liberty outweighs whatever right to life even a hundred thousand potential people have. And it seems reasonable to conclude that the rights of a woman will outweigh by a similar margin whatever right to life a fetus may have by virtue of its potential personhood.

Thus, neither a fetus's resemblance to a person, nor its potential for becoming a person provides any basis whatever for the claim that it has any significant right to life. Consequently, a woman's right to protect her health, happiness, freedom, and even her life,[5] by terminating an unwanted pregnancy, will always override whatever right to life it may be appropriate to ascribe to a fetus, even a fully developed one. And thus, in the absence of any overwhelming social need for every possible child, the laws which restrict the right to obtain an abortion, or limit the period of pregnancy during which an abortion may be performed, are a wholly unjustified violation of a woman's most basic moral and constitutional rights.[6]

POSTSCRIPT ON INFANTICIDE

Since the publication of this article, many people have written to point out that my argument appears to justify not only abortion, but infanticide as well. For a newborn infant is not significantly more personlike than an advanced fetus, and consequently it would seem that if the destruction of the latter is permissible so too must be that of the former. Inasmuch as most people, regardless of how they feel about the morality of abortion, consider infanticide a form of murder, this might appear to represent a serious flaw in my argument.

Now, if I am right in holding that it is only people who have a full-fledged right to life, and who can be murdered, and if the criteria of personhood are as I have described them, then it obviously follows that killing a newborn infant isn't murder. It does *not* follow, however, that infanticide is permissible, for two reasons, In the first place, it would be wrong, at least in this country and in this period of history and other things being equal, to kill a newborn infant, because even if its parents did not want it and would not suffer from its destruction, there are other people who would like to have it, and would, in all probability, be deprived of a great deal of pleasure by its destruction. Thus, infanticide is wrong for reasons analogous to those which make it wrong to wantonly destroy natural resources, or great works of art.

Secondly, most people, at least in this country, value infants and would much prefer that they be preserved, even if foster parents are not immediately available. Most of us would rather be taxed to support orphanages than allow unwanted infants to be destroyed. So long as there are people who want an infant preserved, and who are willing and able to provide the means of caring for it, under reasonably humane conditions, it is *ceteris paribus*, wrong to destroy it.

But, it might be replied, if this argument shows that infanticide is wrong, at least at this time and in this country, doesn't it also show that abortion is wrong? After all many people value fetuses, are disturbed by their destruction, and would much prefer that they be preserved, even at some cost to themselves. Furthermore, as a potential source of pleasure to some foster family, a fetus is just as valuable as an infant. There is, however, a crucial difference between the two cases: so long as the fetus is unborn, its preservation, contrary to the wishes of the pregnant woman, violates her rights to freedom, happiness, and self-determination. Her rights override the rights of those who would like the fetus preserved, just as if someone's life or limb is threatened by a wild animal, his right to protect himself by destroying the animal overrides the rights of those who would prefer that the animal not be harmed.

The minute the infant is born, however, its preservation no longer violates any of its mother's rights, even if she wants it destroyed, because she is free to put it up for adoption. Consequently, while the moment of birth does not make any sharp discontinuity in the degree to which an infant possesses the right to life, it does mark the end of its mother's right to determine its fate. Indeed, if abortion could be performed without killing the fetus, she would never possess the right to have the fetus destroyed, for the same reasons that she has no right to have an infant destroyed.

On the other hand, it follows from my argument that when an unwanted or defective infant is born into a society which cannot afford and/or is not willing to care for it, then its destruction is permissible. This conclusion will, no doubt, strike many people as heartless and immoral; but remember that the very existence of people who feel this way, and who are willing and able to provide care for unwanted infants, is reason enough to conclude that they should be preserved.

NOTES

1. Of course, the principle that it is (always) wrong to kill innocent human beings is in need of many other modifications, e.g., that it may be permissible to do so to save a greater number of other innocent human beings, but we may safely ignore these complications here.

2. John Noonan, "Deciding Who is Human," *Natural Law Forum* 13 (1968): 135.

3. From here on, we will use "human" to mean genetically human, since the moral sense seems closely connected to, and perhaps derived from, the assumption that genetic humanity is sufficient for membership in the moral community.

4. Thomas L. Hayes. "A Biological View," *Commonweal* 85 (March 17, 1967): 677–78; quoted by Daniel Callahan, in *Abortion: Law, Choice and Morality* (London: Macmillan, 1970).

5. That is, insofar as the death rate, for the woman, is higher for childbirth than for early abortion.

6. My thanks to the following people, who were kind enough to read and criticize an earlier version of this paper. Herbert Gold, Gene Glass, Anne Lauterbach, Judith Thomson, Mary Mothersill, and Timothy Binkley.

SUGGESTIONS FOR DISCUSSION

1. In what ways is Noonan's view representative of the Natural Law tradition (see Aquinas, Part I, Chapter 1)? How might Noonan defend his view against the criticism that his appeal to statistics commits the fallacy of deriving an "ought" from an "is" (see Hume, Chapter 2)?

2. What is the basis of Hare's criticisms of pro-choice arguments that appeal to "women's rights," and of antiabortion appeals to the "personhood" of the fetus? In what way is Hare's reformulation of the Golden Rule utilitarian (see Part I, Chapter 4)? How does Hare's interpretation of the Golden Rule differ from Noonan's principle "not to injure another without reason"?

3. How might conflicts between the claimed rights of the woman and those of the fetus be resolved on a principled basis (see Mackie, Part I, Chapter 6)?

FURTHER READING

Brody, B. *Abortion and the Sanctity of Human Life*. Cambridge, Mass.: MIT Press, 1975. (Interpretation, critical analysis; intermediate)

Callahan, D. *Abortion: Law, Choice and Morality*. New York: Macmillan, 1970. (Interpretation, critical analysis; intermediate)

Cohen, M., Nagel, T., and Scanlon, T., eds. *Rights and Wrongs of Abortion*. Princeton: Princeton University Press, 1974. (Interpretation, critical analysis; advanced)

Feinberg, J., ed. *The Problem of Abortion*. 2nd ed. Belmont, Calif.: Wadsworth, 1984. (Interpretation, critical analysis; intermediate)

Grisez, G. *Abortion: The Myths, the Realities and the Arguments*. New York: Corpus Books, 1970. (Interpretation, critical analysis; intermediate)

Noonan, J. T., Jr. *How to Argue About Abortion*. New York: Free Press, 1979. (Interpretation, critical analysis; intermediate)

———. *The Morality of Abortion*. Cambridge, Mass.: Harvard University Press, 1970. (Interpretation, critical analysis; intermediate)

Perkins, R. L., ed. *Abortion*. Cambridge, Mass.: Shenkman, 1975. (Interpretation, critical analysis; intermediate)

Quinn, W. "Abortion: Identity and Loss," *Philosophy and Public Affairs* 13, no 1 (Winter, 1984): 24–54. (Critical analysis; advanced)

Sumner, L. W. *Abortion and Moral Theory*. Princeton: Princeton University Press, 1981. (Interpretation, critical analysis; advanced)

Thomson, J. J. "A Defense of Abortion." *Philosophy and Public Affairs* 1 (Fall 1971): 47–66. (Interpretation, critical analysis; intermediate)

Tooley, M. *Abortion and Infanticide*. New York: Oxford University Press, 1983. (Interpretation, critical analysis; advanced)

12

□

Euthanasia

Murder, or the intentional killing of an innocent person, is wrong; and so it is morally impermissible. Nevertheless, we make exceptions for some sorts of killing: Taking another's life in legitimate self-defense, for example, is permissible, for the victim here is not really innocent. The sophistication of medical technology has made possible the extension of human life; yet, the quality of life is not necessarily sustained when it is extended in this way. *Euthanasia* involves terminating the life of an ailing person in order to prevent his or her further suffering. Thus the question whether euthanasia is in any form morally permissible has become especially acute.

Reasons for Euthanasia Since euthanasia is clearly the intentional taking of life, the person who dies is in the relevant sense innocent. So if any act of euthanasia is to be morally permissible, a candidate must be subject at least to the following conditions: The suffering must be present, persistent, and severe; and death must appear reasonably imminent. The sole reason for terminating the person's life must be to end her or his suffering. The clearest cases involve a candidate's uncoerced request to die, either in person and repeatedly or by way of a Living Will. A *Living Will* is a testament drawn up privately, upon cool and quiet deliberation, prior to the onset of terminal illness or incompetence. It expresses the desired treatment in the case of incompetence, and may include a request for terminating life in case of severely debilitating or painful terminal illness. Standard cases where euthanasia may be an option include the suffering of excruciating pain that can no longer be lessened by drugs (as in advanced forms of bone cancer, say, or where a person has first-degree burns over extensive areas of the body); or a patient in an irreversible coma; or a patient suffering advanced forms of senility. In these cases, prospects for any future well-being and enjoyment are minimal.

Classifications: Kinds of Euthanasia Conscious and clear requests for euthanasia are called voluntary. Voluntary euthanasia is distinguished from both involuntary euthanasia and nonvoluntary euthanasia. *Involuntary euthanasia* occurs where a person, despite severe suffering and faced with the prospect of a painful end, expresses the desire *not* to die but is killed or allowed to die anyway; many people would rightfully take this to be murder. The most complicated cases for the morality of euthanasia are those that are *nonvoluntary*. Here patients are incapable of requesting or indicating a desire for death, or of forming judgments in the matter. Standard cases involve comatose or senile patients incapable of rational thought and leaving no Living Will; or defective newborns like those with Down's syndrome or with extreme brain incapacity. (For theoretical elaboration of the distinction between "voluntary" and "involuntary action," see Aristotle, Part I, Chapter 2.)

Many have considered the distinction between *killing* and *letting die* to be crucial in analyzing the moral status of euthanasia. Thus *active euthanasia* involves killing a patient; that is, causing death by administering some lethal (though humane) treatment such as a drug overdose. *Passive euthanasia* involves letting the patient die by withholding or withdrawing all extraordinary treatment that may prolong life. The cause of death would be whatever ailment naturally afflicts the patient, not any artificially administered treatment. *Extraordinary*—as opposed to *ordinary*—means of prolonging life are means that impose an undue burden both on those providing and on those suffering them. Extraordinary means include a respirator, iron lung, or radiation treatment; ordinary means, food or common antibiotics.

Accordingly, six types of euthanasia may be distinguished: voluntary active and voluntary passive; nonvoluntary active and nonvoluntary passive; involuntary active and involuntary passive. Because involuntary active and involuntary passive forms of euthanasia are extreme and are imposed coercively upon persons against their expressed will, they are generally impermissible.

Permissibility of Euthanasia   So, the moral question of euthanasia may be posed in this way. Is it ever permissible to kill persons or let them die voluntarily or nonvoluntarily for and only for their own benefit? It is usually agreed that if any form is permissible, then only *voluntary passive euthanasia* will be. (The American Medical Association permits discontinuing or withholding only "extraordinary" treatment and only where there is undeniable evidence that the patient is about to die. Any act of killing a patient, no matter what the reason, is considered by the AMA to be unjustifiable.) Further, permissibility will be limited to cases where extraordinary life-prolonging treatment can be withheld or withdrawn. Active euthanasia or failure to administer ordinary treatment is generally considered unacceptable. The Karen Quinlan case provides a problematic example.

State Supreme Court Ruling   At twenty-one years old, Karen Quinlan suffered two inexplicable seizures that left her comatose and irreversibly brain-damaged, though not brain-dead. Her father petitioned the New Jersey courts for the respirator to be removed so that Karen might be allowed to die naturally. Though unable at this time to communicate her preferences, Ms. Quinlan had expressed on three earlier occasions that she never wanted her life to be prolonged by extraordinary means. The lower court refused the petition: it found no constitutional "right to die," only a right to life that would be violated by an act of euthanasia. In 1976 the Supreme Court of New Jersey reversed the decision. Chief Justice Hughes ruled that the question of euthanasia in the case of an incompetent concerns the right of privacy. Hughes addressed the issues in terms of two subsidiary rights: the patient's right not to be invaded physically (by painful medical technology), and the right to independent choice. When the patient is incompetent to choose independently, the following conditions must be met if euthanasia is to be permissible. The patient must be known to have expressed this preference in the past; but failing this, the closest family must judge that the patient would have preferred death, and that this preference is consistent with the opinion of the overwhelming majority in the society. Hughes noted that the right of privacy is effective in euthanasia cases in just the way the U.S. Supreme Court took it to be effective in abortion cases (see *Roe v. Wade*, Part II, Chapter 11; on right-based theories, see Mackie, Part I, Chapter 6).

Readings J. Gay-Williams offers one Natural Law argument and two consequentialist arguments against the permissibility of euthanasia (on Natural Law, see Aquinas, Part I, Chapter 1; on consequentialism, see Chapter 4). The Natural Law argument presumes that euthanasia necessarily undermines human dignity. Dignity is achieved by seeking human goals, and a basic natural goal is human survival. Thus euthanasia is contrary to human nature and so inherently wrong. Gay-Williams appeals to consequences in two ways: First, he argues that even the best medical practitioners sometimes make mistakes, and that the possibility of euthanasia causes patients to give up too readily. He concludes that undertaking euthanasia or "mercy-killing" is contrary to self-interest. Second, Gay-Williams contends that euthanasia as a social policy could lead to callousness in the medical profession and to the widespread social abuse of involuntary euthanasia. He suggests that these possible social effects are too dangerous and undesirable to warrant any euthanasia at all.

Philippa Foot differs from Gay-Williams in holding that human life as such is not inherently good. For Foot, the minimal condition for a good life is having a minimum of basic human goods: A life lacking these goods may be a life not worth living. Nevertheless, Foot insists that a life of greater evil suffered than good enjoyed could be a good life. Only if a person suffered unbearably would one think him "better off dead." Given her background conception of a "good life," Foot analyzes the permissibility of euthanasia in terms of the virtues of justice and charity. Justice concerns what people owe each other in respect of not interfering with their respective rights; charity motivates agents to do good for others beyond anything justice may demand. Principles of justice imply that a patient's right to life sets limits to permissible acts of euthanasia. Both forms of involuntary euthanasia are ruled out; but so also is active nonvoluntary euthanasia, for it violates that part of the right to life which guarantees the duty of noninterference. Passive nonvoluntary euthanasia is not ruled out unless the patient has specifically requested life-preserving action. Charity normally requires that the good of life be preserved. However, charity also serves the good of other persons. So there may be circumstances such that, provided rights are not infringed, active or passive voluntary euthanasia would be morally permissible because charitable. In conclusion, Foot urges conservativism at the level of social policy. She advises against liberalizing euthanasia laws because of prospective abuses and adverse social and moral effects.

James Rachels advances four arguments against the standard view that active euthanasia is impermissible while passive euthanasia is sometimes permissible. Rachels argues, first, that if euthanasia is permissible at all, then active killing will be more humane than passive letting die: suffering is relieved more quickly by killing. However, as Foot points out in criticism of an argument like this, a humane act may be unjust or morally objectionable because it infringes upon a person's rights. Rachels argues, second, that the distinction between active and passive euthanasia rests on the basis of *chance* whether a person may live or die. Chance has no moral relevance, and so the distinction based upon it must be irrelevant from the moral point of view, too. Rachels adds, third, that this distinction between active and passive euthanasia presupposes the distinction between killing and letting die. If the latter distinction is to be morally pertinent in any case, it would have to be so in every appropriate case. Rachels shows that it is not. Rachels's fourth argument turns on the claim that to call euthanasia *passive* is misleading, for there is an act here also—that is, one of *letting die*. He concludes that, if there is any difference between active and passive euthanasia, it lies in their respective consequences, and that here the balance favors active euthanasia. Finally, Rachels illustrates the application of two moral theories to the issue of euthanasia. He shows, first, the utilitarian form an argument for justified mercy-killing would have to assume; and second, how the Golden Rule or Kantian categorical imperative justifies active euthanasia in some cases (on utilitarianism, see Part I, Chapter 4; and on Kant's categorical imperative, see Chapter 3).

New Jersey Supreme Court

In the Matter of Karen Quinlan, an Alleged Incompetent

[The opinion of the Court was delivered by Hughes, Chief Justice.]

The central figure in this tragic case is Karen Ann Quinlan, a New Jersey resident. At the age of 22, she lies in a debilitated and allegedly moribund state at Saint Clare's Hospital in Denville, New Jersey. The litigation has to do, in final analysis, with her life—its continuance or cessation—and the responsibilities, rights, and duties, with regard to any fateful decision concerning it, of her family, her guardian, her doctors, the hospital, the State through its law enforcement authorities, and finally the courts of justice. . . .

New Jersey Supreme Court, 70 *New Jersey Reports* 10 (March 31, 1976).

THE RIGHT OF PRIVACY

It is the issue of the constitutional right of privacy that has given us most concern, in the exceptional circumstances of this case. Here is a loving parent, *qua* parent and raising the rights of his incompetent and profoundly damaged daughter, probably irreversibly doomed to no more than a biologically vegetative remnant of life, is before the court. He seeks authorization to abandon specialized technological procedures which can only maintain for a time a body having no potential for resumption or continuance of other than a "vegetative" existence.

We have no doubt, in these unhappy circumstances, that if Karen were herself miraculously lucid for an interval (not altering the existing prognosis of the condition to which she would soon return) and perceptive of her irreversible condition, she could effectively decide upon discontinuance of the life-support apparatus, even if it meant the prospect of natural death. To this extent we may distinguish [a case] which concerned a severely injured young woman (Delores Heston), whose life depended on surgery and blood transfusion; and who was in such extreme shock that she was unable to express an informed choice (although the Court apparently considered the case as if the patient's own religious decision to resist transfusion were at stake), but most importantly a patient apparently salvable to long life and vibrant health;—a situation not at all like the present case.

... [T]the interests of the patient, as seen by her surrogate, and guardian, must be evaluated by the court as predominant, even in the face of an option *contra* by the present attending physicians. Plaintiff's distinction is significant. The nature of Karen's care and the realistic chances of her recovery are quite unlike those of the patients discussed in many of the cases where treatments were ordered. In many of those cases the medical procedure required (usually a transfusion) constituted a minimal bodily invasion and the chances of recovery and return to functioning life were very good. We think that the State's interest *contra* weakens and the individual's right to privacy grows as the degree of bodily invasion increases and the prognosis dims. Ultimately there comes a point at which the individual's rights overcome the State interest. It is for that reason that we believe Karen's choice, if she were competent to make it, would be vindicated by the law. Her prognosis is extremely poor—she will never resume cognitive life. And the bodily invasion is very great,—she requires 24-hour intensive nursing care, antibiotics, and the assistance of a respirator, a catheter and feeding tube.

Our affirmance of Karen's independent right to choice, however, would ordinarily be based upon her competency to assert it. The sad truth, however, is that she is grossly incompetent and we cannot discern her supposed choice based on the testimony of her previous conversation with friends, where such testimony is without sufficient probative weight. Nevertheless we have concluded that Karen's right of privacy may be asserted on her behalf by her guardian under the peculiar circumstances here present.

If a putative decision by Karen to permit this non-cognitive, vegetative existence to terminate by natural forces is regarded as a valuable incident of her right of privacy, as we believe it to be, then it should not be discarded solely on the basis that her condition prevents her conscious exercise of the choice. The only practical way to prevent destruction of the right is to permit the guardian and family of

Karen to render their best judgment, subject to the qualifications hereinafter stated, as to whether she would exercise it in these circumstances. If their conclusion is in the affirmative this decision should be accepted by a society the overwhelming majority of whose members would, we think, in similar circumstances, exercise such a choice in the same way for themselves or for those closest to them. It is for this reason that we determine that Karen's right of privacy may be asserted in her behalf, in this respect, by her guardian and family under the particular circumstances presented by this record.

DECLARATORY RELIEF

We thus arrive at the formulation of the declaratory relief which we have concluded is appropriate to this case. Some time has passed since Karen's physical and mental condition was described to the Court. At that time her continuing deterioration was plainly projected. Since the record has not been expanded we assume that she is now even more fragile and nearer to death than she was then. Since her present treating physicians may give reconsideration to her present posture in the light of this opinion, and since we are transferring to the plaintiff as guardian the choice of the attending physician and therefore other physicians may be in charge of the case who may take a different view from that of the present attending physicians, we herewith declare the following affirmative relief on behalf of the plaintiff. Upon the concurrence of the guardian and family of Karen, should the responsible attending physicians conclude that there is no reasonable possibility of Karen's ever emerging from her present comatose condition to a cognitive, sapient state and that the life-support apparatus now being administered to Karen should be discontinued, they shall consult with the hospital "Ethics Committee" or like body of the institution in which Karen is then hospitalized. If that consultative body agrees that there is no reasonable possibility of Karen's ever emerging from her present comatose condition to a cognitive, sapient state, the present life-support system may be withdrawn and said action shall be without any civil or criminal liability therefor on the part of any participant, whether guardian, physician, hospital or others. We herewith specifically so hold.

J. Gay-Williams

The Wrongfulness of Euthanasia

My impression is that euthanasia—the idea, if not the practice—is slowly gaining acceptance within our society. Cynics might attribute this to an increasing tendency

From *Intervention and Reflection: Basic Issues in Medical Ethics,* edited by Ronald Munson (Belmont, Calif.: Wadsworth Publishing, 1979). Copyright © 1979 Ronald Munson. Reprinted by permission.

to devalue human life, but I do not believe this is the major factor. The acceptance is much more likely to be the result of unthinking sympathy and benevolence. Well-publicized, tragic stories like that of Karen Quinlan elicit from us deep feelings of compassion. We think to ourselves, "She and her family would be better off if she were dead." It is an easy step from this very human response to the view that if someone (and others) would be better off dead, then it must be all right to kill that person.[1] Although I respect the compassion that leads to this conclusion, I believe the conclusion is wrong. I want to show that euthanasia is wrong. It is inherently wrong, but it is also wrong judged from the standpoints of self-interest and of practical effects.

Before presenting my arguments to support this claim, it would be well to define "euthanasia." An essential aspect of euthanasia is that it involves taking a human life, either one's own or that of another. Also, the person whose life is taken must be someone who is believed to be suffering from some disease or injury from which recovery cannot reasonably be expected. Finally, the action must be deliberate and intentional. Thus, euthanasia is intentionally taking the life of a presumably hopeless person. Whether the life is one's own or that of another, the taking of it is still euthanasia.

It is important to be clear about the deliberate and intentional aspect of the killing. If a hopeless person is given an injection of the wrong drug by mistake and this causes his death, this is wrongful killing but not euthanasia. The killing cannot be the result of accident. Furthermore, if the person is given an injection of a drug that is believed to be necessary to treat his disease or better his condition and the person dies as a result, then this is neither wrongful killing nor euthanasia. The intention was to make the patient well, not kill him. Similarly, when a patient's condition is such that it is not reasonable to hope that any medical procedures or treatments will save his life, a failure to implement the procedures or treatments is not euthanasia. If the person dies, this will be as a result of his injuries or disease and not because of his failure to receive treatment.

The failure to continue treatment after it has been realized that the patient has little chance of benefitting from it has been characterized by some as "passive euthanasia." This phrase is misleading and mistaken.[2] In such cases, the person involved is not killed (the first essential aspect of euthanasia), nor is the death of the person intended by the withholding of additional treatment (the third essential aspect of euthanasia). The aim may be to spare the person additional and unjustifiable pain, to save him from the indignities of hopeless manipulations, and to avoid increasing the financial and emotional burden on his family. When I buy a pencil it is so that I can use it to write, not to contribute to an increase in the gross national product. This may be the unintended consequence of my action, but it is not the aim of my action. So it is with failing to continue the treatment of a dying person. I intend his death no more than I intend to reduce the GNP by not using medical supplies. His is an unintended dying, and so-called "passive euthanasia" is not euthanasia at all.

1. THE ARGUMENT FROM NATURE

Every human being has a natural inclination to continue living. Our reflexes and responses fit us to fight attackers, flee wild animals, and dodge out of the way of trucks. In our daily lives we exercise the caution and care necessary to protect ourselves. Our bodies are similarly structured for survival right down to the molecular level. When we are cut, our capillaries seal shut, our blood clots, and fibrogen is produced to start the process of healing the wound. When we are invaded by bacteria, antibodies are produced to fight against the alien organisms, and their remains are swept out of the body by special cells designed for clean-up work.

Euthanasia does violence to this natural goal of survival. It is literally acting against nature because all the processes of nature are bent towards the end of bodily survival. Euthanasia defeats these subtle mechanisms in a way that, in a particular case, disease and injury might not.

It is possible, but not necessary, to make an appeal to revealed religion in this connection.[3] Man as trustee of his body acts against God, its rightful possessor, when he takes his own life. He also violates the commandment to hold life sacred and never to take it without just and compelling cause. But since this appeal will persuade only those who are prepared to accept that religion has access to revealed truths, I shall not employ this line of argument.

It is enough, I believe, to recognize that the organization of the human body and our patterns of behavioral responses make the continuation of life a natural goal. By reason alone, then, we can recognize that euthanasia sets us against our own nature.[4] Furthermore, in doing so, euthanasia does violence to our dignity. Our dignity comes from seeking our ends. When one of our goals is survival, and actions are taken that eliminate that goal, then our natural dignity suffers. Unlike animals, we are conscious through reason of our nature and our ends. Euthanasia involves acting as if this dual nature—inclination towards survival and awareness of this as an end—did not exist. Thus, euthanasia denies our basic human character and requires that we regard ourselves or others as something less than fully human.

2. THE ARGUMENT FROM SELF-INTEREST

The above arguments are, I believe, sufficient to show that euthanasia is inherently wrong. But there are reasons for considering it wrong when judged by standards other than reason. Because death is final and irreversible, euthanasia contains within it the possibility that we will work against our own interest if we practice it or allow it to be practiced on us.

Contemporary medicine has high standards of excellence and a proven record of accomplishment, but it does not possess perfect and complete knowledge. A mistaken diagnosis is possible, and so is a mistaken prognosis. Consequently, we may believe that we are dying of a disease when, as a matter of fact, we may not be. We may think that we have no hope of recovery when, as a matter of fact, our chances are quite good. In such circumstances, if euthanasia were permitted, we would die needlessly. Death is final and the chance of error too great to approve the practice of euthanasia.

Also, there is always the possibility that an experimental procedure or a hitherto untried technique will pull us through. We should at least keep this option open, but euthanasia closes it off. Furthermore, spontaneous remission does occur in many cases. For no apparent reason, a patient simply recovers when those all around him, including his physicians, expected him to die. Euthanasia would just guarantee their expectations and leave no room for the "miraculous" recoveries that frequently occur.

Finally, knowing that we can take our life at any time (or ask another to take it) might well incline us to give up too easily. The will to live is strong in all of us, but it can be weakened by pain and suffering and feelings of hopelessness. If during a bad time we allow ourselves to be killed, we never have a chance to reconsider. Recovery from a serious illness requires that we fight for it, and anything that weakens our determination by suggesting that there is an easy way out is ultimately against our own interest. Also, we may be inclined towards euthanasia because of our concern for others. If we see our sickness and suffering as an emotional and financial burden on our family, we may feel that to leave our life is to make their lives easier.[5] The very presence of the possibility of euthanasia may keep us from surviving when we might.

3. THE ARGUMENT FROM PRACTICAL EFFECTS

Doctors and nurses are, for the most part, totally committed to saving lives. A life lost is, for them, almost a personal failure, an insult to their skills and knowledge. Euthanasia as a practice might well alter this. It could have a corrupting influence so that in any case that is severe doctors and nurses might not try hard enough to save the patient. They might decide that the patient would simply be "better off dead" and take the steps necessary to make that come about. This attitude could then carry over to their dealings with patients less seriously ill. The result would be an overall decline in the quality of medical care.

Finally, euthanasia as a policy is a slippery slope. A person apparently hopelessly ill may be allowed to take his own life. Then he may be permitted to deputize others to do it for him should he no longer be able to act. The judgment of others then becomes the ruling factor. Already at this point euthanasia is not personal and voluntary, for others are acting "on behalf of" the patient as they see fit. This may well incline them to act on behalf of other patients who have not authorized them to exercise their judgment. It is only a short step, then, from voluntary euthanasia (self-inflicted or authorized), to directed euthanasia administered to a patient who has given no authorization, to involuntary euthanasia conducted as part of a social policy.[6] Recently many psychiatrists and sociologists have argued that we define as "mental illness" those forms of behavior that we disapprove of.[7] This gives us license then to lock up those who display the behavior. The category of the "hopelessly ill" provides the possibility of even worse abuse. Embedded in a social policy, it would give society or its representatives the authority to eliminate all those who might be considered too "ill" to function normally any longer. The dangers of euthanasia are too great to all to run the risk of approving it in any form. The first slippery step may well lead to a serious and harmful fall.

I hope that I have succeeded in showing why the benevolence that inclines us to give approval of euthanasia is misplaced. Euthanasia is inherently wrong because it violates the nature and dignity of human beings. But even those who are not convinced by this must be persuaded that the potential personal and social dangers inherent in euthanasia are sufficient to forbid our approving it either as a personal practice or as a public policy.

Suffering is surely a terrible thing, and we have a clear duty to comfort those in need and to ease their suffering when we can. But suffering is also a natural part of life with values for the individual and for others that we should not overlook. We may legitimately seek for others and for ourselves an easeful death, as Arthur Dyck has pointed out.[8] Euthanasia, however, is not just an easeful death. It is a wrongful death. Euthanasia is not just dying. It is killing.

NOTES

1. For a sophisticated defense of this position see Philippa Foot, "Euthanasia," *Philosophy and Public Affairs* 6 (1977): 85–112. Foot does not endorse the radical conclusion that euthanasia, voluntary and involuntary, is always right.

2. James Rachels rejects the distinction between active and passive euthanasia as morally irrelevant in his "Active and Passive Euthanasia," *New England Journal of Medicine* 292: 78–80. But see the criticism by Foot, 100–103.

3. For a defense of this view see J. V. Sullivan, "The Immorality of Euthanasia," in *Beneficent Euthanasia,* ed. Marvin Kohl (Buffalo: Prometheus Books, 1975), 34–44.

4. This point is made by Ray V. McIntyre in "Voluntary Euthanasia: The Ultimate Perversion," *Medical Counterpoint* 2: 26–29.

5. See McIntyre, 28.

6. See Sullivan, "Immorality of Euthanasia," 34–44, for a fuller argument in support of this view.

7. See, for example, Thomas S. Szasz, *The Myth of Mental Illness,* rev. ed. (New York: Harper & Row, 1974).

8. Arthur Dyck, "Beneficent Euthanasia and Benemortasia," Kohl, op. cit., 117–29.

Philippa Foot

Euthanasia

The widely used *Shorter Oxford English Dictionary* gives three meanings for the word "euthanasia": the first, "a quiet and easy death"; the second, "the means of procuring this"; and the third, "the action of inducing a quiet and easy death." It is a curious fact that not one of the three gives an adequate definition of the word as it is usually understood. For "euthanasia" means much more than a quiet and easy death, or the means of procuring it, or the action of inducing it. The definition specifies only the manner of the death, and if this were all that was implied a murderer, careful to drug his victim, could claim that his act was an act of euthanasia. We find this ridiculous because we take it for granted that in

From *Philosophy and Public Affairs* 6, 2 (1977). This shortened version of the article is reprinted by permission of the author.

euthanasia it is death itself, not just the manner of death, that must be kind to the one who dies.

To see how important it is that "euthanasia" should not be used as the dictionary definition allows it to be used, merely to signify that a death was quiet and easy, one has only to remember that Hitler's "euthanasia" program traded on this ambiguity. Under this program, planned before the War but brought into full operation by a decree of 1 September 1939, some 275,000 people were gassed in centers which were to be a model for those in which Jews were later exterminated. Anyone in a state institution could be sent to the gas chambers if it was considered that he could not be "rehabilitated" for useful work.... These people were killed because they were "useless" and "a burden on society"; only the manner of their deaths could be thought of as relatively easy and quiet.

Let us insist, then, that when we talk about euthanasia we are talking about a death understood as a good or happy event for the one who dies....

...It is easy to say, as if this raised no problems, that an act of euthanasia is by definition one aiming at the *good* of the one whose death is in question, and that it is *for his sake* that his death is desired. But how is this to be explained? Presumably we are thinking of some evil already with him or to come on him if he continues to live, and death is thought of as a release from this evil. But this cannot be enough. Most people's lives contain evils such as grief or pain, but we do not therefore think that death would be a blessing to them. On the contrary life is generally supposed to be a good even for someone who is unusually unhappy or frustrated. How is it that one can ever wish for death for the sake of the one who is to die? This difficult question is central to the discussion of euthanasia, and we shall literally not know what we are talking about if we ask whether acts of euthanasia defined as we have defined them are ever morally permissible without first understanding better the reason for saying that life is a good, and the possibility that it is not always so.

If a man should save my life he would be my benefactor. In normal circumstances this is plainly true; but does one always benefit another in saving his life? It seems certain that he does not. Suppose, for instance, that a man were being tortured to death and was given a drug that lengthened his sufferings; this would not be a benefit but the reverse. Or suppose that in a ghetto in Nazi Germany a doctor saved the life of someone threatened by disease, but that the man once cured was transported to an extermination camp; the doctor might wish for the sake of the patient that he had died of the disease. Nor would a longer stretch of life always be a benefit to the person who was given it. Comparing Hitler's camps with those of Stalin, Dmitri Panin observes that in the latter the method of extermination was made worse by agonies that could stretch out over months.

> Death from a bullet would have been bliss compared with what many millions had to endure while dying of hunger. The kind of death to which they were condemned has nothing to equal it in treachery and sadism.[1]

These examples show that to save or prolong a man's life is not always to do him a service: it may be better for him if he dies earlier rather than later. It must therefore be agreed that while life is normally a benefit to the one who has it, this is not always so.

The judgment is often fairly easy to make—that life is or is not a good to someone—but the basis for it is very hard to find. When life is said to be a benefit or a good, on what grounds is the assertion made?

The difficulty is underestimated if it is supposed that the problem arises from the fact that one who is dead has nothing, so that the good someone gets from being alive cannot be compared with the amount he would otherwise have had. For why should this particular comparison be necessary? Surely it would be enough if one could say whether or not someone whose life was prolonged had more good than evil in the extra stretch of time. Such estimates are not always possible, but frequently they are; we say, for example, "He was very happy in those last years," or "He had little but unhappiness then." If the balance of good and evil determined whether life was a good to someone we would expect to find a correlation in the judgments. In fact, of course, we find nothing of the kind. First, a man who has no doubt that existence is a good to him may have no idea about the balance of happiness and unhappiness in his life, or of any other positive and negative factors that may be suggested. So the supposed criteria are not always operating where the judgment is made. And secondly the application of the criteria gives an answer that is often wrong. Many people have more evil than good in their lives; we do not, however, conclude that we would do these people no service by rescuing them from death.

To get around this last difficulty Thomas Nagel has suggested that experience itself is a good which must be brought in to balance accounts.

> . . . life is worth living even when the bad elements of experience are plentiful, and the good ones too meager to outweigh the bad ones on their own. The additional positive weight is supplied by experience itself, rather than by any of its contents.[2]

This seems implausible because if experience itself is a good it must be so even when what we experience is wholly bad, as in being tortured to death. How should one decide how much to count for this experiencing; and why count anything at all?

Others have tried to solve the problem by arguing that it is a man's desire for life that makes us call life a good: if he wants to live then anyone who prolongs his life does him a benefit. Yet someone may cling to life where we would say confidently that it would be better for him if he died, and he may admit it too. Speaking of those same conditions in which, as he said, a bullet would have been merciful, Panin writes:

> I should like to pass on my observations concerning the absence of suicides under the extremely severe conditions of our concentration camps. The more that life became desperate, the more a prisoner seemed determined to hold onto it.[3]

One might try to explain this by saying that hope was the ground of this wish to survive for further days and months in the camp. But there is nothing unintelligible in the idea that a man might cling to life though he knew those facts about his future which would make any charitable man wish that he might die.

The problem remains, and it is hard to know where to look for a solution. Is there a conceptual connection between *life* and *good*? Because life is not always a good we are apt to reject this idea, and to think that it must be a contingent fact that life is usually a good, as it is a contingent matter that legacies are usually a benefit, if they are. Yet it seems not to be a contingent matter that to save someone's life is ordinarily to benefit him. The problem is to find where the conceptual connection lies.

When are we to say that life is a good or a benefit to a man? The dilemma that faces us is this. If we say that life as such is a good we find ourselves refuted by the examples given at the beginning of this discussion. We therefore incline to think that it is as bringing good things that life is a good, where it is a good. But if life is a good only because it is the condition of good things why is it not equally an evil when it brings bad things? And how can it be a good even when it brings more evil than good?

It should be noted that the problem has here been formulated in terms of the balance of good and evil, not that of happiness and unhappiness, and that it is not to be solved by the denial (which may be reasonable enough) that unhappiness is the only evil or happiness the only good. In this paper no view has been expressed about the nature of goods other than life itself. The point is that on any view of the goods and evils that life can contain, it seems that a life with more evil than good could still itself be a good.

It may be useful to review the judgments with which our theory must square. Do we think that life can be a good to one who suffers a lot of pain? Clearly we do. What about severely handicapped people; can life be a good to them? Clearly it can be, for even if someone is almost completely paralyzed, perhaps living in an iron lung, perhaps able to move things only by means of a tube held between his lips, we do not rule him out of order if he says that some benefactor saved his life. Nor is it different with mental handicap. There are many fairly severely handicapped people —such as those with Down's syndrome (Mongolism)—for whom a simple affectionate life is possible. What about senility? Does this break the normal connection between life and good? Here we must surely distinguish between forms of senility. Some forms leave a life which we count someone as better off having than not having, so that a doctor who prolonged it would benefit the person concerned. With some kinds of senility this is however no longer true. There are some in geriatric wards who are barely conscious, though they can move a little and swallow food put into their mouths. To prolong such a state, whether in the old or in the very severely mentally handicapped is not to do them a service or confer a benefit. But of course it need not be the reverse: only if there is suffering would one wish for the sake of the patient that he should die.

It seems, therefore, that merely being alive even without suffering is not a good, and that we must make a distinction similar to that which we made when animals were our topic. But how is the line to be drawn in the case of men? What is to count as ordinary human life in the relevant sense? If it were only the very senile or very ill who were to be said not to have this life it might seem right to describe it in terms of *operation*. But it will be hard to find the sense in which the men described by Panin were not operating, given that they dragged themselves out to the forest to work. What is it about the life that the prisoners were living that makes us put it on the other side of the dividing line from that of some severely ill or suffering patients, and from most of the physically or mentally handicapped? It is not that they were in captivity, for life in captivity can certainly be a good. Nor is it merely the unusual nature of their life. In some ways the prisoners were living more as other men do than the patient in an iron lung.

The suggested solution to the problem is, then, that there is a certain conceptual connection between *life* and *good* in the case of human beings as in that of animals and even plants. Here, as there, however, it is not the mere state of being alive that can determine, or itself count as, a good, but rather life coming up to some standard of normality. It was argued that it is as part of ordinary life that the elements of good that a man may have are relevant to the question of whether saving his life counts as benefiting him. Ordinary human lives, even very hard lives, contain a minimum of basic goods, but when these are absent the idea of life is no longer linked to that of good. And since it is in this way that the elements of good contained in a man's life are relevant to the question of whether he is benefited if his life is preserved, there is no reason why it should be the balance of good and evil that counts.

It should be added that evils are relevant in one way when, as in the examples discussed above, they destroy the possibility of ordinary goods, but in a different way when they invade a life from which the goods are already absent for a different reason. So, for instance, the connection between *life* and *good* may be broken because consciousness has sunk to a very low level, as in extreme senility or severe brain damage. In itself this kind of life seems to be neither good nor evil, but if suffering sets in one would hope for a speedy end.

The idea we need seems to be that of life which is ordinary human life in the following respect—that it contains a minimum of basic human goods. What is ordinary in human life—even in very hard lives—is that a man is not driven to work far beyond his capacity; that he has the support of a family or community; that he can more or less satisfy his hunger; that he has hopes for the future; that he can lie down to rest at night. Such things were denied to the men in the Vyatlag camps described by Panin; not even rest at night was allowed them when they were tormented by bed-bugs, by noise and stench, and by routines such as body-searches and bath-parades—arranged for the night time so that work norms would not be reduced. Disease too can so take over a man's life that the normal human goods disappear. When a patient is so overwhelmed by pain or nausea that he cannot eat with pleasure, if he can eat at all, and is out of the reach of even the most loving voice, he no longer has ordinary human life in the sense in which the words are used here. And we may now pick up a thread from an earlier part of the discussion by remarking that crippling depression can destroy the enjoyment of ordinary goods as effectively as external circumstances can remove them.

This, admittedly inadequate, discussion of the sense in which life is normally a good, and of the reasons why it may not be so in some particular case, completes the account of what euthanasia is here taken to be. An act of euthanasia, whether literally act or rather omission, is attributed to an agent who opts for the death of another because in his case life seems to be an evil rather than a good. The question now to be asked is whether acts of euthanasia are ever justifiable. But there are two topics here rather than one. For it is one thing to say that some acts of euthanasia considered only in themselves and their results are morally unobjectionable, and another to say that it would be all right to legalize them. Perhaps the practice of euthanasia would allow too many abuses, and perhaps there would be too many mistakes. Moreover the practice might have very important and highly undesirable side effects, because it is unlikely that we could change our principles about the treatment of the old and the ill without changing fundamental emotional attitudes and social relations. The topics must, therefore, be treated separately. In the next part of the discussion, nothing will be said about the social consequences and possible abuses of the practice of euthanasia, but only about acts of euthanasia considered in themselves.

What we want to know is whether acts of euthanasia, defined as we have defined them, are ever morally permissible. To be more accurate, we want to know whether it is ever sufficient justification for the choice of death for another that death can be counted a benefit rather than harm, and that this is why the choice is made.

It will be impossible to get a clear view of the area to which this topic belongs without first marking the distinct grounds on which objection may lie when one man opts for the death of another. There are two different virtues whose requirements are, in general, contrary to such actions. An unjustified act of killing, or allowing to die, is contrary to justice or to charity, or to both virtues, and the moral failings are distinct. Justice has to do with what men *owe* each other in the way of noninterference and positive service. When used in this wide sense, which has its history in the doctrine of the cardinal virtues, justice is not especially connected with, for instance, law courts but with the whole area of rights, and duties corresponding to rights. Thus murder is one form of injustice, dishonesty another, and wrongful failure to keep contracts a third; chicanery in a law court or defrauding someone of his inheritance are simply other cases of injustice. Justice as such is not directly linked to the good of another, and may require that something be rendered to him even where it will do him harm, as Hume pointed out when he remarked that a debt must be paid even to a profligate debauchee who "would rather receive harm than benefit from large possessions."[4] Charity, on the other hand, is the virtue which attaches us to the good of others. An act of charity is in question only where something is not demanded by justice, but a lack of charity and of justice can be shown where a man is denied something which he both needs and has a right to; both charity and justice demand that widows and orphans are not defrauded, and the man who cheats them is neither charitable nor just.

It is easy to see that the two grounds of objection to inducing death are distinct. A murder is an act of injustice. A culpable failure to come to the aid of someone whose life is threatened is normally contrary, not to justice, but to charity. But where one man is under contract, explicit or implicit, to come to the aid of another injustice too will be shown. Thus injustice may be involved either in an act or an omission, and the same is true of a lack of charity; charity may demand that someone be aided, but also that an unkind word not be spoken.

The distinction between charity and justice will turn out to be of the first importance when voluntary and nonvoluntary euthanasia are distinguished later on. . . .

Let us now ask how the right to life affects the morality of acts of euthanasia. Are such acts sometimes or always ruled out by the right to life? This is certainly a possibility; for although an act of euthanasia is, by our definition, a matter of opting for death for the good of the one who is to die, there is, as we noted earlier, no direct connection between that to which a man has a right and that which is for his good. It is true that men have the right only to the kind of thing that is, in general, a good: we do not think that people have the right to garbage or polluted air. Nevertheless, a man may have the right to something which he himself would be better off without; where rights exist it is a man's will that counts not his or anyone else's estimate of benefit or harm. So the duties complementary to the right to life —the general duty of noninterference and the duty of service incurred by certain persons—are not affected by the quality of a man's life or by his prospects. Even if it is true that he would be, as we say, "better off dead," so long as he wants to live this does not justify us in killing him and may not justify us in deliberately allowing him to die. All of us have the duty of noninterference, and some of us may have the duty to sustain his life. Suppose, for example, that a retreating army has to leave behind wounded or exhausted soldiers in the wastes of an arid or snowbound land where the only prospect is death by starvation or at the hands of an enemy notoriously cruel. It has often been the practice to accord a merciful bullet to men in such desperate straits. But suppose that one of them demands that he should be left alive? It seems clear that his comrades have no right to kill him, though it is a quite different question as to whether they should give him a life-prolonging drug. The right to life can sometimes give a duty of positive service, but does not do so here. What it does give is the right to be left alone.

Interestingly enough we have arrived by way of a consideration of the right to life at the distinction normally labeled "active" versus "passive" euthanasia, and often thought to be irrelevant to the moral issue.[5] Once it is seen that the right to life is a distinct ground of objection to certain acts of euthanasia, and that this right creates a duty of noninterference more widespread than the duties of care there can be no doubt about the relevance of the distinction between passive and active euthanasia. Where everyone may have the duty to leave someone alone, it may be that no one has the duty to maintain his life, or that only some people do.

Where then do the boundaries of the "active" and "passive" lie? In some ways the words are themselves misleading, because they suggest the difference between act and omission which is not quite what we want. Certainly the act of shooting someone is the kind of thing we were talking about under the heading of "interference," and omitting to give him a drug a case of refusing care. But the act of turning off a respirator should surely be thought of as no different from the decision not to start it; if doctors had decided that a patient should be allowed to die, either course of action might follow, and both should be counted as passive rather than active euthanasia if euthanasia were in question. The point seems to be that interference in a course of treatment is not the same as other interference in a man's life, and particularly if the same body of people are responsible for the treatment and for its discontinuance. In such a case we could speak of the disconnecting of the apparatus as killing the man, or of the hospital as allowing him to die. By and large, it is the act of killing that is ruled out under the heading of noninterference, but not in every case.

Doctors commonly recognize this distinction, and the grounds on which some philosophers have denied it seem untenable. James Rachels, for instance, believes that if the difference between active and passive is relevant anywhere, it should be relevant everywhere, and he has pointed to an example in which it seems to make no difference which is done. If someone saw a child drowning in a bath it would seem just as bad to let it drown as to push its head under water.[6] If "it makes no difference" means that one act would be as iniquitous as the other this is true. It is not that killing is *worse* than allowing to die, but that the two are contrary to distinct virtues, which gives the possibility that in some circumstances one is impermissible and the other permissible. In the circumstances invented by Rachels, both are wicked: it is contrary to justice to push the child's head under the water—something one has no right to do. To leave it to drown is not contrary to justice, but it is a particularly glaring example of lack of charity. Here it makes no practical difference because the requirements of justice and charity coincide; but in the case of the retreating army they did not: charity would have required that the wounded soldier be killed had not justice required that he be left alive.[7] In such a case it makes all the difference whether a man opts for the death of another in a positive action, or whether he allows him to die. An analogy with the right to property will make the point clear. If a man owns something he has the right to it even when its possession does him harm, and we have no right to take it from him. But if one day it should blow away, maybe nothing requires us to get it back for him; we could not deprive him of it, but we may allow it to go. This is not to deny that it will often be an unfriendly act or one based on an arrogant judgment when we refuse to do what he wants. Nevertheless, we would be within our rights, and it might be that no moral objection of any kind would lie against our refusal.

It is important to emphasize that a man's rights may stand between us and the action we would dearly like to take for his sake. They may, of course, also prevent action which we would like to take for the sake of others, as when it might be tempting to kill one man to save several. But it is interesting that the limits of allowable interference, however uncertain, seem stricter in the first case than the second. Perhaps there are no cases in which it would be all right to kill a man against his will *for his own sake* unless they could equally well be described as cases of allowing him to die, as in the example of turning off the respirator. However, there are circumstances, even if these are very rare, in which one man's life would justifiably be sacrificed to save others, and "killing" would be the only description of what was being done. For instance, a vehicle which had gone out of control might be steered from a path on which it would kill more than one man to a path on which it would kill one.[8] But it would not be permissible to steer a vehicle towards someone in order to kill him, against his will, for his own good. An analogy with property rights illustrates the point. One may not destroy a man's property against his will on the grounds that he would be better off without it; there are however circumstances in which it could be destroyed for the sake of others. If his house is liable to fall and kill him that is his affair; it might, however, without injustice be destroyed to stop the spread of a fire.

We see then that the distinction between active and passive, important as it is elsewhere, has a special importance in the area of euthanasia. It should also be clear why James Rachels' other argument, that it is often "more humane" to kill than to allow to die, does not show that the distinction between active and passive euthanasia is morally irrelevant. It might be "more humane" in this sense to deprive a man of the property that brings evils on him, or to refuse to pay what is owed to Hume's profligate debauchee; but if we say this we must admit that an act which is "more humane" than its alternative may be morally objectionable because it infringes rights.

So far we have said very little about the right to service as opposed to the right to noninterference, though it was agreed that both might be brought under the heading of "the right to life." What about the duty to preserve life that may belong to special classes of persons such as bodyguards, firemen, or doctors? Unlike the general public they are not within their rights if they merely refrain from interfering and do not try to sustain life. The subject's claim-rights are two-fold as far as they are concerned and passive as well as active euthanasia may be ruled out here if it is against his will. This is not to say that he has the right to any and every service needed to save or prolong his life; the rights of other people set limits to what may be demanded, both because they have the right not to be interfered with and because they may have a competing right to services. Furthermore one must enquire just what the contract or implicit agreement amounts to in each case. Firemen and bodyguards presumably have a duty which is simply to preserve life, within the limits of justice to others and of reasonableness to themselves. With doctors it may however be different, since their duty relates not only to preserving life but also to the relief of suffering. It is not clear what a doctor's duties are to his patient if life can be prolonged only at the cost of suffering or suffering relieved only by measures that shorten life. George Fletcher has argued that what the doctor is under contract to do depends on what is generally done, because this is what a patient will reasonably expect.[9] This seems right. If procedures are part of normal medical practice then it seems that the patient can demand them however much it may be against his interest to do so. Once again it is not a matter of what is "most humane."

That the patient's right to life may set limits to permissible acts of euthanasia seems undeniable. If he does not want to die no one has the right to practice active euthanasia on him, and passive euthanasia may also be ruled out where he has a right to the services of doctors or others.

Perhaps few will deny what has so far been said about the impermissibility of acts of euthanasia simply because we have so far spoken about the case of one who positively wants to live, and about his rights, whereas those who advocate euthanasia are usually thinking either about those who wish to die or about those whose wishes cannot be ascertained either because they cannot properly be said to have wishes or because, for one reason or another, we are unable to form a reliable estimate of what they are. The question that must now be asked is whether the latter type of case, where euthanasia though not involuntary would again be nonvoluntary, is different from the one discussed so far. Would we have the right to kill someone for his own good so long as we had no idea that he positively wished to live? And what about the life-prolonging duties of doctors in the same circumstances? This is a very difficult problem. On the one hand, it seems ridiculous to suppose that a man's right to life is something which generates duties only where he has signaled that he wants to live; as a borrower does indeed have a duty to return something lent on indefinite loan only if the lender indicates that he wants it back. On the other hand, it might be argued that there is something illogical about the idea that a right has been infringed if someone incapable of saying whether he wants it or not is deprived of something that is doing him harm rather than good.

Yet on the analogy of property we would say that a right has been infringed. Only if someone had earlier told us that in such circumstances he would not want to keep the thing could we think that his right had been waived. Perhaps if we could make confident judgments about what anyone in such circumstances would wish, or what he would have wished beforehand had he considered the matter, we could agree to consider the right to life as "dormant," needing to be asserted if the normal duties were to remain. But as things are we cannot make any such assumption; we simply do not know what most people would want, or would have wanted, us to do unless they tell us. This is certainly the case so far as active measures to end life are concerned. Possibly it is different, or will become different, in the matter of being kept alive, so general is the feeling against using sophisticated procedures on moribund patients, and so much is this dreaded by people who are old or terminally ill. Once again the distinction between active and passive euthanasia has come on the scene, but this time because most people's attitudes to the two are so different. It is just possible that we might presume, in the absence of specific evidence, that someone would not wish, beyond a certain point, to be kept alive; it is certainly not possible to assume that he would wish to be killed.

In the last paragraph we have begun to broach the topic of voluntary euthanasia, and this we must now discuss. What is to be said about the case in which there is no doubt about someone's wish to die: either he has told us beforehand that he would wish it in circumstances such as he is now in, and has shown no sign of a change of mind, or else he tells us now, being in possession of his faculties and of a steady mind. We should surely say that the objections previously urged against acts of euthanasia, which it must be remembered were all on the ground of rights, had disappeared. It does not seem that one would infringe someone's right to life in killing him with his permission and in fact at his request. Why should someone not be able to waive his right to life, or rather, as would be more likely to happen, to cancel some of the duties of noninterference that this right entails? (He is more likely to say that he should be killed by this man at this time in this manner, than to say that anyone may kill him at any time and in any way.) Similarly someone may give permission for the destruction of his property, and request it. The important thing is that he gives a critical permission, and it seems that this is enough to cancel the duty normally associated with the right. If someone gives you permission to destroy his property it can no longer be said that you have no right to do so, and I do not see why it should not be the case with taking a man's life. An objection might be made on the ground that only God has the right to take life, but in this paper religious as opposed to moral arguments are being left aside. Religion apart, there seems to be no case to be made out for an infringement of rights if a man who wishes to die is allowed to die or even killed. But of course it does not follow that there is no moral objection to it. Even with property, which is after all a relatively small matter, one might be wrong to destroy what one had the right to destroy. For, apart from its value to other people, it might be valuable to the man who wanted it destroyed, and charity might require us to hold our hand where justice did not.

Let us review the conclusion of this part of the argument, which has been about euthanasia and the right to life. It has been argued that from this side come stringent restrictions on the acts of euthanasia that could be morally permissible. Active nonvoluntary euthanasia is ruled out by that part of the right to life which creates the duty of noninterference though passive nonvoluntary euthanasia is not ruled out, except where the right to life-preserving action has been created by some special condition such as a contract between a man and his doctor, and it is not always certain just what such a contract involves. Voluntary euthanasia is another matter: as the preceding paragraph suggested, no right is infringed if a man is allowed to die or even killed at his own request.

Turning now to the other objection that normally holds against inducing the death of another, that it is against charity, or benevolence, we must tell a very different story. Charity is the virtue that gives attachment to the good of others, and because life is normally a good, charity normally demands that it should be saved or prolonged. But as we so defined an act of euthanasia that it seeks a man's death for his own sake—for his good—charity will normally speak in favor of it. This is not, of course, to say that charity can require an act of euthanasia which justice forbids, but if an act of euthanasia is not contrary to justice—that is, it does not infringe rights—charity will rather be in its favor than against.

Once more the distinction between nonvoluntary and voluntary euthanasia must be considered. Could it ever be compatible with charity to seek a man's death although he wanted to live, or at least had not let us know that he wanted to die? It has been argued that in such circumstances active euthanasia would infringe his right to life, but passive euthanasia would not do so, unless he had some special right to life-preserving service from the one who allowed him to die. What would charity dictate? Obviously when a man wants to live there is a presumption that he will be benefited if his life is prolonged, and if it is so the question of euthanasia does not arise. But it is, on the other hand, possible that he wants to live where it would be better for him to die: perhaps he does not realize the desperate situation he is in, or perhaps he is afraid of dying. So, in spite of a very proper resistance to refusing to go along with a man's own wishes in the matter of life and death, someone might justifiably refuse to prolong the life even of someone who asked him to prolong it, as in the case of refusing to give the wounded soldier a drug that would keep him alive to meet a terrible end. And it is even more obvious that charity does not always dictate that life should be prolonged where a man's own wishes, hypothetical or actual, are not known.

So much for the relation of charity to nonvoluntary passive euthanasia, which was not, like nonvoluntary active euthanasia, ruled out by the right to life. Let us now ask what charity has to say about voluntary euthanasia both active and passive. It was suggested in the discussion of justice that if of sound mind and steady desire a man might give others the *right* to allow him to die or even to kill him, where otherwise this would be ruled out. But it was pointed out that this would not settle the question of whether the act was morally permissible, and it is this that we must now consider. Could not charity speak against what justice allowed? Indeed it might do so. For while the fact that a man wants to die suggests that his life is wretched, and while his rejection of life may itself tend to take the good out of the things he might have enjoyed, nevertheless his wish to die might here be opposed for his own sake just as it might be if suicide were in question. Perhaps there is hope that his mental condition will improve. Perhaps he is mistaken in thinking his disease incurable. Perhaps he wants to die for the sake of someone else on whom he feels he is a burden, and we are not ready to accept this sacrifice whether for ourselves or others. In such cases, and there will surely be many of them, it could not be for his own sake that we kill him or allow him to die, and therefore euthanasia as defined in this paper would not be in question. But this is not to deny that there could be acts of voluntary euthanasia both passive and active against which neither justice nor charity would speak.

We have now considered the morality of euthanasia both voluntary and nonvoluntary, and active and passive. The conclusion has been that nonvoluntary active euthanasia (roughly, killing a man against his will or without his consent) is never justified; that is to say, that a man's being killed for his own good never justifies the act unless he himself has consented to it. A man's rights are infringed by such an action, and it is therefore contrary to justice. However, all the other combinations, nonvoluntary passive euthanasia, voluntary active euthanasia, and voluntary passive euthanasia are sometimes compatible with both justice and charity. But the strong condition carried in the definition of euthanasia adopted in this paper must not be forgotten; an act of euthanasia as here understood is one whose purpose is to benefit the one who dies.

In the light of this discussion let us look at our present practices. Are they good or are they bad? And what changes might be made, thinking now not only of the morality of particular acts of euthanasia but also of the indirect effects of instituting different practices, of the abuses to which they might be subject and of the changes that might come about if euthanasia became a recognized part of the social scene?

The first thing to notice is that it is wrong to ask whether we should introduce the practice of euthanasia as if it were not something we already had. In fact we do have it. For instance it is common, where the medical prognosis is very bad, for doctors to recommend against measures to prolong life, and particularly where a process of degeneration producing one medical emergency after another has already set in. If these doctors are not certainly within their legal rights this is something that is apt to come as a surprise to them as to the general public. It is also obvious that euthanasia is often practiced where old people are concerned. If someone very old and soon to die is attacked by a disease that makes his life wretched, doctors do not always come in with life-prolonging drugs. Perhaps poor patients are more fortunate in this respect than rich patients, being more often left to die in peace; but it is in any case a well recognized piece of medical practice which is a form of euthanasia.

No doubt the case of infants with mental or physical defects will be suggested as another example of the practice of euthanasia as we already have it, since such infants are sometimes deliberately allowed to die. That they are deliberately allowed to die is certain; children with severe spina bifida malformations are not always operated on even where it is thought that without the operation they will die; and even in the case of children with Down's syndrome who have intestinal obstructions the relatively simple operation that would make it possible to feed them is sometimes not performed.[10] Whether this is euthanasia in our sense or only as the Nazis understood it is another matter. We must ask the crucial question, "Is it for the sake of the child himself that the doctors and parents choose his death?" In some cases the answer may really be yes, and what is more important it may really be true that the kind of life which is a good is not possible or likely for this child, and that there is little but suffering and frustration in store for him.[11] But this must presuppose that the medical prognosis is wretchedly bad, as it may be for some spina bifida children. With children who are born with Down's syndrome it is, however, quite different. Most of these are able to live on for quite a time in a reasonably contented way, remaining like children all their lives but capable of affectionate relationships and able to play games and perform simple tasks. The fact is, of course, that the doctors who recommend against life-saving procedures for handicapped infants are usually thinking not of them but rather of their parents and of other children in the family or of the "burden on society" if the children survive. So it is not for their sake but to avoid trouble to others that they are allowed to die. When brought out into the open this seems unacceptable: at least we do not easily accept the principle that adults who need special care should be counted too burdensome to be kept alive. It must in any case be insisted that if children with Down's syndrome are deliberately allowed to die this is not a matter of euthanasia except in Hitler's sense. And for our children, since we scruple to gas them, not even the manner of their death is "quiet and easy"; when not treated for an intestinal obstruction a baby simply starves to death. Perhaps some will take this as an argument for allowing active euthanasia, in which case they will be in the company of an S.S. man stationed in the Warthgenau who sent Eichmann a memorandum telling him that "Jews in the coming winter could no longer be fed" and submitting for his consideration a proposal as to whether "it would not be the most humane solution to kill those Jews who were incapable of work through some quicker means."[12] If we say we are *unable* to look after children with handicaps we are no more telling the truth than was the S.S. man who said that the Jews could not be fed.

Nevertheless if it is ever right to allow deformed children to die because life will be a misery to them, or not to take measures to prolong for a little the life of a newborn baby whose life cannot extend beyond a few months of intensive medical intervention, there is a genuine problem about active as opposed to passive euthanasia. There are well-known cases in which the medical staff has looked on wretchedly while an infant died slowly from starvation and dehydration because they did not feel able to give a lethal injection. According to the principles discussed in the earlier part of this paper they would indeed have had no right to give it, since an infant cannot ask that it should be done. The only possible solution —supposing that voluntary active euthanasia were to be legalized—would be to appoint guardians to act on the infant's behalf. In a different climate of opinion this might not be dangerous, but at present, when people so readily assume that the life of a handicapped baby is of no value, one would be loath to support it.

Finally, on the subject of handicapped children, another word should be said about those with severe mental defects. For them too it might sometimes be right to say that one would wish for death for their sake. But not even severe mental handicap automatically brings a child within the scope even of a possible act of euthanasia. If the level of consciousness is low enough it could not be said that life is a good to them, any more than in the case of those suffering from extreme senility. Nevertheless if they do not suffer it will not be an act of euthanasia by which someone opts for their death. Perhaps charity does not demand that strenuous measures are taken to keep people in this state alive, but euthanasia does not come into the matter, any more than it does when someone is, like Karen Ann

Quinlan, in a state of permanent coma. Much could be said about this last case. It might even be suggested that in the case of unconsciousness this "life" is not the life to which "the right to life" refers. But that is not our topic here.

What we must consider, even if only briefly, is the possibility that euthanasia, genuine euthanasia, and not contrary to the requirements of justice or charity, should be legalized over a wider area. Here we are up against the really serious problem of abuse. Many people want, and want very badly, to be rid of their elderly relatives and even of their ailing husbands or wives. Would any safeguards ever be able to stop them describing as euthanasia what was really for their own benefit? And would it be possible to prevent the occurrence of acts which were genuinely acts of euthanasia but morally impermissible because infringing the rights of a patient who wished to live?

Perhaps the furthest we should go is to encourage patients to make their own contracts with a doctor by making it known whether they wish him to prolong their life in case of painful terminal illness or of incapacity. A document such as the Living Will seems eminently sensible, and should surely be allowed to give a doctor following the previously expressed wishes of the patient immunity from legal proceedings by relatives.[13] Legalizing active euthanasia is, however, another matter. Apart from the special repugnance doctors feel towards the idea of a lethal injection, it may be of the very greatest importance to keep a psychological barrier up against killing. Moreover it is active euthanasia which is the most liable to abuse. Hitler would not have been able to kill 275,000 people in his "euthanasia" program if he had had to wait for them to need life-saving treatment. But there are other objections to active euthanasia, even voluntary active euthanasia. In the first place, it would be hard to devise procedures that would protect people from being persuaded into giving their consent. And secondly the possibility of active voluntary euthanasia might change the social scene in ways that would be very bad. As things are, people do, by and large, expect to be looked after if they are old or ill. This is one of the good things that we have, but we might lose it, and be much worse off without it. It might come to be expected that someone likely to need a lot of looking after should call for the doctor and demand his own death. Something comparable could be good in an extremely poverty-stricken community where the children genuinely suffered from lack of food; but in rich societies such as ours it would surely be a spiritual disaster. Such possibilities should make us very wary of supporting large measures of euthanasia, even where moral principle applied to the individual act does not rule it out.

I would like to thank Derek Parfit and the editors of *Philosophy and Public Affairs* for their very helpful comments.

NOTES

1. Dmitri Panin, *The Notebooks of Sologdin* (London, 1976), 66–67.
2. Thomas Nagel, "Death," in James Rachels, ed., *Moral Problems* (New York, 1971), 362.
3. Panin, *Sologdin*, 85.
4. David Hume, *Treatise*, Book III, Part II, Section I.

5. See, for example, James Rachels, "Active and Passive Euthanasia," *New England Journal of Medicine* 292, no. 2 (Jan. 9, 1975): 78–80.

6. Ibid.

7. It is not, however, that justice and charity conflict. A man does not lack charity because he refrains from an act of injustice which would have been for someone's good.

8. For a discussion of such questions, see my article "The Problem of Abortion and the Doctrine of Double Effect," *Oxford Review* 5 (1967); reprinted in Rachels, *Moral Problems,* and J. Gorovitz, *Moral Problems in Medicine* (Englewood Cliffs, N.J.: Prentice-Hall, 1976).

9. George Fletcher, "Legal Aspects of the Decision not to Prolong Life," *Journal of the American Medical Association* 203, no. 1 (Jan. 1, 1968): 119–22. Reprinted in Gorovitz.

10. I have been told this by a pediatrician in a well-known medical center in the United States. It is confirmed by Anthony M. Shaw and Iris A. Shaw, "Dilemma of Informed Consent in Children," *New England Journal of Medicine* 289, no. 17 (Oct. 25, 1973): 885–90. Reprinted in Gorovitz.

11. It must be remembered, however, that many of the social miseries of spina bifida children could be avoided. Professor R. B. Zachary is surely right to insist on this. See, for example, "Ethical and Social Aspects of Spina Bifida," *The Lancet* (Aug. 3, 1968): 274–76. Reprinted in Gorovitz.

12. Quoted by Hannah Arendt, *Eichmann in Jerusalem* (London, 1963), 90.

13. Details of this document are to be found in J. A. Behnke and Sissela Bok, eds., *The Dilemmas of Euthanasia* (New York, 1975), and in A. B. Downing, ed., *Euthanasia and the Right to Life: The Case for Voluntary Euthanasia* (London, 1969).

James Rachels

Active and Passive Euthanasia

The distinction between active and passive euthanasia is thought to be crucial for medical ethics. The idea is that it is permissible, at least in some cases, to withhold treatment and allow a patient to die, but it is never permissible to take any direct action designed to kill the patient. This doctrine seems to be accepted by most doctors, and it is endorsed in a statement adopted by the House of Delegates of the American Medical Association on December 4, 1973:

> The intentional termination of the life of one human being by another—mercy killing —is contrary to that for which the medical profession stands and is contrary to the policy of the American Medical Association.
>
> The cessation of the employment of extraordinary means to prolong the life of the body when there is irrefutable evidence that biological death is imminent is the

From *The New England Journal of Medicine,* 292 (1975). Reprinted by permission of *The New England Journal of Medicine* and the author. Copyright © 1975 Massachusetts Medical Society.

decision of the patient and/or his immediate family. The advice and judgment of the physician should be freely available to the patient and/or his immediate family.

However, a strong case can be made against this doctrine. In what follows I will set out some of the relevant arguments, and urge doctors to reconsider their views on this matter.

To begin with a familiar type of situation, a patient who is dying of incurable cancer of the throat is in terrible pain, which can no longer be satisfactorily alleviated. He is certain to die within a few days, even if present treatment is continued, but he does not want to go on living for those days since the pain is unbearable. So he asks the doctor for an end to it, and his family joins in the request.

Suppose the doctor agrees to withhold treatment, as the conventional doctrine says he may. The justification for his doing so is that the patient is in terrible agony, and since he is going to die anyway, it would be wrong to prolong his suffering needlessly. But now notice this. If one simply withholds treatment, it may take the patient longer to die, and so he may suffer more than he would if more direct action were taken and a lethal injection given. This fact provides strong reason for thinking that, once the initial decision not to prolong his agony has been made, active euthanasia is actually preferable to passive euthanasia, rather than the reverse. To say otherwise is to endorse the option that leads to more suffering rather than less, and is contrary to the humanitarian impulse that prompts the decision not to prolong his life in the first place.

Part of my point is that the process of being "allowed to die" can be relatively slow and painful, whereas being given a lethal injection is relatively quick and painless. Let me give a different sort of example. In the United States about one in 600 babies is born with Down's syndrome. Most of these babies are otherwise healthy—that is, with only the usual pediatric care, they will proceed to an otherwise normal infancy. Some, however, are born with congenital defects such as intestinal obstructions that require operations if they are to live. Sometimes, the parents and the doctor will decide not to operate, and let the infant die. Anthony Shaw describes what happens then:

> ... When surgery is denied [the doctor] must try to keep the infant from suffering while natural forces sap the baby's life away. As a surgeon whose natural inclination is to use the scalpel to fight off death, standing by and watching a salvageable baby die is the most emotionally exhausting experience I know. It is easy at a conference, in a theoretical discussion, to decide that such infants should be allowed to die. It is altogether different to stand by in the nursery and watch as dehydration and infection wither a tiny being over hours and days. This is a terrible ordeal for me and the hospital staff—much more so than for the parents who never set foot in the nursery.[1]

I can understand why some people are opposed to all euthanasia, and insist that such infants must be allowed to live. I think I can also understand why other people

[1]A. Shaw, "Doctor, Do We Have a Choice?" *New York Times Magazine,* Jan. 30, 1972, p. 59.

favor destroying these babies quickly and painlessly. But why should anyone favor letting "dehydration and infection wither a tiny being over hours and days"? The doctrine that says that a baby may be allowed to dehydrate and wither, but may not be given an injection that would end its life without suffering seems so patently cruel as to require no further refutation. The strong language is not intended to offend, but only to put the point in the clearest possible way.

My second argument is that the conventional doctrine leads to decisions concerning life and death made on irrelevant grounds.

Consider again the case of the infants with Down's syndrome who need operations for congenital defects unrelated to the syndrome to live. Sometimes, there is no operation, and the baby dies, but when there is no such defect, the baby lives on. Now, an operation such as that to remove an intestinal obstruction is not prohibitively difficult. The reason why such operations are not performed in these cases is, clearly, that the child has Down's syndrome and the parents and the doctor judge that because of that fact it is better for the child to die.

But notice that this situation is absurd, no matter what view one takes of the lives and potentials of such babies. If the life of such an infant is worth preserving, what does it matter if it needs a simple operation? Or, if one thinks it better that such a baby should not live on, what difference does it make that it happens to have an obstructed intestinal tract? In either case, the matter of life and death is being decided on irrelevant grounds. It is the Down's syndrome, and not the intestines, that is the issue. The matter should be decided, if at all, on that basis, and not be allowed to depend on the essentially irrelevant question of whether the intestinal tract is blocked.

What makes this situation possible, of course, is the idea that when there is an intestinal blockage, one can "let the baby die," but when there is no such defect there is nothing that can be done, for one must not "kill" it. The fact that this idea leads to such results as deciding life or death on irrelevant grounds is another good reason why the doctrine should be rejected.

One reason why so many people think that there is an important moral difference between active and passive euthanasia is that they think killing someone is morally worse than letting someone die. But is it? Is killing, in itself, worse than letting die? To investigate this issue, two cases may be considered that are exactly alike except that one involves killing whereas the other involves letting someone die. Then, it can be asked whether this difference makes any difference to the moral assessments. It is important that the cases be exactly alike, except for this one difference, since otherwise one cannot be confident that it is this difference and not some other that accounts for any variation in the assessment of the two cases. So, let us consider this pair of cases.

In the first, Smith stands to gain a large inheritance if anything should happen to his six-year-old cousin. One evening while the child is taking his bath, Smith sneaks into the bathroom and drowns the child, and then arranges things so that it will look like an accident.

In the second, Jones also stands to gain if anything should happen to his six-year-old cousin. Like Smith, Jones sneaks in planning to drown the child in his bath. However, just as he enters the bathroom Jones sees the child slip and hit his head, and fall face down in the water. Jones is delighted; he stands by, ready to push the child's head back under if it is necessary, but it is not necessary. With only a little thrashing about, the child drowns all by himself, "accidentally," as Jones watches and does nothing.

Now Smith killed the child, whereas Jones "merely" let the child die. That is the only difference between them. Did either man behave better, from a moral point of view? If the difference between killing and letting die were in itself a morally important matter, one should say that Jones's behavior was less reprehensible than Smith's. But does one really want to say that? I think not. In the first place, both men acted from the same motive, personal gain, and both had exactly the same end in view when they acted. It may be inferred from Smith's conduct that he is a bad man, although that judgment may be withdrawn or modified if certain further facts are learned about him—for example, that he is mentally deranged. But would not the very same thing be inferred about Jones from his conduct? And would not the same further considerations also be relevant to any modification of this judgment? Moreover, suppose Jones pleaded, in his own defense, "After all, I didn't do anything except just stand there and watch the child drown. I didn't kill him; I only let him die." Again, if letting die were in itself less bad than killing, this defense should have at least some weight. But it does not. Such a "defense" can only be regarded as a grotesque perversion of moral reasoning. Morally speaking, it is no defense at all.

Now, it may be pointed out, quite properly, that the cases of euthanasia with which doctors are concerned are not like this at all. They do not involve personal gain or the destruction of normal healthy children. Doctors are concerned only with cases in which the patient's life is of no further use to him, or in which the patient's life has become or will soon become a terrible burden. However, the point is the same in these cases: the bare difference between killing and letting die does not, in itself, make a moral difference. If a doctor lets a patient die, for humane reasons, he is in the same moral position as if he had given the patient a lethal injection for humane reasons. If his decision was wrong—if, for example, the patient's illness was in fact curable—the decision would be equally regrettable no matter which method was used to carry it out. And if the doctor's decision was the right one, the method used is not in itself important.

The AMA policy statement isolates the crucial issue very well: the crucial issue is "the intentional termination of the life of one human being by another." But after identifying this issue, and forbidding "mercy-killing," the statement goes on to deny that the cessation of treatment is the intentional termination of a life. This is where the mistake comes in, for what is the cessation of treatment, in these circumstances, if it is not "the intentional termination of the life of one human being by another"? Of course it is exactly that, and if it were not, there would be no point to it.

Many people will find this judgment hard to accept. One reason, I think, is that it is very easy to conflate the question of whether killing is, in itself, worse than letting die, and with the very different question of whether most actual cases of killing are more reprehensible than most actual cases of letting die. Most actual cases of killing are clearly terrible (think, for example, of all the murders reported in the newspapers), and one hears of such cases every day. On the other hand, one hardly ever hears of a case of letting die, except for the action of doctors who are motivated by humanitarian reasons. So one learns to think of killing in a much worse light than of letting die. But this does not mean that there is something about killing that makes it in itself worse than letting die, for it is not the bare difference between killing and letting die that makes the difference in these cases. Rather, the other factors—the murderer's motive of personal gain, for example, contrasted with the doctor's humanitarian motivation—account for different reactions to the different cases.

I have argued that killing is not in itself any worse than letting die; if my contention is right, it follows that active euthanasia is not any worse than passive euthanasia. What arguments can be given on the other side? The most common, I believe, is the following:

"The important difference between active and passive euthanasia is that, in passive euthanasia, the doctor does not do anything to bring about the patient's death. The doctor does nothing, and the patient dies of whatever ills already afflict him. In active euthanasia, however, the doctor does something to bring about the patient's death: he kills him. The doctor who gives the patient with cancer a lethal injection has himself caused his patient's death; whereas if he merely ceases treatment, the cancer is the cause of the death."

A number of points need to be made here. The first is that it is not exactly correct to say that in passive euthanasia the doctor does nothing, for he does do one thing that is very important: he lets the patient die. "Letting someone die" is certainly different, in some respects, from other types of action—mainly in that it is a kind of action that one may perform by way of not performing certain other actions. For example, one may let a patient die by way of not giving medication, just as one may insult someone by way of not shaking his hand. But for any purpose of moral assessment, it is a type of action nonetheless. The decision to let a patient die is subject to moral appraisal in the same way that a decision to kill him would be subject to moral appraisal: it may be assessed as wise or unwise, compassionate or sadistic, right or wrong. If a doctor deliberately let a patient die who was suffering from a routinely curable illness, the doctor would certainly be to blame for what he had done, just as he would be to blame if he had needlessly killed the patient. Charges against him would then be appropriate. It would be no defense at all for him to insist that he didn't "do anything." He would have done something very serious, indeed, for he let his patient die.

Fixing the cause of death may be very important from a legal point of view, for it may determine whether criminal charges are brought against the doctor. But I do not think that this notion can be used to show a moral difference between active and passive euthanasia. The reason why it is considered bad to be the cause of someone's death is that death is regarded as a great evil—and so it is. However, if it has been decided that euthanasia—even passive euthanasia—is desirable in a given case, it has also been decided that in this instance death is no greater an evil than the patient's continued existence. And if this is true, the usual reason for not wanting to be the cause of someone's death simply does not apply.

Finally, doctors may think that all of this is only of academic interest—the sort of thing that philosophers may worry about but that has no practical bearing on their own work. After all, doctors must be concerned about the legal consequences of what they do, and active euthanasia is clearly forbidden by the law. But even so doctors should also be concerned with the fact that the law is forcing upon them a moral doctrine that may well be indefensible, and has a considerable effect on their practices. Of course, most doctors are not now in the position of being coerced in this matter, for they do not regard themselves as merely going along with what the law requires. Rather, in statements such as the AMA policy statement that I have quoted, they are endorsing this doctrine as a central point of medical ethics. In that statement, active euthanasia is condemned not merely as illegal but as "contrary to that for which the medical profession stands," whereas passive euthanasia is approved. However, the preceding considerations suggest that there is really no moral difference between the two, considered in themselves (there may be important moral differences in some cases in their *consequences,* but, as I pointed out, these differences may make active euthanasia, and not passive euthanasia, the morally preferable option). So, whereas doctors may have to discriminate between active and passive euthanasia to satisfy the law, they should not do any more than that. In particular, they should not give the distinction any added authority and weight by writing it into official statements of medical ethics.

The Argument from Mercy

THE UTILITARIAN VERSION OF THE ARGUMENT

. . . The utilitarian argument may be elaborated as follows:

1. Any action or social policy is morally right if it serves to increase the amount of happiness in the world or to decrease the amount of misery. Conversely, an action or social policy is morally wrong if it serves to decrease happiness or to increase misery.
2. The policy of killing, at their own request, hopelessly ill patients who are suffering great pain, would decrease the amount of misery in the world. . . .
3. Therefore, such a policy would be morally right.

The first premise of this argument, (1), states the Principle of Utility, which is the basic utilitarian assumption. Today most philosophers think that this principle is wrong, because they think that the promotion of happiness and the avoidance of misery are not the *only* morally important things. Happiness, they say, is only one among many values that should be promoted: freedom, justice, and a respect for people's rights are also important. To take one example: People *might* be happier if there were no freedom of religion; for, if everyone adhered to the same religious beliefs, there would be greater harmony among people. There would be no unhappiness caused within families by Jewish girls marrying Catholic boys, and so forth. Moreover, if people were brainwashed well enough, no one would mind not having freedom of choice. Thus happiness would be increased. But, the argument continues, even if happiness *could* be increased this way, it would not be right to

From *Matters of Life and Death: New Introductory Essays in Moral Philosophy,* edited by Tom Regan (New York: Random House, 1980). Reprinted by permission of Random House and the author.

deny people freedom of religion, because people have a right to make their own choices. Therefore, the first premise of the utilitarian argument is unacceptable.

There is a related difficulty for utilitarianism, which connects more directly with the topic of euthanasia. Suppose a person is leading a miserable life—full of more unhappiness than happiness—but does *not* want to die. This person thinks that a miserable life is better than none at all. Now I assume that we would all agree that the person should not be killed; that would be plain, unjustifiable murder. Yet it *would* decrease the amount of misery in the world if we killed this person—it would lead to an increase in the balance of happiness over unhappiness—and so it is hard to see how, on strictly utilitarian grounds, it could be wrong. Again, the Principle of Utility seems to be an inadequate guide for determining right and wrong. So we are on shaky ground if we rely on *this* version of the argument from mercy for a defense of euthanasia.

Doing What Is in Everyone's Best Interests   Although the foregoing utilitarian argument is faulty, it is nevertheless based on a sound idea. For even if the promotion of happiness and avoidance of misery are not the *only* morally important things, they are still very important. So, when an action or a social policy would decrease misery, that is *a* very strong reason in its favor. In the cases of voluntary euthanasia we are now considering, great suffering is eliminated, and since the patient requests it, there is no question of violating individual rights. That is why, regardless of the difficulties of the Principle of Utility, the utilitarian version of the argument still retains considerable force.

I want now to present a somewhat different version of the argument from mercy, which is inspired by utilitarianism but which avoids the difficulties of the foregoing version by not making the Principle of Utility a premise of the argument. I believe that the following argument is sound and proves that active euthanasia *can* be justified:

1. If an action promotes the best interests of *everyone* concerned, and violates *no one's* rights, then that action is morally acceptable.
2. In at least some cases, active euthanasia promotes the best interests of everyone concerned and violates no one's rights.
3. Therefore, in at least some cases active euthanasia is morally acceptable.

The Argument from the Golden Rule

"Do unto others as you would have them do unto you" is one of the oldest and most familiar moral maxims. Stated in just that way, it is not a very good maxim: Suppose a sexual pervert started treating others as he would like to be treated himself; we might not be happy with the results. Nevertheless, the basic idea behind the Golden Rule is a good one. The basic idea is that moral rules apply impartially to everyone alike; therefore, you cannot say that you are justified in treating someone else in a certain way unless you are willing to admit that that person would also be justified in treating *you* in that way if your positions were reversed.

Kant and the Golden Rule   The great German philosopher Immanuel Kant (1724–1804) incorporated the basic idea of the Golden Rule into his system of ethics. Kant argued that we should act only on rules that we are willing to have applied universally; that is, we should behave as we would be willing to have *everyone* behave. He held that there is one supreme principle of morality, which he called "the Categorical Imperative." The Categorical Imperative says:

> Act only according to that maxim by which you can at the same time will that it should become a universal law.[1]

Let us discuss what this means. When we are trying to decide whether we ought to do a certain action, we must first ask what general rule or principle we would be following if we did it. Then, we ask whether we would be willing for everyone to follow that rule, in similar circumstances. (This determines whether "the maxim of the act"—the rule we would be following—can be "willed" to be "a universal law.") If we would not be willing for the rule to be followed universally, then we should not follow it ourselves. Thus, if we are not willing for others to apply the rule to *us,* we ought not apply it to *them*.

In the eighteenth chapter of St. Matthew's gospel there is a story that perfectly illustrates this point. A man is owed money by another, who cannot pay, and so he has the debtor thrown into prison. But he himself owes money to the king and begs that *his* debt be forgiven. At first the king forgives the debt. However, when the king hears how this man has treated the one who owed him, he changes his mind and "delivers him unto the tormentors" until he can pay. The moral is clear: If you do not think that others should apply the rule "Don't forgive debts!" to *you,* then you should not apply it to others.

The application of all this to the question of euthanasia is fairly obvious. Each of us is going to die someday, although most of us do not know when or how. But suppose you were told that you would die in one of two ways, and you were asked to choose between them. First, you could die quietly, and without pain, from a fatal injection. Or second, you could choose to die of an affliction so painful that for several days before death you would be reduced to howling like a dog, with your family standing by helplessly, trying to comfort you, but going through its own psychological hell. It is hard to believe that any sane person, when confronted by these possibilities, would choose to have a rule applied that would force upon him or her the second option. And if we would not want such a rule, which excludes euthanasia, applied to us, then we should not apply such a rule to others.

Implications for Christians   There is a considerable irony here. Kant, as we have already noted, was personally opposed to active euthanasia, yet his own Categorical Imperative seems to sanction it. The larger irony, however, is for those in the Christian Church who have for centuries opposed active euthanasia. According to

[1]*Foundations of the Metaphysics of Morals,* 422.

the New Testament accounts, Jesus himself promulgated the Golden Rule as the supreme moral principle—"This is the Law and the Prophets," he said. But if this is the supreme principle of morality, then how can active euthanasia be always wrong? If I would have it done to me, how can it be wrong for me to do likewise to others?

R. M. Hare has made this point with great force. A Christian as well as a leading contemporary moral philosopher, Hare has long argued that "universalizability" is one of the central characteristics of moral judgment. ("Universalizability" is the name he gives to the basic idea embodied in both the Golden Rule and the Categorical Imperative. It means that a moral judgment must conform to universal principles, which apply to everyone alike, if it is to be acceptable.) In an article called "Euthanasia: A Christian View," Hare argues that Christians, if they took Christ's teachings about the Golden Rule seriously, would not think that euthanasia is always wrong. He gives this (true) example:

> The driver of a petrol lorry [i.e., a gasoline truck] was in an accident in which his tanker overturned and immediately caught fire. He himself was trapped in the cab and could not be freed. He therefore besought the bystanders to kill him by hitting him on the head, so that he would not roast to death. I think that somebody did this, but I do not know what happened in court afterwards.
>
> Now will you please all ask yourselves, as I have many times asked myself, what you wish that men should do to you if you were in the situation of that driver. I cannot believe that anybody who considered the matter seriously, as if he himself were going to be in that situation and had now to give instructions as to what rule the bystanders should follow, would say that the rule should be one ruling out euthanasia absolutely.[2]

We might note that *active* euthanasia is the only option here; the concept of passive euthanasia, in these circumstances, has no application.

SUGGESTIONS FOR DISCUSSION

1. Why is Gay-Williams's appeal to "human dignity" in attacking euthanasia a version of Natural Law theory? What consequentialist arguments does he develop against euthanasia? How do the deontological and consequentialist arguments *for* euthanasia outlined by Rachels differ from the arguments *against* euthanasia formulated by Gay-Williams?
2. Does Philippa Foot's concept of virtue differ from that of Aristotle (see Part I, Chapter 1)? How does Foot use the concept of virtue to analyze the permissibility of euthanasia?
3. Is there a right to privacy? If there is, is it sufficiently strong to ground the permissibility of euthanasia, active or passive?

FURTHER READING

Bayles, M., and High, D., eds. *Medical Treatment of the Dying: Moral Issues.* Boston: G. K. Hall and Schenkman, 1978. (Interpretation, critical analysis; intermediate)

---

[2]*Philosophic Exchange* (Brockport, N.Y.) II:1 (Summer 1975): 45.

Beauchamp, T., and Perlin, S., eds. *Ethical Issues in Death and Dying*. Englewood Cliffs, N.J.: Prentice-Hall, 1978. (Interpretation, critical analysis; intermediate)

Behnke, J., and Bok., S., eds. *The Dilemmas of Euthanasia*. Garden City, N.Y.: Anchor Books, 1975. (Interpretation, critical analysis; intermediate)

Downing, A., ed. *Euthanasia and the Right to Death: The Case for Voluntary Euthanasia*. New York: Humanities Press, 1979. (Interpretation, critical analysis; intermediate)

Glover, J. *Causing Death and Saving Lives*. New York: Penguin, 1977. (Interpretation, critical analysis; intermediate)

Grisez, G., and Boyle, J. *Life and Death with Liberty and Justice*. Notre Dame: Notre Dame University Press, 1979. (Interpretation, critical analysis; advanced)

Kohl, M., ed. *Beneficent Euthanasia*. Buffalo: Prometheus Books, 1975. (Interpretation, critical analysis; intermediate)

Ladd, J., ed. *Ethical Issues Relating to Life and Death*. New York: Oxford University Press, 1979. (Interpretation, critical analysis; advanced)

Mappes, T., and Zembaty, J., eds. *Biomedical Ethics*. 2nd ed. New York: McGraw-Hill, 1986. (Interpretation, critical analysis; intermediate)

Steinbock, B., ed. *Killing and Letting Die*. Englewood Cliffs, N.J.: Prentice-Hall, 1980. (Interpretation, critical analysis; intermediate)

Veatch, R. *Death, Dying and the Biological Revolution*. New Haven: Yale University Press, 1976. (Interpretation, critical analysis; intermediate)

13

□

Punishment and the Death Penalty

The basic legal structure of any society undertakes to establish and maintain organization and order. If members of society naturally ordered their social relations and actions to accord with the principles of perfect justice, laws would be unnecessary. For societies less than perfectly just in this way, it is not enough that a basic legal structure merely exist; its laws must be enforced. If a person breaks a law, some effective action must be taken to reimpose order. Failing this, laws would have little effect, and anarchy would reign. Now it is generally agreed that punishment is the appropriate response to law-breaking. We deem liberty a basic value, and punishment deprives persons of liberty in some way or it imposes a hardship. This raises the question of a general justification for punishment. What justifies punishment as the appropriate response to violations of law? In particular, what forms of punishment are most appropriate to given violations of the law? Types of punishment most commonly include public censure, fines, community service, physical suffering, or imprisonment. Thus it is important to inquire whether there are limits to the forms and severity of punishment that the law may impose.

It is within this context of the theory of punishment that the issue of capital punishment or the death penalty must be addressed. On one hand, the death penalty is one punishment among others, and so it is subject to the same form of justification as punishment in general. On the other hand, it is the most extreme form punishment can assume. It especially raises the question whether the institution of capital punishment would exceed the bounds of morality. Thus if it is to be morally permissible in some cases, capital punishment seems to require special justification.

Justifications for Punishment   Theories of justification for punishment generally assume one of two contending forms: *retributivist* or *utilitarian*. The differences between the two theories of punishment reflect differences between deontological and consequentialist moral theories; that is, between those theories that reject and those that appeal to consequences as the basis for determining what is just and what is not (see, respectively, Kant, Part I, Chapter 3; and Chapter 4). The differences between the two views of punishment, and difficulties with each, are analyzed in R. S. Downie's article.

For the *retributivist,* guilt is a necessary and sufficient condition for punishment. Crimes are to be punished; the nature, motive, and degree of the crime determine the appropriate punishment. Punishment is justified insofar as it "fits the crime" or "redresses the moral balance," and it must be "of equal magnitude" to the crime committed. Thus retributivism is backward-looking in its concern to reinstate justice as it existed before the crime took place. It is deontological in ignoring any social utility that punishment may afford. On this view, punishment is considered good in itself, demanded by the dictates of justice despite any valuable consequences it may bring about, and though there may be none. This is considered one of the main failings of retributivism. Where no social usefulness would flow from it, "punishment for punishment's sake" seems excessively moralistic. Another criticism is that punishment is not always the appropriate response to a violation of the law. Failure to convict a "mercy-killer" may be a case in point (on euthanasia, see Part II, Chapter 12). It follows that, though the guilt of an agent is a necessary condition for his or her punishment, it is not sufficient.

Utilitarian theories of punishment attempt to avoid retributivism's difficulties. Here punishment is justified according to the good consequences or social utility it would produce. Utilitarian forms of punishment are prospective: If punishment would not produce future social value in a given case, it would not be required. Utilitarian justifications of punishment are usually of two kinds: reform or deterrence. On the *reformative* view, punishment is to provide a criminal with a socially desirable set of skills and attitudes. In this sense, punishment is to have the end of education, moral and otherwise. Yet it is often countered that, though it is important, reform fails to exhaust the various complex ways the criminal law is intended to affect society. The *deterrent* consideration assumes primacy here. The prospect of punishment is designed to deter potential violators of the law. Potential criminals are supposed to factor in their possible punishment when calculating the projected consequences of their criminal acts. This raises a question of fact as to whether punishment deters in this way. Should some kinds of punishment prove upon examination not to deter as such, they would be unjustified on the deterrence view. The major shortcoming of deterrence theories is that they may justify punishment of innocent persons if this served to deter others from committing crimes. Guilt is not a necessary condition for punishment; nor in fact is it sufficient. This is unfair and contrary to the dictates of justice.

The Permissibility of Capital Punishment   Justifications for the death penalty have assumed both retributivist and utilitarian forms. In the case of retribution, it has been suggested that no punishment so fits the crime of murder as death. In utilitarian terms, it is often argued that the prospect of death is the sole sufficient deterrent of vicious crimes. Again there is a factual question here that is to be resolved by the appropriate empirical studies: Is it true that the prospect of death deters potential murderers? Some have argued that death is warranted for criminals who prove to be beyond reform. These considerations raise two questions. First, are some transgressions of the law so extreme and some criminals so dangerous that no punishment is too severe? Second, and by contrast, are some punishments too unjust—too "cruel and unusual"—to be warranted no matter their social utility?

Supreme Court Rulings The Eighth Amendment (1791) prohibits any punishment that is "cruel and unusual." This clause was drafted primarily to outlaw such inhumane punishments as torture, the rack, the wheel, burning at the stake, and so forth. It is to this clause, and to the "due process" clause of the Fourteenth Amendment (1868), that legal opposition to capital punishment has usually appealed. A narrow majority of the Supreme Court ruled in 1972 that the death penalty as instituted by numerous states at the time was unconstitutional *(Furman v. Georgia)*. Two of the five justices making up the majority considered capital punishment to be inherently cruel and excessive. The remaining three ruled that it was unconstitutional only as the states at the time instituted it. State courts were found to apply the death penalty in an arbitrary way, establishing no standards to determine when a jury may choose capital punishment and when not. One result the Court thought follows from this is the disproportionate and discriminatory sentencing to death of black criminals, in violation of the Fourteenth Amendment.

In *Gregg v. Georgia* (1976), the Supreme Court ruled that the death penalty is not unconstitutional and that it is acceptably administered in the state of Georgia. The Court held that capital punishment is endorsed by a majority in contemporary American society and that it is consistent with the concept of human dignity which is basic to the Eighth Amendment. Though it was admitted that the death penalty is an extreme sanction, it was held to be appropriate in the case of extreme crimes, and so not to be disproportionate punishment. It was also found to serve both retributive and deterrent social purposes. Moreover, in *Furman* the Court had decided that the Georgia statute allowed the death penalty to be arbitrarily applied. Since then, the Georgia legislature had ruled that a jury must find a crime to be characterized by at least one from a list of aggravating factors before the death penalty could be imposed. Consequently, the Court acknowledged in *Gregg* that the death penalty is no longer arbitrarily applied in Georgia.

In a dissenting opinion, Justice Thurgood Marshall contended that if the American public were fully informed, they would find capital punishment unacceptable. Marshall argued that the death penalty is in any case unconstitutional, because it is excessive punishment. It is not necessary as a deterrent, for the alternative of life imprisonment serves equally well; and it is inconsistent with any retributive standard, for it denies the wrongdoer's dignity and worth.

Readings Ernest van den Haag admits that it is an unresolved factual issue as to whether the death penalty deters crime. However, he suggests that the principle of inherent dignity of human life implies the following rule: If human life is to be risked, it is preferable to risk the life of the guilty than that of the innocent. For it is more important to protect prospective victims than to spare murderers. So if imposing the death penalty could conceivably save the lives of future murder victims, there is a moral obligation to impose it. (Note that this argument may presuppose hypothetical guilt for a potential crime before the crime is actually committed.)

In contrast to both retributivist and utilitarian accounts, Thomas Hurka develops a right-based theory of punishment (on right-based moral theories, see Mackie, Part I, Chapter 6). Hurka contends that his right-based theory incorporates the appealing aspects of both retributivist and utilitarian theories, while avoiding their deficiencies. Hurka characterizes persons in terms of natural rights. Each has a right to the most extensive liberty compatible with the like liberty for all. This right entails an enforcement right to use coercion, including some threats and the *minimum* harms necessary, in legitimate self-defense of one's rights. Hurka derives the right to punish from this right to make threats: punishment is justified as the right to inflict harms on others for rights violated. Harms inflicted in punishment cannot exceed the degree of importance of the rights violated. So death cannot be mandated for relatively minor criminal violations of others' rights. For deterrence theories, successful criminal deterrence is both a necessary and sufficient condition for imposing capital punishment. For retributivist theories, necessary and sufficient conditions for the death penalty are that the person is guilty and that the punishment "fit" the class of crime. On Hurka's rights theory, by contrast, the deterrence effect (if factually established) *and* the actual guilt of a criminal in violating the right to life of an innocent person are each individually necessary conditions for instituting the death penalty. In other words, capital punishment is not justifiable without both of these conditions. Yet they would be sufficient to justify capital punishment if and only if they hold conjointly.

Hugo Adam Bedau criticizes both deterrence and retributivist arguments as inadequate to justify capital punishment. He rejects the claim that the death penalty deters capital offenses: very few nonexecuted murderers repeat their crimes, whether or not the death penalty is in effect. Moreover, the death penalty has no noticeably greater deterrent effect than long-term imprisonment. If the same effect is to be achieved by a given punishment as by some other one, but at the expense of less human suffering, then the less extreme punishment is preferable. This renders the death penalty obsolete. Bedau supports this criticism by noting the many hidden costs, both individual and social, that the death penalty carries. The retributivist argument for capital punishment rests upon the principle of retaliation or *lex talionis* (literally, "a life for a life"). This presupposes the principle of just distribution: that severity of punishment is determined by gravity of offense. Bedau argues that only a literal interpretation of the principle of just distribution could support the institution of capital punishment. He contends that no literal-minded interpretation of the principle will be defensible. He concludes that capital punishment cannot be supported by claiming that it institutes just retribution. Bedau insists that we can accept the principle of just retribution to support a schedule of strict and severe punishments, while rejecting *lex talionis* and capital punishment. Finally, he lays out a practical argument against the death penalty in showing that it is applied unequally and arbitrarily to the poor and unprivileged in violation of the Fourteenth Amendment: In the words of a popular slogan, "Those without the capital get the punishment."

Bedau issues a humanistic plea for long-term imprisonment rather than capital punishment. Long-term imprisonment is retributive, socially protective, and a deterrent. In addition, it has a symbolic benefit: There is no need to employ the inhumane means in punishment that were employed in the crime.

R. S. Downie

Justifying Punishment

Traditionally two very general sorts of justification have been offered for the practice of punishment: retributivist and utilitarian. According to the theory of retribution . . . guilt is a necessary and a sufficient condition of the infliction of punishment on an offender. Is the theory plausible?

It might be said against it that it does not reflect actual practice either in the law or in more informal normative orders such as schools or the family. In these institutions we find such practices as the relaxation of punishment for first offenders, warnings, pardons, and so on. Hence, it may seem that actual penal practice is at variance with the retributive theory if it is saying that guilt is a necessary and a sufficient condition of punishment. Only in games, it may be said, do we find a sphere where the infringement of rules is a necessary and a sufficient condition of the infliction of a penalty, and even in games there may be a "playing the advantage" rule.

It is not clear, however, that the retributivist need be disturbed by this objection. He might take a high-handed line with the objection and say that if it is the case that actual penal practice does not reflect his theory then so much the (morally) worse for actual practice. Whatever people in fact do, he might argue, it is morally fitting that guilt be a necessary and a sufficient condition of the infliction of punishment.

A less high-handed line, and one more likely to conciliate the opponents of the retributivist theory, is to say that the statement of the theory so far provided is to be taken as a very general one. When it is said that guilt is a necessary and a sufficient condition of punishment it is not intended that punishment should in every case follow inexorably. There are cases where extenuating circumstances may be discovered and in such cases it would be legitimate to recommend mercy or even to issue a pardon. It is unfair to the retributivist to depict his theory as the inflexible application of rules. There is nothing in the theory which forbids it the use of all the devices in the law and in less formal institutions whereby punishment may in certain circumstances be mitigated. Even the sternest of retributivists can allow for the concept of mercy. Perhaps the objection may be avoided completely if the theory is stated more carefully as: guilt and nothing other than guilt may justify the infliction of punishment. To state the theory in this way is to enable it to accommodate the complex operation of extenuating factors which modify the execution of actual systems of law. But to say this is not yet to explain why guilt and nothing other than guilt may justify the infliction of punishment. Indeed, we might ask the retributivist to tell us why we should punish anyone at all.

From R. S. Downie, *Roles and Values* (London: Methuen and Co., Ltd., 1971). Reprinted by permission.

Retributivists give a variety of answers to this question. One is that punishment annuls the evil which the offender has created. It is not easy to make sense of this claim. No amount of punishment can undo an offense that has been committed: what has been has been. Sometimes metaphors of punishment washing away sin are used to explain how punishment can annul evil. But such ideas can mislead. Certainly, the infliction of punishment may, as a matter of psychological fact, remove some people's *feelings* of guilt. But we may query whether this is necessarily a good thing. Whether or not it is, however, it is not the same as annulling the evil committed.

A second retributivist idea is that the offender has had some sort of illicit pleasure and that the infliction of pain will redress the moral balance. People speak of the criminal as "paying for what he has done" or as "reaping a harvest of bitterness"; the infliction of suffering is regarded as a fitting response to crime. But this view may be based on a confusion of the idea that "the punishment must fit the crime," which is acceptable if it means only that punishment ought to be proportionate, with the idea that punishment is a fitting response to crime, which is not so obviously acceptable. It may be that the traditional *lex talionis* is based on a confusion of the two ideas. At any rate, it is the idea of punishment as the "fitting response" which is essential to the retributivist position.

A third claim sometimes made by the retributivists is that an offender has a right to punishment. This claim is often mocked by the critics of retributivism on the grounds that it is an odd right that would gladly be waived by the holder! It might be thought that the view can be defended on the grounds that the criminal's right to punishment is merely the right correlative to the authority's duty to punish him. Such a defense is not plausible, however, for, even supposing there is a right correlative to a legal authority's duty to punish criminals, it is much more plausible to attribute this right to the society which is protected by the deterrent effect of punishment.

There are two arguments, more convincing than the first, which can be put forward in defense of the view that the offender has a right to punishment. One of these requires us to take the view in conjunction with the premise that punishment annuls evil. If punishment can somehow wash away the guilt of the offender then it is plausible to say that the offender has a right to be punished. The difficulty with this argument, however, is that it simply transfers the problems. It is now intelligible to say that the offender has a right to punishment, but, as we have already seen, it is not at all clear what it means to say that punishment annuls evil.

The other argument invites us to consider what the alternative is to punishing the criminal. The alternative, as we shall shortly see, may be to "treat" him and attempt a "cure" by means of various psychological techniques. Now this would be rejected as morally repugnant by many retributivists, on the grounds that an offender has freely decided to break the law and should be regarded as a self-determining rational being who knew what he was doing. An offender, so described, may be said to have a right to *punishment* (as distinct from psychological treatment, moral indoctrination, or brainwashing in the interests of the State). Such an argument produces a favorable response from many criminals who, when they have served their time in prison, feel that the matter is then over and that they ought to be protected from the attentions of moral doctors and the like. So stated, there may be some truth in the "right to punishment" doctrine, however easy it is for the sophisticated to mock it.

So far we have been concerned to suggest detailed criticism of the retributivist theory. But there are two general criticisms which are commonly made of it at the moment (for it is a most unfashionable theory in philosophical and other circles). The first is that insofar as its claims are intelligible and prima facie acceptable, they are disguised utilitarian claims.

This criticism is valid against certain ways in which retributivists sometimes state their claims. For example, they have sometimes regarded the infliction of punishment as the "emphatic denunciation by the community of a crime." But we might well ask why society should bother to denounce crime unless it hopes by that means to do some good and diminish it. A second example of a retributivist claim which easily lends itself to utilitarian interpretation is that the infliction of punishment reforms the criminal by shocking him into a full awareness of his moral turpitude. The question here is not whether this claim is in fact plausible (criminologists do not find it so) but whether the justification of punishment it offers is essentially retributivist. It seems rather to be utilitarian, and in this respect like the more familiar version of the reform theory we shall shortly examine.

It seems, then, that this criticism does have some force against certain retributivist claims, or against certain ways of stating retributivist claims. But the criticism does not do radical damage to retributivism. Provided the theory is stated in such a way that it is clear that the justification of punishment is necessarily only that it is a fitting response to an offender, then the fact that punishment may sometimes also do good need not count against retributivism. It is, however, an implication of retributivism that it must sometimes be obligatory to punish when punishment is not expected to do any good beyond itself.

It is precisely this implication which is used as the basis for the second criticism of retributivism. This criticism is a straightforward moral judgment, that the theory is morally objectionable in that it requires us to inflict punishment, which is by definition unpleasant and therefore as such evil, for no compensating greater good. The critics therefore invite us to reject the theory as a barbarous residue of old moral ideas.

In the context of philosophical analysis it is important to avoid taking sides in moral argument, as far as this can be done. But it may be worth pointing out that perhaps the great majority of ordinary people have sympathy with some form of retributivism. Contemporary philosophers often appeal to what the "ordinary moral agent" would do or say in certain circumstances, or what the morality of "common sense" would hold on certain topics, but if they make this appeal in settling questions of the justification of punishment they may find that the ordinary person adheres to some form of retributivism. Since there is generally something to be said for an appeal in moral matters to what people ordinarily think, let us consider whether the implication of retributivism is really so morally repugnant.

The implication is that on some occasions it will be obligatory to punish an offender even though this will do no good beyond itself, and that even when some further good is in fact accomplished by the punishment this is irrelevant to its justification. Now it may be that this implication is thought to be morally objectionable because the clause "no good beyond itself" is equated with "no good at all." But a retributivist will claim that the mere fact of inflicting punishment on an offender is good in itself. It is not that a *further* good will result (although it may do so) but that the very fact of the punishment is fitting and to that extent good.

This argument may be made more convincing by an example. Let us suppose that a Nazi war criminal responsible for the cruel torture and deaths of many innocent people has taken refuge in South America where he is living *incognito*. Let us suppose that he has become a useful and prosperous member of the community in which he is living. Let us suppose that the whereabouts of this criminal are discovered and it becomes possible to bring him to justice and punish him. It is very doubtful whether such punishment will have any utilitarian value at all; the criminal will not in any way be "reformed" by treatment, and the deterrence of other war criminals seems an unrealistic aim. We can at least imagine that the punishment of such a criminal will have minimal utilitarian value and may even have disvalue in utilitarian terms. Nevertheless, many people might still feel that the criminal ought to be brought to justice and punished, that irrespective of any further good which may or may not result from the punishment, it is in itself good that such a man should be punished for his crimes. To see some force in this special pleading is to see that retributivism is not completely without moral justification although it can never on its own constitute a complete theory of the justification of punishment.

I have tried to find merits in the retributivist theory because it is frequently dismissed with contempt by philosophers and others at the present time, but we shall now consider theories of the justification of punishment with more obvious appeal. These are all different forms of utilitarianism and they therefore have in common the claim that the justification of punishment necessarily rests in the value of its consequences. There are two common forms of utilitarian justification: in terms of deterrence and in terms of reform.

According to the deterrence form of the utilitarian theory the justification of punishment lies in the fact that the threats of the criminal law will deter potential wrongdoers. But since threats are not efficacious unless they are carried out, proved wrongdoers must in fact have unpleasant consequences visited on them. The increase in the pain of the criminal, however, is balanced by the increase in the happiness of society, where crime has been checked. The theory is modified to account for two classes of people for whom the threats of the law cannot operate; the cases of infants and madmen on the one hand, and on the other hand cases in which accident, coercion and other "excusing conditions" affected the action. In such cases the threats of the law would clearly have little effect and punishment would therefore do no social good.

A deterrent theory of this general sort has often been accepted by utilitarian philosophers from the time of Bentham, but it is frequently criticized. The most common criticism is that it does not rule out the infliction of "punishment" or suffering on the innocent. Utilitarians, that is, argue that where excusing conditions exist punishment would be wasted or would be socially useless. But their argument shows only that the threat of punishment would not be effective in particular cases where there are excusing conditions; the infliction of "punishment" in such cases would still have deterrent values on *others* who might be tempted to break the law. Moreover, people who have committed a crime may hope to escape by pleading excusing conditions and hence there would be social efficacy in punishing those with excuses. Presumably this is the point of "strict liability" in the civil law. But if the deterrent theory commits us to such implications it is at variance with our ordinary views, for we do not accept that the punishment of the lunatic (say) is permissible whatever its social utility.

Utilitarians have sometimes tried to meet this objection by arguing that a system of laws which did not provide for excusing conditions might cause great misery to society. There would be widespread alarm in any society in which no excusing conditions were allowed to affect judicial decisions in criminal cases, and indeed (a utilitarian might argue) such a system might not receive the cooperation of society at large, without which no judicial system can long operate. The utilitarian reply, then, is that while punishment is justified by its deterrent value we must allow excusing conditions since they also have social utility.

It is doubtful, however, whether this reply is adequate. For if excusing conditions are allowed only insofar as they have social utility there remains the possibility that some unusual cases may crop up in which the infliction of suffering or "punishment" on an innocent person would have social utility which would far outweigh the social utility of excusing him. This is not only a logical possibility on the deterrent theory but a very real possibility in communities in which the "framing" of an innocent person might prevent rioting of a racial or religious kind. But this implication of the deterrent theory is at odds with widely accepted moral views. Rather it would be held that the rights of the individual must come before the good of society. This does not mean that the rights of the individual must never be sacrificed to the general good but only that there are certain basic rights, the rights of man, or rights which belong to persons as such, which must never be violated no matter what social good will accrue. It is the weakness of the deterrent version of the utilitarian justification of punishment that it cannot accommodate this truth. Here the deterrent theory contrasts adversely with the retributive theory which does stress the rights of the individual against those of society.

Despite this criticism, however, the deterrent theory cannot be entirely dismissed for it does have relevance at the level of legislation. Whereas it is a failure if it is regarded as an attempt to provide a complete justification of punishment it does succeed in bringing out one of the functions of punishment—that of acting as a deterrent to the potential criminal.

The second conception in terms of which utilitarians try to justify the infliction of punishment is that of "reform." They argue that when a criminal is in prison or in some other detention center a unique opportunity is created for equipping him with a socially desirable set of skills and attitudes. The claim is that such a procedure will have a social utility which outweighs that of conventional punishment.[1] The theory is often based on a psychological or sociological study of the effects of certain kinds of deprivation, cultural starvation, and general lack of

---

[1]This theory must be distinguished from that mentioned in the discussion of retributivism—that conventional punishment reforms by "shocking" the criminal into an awareness of what he has done. Apart from the question of its consistency with the tenets of retributivism this claim does not seem to be supported by the facts; conventional punishment is said by criminologists in fact to increase the criminal's resentment against society.

education on the individual's outlook, and the hope is that these may be put right by re-education or psychological treatment in the period when there would otherwise be conventional punishment.

There are certain oddities about the reform theory if it is intended to be a justification for punishment. The first is that the processes of reform need not involve anything which is painful or unpleasant in the conventional sense. Some critics of the theory would rule it out on that ground alone. In reply, the advocates of the theory might say that insofar as the criminal is *compelled* to undergo reform the process can count as "punishment" in the conventional sense; at least the criminal is deprived of his liberty and that is in itself unpleasant whatever else may happen to him during his period of enforced confinement. A different line of defense might be to concede that reform is not punishment in the conventional sense and to go on to point out that the reform theory is an attempt to replace punishment with a practice which has greater utilitarian justification. According to this line, punishment cannot be justified on utilitarian grounds and the utilitarian must therefore replace punishment with a practice which is justifiable.

There is a second respect in which the reform theory has consequences which are at variance with traditional ideas on punishment. The processes of reform may involve what might be called "treatment." It happens to be true that many advocates of the theory are influenced by psychological doctrines to the effect that the criminal is suffering from a disease of social maladjustment from which he should be cured. Hence, the processes of reform may include more than re-education in the conventional sense; they may involve what is nearer to brain-washing (and from a strictly utilitarian point of view there is everything to be said in favor of this if it is in fact effective). A merit of the retributive theory is to insist that persons as ends in themselves should be protected against undue exposure to the influence of moral "doctors" no matter how socially effective their treatment may be.

The third respect in which the theory departs from traditional ideas is that it gives countenance to the suggestion that the criminal may legitimately be detained until he is reformed. But in some advanced cases of social disease the cure may take some time. And what of the incurables? Here again the retributive theory reminds us of the inhumanity of treating people simply as social units to be molded into desirable patterns.

So far we have considered three oddities of the reform theory, but none of these, of course, invalidates it. The first point simply brings out the nature of the reform theory, and the second and third are hardly implications in the strict sense but merely probable consequences if the practice which the theory reflects is developed in a certain direction. The fatal defect of the theory is rather that it is inadequate as an account of the very many complex ways in which the sanctions of the criminal law are intended to affect society. The reform theory concentrates on only one kind of case, that of the person who has committed an offense or a number of offenses and who might do so again. Moreover, it is plausible only for a certain range of cases in this class; those requiring treatment rather than conventional punishment. But it must be remembered that the criminal law is also intended for those, such as murderers, traitors, and embezzlers, for whom the possibility of a second offense is limited. Moreover, the criminal law serves also to deter ordinary citizens who might occasionally be tempted to commit offenses. The inadequacy of the reform theory lies in its irrelevance to such important types of cases.

It is clear, then, that no one of the accounts of punishment provides on its own an adequate justification of punishment. The retributive theory, which is often taken to be an expression of barbarism, in fact provides a safeguard against the inhumane sacrifice of the individual for the social good, which is the moral danger in the utilitarian theory. Bearing in mind this moral doctrine about the rights of the individual we can then incorporate elements from both the deterrent and the reform versions of utilitarian justification. Only by drawing from all three doctrines can we hope to reflect the wide range of cases to which the criminal law applies.

Justices Potter Stewart, Lewis F. Powell, Jr., and John Paul Stevens

Majority Opinion in *Gregg v. Georgia*

The petitioner, Troy Gregg, was charged with committing armed robbery and murder. In accordance with Georgia procedure in capital cases, the trial was in two stages, a guilt stage and a sentencing stage. . . .

. . . The jury found the petitioner guilty of two counts of armed robbery and two counts of murder.

At the penalty stage, which took place before the same jury, . . . the trial judge instructed the jury that it could recommend either a death sentence or a life prison sentence on each count. . . . The jury returned verdicts of death on each count.

The Supreme Court of Georgia affirmed the convictions and the imposition of the death sentences for murder. . . . The death sentences imposed for armed robbery, however, were vacated on the grounds that the death penalty had rarely been imposed in Georgia for that offense. . . .

We address initially the basic contention that the punishment of death for the crime of murder is, under all circumstances, "cruel and unusual" in violation of the Eighth and Fourteenth Amendments of the Constitution. . . .

The court on a number of occasions has both assumed and asserted the constitutionality of capital punishment. In several cases that assumption provided a necessary foundation for the decision, as the Court was asked to decide whether a particular method of carrying out a capital sentence would be allowed to stand under the Eighth Amendment. But until *Furman v. Georgia* (1972), the Court never confronted squarely the fundamental claim that the punishment of death always, regardless of the enormity of the offense or the procedure followed in

United States Supreme Court, 428 U.S. 153 (1976).

imposing the sentence, is cruel and unusual punishment in violation of the Constitution. Although this issue was presented and addressed in *Furman* it was not resolved by the court. . . . We now hold that the punishment of death does not invariably violate the Constitution. . . .

The death penalty is said to serve two principal social purposes: retribution and deterrence of capital crimes by prospective offenders.[1]

In part, capital punishment is an expression of society's moral outrage at particularly offensive conduct. This function may be unappealing to many, but it is essential in an ordered society that asks its citizens to rely on legal processes rather than self-help to vindicate their wrongs.

> The instinct of retribution is part of the nature of man, and channeling that instinct in the administration of criminal justice serves an important purpose in promoting the stability of a society governed by law. When people begin to believe that organized society is unwilling or unable to impose upon criminal offenders the punishment they "deserve," then there are sown the seeds of anarchy—of self-help, vigilante justice, and lynch law. *Furman v. Georgia* (Stewart, J., concurring).

"Retribution is no longer the dominant objective of the criminal law," but neither is it a forbidden objective nor one inconsistent with our respect for the dignity of men. Indeed, the decision that capital punishment may be the appropriate sanction in extreme cases is an expression of the community's belief that certain crimes are themselves so grievous an affront to humanity that the only adequate response may be the penalty of death.

Statistical attempts to evaluate the worth of the death penalty as a deterrent to crimes by potential offenders have occasioned a great deal of debate. The results simply have been inconclusive. . . .

Although some of the studies suggest that the death penalty may not function as a significantly greater deterrent than lesser penalties, there is no convincing empirical evidence either supporting or refuting this view. We may nevertheless assume safely that there are murderers, such as those who act in passion, for whom the threat of death has little or no deterrent effect. But for many others, the death penalty undoubtedly is a significant deterrent. There are carefully contemplated murders, such as murder for hire, where the possible penalty of death may well enter into the cold calculus that precedes the decision to act. And there are some categories of murder, such as murder by a life prisoner, where other sanctions may not be adequate.

The value of capital punishment as a deterrent of crime is a complex factual issue the resolution of which properly rests with the legislatures, which can evaluate the results of statistical studies in terms of their own local conditions and with a flexibility of approach that is not available to the courts. Indeed, many of the post-*Furman* statutes reflect just such a responsible effort to define those crimes and those criminals for which capital punishment is most probably an effective deterrent.

In sum, we cannot say that the judgment of the Georgia Legislature that capital punishment may be necessary in some cases is clearly wrong. Considerations of federalism, as well as respect for the ability of a legislature to evaluate, in terms of its particular State, the moral consensus concerning the death penalty and its social utility as a sanction, requires us to conclude, in the absence of more convincing evidence, that the infliction of death as a punishment for murder is not without justification and thus is not unconstitutionally severe.

Finally, we must consider whether the punishment of death is disproportionate in relation to the crime for which it is imposed. There is no question that death as a punishment is unique in its severity and irrevocability. When a defendant's life is at stake, the Court has been particularly sensitive to insure that every safeguard is observed. But we are concerned here only with the imposition of capital punishment for the crime of murder, and when a life has been taken deliberately by the offender,[2] we cannot say that the punishment is invariably disproportionate to the crime. It is an extreme sanction, suitable to the most extreme crimes.

We hold that the death penalty is not a form of punishment that may never be imposed, regardless of the circumstances of the offense, regardless of the character of the offender, and regardless of the procedure followed in reaching the decision to impose it.

1. Another purpose that has been discussed is the incapacitation of dangerous criminals and the consequent prevention of crimes that they may otherwise commit in the future.

2. We do not address here the question whether the taking of the criminal's life is a proportionate sanction where no victim has been deprived of life—for example, when capital punishment is imposed for rape, kidnapping, or armed robbery that does not result in the death of any human being.

Justice Thurgood Marshall

Dissenting Opinion in *Gregg v. Georgia*

In *Furman v. Georgia* (1972) (concurring opinion), I set forth at some length my views on the basic issue presented to the Court in [this case]. The death penalty, I concluded, is a cruel and unusual punishment prohibited by the Eighth and Fourteenth Amendments. That continues to be my view. . . .

In *Furman* I concluded that the death penalty is constitutionally invalid for two reasons. First, the death penalty is excessive. And second, the American people, fully informed as to the purposes of the death penalty and its liabilities, would in my view reject it as morally unacceptable. . . .

Even assuming, however, that the post-*Furman* enactment of statutes authorizing the death penalty renders the prediction of the views of an informed citizenry an uncertain basis for a constitutional decision, the enactment of those statutes has no bearing whatsoever on the conclusion that the death penalty is unconstitutional

United States Supreme Court, 428 U.S. 153 (1976).

because it is excessive. An excessive penalty is invalid under the Cruel and Unusual Punishments Clause "even though popular sentiment may favor" it. The inquiry here, then, is simply whether the death penalty is necessary to accomplish the legitimate legislative purposes in punishment, or whether a less severe penalty—life imprisonment—would do as well.

The two purposes that sustain the death penalty as nonexcessive in the Court's view are general deterrence and retribution. . . . The available evidence, I concluded in *Furman,* was convincing that "capital punishment is not necessary as a deterrent to crime in our society." . . .

. . . The evidence I reviewed in *Furman* remains convincing, in my view, that "capital punishment is not necessary as a deterrent to crime in our society." The justification for the death penalty must be found elsewhere.

The other principal purpose said to be served by the death penalty is retribution. The notion that retribution can serve as a moral justification for the sanction of death finds credence in the opinion of my Brothers Stewart, Powell, and Stevens. . . . It is this notion that I find to be the most disturbing aspect of today's unfortunate [decision].

The concept of retribution is a multifaceted one, and any discussion of its role in the criminal law must be undertaken with caution. . . .

The . . . contentions—that society's expression of moral outrage through the imposition of the death penalty pre-empts the citizenry from taking the law into its own hands and reinforces moral values—are not retributive in the purest sense. They are essentially utilitarian in that they portray the death penalty as valuable because of its beneficial results. These justifications for the death penalty are inadequate because the penalty is, quite clearly I think, not necessary to the accomplishment of those results.

There remains for consideration, however, what might be termed the purely retributive justification for the death penalty—that the death penalty is appropriate, not because of its beneficial effect on society, but because the taking of the murderer's life is itself morally good. . . .

. . . The mere fact that the community demands the murderer's life in return for the evil he has done cannot sustain the death penalty, for as Justices Stewart, Powell, and Stevens remind us, "the Eighth Amendment demands more than that a challenged punishment be acceptable to contemporary society." To be sustained under the Eighth Amendment, the death penalty must "compor[t] with the basic concept of human dignity at the core of the Amendment"; the objective in imposing it must be "[consistent] with our respect for the dignity of [other] men." Under these standards, the taking of life "because the wrongdoer deserves it" surely must fail, for such a punishment has as its very basis the total denial of the wrongdoer's dignity and worth.

The death penalty, unnecessary to promote the goal of deterrence or to further any legitimate notion of retribution, is an excessive penalty forbidden by the Eighth and Fourteenth Amendments. I respectfully dissent from the Court's judgment upholding the [sentence] of death imposed upon the [petitioner in this case].

Ernest Van Den Haag

On Deterrence and the Death Penalty

. . . If we do not know whether the death penalty will deter others [in a uniquely effective way], we are confronted with two uncertainties. If we impose the death penalty, and achieve no deterrent effect thereby, the life of a convicted murderer has been expended in vain (from a deterrent viewpoint). There is a net loss. If we impose the death sentence and thereby deter some future murderers, we spared the lives of some future victims (the prospective murderers gain too; they are spared punishment because they were deterred). In this case, the death penalty has led to a net gain, unless the life of a convicted murderer is valued more highly than that of the unknown victim, or victims (and the non-imprisonment of the deterred non-murderer).

The calculation can be turned around, of course. The absence of the death penalty may harm no one and therefore produce a gain—the life of the convicted murderer. Or it may kill future victims of murderers who could have been deterred, and thus produce a loss—their life.

To be sure, we must risk something certain—the death (or life) of the convicted man, for something uncertain—the death (or life) of the victims of murderers who may be deterred. This is in the nature of uncertainty—when we invest, or gamble, we risk the money we have for an uncertain gain. Many human actions, most commitments—including marriage and crime—share this characteristic with the deterrent purpose of any penalization, and with its rehabilitative purpose (and even with the protective).

More proof is demanded for the deterrent effect of the death penalty than is demanded for the deterrent effect of other penalties. This is not justified by the absence of other utilitarian purposes such as protection and rehabilitation; they involve no less uncertainty than deterrence.[1]

Irrevocability may support a demand for some reason to expect more deterrence than revocable penalties might produce, but not a demand for more proof of deterrence, as has been pointed out above. The reason for expecting more deterrence lies in the greater severity, the terrifying effect inherent in finality. Since it seems more important to spare victims than to spare murderers, the burden of proving that the greater severity inherent in irrevocability adds nothing to deterrence lies on those who oppose capital punishment. Proponents of the death penalty

From the *Journal of Criminal Law, Criminology and Police Science* 60, 2 (1969): 146–7. Reprinted by special permission of Northwestern University School of Law.

[1]Rehabilitation or protection are of minor importance in our actual penal system (though not in our theory). We confine many people who do not need rehabilitation and against whom we do not need protection (e.g., the exasperated husband who killed his wife); we release many unrehabilitated offenders against whom protection is needed. Certainly rehabilitation and protection are not, and deterrence is, the main actual function of legal punishment if we disregard nonutilitarian purposes.

need show only that there is no more uncertainty about it than about greater severity in general.

The demand that the death penalty be proved more deterrent than alternatives cannot be satisfied any more than the demand that six years in prison be proved to be more deterrent than three. But the uncertainty which confronts us favors the death penalty as long as by imposing it we might save future victims of murder. This effect is as plausible as the general idea that penalties have deterrent effects which increase with their severity. Though we have no proof of the positive deterrence of the penalty, we also have no proof of zero, or negative effectiveness. I believe we have no right to risk additional future victims of murder for the sake of sparing convicted murderers; on the contrary, our moral obligation is to risk the possible ineffectiveness of executions. However rationalized, the opposite view appears to be motivated by the simple fact that executions are more subjected to social control than murder. However, this applies to all penalties and does not argue for the abolition of any.

Thomas Hurka

Rights and Capital Punishment

Discussions of the morality of capital punishment, and indeed discussions of the morality of punishment in general, usually assume that there are two possible justifications of punishment, a deterrence justification associated with utilitarianism and other consequentialist moral theories, and a retributive justification associated with deontological moral theories. But now that rights-based theories are attracting the increasing attention of moral philosophers it is worth asking whether these theories may not employ a different justification of punishment, with different consequences for the morality of particular forms of punishment. I will argue that rights theories do employ a different justification of punishment, and that this justification combines many of the attractive features of the deterrence and retributive justifications while avoiding their unattractive features. In particular, I will argue that the rights-based justification has more attractive consequences for the morality of capital punishment than either the deterrence or retributive justifications.[1]

Rights-based moral theories hold that persons have certain natural rights, and the fact that these rights are natural is often expressed by saying that persons would possess them "in the state of nature." Among the rights which persons are usually said to possess in the state of nature is the right to punish those who violate the rights of others. In section 7 of the *Second Treatise,* Locke says that the state of

From *Dialogue* XXI, 4 (December 1982). Reprinted by permission.

nature has a Law of Nature to govern it, and that "everyone has a right to punish the transgressors of the Law to such a Degree, as may hinder its Violation."[2] Nozick too includes a right to punish among those he grants in *Anarchy, State, and Utopia*, quoting Locke's description of this right with approval, and devoting an entire section to a discussion of "the right of all to punish."[3] If persons have a right to punish in the state of nature, then they are permitted to punish the violators of rights if they want to, but they are also permitted to refrain from punishing them if they do not want to. . . .

The right to punish which persons have in the state of nature is not a primitive right, but derives from another more general right which they possess. Whenever persons in the state of nature have a natural right they also have the right to *enforce* that right, that is, the right to use coercion against other persons to prevent them from violating it.[4] The most familiar form of coercion is the use of force, and persons in the state of nature therefore have the right to use force to defend themselves against would-be violators of their rights, and also to defend third parties. But this right of self- (and other-) defense is not the only enforcement right which they possess. The making of threats is also a form of coercion, and persons in the state of nature therefore also have the right to threaten others with certain harms if they succeed in violating their rights, or succeed in violating the rights of third parties. It is from this second enforcement-right that the right to punish derives. If persons in the state of nature have the right to threaten others with harms if they succeed in violating rights, then they surely also have the right to inflict these harms on them once the relevant rights have been violated. But this is just what the right to punish is: a right to inflict harms on persons who have successfully violated the rights of others.[5]

Although Locke and Nozick include a right to punish among those possessed in the state of nature they do not provide any justification of this right. They do not show *why* rights theories should contain a right to punish, or even why they should contain enforcement rights in general, but simply include these rights on a list of those possessed in the state of nature. There is one kind of rights theory, however, which in a somewhat stricter usage of the term than is usual I will call a "libertarian" rights theory, which can provide such a justification. A libertarian rights theory holds that there is really only one natural right, namely the equal right of all persons to the most extensive liberty compatible with a like liberty for other persons, and that all other natural rights are species or instances of the right to liberty. They are all rights to exercise liberty in certain specified areas, and impose on other persons the duty not to interfere with liberty in those areas.[6] Because these rights are instances of a right to the *most extensive* liberty we are to identify them by identifying the most extensive right to liberty possible. Comparing the extent of different liberties in the way this requires involves some obvious difficulties, but the following should be uncontroversial. If one liberty contains another as a proper part, so that exercising the second liberty always involves exercising the first, but exercising the first liberty does not always involve exercising the second, then the first liberty is more extensive than the second (some examples: the liberty to buy property in Canada is more extensive than the liberty to buy property in Alberta, for it contains it as a proper part; the liberty to move either of one's arms freely is more extensive than the liberty to move one's left arm freely, for it contains it as a proper part, and so on). But this is all we need to show why a libertarian rights theory has to contain enforcement rights. Let us imagine that we have discovered that L is the most extensive liberty not containing the liberty to do any enforcing such that every person can have an equal right to exercise all the liberties in L, and no one person's right conflicts with that of any other. Then in deciding whether to grant enforcement rights we are deciding whether to add to L the liberty of removing from other persons the liberty of removing liberties in L from other persons. We have every reason to do this and no reason not to. If we add this liberty —and it is once again best described as the liberty to remove from other persons the liberty of removing liberties in L from other persons—we will be creating a new liberty L^1, which contains L as a proper part, and is therefore more extensive than it. But at the same time we will not be subtracting liberties from any other person's liberty L. Although the liberty we are adding conflicts with some liberties of other persons all these are liberties which have already been excluded from L, and have therefore already been excluded from the protection of their natural right to liberty. Allowing enforcement rights enables us to extend the scope of everyone's right to liberty—which is just what a libertarian rights theory requires us to do—without detracting in any way from the right to liberty of others. And if this is the case, then a libertarian rights theory can give exactly the same justification for these rights as for any other rights it grants.

This justification of enforcement rights, which I have presented so far in a fairly abstract way, applies most directly to the right of self- (or other-) defense. If we give persons the right to use force to prevent rights violations then we are obviously extending the scope of their right to liberty without limiting the right to liberty of anyone else, for no one has the right to violate rights. But it also applies to the right to make and carry out threats which lies behind the right to punish. When we threaten a person with harms if he successfully violates rights we do not remove from him the liberty of violating rights as such. But we do remove from him the more complex liberty of violating rights and not having those harms inflicted on him afterwards. If he does not have the right to exercise the simple liberty he does not have the right to exercise the more complex one either, and in giving other persons the right to remove the more complex liberty from him a libertarian rights theory is once again extending the scope of their right to liberty without in any way detracting from his.

Because it derives the right to punish from a right to make certain threats, the rights-based justification has two attractive consequences which also follow from the retributive justification. The first is that it is never permissible to punish persons who have not violated, or who have not been found by reliable proceedings to have violated, the rights of other persons. Guilt, in other words, is a necessary condition of the permissibility of punishment on the rights-based view. The reasoning leading up to this consequence should be fairly evident. The right to use coercion to prevent others from violating rights only entitles us to make a very specific threat, namely the threat to inflict certain harms on them if they actually succeed in violating rights, and we could not claim to be carrying out this threat if we inflicted harms on someone whom we did not have reliable reasons to think had violated rights. This first consequence also follows from the retributive justification, but it is a well-known objection to the deterrence justification that no such consequence follows from it. Critics of the deterrence justification often point out that it could license the framing and "punishment" of an innocent man if this would be sufficiently effective in deterring future crimes. The rights-based justification is not open to this objection for it holds, along with the retributive justification, that guilt is always a necessary condition of the permissibility of punishment. The second consequence is that it is never permissible to punish persons for rights violations unless our intention to punish persons for those violations has been publicly announced in the past. The reasoning leading up to this consequence should also be evident. If punishment is only permissible because it is the carrying out of a permissible threat, then it is only permissible when that threat has actually been made. Punishments for the violation of secret laws, or for the violation of retroactive laws, are never permissible on the rights-based view, though we can easily imagine circumstances in which they would be permissible and even required on the deterrence view, and perhaps even on some retributive views as well.

The rights-based justification, then, has some attractive consequences in common with the retributive justification for the question when punishment is permissible. But when it turns to the question of how much punishment is permissible, or how severe a punishment is permissible, it has some consequences in common with the retributive justification and some in common with the deterrence justification. The important thing to realize here is that the enforcement rights which persons have in the state of nature are not unqualified. They are subject to at least two qualifications, and these qualifications place limits on the severity of the punishments which they may inflict in the state of nature, and which their governments may inflict in civil society. To set out these qualifications I will begin by examining some particular cases involving self-defense where I think their intuitive attractiveness is especially evident, and then give them a theoretical justification. I will conclude by showing what the implications of these qualifications are for questions about the morality of punishment, and in particular for questions about the morality of capital punishment.

Let us begin by imagining the following case. One person X is trying to violate a fairly unimportant right of another person Y, say, the right not to be tickled, and Y is considering how to prevent this. Y is not nearly as strong as X, so he cannot hope to stop X just by resisting him physically. Nor will any threat of Y's deter X. But Y does have in his hands a pistol with which he can kill X. If killing X is the only way Y can prevent X from violating his right not to be tickled, is it permissible for Y to use his pistol?... We would insist that there is an upper limit on the amount of coercion persons can use to enforce their rights, and that this limit is lower the less important the rights are which they are enforcing. For Y to kill X just to prevent him from tickling him is for Y quite clearly to overstep a limit which is, in the case of a very unimportant right like the right not to be tickled, very low indeed.

Reflection on this case suggests what I will call an *upper limit* qualification on persons' enforcement rights. The most natural way for a rights theory to express this qualification is as follows. Although Y's right to enforce his right to ϕ entitles him to act in ways which would otherwise involve violating some rights of X's, it does not entitle him to act in ways which would otherwise involve violating any rights of X's which are more important than his own right to ϕ. In the course of enforcing his right to ϕ Y can act in ways which would otherwise involve violating

X's right to ϕ, or any rights of X's which are less important than his right to ϕ. So if X is trying to kill him Y can kill X in self-defense, or assault him or tie him up. But he cannot act in ways which would otherwise involve violating any rights of X's which are more important than his right to ϕ....

Now let us imagine another case. X is attacking Y with the intention of killing him, and Y is considering how to prevent this. He has in one hand a pistol, with which he can kill X, and in the other hand a tranquilizer gun, with which he can sedate X long enough to make his escape but with which he will not do X any permanent damage. The two weapons will be equally effective in repelling X's attack and Y knows this. Is it permissible for Y to use his pistol and kill X? Although Y's killing X would not violate the upper limit qualification I think most of us would agree that it is not permissible. We would insist that there is another limitation on the amount of coercion Y can use to enforce his rights, one which requires him never to use more than the minimum amount of coercion necessary to prevent the violation of his rights. In this case Y's killing X would involve more than the minimum amount of coercion, for he can also use the tranquilizer gun on X, and killing him is therefore impermissible.

This second case suggests another qualification on persons' enforcement rights, one which I will call a *minimum necessary* qualification, and which is most natural for a rights theory to express as follows. Although Y's right to enforce his right to ϕ sometimes entitles him to act in ways which would otherwise involve violating X's right to ψ, it only does so when it is not possible for Y to prevent the violation of his right to ϕ just as effectively by acting in ways which would otherwise involve violating only rights of X's which are less important than his right to ψ. (If it is possible for Y to prevent the violation of his right to ϕ by acting in ways which would not otherwise involve violating any of X's rights, e.g., by running away, this qualification requires him to run away.)....

In discussing the upper limit and minimum necessary qualifications I have made extensive use of the notion of the *importance* of a natural right, and there will no doubt be questions about exactly what this notion involves. In speaking of the importance of a right I have intended in the first place to speak of something intuitive. We all have, I trust, an intuitive sense that the right to life is more important than the right not to be physically assaulted, which in turn is more important than the right not to be tickled. But the notion can also be given a formal representation in a libertarian rights theory of the kind we have been discussing. If every right is an instance of the right to liberty, then it seems natural to say that one right is more important than another whenever it is a right to a more extensive liberty than the other. And although comparing the extent of some liberties raises obvious difficulties the following should once again be uncontroversial. If one liberty contains another as a proper part, so that exercising the second liberty always involves exercising the first, but exercising the first liberty does not always involve exercising the second, then the first liberty is more extensive than the second. The ranking procedure which these two suggestions yield is perhaps most usefully put as follows: one right is more important than another whenever violating the first right always involves violating the second, but violating the second right does not always involve violating the first (an example: the right to buy property in Canada is more important than the right to buy property in Alberta because preventing a person from buying property in Canada always involves preventing him from buying it in Alberta, but preventing him from buying it in Alberta does not always involve preventing him from buying it in Canada.) This ranking procedure does not generate anything like a complete ordering over rights. It only generates a partial ordering, but the ordering is not so partial as to be useless. It has, for instance, some clear results about a number of rights that are important for questions about self-defense. It holds that the right not to be both tied up and beaten is more important than the right simply not to be tied up, that the right not to have both arms broken is more important than the right not to have one's left arm broken, and that the right not to have property valued at $100 destroyed is more important than the right not to have property valued at $1 destroyed. It also has some clear results about a number of rights that are important for questions about punishment. It holds that the right not to be imprisoned for ten years is more important than the right not to be imprisoned for five years, and that the right not to be fined $100 is more important than the right not to be fined $1. Most importantly for our concerns, however, it has clear results about the right which is most centrally involved in questions about capital punishment, namely the right to life. On a libertarian view the right to life is the right to exercise the liberty of choosing life over death, and imposes on others the duty not to remove that liberty, as they would do if they forcibly chose death for us. But this means that the right to life has to be the most important natural right there is. Choosing life is choosing to exercise all the liberties we do exercise when we are alive, while choosing death is choosing to exercise no further liberties at all. A person who removes the liberty of choosing life from us is therefore removing all our other liberties from us. In violating our right to life he is violating all our other rights as well, for he is leaving us in a position where we can never exercise those rights again. Although the proper part ranking procedure has clear results in these areas it does not have clear results in certain others. It does not say anything determinate about the relative importance of property rights and rights not to be physically assaulted, for instance, or of property rights and rights not to be imprisoned. These gaps in the ordering it generates weaken but they do not prevent the operation of the upper limit and minimum necessary qualifications. If property rights and rights not to be physically assaulted are unranked with respect to each other then neither is more important than the other, and persons may if necessary use force against others to prevent them from destroying their property, and destroy others' property to prevent them from assaulting them. Far from being an unwanted result this is one which I think we ought to welcome, for our intuitions seem to support the view that in most cases these two forms of self-defense are, if necessary, permissible. . . .

Having discussed the upper limit and minimum necessary qualifications in a general way let us now see what their implications are for questions about punishment. The qualifications place limits on the severity of the punishments which persons are permitted to inflict in the state of nature, and which their governments are permitted to inflict in civil society. It follows from the upper limit qualification that they are never permitted to inflict punishments which infringe rights that are more important than the ones which the offender has violated, and which they are therefore enforcing. And it follows from the minimum necessary qualification that they are never permitted to inflict punishments which infringe rights that are more important than is necessary to prevent further violations of the right which they are enforcing. If two punishments will be equally effective in deterring violations of this right, they have a duty to impose the less severe punishment; and if no punishments will be effective in deterring violations, they have a duty to impose no punishment at all.…

Of these two consequences the one which follows from the upper limit qualification also follows from many versions of the retributive justification. Many retributive theorists also hold that there is an upper limit on the severity of the punishments we can inflict for certain crimes, and that we do wrong if we exceed this limit. But no such consequence follows from the deterrence justification. The deterrence justification permits and even requires as severe a punishment as will best promote the overall good of society, and this punishment can sometimes be very severe indeed. It might well be the case that capital punishment would be an effective deterrent to the crime of shoplifting, and that the benefits to society as a whole of the huge reduction in shoplifting resulting from its imposition would far outweigh the harms to the one or two individuals foolish enough to be caught and executed for shoplifting. Most of us do not think, however, that it could ever be permissible to impose capital punishment for the crime of shoplifting, and take it to be a serious objection to the deterrence justification that it could sometimes require it. The consequence which follows from the minimum necessary qualification also follows from the deterrence justification, but it does not follow from the retributive justification. The retributive justification can require us to impose severe punishments when no further rights violations will be prevented by them, and indeed when no further social good will result from them at all. Some retributive theorists like Kant have of course revelled in this fact, but I think most of us find it repugnant. We think that punishment is only permissible when it does something to promote social good, and take it to be a serious objection to the retributive justification that it requires it even when it does nothing to promote social good.

What are the consequences of the rights-based justification for the special case of capital punishment? Capital punishment infringes the right to life of a criminal, and the right to life is the most important right there is. This means that, given the upper limit qualification, the rights-based justification will only allow capital punishment to be imposed on persons who have violated the right to life of another, that is, it will only allow capital punishment to be imposed for the crime of murder. At the same time, however, given the minimum necessary qualification, the rights-based justification will only allow capital punishment to be imposed for the crime of murder if there is no other less severe punishment which is equally effective at deterring murder. Extensive criminological studies have failed to produce any evidence that capital punishment is a more effective deterrent to murder than life imprisonment, and the rights-based justification will therefore hold that, until such evidence is produced, the imposition of capital punishment for any crime at all is impermissible.[7] This is in my view an attractive consequence, and it is one which also follows from the deterrence justification. But it is not bought at the cost of the many unattractive consequences of the deterrence justification. Many of us believe that if capital punishment is not an effective deterrent to murder then it ought not to be imposed. But we would not want this view to commit us to the simple deterrence justification, with all the unattractive consequences which that justification has. We would not want it to commit us to the view that capital punishment could be a permissible or even a required punishment for shoplifting, and we would not want it to commit us to the view that it could be permissible or even required to frame and "punish" an innocent man. The rights-based justification allows us to give some weight to the question of deterrence in assessing the morality of capital punishment, without giving it the overwhelming weight which it has in the deterrence justification.

Perhaps the distinctive consequences of the rights-based justification for the morality of capital punishment can best be summarized as follows. Assuming that a retributive calculus will find capital punishment a "fitting" punishment for the crime of murder, the retributive justification holds that it is a necessary and sufficient condition for the permissibility (and even requiredness) of imposing capital punishment on a person that he be guilty of murder. The rights-based justification agrees that this is a necessary condition but denies that it is sufficient; for a punishment to be permissible, it maintains, it must have some independent deterrent effect. The deterrence justification, by contrast, holds that it is a necessary and sufficient condition for the permissibility (and even requiredness) of imposing capital punishment on a person that this punishment have some independent deterrent effect. The rights-based justification once again agrees that this is a necessary condition but denies that it is sufficient; for a punishment to be permissible the person who undergoes it must be guilty of a crime, and guilty of a crime which violated rights at least as important as those which his punishment will infringe. In the rights-based justification conditions which are individually both necessary and sufficient in the deterrence and retributive justifications are made individually necessary but only jointly sufficient, and for this reason the rights-based justification can be said to combine the attractive features of the other two justifications while avoiding their unattractive features. The view that the conditions focused on by the deterrence and retributive justifications are individually necessary but only jointly sufficient for the permissibility of punishment has of course been defended by a number of philosophers. But I think it is only in the context of a rights-based moral theory that this view can be given a theoretical justification, and the attractive features of the deterrence and retributive justifications combined in a manner that is principled rather than *ad hoc*.

NOTES

1. Some philosophers have argued that we should apply the deterrence justification to the institution of punishment and the retributive justification to particular acts within this institution; for classic statements of this "mixed" view see John Rawls, "Two Concepts of Rules," *Philosophical Review* 64 (1955): 3–32, and H. L. A. Hart, "Prolegomenon to the Principles of Punishment," in his *Punishment and Responsibility* (Oxford, 1968), 1–13. But these arguments seem to me to rely on a dubious distinction between an institution and the acts of which it is composed. The rights-based justification I will defend has many of the same attractive consequences as this mixed view without relying on its dubious assumptions about institutions.

2. John Locke, *Two Treatises of Government,* 2d ed., ed. Peter Laslett (New York, 1967).

3. Robert Nozick, *Anarchy, State, and Utopia* (New York, 1974), 10, 137–42.

4. On this see H. L. A. Hart, "Are There Any Natural Rights?" *Philosophical Review* 64 (1955): 175–91.

5. Enforcement rights are often said to include not only a right of self- (and other-) defense and a right to punish but also a right to exact compensation, where this right to exact compensation is sometimes exercised alongside the right to punish and sometimes exercised when it would be wrong to punish. The right to exact compensation, however, need not be regarded as a separate enforcement right. If we say that alongside their ordinary rights persons have more complex rights not to be harmed without compensation being paid them afterwards, we can say that exacting compensation prevents the violation of these rights in exactly the same way that self-defense prevents the violation of simpler rights....

6. A libertarian rights theory of this kind is presented in Immanuel Kant, *The Metaphysical Elements of Justice: Part 1 of the Metaphysics of Morals,* John Ladd, trans. (Indianapolis, 1965), and discussed by Hart in "Are There Any Natural Rights?"

7. As is often pointed out, the studies have not produced evidence that capital punishment is *not* a deterrent to murder either. But the onus of proof in this question is surely on the defenders of capital punishment to show that it is.

Hugo Adam Bedau

Capital Punishment

CAPITAL PUNISHMENT AND SOCIAL DEFENSE

PREVENTING VERSUS DETERRING CRIME

The analogy between capital punishment and self-defense requires us to face squarely the empirical questions surrounding the preventive and deterrent effects of the death penalty. Executing a murderer in the name of punishment can be seen as a crime-*preventive* measure just to the extent it is reasonable to believe that if the murderer had not been executed he or she would have committed other crimes (including, but not necessarily confined to, murder). Executing a murderer can be seen as a crime *deterrent* just to the extent it is reasonable to believe that by the example of the execution other persons would be frightened off from committing murder. Any punishment can be a crime preventive without being a crime deterrent, just as it can be a deterrent without being a preventive. It can also be both or neither. Prevention and deterrence are theoretically independent because they operate by different methods. Crimes can be prevented by taking guns out of the hands of criminals, by putting criminals behind bars, by alerting the public to be less careless and less prone to victimization, and so forth. Crimes can be

From *Matters of Life and Death: New Introductory Essays in Moral Philosophy,* 2nd ed., edited by Tom Regan (New York: Random House, 1986). Copyright © 1986 Random House, Inc. Reprinted by permission of the author and publisher.

deterred only by making would-be criminals frightened of being arrested, convicted, and punished for crimes—that is, making persons overcome their desire to commit crimes by a stronger desire to avoid the risk of being caught and punished.

THE DEATH PENALTY AS A CRIME PREVENTIVE

Capital punishment is unusual among penalties because its preventive effects limit its deterrent effects. The death penalty can never deter the executed person from further crimes. At most, it can prevent a person from committing them. Popular discussions of the death penalty are frequently confused because they so often assume that the death penalty is a perfect and infallible deterrent so far as the executed criminal is concerned, whereas nothing of the sort is true. What is even more important, it is also wrong to think that in every execution the death penalty has proved to be an infallible crime preventive. What is obviously true is that once an offender has been executed, it is physically impossible for that person to commit any further crimes, since the punishment is totally incapacitative. But incapacitation is not identical with prevention. Prevention by means of incapacitation occurs only if the executed criminal would have committed other crimes if he or she had not been executed and had been punished only in some less incapacitative way (e.g., by imprisonment).

What evidence is there that the incapacitative effects of the death penalty are an effective crime preventive? From the study of imprisonment, parole, release records, this much is clear: If the murderers and other criminals who have been executed are like the murderers who were convicted but not executed, then (1) executing all convicted murderers would have prevented many crimes, but not many murders (less than one convicted murderer in five hundred commits another murder); and (2) convicted murderers, whether inside prison or outside after release, have at least as good a record of no further criminal activity as any other class of convicted felon....

THE DEATH PENALTY AS A CRIME DETERRENT

Determining whether the death penalty is an effective deterrent is even more difficult than determining its effectiveness as a crime preventive. In general, our knowledge about how penalties deter crimes and whether in fact they do—whom they deter, from which crimes, and under what conditions—is distressingly inexact. Most people nevertheless are convinced that punishments do deter, and that the more severe a punishment is the better it will deter. For half a century, social scientists have studied the questions whether the death penalty is a deterrent and whether it is a better deterrent than the alternative of imprisonment. Their verdict, while not unanimous, is nearly so. Whatever may be true about the deterrence of lesser crimes by other penalties, the deterrence achieved by the death penalty for murder is not measurably any greater than the deterrence achieved by long-term imprisonment. In the nature of the case, the evidence is quite indirect. No one can identify for certain any crimes that did not occur because the would-be offender was deterred by the threat of the death penalty and could not have been deterred by a less severe threat. Likewise, no one can identify any crimes that did occur because the offender was not deterred by the threat of prison even though he would have been deterred by the threat of death. Nevertheless, such evidence as we have fails to show that the more severe penalty (death) is really a better deterrent than the less severe penalty (imprisonment) for such crimes as murder.

If the conclusion stated above is correct, and the death penalty and long-term imprisonment are equally effective (or ineffective) as deterrents to murder, then the argument for the death penalty on grounds of deterrence is seriously weakened. One of the moral principles identified earlier now comes into play. It is the principle that unless there is a good reason for choosing a more rather than a less severe punishment for a crime, the less severe penalty is to be preferred. This principle obviously commends itself to anyone who values human life and who concedes that, all other things being equal, less pain and suffering is always better than more. Human life is valued in part to the degree that it is free of pain, suffering, misery, and frustration, and in particular to the extent that it is free of such experiences when they serve no purpose. If the death penalty is not a more effective deterrent than imprisonment, then its greater severity is gratuitous, purposeless suffering and deprivation. Accordingly, we must reject it in favor of some less severe alternative, unless we can identify some more weighty moral principle that the death penalty protects better than any less severe mode of punishment does. Whether there is any such principle is unclear.

A COST/BENEFIT ANALYSIS OF THE DEATH PENALTY

A full study of the costs and benefits involved in the practice of capital punishment would not be confined solely to the question of whether it is a better deterrent or preventive of murder than imprisonment. Any thoroughgoing utilitarian approach to the death-penalty controversy would need to examine carefully other costs and benefits as well, because maximizing the balance of all the social benefits over all the social costs is the sole criterion of right and wrong according to utilitarianism.... Let us consider, therefore, some of the other costs and benefits to be calculated. Clinical psychologists have presented evidence to suggest that the death penalty actually incites some persons of unstable mind to murder others, either because they are afraid to take their own lives and hope that society will punish them for murder by putting them to death, or because they fancy that they, too, are killing with justification analogously to the lawful and presumably justified killing involved in capital punishment. If such evidence is sound, capital punishment can serve as a counterpreventive or even an incitement to murder; such incited murders become part of its social cost. Imprisonment, however, has not been known to incite any murders or other crimes of violence in a comparable fashion. (A possible exception might be found in the imprisonment of terrorists, which has inspired other terrorists to take hostages as part of a scheme to force the authorities to release their imprisoned comrades.) The risks of executing the innocent are also part of the social cost. The historical record is replete with innocent persons arrested, indicted, convicted, sentenced, and occasionally legally executed for crimes they did not commit. This is quite apart from the guilty persons unfairly convicted, sentenced to death, and executed on the strength of perjured testimony, fraudulent evidence, subornation of jurors, and other violations of the civil rights and liberties of the accused. Nor is this all. The high costs of a capital trial and of the inevitable appeals, the costly methods of custody most prisons adopt for convicts on "death row," are among the straightforward economic costs that the death penalty incurs. Conducting a valid cost/benefit analysis of capital punishment is extremely difficult, and it is impossible to predict exactly what such a study would show. Nevertheless, based on such evidence as we do have, it is quite possible that a study of this sort would favor abolition of all death penalties rather than their retention.

WHAT IF EXECUTIONS DID DETER?

From the moral point of view, it is quite important to determine what one should think about capital punishment if the evidence were clearly to show that the death penalty is a distinctly superior method of social defense by comparison with less severe alternatives. Kantian moralists ... would have no use for such knowledge, because their entire case for the morality of the death penalty rests on the way it is thought to provide a just retribution, not on the way it is thought to provide social defense. For a utilitarian, however, such knowledge would be conclusive. Those who follow Locke's reasoning would also be gratified, because they defend the morality of the death penalty both on the ground that it is retributively just and on the ground that it provides needed social defense.

What about the opponents of the death penalty, however? To oppose the death penalty in the face of incontestable evidence that it is an effective method of social defense violates the moral principle that where grave risks are to be run, it is better that they be run by the guilty than by the innocent.... If opposition to the death penalty is to be morally responsible, then it must be conceded that there are conditions (however unlikely) under which that opposition should cease.

But even if the death penalty were known to be a uniquely effective social defense, we could still imagine conditions under which it would be reasonable to oppose it. Suppose that in addition to being a slightly better preventive and deterrent than imprisonment, executions also have a slight incitive effect (so that for every ten murders an execution prevents or deters, it also incites another murder). Suppose also that the administration of criminal justice in capital cases is inefficient, unequal, and tends to secure convictions and death sentences only for murderers who least "deserve" to be sentenced to death (including some death sentences and a few executions of the innocent). Under such conditions, it would still be reasonable to oppose the death penalty, because on the facts supposed more (or not fewer) innocent lives are being threatened and lost by using the death penalty than would be risked by abolishing it. It is important to remember throughout our evaluation of the deterrence controversy that we cannot ever apply the principle ... that advises us to risk the lives of the guilty in order to save the lives of the innocent. Instead, the most we can do is weigh the risk for the general public against the execution of those who are *found* guilty by an imperfect system of criminal justice. These hypothetical factual assumptions illustrate the contingencies upon which the morality of opposition to the death penalty rests. And not only the morality of opposition; the morality of any defense of the death penalty rests on the same contingencies. This should help us understand why, in resolving the morality of capital punishment one way or the other, it is so important to know, as well as we can, whether the death penalty really does deter, prevent, or incite crime, whether the innocent really are ever executed, and how likely is the occurrence of these things in the future.

HOW MANY GUILTY LIVES IS ONE INNOCENT LIFE WORTH?

The great unanswered question that utilitarians must face concerns the level of social defense that executions should be expected to achieve before it is justifiable to carry them out. Consider three possible situations: (1) At the level of a hundred executions per year, each additional execution of a convicted murderer reduces the number of murder victims by ten. (2) Executing every convicted murderer reduces the number of murders to 5,000 victims annually, whereas executing only one out of ten reduces the number to 5,001. (3) Executing every convicted murderer reduces the murder rate no more than does executing one in a hundred and no more than does a random pattern of executions. . . .

Since no adequate cost/benefit analysis of the death penalty exists, there is no way to resolve these questions from that standpoint at this time. Moreover, it can be argued that we cannot have such an analysis without already establishing in some way or other the relative value of innocent lives versus guilty lives. Far from being a product of cost/benefit analysis, a comparative evaluation of lives would have to be available to us before we undertook any such analysis. Without it, no cost/benefit analysis can get off the ground. Finally, it must be noted that our knowledge at present does not approximate to anything like the situation described above in (1). On the contrary, from the evidence we do have it seems we achieve about the same deterrent and preventive effects whether we punish murder by death or by imprisonment. . . . Therefore, something like the situation in (2) or in (3) may be correct. If so, this shows that the choice between the two policies of capital punishment and life imprisonment for murder will probably have to be made on some basis other than social defense; on that basis alone, the two policies are equivalent and therefore equally acceptable.

CAPITAL PUNISHMENT AND RETRIBUTIVE JUSTICE

. . . [T]here are two leading principles of retributive justice relevant to the capital-punishment controversy. One is the principle that crimes should be punished. The other is the principle that the severity of a punishment should be proportional to the gravity of the offense. They are moral principles of recognized weight. No discussion of the morality of punishment would be complete without taking them into account. Leaving aside all questions of social defense, how strong a case for capital punishment can be made on their basis? How reliable and persuasive are these principles themselves?

CRIME MUST BE PUNISHED

Given the general rationale for punishment sketched earlier . . . there cannot be any dispute over this principle. In embracing it, of course, we are not automatically making a fetish of "law and order," in the sense that we would be if we thought that the most important single thing to do with social resources is to punish crimes. In addition, this principle need not be in dispute between proponents and opponents of the death penalty. Only those who completely oppose punishment for murder and other erstwhile capital crimes would appear to disregard this principle. Even defenders of the death penalty must admit that putting a convicted murderer in prison for years is a punishment of that criminal. The principle that crime must be punished is neutral to our controversy, because both sides acknowledge it.

It is the other principle of retributive justice that seems to be a decisive one. Under the principle of retaliation, *lex talionis,* it must always have seemed that murderers ought to be put to death. Proponents of the death penalty, with rare exceptions, have insisted on this point, and it seems that even opponents of the death penalty must give it grudging assent. The strategy for opponents of the death penalty is to argue either that (1) this principle is not really a principle of justice after all, or that (2) to the extent it is, it does not require death for murderers, or that (3) in any case it is not the only principle of punitive justice. As we shall see, all these objections have merit.

IS MURDER ALONE TO BE PUNISHED BY DEATH?

Let us recall, first, that not even the biblical world limited the death penalty to the punishment of murder. Many other nonhomicidal crimes also carried this penalty (e.g., kidnapping, witchcraft, cursing one's parents). In our own nation's recent history, persons have been executed for aggravated assault, rape, kidnapping, armed robbery, sabotage, and espionage. It is not possible to defend *any* of these executions (not to mention some of the more bizarre capital statutes, like the one in Georgia that used to provide an optional death penalty for desecration of a grave) on grounds of just retribution. This entails that either such executions are not justified or that they are justified on some ground other than retribution. In actual practice, few if any defenders of the death penalty have ever been willing to rest their case entirely on the moral principle of just retribution as formulated in terms of "a life for a life." (Kant seems to have been a conspicuous exception.) Most defenders of the death penalty have implied by their willingness to use executions to defend not only life but limb and property as well, that they did not place much value on the lives of criminals when compared to the value of both lives and things belonging to innocent citizens.

ARE ALL MURDERS TO BE PUNISHED BY DEATH?

The abstract principle that the punishment of death best fits the crime of murder turns out to be extremely difficult to interpret and apply.

If we look at the matter from the standpoint of the actual practice of criminal justice, we can only conclude that "a life for a life" plays little or no role whatever. Plea bargaining (in which a person charged with a crime pleads guilty in exchange for a less severe sentence than he might have received if his case went to trial and he was found guilty), even where murder is concerned, is widespread. Studies of criminal justice reveal that what the courts (trial or appellate) in a given jurisdiction decide on a given day is first-degree murder suitably punished by death could just as well be decided in a neighboring jurisdiction on another day either as second-degree murder or as first-degree murder but without the death penalty. The factors that influence prosecutors in determining the charge under which they will prosecute go far beyond the simple principle of "a life for a life." Cynics, of course, will say that these facts show that our society does not care about justice. To put it succinctly, either justice in punishment does not consist of retribution, because there are other principles of justice; or there are other moral considerations besides justice that must be honored; or retributive justice is not adequately expressed in the idea of "a life for a life"; or justice in the criminal justice system is beyond our reach.

IS DEATH SUFFICIENTLY RETRIBUTIVE?

Those who advocate capital punishment for murder on retributive grounds must face the objection that, on their own principles, the death penalty in some cases is morally inadequate. How could death in the electric chair or the gas chamber or before a firing squad or on a gallows suffice as just retribution, given the savage, brutal, wanton character of so many murders? How can retributive justice be served by anything less than equally savage methods of execution? From a retributive point of view, the oft-heard exclamation, "Death is too good for him!" has a certain truth. Are defenders of the death penalty willing to embrace this consequence of their own doctrine?

If they were, they would be stooping to the methods and thus to the squalor of the murderer. Where the quality of the crime sets the limits of just methods of punishment, as it will if we attempt to give exact and literal implementation to *lex talionis,* society will find itself descending to the cruelties and savagery that criminals employ. What is worse, society would be deliberately authorizing such acts, in the cool light of reason, and not (as is often true of vicious criminals) impulsively or in hatred and anger or with an insane or unbalanced mind. Moral restraints, in short, prohibit us from trying to make executions perfectly retributive. Once we grant that such restraints are proper, it is unreasonable to insist that the principle of "a life for a life" nevertheless by itself justifies the execution of murderers....

DIFFERENTIAL SEVERITY DOES NOT REQUIRE EXECUTIONS

What, then, emerges from our examination of retributive justice and the death penalty? If retributive justice is thought to consist in *lex talionis,* all one can say is that this principle has never exercised more than a crude and indirect effect on the actual punishments meted out by society. Other principles interfere with a literal and single-minded application of this one. Some homicides seem improperly punished by death at all; others would require methods of execution too horrible to inflict; in still other cases any possible execution is too deliberate and monstrous given the nature of the motivation culminating in the murder. In any case, proponents of the death penalty rarely confine themselves to reliance on nothing but this principle of just retribution, since they rarely confine themselves to supporting the death penalty only for all murders.

But retributive justice need not be thought of as consisting in *lex talionis.* One may reject that principle as too crude and still embrace the retributive principle that the severity of punishments should be graded according to the gravity of the offense. Even though one need not claim that life imprisonment (or any kind of punishment other than death) "fits" the crime of murder, one can claim that this punishment is the proper one for murder. To do this, the schedule of punishments accepted by society must be arranged so that this mode of imprisonment is the most severe penalty used. Opponents of the death penalty need not reject this principle of retributive justice, even though they must reject a literal *lex talionis*.

EQUAL JUSTICE AND CAPITAL PUNISHMENT

During the past generation, the strongest practical objection to the death penalty has been the inequities with which it has been applied. As the late Supreme Court Justice William O. Douglas once observed, "One searches our chronicles in vain for the execution of any member of the affluent strata of this society." One does not search our chronicles in vain for the crime of murder committed by the affluent. All the sociological evidence points to the conclusion that the death penalty is the poor man's justice; hence the slogan, "Those without the capital get the punishment." The death penalty is also racially sensitive. Every study of the death penalty for rape (unconstitutional only since 1977) has confirmed that black male rapists (especially where the victim is a white female) are far more likely to be sentenced to death and executed than white male rapists. Convicted black murderers are more likely to end up on "death row" than are others, and the killers of whites (whether white or nonwhite) are more likely to be sentenced to death than are the killers of nonwhites.

Let us suppose that the factual basis for such a criticism is sound. What follows for the morality of capital punishment? Many defenders of the death penalty have been quick to point out that since there is nothing intrinsic about the crime of murder or rape dictating that only the poor or only racial-minority males will commit it, and since there is nothing overtly racist about the statutes that authorize the death penalty for murder or rape, capital punishment itself is hardly at fault if in practice it falls with unfair impact on the poor and the black. There is, in short, nothing in the death penalty that requires it to be applied unfairly and with arbitrary or discriminatory results. It is at worst a fault in the system of administering criminal justice. (Some, who dispute the facts cited above, would deny even this.) There is an adequate remedy—execute more whites, women, and affluent murderers.

Presumably, both proponents and opponents of capital punishment would concede that it is a fundamental dictate of justice that a punishment should not be unfairly—inequitably or unevenly—enforced and applied. They should also be able to agree that when the punishment in question is the extremely severe one of death, then the requirement to be fair in using such a punishment becomes even more stringent. There should be no dispute in the death penalty controversy over these principles of justice. The dispute begins as soon as one attempts to connect the principles with the actual use of this punishment.

In this country, many critics of the death penalty have argued, we would long ago have got rid of it entirely if it had been a condition of its use that it be applied equally and fairly. In the words of the attorneys who argued against the death penalty in the Supreme Court during 1972, "It is a freakish aberration, a random extreme act of violence, visibly arbitrary and discriminatory—a penalty reserved for unusual application because, if it were usually used, it would affront universally shared standards of public decency." It is difficult to dispute this judgment, when one considers that there have been in the United States during the past fifty years about half a million criminal homicides but only about 3,900 executions (all but 33 of which were of men).

We can look at these statistics in another way to illustrate the same point. If we could be assured that the nearly 4,000 persons executed were the worst of the bad, repeated offenders incapable of safe incarceration, much less of rehabilitation, the most dangerous murderers in captivity—the ones who had killed more than once and were likely to kill again, and the least likely to be confined in prison without chronic danger to other inmates and the staff—then one might accept half a million murders and a few thousand executions with a sense that rough justice had been done. But the truth is otherwise. Persons are sentenced to death and executed not because they have been found to be uncontrollably violent or hopelessly poor confinement and release risks. Instead, they are executed because they have a poor defense (inexperienced or overworked counsel) at trial; they have no funds to bring sympathetic witnesses to court; they are transients or strangers in the community where they are tried; the prosecuting attorney wants the publicity that goes with "sending a killer to the chair"; there are no funds for an appeal or for a transcript of the trial record; they are members of a despised racial or political minority. In short, the actual study of why particular persons have been sentenced to death and executed does not show any careful winnowing of the worst from the bad. It shows that the executed were usually the unlucky victims of prejudice and discrimination, the losers in an arbitrary lottery that could just as well have spared them, the victims of the disadvantages that almost always go with poverty. A system like this does not enhance human life; it cheapens and degrades it. However heinous murder and other crimes are, the system of capital punishment does not compensate for or erase those crimes. It only tends to add new injuries of its own to the catalogue of human brutality.

Conclusion

Our discussion of the death penalty from the moral point of view shows that there is no one moral principle the validity of which is paramount and that decisively favors one side of the controversy. Rather, we have seen how it is possible to argue either for or against the death penalty, and in each case to be appealing to moral principles that derive from the worth, value, or dignity of human life. We have also seen how it is impossible to connect any of these abstract principles with the actual practice of capital punishment without a close study of sociological, psychological, and economic factors. By themselves, the moral principles that are relevant are too abstract and uncertain in application to be of much help. Without the guidance of such principles, of course, the facts (who gets executed, and why) are of little use, either.

My own view of the controversy is that, given the moral principles we have identified in the course of our discussion (including the overriding value of human life), and given all the facts about capital punishment, the balance of reasons favors abolition of the death penalty. The alternative to capital punishment that I favor, as things currently stand, is long-term imprisonment. Such a punishment is retributive and can be made appropriately severe to reflect the gravity of the crime. It gives adequate (though hardly perfect) protection to the public. It is free of the worst defect to which the death penalty is liable: execution of the innocent. It tacitly acknowledges that there is no way for a criminal, alive or dead, to make complete amends for murder or other grave crimes against the person. Last but not least, it has symbolic significance. The death penalty, more than any other kind of killing, is done by officials in the name of society and on its behalf. Yet each of us has a hand in such killings. Unless they are absolutely necessary they cannot be justified. Thus, abolishing the death penalty represents extending the hand of life even to those who by their crimes have "forfeited" any right to live. It is tacit admission that we must abandon the folly and pretense of attempting to secure perfect justice in an imperfect world.

Searching for an epigram suitable for our times, in which governments have waged war and suppressed internal dissent by using methods that can only be described as savage and criminal, Camus was prompted to admonish: "Let us be neither victims nor executioners." Perhaps better than any other, this exhortation points the way between forbidden extremes if we are to respect the humanity in each of us.

SUGGESTIONS FOR DISCUSSION

1. Construct a utilitarian argument (see Part I, Chapter 4) for capital punishment. How would this argument differ from a Kantian justification of the death penalty (see Chapter 3)? Is either argument convincing?

2. Are all right-based arguments (see Mackie, Part I, Chapter 6) for capital punishment necessarily inconsistent, and so self-defeating?

3. How would Hobbes justify punishment (see Part I, Chapter 2)? Would the same kind of argument also justify capital punishment?

FURTHER READING

Acton, H. B., ed. *The Philosophy of Punishment*. London: Macmillan, 1969. (Interpretation, critical analysis; intermediate)

Bedau, H. A., ed. *The Death Penalty in America*. 3rd ed. New York: Oxford University Press, 1982. (Interpretation, critical analysis; intermediate)

Berns, W. *For Capital Punishment*. New York: Basic Books, 1979. (Interpretation, critical analysis; intermediate)

Black, C. L. *Capital Punishment: The Inevitability of Caprice and Mistake*. New York: W. W. Norton, 1974. (Interpretation, critical analysis; introductory)

Ezorsky, G., ed. *Philosophical Perspectives on Punishment*. Albany: SUNY Press, 1972. (Interpretation, critical analysis; advanced)

Feinberg, J., and Gross, H., eds. *Punishment: Selected Readings*. Belmont, Calif.: Dickinson, 1975. (Interpretation, critical analysis; advanced)

Goldinger, M., ed. *Punishment and Human Rights*. Cambridge, Mass.: Schenkman, 1974. (Interpretation, critical analysis; intermediate)

Hart, H. L. A. *Punishment and Responsibility*. New York: Oxford University Press, 1968. (Interpretation, critical analysis; advanced)

Honderich, T. *Punishment: The Supposed Justifications*. Baltimore: Penguin Books, 1968. (Interpretation, critical analysis; intermediate)

Lyons, D. *Ethics and the Rule of Law*. New York: Cambridge University Press, 1984. *(Survey, critical analysis; introductory)*

McCafferty, J., ed. *Capital Punishment*. New York: Lieber-Atherton, 1972. (Interpretation, critical analysis; intermediate)

Murphie, J. G. *Retribution, Justice and Therapy*. Dordrecht: D. Reidel, 1979. (Interpretation, critical analysis; advanced)

Richards, D. A. J. *The Moral Criticism of Law*. Encino, Calif.: Dickenson, 1977. (Interpretation, critical analysis; advanced)

Van den Haag, E., and Conrad, J. P. *The Death Penalty: A Debate*. New York: Plenum, 1983. (Interpretation, critical analysis; intermediate)

14

□

Political Violence

Violence and Freedom Violence cuts across cultures and pervades political systems of virtually every persuasion. Repressive societies use violence to assert and maintain effective social control. Those societies that are relatively more open often face a dilemma concerning freedom. Emphasis upon individual liberties encourages free expression; however, individual freedoms conflict, and at the extreme violence is invoked by individuals "to resolve" disputes. The dilemma consists in the fact that freedom gives rise to violence, while such use of violence undermines the fabric of freedom. So freedom of expression is usually restricted by the Harm Principle: acts are permissible only if they are not harmful to others. (For an elaboraton of the Harm Principle, see Mill, Part I, Chapter 4; and Part II, Chapter 9.) Violent acts are usually considered to be morally impermissible, virtually by definition.

The Concept of Violence Some philosophers have argued that the moral status of violence should not be reduced to a matter of definition: an acceptable definition of violence ought to leave open the question of its moral permissibility. Violence will be defined, accordingly, as the forceful physical or psychological attack upon person(s) or property. The aims of violent attack or abuse are various, but they need not be specified by definition. All forms of violence involve force; they intend intimidation and harm, if only to bring about some claimed good; and they are for the most part coercive. Clearly, force, intimidation, and coercion can be effected without violence. One may argue a political or philosophical point forcefully, intimidate by conveying information, and coerce by careful manipulation. Violence may be threatened so as to force, intimidate, or coerce persons to do other than they would freely choose. Threats of this kind are normally called violent as well. Further, *doing* violence differs in a subtle way from violence *per se* We may do violence to a language, say, or to someone's ideas without using violence or being violent. The wider notion of "violating rules of propriety" perhaps captures the senses of both "doing violence" and "being violent." Again, violence differs from power. One may exercise power violently; yet knowledge, for example, may empower without rendering its possessor violent.

Morality and Violence   In posing the question whether violence in any of its forms may be morally permissible, we should distinguish between three general types of violence: interpersonal, social, and political. *Interpersonal violence* of one individual against another for personal effect (for example, a mugging) is ruled immoral by the Harm Principle. *Social violence* is a function of legitimating structural norms. Though socially legitimated by the system's norms, the violence may be morally impermissible. Thus Marx's notions of alienated labor (see Part I, Chapter 5), physical and psychological abuse of women, and vigilantilism may be systemically legitimate forms of violence. Nevertheless, they are morally unacceptable. More problematically, pornography (see Part II, Chapter 9) and the sport of boxing are considered by some to fall in this category.

Political violence involves the use of force against persons or things to enforce or change questionable political practices or to bring about deceitful political ends. This use of force is often destructive and prohibited by law. Political violence may be expressed in various forms: riotous protest, excessive use of repressive force by the military or police "to secure order"; massive psychological propaganda; invasion or imposed control of an otherwise sovereign territory; revolution or terrorism. Political violence, in short, is force undertaken for political ends. The readings in this section address the question whether political violence of any kind is morally justifiable. As Hobbes foresaw, this question goes to the heart of what is a just society (see Part I, Chapter 2).

Readings   Paul Wilkinson contends that virtually the only condition under which political violence may be justified is when the majority of a population suffers massive repression at the hands of a despotic minority regime. Repression must include denial of basic civil rights (voting, equality before the law, political expression, etc.); and all available channels of protest must have been exhausted. Here the minority imposes itself upon the majority in violent fashion; so the majority can legitimately resist by force of a "just rebellion." Wilkinson maintains, however, that in a liberal-democratic state *minority* rights are actively promoted and protected. He insists that a liberal-democratic state nearly always makes available to minorities channels of protest, pressure, and reform to alleviate their grievances. (On the rare occasions when a liberal-democratic state fails to protect minority rights, as in the case of American-Japanese imprisonment during World War II, Wilkinson admits that a case may be made out for the use of counterviolence.) Yet political violence exercised by some group in service of its own narrow political ends can never be morally justified. Should a minority fail to convince the majority through legitimate channels—persuasion, negotiation, voting, lobbying, or peaceful protest—it must abide by the majority decision. Accordingly, Wilkinson attacks terrorist acts as criminal. He concludes that the liberal-democratic state is justified in using force to repress all acts endorsed by the ideology of terrorisim, as well as any violent expression of minority civil disobedience.

C. A. J. Coady takes issue with the assumption that terrorism is an ideology. He characterizes it as a *tactic* involving intentional killing or severe harming of noncombatants (innocents). Thus Coady thinks that members of the armed forces cannot be objects of terrorist attack. They are participants, rather, in activities akin to war. However, members of a nation's armed forces can engage in terrorist attacks directed at innocent or unengaged civilians, whether its own or those of another nation.

Coady insists that the same moral standards be used to assess the justifiability of state violence (to repress or to engage in war), revolutionary violence, and terrorism. He rejects utilitarianism or the appeal to beneficial consequences (see Part I, Chapter 4) as the standard for assessing justifiability, in favor of an "internal"—roughly, deontological (see Kant, Chapter 3)—account. Coady considers the permissibility of political violence along the lines of "just war" theory. He distinguishes between the justifiability *of* a war *(jus ad bellum)* or revolution and the justifiability of means *in* fighting a war *(jus in bello)* or revolution. Though a war or revolution may be morally acceptable, Coady argues that it is never permissible as a means to target noncombatants. He draws a useful distinction between two general objects of revolutionary violence: violence directed at legitimate targets, including combatants, if the revolution is justified; and violence directed exclusively or primarily at noncombatants. The latter, Coady thinks, is always impermissible; the former is morally permissible. Terrorism is aimed at objects of an impermissible sort. It sets out to achieve its ends by attacking morally illegitimate targets, and in excessive ways. Coady concludes that terrorism should be universally condemned. Nevertheless, he finds that some forms of both state and revolutionary violence are permissible, while some are not.

Virginia Held distinguishes between three structural forms that justification of violence might assume: political, legal, moral. *Political* justifications of violence are usually utilitarian: a violent act will be justified within a political system if it is generally considered to have consequences contributing to improvement of the political system. State or antistate violence will be politically acceptable if it meets the following conditions: It must not lead to further violence; it must directly generate generally approved political consequences; and there must exist no effective alternative means to bring about these ends. A *legal* system depends very largely upon a set of deontologically based rules, which are considered to have inherent worth and are not valuable because of any social utility they may produce. Legal rules must exclude the use of violence to achieve ends, save for self-defense and for law enforcement narrowly conceived. Legal systems almost invariably exclude subversive or terrorist acts.

Though an act of violence may be politically and legally indefensible, it might be *morally* justified. This will be the case for Held under two conditions. First, it must not generate further violence; and second, it must bring about morally justifiable better consequences or it must be the only viable alternative prescribed by a valid moral rule. Thus the *moral* justifiability of political violence will be established on the basis of both deontological rules and political consequences. Violence will be morally acceptable, Held thinks, to defend ourselves from those trying violently to prevent us from entering into cooperative, permissible moral relations. But it will also be acceptable to defend our rights to express why we think others ought to enter into such relations with us, when these rights are under violent attack. Violence cannot be justified to force others to cooperate with us. Unlike Coady, Held holds that terrorism, in cases where no alternative is available, could be morally justifiable. She agrees with Coady, however, that violence is never permissible if it involves the unnecessary and random killing of innocents. In any case, nonviolent means to political ends will always be preferable to violent ones.

An alternative suggestion is implicit in the views discussed here. In generally rejecting violence, we are encouraged to examine much more thoroughly the possibilities of *nonviolence* as a moral means to achieving political goals. The overwhelming forces of both nuclear and nonnuclear destruction now threatening life, liberty, and property perhaps impress upon us a compelling duty of political morality to examine the forms and viability of nonviolent social and political practice.

Paul Wilkinson

Terrorism and the Liberal State

CAN POLITICAL VIOLENCE EVER BE MORALLY JUSTIFIED IN A LIBERAL STATE?

To partially explain acts of political violence is not necessarily to justify them. Under what circumstances, if any, is resort to political violence justified within an operative liberal democracy? The categorical "no" given by T. H. Green in his *Lectures on Political Obligation* in answer to this question is too facile, too much a product perhaps of that smug complacency of Victorian England which . . . was also reflected in the writings of Mill. Perhaps we should forgive the natural pride of the mid and late Victorians in what they generally regarded as their model of progressive constitutional democracy. But, alas, there are large pockets of injustice, discrimination, under-privilege and exploitation in even the greatest of democracies. And can we really say to those who do not enjoy *basic* civil rights (e.g., the franchise, equality under the law), "You who are outside the political community of citizens yet dwell and labor in our midst have no moral right to take direct action to secure democratic rights"? Had the slaves of the American South no moral right to rebel against their owners and the system that exploited them? Those who are the subjects of a liberal state, but who are not admitted to its rights of citizenship, cannot be morally bound to obedience to the state. They are not bound by political obligation for they have not been accorded any rights by the state.

It may be objected that a state in which the majority does not enjoy citizenship is not in any case a liberal democracy in the true sense of these terms. It may be that a ruling group, as is the case with the whites of South Africa, accord

From *Terrorism and the Liberal State,* 2nd ed. (New York: New York University Press, 1986). Reprinted by permission of New York University Press and Macmillan (U.K.). Copyright © Paul Wilkinson.

themselves the rights of an Athenian minority confining democratic procedures and participation to their own minority affairs. But it does not follow that in such conditions the subject majority population owes any duty of obedience to their rulers, whatever massive resources the latter may employ to coerce their obedience. It may be argued that on prudential grounds the majority may be well advised to avoid confrontation when the forces of the state enjoy a huge power advantage. Majority leaders need to weigh the chances of victory for their just rebellion against the possible loss of life that might ensue from defeat and retribution at the hands of the régime.

In strict terms, where a majority is subjected to tyrannical or despotic rule by a minority the minority is imposing its sovereignty by violence and therefore can be legitimately opposed by the force of just rebellion or resistance by the majority. By definition such a purely coercive régime cannot be a lawful liberal democratic state, and therefore majority opposition to it cannot be regarded as seditious or violent according to the liberal democratic principle we have earlier defined [universal rights of democratic participation and democratic majoritarianism, rule of law and judicial independence].

There are at least two sets of circumstances, however, in which a *prima facie* case can be made for the morally justifiable resort to political violence by a minority within a liberal democratic state. Firstly, there is the case of the minority whose basic rights and liberties are denied or taken away by arbitrary action of the government or its agencies. A clearcut example is the case of the U.S. citizens of Japanese descent illegally interned by the U.S. authorities in clear violation of the Constitution. The second case arises when one minority is attacked by another minority and does not receive adequate protection from the state and its forces of law and order. In such circumstances the attacked minority community may have little alternative but to resort to violence as a result of the gross ineptitude or dereliction of the state. Fortunately such conditions have been the exception rather than the rule in most Western liberal democracies.

When, as is generally the case in liberal democracies, aggrieved minorities enjoy full protection and rights of participation in the liberal state, and their enjoyment of these rights is not under attack either by the state or by other groups or factions, violence for political ends *cannot* be morally justified. It can never be right for minorities—however intensely they may desire to realize particular aims or to redress specific grievances—to use violence to try to coerce the majority or the government into submitting to their demands. They are entitled to use to the full the normal channels of democratic argument, opposition and lobbying through the political parties, pressure groups, the media and peaceful protest. But they must limit themselves to persuasion, negotiation, and peaceful bargaining. And if persuasion through the ballot box, lobbying, and peaceful demonstration ultimately fail to win the minority's objectives, then, according to the tested principles of liberal democracy, they must abide by the democratic decision of the majority.

But one critic asks:

> Suppose the minority is *permanent* and therefore cannot use the political system for its own benefit, or at least not to the same extent as the majority? Is it not, then, entitled to use extra-legal means to get its way?[1]

If only because the very posing of these questions reveals a basic ignorance of the nature of liberal democracy as well as its political theory which is alas all too common, it is necessary to deal with them. Every large modern democracy contains scores of "permanent minorities" in the sense that there are many who belong to minority ethnic groups, minority religions, minority language groups, minority political parties, and an almost infinite number of special occupational, professional, and industrial interest groups. But by the very nature of liberal democracy these minorities coalesce and participate in, and vote for, major political parties with more general aims, parties which may form the government or become part of the governing coalition. Thus in theory and practice it is open to every citizen in a liberal democracy, regardless of any minority status that they enjoy in their non-political lives, to become part of the political majority.

Moreover, in any operative liberal democracy no law-abiding minority, however non-conformist and unpopular it may be among opposed groups or society at large, need fear for its right to exist and to campaign for its beliefs, or for the individual civil rights of its members. And by the same token members of minority groups are bound to abide by the laws of the liberal democracy in which they enjoy the benefits of citizenship. As argued above, it is only when a minority can show that it is denied basic civil rights, denied the right to vote, denied equality before the law, discriminated against as a minority group in respect of rights and freedoms, that a case can be made for direct action such as mass civil disobedience. Even in such rare circumstances as these, it would be necessary to show that all peaceful methods of persuasion and pressure had been exhausted before one could reasonably justify the use of direct action which could lead to violent confrontation, with all the unpredictable consequences and potentially greater evils this might bring in its train. It should be obvious enough that no liberal democracy could survive very long if every minority group that found itself unable to dominate the system felt entitled to use violence and other extra-legal means to get its way. Protestors impatient for confrontation should recall the warning in *King Lear:* "striving to better oft we mar wat's well."

A rather more subtle and sophisticated attack on the liberal democratic view of violence defended above has been mounted by recent writers. These theorists stoutly disclaim any sympathy with those extremists of left or right who wish to destroy liberal democracy. Nor do they have any truck with the views of those like Sartre and Fanon who assert that revolutionary violence is in itself "liberative" and "cathartic." Yet although those who wish to radically revise the liberal democratic theory of violence admit that violence is an evil, they seek to persuade us that, under certain conditions, it is an entirely warranted and sometimes a uniquely effective way of achieving political objectives, even within the framework of liberal democracy.[2]

[Ted] Honderich concludes that instrumental violence to redress inequality and reduce suffering is legitimate in a liberal democracy, provided: (a) that it has a reasonable prospect of alleviating more suffering than it causes, and (b) that there is no alternative method of alleviation possible. A recent proponent of the case for what he terms as "democratic violence" as an acceptable "form of politics" ignores Honderich's caveat (b), but adds two main practical requirements if violence is to be an effective form of politics: (1) its users must form part of a broader political movement, and be able to remain part of it, notwithstanding their involvement in violence, (2) the act of violence must be used to convey a relatively straightforward message that is not obliterated by the act itself.[3]

Is the revisionist justification for "democratic" violence convincing? Or is it based on a fundamental misunderstanding of liberal democratic principles? For a number of reasons, it can be argued, the attempt to justify and even to commend the use of violence for political ends in a liberal democracy is dangerously misguided. First, the revisionists show no appreciation of the importance and the inherent fragility of the rule of law, which is a keystone of any democratic system. In any operative liberal democracy the rule of law is a guarantor that the basic rights and freedoms of every member of society will be protected and upheld. Acts of violence systematically committed for political ends tend inevitably to undermine the authority and effectiveness of the forces of law and order, on which the very poorest and weakest in society ultimately depend for their security. Once one aggrieved minority decides it is justified in resorting to violence and is seen not only to get away with it but also to achieve tangible rewards, will not every other group that wants to claim it is dissatisfied with the distribution of wealth, power, status, influence, etc. take up the same tactic? And would this not inevitably lead ultimately to the breakdown of the rule of law which depends, in a democracy, on the tacit consent and cooperation of most of the population most of the time? Is this not a recipe for anarchy?

And who is to decide for a particular group when the level of suffering or harm to that group has reached a point where alleviation through violence would be justified? Who are the political geniuses who will be able to balance precisely the harm that will be caused by the violence against the harm caused by the continuation of the status quo? Mistaken assumptions about the future could be tremendously costly. Riots such as those in Brixton and Toxteth (1981) and Handsworth (1985) show it is impossible to control the dangerous and volatile force of collective violence. If the recommendations of Lord Scarman's wise Report on the Brixton disorders (1981) advocating improvements in community policing, community relations, and regeneration and youth employment opportunities for deprived inner city areas are not urgently and fully implemented more tragic and destructive riots will occur. These orgies of violence inflict greatest damage on the deprived areas where they occur, running out of control, and provoking counter-violence and escalation.

But there is an even more fundamental error in the revisionists' position. It implies that violence is a final and unavoidable resort of the desperate, that there are no other methods of campaigning to reduce their powerlessness or deprivation available to them. But in a liberal democratic state, by definition, there will *always* be peaceful channels of protest, pressure, and reform. Legislators, governments, and public opinion expect to be constantly lobbied and criticized. Any study of policies, decisions, and the legislative process in Western states shows how the political systems constantly reflect these influences at work. If lobbying the legislature and government department does not succeed, an aggrieved group can attempt to get their message through the mass media. Peaceful demonstrations, marches, rallies, and public meetings are all avenues for gaining publicity and reaching a much larger audience via mass media coverage. Well-organized campaigns will also frequently attempt to enlist the support of foreign organizations, opinion, and governments, where this offers possibilities of bringing pressure to bear on a target government or public. No serious political scientist looking at the political life of Western democracies in the 1980s would find it easy to believe the claim that violence is the *only method* open to the powerless and aggrieved to get their message across in the liberal democracies. On the contrary, a great deal of evidence is available showing that the use or advocacy of violence for political ends is positively counterproductive in influencing mainstream opinion and policymakers in these societies.

The defenders of so-called "democratic" violence are surely romanticizing if they believe that, for example, trade unionists, religious minorities, and other groups today are engaged in struggles for fundamental civil rights comparable to those of the nineteenth-century birth-pangs of modern democracy. In the pluralist and open liberal societies of the West today, political violence is not only outmoded: it is a potentially dangerous weapon which threatens the basic human rights of other citizens and minorities, and which can very seriously damage the fabric of liberal democratic politics and the rule of law.

Except in the very extreme and rare cases we have already identified, therefore, political violence in a liberal democratic state must be regarded as intolerable. If violence becomes the accepted or normal means for groups to gain political objectives within a state one can say goodbye to liberal democracy. To be effective a liberal state must not foster civil violence: it must conquer it. . . .

TERRORISM AND CRIMINALITY

It is precisely because terrorists, by definition, follow a systematic policy of terror, that their acts are analogous to crimes. The very notion of crime, even in the most primitive legal systems, implies the moral responsibility of individuals for their actions and hence for any violation of the legal code. We cannot make a general rule that terrorists are to be exempted from criminal responsibility unless we are either prepared to plead their irresponsibility on the grounds of insanity or are willing to allow the whole moral and legal order to be undermined by deferring to the terrorist. In most legal systems the typical acts of terrorist groups (such as bombings, murders, kidnapping, wounding, and blackmail) constitute serious offenses under the prevailing codes. Without exception murder is punishable under the legal code of all states. As terrorism involves systematic cold-blooded murder it is particularly repugnant to the Judaeo-Christian tradition and to all societies which are deeply infused with human values.

It is still widely held that the divine injunction against murder (the Sixth Commandment) is an absolute imperative which allows only four special cases of exception: (i) murder committed in the course of a just war on behalf of one's country (a pacifist would, of course, object to this exception on conscientious grounds); (ii) judicial execution in punishment for the crimes of murder or treason (a principled abolitionist would deny this ground); (iii) murder committed in the course of a just rebellion against tyrannical rule or foreign conquest; and (iv) in self-defense against violent attack. Clearly there is a world of difference between justification for specific acts of murder and justification for a systematic policy of indiscriminate murder as a means to a political end. Even if the terrorists claim, as they commonly do, that they are waging a just war or a just rebellion in terms of the classical criteria laid down by theologians and moral philosophers, they do not thereby succeed in providing ethical justification for their deliberate choice of systematic and indiscriminate murder as their sole or principal means of struggle. It would be a logical absurdity to try to justify terrorism in terms of an ethic founded on the sanctity of individual human life. Hence terrorists claim to act according to a higher "revolutionary morality" which transvalues everything in terms of the revolutionary struggle.

This terrorist revolutionary morality takes many different forms and is informed by a confusing and often self-contradictory collection of self-justificatory beliefs, myths, and propaganda. . . . The point I wish to establish here, however, is that if we attach any meaning and value to our Western Judaeo-Christian, liberal, and humanist values, and the ethical and legal systems that have been shaped by this tradition, we must logically recognize the criminal nature of terrorism. Terrorism is more than simply a manifestation of psychopathology, and more than a symptom of social discontent, oppression, and injustice—though it may be both of these things as well. It is also a moral crime, a crime against humanity, an attack not only on our security, our rule of law, and the safety of the state, but on civilized society itself.

The terrorist speaks a different language of justification, and for him the arguments from ethical and humanitarian principle are dismissed as sentimental and bourgeois irrelevancies. Defiantly and proudly they place themselves outside and "above" the law. Hence, . . . the apparently close bonds between terrorists and bandits (whom Bakunin regarded as the natural and original revolutionaries). Hence also the intimate organizational, financial, and logistic links between terrorist movements and criminal sub-cultures.

Yet there remains a significant difference between them in that the terrorist, unlike the criminal, insists on the revolutionary legitimacy and historical necessity and significance of his acts. If captured and brought to trial the terrorist thus typically refuses to recognize the legitimacy and legality of the courts: in his eyes the judiciary is simply the contemptible creature of an irredeemably rotten order. There can thus be no meaningful dialogue between them. . . . [T]errorists generally claim that their own acts dispense justice and punishment according to a higher law of revolution: terrorists claim to extirpate the crimes of the state.

Revolutionary terrorists make war on legality and hence their "criminality" is an essential part of their self-definition. They regard the law and its agents as both symbol and embodiment of the "oppressions" and "injustices" they wish to remove. Echoing Kropotkin they would claim "everything is good for us which falls outside legality." Yet the awesome consequences of this nihilistic rejection of all ethical and legal constraints are that the professional terrorists become totally corrupted and criminalized by their obsessive absorption in assassination, massacre and destruction. Terrorism tends to brutalize those involved in its planning and perpetration. A cult of bombs and guns is created and headstrong youths can become so hooked on the life of terrorist murder that they perform their tasks in a kind of sacrificial ecstasy. It must be recognized that just as there are war crimes and war criminals guilty of crimes against humanity, there are also revolutionary crimes against humanity. Revolutionary terrorists are those who choose to devote themselves to the macabre specialisms of revolutionary criminality.... Thus the inherently criminalizing effects of terrorist conspiracy upon the personalities of revolutionaries may, and frequently do, threaten the very survival of the cause. And yet the more dependent the terrorist secret society becomes upon intimidation, blackmail, and trickery to coerce and control its own members, the more difficult it becomes for its members to break free of the circle of criminality, mutual suspicion, and deception.

NOTES

1. Robert Skidelsky, "Points of No Return," The *Spectator*, Oct. 1977.
2. David Miller, "Use and Abuse of Political Violence," *Political Studies* (September 1984): 401–19.
3. Ibid., 417.

C. A. J. Coady

The Morality of Terrorism

Throwing a bomb is bad,
Dropping a bomb is good;
Terror, no need to add,
Depends on who's wearing the hood.[1]

There is a strong tendency in the scholarly and sub-scholarly literature on terrorism to treat it as something like an ideology. There is an equally strong tendency to treat it as always immoral. Both tendencies go hand in hand with a considerable degree of unclarity about the meaning of the term "terrorism." I shall try to dispel this unclarity and I shall argue that the first tendency is the product of confusion and that once this is understood, we can see, in the light of a more definite analysis of terrorism, that the second tendency raises issues of inconsistency, and even hypocrisy. Finally, I shall make some tentative suggestions about what categories of target may be morally legitimate objects of revolutionary violence, and I shall discuss some lines of objection to my overall approach.

The tendency to think of terrorism as an ideology is no doubt encouraged by superficial verbal resemblances—so many expressions ending in "-ism" are words

This is a considerably shortened version of the author's paper, "The Morality of Terrorism," which appeared in *Philosophy* 60, 1 (1985): 47–69. Reprinted by permission of Cambridge University Press and the author. Copyright © 1985 The Royal Institute of Philosophy.

for ideologies or systems of belief—but reflection indicates that the "-ism" ending here refers to no more than the relatively systematic nature of a method or a tactic. . . .

. . . [F]ar from being an ideology, or long-range goal of action, terrorism, or what many people would regard as terrorism, is . . . a technique in the service of such a goal. This is hardly surprising for terror is a form of violence and violence is primarily a means. It must of course be conceded that just as there are those who treat violence generally as *almost* an end in itself so there are those who do the same for terrorism. . . .

Let us acknowledge then that there are warriors who treat war as self-justifying and terrorists who treat terror as self-justifying but let us ignore them as aberrational. Such aberrations need their own discussion but shall not find it here. It may be possible to argue that those who begin by treating war or terror as means inevitably finish up treating them as ends; this is an important line of moral criticism but it contains the implicit concession that the activities can seem justifiable as means, and since this is how they are usually defended, this is how they should, in the first instance, be examined.

This is precisely the way discussions of the morality of war often proceed. Clausewitz's dictum, "War is the continuation of policy by other means," is announced and then a debate ensues as to the efficiency of war in promoting those policy objectives. As reflection on the morality of war has developed in the past and also increasingly in recent years, this stark utilitarian formula has been perceived to be inadequate. It has seemed clear to many that some means that would be effective in producing the desired policy objectives are morally inadmissible or at least dubious—for instance, introducing deadly poison into the enemy's civilian water supply to facilitate the defeat of his troops. Many believe, in my view rightly, that the obliteration bombing of enemy cities is equally reprehensible even if one's cause is right and it can be shown that the bombing hastens one's achievement of victory and reduces one's own casualties. All of this is related to questions traditionally discussed in just war theory under the category of the *jus in bello*.[2] . . . But the terminology is not my concern here. The crucial point is merely that when violence is viewed as a means to certain ends (believed to be) of importance then there are broadly three ways of assessing its morality. One is to reject it on the ground that the use of violence (or at any rate, severe violence) in the pursuit of good ends is never morally licit; this is the pacifist position.[3] A second is to assess the violence solely in terms of its efficiency in contributing to the achievement of the good ends; this is the utilitarian response.[4] A third is to assess the violence, partly in terms of its efficiency, but more significantly in terms of the sort of violence it is, most particularly whether it is directed at morally appropriate targets but also whether it is barbaric or grotesque or disproportionate. (This last feature may fit into a purely utilitarian framework depending upon how it and the framework are described.) This third response I shall call the internal viewpoint since it does not treat the morality of the violence externally solely in terms of its consequences. It will of course be sensitive to consequences but not as the sole moral consideration. We should note that it is a significant part of this outlook to be concerned that non-combatants be afforded a moral immunity from direct military attack. In what follows, the pacifist position, important though it is, will be gently set aside because I am interested in comparisons between those who justify violence by the State (notably warfare) in pursuit of its goals and those who justify violence by non-State groups in pursuit of their goals. It is in the context of such justificatory endeavour that the moral problem of terrorism should be placed.

Before proceeding further along these lines it is appropriate to turn briefly to definitional matters. If terrorism is a method there is still the question, what method? It is clear . . . that the term "terrorism" (or just "terror") can be used more or less narrowly and it is unlikely that the term in "ordinary" political parlance has any particularly definite sense since it has arisen and continues to be employed in contexts of a highly emotional, partisan, even hysterical nature. The semantic confusion generated by such contexts seems about equally distributed between supporters and opponents of terrorism but it is possible to discern in the welter of accusation, complaint, and exposition an outline on which the different concerns and anxieties converge. I shall attempt to bring this outline into focus by defining the concept in terms which capture much of what seems to exercise people in their worries about terrorism and which allow me to continue my exploration of analogies between warfare and other forms of political violence. I think that it also does justice to the historical evolution of the term. . . .

. . . [T]he definition of a terrorist act would go as follows: "A political act, ordinarily committed by an organized group, which involves the intentional killing or other severe harming of non-combatants or the threat of the same or intentional severe damage to the property of non-combatants or the threat of the same." The term "terrorism" can then be defined as the tactic or policy of engaging in terrorist acts.

Certain consequences of this definition need to be noted:

There is no explicit reference to some features of terrorist activity which commentators have regarded as important, for instance, the sort of wider effects it typically aims to produce, such as publicizing a forgotten cause, provoking an over-reaction from the enemy, intimidating some group who may or may not be the group under direct attack, and so on. These features are important but I do not propose to treat such specific political objectives as part of the definition. The more general reference to "a political act" is here advantageously vague because it does not restrict the political uses to which the terrorist tactic may be turned and it rightly allows for empirical investigation to determine what various groups use terrorism for. It might however be claimed that there is one very general effect of terror tactics that deserves to be written into the definition, namely, the effect of fear. The distinctive point of terrorism as a tactic, it will be said, is to terrorize, to spread fear and so destabilize social relations. This claim contains an insight into the sociology of terrorism but I do not think it should be made a matter of definition. . . . My reasons are threefold. In the first place, stress upon this effect tends to preclude any serious concern with the more intrinsic issue of the type of methods used (as it may be) to generate the fear. . . . Secondly the fear effect seems to some degree associated with all uses of political violence, including open warfare where civilian populations are involved though not directly attacked. Thirdly, intimate as the fear effect may be, it does nevertheless seem possible that terrorist attacks should give rise, not to the spread of fear and demoralization, but to defiance and a strengthening of resolve. It would be a defective definition which was forced to treat such attacks as thereby non-terrorist even though they had deliberately encompassed, let us say, the deaths of children. This last point has a further implication for the definition in terms of fear because if we seek to meet the counter-example by referring in the definition to an intention to spread fear rather than to actual production of it then we face the different problem, already mentioned, that we are prejudging an empirical investigation into the specific motives of those who choose to attack non-combatants. . . . Those readers who agree with me that the attack upon non-combatants is the crucial definitional feature but are more impressed by the fear-creation motive than I am could amend the definition to include a subsidiary reference to the common presence of such motivation. The phrase "and commonly involving the intention to create or maintain widespread fear" could then be inserted after the phrase "an organized group." Such a guarded and secondary reference to the fear effect would not materially affect the course of our discussion. I shall further discuss some of the issues raised by the relations between fear and terrorism at the end of this paper.

As defined, terrorism is not a tactic restricted to revolutionaries or other non-governmental groups. Doubtless many people would be surprised at the idea that governments and authorized governmental instrumentalities do or can use terrorist methods for their political purposes but such surprise is usually the product of naivete or prejudice. Certainly if we see terrorism as a particular kind of employment of political violence (and this seems a central strand in all the varied and often confused uses of the expression) then we should surely be impressed by analogies and identities between methods used rather than dissimilarities between the powers and standings of the agents using them. Otherwise we run the risk of treating the term "terrorism" the way some people treat the term "obstinacy," as a state into which only others can lapse; the parallel state in their own case being described as "strength of purpose." There is, of course, no need to deny that the use of terror by non-State groups rather than by the State raises special theoretical issues and I shall have something to say about this later. . . .

I have made no use of the notion of indiscriminate violence which often figures in definitions or discussions of terrorism. I have avoided this because I think that it is confusing. There is a sense in which I agree with the idea that terrorism involves indiscriminate violence, namely, the sense in which it fails to discriminate between combatant and non-combatant targets. . . . On the other hand, many writers use "indiscriminate" to convey the idea that terrorism is quite irrational in that the terrorist weapon is used in an undiscriminating way, as it were, wildly and pointlessly. This need not be true at all of attacks upon non-combatants or their property and there is usually a good deal of thought and selection going into the terrorist technique employed. . . .

I have stressed the contrast between the utilitarian and internal approaches to the morality of violence because it seems to me that many condemnations of terrorism are subject to the charge of inconsistency, if not hypocrisy, because they insist on applying one kind of morality to the State's use of violence in war (either international or civil or anti-insurgency) and another kind altogether to the use of violence by the non-State agent (e.g., the revolutionary). For one's own State a utilitarian standard is adopted which morally legitimates the intentional killing of non-combatants so that such acts of State terrorism as the bombing of Dresden are deemed to be morally sanctioned by the good ends they supposedly serve. The same people, however, make the move to higher ground when considering the activities of the rebel or the revolutionary and judge his killing of non-combatants by the internal standard. In the case of the revolutionary, the thought is that even if his cause is just and his revolution legitimate, his methods are morally wrong because of what they are or involve. In the case of the State or its instrumentalities this thought is quietly abandoned and replaced by those utilitarian considerations which are denied to the revolutionaries.

Consistency may be achieved in either of two ways: by adopting the utilitarian response to both kinds of case or the internal response to both kinds of case. I would myself urge the second type of consistency and object to the technique of terrorism as immoral wherever and whenever it is used or proposed. Does this amount to the moral rejection of both war and armed revolution? This is a serious issue precisely because both modern war and modern revolution have become so committed to tactics and strategies which are terrorist. In war, the bombing of civilian populations is the most striking example but there are other techniques such as the defoliation of forests, the destruction of crops, the destruction of villages, the slaughter of villagers, and forced resettlement of populations which either are terrorist or involve terrorism. In revolutionary warfare the recourse to such weapons as letter bombs, bombs in public places, hijacking of civilian transportation and threats to kill passengers, random killings or maimings, and so on are familiar. If such procedures are really intrinsic and inevitable then wars and revolutions stand under moral condemnation; this is perhaps the real challenge of modern pacifism. I am not myself persuaded (quite or yet) of the inevitability so let us now suppose that wars and revolutions can be waged without recourse (or with only marginal, as it were, accidental recourse) to terrorism.

. . . [L]et me just stress the basic insight behind the prohibition on killing or attacking non-combatants. This is that we can only be justified in killing someone (leaving aside the difficult case of capital punishment) if they are actually engaged in prosecuting an attack upon us or others or engaged in some similar project involving the infliction of gross injustice. They then become legitimate targets for our essentially defensive violence. Now there will be those not actually firing a gun who will still be implicated in a chain of agency under the description "prosecuting the attack" or some very similar description at whom it will be right to direct violence, e.g., a man bringing bullets to the gunman. Hence, the target area can be reasonably enlarged beyond the man with the gun but it is just absurd to enlarge it to include whole nations or even very considerable sections of them. This enlargement cannot be made to work simply by showing that there are various sustaining causal connections between certain groups and those who are the obvious combatants. Soldiers could not fight without food but this does not make combatants of the farmers who supply them with food as part of the business of sustaining their fellow countrymen. The farmer's activities are essentially directed toward nourishing the soldier *qua* man not *qua* soldier and he is not a combatant even if in his heart he supports the war (just as the soldier *is* a combatant even if he is a conscript who hates what he is doing). Similarly for the medicos who try to heal and repair the men who are soldiers and for the mothers without whose contribution those men who are soldiers would not have been born. More generally in any nation at war there will be countless numbers of citizens who are not engaged in prosecuting the harmful activities which constitute the just grievance which entitles another country to take up arms. Most of the population of children, women, and the aged fall into this category, as do most of the artisans and professional people and workers who are not directly involved in such war-related industries as the production of armaments. Of course, there may be soldiers who are pacifist conscripts determined not to shoot when the battle begins just as there may be elderly civilian ladies who are dedicated political agents taking some very active part in the war campaign but here, as elsewhere in the discussion of public morality, the idea of reasonable expectation is important and, prior to specific information to the contrary, it is reasonable to view soldiers with guns as engaged in prosecuting the attack and elderly civilian ladies as not. . . .

One of the ironies of the attempt by supporters of State violence to undermine the combatant/non-combatant distinction is that some supporters of revolutionary violence have learned from them and equally speciously argue that in revolutionary struggle it is impossible to distinguish combatants and non-combatants among the "enemy." Here the supposedly unified enemy is often a class rather than a nation but in either case the notion of "collective guilt" or "collective combatant status" is very dubious, although those who say that the distinction is useless in war should be more sympathetic to the revolutionaries' theoretical position than they are. None the less there are interesting and rather tricky questions raised by transferring the notions of combatant and non-combatant from the context of formal international war to the area of conflict within the State. Before looking more fully at this however there is one point that should be briefly addressed.

It may be urged against much of what I have said that it assumes, especially in its parallels between war and revolution, that a revolution can be morally justified. It is this assumption that is highly debatable for it may be said that citizens can never be morally justified in bringing violence to bear against their rulers. In reply I would urge that *if* it is possible for some wars to be morally justifiable then it is hard to resist the extension of the justificatory patterns to the case of revolution. Certainly some regimes seem to have committed such wrongs against their own populations or against sub-groups within those populations as to create at least a *prima facie* case for violent redress. Nazi Germany and Uganda, under Amin, seem to present such cases; moreover, armed underground resistance to Nazi occupation forces in countries like France whose leaders signed a formal surrender treaty seem to bring us close to the revolutionary pattern and this was generally approved of by many people who are opposed to revolutionary violence in other contexts. It may be said that a moral case for revolution can exist against a dictatorship but never against a democracy. As a convinced democrat, I am sensitive to the force of this rejoinder but find its force blunted by two considerations. The first is that many basically non-democratic political societies have democratic trappings. South Africa, for instance, is frequently classed as a democracy because it has democratic forms for a section of its population but the restricted franchise surely disqualifies it from the protection of any argument against revolution based upon politically relevant properties of democracies. The second is that, ever since Tocqueville, political theorists have been aware of the problems posed by majority tyranny over minorities and by the deep and serious injustices that democratic legal machinery can countenance—the situation in Northern Ireland is not irrelevant here. In any event most revolutionary activity today goes on in countries, like many of those in South America, which make small pretense of being democratic.

The general theory of the just revolution needs more development but I want to press the issue about how such revolutions should be conducted and in particular who are the combatants and non-combatants. Let me begin with the point that revolutionaries themselves do not always have trouble distinguishing broadly between combatants and non-combatants though, of course, there are gray areas. To take an example used by Michael Walzer, the play by Albert Camus, entitled *The Just Assassins*, is based upon an actual episode in Russia early this century in which a group of revolutionaries decided to assassinate a tsarist official, the Grand Duke Sergei, a man personally involved in the suppression of radical activity. The man chosen to do the killing hid a bomb under his coat and approached the victim's carriage but when he got close he realized that the Grand Duke had two small children on his lap so he abandoned the attempt and Camus has one of his comrades say, in accepting the decision, "Even in destruction there's a right way and a wrong way—and there are limits."[5]

Similarly, if one reads Guevara's *Bolivian Diary*, one is struck by the care with which targets are discriminated even to the point where captured government soldiers and agents are given a political lecture and then released (the guerillas not having the facilities to imprison captives).[6] ... The Cypriot revolutionary, General George Grivas, showed his sensitivity to the distinction in his memoirs when he wrote of the EOKA campaign, "We did not strike, like the bomber, at random. We shot only British servicemen who would have killed us if they could have fired first, and civilians who were traitors or intelligence agents."[7] Whether Grivas truly described EOKA practice is less important for our discussion than his acknowledgment of the possibility and desirability of directing revolutionary violence at morally legitimate targets.

In a just revolution then who are the combatants from a revolutionary's point of view? To begin with there are those who directly employ violence to perpetrate the injustices against which the revolution is aimed: the army or elements of it, the police or elements of it,[8] the secret police, foreigners directly involved in assisting the governmental forces in prosecuting the injustices, informers, and the politicians who are directing the "oppression" complained of.... If the politicians can be shown to be in a chain of agency directing the tyrannical behavior which justifies the revolution then they seem to be legitimate targets. Let us suppose the IRA's revolutionary activity in Northern Ireland to be justified. Its use of bombs on railways and in pubs would clearly be illegitimate and a case of terrorism since such attacks necessarily fail to discriminate between combatants and non-combatants. Similarly with the killing of Mountbatten and the others on his boat since not only were they innocent but so surely was Mountbatten.... By contrast, there is at least the beginning of a case for the assassination of the Conservative spokesman on Northern Ireland, Airey Neave—not, I think, sufficient but at least addressed to considerations which have some relevance. A more clear-cut case is provided by the kidnap–killing of the American Public Safety Adviser, Dan Mitrione, in Uruguay in 1970. Mitrione had been sent to Uruguay to assist in the suppression of the Tupamaros insurgency. There is considerable evidence that he had an important role in the torture campaign waged against Uruguay's political prisoners. It would be absurd to regard his position as that of an uninvolved diplomat though this was how he was initially portrayed in the Western media at the time of his death.[9]

Distinctions of this kind between targets of revolutionary violence are not only important for the revolutionaries from the point of view of how they should behave but also for observers concerned with describing their behavior. The fact is of course that most observers, and especially the press, describe any revolutionary as a terrorist and virtually any revolutionary use of violence as terrorism, including even the killing of soldiers. At least this is so throughout most of the Western media with respect to revolutionary violence directed against established governments in what is often called "the Free World". The revolutionaries in Afghanistan, on the other hand, are seldom if ever referred to as terrorist in the Western press though I doubt that their tactics display more concern for moral scruple than those employed in Belfast or El Salvador. The assumption underlying this linguistic habit is of course that revolutions against us and our allies are unjustified whereas revolutions against our ideological enemies are invariably justified. The same assumption, with suitably adjusted referents for the indexical elements, guides the reporting of the Soviet bloc press.

Whatever the naivete or cynicism of this assumption it does raise interesting theoretical issues since if we assume that some given revolutionary campaign is unjustified then we would seem to have some reason to make light of any distinction between the targets selected by the rebels. After all if a revolution is unjustified then any killing done in its name is unjustified whether of combatants or non-combatants. There is a point of connection here with just war theory since it would seem that we can make a precisely similar point about an unjustified war. Let us revert to the just war terminology mentioned earlier and refer to those considerations which morally justify the resort to arms in the first place as the *jus ad bellum* and those considerations which place moral constraints upon how the war is waged as the *jus in bello*. Terrorism is morally condemned under the *jus in bello* and it is sometimes held that the *jus in bello* and *jus ad bellum* are independent. Michael Walzer has, for instance, claimed that the "two sorts of judgments are logically independent. It is perfectly possible for a just war to be fought unjustly and for an unjust war to be fought in strict accordance with the rules."[10] I have argued against the first kind of independence elsewhere[11] and shall now merely reaffirm that it is imperilled by the thought that what the *jus ad bellum* justifies is a certain course of action *the nature of which* is partially specified by the means which are proposed or involved and which in turn fall under the judgment of the *jus in bello*. I want rather to focus here on the second kind of independence, the idea that an unjustified war can be fought in accordance with the moral rules of *jus in bello*. There is a sense in which this is clearly possible both for a war or for a revolution but there is also a sense in which, as I have already said, *all* the killing done by the warriors whose cause is unjust is itself unjustified so that the thought can easily arise that the victims in uniform are as much sinned against as any civilians killed in defiance of the *jus in bello* and the war conventions associated with it.

Is this thought correct? Almost but not quite. There is substantial truth in it but it tends to obscure something important, namely, that whatever the objective facts about a given State's justification in going to war its soldiery are likely to believe that they have good moral reason for trying to wound or kill enemy soldiers whereas, even subjectively, they will not be in the same position *vis-à-vis* the enemy's civilian population. This consideration has quite wide scope for it ranges from matters to do with trust in one's national leaders to quite specific issues to do with shooting back when you are shot at. All of these involve important questions of responsibility with which I cannot now deal but, taken in conjunction with the fact that it may often be a very difficult matter to determine which, if either, side in a war is justified in fighting, they make it intelligible that in the case of warfare, at least, we should continue to insist upon some moral differentiation between killing combatants and non-combatants even by those who are waging an unjust war. Such an insistence should not however be at the expense of the genuine insight contained in the idea that the killing of combatants in an unjust war is morally problematic. Of course, for our purposes, we have had to simplify a great deal and ignore many interesting complexities and difficulties posed by actual war situations where it may be that a war is unjustified on both sides or may appear to be justified on both or may begin as unjust and become just and so on.

What is the lesson of this digression for our discussion of terrorism and revolutionary violence? Surely this, that we should continue to make a distinction between two broad types of revolutionary violence, that which is directed at what would be legitimate targets if the revolution were justified and that which is directed at non-combatants. We should reserve the term "terrorism" only for the latter and it can be unequivocally condemned. Violence of the former kind stands or falls morally by the judgment of the overall legitimacy of the revolutionary activity. Does this open the way to condoning far too many acts of political violence which understandably cause such widespread shock and distress? It all depends. If you think that violent revolutionary struggle is readily justifiable, an easy moral option, then you should be prepared for the consequences and have a realistic appreciation of what you are supporting. If, on the other hand, you think that violent revolution is sometimes, but only seldom, justifiable then the killings you condone will be far more restricted. (You can vehemently condemn the killing of Aldo Moro without regarding it as terrorist.) My own view is that violent revolution, like war, is only rarely justifiable though one's sympathies may often be more with the rebels because of their genuine and unlikely-to-be-remedied grievances. . . .

Finally, let me return . . . to the connection between terrorism and fear. . . . I reject . . . the suggestion that terrorism should be defined wholly or partly in terms of the creation or spread of fear but there is no doubt that *one* of the reasons why people are so disturbed by terrorist activities is that they find such activities deeply undermining of social realities with which their lives are enmeshed and which provide a background of normalcy against which they can go about their ordinary living. (No doubt this is less important when their "ordinary" lives are already dominated by fear and oppression.) From the perspective of this paper there is no reason to deny any of this. Indeed my account of terrorism goes far toward explaining why this should be so since the method of terror is to attack those who have reason to think of themselves as uninvolved. It is also true, however, that any form of covert warfare, no matter how discriminating, will lead to the breaking down of normalcy conditions though not so dramatically as terrorism. Any form of low-intensity warfare (to use the jargon) will make familiar figures such as policemen, soldiers, and politicians into targets; it will lead to the killing of apparently innocent people who are, in reality, informers, secret police, or foreign political advisers; it will result in some mistaken or accidental killing or injuring of genuine non-combatants and itself create an atmosphere of suspicion. Here we have another potent source of the confusion between terrorism and other forms of revolutionary violence but confusion it remains, however understandable, for the terrorist seeks to gain his ends by deliberately attacking those who are not morally legitimate targets. . . .

I have throughout had to adopt many simplifications and approximations. One such is the implication that all revolutionary war is of a piece in style, tactic, and strategy; another is that all sub-State political violence of an organized kind is *revolutionary* where plainly it is not; another that "secret war" makes unambiguous sense; another that revolutionary war is always conducted within the national confines of the State which is the principal target but, of course, there is trans-national revolutionary activity and trans-national terrorism. Finally there is clearly room for dispute about the criteria for distinguishing combatant and non-combatant both in war and, even more awkwardly, in revolutionary contexts. I am not particularly enamored of the words "combatant" and "non-combatant"; in some ways, it might be clearer to speak of legitimate and non-legitimate targets but whichever usage appeals there are still problems of detail and principle in spelling out the notion of a chain of agency, which seems to be central to the distinction. This is an important and difficult task which I must leave to another occasion. In the present context, I will be happy enough if it can be agreed that the distinction exists and has the role I attribute to it and that clear cases can be described on either side of the divide.

NOTES

1. Roger Woddis, "Ethics for Everyman," from *The New Oxford Book of Light Verse*, chosen and edited by Kingsley Amis (Oxford University Press, 1978), 292.

2. Cf. Michael Walzer, *Just and Unjust Wars* (London: Allen Lane, 1978): Barrie Paskins and Michael Dockrill, *The Ethics of War* (London: Duckworth, 1979); James Turner Johnson, *Ideology, Reason and the Limitation of War* (Princeton: Princeton University Press, 1975).

3. Here I simplify somewhat for purposes of exposition. What I sketch is certainly a pacifist position but some pacifists would accept the use of severe police violence within a legal framework but reject what they see as the basically unconstrained violence of war. For a good discussion of some of the issues to do with pacifism see Jenny Teichman, "Pacifism," *Philosophical Investigations* 4 (Jan. 1982).

4. This is again shorthand but I think reasonable shorthand. In a fuller discussion we should distinguish that utilitarianism which looks to justify violence by its promotion of narrowly military goals and that which takes a wider view of the goods in question. There is also the question of rule-utilitarianism. If rule-utilitarianism can be shown to be a genuine

alternative to act-utilitarianism as a form of utilitarianism then perhaps some version of it would blur the line between the second and third responses.

5. Walzer, op. cit. 199.

6. Che Guevara, *Bolivian Diary*, trans. Carlos P. Hansen and Andrew Sinclair (London: Jonathan Cape/Lorrimer, 1968). For a few such incidents see 67, 77, and 92.

7. Quoted in Robert Taber, *The War of the Flea* (London: Paladin, 1972), 106.

8. The importance of discrimination here is illustrated by the example of the Jewish revolutionaries who assassinated Lord Moyne in Cairo in 1944 but refused to kill an Egyptian policeman whom they did not regard as an agent of British imperialism in Palestine even though this refusal led to their capture. See Walzer, op. cit., 199.

9. For a sober assessment of allegations about Mitrione's role see A. J. Langguth, *Hidden Terrors* (New York: Pantheon Books, 1978), especially 250–54.

10. Walzer, op. cit., 21.

11. C. A. J. Coady, "The Leaders and the Led," *Inquiry* 23 (Sept. 1980), 286.

Virginia Held

Violence, Terrorism, and Moral Inquiry

. . . In developing the arguments of this paper, I shall concentrate on the question of the justifiability of violence. I shall then briefly consider whether the arguments apply also to terrorism, and if not, why not. And I shall then consider the implications for moral inquiry that the discussion may suggest.[1]

VIOLENCE

It is sometimes suggested that violence is by definition wrong, but to maintain this is not a satisfactory position. It is easy enough to think of examples of acts of violence of which it is meaningful to ask whether they were wrong or not. One of the clearest examples would be the 1944 bomb plot against Hitler. To answer questions about the justifiability of acts of violence requires that the issues not be construed as ones which can be settled merely by appealing to a definition.

Violence can be defined as action, usually sudden, predictably and coercively inflicting injury upon or damage harming a person.[2] The threat of such action is a violent threat. Property damage is sometimes called "violence" by those who deplore it, but should only be included insofar as it risks injury or harm to persons.[3]

Some hold that failures to act can also be instances of violence,[4] as when persons are harmed by being deprived of food. But it might be more accurate to see the violence involved as the injury inflicted when those who are deprived attempt to change their position. And failures to act can certainly be morally outrageous

From *The Monist* (1984): 605–26. Reprinted by permission of the author and editor.

without being violent. To starve a person slowly may be as blameworthy as, or sometimes even more blameworthy than, killing the person quickly. But it is not more violent.

Harm can be inflicted through psychological as well as physical pressure, and the injury caused by violence may be physical or psychological.

A dissident who blows up a car, intentionally killing its occupants, is violent. The police who capture him with guns threaten violence to do so. If he is wounded or killed in the capture, violence has been used against him. A competent doctor operating on a patient is not inflicting harm. An honest tennis player injuring another does not do so predictably. Automobile driving predictably risks injury, but to the extent that it is voluntarily engaged in, it does not do so coercively.

Violence is distinct from force and coercion, since force may be used to coerce without violence, and coercion is not always violent, though violence is always coercive.[5] Force is power to cause someone to do something against his or her will. Coercion is the activity of causing someone to do something against his or her will,[6] whether that will is actual, or what the person would will if the person knew what was going to happen to him or to her or to others, and still had what could be described as a capacity to will.

The use of force to coerce may often be justified where the use of violence for the same purpose would not be. For instance, a parent may coerce a child to surrender a dangerous object by gently forcing the child's fingers open, where to retrieve the object by a violent blow would not be justified.

If we agree with Plato that it can never be right to injure or harm anyone, we will be back with the view, rejected at the outset, that violence is by definition unjustifiable. But we can retain a meaning of "inflicting injury" which is descriptive, and morally indeterminate, and that does not allow us to call every form of causing pain a kind of violence. To injure someone in self-defense, or in the upholding of a just law, may be not only a legally allowed but a morally justifiable case of injuring.

The legal rules of almost any legal system permit the use of violence to preserve and enforce the laws, whether these laws are just or not, but forbid most other uses of violence. Where laws are morally unjustified, the use of violence to uphold them will be morally unjustified even if legally permitted. And sometimes legal rules permit the use of violence to uphold highly corrupt and harmful political power. Violence is also often used in the enforcement of law in excess of what might be needed for this purpose, and in excess of what the law allows.

In an improving political system, violence not allowed by law will seldom be found legal by new judicial decisions, so we can rarely speak of illegal violence as coming to be *legally* justified, at least not without becoming, first, politically acceptable. But it is not unusual for illegal violence to become politically justified in the sense that within the political system it will come to be taken as justified. Let's examine these issues.

If we have made a higher-level moral judgment that a given political system is worthy of existence, or that it is satisfactory enough for us to consider ourselves to be members of it, that it ought to be changed rather than destroyed, but that it cannot be adequately changed within its existing legal forms and legally allowed political processes, we may consider engaging in acts of violence which are illegal but which will come to be seen as justifiable on political grounds. And if we consider a given political system so thoroughly corrupt and productive of harm that it cannot be repaired, we may consider whether we would be morally justified in engaging in violence to rid human beings of the violence it inflicts or to express our outrage.

POLITICAL VIOLENCE

To consider whether violence can be politically justified we need to distinguish political violence from other forms of violence. We may say that political violence is violent action against individuals or groups for political or social reasons. Usually, we can consider any attacks upon public officials to be instances of political violence, unless they are for obviously personal non-political reasons. And when agents of government employ violence beyond what is needed for the enforcement of justifiable law, this is political violence.

For an act of violence to be justifiable within a political system, it must at least be an act of political violence. But can any of *these* acts be justified *within* a political system? Or can they be justified only by appeal to moral considerations in opposition to what the political system will approve?

The legal rules of almost any political system are likely to rule out the use of violence as a means of interpersonal and intergroup conflict in favor of other forms of interaction: voting, political and economic pressure, lobbying, judicial decision, executive decree, etc., all of which involve power, and some of which involve force, but none of which need involve violence.

From the legal point of view, it would be hard to maintain that acts of violence on other grounds than self-defense narrowly conceived and law enforcement are ever justifiable within a political system. But such a view assumes that the legal system is above political control, is more inclusive than the political system, and that both may only be changed in ways which the legal system declares allowable. The legal system may still be subject to moral criticism, but if it is subject only to moral criticism, it may, as a system, be changed only internally, according to its own rules, or as a result of moral influence, which may be inordinately weak.

In a world in which moral persuasion would exercise considerably more power than it does at present, this might be the appropriate hierarchy: the political system subsumed under the legal, and the legal under the moral. But it is hard to suppose that this is always the appropriate hierarchy for the world as we know it, since many legal systems represent as finite a stage of moral understanding as the political systems to which they are attached, and they sometimes represent attitudes frozen into law which are unsuited to a new situation. There is a sense in which law records and embodies political decisions already made and although we should not assume that whatever is later in time is morally superior, we need not assume, especially in realms as much in need of change as most legal and political ones, that it is never so.

If we do not, then, give priority to legal judgments over political judgments, although we may give priority to moral judgments over both, can we consider some acts of political violence justifiable within a political system? . . .

Let us suppose, then, that an intentional act of political violence, Vp, does not lead to additional, more extensive, unintended violence, and does produce what can be taken to be, in a sense to be considered, good results. What can be meant by holding the judgment "Vp was justifiable" valid within political system P?

We may well argue that one of the primary functions of a political system is the validation of political positions as justifiable or non-justifiable, just as one of the primary functions of a legal system is the validation of legal claims as justifiable or non-justifiable. The grounds upon which a judgment may be valid may be different in the two systems, but both provide a method of deciding between conflicting claims.

If an act not permitted by existing laws but concerning which there are strongly felt conflicting positions turns out to have results which are generally considered to contribute to the well-being of the political system, the act will be considered justifiable within this system. And if we can make a decision at a moral level that the continued well-being of that political system is at least better than its destruction, then the act, even if it is an act of violence, may not only be *considered* justifiable within a political system, but may be politically justifiable. . . .

Hannah Arendt considered all justification to depend upon future consequences: "Legitimacy, when challenged, is claimed by an appeal to the past, while justification relates to an end which lies in the future. Violence can be justifiable, but it never will be legitimate."[7] I do not share the view that justification is only possible in terms of future outcome; political justification is more often arrived at this way because of the nature of political systems, but legal justification is and should be more often arrived at by appealing to the past and to deontological principles because of the nature of legal systems.[8] Violence on other grounds than self-defense and law enforcement is not in fact found justifiable or legitimate by most advanced legal systems because an acceptable set of legal rules should rule it out. But this is not a requirement for every legal system, as some have allowed violent revenge carried out by private individuals, and others have permitted an excessive use of violence to be used in enforcing their rules. And within certain political systems, violence might be justified by reference to a prior political rule recommending it in certain circumstances. That a promising political system struggling for survival may occasionally be justified in taking violent measures against corrupt opponents is a political rule sometimes conceded, however reluctantly, by others than pure Machiavellians. So we cannot say that *only* the future can justify violence, though political violence should normally be judged by its results.

Political justification, I wish to argue, presupposes the existence of a political system with methods of deciding between conflicting claims, just as legal justification presupposes the existence of a legal system.

Within various established political systems now in existence, some acts of violence seem to be capable of being found justifiable if they have the following characteristics:

(1) They do not lead to additional, more extensive violence.

(2) They directly and promptly bring about political consequences which are more decisively approved within the political system than the actions were disapproved.

(3) No effective alternative means of bringing about these consequences were possible. Perhaps acts of violence can be justifiable on other grounds as well; I am trying to suggest characteristics such that, if an act has them, it is justifiable. I intentionally evade the language of necessary and sufficient conditions.

A few words about (1) above: it is not meant to require that other acts of violence not occur, since the same kinds of reasons or causes that lead to one act of violence may lead to another, but it suggests that each act needs to be justified independently, and that a given act of political violence has this characteristic only if *it* does not produce further, more extensive violence.

Since violence is the inflicting of injury and damage rather than the creation of any political good, we may say that the only consequences it is in fact capable of producing, in (2) above, are negative ones: the harm to or the destruction or removal of some person or power or obstacle. But sometimes this is a result that will be widely approved, and that will make possible further good consequences. And we can further note that although political systems ought to develop in ways such that characteristic (3) is, in fact, *never* present, until they do, violence can sometimes be politically justifiable.

Whenever the conditions are present that would give what Joan Bondurant calls "the process of creative conflict"[9] a chance of successes, it should be favored. The Gandhian method of winning over one's opponents through non-violent pressure may well be more effective than violence in undermining the attachment people have to mistaken views. But one should not ask peoples willingly to accept genocide, even if one believes—and it would be a position for which little evidence could be marshalled—that the world would be so shocked it would be the last case of genocide. And one should not assume that non-violent protest is always worth the risk. Walter Laqueur believes that "civil disobedience would not have had the slightest effect in Nazi Germany; Gandhi was quite mistaken when he recommended it."[10] He may be mistaken. Joan Bondurant points out that "had the Jews offered satyagraha against the Nazi regime their losses could scarcely have been greater.... Had the Jews of Germany been schooled in the art of satyagraha, an organized effort of satyagraha might have got underway. The chances for success are certainly as great as the chances for violent revolution under the modern police-state system."[11] But if the empirical judgment is made that those preventing the alternative means in characteristic (3) from being available are totally unlikely to change, then refraining from violence might be harder to justify than resorting to it. . . .

Before contemporary advocates of violence take heart from the kind of analysis here presented, it should be noted that on this analysis of political justification, the violent actions justified within a political system may be those taken in behalf of the system against a dissident individual or group, as well as those taken against established power by those who would reform it. For violence to be politically justifiable, it must be justifiable in some sense within a political system, though the system may change dramatically. The judgment will be made by the system itself.

CAN VIOLENCE BE MORALLY JUSTIFIABLE?

Just as there is some civil disobedience that will be found legally justifiable by future judicial decisions about constitutionality, and some which will never be found legally justifiable within a given legal system but is still morally justifiable, so there can be violence aimed at changing a political system that will be found acceptable within that system, and also violence aimed at changing a system that, though it will never be found politically justifiable by that system, may nevertheless be morally justifiable. An example might be a violent political protest against the jailing of political opponents in a state which will never reform itself in such a way as to find the protest justifiable.

If an individual has no sincere expectation that her act of political violence may be found justifiable within the political system in which she takes it, dependent as that system must be for its very existence on certain configurations of prevailing power, she may consider whether the action can be morally justifiable. An act of political violence may be morally justifiable, I think, if it has the following characteristics:

1. It does not lead to additional, more extensive violence.

Either,

2. It directly and promptly brings about consequences which are, in terms of a justifiable moral system, of sufficient greater moral good than evil to outweigh the violence itself, and no effective alternative means of bringing about these consequences are possible;

Or,

3. It is prescribed by a moral rule or principle which is valid and applicable to a situation before the individual, and no alternative way of fulfilling this rule is possible.

It is apparent from the foregoing that I have included reference to a deontologically based rule among the grounds for moral justification, and excluded reference to any such rule from the grounds for political justification. This reflects the view that political justification presupposes the existence of a political system with the power to make its decisions effective for the members of that system, and that political justification depends upon an examination of consequences more significantly than it depends upon reference to deontologically grounded rules. Legal justification presupposes the existence of a legal system capable of effectively enforcing its decisions, but depends upon reference to deontologically grounded rules more significantly than upon estimations of consequences. Moral justification, in contrast, depends upon both deontologically based rules and an examination of consequences, and proceeds by an activity loosely analogous to the scientific activity of constructing hypotheses and subjecting them to tests. Moral justification presupposes the existence of a moral system in some sense, but not in the sense of being able to impose and enforce its decisions. A moral system should be authoritative because it is able to win the voluntary assent of free moral agents in a way comparable to that by which a scientific system gains authority by winning the acceptance of free and impartial inquirers. Conflicts between moral systems, obviously rife at present, should be settled by argument and persuasion on the basis of sincere and impartial deliberation and extensive moral experience. But some states refuse to allow this process to occur. Though it can proceed to some extent even under conditions of repression, it ought to be enabled to develop freely.

If the effectiveness of a moral system should depend upon its power to win voluntary agreement, one may wonder whether any moral rule can ever prescribe a violent act, or any good consequences justify such as act.

Kant argued that "everyone may use violent means to compel another to enter into a juridical state of society."[12] But we might agree that a state, with legal provisions allowing violence in self-defense but forbidding it generally, would be better and stronger if founded on agreement rather than on forcible imposition. Those who agree might use violence to defend themselves *against* those who do not, but this would be collective self-defense, not imposing a legal system on those who do not accept it.

The most plausible view, then, might be that we are not justified in using violence to force others to cooperate with us, but that we may defend ourselves against those who prevent us from entering into cooperative, morally justifiable relations. And we may use violence to defend our moral rights to express our views on why others ought to join in arrangements for the resolution of conflict through argument and political decision rather than through violence.

When there is no viable alternative way to defend our moral rights to free expression or to be given a hearing, violence may be morally justifiable. This view reflects the primacy that is often felt for the moral rights of freedom of thought, of expression, of conscience.

VIOLENCE AND THE SELF

The argument is made, particularly by Sartre and by Fanon, that violence can contribute significantly to the psychological health of the oppressed. They argue that through the commission of a violent act, a subjugated person can come to recognize his human freedom. . . .

One may respond that the capacity to say "no" to the command of one's oppressor may indeed be an essential part of the process by which a person becomes aware of her freedom, but that the form of the refusal need not therefore be violent. It may even be asserted that the awareness of freedom is greater when a person recognizes that she possesses a capacity for violent action, and also a capacity to refrain from using it. She may become conscious of a higher degree of freedom by defying those who taunt her to prove herself through violence as well as by defying those who oppress her.

If, however, an existing political system refuses to allow the expression of moral arguments designed to transform it, and if an act of political violence can constitute such an expression, it may be morally justifiable. There will be grave danger that any violent political act will cause unforeseeable consequences, and even graver danger that a violent action intended to change a political system will instead be seen as, and unleash the responses that would attend, an action intended to destroy that system. Then the consequence may be to entrench repression rather than to shake it. If any such acts are to have any chance of achieving their purposes it will be necessary to evolve tacit rules to keep them within bounds and make their intentions clear. As in the case of civil disobedience, there will have to be an understanding of the possible moral sincerity of both the actor and those members of the political system faced with responding to such action, both of whom may be acting in accordance with what they conscientiously consider to be their moral obligations. In the case of civil disobedience, the sincerity of the actor can sometimes be demonstrated by his willingness to limit himself to non-violent actions. Sometimes, but not always, a willingness to accept the penalty which the legal system decides upon, or to perform the action in public, can contribute to a demonstration of sincerity.[13] Comparable evidence of sincerity is much more difficult to offer in the case of violent action that is not justifiable within the political system, but it is not impossible. The provision of fair warning to minimize unnecessary injury, the offering of unmistakable evidence of restraint that the violence can be ended in as disciplined a way as it is being taken, may all contribute.

When those to whom a political system fails to give a voice constitute a large number of that system's members, the argument may be persuasive that an act of violence which warns that system of possible danger to itself, may have to be justifiable within that political system or it will not be justifiable at all. But when those to whom a political system denies a voice are too small a minority or too powerless to represent a significant threat to the existence or even the health of that system, the requirement that for an act of violence to be morally justifiable it must also be politically justifiable, may be mistaken. Political systems have been known to be long-lived, though highly immoral.

Quite clearly, the world should be such that violent but illegal actions are *never* morally justifiable. Persuasion and argument should always be the forms through which moral judgment succeeds in being authoritative for political actions. Political systems should be such as to provide the forums within which moral argument can take place, and to transform the clash of forces behind the arguments into an interaction of minds, wills, and political power rather than of violent actions.

Polemarchus' observation to Socrates on the road from Piraeus is, however, still with us: you cannot persuade those who will not listen.[14]

Although it is almost never the case, if an act of violence is the only way to open the possibilities for persuasion and argument through non-violent forms, to channel intractable conflicts into intellectual, political and legal processes of resolution, or to express non-acceptance of the despicable acts of evil regimes, it may be morally justifiable. War to end war has been a miserable failure; violence to end violence is no less likely to fail. But the requirements for an act of violence to be morally justifiable may not be impossible to meet, logically or empirically.

DESTRUCTION OF THE STATE

If we decide, finally, at the moral level that efforts to transform an existing state through legal means, through civil disobedience or political strikes,[15] or through the kind of violence that may be politically justifiable, or morally justifiable to gain a hearing or to express opposition to torturers and tyrants, are all futile or impossible, a moral decision may be made that the very existence of a given state is unacceptable. Can violence to destroy a state and to defend a new one being brought into existence then be morally justifiable? Account will need to be taken of the possibilities of uncontrolled violence and vicious repression, as the system seeks to defend its existence and as its attackers increase their stake in success. Assessment should continually be made of the chances for new non-violent measures to bring about the changes sought, after every breakdown of such measures. The inability of destruction to provide, of itself, any better alternative system, should never be forgotten. Nevertheless, in some circumstances, violent action may result in less violence than otherwise, and may, I think, be justified.

If one believes that it may be morally justifiable to punish criminals, the same sorts of arguments would provide moral justification of the "punishment" on moral grounds of tyrants and torturers where existing law and political power allow them otherwise to go unpunished. Even though there may be, in a given situation, no realistic expectation of vindication within a given political system, the victims or intended victims or defenders of such victims of torture or of political violence carried out by tyrants may be morally justified in trying to assure that those who commit evil deeds cannot do so without cost to themselves. Violence to punish torturers and tyrants may be more justifiable than violence to uphold unjust regimes. And where no other way exists to punish the violent and immoral use of power, violence to do so may be justified if punishment ever is, though one may well doubt that punishment can ever be justified.

Of course there is the danger that those judging whether a given case of torture or tyranny deserves punishment are making a mistaken judgment, but we must allow for the possibility that such judgments are correct. We should not make the faulty assumption that those with political power are always more nearly right than those without it.

And although these should never be the only choices, where the choice that cannot be escaped is between supporting violently evil regimes and supporting those who use violence against them, we will be responsible either way for excusing violence. And whether we do or do not choose the less wrongful use of it will be a necessary aspect of determining whether the act of violence we excuse is or is not morally justifiable. Narrow descriptions of the acts themselves, stripped of their contexts, of the intentions with which they are performed, and of their place in the progression or diversion of social movements, cannot provide the basis for adequate moral judgment. Whether the violence is used to maintain repression and exploitation or to bring about a respect for human rights will make a difference....

As existing governments increase their knowledge of the degrees of repression that may contain opposition without provoking full-scale rebellion, and as the weapons of violence increase in destructiveness and the forms of violence become ever more sophisticated and insidious, resorting to violence becomes ever more dangerous. Occasionally, morality may recommend the destruction of a state. But we can reject any number of aspects of the states we are in—and no morally responsible person can fail to do so under most present conditions—without acting to destroy the state itself.

CAN TERRORISM BE JUSTIFIED?

Do the arguments I have considered concerning violence apply also to terrorism? Terrorism is sometimes defined as "the systematic use of murder, injury, and destruction" to create terror and despair through "indiscriminate" attacks in which "no distinction" is made that might exempt the innocent from being targets of such attacks.[16] Terrorists are sometimes said to "sacrifice all moral and humanitarian considerations for the sake of some political end."[17] If terrorism is defined this way, we may be unable even to raise the question of whether it could be justifiable. As with violence, the question should be open, not shut by definition. Any adequate definition of terrorism must be able to include terrorism carried out by a government as well as by its opponents. If, as some report, terrorist acts "are often viewed in many Third World countries as noble acts of 'freedom fighters,' "[18] we should be able to examine the reasons without having precluded them by definitional fiat.

Robert Young, in an article on terrorism, agrees with most definitions that terrorism is "intimidatory in intent,"[19] but does not agree that terrorist attacks need be "indiscriminate." The targets of terrorism may be the armed forces, the police, and those with political power responsible for repression. Although surprise is "central to the potency of terrorism,"[20] this is not inconsistent with warnings to minimize harm to the innocent. In Young's view, terrorism should only be a tactic of last resort where other means of political action are not available. However, as part of an ideological "program of revolutionary struggle," it may be justified, he thinks, as certain wars can be. Its casualties and violence are very limited compared to war. A program including terrorist acts may in his view be the only realistic means to counter state-inspired terrorism, and, if its cause is just and success likely, terrorism may thus be justified.

In one of the most comprehensive discussions, Grant Wardlaw defines political terrorism as "the systematic threat of violence to secure political goals."[21] The purposes may be very varied: "Whilst the primary effect is to create fear and alarm the objectives may be to gain concessions, obtain maximum publicity for a cause, provoke repression, break down social order, build morale in the movement or enforce obedience to it. Several of the objectives may be accomplished simultaneously be a single incident."[22]. . .

Interestingly, those who defend terrorism often employ arguments familiar from "just war" discussions. John Dugard writes that "the Third World argument is based largely on a Western philosophical tradition: that of the 'just war.' "[23] He points out that many states "including the major Western powers, have on occasion engaged in acts of terror against civilian populations which completely overshadow the acts of terror committed by national liberation movements. . . ."[24] While prohibitions against state terrrorism remain unenforced, "it is asking too much," he thinks, "of Third World countries to collaborate in the suppression of the most effective means to counter terror available to national liberation movements."[25]

We might conclude that *if* war can be justified, terrorist acts can be also, if they have certain characteristics. But if terrorism includes, not by definition but in fact, the unnecessary killing of the innocent, it is at least not more justified than war in doing so, though the scale may be smaller. And if comparable good results can be accomplished with far less killing, an alternative to war that would achieve these results through acts intrinsically no worse than those that occur in war would be more justifiable.

But it is almost always possible to show that as limited terrorism is better than war, less violent alternatives to terrorism are better than terrorism, and non-violent pressures are better than violent ones. We might agree that the causing of war, whether through aggression, violent repression, the extermination or expulsion of unwanted populations, or by depriving people of the means to maintain life, is the ultimate crime of violence. If war to prevent the success of those who cause war can be justified, lesser uses of terror and violence can also, sometimes, be justified. But the more tyrants and torturers depend on the support of those around them, the better may be the chances of eroding that support through non-violent pressure. The opponents of evil should not have to sacrifice their lives. But those who use violence must also be prepared to risk their lives.[26] To risk one's life in non-violent protest, if the risk is no greater, and the chance of success and the rightness of the cause are only no less, is surely more justifiable.

EXPERIENCE AND MORAL INQUIRY

What can discussions such as these indicate about the ways in which we ought to conduct moral inquiry? They show, I think, that an adequate treatment of the problems involved requires consideration of both their deontological and consequentialist aspects. We must be able to assess the rightness or wrongness of an act which is an instance of a moral rule such as "resist violent oppression," even if it has no further good or bad consequences. We should be able to consider whether such an act is justifiable when its effects are unknowable. But we must also be able to evaluate many acts of violence on the basis of the good or bad consequences they bring about. And here the very great importance of reliable empirical estimates and findings is clear. We need to know far more than we seem to about the actual results of violence and its alternatives, and to be able to compare realistically the expectable outcomes of non-violent *vs.* violent efforts. Such empirical information is certainly insufficient for even our consequentialist moral judgments, since we also need to have adequate views on why we should hold various consequences good or bad and how good or bad to consider them. And it is certainly of no help in determining the deontological justifiability of acts of violence. But we might more easily agree on the overall moral conclusions of our deliberations if we could agree on the empirical components.

On the other hand, discussions such as these may suggest that we can make considerable progress in understanding what we think we ought to hold concerning violence and terrorism without being able to settle the disputes between the standard ethical or meta-ethical theories available, such as Kantian morality, or utilitarianism, or intuitionism, though we might be able to reject emotivism as unable to account for the ways in which the discussions make sense. We should recognize how attention to such actual problems might inform and improve our moral theories and our views of how to conduct moral inquiry. . . .

In the progress of scientific inquiry there is no substitute for observation. In some comparable way, there is, in my view, in the conduct and possible progress of moral inquiry, no substitute for the experience of making moral choices, as human beings sincerely trying to be morally conscientious and responsible.[27] Attention to many actual moral problems and to the ways in which conscientious persons try to deal with them can illustrate this conclusion.

NOTES

1. For further discussion of moral inquiry, see Virginia Held, *Rights and Goods: Justifying Social Action* (New York: Free Press, Macmillan, 1984).

2. The discussions of more complex and refined definitions in *Violence,* edited by Jerome A. Shaffler (New York: McKay, 1971) are helpful. See also Francis C. Wade, "On Violence," *Journal of Philosophy* LXVIII: 12 (June 17, 1971), and Joseph Betz, "Violence, Garver's Definition and a Deweyan Correction," *Ethics* 87:4 (July 1977). I shall concentrate in this paper on questions of justification rather than explore those of definition.

3. For arguments concerning what our moral rights to property should and should not include, see Virginia Held, ed., *Property, Profits, and Economic Justice* (Belmont, Calif.: Wadsworth, 1980). What, from a moral point of view, our "property" is taken to include may affect whether we are "harmed" by its destruction. I shall not in this paper explore the meaning of "harm."

4. See John Harris, "The Marxist Conception of Violence," *Philosophy and Public Affairs* 3, no. 4 (Winter 1974): 192–220. Harris shows why "the moment we realize that harm to human beings could be prevented, we are entitled to see the failure to prevent it as a cause of harm" (204–205). And he defends Engels's view that violence "has been committed if thousands of workers have been deprived of the necessities of life or if they have been forced into a situation in which it is impossible for them to survive" (Frederick Engels, *The Condition of the Working Class in England,* trans. and ed. Henderson and Chaloner (Oxford: Oxford University Press, 1958, 108).

5. Are hockey, football, and boxing, then, when voluntarily engaged in, not violent sports? I find this a difficult question. I think that player A does not commit an act of violence in tripping, tackling or punching player B, if both are voluntarily playing the game by the rules. But since the outcomes of such acts may be so similar to what they would have been had the acts been acts of violence, it may be appropriate to call such *sports* violent. And players performing such acts against the rules are acting coercively, and hence, here, violently.

6. See Virginia Held, "Coercion and Coercive Offers," in J. Roland Pennock and John W. Chapman, eds., *Coercion: Nomos XIV* (New York: Atherton, 1971).

7. Hannah Arendt, "Civil Disobedience," *The New Yorker*, Sept. 12, 1970, 19.

8. For further discussion, see Virginia Held, *Rights and Goods*, and "Justification: Legal and Political," *Ethics* 86:1 (Oct. 1975): 1–16.

9. Joan Bondurant, *Conquest of Violence* (Berkeley: University of California Press, 1965), viii.

10. Walter Laqueur, "The Anatomy of Terrorism," in *Ten Years of Terrorism, Collected Views*, eds. Jennifer Shaw, E. F. Gueritz, and A. E. Younger, Royal United Services for Defense Studies (London: Crane, Russak & Co., 1979), 20.

11. Joan Bondurant, see n9 above, 227.

12. Immanuel Kant, *The Metaphysical Elements of Justice*, trans. John Ladd (New York: Liberal Arts, 1965) 76–77.

13. See Virginia Held, "Civil Disobedience and Public Policy," in *Revolution and the Rule of Law*, ed. Edward Kent (Englewood Cliffs, N.J.: Prentice-Hall, 1971), and Virginia Held, "Consent and Civil Disobedience" in *Archiv für Rechts- und Sozial-philosophie*, Nr. 12 (Wiesbaden: Franz Steiner Verlag, 1979).

14. Plato, *The Republic*, 328.

15. See Virginia Held, "On Understanding Political Strikes," in *Philosophy and Political Action*, eds. V. Held, K. Nielsen, and C. Parsons (New York: Oxford University Press, 1972).

16. Paul Wilkinson, "The Laws of War and Terrorism," in *The Morality of Terrorism, Religious and Secular Justifications*, eds. David C. Rapoport and Yonah Alexander (New York: Pergamon Press, 1982), 310–11. See also Michael Walzer, *Just and Unjust Wars* (New York: Basic Books, 1977), especially ch. 12.

17. Paul Wilkinson, *Political Terrorism* (London: Macmillan, 1974), 17.

18. John Dugard, "International Terrorism and the Just War," *Stanford Journal of International Studies* XII, 21–37: 77.

19. Robert Young, "Revolutionary Terrorism, Crime and Morality," *Social Theory and Practice* 4, no. 3 (Fall 1977): 288.

20. Ibid., 289.

21. Grant Wardlaw, *Political Terrorism* (Cambridge: Cambridge University Press, 1982), 13.

22. Ibid., 41–42.

23. John Dugard, see n18 above, 77.

24. Ibid., 91.

25. Ibid.

26. See Joan Bondurant, n9 above, ch. VI.

27. For further discussion, see Virginia Held, "The Political 'Testing' of Moral Theories," *Midwest Studies in Philosophy* VII (1982): 343–63, and *Rights and Goods*, chs. 3 and 15.

SUGGESTIONS FOR DISCUSSION

1. Define political violence. Distinguish between power, coercion, revolutionary violence, reactionary violence, and terrorism.

2. Can political violence be justified, if at all, only in terms of consequences?

3. Develop a deontological (see Part I, Chapter 3), a consequentialist (Chapter 4), and a right-based (see Mackie, Chapter 6) argument for the preference of nonviolent over violent political action. Are these arguments sufficiently strong to commit us to opposing all forms of political violence?

FURTHER READING

Clor, H. M. *Civil Disorder and Violence.* Chicago: Rand McNally, 1972. (Interpretation, critical analysis; intermediate)

Coady, C. A. J. "The Idea of Violence." *Philosophical Papers* 14 (May 1985): 1–14. (Interpretation, critical analysis; advanced)

Fanon, F. *Wretched of the Earth*. Harmondsworth: Penguin, 1967. (Critical analysis; advanced)

Harris, J. "The Marxist Conception of Violence." *Philosophy and Public Affairs* 3, no. 4 (Winter 1974): 192–220. (Interpretation, critical analysis; advanced)

Held, V., Nielsen, K., and Parsons, C., eds. *Philosophy and Political Action*. Oxford: Oxford University Press, 1972. (Interpretation, critical analysis; advanced)

Honderich, T. *Political Violence*. Ithaca, N.Y.: Cornell University Press, 1976. (Interpretation, critical analysis; advanced)

Hughes, M. "Terrorism and National Security." *Philosophy* 57 (January 1982), 5–25. (Interpretation, critical analysis; advanced)

Kuper, L. *Genocide*. New Haven: Yale University Press, 1981. (Critical analysis; intermediate)

Laqueur, W. *Terrorism*. London: Weidenfeld and Nicolson, 1977. (Critical analysis; intermediate)

Nagel, T. "Ruthlessness in Public Life." In *Mortal Questions*. Cambridge: Cambridge University Press, 1979. (Critical analysis; advanced)

Norton, A. H., and Greenber, M. H. *International Terrorism: An Annotated Bibliography and Research Guide*. Boulder: Westview, 1979.

Paskins, B., and Dockrill, M. *The Ethics of War*. London: Duckworth, 1979. (Interpretation, critical analysis; advanced)

Rapoport, D., and Alexander, Y., eds. *The Morality of Terrorism: Religious and Secular Justifications*. New York: Pergamon Press, 1982. (Interpretation, critical analysis; intermediate)

Schmid, A. P., *Political Terrorism: A Research Guide to Concepts, Theories, Data Bases and Literature*. Amsterdam: North Holland Publishing, 1983.

Shaffer, J. A., ed. *Violence*. New York: D. McKay, 1971. (Interpretation, critical analysis; advanced)

Sorel, G. *Reflections on Violence*. London: George Allen and Unwin, 1925. (Interpretation, critical analysis; intermediate)

Wade, F. C. "On Violence." *Journal of Philosophy* LXVIII, 12 (1971): 369–77. (Interpretation, critical analysis; advanced)

Walzer, M. *Just and Unjust Wars*. London: Allen and Unwin, 1978. (Interpretation, critical analysis; advanced)

Wardlaw, G. *Political Terrorism*. Cambridge: Cambridge University Press, 1982. (Interpretation, critical analysis; advanced)

Wilkinson, P. *Terrorism, and the Liberal State*. New York: New York University Press, 1986. (Interpretation, critical analysis; intermediate)

Williams, B. "Politics and Moral Character" In *Moral Luck*. Cambridge: Cambridge University Press, 1981. (Interpretation, critical analysis; advanced)

Young, R. "Revolutionary Terrorism, Crime and Morality." *Social Theory and Practice* 4, no. 3 (Fall 1977): 287–302. (Interpretation, critical analysis; advanced)

Glossary

NOTE: The glossary consists of brief definitions and explanations of key terms appearing either in the introductions or readings. *Italicized* words are cross-referenced in the glossary.

Abortion   The termination of a pregnancy prior to birth, resulting in the death of the fetus. A miscarriage is a spontaneous abortion that is not caused by the pregnant woman or anyone else. An induced abortion is caused by someone other than the pregnant woman, usually at her request; while a self-induced abortion is caused by the pregnant woman on her own.

Absolutism   The theory that there are invariant and objective moral truths or rules. Absolutists may nevertheless hold that there are sometimes exceptions to the absolute moral rules or principles. This theory is contrasted with *relatvism*.

Affirmative action   Any policy or program the aim of which is to institute greater social equality, especially of opportunity, for women and racial minorities. Affirmative action programs include widening the applicant pool for jobs, promotions, and college admissions, advertising widely and in nondiscriminatory ways, using nondiscriminatory categories and criteria in hiring, promotions, and admissions, and *preferential treatment*.

Agent   Any person who acts, has acted, or is contemplating action. A moral agent is one bearing moral qualities of responsibility, and may be judged accordingly as good or bad, virtuous or vicious, just or unjust.

Alienation   The hostile separation or estrangement of an *agent* from features of the social or natural environment, or from the agent's own state of mind. Marx considered all the aspects of alienation to be functions of the worker's role in capitalist economic production and relations.

Altruism   Any action that aims at producing good for another for the other person's sake. It is usually contrasted with *egoism*.

A posteriori   *Judgments* or *principles* the *justification* for which is *empirical* or factual, and which are said to be acquired by the sense-impressions.

A priori *Judgments* or *principles* the validity of which is independent of any sense-impressions or *empirical justification*. The term is used more generally to designate anything knowable by reason alone, or anything that is nonempirical.

Autonomy The capacity of the *will* to command a (moral) law for itself, and to follow it. For Kant, moral action is always autonomous or self-imposed. Autonomy is the precondition for moral responsibility. (See *Heteronomy*.)

Capital punishment Punishment by death for having committed crimes of the worst order ("capital crimes").

Categorical imperative For Kant, this is the basic *principle* of morality. It is the supreme law of self-legislating, rational beings. It commands unconditional obedience to the practical moral law formulated by reason. It obliges or binds any rational agent to act as the moral law commands and only for the sake of the moral law. Kant contrasts this with the *hypothetical imperative*.

Consequentialism The class of ethical theories that determines the morality or immorality of any act, policy, principle, or institution on the basis solely of its consequences or outcomes. (See *Utilitarianism*.)

Contractarianism (contractualism) The theory that moral rules are established and justified by a hypothetical (or implicit) agreement or contract between *agents* upon whom the rules would then be binding. (See *Social contract*.)

Critical analysis Discussion and assessment of the strengths and weaknesses of a given argument.

Cultural relativism The theory that moral values or standards are thought to be conditioned by (or relative to) the particular culture in which they arise, and so hold only for that culture. On this view, there are no absolute or universal moral standards. (See *Absolutism; Relativism*.)

Deontology The set of theories that rejects the claim that moral values like rightness or wrongness are to be defined in terms of the production of goodness or badness. Most commonly attributed to Kant, it is the study of *duty* as the basic moral concept, and of the moral concepts derivative from duty.

Descriptive ethics A description of the ethical values, practices, and customs of a particular society at a particular time. (See *Metaethics; Normative ethics*.)

Duty An act that an *agent* is morally obliged or bound or ought to do, in contrast with what one may find pleasing or have an inclination to do.

Egalitarianism The view that all humans are equal, and so that they should be treated equally in terms of *liberties* or *rights* or respect or opportunities or distributions.

Egoism

Ethical egoism The theory that persons ought to act only from self-interest.

Psychological egoism A view about the actual psychological motivations of humans. It claims that the effective, though possibly hidden, motive of all voluntary acts is a desire for one's own welfare. So one can be a psychological egoist without being an ethical egoist.

Empirical Of or pertaining to experience of actual facts.

Ethical theory (normative)   A set of principles or rules more or less systematically related that provides criteria for determining what one ought to do and for evaluating actions.

Ethical relativism   The view that an act, rule, or practice which is right for one society, culture or individual may actually be wrong for another.

Eudaimonia   For Aristotle, this is the highest good in life, or happiness or well-being. It is not pleasure.

Euthanasia   Literal Greek meaning: a good death. It is commonly used as a synonym for "mercy killing" or, less often and in a more restricted sense, for "letting someone die."

Felicific   Making happy; giving rise to happiness or pleasure. In Bentham, the felicific calculus is used interchangeably with the hedonic calculus. (See *Hedonism*.)

Fornication   Any sexual intercourse outside the marriage relation. The term implies moral disapprobation.

Golden Rule   Do unto others as you would want others to do unto you; or Do not unto others what you would not want done to you.

Hedonism   The theory that the only *intrinsic good* or value in human life is pleasure or happiness. On the hedonic or *felicific* calculus, the value of all things is to be measured in terms of the pleasure or happiness they promote. An action is considered moral if it generates the greatest happiness or pleasure, or the least amount of pain, among the conceivable alternatives.

Heteronomy   The character of a *will* that is determined to act by motivations external to itself, like desires or inclinations. For Kant, heteronomous acts have no moral worth, and in that sense are sharply contrasted with *autonomous* acts.

Hypothetical imperative   For Kant, any command to action for an *agent* that is conditional or dependent upon the goals aimed at. In general, it commands one to act on the basis of self-interest or prudence (for the sake of fulfilling happiness). It is contrasted with the unconditional or morally obligatory command of the *categorical imperative*.

Incontinence (Weakness of the Will)   The state of human character such that the *agent* does wrong knowingly, yet is incapable of restraint. It is the moral condition in which the agent's rational deliberation or will is overridden or consumed by desire. Aristotle's term for it is *akrasia*.

Innate properties   Properties or characteristics of humans that are claimed to be given at birth; properties that all human beings are supposed to possess by nature and universally.

Interpretation   A detailed reconstruction and explanation of given arguments.

Intrinsic good   The goodness of something in itself, the goodness of which is not conditional upon any property external to the thing.

Intuitionism   The theory that moral values can be known only by a moral insight or faculty of moral intuition. Moral values like rightness and wrongness are considered to be *objective;* the ability to intuit them is deemed inherent in everyone.

Judgment A decision or conclusion about an action, belief, *rule,* or *principle.*

Justification Providing convincing and independent reasons in support of a *judgment.*

Libertarianism The theory that endorses exercise of the greatest possible unrestrained social, political, and economic *liberty.*

Liberty The unrestricted *right* to choose between alternative actions, aims, or ends; the right not to be restricted in pursuing the objects of one's desires; the freedom from external constraint ("negative liberty"); the freedom to act on one's choices ("positive liberty").

Maxim For Kant, a general principle of action upon which the *agent* actually acts or is considering acting, which specifies the action to be performed. The maxim is stated in general terms as though it were the agent's policy to act this way whenever appropriate circumstances arise.

Metaethics The analysis of the concepts, methods, and logical structure of ethical reasoning, of moral *judgments* and their *justification,* and of the meanings of moral terms. (See *Descriptive ethics; Normative ethics.*)

Moral sense For Hume, that special moral feeling or emotion that causes *agents* to approve of some actions or circumstances and to disapprove of others.

Natural law A moral *principle* or standard established by the nature of things or by God, to which human laws and actions ought to conform. For Hobbes, by contrast, it is that general rule discovered by reason which forbids human beings doing anything that would threaten their own lives.

Naturalistic fallacy The view, claimed by G. E. Moore to be a fallacy or mistake in reasoning, of defining moral concepts in terms of nonmoral ones, or of deducing moral conclusions from nonmoral premises.

Necessary condition *Y* is a necessary condition for *X* if and only if *X* cannot pertain unless *Y* pertains. (See *Sufficient condition.*)

Normative ethics The inquiry into the norms or standards of moral behavior, and their *justification.* Normative ethics sets out to establish how human *agents* ought morally to conduct their lives, and to evaluate how they in fact do. (See *Metaethics; Descriptive ethics.*)

Objectification For Marx, the act of fixing as unchangeable the given relations of the current production process.

Objective right/good The right or good established independent of what any *agent* subjectively considers it right or good to do; it is what would be right or good for any agent in the circumstances to do.

Obligation The necessity or requirement an *agent* has to do some specified act. Moral obligation or *duty* is considered by some to be conditional upon desiring an end like happiness; by others, such as Kant, it is considered to be *categorical* or unconditional. Unconditional moral obligations impose duties upon agents independent of any consideration external to the nature of the act contemplated, such as the happiness or benefits it may cause.

Offense Principle. The *principle* that restriction of a person's *liberty* can be justified to prevent offense to others.

Passion For Hume, a feeling or emotion.

Perversity On the narrow, technical interpretation, it is any sexual act incapable by its nature of ending in reproduction. On a wider interpretation, it means simply any abnormal or uncommon sexual acts.

Preferential treatment The policy of hiring, promotion, or admission of minorities and women primarily because of their group membership. The aims of any such policy are to eliminate discriminatory employment, seniority, or admissions patterns, and to effect greater social justice.

Prima facie **duties** *Agents'* self-evident *obligations* or *duties* that are binding provided no higher *prima facie* duty obligates them in the given circumstances. For example, benevolence or doing good to another for the other person's sake is a *prima facie* duty. It obliges the agent to act accordingly provided it does not violate a more compelling *prima facie* duty, say, the duty not to harm others.

Principle A general statement that serves as the basis for justifying, evaluating, or guiding beliefs, acts, or moral rules.

Promiscuity Multiple sexual relations.

Relativism The view that moral values are conditional upon or relative to individuals or to groups or to cultures (societies). Values are taken to be conditional upon the particular social formation in which they arise. (See *Cultural relativism; Ethical relativism; Absolutism.*)

Respect For Persons (Principle of) The *principle* that persons are owed respect as autonomous agents.

Reverse discrimination The claim that policies of *preferential treatment,* in which racial minorities or women are hired, promoted, or admitted to colleges primarily on the basis of their race or sex, discriminate in reverse against those who are thus denied equal opportunity (namely, white males). (See also *Preferential treatment; Affirmative action.*)

Rhetoric The art and power of persuasion. Techniques of rhetoric were of particular concern to Plato's antagonists, the Sophists of Greece, and later to the Romans.

Right That which is valuable or proper. A right is that for which one has a justifiable claim or demand, often a *liberty* or power, which is authorized by those in a position to do so. Human or civil rights are those claims to which individuals are entitled in virtue of being human or citizens.

Rule General guides governing what ought or ought not to be done for a class of cases. (See *Principle.*)

Slave morality Nietsche's term for any code of values that enthrones *duty,* passivity, control of emotions, or acceptance of tradition and authority. It is a system of thought designed to maintain control of the oppressed and to instill in them fear of change.

Social contract   The original implicit agreement by which, according to some modern philosophers, individuals are united in forming the state. Civil society and its power are justified, and political, legal, and moral values are binding, insofar as they are implicitly or hypothetically agreed to by the parties to the contract. (See *State of nature; Contractarianism.*)

State of nature   For Hobbes and Rousseau, a hypothetical situation in which people live without government or positive law. The concept is used as a premise in the argument to justify fundamental principles of morality, law, and political structure. (See *Social contract; Contractarianism.*)

Stoicism   The theory, important in antiquity, that every person must follow the rational will of the universe and act consistent with the divine laws of nature; and that all persons must accept and act in keeping with their proper place in the scheme of the universe.

Sufficient condition X is a sufficient condition for Y if, whenever X occurs, Y will also occur. Nevertheless, Y can occur without X occurring. (See also *Necessary condition.*)

Survey   A general summary or overview of the main points of the argument at issue.

Teleological ethics   The set of theories holding that the moral worth of an act is determined by whether the act achieves its proper end, aim, or goal.

Utilitarianism   The theory that holds that the measure of moral rightness or wrongness is whether an act, rule, or policy maximizes utility. In the work of Bentham and Mill utility is interpreted as happiness or pleasure; more recently, it has been interpreted as preferences, interests, welfare, or benefits. (See *Hedonism; Felicific.*)

  Act-utilitarianism   The theory that one ought morally to undertake only those acts which maximize utility.

  Ideal utilitarianism   The theory that the moral rightness or wrongness of an act is determined by whether it adds to the greatest total amount of good or not, where good is not limited to pleasure but includes other *intrinsic goods.*

  Rule-utilitarianism   The theory that moral *rules* are to be chosen that maximize utility, and that to act morally one must follow the rules.

Virtues(s)   For Aristotle, excellent states of character established by the rational faculty, and by which human conduct is habitually to be directed if it is to be moral.

Will, general   For Rousseau, the faculty of willing ascribed to the general (political) collective (i.e., the state). The general will is usually opposed to the wills of isolated individuals, or to the wills of a group of individuals not bound by a coherent principle.

Will, good   For Kant, the self-conscious resolve to act in a way that is morally right, and only because it is morally right. A will is not good because of any beneficial consequences it may have; it has *intrinsic* moral worth. The good will is the only thing that is good without qualification; it is necessary for the production of any other good, including happiness.

Index

Hume, David, 73–75, 100, 102, 103, 131
  Treatise of Human Nature, A, 82–95
Hurka, Thomas, 423–24
  Rights and Capital Punishment, 436–43
hypothetical imperatives, 101

ideal rule-utilitarianism, 134–35
imperatives, 101
  categorical, 101–102
  hypothetical, 101
incontinence (weakness of the will), 16
infanticide, 385–86
injustice, 14, 17
  Hobbes on, 72
interpersonal violence, 456
*Introduction to the Principles of Morals and
    Legislation, An* (Bentham), 136–44
intuitionism, 12
  moral, 180–81
Is Racial Discrimination Special? (Levin),
    264–71
*Is the Favoring of Women and Blacks in
    Employment and Educational
    Opportunities Justified?* (Katzner),
    272–80

judgments
  ethical, 2
  moral, 2
justice, 2, 12
  Aristotle on, 17
  distributive, 17, 225–57
  Hobbes on, 72
  rectificatory, 17, 225
  Sophists and, 13–14
justification, 3
Justifying Punishment (Downie), 425–31

Katzner, Louis, 260–61
  article by, 272–80
Kant, Harold S., 318, 319
Kant, Immanuel, 11, 100–103, 133, 182
  Groundwork of the Metaphysic of Morals,
    111–29

law
  Aquinas' conception of, 18
  natural, 12
laws, 6
legal moralism, 292
legal paternalism, 292

Leviathan (Hobbes), 76–82
Levin, Michael E., 260
  Is Racial Discrimination Special?, 264–71
Liberalism and Pornography (Clark),
    299–306
liberty, 225–26
  Mill on, 156–58
living will, 388
Locke, John, 226
Lying, 102

MacIntyre, Alasdair, 5, 185–86
  *Virtues, The Unity of a Human Life, and
    the Concept of a Tradition,* 211–18
Mackie, J. L., 181–82, 354
  *Can There Be a Right-Based Moral
    Theory?* 192–200
Marshall, Thurgood, 423
  dissenting opinion in *Gregg v. Georgia,*
    433–34
Marx, Karl, 160–62
  Economic and Philosophical Manuscripts,
    163–69
  German Ideology, The, 169–72
masturbation, 328, 330, 343
  pornography and, 317–18
  Vatican declaration on, 338–39
McGary, Howard, Jr., 261
  *Reparations, Self-Respect, and Public
    Policy,* 280–88
metaethics, 2–3, 180
Mill, John Stuart, 131–35, 292, 321
  On Liberty, 156–58
  Utilitarianism, 144–56
moral bargaining, 184
moral conflict, 5
moral critics, 12
moral intuition, 180
moral principles, 6
moral theories, 11, 223
moralism, legal, 292
morality, 2
  master, 162, 163
  sexual, 327–51
  slave, 162–63
Morality and the Wealth of the Body Politic
    (Beauchamp), 345–51
Morality of Terrorism, The (Coady),
    464–73
Morals by Agreement (Gauthier), 201–10
morals offenses, 291

Ruddick, Sara, 330–31
  Better Sex, 340–45
rule-utilitarianism, 134–35

sadism, 341
Sartre, Jean Paul, 343
scientific theory, 223
self-love, 98
sex discrimination, 258–88
sexual morality, 327–51
sexual relations, 19
social contract, 12, 75, 98–99, 226
  theories, 12
Social Contract, The (Rousseau), 103–110
social violence, 456
socialism, 226, 227, 241–55
socialization, 99
Socrates, 13, 14, 16, 133
sodomy, 329–30
  Bowers v. Hardwick, 329, 331–34
Sophists, 13–14
Stanley v. Georgia, 297
Stevens, John Paul, majority opinion in
  Gregg v. Georgia, 431–33
Stewart, Potter, majority opinion in *Gregg v.
  Georgia,* 431–33
stoicism, 17
Summa Theologica (St. Thomas Aquinas),
  60–68
sympathy, Hume's theory of, 74–75

teleology, 15
terrorism, 456, 457, 458–85
Terrorism and the Liberal State
  (Wilkinson), 458–64
Theory of Justice, A (Rawls), 235–41
Thrasymachus, 13–14
Treatise of Human Nature, A (Hume),
  82–95

University of California v. Bakke, 261–63
utilitarianism, 11, 12, 131–35
  act-, 134
  aggregate, 135

utilitarianism (*cont.*)
  average, 135
  classical, 131–32, 135
  hedonic, 135
  preference, 135
  rejection of, 180
  revised, 132–35
  rule-, 134–35
Utilitarianism (Mill), 144–56
utility, Bentham's principle of, 131

value, 4
Vatican Declaration on Some Questions of
  Sexual Ethics, 334–39
violence
  interpersonal, 456
  political, 455–85
  social, 456
Violence, Terrorism, and Moral Inquiry
  (Held), 473–85
virtue
  Aristotle on, 15
  Sophists' view of, 13
virtue theories, 12
virtues, 185–86
*Virtues, the Unity of a Human Life, and the
  Concept of a Tradition* (MacIntyre),
  211–18
voyeurism, 341

Warren, Mary Anne, 355, 357
  *On the Moral and Legal Status of
  Abortion,* 379–86
What Makes Right Acts Right? (Ross),
  186–92
White, Byron, 330
  majority opinion in *Bowers v. Hardwick,*
  331–33
Wilkinson, Paul, 456
  Terrorism and the Liberal State, 458–64
will
  general, 99
  good, 101
will-to-power, 163